Class formation and
urban-industrial society

Class formation and urban-industrial society
Bradford, 1750–1850

THEODORE KODITSCHEK

University of Missouri, Columbia

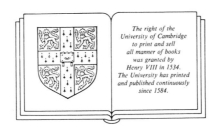
*The right of the
University of Cambridge
to print and sell
all manner of books
was granted by
Henry VIII in 1534.
The University has printed
and published continuously
since 1584.*

CAMBRIDGE UNIVERSITY PRESS

Cambridge

New York   Port Chester   Melbourne   Sydney

Published by the Press Syndicate of the University of Cambridge
The Pitt Building, Trumpington Street, Cambridge CB2 1RP
40 West 20th Street, New York, NY 10011, USA
10 Stamford Road, Oakleigh, Melbourne 3166, Australia

First published 1990

Printed in Canada

Library of Congress Cataloging-in-Publication Data
Koditschek, Theodore.
Class formation and urban-industrial society : Bradford, 1750–1850 /
Theodore Koditschek.
p.   cm.
ISBN 0-521-32771-7
1. Social classes – England – Bradford – History. 2. Middle classes –
England – Bradford – History. 3. Working class – England – Bradford
– History. 4. Urbanization – England – Bradford – History. 5. Bradford
(England) – Social conditions.   I. Title.
HN400.S6K63   1990
305.5′09428′17 – dc19
89-17484
CIP

British Library Cataloguing in Publication Data
Koditschek, Theodore
Class formation and urban-industrial society : Bradford, 1750–1850.
1. Greater Manchester (Metropolitan County). Bradford. Social life, history
I. Title
942.7′33

ISBN 0–521–32771–7   hard covers

To the memory of my mother and my father

Contents

Acknowledgments

Although the Bradford bourgeoisie regarded itself as a group of self-made individuals who were sole authors of all that their enterprise produced, those who study them and the world they thought they had created can be under no such illusions. My own substantive intellectual debts to predecessors are discharged in my footnotes, but I also want to acknowledge those individuals and institutions whose help at various points either made this book possible, facilitated its progress, or improved its quality.

To begin with, I must acknowledge the assistance of all those libraries and librarians, archives and archivists, who not only enabled me to do my research but often provided a pleasant environment in which to work. Special thanks must go to the staffs of the British Library, the University of London Institute for Historical Research, to David James and his staff at what has now become the Bradford Archives, and to Elvira Wilmott and her staff in the Local History Department of the Bradford Central Library.

Two fellowships, one from the American Council of Learned Societies and the other from the Princeton University History Department's Shelby Cullom Davis Postdoctoral Fund, relieved me of teaching responsibilities at a critical moment when a just-completed dissertation was evolving into a very different kind of book.

Research assistance in transcribing some of the data for statistical analysis was provided by Cate Tallman-Evans. Janet White helped make the figures camera ready. Michael Bellesilles, Kate Dornhuber, Penny Livesay, Pat Cooper, and the secretarial staff of the History Department at Virginia Polytechnic Institute and State University provided assistance in typing and retyping the manuscript. I would also like to thank Harold Livesay, then Head of the Virginia Tech History Department, for doing everything in his power to provide me with optimal working conditions during my year there as a Visiting Fellow in 1986–87. At Worcester Polytechnic Institute, the Humanities Department granted me a reduced teaching load during the spring of 1989, as the book was going to press. Finally, I would like to thank Sharon Fleming for preparing the index.

A number of scholars read and criticized all or part of earlier drafts of the manuscript. In addition to giving me much appreciated encouragement, Cynthia Bouton, David Cannadine, Dina Copelman, Christine Heyrman,

Michael Johnson, Lynn Lees, Arno Mayer, Jerrold Seigel, Jonathan Wiener, Martin Wiener, and several anonymous reviewers all made suggestions that have improved the final work. Special thanks in this regard must go to John Gillis, who first introduced me to British social history as an undergraduate and who has followed the progress of my work with great interest ever since. Lawrence Stone, my dissertation adviser, has also supported this project since its inception. By his encouragement of my early intellectual efforts and by the formidable example of his own classic studies in social history, he has emboldened me to be ambitious and to make the commitment of time, thought, and energy that a large-scale work of social and historical synthesis requires.

At Cambridge University Press, my editor, Frank Smith, has been an unfailing source of encouragement and patience during my final four years of work on this book. He and his assistant Sara Ominsky labored diligently to facilitate the pruning of the superfluous overgrowth that marred the first draft. The expert copyediting of Robert Racine has enabled me to make a number of additional stylistic improvements.

The final stages of editorial revision and production are always a difficult time for an author. In my case, they were compounded by a succession of disruptive moves. I was, therefore, fortunate to have found four fellow travelers during this period, Susan Bordo, Tom Kemp, Ruth Smith, and Sarah Whites-Koditschek, who gave me friendship, reassurance, and intellectual diversion at a time when it was too late for me to benefit from anything else.

Finally, I want to thank my wife, LeeAnn Whites, fellow traveler and fellow historian, who has provided assistance in every category for which I have acknowledged the help of others. Nevertheless, her greatest contribution to my work has been her dedication to her own. Through our intellectual partnership, I have learned much of what I know about class and gender formation and about the power of history to dispel those illusions that so often obscure the true nature of social relationships.

Abbreviations

The following abbreviations appear in notes:

BA, Bradford Antiquary
BO, Bradford Observer
BOB, Bradford Observer Budget
HO, Public Records Office, Home Office Papers
OS, Ordnance Survey Map
PP, Parliamentary Papers

Introduction

This book examines the process of capitalist class formation as it occurred in the industrial city of Bradford, England, between 1750 and 1850. Although few historians of modern Britain would deny the existence of social classes, there has been considerable disagreement about how to define them and about their role in the historical transformations of the age. For most British historians, class is but one aspect of a diffuse social reality that their subjects experienced and sometimes expressed. Following Max Weber or their own reading of the evidence, they acknowledge class as one of several diverse social forces and identities but deny any necessary connection between particular class positions and forms of consciousness and refuse to grant "class" any conceptual privilege when framing their explanations of historical change.[1]

However, for a significant minority of British historians, class has played a more central explanatory role. Usually following Karl Marx, with a very different reading of the evidence, these scholars see class formation as the most important product of industrial-capitalist development and usually envision class conflict as the most decisive experience through which the pattern of modern social and political history has been shaped.[2] During the 1950s, 1960s, and 1970s, this Marxist or neo-Marxist approach was revitalized by the emergence of a "new social history" whose accumulating body of research and writing began to pose an increasingly formidable challenge to the orthodoxies of the academic mainstream. Emphasizing the significance of social change and conflict, and focusing on the experience of the exploited and oppressed, this new scholarship began to undermine the dominant vision of history as a continual quest for social order and stability undertaken by political and economic elites. Out of this combination of empirical interest in the history of the downtrodden and a newfound theoretical sophistication in approaching the dynamics of large-scale change, there emerged two generations of labor historians who sought to find in the reconstruction of the

---

[1] Max Weber, "Class, Status, and Party," in H. H. Gerth and C. Wright Mills, eds., *From Max Weber* (New York, 1946), 180–96.
[2] Harvey Kaye, *The British Marxist Historians* (Cambridge, 1984).

1

working-class experience a new and more powerful interpretive framework for understanding the development of society as a whole.[3]

As is well known, this new school of labor and social historians produced a large volume of research that culminated early in a string of seminal articles by E. J. Hobsbawm and E. P. Thompson and in the latter's grand synthesis *The Making of the English Working Class*.[4] In this book, it is class formation, rather than industrial expansion or political liberalization, that serves as the central theme around which the entire panorama of modern history unfolds. Here, Thompson retells the tale of early-nineteenth-century social transformation in terms of the transmutation of a diverse collection of local artisanal communities, under the impact of capitalist penetration, into an increasingly organized national working class. To Thompson, this raising of "collective self-consciousness [was] the great spiritual gain of the Industrial Revolution against which the disruption of an older and in many ways more humanly comprehensible way of life must be set."[5]

Notwithstanding his focus on working-class formation, Thompson was "conscious, at times, of writing against the prevailing orthodoxies" of official Marxism. According to him, class was not "a 'structure' or even a 'category' but . . . something which in fact happens (and can be shown to have happened) in human relationships."[6] The class experience was "largely determined by the productive relations into which men are born or enter involuntarily." But if class was the driving force of history, it was not some metaphysical motor transmitting its energy from a historicist beyond. "If the experience appears as determined, class consciousness does not." Class consciousness,

---

[3] Until the 1950s, British labor history had been, with some notable exceptions, an intellectual backwater whose primarily hagiographic, antiquarian, or institutional orientation had largely neglected the workers' place in the broader historical stream. E. J. Hobsbawm, *Worlds of Labor* (London, 1984), 1–14; idem, "From Social History to the History of Society," in M. W. Flinn and T. C. Smout, eds., *Essays in Social History* (Oxford, 1974).

[4] See particularly, E. J. Hobsbawm, *Labouring Men* (London 1964); *Primitive Rebels* (New York, 1965); E. P. Thompson, *The Making of the English Working Class* (New York, 1963); "Time, Work Discipline and Industrial Capitalism," *Past and Present*, 38 (1967); "The Moral Economy of the English Crowd in the Eighteenth Century," *Past and Present*, 50 (1971); and "Patrician Society, Plebeian Culture," *Journal of Social History*, 7 (1974). Also of considerable importance are the essays in Asa Briggs and John Saville, eds., *Essays in Labour History*, vol. 1 (London, 1960); Asa Briggs, ed., *Chartist Studies* (London, 1959); and the best work of J. F. C. Harrison, *Learning and Living* (London, 1961); idem, *The Quest for the New Moral World, Robert Owen and the Owenites in Britain and America* (New York, 1969).

[5] Thompson, *English Working Class*, 830.

[6] "Class happens," Thompson continues, "when some men, as a result of common experiences (inherited or shared), feel and articulate the identity of their interests as between themselves, and as against other men whose interests are different from (and usually opposed to) theirs." Thompson, *English Working Class*, 9.

the means whereby "these experiences are handled in cultural terms," was indeed "an active process which owes as much to agency as to conditioning."[7]

Although granting the operation of "a logic in the responses of similar occupational groups undergoing similar experiences," Thompson insisted that each instance of the class relationship had to be interpreted historically, rather than specified theoretically in terms of an invariant developmental law. Though it may be a social identity that promotes abstraction, "class," Thompson recognized, acquires its meaning only insofar as it is "embodied in people in a real context." To succeed in achieving any general class consciousness they had first to be participants in a concrete community whose members not only shared common forms of oppression, but were bound together by the act of forging a joint response.[8]

In the quarter century since Thompson's synthesis was published, his pathbreaking conceptualization of the process of working-class formation has had a profound impact on his own and a younger generation of social historians who have produced a series of studies refining and reformulating the Thompsonian paradigm and applying it to earlier and later times.[9] Yet in the midst of this barrage of specialized studies, there have been virtually no full-scale attempts to reconsider the process of class formation as a whole.[10] This is unfortunate since, for all its intellectual power and vitality, the original Thompsonian formulation is, in certain respects, flawed.

[7] Thompson, *English Working Class*, 9–10. To understand Thompson's theoretical position it is necessary to recognize that he is not only a Marxist who criticizes capitalism, but an anti-Stalinist who (at least since 1956) has vigorously opposed positivist or structuralist readings of Marxism and has sought to offer an alternative humanist and voluntarist reading of his own. See his *The Poverty of Theory and Other Essays* (London, 1978).

[8] Hence, Thompson's oft quoted assertion that "class is defined by men as they live their own history, and, in the end, this is its only definition." *English Working Class*, 11.

[9] The most important of these in the field of British history are Dorothy Thompson, *The Chartists* (London, 1984); John Foster, *Class Struggles and the Industrial Revolution* (London, 1974); Iorwerth Prothero, *Artisans and Politics in Early Nineteenth Century London* (Folkstone, 1979); Richard Price, *Masters, Unions, and Men: Work Control in Building and the Rise of Labour, 1830–1914* (Cambridge, 1980); Gareth Stedman Jones, *Outcast London* (London, 1984); idem, *Languages of Class* (Cambridge, 1983); and the essays in Royden Harrison and Jonathan Zeitlin, eds., *Divisions of Labour: Skilled Workers and Technological Change in Nineteenth Century Britain* (Champaign, Ill., 1985).

[10] R. S. Neale, in *Class and Ideology in the Nineteenth Century* (London, 1972), and again in *Class in English History, 1680–1950* (Oxford, 1981), and *Writing Marxist History* (Oxford, 1985), proposed an alternative five-class model that has suffered a not entirely undeserved historiographical neglect. The only other sustained effort to explain the overall development of British society in terms of the logic of class relations is Harold Perkin's shrewd, but idiosyncratic *The Origins of Modern English Society, 1780–1880* (London, 1969), which abandons Thompson's Marxist categories in favor of a more eclectic approach. Perkin's early chapters on eighteenth-century society and the causes and consequences of industrialization are the most original and insightful. His actual class analysis, although

Almost from the outset critics have attacked it on numerous counts, disputing that an English working class was really "made" by the time of the Reform Act and questioning how Thompson would handle the developments of subsequent periods, particularly those of the middle and late Victorian era when the working-class radicalism with which his account culminates was replaced by a fatalistic quiescence on the part of the majority and an increasingly active accommodation with capitalism among at least a substantial section of the skilled.[11] Moreover, since the trajectory of twentieth-century working-class development seems to follow this subsequent pattern of incorporation and accommodation more closely than the early-nineteenth-century pattern of anticapitalist revolt, it is the former rather than the latter that may be taken as most characteristic of mature class relations and, therefore, as most urgently in need of being explained.

However, not everyone has accepted Thompson's portrayal of early-nineteenth-century working-class radicalism, and his arguments about proletarian cohesion and militance have been challenged even in his own chronological frame. According to R. Currie and R. M. Hartwell, Thompson's working class, as his own extensive evidence can be made to show, was "rich in conflict" between artisans, factory workers, and the laboring poor. In their view, "even after 850 pages," the notion of a single self-conscious class of workers "united by common experiences, remains . . . a

---

offering many valuable insights into the relation between class and ideology that I have tried to develop in my own work suffers, in the end, from a misconception of both. Defined in terms of source of income rather than relationship to production, Perkin's classes are arbitrary constructs that follow no discernable logic of interaction. Had his notion of class been purely descriptive, this might have posed no problem, but since it constitutes the explanatory framework on which his whole account rests, it leads him into a series of inconsistencies. He begins by telling us that "the great conflicts of the age were all at bottom struggles for income." (p. 219). A page later, however, we are informed that "the primary conflict in the newly born class society . . . was a struggle between ideals." Therefore, "the class which was most successful in this educational and moral struggle" would succeed in imposing "its ideal upon others" and emerge victorious in material terms. This muddling of cause and effect can be directly attributed to Perkin's failure to recognize that class, at least as an explanatory concept, cannot be located directly in the arenas in which we seek its manifestations (such as source of income or ideological consciousness), but must ultimately be rooted in the underlying social relations wherein a society and the material resources that sustain it are originally produced. For a perceptive critique of Perkin and an extended discussion of the secondary literature see, R. J. Morris, *Class and Class Consciousness in the Industrial Revolution, 1780–1850* (London, 1979), esp. 12–14.

[11] "How," asks Perry Anderson, "could the English Working Class have been made in the 1830's if it later underwent this astonishing transformation?" *Arguments Within English Marxism* (London, 1980), 45.

myth, a construct of determined imagination and theoretical presuppositions."[12] But even Marxists who share Thompson's "theoretical presuppositions" are sometimes troubled by what they see as his unwarranted conflation of different occupational traditions and experiences and his insufficient attention to the mode of production in which these experiences and traditions were shaped. According to some critics, the fact that capitalist productive relations developed so slowly and unevenly in England makes it only more natural that workers in different sectors of the economy would come to class consciousness at differing rates. Thompson, however, is said to have ignored the subtleties of this process so that, according to Perry Anderson, "the objective forces" of capitalist exploitation constitute "a dreadful backcloth to the book rather than a direct object of analysis in its own right."[13]

Most damaging, however, to the Thompsonian paradigm is that other social historians have offered alternative frameworks for interpreting popular culture and consciousness that seem to reflect greater sensitivity to these internal divisions within the workers' ranks. Geoffrey Best, who declared himself "prepared to accept a Marxist structure of indelible class antagonisms if I have to," concluded that it was not class but respectability – the ability to master one's own wayward instincts and to remain independent of external manipulation and control – that "was the sharpest of all lines of social division ...a sharper line by far than that between rich and poor, employer and employee, or capitalist and proletarian." Some Marxists have attempted to accommodate such objections by attributing the prevalence of respectability among certain types of workers to the existence of a labor "aristocracy" whose special privileges predisposed them to being co-opted and bought off.[14] However, in a work force that was distributed along a broad continuum of specific relations to the production process, there is little foundation, either empirical or theoretical, for so sharp a distinction to be made. Moreover, the aspiration toward respectability extended much farther downward than any reasonable criteria of labor aristocrats would allow. Finally, unrespectability was by no means synonymous with rebelliousness or class

---

[12] R. M. Hartwell and R. Currie, "The Making of the English Working Class?" *Economic History Review,* 18:3 (1965).

[13] Anderson, *English Marxism,* 35.

[14] G. F. A. Best, *Mid-Victorian Britain, 1850–75* (New York, 1971), xv, 260; Hobsbawm, *Labouring Men,* 321–70; Robert Gray, *The Aristocracy of Labour in Nineteenth Century Britain* (London, 1981); J. Field, "British Historians and the Concept of the Labour Aristocracy," *Radical History Review,* 19 (1978–9); H. F. Moorehouse, "The Marxist Theory of the Labour Aristocracy," *Social History,* 3 (1978); A. Reid, "Response to Moorehouse," *Social History,* 3 (1978).

consciousness, since many workers of this type were prone to being either quiescent or differential, and it was from the ranks of the respectable that the most articulate and consistently radical Victorian working people were drawn.[15]

Much more plausible than the neo-Marxist theory of labor aristocracy is Brian Harrison's argument that such divisions within popular culture were rooted in divergent patterns of consumption and leisure at least as much as in different experiences of work. By insisting on the enduring significance of plebeian traditions of religion and recreation, which predated the advent of capitalist production and operated according to a different logic in another sphere, Harrison is simply following Thompson's example. Yet unlike Thompson, who envisions these as forces unifying the workers, he sees them as more often setting workers culturally at odds, aligning different proletarian sections with different and equally divided elite groups. So compelling is some of the evidence for these cultural bifurcations, cutting across and often blunting the influence of class lines, that even historians initially lured by the promise of the Thompsonian approach sometimes found themselves concluding that, not class, but other forms of consciousness exercised a dominant influence on the majority of ordinary working-class women and men.[16]

Thus Thomas Laqueur has shown the important role played by Sunday schools in educating and integrating working-class children from all social levels, teaching them the values of self-discipline and respectability that would be required of them in the new urban-industrial world. Conversely, Patrick Joyce contends that the culture of the factory, as it became the dominant mode of production in the industrial North, so far from fostering a militant class consciousness, set in motion "the mechanics of social stability and class domination and ... the emergence of feelings sufficiently deep-rooted to be called deference."[17] Although it may be difficult to reconcile Joyce's deferential factory laborers with the striving toward independence and respectability of Laqueur's working class, both agree in viewing militant class consciousness as a minority phenomenon whose significance was diminishing rather than increasing as industrial-capitalist society matured.

Such empirical reexaminations have led some of the most theoretically minded social historians of the rising generation completely to abandon the concept of class. Thus Craig Calhoun, in the most thorough and searching of the Thompson critiques, has argued that the artisanal radicals who are

---

[15] Henry Pelling, *Popular Politics and Society in Late Victorian Britain* (London, 1968), 37–61; Brian Harrison, *Peaceable Kingdom* (Oxford, 1982), 157–216.

[16] Harrison, *Peaceable Kingdom*, 123–56.

[17] Patrick Joyce, *Work, Society, and Politics: The Culture of the Factory in later Victorian England* (New Brunswick, 1980), xiv; Thomas Laqueur, *Religion and Respectability: Sunday Schools and Working Class Culture, 1780–1850* (New Haven, Conn., 1976).

the heroes of the story were not pioneers of mature class consciousness, but "reactionary radicals" whose communitarian populism actually represented the last gasp of a traditional preindustrial world.[18] Most recently, William Reddy has gone even farther, contending that it is "quite possible to account for the whole of English social history down through 1850 without invoking class interest" and that "it is necessary to do so for the simple reason that the result is less approximate, less fuzzy, truer to the documents, than an approach that depends on the old scenario of class conflict."[19]

We need not endorse these calls to abandon class as a historical concept to acknowledge real problems in Thompson's handling of it and to see that, if it is to be reformulated more satisfactorily, his conflation of theory with history must be rethought. Precisely because class is the critical focal point for theoretically informed history, the impulse to reduce the former to the latter (or vice versa) must be resisted in favor of a dialectical approach. Class is, indeed, a real force in history, but the historian should not expect to encounter it empirically in its pure theoretical form. What historians see when they survey their evidence is a much more complex and less clear-cut social formation in which the classes that the logic of productive relations dictate are, to a greater or lesser degree, fractured, distorted, and perhaps even contraindicated by the concrete, contingent, historical settings and sequences in which the class abstractions are enmeshed.[20]

Marx himself, though he never explicitly articulated them, seems to have been well aware of the implications of having located class in a no-man's-land between theory and history in order to use it to perform a mediating role. At first sight it may seem odd that a concept so obviously central to historical materialism should have been given so little analysis and explication in Marx's most important theoretical works. In fact, the concept of class appears most explicitly in his historical writings, most notably in his empirical narratives of the rise and fall of the second French Republic, in which he provides an extended examination of an actual social formation in its relation to the abstract productive relations of class. What Marx finds in these studies of mid-nineteenth-century French society is neither a "pure" proletariat or

---

[18] Craig Calhoun, *The Question of Class Struggle* (Chicago, 1982), 60–94.

[19] William Reddy, *Money and Liberty in Modern Europe: A Critique of Historical Understanding* (Cambridge, 1987), 195. See also Gertrude Himmelfarb, *The Idea of Poverty: England in the Early Industrial Age* (New York, 1983), for the most sustained effort to displace the concept of class from the explanatory center of nineteenth-century British social history, essentially by positing "the problem of poverty" in its stead.

[20] Nicos Poulantzas, *Political Power and Social Classes* (London, 1973); Anthony Giddens, *The Class Structure of the Advanced Societies* (London, 1973). See also George Lukacs, *History and Class Consciousness* (Cambridge, Mass., 1971), 46–82.

a "pure" bourgeoisie. On the contrary, he depicts a much more complex constellation of empirically constituted social entities whose relationship to capitalism is, to some degree, tempered by the particularities of French history, either because it represents the postrevolutionary remnant of some precapitalist social group, or because it represents a group required by capitalism, which capitalist productive relations have not yet brought within their totalizing grip.[21]

When we apply a comparable class analysis to the society of of early-nineteenth-century Britain, where industrial capitalism was more developed than in contemporary France, it becomes evident that Thompson's account of working-class formation is far more plausible than his critics would have us believe; for Thompson makes no attempt to reconstruct the historical experience of all English workers but concentrates on that particular section of beleaguered artisans whose existence predated industrial capitalism but who bore the full brunt of its proletarianizing effect. Yet because of the centrality of these artisans' experience to the larger historical fate of their class, his book goes far toward earning its title despite the limited empirical range of its research.

Certainly, Thompson's critics err in dismissing his subjects as a small, backward-looking, anachronistic minority out of phase with the larger trends

---

[21] Karl Marx, *Class Struggles in France* (Moscow, 1972); idem, *The Eighteenth Brumaire of Louis Bonaparte* (New York, 1963). Marx's abstraction, in theoretical works like *Capital*, from the concrete social formations that he investigates empirically in his studies of France, has generally been treated by subsequent commentators as though it were an exercise in the construction of Weberian ideal types. This distorts Marx's basic purpose and disregards his most profound theoretical achievement, which was to see that the abstract logic of capitalist development is not only an explanatory scheme constructed by the investigator, but an actual force within history that impinges, if not always completely or unambiguously, on the behavior and consciousness that his subjects display. In Marx's view, it is precisely this unique transforming power of capitalism, its ability to impart "abstraction" into the fabric of events, which makes it an epoch in human history. By forcing those who operate within its framework to project concrete acts of labor and objects of utility into a generalized, exchangeable, commodity form, Marx recognized that capitalism had opened the way for entirely new forms of social organization in which (for better or worse) relationships that had hitherto been enacted within the limited frame of particular communities could henceforth occur on an increasingly globalized, species-wide scale.

Unfortunately, Marx's insight into this capitalist dialectic of abstraction was not matched by an equivalent commitment to detailed historical examination of the reasons why it has, in actual practice, been impeded, modified, and occasionally reversed. Subsequent thinkers in the Marxist tradition have done little to rectify this imbalance, so that today there are a surfeit of improvements on and exegeses of Marxist theory (which, as theory, may scarcely need them), combined with a dearth of sensitive empirical studies to reconcile it with the real historical patterns that have emerged in the actual capitalist world.

of contemporary working-class life. The textile handicraftsmen who provide him with his central paradigm alone, encompassed, during the 1830s, about one-sixth of the adult male work force.[22] Enormously extended and inflated by the introduction of factory spinning, they were then proletarianized and ultimately destroyed by the forces of capitalist development and growth.[23] Moreover, the proletarianization to which the textile handicraftsmen were so dramatically subjected was also experienced with greater or lesser virulence by other working-class social groups. As Thompson and Iorwerth Prothero have demonstrated, at least sections of virtually every large artisanal trade – shoemaking, tailoring, masonry, cabinetmaking, and shipbuilding – were periodically beset by the same pressures – breakdown of apprenticeship, competition in the labor market, wage undercutting, and violent fluctuations in trade – that had undermined the textile handicraftsmen, despite the fact that, during the years before midcentury, their occupations were relatively free of major industrial reorganizations and substantial infusions of technological change.[24]

Although this sort of analysis largely excludes women, agricultural laborers, factory workers, mechanics, and craftsmen in the luxury trades, a case could be made that, at least until 1850, the Thompsonian paradigm is partly applicable to the majority of the adult male working class. Certainly, to characterize his subjects as "reactionary radicals," nostalgic for the mythical communitarianism of a bygone age, obscures a central virtue of Thompson's analysis. In separating the "backwardness" of their culture from the "modernity" of their experiences, it diminishes the novelty and historical significance of what they were about. "True enough," Thompson acknowledges, "one direction of the great agitation of the artisans was to *resist* being turned into a proletariat." But "when they knew that this cause was lost ... they reached out again in the Thirties and Forties and sought to achieve new and only imagined forms of social control."[25]

More tellingly, it can be objected that this active experience of proletarianization, as opposed to a more passive subsistence in the proletarian state, was a peculiar characteristic of early capitalism – the unique product of a temporary, transitional stage. There is considerable force in this objection, for capitalist societies that successfully reach maturity invariably do develop levels of social and political complexity both within and, even more, beyond the workplace, which sometimes defy analysis in dualistic class terms. However, the history of capitalism also shows that proletarianization is an ongoing

---

[22] Thompson, *English Working Class*, 311; J. H. Treble, *Urban Poverty in Britain, 1830–1914* (London, 1979), 28.

[23] Thompson, *English Working Class*, 260–1, 269–314.

[24] Thompson, *English Working Class*, 234–68; Prothero, *Artisans and Politics*, 210–31.

[25] Thompson, *English Working Class*, 831.

process, stabilizing in one place only to erupt anew and penetrate somewhere else.[26] Perhaps even more significantly, it has come to constitute a far more pervasive paradigm for the undermining of personal autonomy in a modern "mass" society in which formally free individuals find themselves subjected in practice to ever more intrusive and compulsory forms of personal surveillance and control.[27]

Doubtless, it is necessary to distinguish this ongoing, incremental encroachment into individual autonomy and the labor process from the explosive traumas of early industrial capitalism when proletarianization in the workplace not only was experienced with frightful intensity, but was overlaid by devastating environmental dislocations such as immigration and the transmutation of a traditional rural village existence into a modern, depersonalized, urban way of life. But this simply illustrates the stricture that Thompson's story, as he himself would be the first to admit, must be treated as an exemplary tale, rather than as a universal model of class formation to be applied indiscriminately in any time or place.

Curiously, for all the criticism of Thompson's treatment of the workers, no one has noticed the ways he has limited his class analysis by entirely neglecting the bourgeoisie. Yet surely we are compelled to draw this conclusion from his own dictum that class is a relationship and not a thing. Perhaps his invocation of working-class agency lacks full conviction not because it romanticizes the proletariat, but because it ignores the agency of bourgeois capitalists who had a profound impact on the way the working class was made. From Thompson we learn much about the oppression of capitalism but little about the oppressors who inflicted it as if they did not also act out of a culture, consciousness, and ideology of their own.

---

[26] Thus toward the end of the nineteenth century when the mid-Victorian boom had run its course, a new wave of industrial reorganization and technological transformation subjected a new round of workers to the experience of deskilling – including some in those very privileged occupations that the first Industrial Revolution had originally raised up. Any reader of the daily newspaper will know that the process continues to this day. Hobsbawm, *Labouring Men*, 380–1; Harry Braverman, *Labor and Monopoly Capital: The Degradation of Work in the Twentieth Century* (New York, 1974).

[27] For the proliferation of new and increasingly intrusive forms of personal discipline throughout modern society see the works of Michel Foucault, especially, *Discipline and Punish* (New York, 1979). Foucault, however, would probably want to subsume the proletarianization of labor, which Marxism regards as paradigmatic, into a subinstance of what he regards as a deeper and less easily challengeable process of bodily control and surveillance that he sees as taking on a new level of significance and intensity with the onset of the modern age. For an assessment by Foucault of his relationship to Marxism see P. Rabinow, ed., *The Foucault Reader* (New York, 1984), 51–3.

In fact, Thompson seems to think they did not, for the social entity against which his workers define themselves is not a coherent class, but a loose, defensive coalition of landlords, industrialists, and government officials whose union is contingent, fueled by a common interest in the protection of property and a common fear of popular revolt. Depicting a convergence of old elites selfishly embracing political economy with new elites anxiously joining their counterrevolutionary crusade, Thompson concludes that "the years between the French Revolution and the Reform Bill...had seen the formation of a middle class 'class consciousness' more conservative, more wary of idealist causes...more narrowly self-interested than that of any nation."[28] With this curt dismissal, the man who taught us to reject the structuralist vision of history as "a process without a subject" commits himself to a history of capitalism without the bourgeoisie.[29]

In fairness to Thompson, it must be acknowledged that this neglect or outright denial of bourgeois class agency has been characteristic of historians as a group. Perhaps in reaction against facile claims made by a more "Whiggish" generation of earlier historians, modern scholars have grown wary of all generalizations about the subject, well aware that there is scarcely a period of history in which someone has not sighted a rising bourgeoisie.[30] Even as regards the nineteenth century, a bourgeois era if there ever was one, we hear much talk of bourgeois art, literature, culture, ideology, and politics, but very little mention of a bourgeoisie. As an adjective, the word has become a historiographical catchall, attaching to almost everything in general without clearly denoting the distinct reality of any social group. It is as though, under the weight of a bourgeois society, the bourgeoisie, as a class, has disappeared.[31]

For some historians, like Martin Wiener, consciousness of Britain's current economic infirmities has heightened awareness of the apparent invisi-

---

[28] Thompson, *English Working Class*, 820.

[29] E. P. Thompson, *The Poverty of Theory* (London, 1978), 73–103.

[30] J. H. Hexter, "The Myth of the Middle Class in Tudor England," *Reappraisals in History* (New York, 1961).

[31] The most notable examples of this genre, which depicts mid-Victorian bourgeois society without a bourgeoisie, are, for England, G. M. Young, *Victorian England: Portrait of an Age* (London, 1936); W. L. Burn, *The Age of Equipoise* (New York, 1965); Walter Houghton, *The Victorian Frame of Mind* (New Haven, Conn., 1957); and Best, *Mid-Victorian Britain;* for France, Theodore Zeldin, *Ambition and Love* (Oxford, 1979). Only E. J. Hobsbawm, *Age of Capital: 1848–1875* (New York, 1975), treats the period in a way that class does not disappear. Even the handful of studies that focus on the bourgeoisie itself, such as Adeline Daumard, *Les bourgeois de Paris aux XIXe siecle* (Paris, 1970), and Peter Gay, *The Bourgeois Experience: Victoria to Freud,* vol. 1, *Education of the Senses* (Oxford, 1984) and vol. 2, *The Tender Passion* (Oxford, 1986), are strikingly innocent of any theoretically explicit notion of class.

bility of the nineteenth-century bourgeoisie. Portraying it as a class that abandoned its commitment to active entrepreneurship in favor of a passive, rentier, aristocratic identity and style, Wiener sees, in the erosion of nineteenth-century bourgeois class consciousness, the origins of the "English disease."[32] Certainly not all historians share Wiener's reading of the late Victorian era as the triumph of the aristocratic ideal, but even those who would affirm the bourgeoisie's bourgeois character have difficulty in establishing what that was.

What makes the nineteenth-century bourgeoisie so difficult to characterize is that, even more than the working class, it was composed of a wide range of subgroups. Perhaps few would assume (as Thompson appears to) that it should be stretched to include all property owners including the postfeudal landed class. Yet even if landed aristocrats are treated as a separate class, there remain a wide range of large and small proprietors – from multimillionaire bankers and merchants, prosperous manufacturers, farmers, professionals, and urban rentiers, down to the vast mass of petty shopkeepers and retailers – to be included within the bourgeoisie.

As the work of W. D. Rubenstein has indicated, there were extraordinarily wide variations in wealth and cultural orientation even among the urban bourgeois elites. Large merchants and bankers, usually centered in London and oriented toward international trade, insurance, and high finance, continued to overshadow and disdain parvenu provincial industrialists who were relatively isolated from establishment circles until the very end of the Victorian age.[33] Professionals, though clearly belonging to the bourgeois spectrum, also constituted a distinct group. Not only did they have their own particular interests, but sometimes they exhibited an entirely distinctive outlook on the world.[34]

Finally, the broad ranks of petit bourgeois shopkeepers and small proprietors, the urban peasantry as John Vincent has called them, occupied a unique place in the social structure, sharing many common interests and values with their bourgeois superiors, but experiencing a level of economic insecurity that often gave them (though they often preferred not to acknowledge it) more in common with the urban working class.[35] So varied was the diverse assortment of "people who might [in the nineteenth century] be

[32] Martin Wiener, *English Culture and the Decline of the Industrial Spirit, 1850–1980* (Cambridge, 1981).

[33] W. D. Rubenstein, "The Victorian Middle Classes: Wealth, Occupation, and Geography," *Economic History Review*, 30:4 (1977); "Wealth, Elites, and the Class Structure of Modern Britain," *Past and Present*, 76 (1977); *Men of Property: the Very Wealthy in Britain Since the Industrial Revolution* (New Brunswick, 1981).

[34] Perkin, *Modern English Society*, 252–70, 319–39.

[35] John Vincent, *Pollbooks: How the Victorians Voted* (Cambridge, 1967), 25; G. Crossick, ed., *The Lower Middle Class in Britain* (London, 1977).

called middle class" that Professor Kitson Clark, at one point, despaired "that any general statement that purports to include them all must be fallacious, any common denominator credited to them all must be delusion".[36]

To make sense of this diverse collection of social strata, to see the bourgeoisie as more than a loose descriptive category, to understand it as a coherent and historically purposive social class, it will be necessary to focus on the experience of that section, that is, the entrepreneurial capitalists who, like Thompson's proletarianized artisans among the workers, stood on capitalist productive relations' cutting edge. However, historians who undertake to do this find themselves at a serious disadvantage since the Marxist historical and theoretical tradition, which offers so much guidance in studying workers, is remarkably silent on the subject of the capitalist bourgeoisie. In contrast to the veritable cottage industry, which has developed around the making of the English working class, contemporary scholarship has, until recently, produced virtually nothing on the class formation of the English bourgeoisie.[37]

This imbalance in the work of contemporary students of class formation is, to some extent, traceable back to Marx himself. "The bourgeoisie," he and Engels argued in *The German Ideology*, "develops only gradually, splits according to the division of labor into various functions, and finally absorbs all propertied classes it finds in existence."[38] Appearing to offer scriptural authority to the Thompsonian position, in this passage they conclude, "The separate individuals form a class only insofar as they have to carry on a common battle against another class; otherwise they are on hostile terms with one another as competitors." Unlike the workers, who were to be the active agents of history, then, the bourgeoisie, though objectively a class in its relation to production, never fully became a class-for-itself, since it appears to have been capable of acting collectively only defensively, in a negative sense.[39]

There is, however, another strand in Marx's argument that portrays the

[36] G. N. Kitson Clark, *The Making of Victorian England* (London, 1962), 6.

[37] In addition to Asa Briggs, "Middle Class Consciousness in English Politics, 1780–1846," *Past and Present*, 10 (1957); idem, "The Language of Class in Early Nineteenth Century England," in *Essays in Labor History;* a number of recent works have begun to shed some light on the process of bourgeois class formation, although none of them have, so far, directly taken the problem on. In particular, see J. Seed, "Unitarianism, Political Economy, and the Antinomies of Liberal Culture in Manchester, 1830–50," *Social History*, 7:1 (1982); R. J. Morris, "The Middle Classes and British Towns and Cities of the Industrial Revolution, 1780–1870," in D. Fraser and A. Sutcliffe, eds., *The Pursuit of Urban History* (London, 1983); Anthony Howe, *The Cotton Masters, 1830–60* (Oxford, 1984); and Lenore Davidoff and Catherine Hall, *Family Fortunes; Men and Women of the English Middle Class, 1780–1850* (London, 1987).

[38] Karl Marx and Friedrich Engels, *The German Ideology* (New York, 1947), 69.

[39] Ibid.

class character of capitalists in a different light. To be sure, in *Capital* we are again reminded that, "except as personified capital, the capitalist has no historical value." However, insofar "as he is personified capital," it turns out he can do quite a lot. "Fanatically bent on making value expand itself, he ruthlessly forces the human race to produce for production's sake; he thus forces the development of the productive powers of society, and creates those material conditions which alone can form the basis of a higher form of society."[40] Thus in their most balanced and comprehensive assessment, Marx and Engels conclude:

> The bourgeoisie historically has played a most revolutionary role in history... wherever it has got the upper hand [it] has put an end to all feudal, patriarchal, idyllic relations. It has pitilessly torn asunder the motley feudal ties that bound man to his 'natural superiors,' and has left remaining no other nexus between man and man than naked self-interest, than callous 'cash payment.' It has drowned the most heavenly ecstasies of religious fervor... in the icy water of egotistical calculation. It has resolved personal worth into exchange value and in the place of the numberless indefeasible chartered freedoms, has set up that single, unconscionable freedom – Free Trade. In one word, for exploitation, veiled by religious and political illusions, it has substituted naked, shameless, direct, brutal exploitation.[41]

If, for Marx the theorist, the proletariat was to be the imagined agent of the classless, socialist society of the future, for Marx the historian, it was the bourgeoisie who acted as the actual agent of the class-bound, alienated, capitalist society of his own day. And if the working class was to learn its positive class mission negatively, through struggle against bourgeois capitalist tyranny, then it was, in part, because the bourgeoisie itself had already pointed the way forward with its own positive sense of class mission, forged in the course of a long historical struggle against the tyranny of the feudal aristocracy.

In fact, as Marx himself admitted, "no credit is due me for discovering either the existence of classes or the struggle between them," because, long before him, bourgeois historians and political economists had traced quite effectively the rise and struggles of their own.[42] In an account of class formation that Marx himself adapted, and that remains, at least in broad outline, the model still employed by economic historians today, these men traced the development of the bourgeoisie and its antiaristocratic challenge by linking both in the economic spread of the capitalist marketplace, a process that facilitated the emergence of the bourgeoisie as a distinctive social group.

[40] Karl Marx, *Capital* (Moscow, 1954), 1:555.

[41] Karl Marx and Friedrich Engels, *The Communist Manifesto* (New York, 1948), 11.

[42] Karl Marx and Friedrich Engels, *Selected Correspondence, 1846–1895* (Westport, Conn., 1975), 57.

At the core of this account is the recognition that, long before full-blown capitalism triumphed as a dominant mode of production, it had gestated slowly within the historical framework of feudalism as a more limited system of market exchange. Gradually penetrating the subsistence economy of the feudal manor, medieval commerce broke the stranglehold of local self-sufficiency and facilitated a social and economic division of labor that promoted growing levels of economic prosperity and geographical differentiation between countryside and town. As demand for luxury articles proliferated, urban mercantile and manufacturing centers spread. Offering freedom from the feudal constraints of serfdom and lordly domination, these cities became magnets for the most enterprising and ambitious who sought to rise above their inherited place. Insofar as a modest surplus could be squeezed out of agriculture, this urban sector was able to expand. Gradually, old trade routes were reopened, money found its way back into circulation, living standards began to rise, and more immigrants spilled into the cities as population levels grew.[43]

But for all that cities and commerce were solvents of feudalism, throughout the Middle Ages and much of the early modern period, they remained profoundly isolated entities, existing in the interstices of an overwhelmingly traditional agrarian world. The spread of capitalist commercial relations did not necessarily bring capitalist techniques of production, and the imbalances between burgeoning population levels and inadequately increasing production yields inevitably produced a Malthusian crisis and a downward spiral to the barbarism and backwardness that had plagued medieval society from the start. Unable to break out of the cycle of violence and insecurity that characterized the larger environment in which they lived, cities and the burghers who inhabited them were forced back on the feudal logic of dependence that pervaded the medieval countryside. Burghers, who consolidated their position, incorporated themselves into chartered companies and contracted with feudal suzerains to defend them against the twin threats of armed marauders, who would rob or destroy them, and parvenu interlopers, who would compete for their share of a limited economic pie.[44]

Determined, at all costs, to protect their position, these chartered companies obtained economic monopolies and political privileges from feudal

[43] Henri Pirenne, *Medieval Cities* (Princeton, N.J., 1925); R. S. Lopez, *The Commercial Revolution of the Middle Ages* (Cambridge, 1976); J. Merrington, "Town and Country in the Transition to Capitalism," in R. H. Hilton, ed., *The Transition from Feudalism to Capitalism* (London, 1978).

[44] Pirenne, *Medieval Cities*, 170–212; Max Weber, *Economy and Society* (Berkeley, 1978), 2:1212–62; George Unwin, *Industrial Organization in the Sixteenth and Seventeenth Centuries* (Oxford, 1904), 9–19; F. Pollock and F. W. Maitland, *The History of English Law*, vol. 1 (Cambridge, 1968), 634–88; Quentin Skinner, *The Foundations of Modern Political Thought*, vol. 1 (Cambridge, 1978), 11.

authorities in return for payments of grants or taxes. As the freedom of the city was thus transmuted into the privilege of the *Burgherrecht,* the same principle of inherent hierarchy that pervaded feudalism began to inform the social structure of the urban world. Even those outside the corporatist framework found themselves drawn, despite their best intentions, into the logic that its primacy implied. New strata of entrepreneurially minded insurgents could and did overthrow established burghers or supplant old cities either by carving out entirely new markets or capturing existing ones by producing and selling cheap. At such moments, medieval parvenus appeared quite progressive – as burghers who were prepared to win their triumph under bourgeois conditions rather than seeking it furtively through a feudal back door. However, before the nineteenth century, such conditions existed only intermittently, before the sixteenth century, scarcely at all. Forced to seek their freedom within the framework of the *Burgherrecht,* or the city-state republic, and to conceive their mission entirely in local terms, their struggle against vested interests was usually too narrowly rooted in their own self-interest to remain long equated with the common good. Invariably, success in overthrowing the existing oligarchy was followed by the establishment of a new one, which quickly acquired privileges and monopolies of its own.[45]

Thus although medieval burghers became a separate estate of society and, at times, with their endless cycle of innovation and consolidation, even created the illusion of a perpetually rising bourgeoisie, they remained, fundamentally, a group divided into separate cities, corporations, and social strata whose common location within the social and economic structure only exacerbated mutual jealousies and prevented the emergence of a sense of universal purpose that is the hallmark of a presumptively ascendant elite. Since the burgher was a man whose collective identity was always limited to a specific community existing in a particular time and place, since his "rights" were something that this community held as a monopoly, they could not be universalized and still remain his own. Yet the rights of man were latent in the privileges of the municipality just as the conservative burgher contained the historical kernel out of which the liberal bourgeoisie would grow. However, these possibilities could be realized only after the isolated world of medieval and early modern cities gave way, in the period covered by this book, to a modern urban-industrial society in which capitalism assumed center stage as the dominant mode of production and ceased to appear merely as an interstitial mechanism of exchange.

Although the transition to a capitalist society can be traced back as far as the sixteenth century, it was not until the 1750–1850 period that the new

---

[45] Vilfredo Pareto, *The Rise and Fall of the Elites* (Totowa, N.J. 1968).

mode of production decisively took hold, spreading from agriculture, where, in England, it had gained an early foothold, to industry, where it unleashed a dynamic of self-sustaining economic and demographic growth.[46] During these years, Britain's main manufacturing industries – textiles, transportation, and metallurgy – underwent large-scale mechanization, industrial reorganization, and proletarianization of the work force, which opened the way for quantum productivity leaps.[47]

To be sure, these developments did not completely transform the entire economy or society and, even in 1850, these three modernized sectors employed only about a quarter of the work force and generated about the same proportion of the national income.[48] But as Professor Landes aptly put it, "Beneath this [slowly changing numerical] surface, the vital organs were being transformed; and though they weighed but a fraction of the total – whether measured by people or by wealth – it was they that determined the metabolism of the entire system."[49] After 1846, when the state repudiated economic protectionism in principle, the entire economy was gradually exposed to the same relentless competition that had hitherto been felt primarily

---

[46] A full examination of this transformation, of which the 1750–1850 period represents only the final stage, would require at least one book in itself. For studies that touch on aspects of the early stages of this process when the transition out of feudalism first occurred (broadly speaking, the period up to 1660), see Maurice Dobb, *Studies in the Development of Capitalism* (New York, 1947); R. H. Hilton, ed., *Feudalism to Capitalism;* Immanuel Wallerstein, *The Modern World System*, vol. 1 (New York, 1974); vol. 2 (New York, 1980); T. H. Aston and C. H. E. Philpin, eds., *The Brenner Debate: Agrarian Class Structure and Economic Development in Pre-Industrial Europe* (Cambridge, 1985); Robert Brenner, "The Origins of Capitalist Development: A Critique of Neo-Smithian Marxism," *New Left Review*, 104 (1977); Perry Anderson, *Lineages of the Absolutist State* (London, 1974), and Christopher Hill, *The Century of Revolution* (Edinburgh, 1972). For particularly useful examinations of the issues involved in the actual genesis of capitalist productive relations in English agriculture and industry during the eighteenth and early nineteenth centuries see Maxine Berg, *The Age of Manufactures* (Oxford, 1985); Phyllis Deane, *The First Industrial Revolution* (Cambridge, 1965); E. J. Hobsbawm, *Industry and Empire* (London, 1968); F. F. Mendels, "Proto-industrialization, the First Phase of the Industrialization Process," *Journal of Economic History*, 32:1 (1972); G. E. Mingay, *Enclosure and the Small Farmer in the Age of Industrial Revolution* (London, 1968); and Perkin, *Modern English Society.*

[47] See statistics in Phyllis Deane and W. A. Cole, *British Economic Growth, 1688–1945* (Cambridge, 1962), 166, 182–241; and B. R. Mitchell, *Abstract of British Historical Statistics* (Cambridge, 1962), 60–1.

[48] David Cannadine, "The Present and the Past in the English Industrial Revolution," *Past and Present*, 103 (1984); Raphael Samuel, "The Workshop of the World: Steam Power and Hand Technology in Mid-Victorian Britain," *History Workshop*, 3 (1977); N. F. R. Crafts, *British Economic Growth During the Industrial Revolution* (Oxford, 1985); Deane and Cole, *British Economic Growth*, 212, 226, 233; Mitchell, *British Historical Statistics*, 60.

[49] David Landes, *The Unbound Prometheus, Technological Change and Industrial Development in Western Europe, 1750 to the Present* (Cambridge, 1969), 122.

in the industrial core. Thereafter, it was only a matter of time before the productive and market forces that had revolutionized these leading sectors would set the terms for most aspects of British socioeconomic life.

Hand in hand with the triumph of a new mode of production came the emergence of a predominantly urban environment as, by midcentury, Britain also became the first major country in which fewer people lived in the countryside than in cities and towns. Although cities long predated industrial capitalism and, even in the nineteenth century, preindustrial cities like preindustrial forms of manufacturing continued to exist, the urbanization of the overall society became possible only within the context of an increasingly industrial-capitalist world.[50] Of course, even in the new industrial cities, where the mode of production was being directly transformed, the economic process of industrialization and the environmental process of urbanization must be recognized as analytically distinct. Nevertheless, as this book will demonstrate, in practice they were intertwined inextricably, feeding, reinforcing, and compounding one another in what appeared, at least before midcentury, to be a single urban-industrial revolution at work on both fronts.[51]

It is within the context of this urban-industrial revolution that we must locate not only the proletarianization of the workers, but the ascent of a new entrepreneurial bourgeoisie. Like Thompson's beleaguered artisans among the workers (albeit at the opposite extreme), these entrepreneurs, because

[50] The connection between industrial capitalism and the emergence of an urban society can be seen in the early-nineteenth-century census statistics that show that although England's overall urban population grew by 288 percent, much of this growth was concentrated in the new, northern provincial cities where the Industrial Revolution was taking place. These cities increased their share of the urban population from 28 percent in 1801 to 32 percent in 1851, as compared with the traditional, often southern, metropolitan and mercantile centers, whose share of the total urban population fell from 62 percent to 41 percent. Calculated from information in Adna Weber, *The Growth of Cities in the Nineteenth Century* (New York, 1899), 43.

[51] For the relationship between urbanism, capitalism, and modern society see Friedrich Engels, *The Condition of the Working Class in England* (Moscow, 1973); and Lewis Mumford, *The Culture of Cities* (New York, 1938); and his later *The City in History* (New York, 1961). Other key contributions are R. E. Park, E. W. Burgess, and R. D. McKenzie, *The City* (Chicago, 1925); Louis Wirth, *On Cities and Social Life* (Chicago, 1964); Ferdinand Toennies, *Community and Society* (Ann Arbor, 1957); Georg Simmel, *On Individuality and Social Forms* (Chicago, 1971); and Manuel Castells, *The Urban Question: A Marxist Approach* (Cambridge, Mass., 1977). For the general history of urbanization in modern Britain see Peter Clark, ed., *The Early Modern Town* (New York, 1976); P. J. Corfield, *The Impact of English Towns, 1700–1800* (Oxford, 1982); C. W. Chalklin, *The Provincial Towns of Georgian England* (Montreal, 1974); P. J. Waller, *Town, City, and Nation, England, 1850–1914* (New York, 1983); Asa Briggs, *Victorian Cities* (New York, 1963); and M. Wolff and H. J. Dyos, eds., *The Victorian City: Image and Reality*, 2 vols. (London, 1973).

of their critical position in capitalist production, became, in the words of Harold Perkin, "the ideal citizen[s] of the middle class."[52] In a manner quite similar to Thompson's class-conscious activists and very different from that of the traditional preindustrial burghers, these new industrial entrepreneurs found themselves strategically placed to stake out a distinctively bourgeois ideological standpoint that could be embraced with greater or lesser enthusiasm by other sections of the bourgeoisie.

Often Dissenters in religion and radical liberals in politics, as well as upstarts in economic terms, these parvenu, provincial, entrepreneurial capitalists were largely excluded both locally and nationally from the networks of economic privilege and political authority that were monopolized by the established Anglican Tory elites. Like their medieval and early modern historical predecessors, these entrepreneurs resented the aristocratic oligarchy that shut them out. But unlike previous parvenus who had been content merely to join or supplant the old establishment, these new industrial capitalists initiated reform movements to abolish every economic monopoly and to end the reign of oligarchic privilege for good. Overlaid upon the movement of entrepreneurial burghers for control of their cities was now, for the first time, the national movement of a capitalist bourgeoisie for hegemony in society at large.[53]

As agents of the urban-industrial capitalist transformation, it was only natural that these men should seek to universalize throughout the whole of society the logic of competitive individualism by which they had risen up. Convinced that their own self-interest was synonymous with that of the larger community, they invoked the new enlightenment ideology of science and reason along with the older truths of religion to demonstrate that their own social vision based on freedom in the marketplace was intellectually, morally, economically, and politically superior to the corrupt and irrational system of aristocratic domination and monopolist control. It was, they argued, in the interests of all people to join them in their attack on the establishment and to legitimate their own claims to power.

Thus the liberal struggle against aristocratic anachronism was portrayed not as the industrial capitalists' special interest, but as the cause of every productive citizen who would naturally rally to the cause of progress by eliminating the artificial fetters that had hitherto kept them down. If industrial entrepreneurs were the natural leaders of this insurgency, it was not in their

---

[52] Perkin, *Modern English Society*, 221.

[53] Derek Fraser, *Urban Politics in Victorian England* (Leicester, 1976); idem, *Power and Authority in the Victorian City* (Oxford, 1979). For some relevant local studies see E. P. Hennock, *Fit and Proper Persons* (London, 1973); Conrad Gill, *History of Birmingham*, vol. 1 (Oxford, 1952); A. Redford, *The History of Local Government in Manchester* (London, 1939); A. T. Patterson, *Radical Leicester* (Leicester, 1954); and Foster, *Class Struggles*.

limited capacity as a class or class fraction, but because, as the agents of the
capitalist productive revolution, the logic of their particular social position
forced them to act as the representatives of the people at large. "A determinate class," to make the point in Marx's language – a particular section
of civil society – was now, for the first time in history, seeking "from its
particular situation," to find not merely its own emancipation, but "a general
emancipation of society as a whole."[54] Perhaps in our own enduring image
of the nineteenth century as a bourgeois society without a bourgeoisie, we
can read a measure of its success.

Of course, as several recent historians remind us, it is a great mistake
simply to conflate the experience of nineteenth-century Britain with that of
its industrial entrepreneurs. The social formation of midcentury Britain,
though closer to the abstract industrial capitalist paradigm than that which
prevailed in contemporary France, left industrial entrepreneurs a distinct
minority even within their own class. Notwithstanding their economic significance, they continued to be overshadowed in terms of wealth not only
by the landed aristocracy, but by the London-based commercial elites who
benefited from the growth of industry although they operated outside the
industrial sphere.[55] It is, therefore, not surprising that those great political
moments like the 1832 Reform Act or the 1846 Corn Law repeal, once
taken as hallmarks of bourgeois supremacy, were, in fact, more ambiguous
triumphs that left large portions of the Old Regime substantially intact.[56]
But perhaps the New Regime was not so urgently required if, as became
increasingly evident after 1850, the Old Regime was willing to govern in its
name. Bourgeois aspirations toward hegemony would not be abandoned, but
bourgeois liberals did not need to elevate a new clique of rulers before they
had completely built the new society to be ruled.

In this sense, the nineteenth-century bourgeoisie's real failure was not
the incompleteness of its demolition of aristocratic dominance, but its inability, at least before midcentury, fully to secure the new urban-industrial
capitalist environment, which its own economic initiative had done so much
to create; for as Marx and many others have noted, the idea that bourgeois
entrepreneurs would automatically emancipate society in the act of eman-
cipating themselves was a myth fostered by the illusion that the conditions
of the capitalist could be extended to all inhabitants of his world. Turning
an eye to the workers for whom the reign of free-market competition brought,
not achievement and self-reliance, but poverty and dispossession, Marx

---

[54] Karl Marx, *Contribution to a Critique of Hegel's Philosophy of Right* (Cambridge, 1970),
139–40. See also Lukacs, *History and Class Consciousness*, 62–8.

[55] Rubenstein, "Wealth, Elites, and Class Structure."

[56] Norman Gash, *Politics in the Age of Peel* (New York, 1971).

noted that within "the self-same relations in which there is a development of the productive forces, there is also a force producing repression."[57]

Looking at the environmental impact of urbanization within the framework of industrial capitalism, Tocqueville noted the same dual dynamic at work. "Here humanity attains its most complete development and its most brutish; here civilization works its miracles and civilized man is turned back almost into a savage."[58] The same urban-industrial revolution that created the world's first fully capitalist bourgeoisie also created that class of proletarianized workers about whom Thompson so eloquently wrote. Rejecting the liberal entrepreneurial vision of a fully competitive individualist world, they drew on the preindustrial plebeian culture of community to create, in response to capitalist exploitation, an alternative collectivist vision of their own.

It is this double-edged dynamic of class formation, focusing on the dialectical interaction of an industrial proletariat and bourgeoisie simultaneously in formation, that constitutes the subject of this book. The problem is tackled through a detailed examination of the evolution of social group relations in Bradford, one of the most important early industrial textile cities, which, by 1850, had become the international center of the worsted trade. With a population of 100,000 and an immediate hinterland at least as large, Bradford then stood as the core of a distinctive economic region, the West Yorkshire worsted district, which was one of the nation's most important industrial areas and, after Lancashire cottons, the second most dynamic sector within the textile trade.[59] Like better known and more exhaustively researched urban-industrial centers such as Manchester, Leeds, and Birmingham, Bradford was large enough and important enough to be a major center of economic, social, and political activity. Unlike them, however, it was not so large and unwieldy as to preclude comprehensive investigation by a historian working alone.

Even so, a single city, however significant, may seem an inadequate framework in which to locate an abstract social identity like class. Yet if class consciousness is, by definition, universalistic, seeking to interpret and trans-

---

[57] Karl Marx, *The Poverty of Philosophy* (New York, 1963), 122–3.

[58] Alexis de Tocqueville, *Journeys to England and Ireland* (New Haven, Conn., 1958), 107–8.

[59] J. G. Jenkins, ed., *The Wool Textile Industry in Great Britain* (London, 1972). According to Donald McCloskey, "The Industrial Revolution: A Survey," in D. M. McCloskey and R. C. Floud, eds., *The Economic History of Britain Since 1700* (Cambridge, 1981), 1: 114, between 1780 and 1850 the worsted industry experienced a 1.8 percent average annual rate of increase in productivity – a rate exceeded only by the cotton and shipping industries.

form the world, its formation, as Thompson reminds us, is a concrete historical process that evolves within the life of an actual human community,
generating its wider social solidarities out of common experiences that can
be felt on a more immediate and comprehensible plane. Here, at the level
of direct human experience, where his subjects themselves acted and lived,
the historian can trace the precise interconnections between the objective
social and economic circumstances in which they found themselves and the
cultural and ideological responses that they made. Here, the ideal of "total
history," which, when elevated to the highest level of generality, easily degenerates into truism and vacuity, can be realized through a precise empirical
reconstruction, within a specific community, of the complex and constantly
interrelated forces of economic, social, and political change.

Hence, beyond the methodological constraints of the historian, the most
powerful justification for focusing the analysis of class formation on a single
city comes from the character and consciousness of our subjects themselves;
for in the nineteenth century, the individual city was the locus of its inhabitants' economic and social identity to a degree that, today, we too easily
forget. Living as we do in an age of fully triumphant capitalism, inescapable
in penetration and limitless in scope, we have grown accustomed to a much
more sprawling, formless, and undifferentiated urban pattern, underwritten
by the technology of electrification, mass communication, and the auto-
mobile. Here, urbanization engulfs the entire society and the very distinction
between town and country fades into oblivion as well-defined individual
communities almost cease to exist. However, in the nineteenth century, with
its uneven pattern of economic development, when industrial capitalism
penetrated unequally into different productive spheres, urbanization was
discontinuous and intermittent as the prevailing technology of the steam
engine and the railroad tended to reinforce, and even intensify, the preindustrial pattern that concentrated urban populations and specific industries
in well-defined cities and towns.[60]

It was, as Asa Briggs reminds us, "an age of great cities," when Manchester, Birmingham, London, or Chicago could shock the world with their novel
problems and possibilities that seemed to make each one successively the
symbol of an age.[61] Certainly, the Victorians saw their cities not as arbitrary
geographical constructs but as living organisms whose development was
inextricably bound up with their own. Even the openness of the newest of

[60] Briggs, *Victorian Cities*, 13–9; Castells, *The Urban Question*.

[61] No doubt, Briggs, *Victorian Cities*, 59, goes too far when he proposes to write the urban
history of nineteenth-century Britain through collected biographies of several separate
towns, but his error is less than that of John Foster, who assumes that in a capitalist
society, the individual city "is never more than an arbitrary bite out of a larger political
system." *Class Struggles*, 3.

these cities, the very thinness of their historical roots, could foster a sense of identity among inhabitants many of whom were immigrants, mobile and ambitious people with a common eagerness to get ahead. But tradition, whether real or invented, duly exerted its hallowing effect, giving people whose lives were often extraordinarily disrupted a sense of place to which they could belong.[62]

Here, the persistence of the medieval system of borough political organization well into the urban-industrial age provided a ready-made civic focus for nineteenth-century urbanites in whom the mentality of the traditional burgher had not yet been entirely effaced.[63] In these nineteenth-century cities, national and municipal politics were as inseparable as the two sides of a coin. The bourgeois parvenu who demanded reform of Parliament was not likely to ignore the local oligarchy that ruled his own town. It was a long experience of rooting out local restrictions, monopolies, and apprenticeship regulations that often conditioned his assault on national monopoly when he demanded repeal of the agrarian Corn Laws. Disestablishment of the church was, by definition, a national issue, but long before it was put on the parliamentary agenda, it had been fought out in urban vestries all over England and Wales. Here we see the struggle for free trade in religion, in politics, and, of course, in commodities being elevated from a series of unrelated grievances into an abstract ideology of universal liberty by a concrete historical process in which its particular manifestations are explored simultaneously at every level and in every sphere.

Convincing workers to share in this liberal vision of a voluntary urban community based on bourgeois principles of competitive individualism was, of course, a much more difficult task. As we have already noted, theirs was a very different and much more alienating experience of urban-industrial capitalism. Indeed, the locus of class struggle was much less likely to appear to them in a civic assault on political oligarchy than in resistance to the economic exploitation inherent in the wage–labor relationship itself. As Engels powerfully demonstrated in his *Condition of the English Working Class*, urbanization, so far from offering workers a new focus of identity, merely reproduced, in the form of environmental squalor, the degradation that had first affected them in their relationship to work.[64] Consequently, the new forms of community that they created in the capitalist city tended to be very

---

[62] E. J. Hobsbawm and T. Ranger, eds., *The Invention of Tradition* (Cambridge, 1983).

[63] John Vincent, no doubt, exaggerates when he argues that "elections considered as national politics were frivolous and primitive, considered as local politics serious and rational," but he is not far wrong in detecting about the Victorian urban borough more than a whiff of the ancient Greek city-state. *The Formation of the British Liberal Party* (New York, 1966), xxix.

[64] Engels, *Condition of the Working Class in England*.

different from those characteristic of the bourgeoisie, centering on the slum neighborhood, the beershop, the trade union, and the mass meeting much more than on the chapel, the exchange, or the municipal town hall.

And yet the tenacity of the popular culture of self-help and respectability, on which Thompson's critics are prone to dwell, shows that the workers' urban-industrial reality was even more complex. Although by no means necessarily bourgeois in character and often reinforcing workers' desire for independence as a class, this cultural strain of worker respectability clearly did succeed, especially after the economic improvement and stabilization of social relationships at midcentury, in bringing a substantial section of urban workers within bourgeois liberalism's conceptual frame.

In this book we will trace the origins of this mid-Victorian liberal consensus in the experience of class conflict during the early Victorian age, for it is argued that the 1830s and 40s constituted a period of crisis in the history of class relations when both entrepreneurial bourgeoisie and dispossessed proletariat were forced, in the crucible of conflict, to perceive more realistically both the limits and possibilities of the urban-industrial capitalist environment that they shared. Coming face to face with its strength and resiliency as a social and economic system, workers learned, not only the apparent futility of trying to destroy capitalism outright, but also the potential benefits that might accrue to them even as wage earners if they learned to play by its rules.[65]

Conversely, bourgeois liberals were forced to acknowledge the necessity of actually creating the conditions of freedom and progress that their ideology had hitherto abstractly espoused. Here it was necessary to sort out those elements of competitive capitalism that were necessary for the functioning of the system from those that might be modified or completely transformed. In particular, it will be argued, once the distinction between industrial exploitation and environmental dysfunction was made, it became possible to consider ways of cushioning the former by alleviating the latter and reconstituting the liberal political cause of civic liberalization by linking it to a program of urban social reform.

In tracing this relational dynamic of class formation, Bradford is not presented as a typical case. Even if such a thing existed, the town's value, for our purposes, lies in its very uniqueness as the fastest-growing city in

---

[65] Hobsbawm, *Labouring Men*, 405–36; Harrison, *Peaceable Kingdom*, 123–56; R. Harrison, *Before the Socialists: Studies in Labour and Politics, 1861–1881* (London, 1965), 78–136; Asa Briggs, *Victorian People* (Chicago, 1955), 168–231; S. Pollard, "Nineteenth Century Co-operation: From Community Building to Shopkeeping," in *Essays in Labour History* 74–112; Trygve Tholfsen, *Working Class Radicalism in Mid-Victorian England* (London, 1976); idem, "The Transition to Democracy in Victorian England," *International Review of Social History*, 6 (1961).

early-nineteenth-century England and the center of its second most dynamic export industry. Here within this well-defined local setting, the forces of industrial-capitalist transformation were unusually powerful, whereas the inertia of traditional economic forms was particularly weak. The result was the local emergence of a social formation in which the classes actually encountered in empirical investigation, although by no means necessarily fated to the destiny which Marx predicted, were, in their actual social composition, remarkably close to those abstractly posited in his theoretical works.

Here the traditional urban oligarchy, itself composed mainly of established industrialists or their descendants, mounted an Anglican Tory defense of privilege that proved remarkably inconsistent and weak. Increasingly out of step with the urban-industrial environment, it was swamped both economically and demographically by a new generation of liberal entrepreneurial insurgents who stood on competitive capitalism's cutting edge. Achieving within midcentury Bradford the undisputed social and political ascendancy that still eluded them on the national plane, these new elites saw their triumph suddenly crumble into disaster as the urban-industrial environment that they had taken to be a realm of freedom and progress was rent with economic crisis, environmental disaster, and class conflicts with the workers far more violent and debilitating than in other places where the march of progress had been less swift. But this intense experience of social dysfunction and confrontation only threw the need for reconciliation and restabilization equally sharply into relief. Hence, during the 1840s, even before the economic crisis had been resolved, new political forms and social relations were being developed, which, in retrospect, can be seen as the precursors of those that would become dominant in the mid-Victorian age.

In sum, the history of Bradford represents an extreme case of developments that were transforming the entire nation. Examining them in sharp focus through the narrowing lens of Bradford may help to suggest the broad parameters within which the wider transformation took place. No doubt those who are preoccupied with typicality will point out that, in other parts of nineteenth-century Britain, class formation was a much hazier process in which conflicts were less virulent and continuities were more pronounced. All this is entirely true. But every place is, in its own way, atypical, and if we reduce complex historical processes to their lowest common denominator – to that which every instance of them reveals – we will not be left with much worth writing about.

Amidst a wealth of recent scholarship and journalism that argues for the incompleteness of Britain's industrial-capitalist revolution, the default of its legacy of bourgeois liberalism, and the gentrification of its industrial bourgeoisie, it is salutary to focus on a case like Bradford where industrial capitalism triumphed unconditionally, and the failure of bourgeois liberalism can only be attributed to the very embarrassments and extremities of its success. From this perspective, the subsequent bankruptcy of late-nineteenth- and twentieth-century bourgeois liberalism (insofar as this has actually taken place) begins to seem less attributable to the survival of preindustrial atavisms, than to the appearance of internal contradictions inherent within the original bourgeois liberal project. As they worked themselves out in urban-industrial settings like Bradford, these contradictions manifested themselves in the form of class conflicts – between capitalists (and those who joined them in defense of private property) and the workers by whose labor this property was produced.

Of course, class and class conflict are not the only significant forces at work in an industrial capitalist society and it would be an error to exaggerate their historical role. But this is not a serious danger in a field like British history, which characteristically presents itself as a record of continuities, built on the foundations of an enduring national consensus that has repeatedly averted sharp breaks and destructive social conflicts by a gadualist, evolutionary accommodation to change. For generations, British historians have gloried (and occasionally despaired) in what Elie Halévy, one of the most distinguished among them, once called, with some justice, "the miracle of modern England, anarchist but orderly," which made possible an experience of "extraordinary stablility...through a period of revolutions and crises."[66]

By highlighting the extremity of these "revolutions and crises," the history of an advanced industrial city like Bradford affords a partial, but indispensable, laboratory for exploring the dynamics of class conflict and division that is obscured by the reification of "extraordinary stability" but that constitutes, this book argues, the historical foundation on which the real process of stabilization was built. Here, in the crucible of extreme social crisis we are enabled to penetrate the finished facts of consensus to see their true origins in a painful dialectic of struggle and change. Here, class conflict, precisely because it was so traumatic and disruptive, also proved in the end to be historically creative, opening the way for new reformist stabiliy to the larger industrial capitalist society of which nineteenth-century Bradford was an early prototype.

[66] Elie Halévy, *England in 1815* (London, 1949), 387. See also Gareth Stedman Jones, "History; The Poverty of Empiricism," in Robin Blackburn, ed., *Ideology in Social Science* (Glasgow, 1972) 96–115; Clark, *Victorian England*, 11, 275–89; Burn, *Age of Equipoise*, 15–52.

PART I

From traditional community to industrial city: Bradford: 1750–1850

1

Protoindustrialization in Bradford: 1750–1810

Before the middle of the eighteenth century, Bradford was a small market town of about four thousand inhabitants whose main function was to serve the simple economic and cultural needs of two or three dozen isolated farming and weaving villages that nestled among the surrounding Pennine foothills. Its location at the junction of three valleys had long made it a natural center of religious, social, and market activity for the entire area, although the pull of Leeds, Wakefield, and Halifax could be felt on the margins. Unlike these larger, more cosmopolitan commercial centers however, traditional Bradford remained geographically and socially rooted in its immediate hinterland.[1]

For physical as well as historical reasons, the hills between Airedale and the Lancashire border had always formed a distinctive region. Set off on three sides from the more accessible lowlands of Lancashire, South Yorkshire, and the Vale of York, Bradford-dale, with its rugged topography and often uninviting climate was relatively cut off from strong outside links. The landscape of the region set its tone: craggy outcroppings of millstone grit, flagstone, and sandstone; dark rising woodlands and narrow fields; drab moorland plateaus; and cold, windy mists that descended from the dank highlands. All these features created an aura of beleaguered inhospitality and fostered an atmosphere of elemental struggle for survival requiring adaptability and hard work. Even the mythical Yorkshire character, with its rough-edged, blunt reserve and its quiet ingenuity, might have been hewn out of the local landscape.[2]

It is, however, as an economic unit that the region stands out most plainly. Here the characteristically poor soils and wet climate, especially in the high-

---

[1] C. Richardson, *A Geography of Bradford* (Bradford, 1976), 48–51; J. N. Dickons and R. Poole, *Kirkgate Chapel Souveneir* (Bradford, 1911), 47; John James, *History and Topography of Bradford* (Bradford, 1841), 1–20.

[2] Gary Firth, "The Genesis of the Industrial Revolution in Bradford," (Bradford, Ph.D. dissertation, 1975), 1–6; Edward Baines, *Yorkshire Past and Present*, vol. 1. (London, 1875); William Scruton, *Old Bradford Views* (Bradford, 1897); Emily Brontë, *Wuthering Heights* (New York, 1959); Richardson, *Geography*, 1–46.

land areas, necessitated a dispersed pattern of settlement with a low level of population density and a heavily pastoral, fundamentally subsistence type of agriculture that made early modern Bradford-dale very different from other parts of England at the time. In particular, there was little evidence locally of the highly organized and profitable system of agricultural capitalism, which was increasingly dividing rural society in southern England into three classes – landlords, capitalist farmers, and wage laborers.[3]

Climatic conditions made wheat cultivation virtually impossible. Geography, the physical difficulties of transport, and the limited size of local markets all diminished the prospects for cash cropping of any other type. Even dairying, gardening, and animal grazing tended to remain essentially on a subsistence level. With agriculture dispersed and, at best, marginally profitable, the large gentry and capitalist farmers, so ubiquitous in the South, were less numerous and dominant. There were one or two dozen large landowners in the area, particularly in the south and west. However, within Bradford proper and throughout much of its hinterland, arable or semiarable land was dispersed in small owner-occupier freeholds or copyholds, almost all of which were under fifty acres, many as small as five or six. A study of probate inventories from nearby Keighley between 1689 and 1710 shows that the average value of farm goods and equipment was £49 as compared with £119 in the Yorkshire wolds. In Keighley, 93 percent of the farmers died with agricultural goods worth less than £100.[4]

Given the small size of individual farmsteads, mostly clustered together in villages or strung out along the valleys, it was the vast highland tracts of desolate wasteland, as much as individual plots, that enabled the region's inhabitants to survive. Largely unenclosed before the late eighteenth century and used in common by villagers of all types, these open lands played an essential part in the traditional cottage economy, not only affording a source of fuel and an extra cushion of subsistence, but permitting the development of a fairly extensive cattle and sheep husbandry, which helped to compensate for the poverty of the arable soils.[5]

Paradoxically, it was the very backwardness of agriculture in Bradford-dale that set the stage for more complex economic forms to emerge. The availability of land for sheep grazing and the smallholders' unfulfilled subsistence needs encouraged sideline involvement not only in woolgrowing and marketing, but increasingly in cottage textile manufacturing too. In the ex-

[3] Firth, "Genesis," 2–4.
[4] Arthur Young, *A Six Month Tour of the North of England*, vol. 1 (London, 1771); R. Brown, *General View of the Agriculture of the West Riding* (Edinburgh, 1799), 7, 8, 16; ibid., 73; M. L. Baumber, *A Pennine Community on the Eve of the Industrial Revolution: Keighley and Haworth between 1660 and 1740* (Keighley, 1977), 24.
[5] Firth, "Genesis," 37–47.

pansive climate of the sixteenth century, this local woolen-spinning and weaving domestic industry proliferated as market opportunities grew. However, during the seventeenth century, when trade contracted with the onset of depression, depopulation, epidemic, and war, the indigenous cottage manufactures began to stagnate.[6]

The economic crises characteristic of this era seemed to set limits beyond which a traditional cottage industry could not go. Probate inventories from Bradford in the 1610s show that, even among established yeoman-clothiers, cattle and farm implements continued to constitute at least half of real goods. More often forced into a sideline of household manufacturing than attracted by real prospects of enrichment and gain, the small farmer-weavers and clothiers of this period were only marginally integrated into the marketplace and remained essentially isolated in a backward economy that gave little indication of great transformations ahead.[7]

The process of protoindustrialization

Between 1700 and 1750, however, all this suddenly began to change. By 1810, Bradford had become a major textile manufacturing center on the verge of a full-scale urban-industrial revolution that would, forty years later, have transformed it into the international center of the worsted trade. The onset of this initial protoindustrial stage of development during the first half of the eighteenth century was inextricably connected with the abandonment of traditional short-staple woolen cloth manufacture in Bradford-dale and the redirection of the indigenous cottage industry toward the production of a new type of long-staple worsted stuff good.[8]

Although worsted products were not unknown during the Middle Ages, the industry really began in the second half of the sixteenth century when

[6] Herbert Heaton, *The Yorkshire Woolens and Worsted Industries* (Oxford, 1920), 45–215.

[7] W. B. Crump, "The Yeoman Clothier of the Seventeenth Century: His Home and Loom Shop," *BA*, 5 (1933), 217–39.

[8] John James, *History of the Worsted Manufacture in England* (London, 1857), 199–331. In this book, the term "protoindustrial" is used to refer to that stage of socioeconomic development in Bradford during which capitalist wage–labor relations were first organized through the putting-out system and coexisted with what remained, in key respects, a traditional, essentially preindustrial social framework characterized by domestic, handicraft modes of production and a semirural ecology of village life. My use of the term follows that of F. F. Mendels, "Proto-industrialization, the First Phase of the Industrialization Process," *Journal of Economic History*, 32 (1972), who first coined it, and that of Peter Kreidte, Hans Medick, and Jurgen Schlumbohm, *Industrialization before Industrialization, Rural Industry in the Genesis of Capitalism* (Cambridge, 1981), which refines and expands Mendels's original ideas.

about 1,200 Dutch weavers and their families fleeing Catholic persecution settled in Norwich and introduced their "new draperies," which quickly revived the economic fortunes of that town. Because they were more sophisticated, more versatile, and in many instances less expensive than traditional fabrics of linen, silk, or wool, these new worsted draperies became immensely popular among the growing class of consumers who sought items more fashionable than crude peasant fustians but more affordable than the choicest luxury cloths. As a result, throughout the seventeenth century, even during depressions when overall trade levels fell, the worsted trade was generally able to retain its prosperity by progressively increasing its market share.[9]

By 1700, the expansion of British worsteds had made Norwich the second largest city in England and continued to underwrite its prosperity for the next hundred years. Nevertheless, as manufacturing developed in East Anglia, all the main processes outside of spinning became highly organized in restrictive corporatist guilds. As a result, East Anglian industry was far from maximizing cost efficiencies and became increasingly dependent on the effective monopoly of domestic markets that protectionist legislation enabled it to maintain.[10] Hence, it became increasingly apparent to aggressive clothiers and woolstaplers in Yorkshire that, notwithstanding their distance from both the appropriate fleeces and major centers of textile demand, the presence in their region of cheap cottage labor created opportunities for worsted production, particularly in the plainer, low-priced products that were destined for the emerging, unsophisticated but highly volatile markets of America and the southern European fringe.[11]

Nevertheless, this proliferation of worsted manufacturing in the West Riding remained concentrated during the eighteenth century in the poorer highland backwaters, especially in the regions surrounding Bradford and Halifax. In the older, arable lowland cloth districts, the local economy expanded more modestly entirely through a revival of the older woolen trade.[12] Here protoindustrial development not only occurred much more slowly, but as Patricia Hudson and others have persuasively argued, was unaccompanied

[9] James, *Worsted Manufacture*, 104–98.

[10] James, *Worsted Manufacture*, 199–258; P. Corfield, "A Provincial Capital in the Late Seventeenth Century: The Case of Norwich," in Peter Clark, ed., *The Early Modern Town* (London, 1976) 223–72.

[11] James, *Worsted Manufacture*, 199–202, 227–30, 254–7; Heaton, *Yorkshire Woolens*, 264–87.

[12] Pat Hudson, "Proto-industrialization; The Case of the West Riding Wool Textile Industry in the Eighteenth and Early Nineteenth Centuries," *History Workshop*, 12 (1981); idem, "From Manor to Mill: The West Riding in Transition" in Maxine Berg, Pat Hudson, and Michael Sonenscher, eds., *Town and Country before the Factory* (Cambridge, 1983), 124–44.

by the striking changes in social structure that worsted-based protoindustrialization in Bradford was to bring, for woolen production, even as its volume expanded, remained generally small scale and decentralized. The 1,200 individual yeoman-clothiers who gathered at the Leeds Cloth Hall on market day operated largely from a domestic base. Often financing the purchase of tools and raw materials by mortgaging their landholdings, which remained the focus of their economic life, these small clothiers worked at home where they drew on the labor of their wives and children, perhaps supplemented by a hired journeyman and an apprentice or two. Although the practice of putting out surplus work to poorer neighbors was not uncommon, it tended to be arranged on an ad hoc, personalized basis. Rarely did it evolve into full-time wage labor on the part of cottagers who still aspired to the status of independent producers and who generally continued to own their own equipment and looms.[13]

By contrast, the more dynamic worsted protoindustry that emerged in the Bradford–Halifax up-country was organized much more capitalistically from the start. Because worsteds were produced for foreign markets and required long staple wools that could not be locally grown, they could be manufactured and marketed on a competitive footing only through the agency of complex, stratified forms of economic organization that would seem ill-suited to the simple egalitarian society of small producers that, throughout the West Riding, had traditionally prevailed.[14]

Seen in this light, the salient question is not why the worsted industry failed to catch on in the lowland districts but why the up-country inhabitants of Bradford-dale ever took it up. The answer, insofar as the evidence permits one, seems to be that these highland villagers abandoned the more stable, small-scale, indigenous woolen industry because of their increasing inability to gain a subsistence from the soil.[15] As we have seen, the infertility of highland agriculture had always constrained local living standards and imposed a fragile equilibrium between population and resources. In the late Middle Ages, pastoralism, together with cottage spinning and weaving, had raised the threshold of subsistence. Since then, generations of low fertility and high mortality together with periodic bursts of waste reclamation had enabled economic viability to be maintained. Even the long-standing practice of partible inheritance could prevail amidst this balance of demographic limitation with snail's-pace growth. However, during the expansive epi-

[13] Heaton, *Yorkshire Woolens*, 285–7; Hudson, "Proto-industrialization"; R. G. Wilson, *Gentleman Merchants: The Merchant Community in Leeds, 1700–1830* (Manchester, 1971), 53–89; R. M. Hartwell, "The Yorkshire Woolen and Worsted Industry, 1800–1850," (Oxford, D. Phil. dissertation, 1955), 292–5.

[14] Hudson, "Proto-industrialization." James, *Worsted Manufacture*, 199–203; 267–8.

[15] Hudson, "Proto-industrialization."

demic-free decades after 1700, the ecological limits of this system were reached, and the size of individual landholdings began to shrink. Whereas the average value of agricultural holdings in Keighley had been £49 between 1689 and 1710, during the 1731–50 period it fell to £36.[16]

It is within the context of these diminishing prospects for economic independence that the rise of worsted protoindustrialization in Bradford-dale must be set. Increasingly unable to eke out a living from agriculture, inhabitants embraced this more intensive, market-driven form of textile production that, for all its greater volatility and tendency to reduce them to the status of wage laborers, did promise an alternate means of support for families who could no longer sustain themselves from the soil. Conversely, a new, aggressive breed of clothier emerged. Although the capital resources necessary for initial entry into worsted production and marketing was beyond the individual means of such men, the presence of a few wealthy woolstaplers who were prepared to help finance their activity through the provision of credit on the sale of raw wool made it possible, as Dr. Hudson has demonstrated, for local clothiers to initiate putting-out operations on a shoestring.[17]

Those who were able to navigate the complexities of these uncharted waters and to maximize the opportunities for radically reducing production costs, could, at least so long as export markets remained buoyant, not only repay creditors out of inflated profits, but accumulate a healthy surplus and expand. M. T. Dickinson's study of Yorkshire clothier probate inventories shows that, even in the 1720–60 period, the average value of movable property of those involved in the worsted trade was twice that of those in the woolen trade at time of death.[18]

Indeed, the success of the new worsted protoindustry and of those who profited from it became the single most important factor in the further evolution of the social structure on which it thrived. Increasing economic dependence on textiles made possible a further subdivision of plots, opening the way after 1750 for a demographic upsurge throughout the West Riding that preceded its national counterpart by thirty years. Between 1750 and

[16] Baumber, *Pennine Community*, 34.
[17] The critical role of credit in capital formation has been treated exhaustively by Pat Hudson in "The Genesis of Industrial Capital in the West Riding Wool Textile Industry, c. 1770–1850," (York, D. Phil. dissertation, 1981), especially 224–67, 331–72, and 394–425. This dissertation has subsequently been published in slightly revised form as *The Genesis of Industrial Capital* (Cambridge, 1986).
[18] Hudson, "Industrial Capital," 63–84.

1780, when the average annual rate of natural increase for England and Wales was 0.75 percent, in the West Riding it shot up by 1.7 percent on average annually, doubling the regional population in the space of fifty years.[19]

There is now a widespread consensus among demographers that the bulk of this dramatic increase was caused by rising fertility, with declining mortality through improved health and sanitation playing, at most, a contributory role.[20] In truth, the very structure of worsted protoindustry created powerful incentives to reverse traditional strategies of late marriage and small families and to produce offspring at an unprecedented rate. Because it required four spinners to produce enough yarn for a single weaver, and eighteen weavers and spinners to process one comber's output of raw wool, families that sought to maximize their efficiency as productive units would place a premium on large numbers of children to undertake the tedious, low-paid, and extremely labor-intensive spinning work.[21]

Of course, large families with numerous offspring only intensified cottagers' dependence on wage labor in textiles as it resulted in a further subdivision of plots. By 1793, Robert Brown reported that textile producers locally had "little if any pretensions to the character of farmers." Even among manufacturers, "a homestead, a sufficient quantity of meadow and of pasture for the support of a horse and cow, with now and then a corn-field form, with few exceptions, the extent of their speculations into agriculture." By 1811, census figures indicated an average density of 1.6 persons per acre throughout Bradford's rural hinterland, which suggests that most villagers now had access to little more than garden plots.[22]

The deepening dependence of Bradford-dale's inhabitants on domestic industry and wage labor after 1750, itself the product of the protoindustrial dynamic, created an environment in which protoindustrialization was able to expand. By 1772, it was estimated that the Yorkshire worsteds employed 84,000, or about 17,000 families, at least a third of whom would have worked

[19] Phyllis Deane and W. H. Cole, *British Economic Growth, 1688–1955* (Cambridge, 1962), 103.

[20] E. A. Wrigley, "The Growth of Population in Eighteenth Century England: A Conundrum Resolved," *Past and Present*, 98 (1983).

[21] James, *Worsted Manufacture*, 281. The effects of protoindustrialization on plebeian fertility is discussed more generally in David Levine, *Family Formation in an Age of Nascent Capitalism* (New York, 1977); "Production, Reproduction, and the Proletarian Family England, 1500–1850," and Charles Tilly, "Demographic Origins of the European Proletariat," in David Levine, ed., *Proletarianization and Family History*, (Orlando, Fla., 1984); and in Hans Medick, "The Proto-industrial Family Economy," in Kriedte, Medick, and Schlumbohm, *Industrialization before Industrialization*.

[22] PP (1812, XI), 413–4, quoted in Hartwell, "Yorkshire Woolens," 295.

for the 400 clothiers who attended the new Bradford Piece Hall.[23] Favorable as this environment was for the run-of-the-mill worsted clothier whose business prospered, its greatest beneficiaries were the handful of spectacularly successful putting-out capitalists who emerged after 1750, men like John Hustler, Edmund Peckover, George Kellet, Thomas Hardcastle, and James Garnett. Whether woolstaplers who branched out into stuffmaking or clothiers who grew successful enough profitably to procure their own wool, these men generally fused mercantile and manufacturing activities together, speculating in raw material while simultaneously managing their own far-flung networks of hundreds of individual cottage laborers.[24]

Having reached this threshold of development and complexity, the Yorkshire worsted industry, which had begun by supplementing the superior Norwich product lines, began to supplant East Anglia as the worsted capital of the world. Intensely corporatist in organization and orientation, and dependent on the rigidly protected home consumer trade, the Norwich industry found its position deteriorating as the spectacular rise of the Lancashire cotton industry eroded traditional domestic markets, and established urban merchants and artisans found themselves unable to compete with cost-cutting Yorkshire counterparts in the volatile but dynamic arena of foreign demand. By the 1770s, a turning point seems to have been reached as East Anglia's worsteds, valued at £1,200,000, were, for the first time, surpassed by those of Yorkshire, now valued at £1,400,000.[25]

With their privileged trading companies, their genteel urban lifestyles, their costly civic ambitions and extravagant political intrigues, the Norwich mercantile establishment, now in its third or fourth generation, was in no position to compete with these rude first-generation Yorkshire counterparts who possessed an insuperable advantage in having access to a dispersed, unorganized, rural labor force with relatively simple expectations and needs. "Frugal and industrious, sustaining himself and family principally with oatmeal, porridge, oat bread and milk," the Yorkshire cottage worker was sufficiently proletarianized to be dependent on wage labor, but still possessing enough of a subsistence cushion to enable him to work for a substandard wage. By contrast, production in East Anglia was organized on the basis of

[23] W. Cudworth, *Rambles Round Horton* (Bradford, 1886), 32; James, *Worsted Manufacture*, 283–6; Firth, "Genesis," 451.

[24] E. M. Sigsworth, *Black Dyke Mills* (Liverpool, 1958), 11–17; Heaton, *Yorkshire Woolens*, 296–301; PP (1806, III), 8–9; James, *History of Bradford*, 272–5; idem, *Worsted Manufacture*, 297, 323–5; Hartwell, "Yorkshire Woolens," 70–89; Hudson, "Industrial Capital," 232–61.

[25] Heaton, *Yorkshire Woolens*, 275; Sigsworth, *Black Dyke*, 11–17; J. H. Clapham, "The Transference of the Worsted Industry to the West Riding," *Economic Journal*, 20 (1910), 195–6.

a skilled, well-paid urban combing and weaving artisanate that was organized in guildlike corporations that kept up customary wage levels, regulated the labor process, and protected members' relatively comfortable lifestyle.[26]

Because they were contemptuous of the stigma of manual labor, the Norwich merchants not only tolerated these worker organizations, but actually relied on them to manage the details of manufacture that were beneath their own dignity. Viewing production from the vantage of commerce and conceptualizing profit in monopolistic terms, they had always specialized in the provision of a small volume of high-priced goods for a luxury market and showed little concern over the spread of the primary manufacturing processes to the cottage industries of the North.[27] By contrast, the new breed of Yorkshire clothiers were much less trammeled by corporatist traditions and apprenticeship regulations. Consequently, they operated in a far more competitive business environment, which involved them more directly in production from the start. Their ability to organize and control their putting-out operations constituted the only basis on which they could hope to gain a competitive edge. They understood that, under conditions of rapid market expansion, the surest road to profit maximization lay not in maintaining high prices, but in reducing labor costs and shifting the locus of return from the skilled arena of luxury consumption to the primary processes of the plainer commodities that could be produced on a large scale for mass demand.[28]

Hence, the concentration of hitherto dispersed cottage workers within the walls of a factory and the replacement of their hand labor as far as possible by mechanical means and motive power was no more than a logical next step for the Yorkshire capitalists in their general strategy of expanding output by reducing unit cost. Whereas Yorkshire's multitude of fast-flowing streams facilitated the siting of early water-powered factories and enhanced the region's potential to serve as industrial pioneer, it was the West Riding social structure, much more than its climate, that encouraged mechanization.[29]

The laboriousness of hand spinning constituted the most serious bottle-

---

[26] M. F. Pritchard, "Decline of the Norwich Worsted Trade," *Economic History Review*, 3 (1951); James, *Worsted Manufacture*, 208–51; idem, *Continuations and Additions to the History and Topography of Bradford* (Bradford, 1866), 84; Heaton, *Yorkshire Woolens*, 290–3.

[27] Clapham, "Transference"; James, *Worsted Manufacture*, 152–206; J. T. Evans, "The Decline of Oligarchy in Seventeenth Century Norwich," *Journal of British Studies*, 14: 1 (1974).

[28] Karl Marx, *Capital* (Moscow, 1954), 1:294–475; Wade Hustwick, "An Eighteenth Century Woolstapler," *Journal of Bradford Textile Society* (Bradford, 1956–7); F. Atkinson, *Some Aspects of the Eighteenth Century Woolen and Worsted Trade in Halifax* (Halifax, 1956); Heaton, *Yorkshire Woolens*, 311.

[29] Clapham, "Transference."

neck that putting-out capitalists had to face. During the boom of 1782–92, when the cessation of hostilities reopened the American trade, this problem became increasingly serious and large employers had to move farther and farther into the north Yorkshire countryside to find a sufficient complement of cottage spinners to fill markets and to keep their weavers and combers in work.[30] As early as 1784, the first worsted spinning mill was erected, and ten years later at least five others were in operation. Although initially unable to produce the finer threads that continued to be spun by hand, factory spinning spread during the 1790s and 1800s as the difficulties of adapting the technology to the peculiar properties of long wool fibers were resolved. Since all these early factories were dependent on water power, they were all located in the rugged hinterland in close proximity to mountain streams. The first factory in Bradford proper, Robert Ramsbotham's Holme mill, was not built until 1800. By 1815 although the town boasted six mills with a total of 250 h.p., the majority of all spinning mills were still, like the cottage industry, dispersed throughout the rural hinterland.[31]

Indeed, these early spinning mills, so far from undermining the prevailing social structures, opened the way for a vast expansion of domestic combing and weaving, which actually gave the putting-out system of cottage manufacturers a new and intensified lease on life. The mechanization of spinning, traditionally a female and adolescent occupation, did little to break up the traditional family economy although the expansion of other textile handicrafts that opened up new opportunities for adult men did a great deal to intensify and extend its range. It is a remarkable characteristic of protoindustrial development that, even in its final stages, it was not accompanied by any notable degree of urbanization or concentration in the center of towns. To be sure, the population of Bradford Township rose from 4,506 in 1780 to 7,767 in 1811, but the average annual rate of increase that this represents (2.3 percent) was probably less than that for the nearby hinterland (estimated at about 3 percent), where most of the population continued to work and live. Here, surrounded by open fields and garden plots, even the most vulnerable handloom weavers and combers, who had become entirely dependent on wages to survive, continued to work in their own cottages and, with the assistance of their wives and children, raised some of their own food, baked their own bread, and brewed their own beer.[32]

---

[30] As manufacturers became increasingly dependent on distant shopkeepers, agents, and other intermediaries to supervise their spinners, their alarm over losses from embezzlement and faulty work rose. This only increased incentives to adapt Arkwright's water frame to the specifications of worsted yarn. James, *Worsted Manufacture*, 293–7, 306, 311–15, 322–5.

[31] James, *History of Bradford*, 273–5; idem, *Worsted Manufacture*, 327–8; Firth, "Genesis," 402–10.

[32] Ivy Pinchbeck, *Women Workers and the Industrial Revolutions, 1750–1850* (New York,

Only in the second quarter of the nineteenth century, with the spread of mechanization to the remaining worsted processes and their concentration in the steam-powered factories of the urban downtown, was the traditional social and economic organization finally eliminated as the overall mode of production was completely transformed. Although hindsight attests to the significance of the technical innovations that initiated factory production, the introduction of mechanized spinning into the Yorkshire worsted region was, in many ways, an anticlimactic event.[33]

Since most of the early factory owners were already quite wealthy putting-out capitalists and the fixed-capital requirements of textile mills and machinery were, in any case, relatively low, the initial transition to power spinning did not itself make any extraordinary demands on capital formation. In the Bradford area, some of the early mills were valued at under £500 for insurance purposes. In 1800, the average valuation was £1,400 and this rose only to £2,400 ten years later. Before 1815, no worsted mill was worth more than £6,000.[34]

According to Dr. Hudson, machinery was often purchased secondhand, although a new steam engine could be had for £850, excluding millwrights costs. Even as late as 1850, circulating capital still constituted at least two-thirds of production costs in the fully mechanized industry. Since most of the early millowners were already large clothiers and woolstaplers with substantial work forces and assets, early factory building cannot have been much of a strain on resources, especially since initial outlays were likely to be recouped quite rapidly through dramatic increases in volume or even windfall profits, which might temporarily accrue.[35] Thus the initial shift to factory spinning in Yorkshire simply enhanced a developmental trajectory that had been implicit in protoindustrialization from the start. Introducing the logic of capitalism into the farming and weaving villages of the West Riding, the protoindustrial process increasingly bifurcated the community into a small entrepreneurial elite who grew increasingly wealthy and a large majority who found themselves increasingly proletarianized.

Nevertheless, before 1815, this trend toward class bifurcation, indeed,

[32] Ivy Pinchbeck, *Women Workers and the Industrial Revolutions, 1750–1850* (New York, 1969), 129–56; James, *History of Bradford*, 409–11; Heaton, *Yorkshire Woolens*, 290–3; F. M. Eden, *The State of the Poor* (London, 1797), 810–11; Joseph Lawson, *Letters to the Young on Progress in Pudsey*, (Stanningley, 1887), 26–38; PP (1806, III), 9, 447; (1812, XI), 407–26.

[33] Paul Mantoux, *The Industrial Revolution in the Eighteenth Century* (London, 1961), 25–44, 189–270; Phyllis Deane, *The First Industrial Revolution* (Cambridge, 1965); Maxine Berg, *The Age of Manufactures* (London, 1985), 15–55, 198–263; Hudson, "Industrial Capital," 141–65.

[34] Firth, "Genesis," 190–3.

[35] Hudson, "Industrial Capital," 102, 226, 291, 294, 315; Firth, "Genesis," 190–3, 388–405; E. M. Sigsworth, "William Greenwood and Robert Heaton," *Journal of the Bradford Textile Society* (Bradford, 1951–2); PP (1842, IX), 1–33.

the entire dynamic of capitalist development on which it was based, continued to be manifested within a protoindustrial framework, which preserved the traditional household, handicraft mode of production and its concomitant ecology of relatively dispersed communal village life. Moreover, just as this protoindustrial pattern of development did not totally transform the way that ordinary villagers worked and lived, it did not transform the capitalists that it created into a remorselessly competitive, fully entrepreneurial class; for after carving out their place in international worsted markets and leaving their East Anglian rivals in the shade, the Yorkshire capitalists, especially the dozen or so who had grown most wealthy, began to resist the impulses toward profit maximization that they or their parents had initially displayed. Because textiles remained intensely competitive, the search for less risky investment outlets meant that, especially in the decades after 1775, they would absorb a gradually diminishing proportion of the profits that worsted enterprise had generated in the first place.[36]

There are many reasons why, during the late eighteenth century, such a search for alternative investments should have occurred. In the first place, as the original entrepreneurs grew older, retired, or sought to establish their children and make provision for the disposal of their estates, it was considered desirable to divert savings into more passive forms of investment that were more liquid (if potentially less lucrative) than the worsted industry or were acknowledged to be more genteel. Moreover, depression and war during the late 1770s, the mid-1790s, and for nearly a decade after 1802 slowed the expansion of worsted exports, setting limits to the amount of new capital that the trade could absorb. Between 1772 and 1815, the volume of raw wool processed in Yorkshire rose at an annual rate of 1.5 percent per year, a rate far lower than that which had prevailed earlier in the century and less than a tenth of the rate that was achieved between 1815 and 1850, when full-scale industrialization took hold.[37]

At the same time that textiles were beginning to look less desirable to established capitalists, the attraction of investing in local economic improvement grew. As late as 1750, Bradford-dale remained an extremely isolated, mountainous backwater that lacked the transport, communication, and financial infrastructure that would be necessary to sustain modern economic life. A traveler who wished to convey bulky goods to or from town or throughout the region would have to devote considerable money and energy to finding adequate transportation. Even if he succeeded in reaching his destination, the absence of convenient commercial facilities might make it an uncongenial place to conduct business and, if this was not a sufficient discouragement,

---

[36] See Chapter 5.
[37] Calculated from information in James, *Worsted Manufacture*, 284, 370, 376, 513.

then the difficulty of obtaining credit or the insufficiency of local coin or bills of exchange might make it impossible to conclude business at all.[38]

As the volume of Bradford's textile trade increased, these obstacles became increasingly problematic, putting businessmen at a competitive disadvantage and jeopardizing future development of the region. Perhaps the diversion of investments away from the export-oriented textile trade toward transport, land, and commerce delayed the onset of full-scale urban-industrial revolution in Bradford, but without the economic and physical infrastructure that in the late eighteenth and early nineteenth century this created, such a revolution could never have taken place.

Protoindustrialization and regional economic development

Of all the impediments to the overall economic development of the region, transport inadequacies posed the most formidable challenge. As early as 1734, a joint-stock company had been organized locally to carve a series of turnpikes through the rugged topography that separated Bradford, Halifax, and Leeds. During the next twenty years, five other turnpikes were either built or projected to link the town with Huddersfield, Wakefield, Harrogate and Keighley as well as with the villages of its own hinterland.[39]

Although such projects were expensive, they could be turned into profitable businesses by charging user fees. With their promise of 4.5 percent annual dividends, these turnpikes provided highly stable and liquid investment alternatives through which local capitalists could assure themselves a modest income while laying the foundations for wider regional economic growth. Not surprisingly, the common people who could not afford the tolls resented and occasionally rioted against these turnpikes. But clothiers and other businessmen gladly paid for the service of quicker and easier travel, which invariably saved them much more than it cost.[40]

For the transport of heavy goods, however, turnpikes remained inadequate. To deal with this problem a group of local capitalists got together in the 1760s and, with the assistance of some outside investors, financed the construction of a long canal that would cross the Pennines and connect Liverpool with Leeds and the Aire River. The Aire then led to Hull and provided links with the midlands via the Trent. The substantial Bradford woolstapler John Hustler and gentleman investor Abraham Balme were

---

[38] Richardson, *Geography*, 47–60; S. O. Bailey, "Plans of Bradford," *BA* n.s. 2 (1905).

[39] Richardson, *Geography*, 47.

[40] Firth, "Genesis," 209–214.

among the leading promoters of this complex scheme. When they succeeded in getting the larger project underway, they raised another £6,000 from twenty-eight local subscribers to construct a canal extension that would directly connect Bradford with the primary artery. The opening of this canal in 1774 probably did more than any other single development to secure the economic future of the town.[41]

Hustler and Balme were the most substantial of a new generation of shrewd investors who sought opportunities for profit on a broad range of economic fronts. In the course of his lifetime, Balme tried his hand at nearly every economic venture that the region had to offer – from wool, to marriage, to fertilizer, to coal, in that order. Through successive acquisitions of land at each stage, he was able to retire to a country estate. Hustler's activities were even more far-reaching. Despite his commitments to woolstapling and to the canal, he found time and money to help found a lime kiln company and to take the leading role in financing the construction of Bradford's first piece hall in 1773, where clothiers could meet their customers in relative comfort while the quality and price of goods could openly be compared. Hustler was so successful that, by his son's death in 1842, the family had accumulated £250,000.[42]

The growing demand for bills of exchange and commercial credit created an incentive for other wealthy textile traders to go into banking as a sideline. At first this was done on an informal basis, but in 1777, Bradford's first banking partnership was established with a working capital of £3,000. This proved insufficient and the venture went bankrupt. However, in 1803, a new bank was founded by a group of Quakers with assistance from the ubiquitous Hustler estate.[43]

Even agriculture, the most backward sector of the local economy, was partly drawn into the vortex of protoindustrial development. Population increase, in particular, created a more lively demand for dairy products, which were well suited to the small farms that characterized the region. Greater profitability stimulated agricultural improvement, and new enclosures were initiated during the decades after 1770. Between then and 1830, sixteen enclosure acts were passed, involving 14,796 acres within the region, much of it highland waste that was being brought into cultivation for the first time.[44]

Along with this increase in agricultural productivity went the development

[41] Ibid., 196–204; Richardson, *Geography*, 50; Hustwick, "Woolstapler."
[42] James, *History of Bradford*, 155; Hustwick, "Woolstapler"; Sigsworth, *Black Dyke*, 26–9.
[43] Firth, "Genesis," 169–81; Hudson, "Industrial Capital," 451–93; William Cudworth, "The First Bradford Bank," *BA*, n.s. 2, (1905), 231–7; *Bradford Old Bank Ltd. Centenary Souvenir* (Bradford, 1903).
[44] Firth, "Genesis," 37–46; Richardson, *Geography*, 35–9.

of more sophisticated facilities for marketing and distribution. The old weekly medieval market and triennial Bradford Fair were no longer sufficient to meet the needs of a growing population. With his usual business acumen, John Hustler realized that a permanent market would constitute an excellent investment. However, his plans were blocked by Lord of the Manor John Marsden, who held the market rights. However, when Benjamin Rawson purchased the manorial rights in 1795, he opened a biweekly market on New Street and later a daily covered market on Darley Street that still bears his name. Meanwhile, five butchers, twenty grocers, and nineteen shopkeepers had settled in the town, and by 1815, their numbers had approximately doubled.[45]

The local gentry and larger landholders, most of whom lived in the hinterland, had an important role to play both in agricultural improvement and in market development. Bringing their substantial wealth and social prestige to bear on improvements that involved their landed property, they too were able to benefit from protoindustrialization and to fatten their rent-rolls by enhancing the value of their land. Nowhere was this symbiosis between landowners and emergent capitalists more evident than in the development of an iron industry on the region's fringe. Tapping the rich deposits of iron and coal that ran along Bradford-dale's southwestern borders, they created a thriving mining and founding industry that, during the preurban, protoindustrial age, briefly rivaled the worsted trade as the region's most dynamic economic sphere.

Coal and iron mining and founding were initiated in the early eighteenth century by several local landowners, such as Edward Leedes of Rookes Hall and Walter Spencer-Stanhope of Thornton, who had reason to believe that valuable deposits lay underneath their land. However, these men were either unwilling or unable to direct the necessary resources to initiate refining operations, and nothing was accomplished until the 1780s when capitalist investors formed two substantial partnerships.[46] The first of these was the nucleus of what, in 1844, officially became the Bowling Iron Company. Its initial capital of £3,500 was divided into ten shares, eight of which were owned by the Sturgeses, a Wakefield iron-founding family, and one by a Leeds iron merchant, Richard Paley. In 1784, they set up a foundry in Bowling, and in 1788, they began smelting. However, it was not until 1794 that the company found its permanent site.[47]

Meanwhile, in 1789, the Low Moor Iron Company was formed in

[45] Firth, "Genesis," 114–50; William Scruton, *Pen and Pencil Pictures of Old Bradford* (Bradford, 1889), 118–119, 179; *Universal British Directory* (London, 1792).

[46] Firth, "Genesis," 237–69.

[47] Hilary Long, "The Bowling Ironworks," *Industrial Archaeology*, 2 (1968), 171–7; William Cudworth, *Histories of Bolton and Bowling* (Bradford, 1891), 175, 207–8.

North Bierley, just outside of Bowling, when Edward Leedes' estate came on the market after his bankruptcy and suicide. Leedes had been unable to develop the estate's mineral resources but his successor, Rev. Joseph Dawson, was. He formed a partnership to purchase the manor for £33,200 and to establish mines and foundries with two local Anglican capitalists, Richard Hird and John Hardy, together with a few smaller partners who soon sold out.[48] Hardy was a Bradford solicitor who had served as estate steward to Walter Spencer-Stanhope. He learned the arts of entrepreneurial speculation and management while practicing them for his employer, later turning them to his own account, and ultimately founding a far greater dynasty of his own. Directed by Hardy's management skills and Dawson's mineralogical expertise, the Low Moor works grew to an enormous scale, with an annually employed capital increasing from £52,000 in 1793 to £250,000 in 1818. Throughout the nineteenth century they remained in the hands of four families, the Hardys, the Dawsons, the Hirds, by inheritance, and the Wickhams, by marriage to the Hirds. These dynasties, with their wealth and social standing, maintained a quiet presence in nineteenth-century Bradford's urban background, furnishing together no fewer than three of the town's Tory M.P.s.[49]

More directly involved in the development of the town were the partners of the Bowling Company, whose plant lay within the borders of the future borough. In 1796, the company leased ninety acres from Sir Francis Lindley Wood, the owner of the Bowling Hall Manor. The Woods, who were later to become viscounts and then earls of Halifax, were a nationally prominent Yorkshire gentry family. They welcomed the income that mining and smelting brought, and when the estate became too fouled with workings and slag heaps, Sir Charles moved away to Hemsworth Hall in Barnsley.[50]

The Bowling works began by producing household goods, but like Low Moor, their future was assured with the outbreak of war in 1793. Both firms became major armaments contractors, producing large quantities of howitzers, cannons, and shot. By 1804, twenty years after its foundation, the capital value of the Bowling works had increased twenty-four-fold to £85,000.[51] By then, John Sturges, Jr., and J. G. Paley, children of the original partners, had become very active in the management of the enterprise, taking

[48] Charles Dodsworth, "The Low Moor Ironworks," *Industrial Archaeology*, 8:2 (1971), 121–64.

[49] William Cudworth, *Round About Bradford* (Bradford, 1876), 55–65; anon., *Fortunes Made in Business* (London, 1884), 1: 90–128.

[50] Cudworth, *Bolton and Bowling*, 175–80, 207.

[51] Calculated from Firth, "Genesis," 178; Cudworth, *Bolton and Bowling*, 204–11.

on two men who had originally apprenticed with a prominent local solicitor, Thomas Mason, who married Paley's sister-in-law, and Joshua Pollard, a failed worsted spinner who married Sturges's daughter and became works manager.[52]

In the two decades before 1815, then, the iron industry made inroads into the economic dominance of the worsted trade. During the war, which reduced textile exports, iron founding was probably a more profitable investment although its highly capital-intensive plant requirements and substantial economies of scale meant that it could be entered only by those who had a sizable capital to invest. Yet those who could finance an iron foundry or who had engineering skills might find metallurgy the most attractive way of accumulating capital, as is illustrated by the career of Henry Leah.

Leah was a hard-driving shrewd businessman who was reputed to eat his dinner on the job. His efforts paid off, for, although he began his career as chief clerk at the Bowling Ironworks for an annual salary of £150, he died in 1846 with a fortune of £500,000. He soon left the Bowling Company to manage a brewery and later helped to found the Bradford Ironworks and Gasworks Companies. But his biggest coup was in purchasing the small, ailing Bierley Ironworks, which he reorganized and turned into a success. Throughout his career he was involved in land and building speculation in various parts of Bradford, and he erected many of the town center buildings along Piccadilly across from the Wool Exchange. Leah's death, a year before Bradford was incorporated, robbed him of the honor for which he seemed slated – of becoming the new town's first mayor.[53]

The making of a gentleman-capitalist elite

Unlike the mid-nineteenth-century entrepreneurs who would succeed them, Bradford's leading capitalists of the late protoindustrial period were never totally dependent for their profits on the intensely competitive worsted trade. Supplementing and sometimes supplanting textile entrepreneurship with regional development, land speculation, and mining or ironfounding, men like Leah, Pollard, Sturges, Paley, Hardy, and Hustler developed diverse, balanced investment portfolios that enabled them to secure themselves as elites. Indeed, as their behavior indicated, such men never wholly identified with their economic functions as capitalists, but aspired to more detached

---

[52] William Cudworth, *Historical Notes on the Bradford Corporation* (Bradford, 1881), 44. For Hailstone see idem, *Horton*, 58–9; idem, *Bolton and Bowling*, 214, 217–21.

[53] Cudworth, *Bolton and Bowling*, 229–30; *BO*, June 11, 1846.

and cultivated roles as gentlemen after their wealth and social preeminence had increased. In this respect, they simply reflected the prevailing values of the aristocratic society in which they lived, for capitalist enterprise in the eighteenth century, though certainly acknowledged as a legitimate means to make money, was not envisioned as an intrinsically honorable activity nor recognized as a socially redemptive end in itself. Despite their own experience of upward mobility and their involvement in economic development, such men tended to see legitimate authority very conservatively, as something that inhered in certain individuals and ought to be distributed along hierarchical lines.[54] Here, too, they simply reflected the fundamentally rural and traditional world in which they still lived – a world where, protoindustrialization notwithstanding, most people continued to live together in longstanding village communities and in household units that merged reproduction with work. Here, in the context of small-scale social units, power remained personal in character, and no style of social leadership that was not fundamentally aristocratic could have secured widespread popular legitimacy and respect.

Yet to assume the traditional mantle of the aristocratic gentleman, Bradford's rising protoindustrialists had to adapt it to the economic requirements of the capitalist enterprise from whose profits their incomes were obtained. Of course, a synthesis between the social roles of the gentleman and the economic functions of capitalism had, to some degree, already been established in England by the landed elite who had long tried to reconcile genteel behavior and honorable status with astuteness and acquisitiveness in the economic realm.[55] Nevertheless, because the economic role of the landed gentleman was, in the first instance, passive, rooted in his position as a property-owning rentier, he had the luxury of keeping his distance from the bustle of the marketplace, generally involving himself directly only in those forms of enterprise that flowed from the demands of improving his own estate.

Insofar as the new protoindustrialists were willing or able to transfer resources from risky into safer and more passive investment forms, they too could hope to build a viable identity as gentlemen on the foundations of an increasingly rentier-capitalist role. However, for most, it was necessary to remain active in competitive enterprises where concern with practical man-

---

[54] For general discussions of the aristocratic character of eighteenth-century English elites see Harold Perkin, *The Origins of Modern English Society* (London, 1969); Lewis Namier, *England in the Age of the American Revolution* (London, 1930), 3–4; and Peter Laslett, *The World We Have Lost* (London, 1971).

[55] Wilson, *Gentlemen Merchants*; Firth, "Genesis," 5–61, 231–353. For the historical roots of this synthesis, see Lawrence Stone, *The Crisis of the Aristocracy, 1558–1641* (London, 1965).

agement and profitability were likely to undercut the possibilities for leisure and detachment that went hand in hand with an aristocratic pose. Thus, while capitalism and gentility may not have been inherently incompatible, a certain tension between them inevitably arose.[56]

This tension revealed itself most visibly in the ambiguities experienced by protoindustrialists who imitated aristocratic residential styles. Unlike the region's landed gentry, whose houses were dispersed throughout the countryside, usually in a manorial center where the family had held its ancestral seat, most capitalists were forced by the demands of merchandizing and production to live within proximity of the town. Nevertheless, few sought to cultivate a genuinely urban lifestyle. Instead of constructing residences in Bradford's small but growing downtown district, most tended to settle in the two or three dozen minor mansions and substantial farmhouses that were scattered within a radius of two miles. Most of these miniature, pseudogentry establishments included a small park or at least a garden, often with an adjoining farm that could be let out. When the stock of suitable residences was exhausted, some of the wealthier of the protoindustrialists, such as John Hustler, bought large plots and constructed their own villas from scratch.[57]

Nevertheless, as Bradford's hinterland became developed and as the density of shops, cottages, dairy farms, ironworks, and country mills grew, even the old estates, Manningham, Horton, Bowling, and Tong Halls, lost their character as manorial centers dominating township life, and began to resemble the purely residential villas where the protoindustrial capitalists lived.[58] In these eighteenth-century patterns of residence we can see a metaphor for the larger social process of elite development, through which the small, indigenous gentry was, at least passively, enlisted in the protoindustrial process while the protoindustrialists metamorphosed in the decades after 1770 into a new, gentleman-capitalist elite.

Religion played a critical role in this change. During the dark years of the seventeenth century, a wave of puritanism had swept the West Riding insuring widespread support during the 1640s and 1650s for the parliamentarians in the Civil War. Although Dissent was less open after the Restoration and had been largely dissipated by the turn of the century, most of Bradford-dale's villages still possessed small Dissenting congregations. In Bradford itself, organized groups of Quakers and Presbyterians both persisted. By 1743, when they had reached their nadir, an Episcopal visitation

[56] Adam Smith, *The Wealth of Nations* (New York, 1937), 47–55; John Foster, *Class Struggles and the Industrial Revolution* (London, 1974), 161–202.

[57] *Bradford Old Bank;* Cudworth, *Bolton and Bowling,* 230–2.

[58] Cudworth, *Bradford Corporation,* 13; Lawrence Stone, "Social Mobility in England, 1500–1700," *Past and Present,* 33 (1966).

estimated that Nonconformists still constituted one-sixth of the local population.[59]

Whether these religious groups attracted individuals who were enterprising and ambitious or whether concentration on, and success in, business was itself a product of the Nonconformist experience is a question on which the evidence sheds little light. Certainly, the puritan values of worldly asceticism, as well as the social ostracism and ethos of mutual assistance that characterized sectarian life, must have set Nonconformists apart from their neighbors and given them both the impulse and opportunity for worldly success. In any case, while some of the new protoindustrialists were Anglicans, Quakers such as John Hustler, Edmund Peckover, Benjamin Seebohm, William Maud, or Charles Harris, and Presbyterians like Joseph Dawson, James Aked, or Abraham Sharp were disproportionately prominent within their ranks. During the course of the eighteenth century as their numbers and religious activism decreased, the wealth of the leading members of these two congregations rose dramatically.

Influenced by the liberal ideals of the enlightenment, many of these men abandoned the ultra-Calvinism of their ancestors and recast the puritan legacy of theological skepticism in a less apocalyptic, more philosophical way.[60] Not surprisingly, the broad-minded spirit of inquiry instilled by their religion and the ingrown sense of fraternity that emerged within their ranks made such congregations almost perfect breeding grounds for the sort of innovative, improving, rationalistic businessmen who could bring scientific knowledge and logical analysis to bear on the concrete problems that practical entrepreneurship posed.

Moreover, the elevated tone and calm rationalism cultivated by Quakers and Presbyterians eventually worked to stimulate a latitudinarian temper within the eighteenth-century Anglican church. By the 1700s, Anglican elites not only began to socialize with the Dissenters, but seemed ready to embrace elements of their philosophical creed. Throughout the region there was an explosion of elite interest among all denominations in natural science, political economy, and local antiquarian research. While Bradford was too small to generate its own lunar or philosophical society, a similar function was performed by other institutions that momentarily elevated the cult of enlightenment and reason into something approaching an upper-class fad.[61]

In 1774, a circulating library was founded with seventy-two subscribers

---

[59] J. H. Turner, *Nonconformity in Idle: with the History of Airedale College* (Bradford, 1876), 9–47; Firth, "Genesis," 222.

[60] James, *History of Bradford*, 224–37; Scruton, *Pen and Pencil Pictures*, 54; Firth, "Genesis," 222–8; A. Cobden-Smith, *Historical Sketches of Chapel Lane Chapel* (Bradford, 1889), 54; H. R. Hodgson, *The Society of Friends in Bradford* (Bradford, 1926).

[61] Gerald Cragg, *The Church and the Age of Reason* (London, 1960), 257–73.

and, by the end of the century, two booksellers had appeared to serve the reading public of the town. The old Bradford Grammar School, which dated from 1662, had grown rather hidebound but, in 1784, Rev. Edward Baldwyn, an intelligent and acerbic Oxford clergyman with strong liberal leanings, was appointed headmaster. His presence was undoubtedly a progressive influence as he introduced an entire generation of local Anglican gentlemen to a bold, optimistic, near deistic creed.[62]

A striking, if slightly exaggerated, example of the character type produced by old Dissent can be seen in the Rev. Joseph Dawson, a Presbyterian minister who, early in life, developed pronounced deistic and Unitarian leanings. Although devout, Dawson preferred the scientific investigation of mineral properties and investment in coal mining to the performance of his pastoral duties. As a founding partner of Low Moor Ironworks, he became an active, and ultimately a wealthy, capitalist. His abstract philosophical liberalism notwithstanding, Dawson eventually began to move in more conservative social circles and his children assimilated into the local gentry itself.[63]

It did not take Bradford's Anglican elites long to recognize that such men, so far from posing a threat, could be useful, even indispensable, business partners in large-scale enterprises or in improvement schemes that required vision and technical expertise. When the subversive political implications of Old Dissent were stripped away by its members' acquisition of wealth and property, its residue of optimistic rationalism proved easily assimilable to the orderly divinity of the eighteenth-century church. A generation later, the leading Quakers and Presbyterians of the early nineteenth century had lost all remaining inhibitions about cultivating connections with the Anglican establishment whereas Anglicans welcomed them, with few reservations, into the inner social circles of the local elite.[64]

Yet, even as Rev. Baldwyn's religious liberalism was taking hold of the establishment, a new grassroots evangelical movement inspired by the preaching of John Wesley was sweeping through the protoindustrial population as a whole. Rejecting both the detachment of rationalistic religion as well as what they believed to be the worldliness of the existing chapels and church, the Wesleyans sought a more methodical and emotional kind of

---

[62] Peter Mathias, "Who Unbound Prometheus," in A. E. Musson, ed., *Science, Technology, and Economic Growth in the Eighteenth Century,* (London, 1972); William Claridge, *Origin and History of Bradford Grammar School* (Bradford, 1882); "Incidents in the Life of the Rev. Edward Baldwyn," *BA,* o.s. 1 (1888).

[63] Anon., *Fortunes Made in Business,* 1: 90–128; T. Jervis, *Address at the Interment of Joseph Dawson of Royds Hall,* (London, n.d.); Turner, *Nonconformity in Idle,* 46–7.

[64] Hustwick, "Woolstapler"; John Simpson, *The Journal of Dr. John Simpson of Bradford, 1825* (Bradford, 1981).

piety that harkened back, albeit with a more promiscuous theology, to the old puritan preoccupations with personal salvation and faith. While Wesleyan Methodism, as it came to be called, clearly began as a popular movement and continued to cling to its early plebeian roots, its emphasis on self-discipline and unstinting labor made it an excellent vehicle through which ambitious young men could gain succor and psychological reinforcement in their efforts to achieve social and economic success.[65]

A disproportionate number of the new upwardly mobile, protoindustrial entrepreneurs were Methodists, especially those such as John Hardy, John Rouse, Samuel Margerison, Edward Ripley, James Garnett, Richard Thorton, William Hainsworth, Nathaniel Dracup, John Murgatroyd, Richard Fawcett, and William Cheesborough who originally came from more humble social backgrounds than most of their Quaker, Presbyterian, and Anglican counterparts. Such men tended to limit their economic activities to retailing and the textile trades, leaving the large-scale projects to more established types. Because their task on the road to success necessitated the gradual accumulation of profits from small enterprise in a single occupation, they found the austere discipline of Methodism more appropriate than the philosophical faith of the secure as a way of mobilizing their energies for strenuous effort and of setting themselves culturally apart from the masses of ordinary men and women.[66]

When Bradford's Methodist movement had first erupted in the 1740s the Anglican establishment had responded with great hostility. They saw little difference between these rude, plainspoken Wesleyan populists and the itinerant radicals they had learned to fear a century earlier. At first the authorities tried to prevent the early Methodist leaders from preaching their unauthorized creed, imprisoning the most charismatic local preacher, John Nelson, and impressing him in the Navy to separate him from his flock.[67] However, it was not long before Bradford's Anglican elites began to recognize the conservative character of Methodism and to see how it might be enlisted to play a socially stabilizing, even counterrevolutionary, role protecting the establishment from the consequences of its own religious indifference and spiritual elitism. John Wesley himself played an important role in centralizing and subduing the movement that came to bear his name. Visiting Bradford

---

[65] J. D. Walsh, "The Origins of the Evangelical Revival," in G. U. Bennett and J. D. Walsh, eds., *Essays in Modern English Church History* (London, 1966).

[66] An analysis of the occupation of the trustees of the two original Wesleyan chapels shows this clearly. Out of thirty-six separate individuals, seven were merchants or woolstaplers, twelve were retailers, five were textile manufacturers, four were professionals, three were in other manufactures, two were iron founders, and one was a worker.

[67] J. N. Dickons, "Kirkgate Chapel and Its Association with Methodism," *BA*, n.s. 5. (1933), 69–79.

every year, he attracted thousands of listeners wherever he preached. His uneasy efforts, first to convert, and then to discipline his often stubbornly independent-minded adherents, won him the respect and trust of local Anglican elites. Eventually they came to see him as an indispensible ally in combating popular irreligion and in providing a safety valve through which the enthusiasm of the masses could harmlessly be discharged.[68]

The Wesleyans, in their turn, were careful to pay due respect to church authority, encouraging their brethren to attend Anglican communion after chapel. Furthermore, as the leading Methodists became increasingly wealthy and powerful, they gravitated more closely toward the established church. As Wesley was painfully aware, the worldly prosperity to which Methodism seemed so conducive inevitably dulled the spiritual intensity of the successful Methodist and eroded the foundations of his spiritual fervor.[69]

As the Wesleyans began to move closer to the Anglican establishment, the church adopted a modified variant of the Methodists' evangelical approach. This linkage was first effected by Rev. William Grimshaw, perpetual curate of Haworth between 1742 and 1763 whose furious efforts to elevate prevailing levels of morality in the district led him to become friends with Wesley and employ some of the same techniques. With the accession of the evangelical Rev. John Crosse to the vicarate of Bradford in 1784, the activist, emotional tone inspired by Wesleyanism infiltrated, albeit in relatively restrained and decorous fashion, into the very heart of the local church. Indeed, Crosse saw a modest dose of evangelical enthusiasm as an indispensable counterweight to the dominant strain of religious rationalism that ignored the spiritual preoccupations of the masses while potentially nurturing theological heterodoxy among elites.[70]

The church's ability to absorb these outside influences, incorporating them so as to temper each other in a way that would revitalize itself, was an indispensable part of the creation of an elite that could aspire to gentlemanly ideals and values without losing touch with the realities of capitalist life. So long as progress was mediated by customary values and sanctified by venerable institutions like the established church, it could pose no danger to the cause of true conservatism and no affront to the ultimate values of the status quo. Grounding progress on a bedrock of traditionalism, eighteenth-century Anglicanism seemed to offer a framework for elite intellectual and

[68] W. W. Stamp, *Historical Notices of Wesleyan Methodism in Bradford* (Bradford, 1841), 17–21.

[69] John Wesley, "Thoughts on Methodism," quoted in D. D. Thompson, *John Wesley as a Social Reformer* (New York, 1898), 32–3.

[70] W. H Dixon and J. Locke, *A Man of Sorrow: The Life and Times of Rev. Patrick Bronte* (London, 1979), 213–8; W. Morgan, *Rev. John Crosse: The Parish Priest* (London, 1841), 55–146; Dickons, "Kirkgate Chapel," 214.

economic development without opening the floodgates for radical disruption and social change. With its sober spirit of undogmatic pragmatism, reconciling diverse, even contradictory, impulses within the secure foundations of an inherited faith, Anglicanism, without wholly losing its character as a distinctive religion, virtually evolved into the sort of secular elite culture in which the gentleman and the capitalist could fuse.[71]

[71] G. F. A. Best, *Temporal Pillars* (Cambridge, 1964), 11–77.

2

The crisis of the traditional community

As the preceding chapter has demonstrated, the ambiguous character of protoindustrialization in eighteenth-century Bradford-dale set the stage for an ambivalent culture to emerge. Because the inexorable dynamic of capitalist economic development had not yet burst the social frameworks of domestic household and village community, it remained compatible with many traditional cultural forms and institutions. During the second half of the eighteenth century, continued protoindustrial expansion put this traditional culture under great pressure, but until 1815, it was able to survive.

Protoindustrialization and the traditional community

Centuries of geographical isolation and economic backwardness in Bradford-dale combined with the relative barrenness of the native soil had long fostered a distinctive regional popular culture that proved extremely resilient, even in the face of socioeconomic change. Fundamentally preliterate and, in some respects, pre-Christian, this popular culture was the product of a world of few social distinctions, minimal division of labor above the level of the household, and little centralized knowledge or political authority. For those who lived their entire lives in this environment, the church, the state, and even the gentry could be viewed almost as foreign impositions.[1] Even as late as the mid-nineteenth century, in those hinterland villages like Idle or Allerton, which urban industrial development had only begun to reach, the atmosphere remained "decidedly clannish," and "the inhabitants in all stations of life are in a relationship of almost family intimacy," sharing a sense of collective solidarity and autonomy that almost impels the historian toward an anthropological approach.[2]

[1] During the sixteenth century, Archbishop Grindal had complained that, in this dark corner of the land, even gentlemen were "not well affected towards Godly religion while among the common people many superstitious practices remain." W. Smith, ed., *Old Yorkshire* (London, 1883), 4:226.

[2] William Cudworth, *Round About Bradford* (Bradford, 1876), 379; Anon., "Yorkshire Life

53

By all accounts, the area was rich in traditional folklore, and villagers spent their lives amidst a world where dangerous goblins, boggards, and spirits were ubiquitous and had to be expiated in ritualistic ways. So far from being seen as inconsistent with Christianity, such beliefs and practices were inextricably intertwined with nominally Christian forms. In Pudsey, skepticism about witchcraft was denounced by villagers as "atheistic." Legends, which would later be believed only by children, carried normative messages that then set ethical standards even for adults. The Guytrash, for example, an apocryphal monster who roamed nightly through Horton's streets, acted as a check on nocturnal behavior and encouraged people to stay at home. Even those who were inclined to scoff at the Guytrash might well tremble at the prospect of encountering Fair Becca, the ghost of a local woman brutally murdered by her husband who vowed that "she would come again as long as the holly grew green."[3]

This web of oral culture wove apocryphal myths and ancient proverbs into a pattern of knowledge that, like the community that absorbed it, was resistant to formal differentiation or monopolization by an educated, professional elite. No doubt, popular reliance on folk medicine was, in part, the result of a dearth of certified practitioners, but even if they had been given a choice, the inhabitants of Baildon might still have patronized James Steel, "a practitioner of the real village type – skillful, affable, jocular and possessing a rare fund of village lore," or Mrs. Wharton, a widely renowned bonesetter who gave not only free services, but sometimes even money to the poor.[4]

At an even lower social level, the region abounded in wise men, fortune tellers, white witches, and faith healers who formed the medical counterparts to the swarm of itinerant preachers, self-taught ranters, and self-proclaimed prophets who proliferated in the spiritual sphere. As late as 1807, one witch, George Mason, died with a practice worth several hundred pounds, whereas Hannah Green, an even more successful competitor, bequeathed £1,000 to her daughter so that the family business could be carried on.[5] A few years earlier, a scandal had broken out when John Hepworth's cure for a poor weaver who had consulted him backfired badly. To exorcise the evil spirit

and Character," *Temple Bar*, (Mar. 1868). For a survey of the anthropological approach to the history of this period, see Peter Burke, *Popular Culture in Early Modern Europe* (New York, 1978).

[3] E. P. Thompson, "The Moral Economy of the English Crowd," *Past and Present*, 50 (1971); James Obelkevich, *Religion and Rural Society: South Lindsey, 1825–75* (Oxford, 1976), 254–312; Joseph Lawson, *Letters to the Young on Progress in Pudsey* (Stanningley, 1887), 45–7; William Cudworth, *Rambles Round Horton* (Bradford, 1886), 171–2; William Scruton, *Pen and Pencil Pictures of Old Bradford* (Bradford, 1889), 203.

[4] Cudworth, *Round About Bradford*, 50, 322, 340.

[5] K. V. Thomas, *Religion and the Decline of Magic* (New York, 1971); John James, *History and Topography of Bradford* (Bradford, 1841), 162.

haunting his patient, Hepworth poured "human blood mixed with hair into a large iron bottle, corked it up tightly and put it into the fire." The results of this procedure was that the bottle exploded, killing the patient.[6]

Even official functions were often, de facto, assumed by the local community itself. This was particularly true in the outlying hinterland villages, far from the reach of either magistrates or church. However, even in Bradford town, official justice depended not only on the tacit sanction of the populace, but on their active participation as an organized mob. "Criminals," one antiquarian reported, "were flogged at cart tail. . . . A pillory was set up at the bottom of Westgate where the market was held . . . people were allowed to throw eggs or potatoes but not stones." Naturally, this popular impulse to defend the moral equilibrium did not always limit itself to the official letter of the law. "Riding the stang," a local variant of rough music, was a common practice in many villages, providing a means of regulating unorthodox behavior and of keeping sexual transgressors at bay.[7]

When written statute came into conflict with this unofficial plebeian moral code, it was sometimes an open question which of the two would prevail. Traditional Yorkshire ballads reveal that the genre of the outlaw hero (whether in the form of Robin Hood, or some lesser-known figure) was extremely popular and framed a code of ethics, handed down from generation to generation, which emphasized the rights of the poor. Crimes like poaching were considered legitimate, and in Pudsey, at least, were regularly practiced by the most respectable and enterprising men of the village.[8] In Bradford, when woolcombers were flogged for crimes against property such as embezzlement of wool, the authorities might be loath to invoke the crowd to carry out the sentence for fear that the criminal might be freed instead.[9]

As E. P. Thompson has persuasively argued, such events were never isolated incidents but reflected the existence of an underlying moral economy that specified that all community members, by mere virtue of their existence, were entitled to an opportunity to gain a livelihood and were subject to equal standards of justice. Like bread riots, these crowd actions were not random outbursts of collective violence but studied interventions designed to protect

---

[6] Cudworth, *Round About Bradford*, 48, 89, 344; James, *History of Bradford*, 162; J. H. Turner, *Nonconformity in Idle: with the History of Airedale College* (Bradford, 1876), 44.

[7] Douglas Hay, "Property and Authority and the Criminal Law," Hay et al., *Albion's Fatal Tree: Crime and Society in Eighteenth Century England* (New York, 1975) 17–63; Gary Firth, "The Genesis of the Industrial Revolution in Bradford," (Bradford, Ph.D. dissertation, 1976), 71; William Henderson, *The Folklore of the Northern Counties* (London, 1879), 29; John James, *Continuations and Additions to the History and Topography of Bradford* (Bradford, 1866), 89; *BO*, July 31, 1845.

[8] Lawson, *Progress in Pudsey*, 116–20; C. J. Davidson-Ingledew, *The Ballads and Songs of Yorkshire* (London, 1860); E. P. Thompson, *Whigs and Hunters* (New York, 1975).

[9] *BOB*, Dec. 7, 1907.

community members either against the imposition of outside authorities or the tyranny of market forces when these were deemed to be working against the interests of the local community at large.[10]

However, for the most part, at least before the eighteenth century, these local communities were left to define and to regulate themselves. Spared the rigors of the demonstration or the bread riot, communal solidarity was usually manifested less explosively in a series of recurrent rituals like "riding the parish" boundary, which delineated it in space, or seasonal wakes and feasts, which demarcated collective time. Like all preindustrial agrarian communities, village life was deeply intertwined with the natural periodicities imposed on human culture by the sun and the soil. Hence, the community revealed itself most explicitly through its calendar of recurrent fairs and festivities in which it ritualistically marked the passage of the seasons, the routines of labors, and ultimately, the stages of life.[11]

Similarly, the same kind of communal manifestations that demarcated the seasonal cycle also figured in the collective celebration of important milestones in the lifecycle of individual community members. Birth, death, and other life changes were not private family events but important rites of passage in which the entire village would be more or less involved. This was particularly true in the case of marriage in which it was especially important that individual choices be sanctioned by gestures of collective assent.[12]

Such was the communitarian village legacy inherited by Bradfordians in the eighteenth century – a form of life that was, at once, narrow and claustro-

---

[10] Thompson, "Moral Economy"; E. J. Hobsbawm, *Primitive Rebels* (New York, 1965); George Rude, *The Crowd in History: A Study of Popular Disturbances in France and England, 1730–1848* (New York, 1964).

[11] E. P. Thompson, "Time, Work Discipline, and Industrial Capitalism," *Past and Present*, 38 (1967). Emile Durkheim, *The Elementary Forms of the Religious Life* (London, 1976).

As the antiquarian William Cudworth suggested, these traditional villagers were "a people best seen in character when their 'feasts' 'rushes' 'tides' and ' thumps' are on." Throughout the region a host of customary celebrations, not only for Christmas and Easter, but for harvest and Martinmas were held to affirm the vitality of community by marking the temporal divisions of its working year. The regional marketing of cattle and agricultural produce that occurred biannually at the Bradford Fair became another occasion when festive celebrations reinforced, or at least reflected, bonds that had been forged in the relations of work. In the case of Whitsuntide, the grandest of all these traditional celebrations, a mildly bacchanalian rite of spring, it was not trade, but courtship that provided the excuse for villagers to gather from miles around for games and entertainment. M. C. F. Morris, *Yorkshire Folk Talk* (London, 1892), 214–15; Firth, "Genesis," 150–2; Smith, ed., *Old Yorkshire*, 1:131.

[12] In Denholme, whenever a couple got married, the whole village was called out by a

phobic but, at the same time, essentially habitable and secure. During the course of the eighteenth century, however, as economic development quickened and population levels grew, relations between community members became increasingly problematic or impersonal, and such spontaneous manifestations of collective solidarity must have come to seem increasingly formulaic and strained. The local community itself was becoming a more complex, socially fluid, and class-divided social environment in which the abstract ebb and flow of the capitalist marketplace was replacing the concrete cycle of sun, seasons, and life-cycle as the primary rhythm of collective life. Yet although these changes in the character of the protoindustrial community must be registered, it is important not to exaggerate their significance or scope. This can be seen by examining the downtown precincts of Bradford proper, where the forces of commercial expansion were most concentrated and intense. Even here, the extraordinary increase in the volume and variety of economic activity serves, if anything, only to highlight how little protoindustrialization altered the physical and environmental structures of the town; for although Bradford was becoming an economic focus of regional trade and commerce, it was not becoming a center of population settlement at anything like a comparable rate.

In 1775, the town proper consisted of only three streets. Over the next quarter century, the slow expansion of downtown settlement contrasted markedly with the vigorous pattern of dispersed regional economic and demographic growth. The map of Bradford in 1802 differed little from the plan of twenty-seven years before. Two new streets had been added, and the density of houses and shops was beginning to thicken, but the entire downtown area still amounted to less than fifty acres, housing a population of only about three thousand. Even here, the mark of the surrounding rural society could scarcely be ignored or escaped. The ramshackle buildings, rustic faces, quaint mannerisms, and broad dialects that visitors noted on the town's narrow streets immediately betrayed the hold of traditional customs and values amidst the bustle of a market day.[13] Most significantly, however, the integration of home with workplace, so characteristic of the rural village economy, still remained

serenading band. After breakfast at the bridegroom's, the procession marched six miles to the Bradford Parish Church. After vows had been exchanged, they all returned by way of the Pack Horse Inn and the day's events were capped by games of ribbon races such as accompanied weddings throughout Yorkshire. See Lawson, *Progress in Pudsey*, 10–20; Henderson, *Folklore*, 37–41; John Wood, *Autobiography* (Bradford, 1877), 23–6. For a general discussion of marriage rituals in early modern England see John Gillis, *For Better, For Worse, British Marriages, 1600 to Present* (Oxford, 1985), 55–83.

[13] T. Jeffrys, "The County of York Surveyed," (map, 1775); J. Johnson, "Map of Bradford," (map, 1802); William Cudworth, *Historical Notes on the Bradford Corporation* (Bradford, 1881), 12; Firth, "Genesis," 131; Scruton, *Pen and Pencil*, 104–8, 223–32, 244–50; *PP* (1812, XI), 407–26.

the norm. Most workshops remained small and artisanal in character, and apprentices sometimes lived in the master's household. Large industrial enterprises were the exception rather than the rule, and they were often run, as far as possible, along household lines.[14]

If eighteenth-century Bradfordians worked and played, made love and money in the same places, they also lived at close quarters with one another. As neighbors, people of different ranks and income levels constantly mingled on the street, at the market, or in the church. Invariably, large houses were jumbled together amidst a welter of cottages and shops. An 1805 rate book reveals a pattern of a half dozen large and small properties alternating with one another along the same street.[15] This propinquity between the upper and lower orders within the community did not so much undercut the social hierarchy as make it more visible and acceptable. Rank was no abstract and impersonal quality. The village atmosphere ensured that it was always defined by particular faces and particular names. In nearby Horton, these personal bonds remained so powerful that surnames were customarily neglected in most interactions between inhabitants, regardless of their individual social position or wealth. Villagers with the same Christian name were distinguished by a patronymic that expressed their ancestry rather than by a family label: Bob Illingworth became Bob o' John's o' Sam's.[16]

Yet community, however resilient, was by no means unchanging. Under the impact of protoindustrialization, it was inevitable that eighteenth-century Bradford would come to constitute an increasingly complex, dynamic, and ultimately unstable community in which there could no longer be any spontaneous consensus as to the values or symbols that stood at the center of its members' collective life.

No doubt, the most obvious physical symbol of community was the edifice of the ancient parish church, which, towering above the shops and dwelling-

---

[14] In fact, Bradford's first spinning machinery was originally set up in the house of its proprietor, James Garnett, before being transferred to a factory. Cudworth, *Bradford Corporation*, 12, 13; "Bradford and its Founders," *BOB*, May 19, 1906.

[15] This rate book is printed in Cudworth, *Bradford Corporation*, 27–33. Since the houses listed are printed street by street, there is every reason to believe that they are ordered house by house. On Westgate, the property of a woolstapler, Richard Slater, rated at £64 was adjoined by Abraham Smith's worth £5. Peter Wells's at £29 was next to William Cavitt's at £6. On Mill bank, Jonas Jenning's at £240 was next to Richard Brown's at £4. Whereas on Ivegate, John Blesard's worth £64 was next to James Sugden's worth £6. The examples could be multiplied. Only on Kirkgate, near the church, and at the top of Horton Road were there disproportionate concentrations of elites, and only New Market Street seems to have been filled entirely with small- or middling-sized houses. See also Scruton, *Pen and Pencil*, 220–2.

[16] Cudworth, *Horton*, 10, 163; *BO*, Oct. 11, 1855.

houses, had, since its construction in 1458, served as the almost inevitable center for the enactment of Bradford's public life. For centuries, its bell had tolled the important events of war and peace, while its registers had recorded the commonplace ones of marriage, birth, and death, and its vestry had housed the most authoritative local governmental institution, which elected officers, supervised relief, and took communal decisions of every sort. Even after death, Bradfordians would be buried in the churchyard, where a stone inscription would remind future generations that they had lived.[17]

If the symbolism of the church's exterior linked the future with the past, conjuring up in the minds of inhabitants an image of the history of their town, inside, its seating plan mapped the social hierarchy of the present, putting it on weekly display. The range of pews, graded by elegance and proximity to the altar, were often attached to corresponding parcels of landed property into which the parish was divided. Up to a point, one's place in the church denoted one's status in the community, changing with gains or losses in property and public esteem. Even the poor had their place if they chose to attend – a gesture that had traditionally been encouraged by the practice of distributing relief on Sunday after divine service.[18]

Of course, because it was also a religious organization, the communality of the church had become somewhat problematic since it had, since the seventeenth century, ceased to encompass the spiritual community as a whole. Nevertheless, religious Nonconformity notwithstanding, no eighteenth-century Methodist, Quaker, or Presbyterian would openly have questioned the right of the church to dominate the secular life of the parish, to levy tithes and church rates on everyone, or even to impose penalties on the minority of conscience that could afford to pay the price of dissent; for religious heterodoxy, although the right of individuals, was not the community's natural state of being and had to be purchased at the expense of disabilities in the civil sphere.[19]

In fact, since the economic ascent of Bradford's leading eighteenth-century Nonconformists was diminishing the social and political significance of sectarian distinctions, if wealthy Dissenters remained aloof from the church as a spiritual institution, they rallied in growing numbers to the broad secular culture that was nourished within the Anglican fold. Indeed, the real challenge to the church's ability to serve as a focus of eighteenth-century community life came, not from the principled opposition of Dissenters, but from the indifference and hostility of the protoindustrial masses, who were

[17] William Scruton, *Old Bradford Views* (Bradford, 1897); Firth, "Genesis," 71–3.
[18] Cudworth, *Bradford Corporation*, 4; W. Robertshaw, "Bradford Church Pews," *BA*, n.s. 7 (1952), 49–53.
[19] Lawson, *Progress in Pudsey*, 89; Obelkevich, *Religion and Rural Society*, 143–82.

not so much disaffected by its doctrinal positions as estranged from what they perceived as its secular character as an establishment for elites.

Although it is impossible to gauge levels of popular identification with, or even attendance at, Bradford's pre-eighteenth-century church, there is evidence that the social strains and divisions of protoindustrial capitalism encouraged many common people to regard it as a bastion of privilege that not only ignored their spiritual preoccupations, but actively relegated them to a servility within its social structure while ideologically legitimizing their increasingly marginal economic roles. "The whole State Church machinery," in the words of one nearby villager, "seemed a harsh, cruel, vindictive, and slavish affair, without a redeeming feature to win the reverence and affection of one not unmanned by cowardice; and we could not help but thinking that if it were not the State Church, patronized by the rich and mighty as well as the cheapest one afloat, very few would have paid attention to it."[20]

In becoming a religion of gentlemen-capitalists, Anglicanism seemed to lose whatever allegiance it may have once inspired among a struggling populace whose spiritual welfare apathetic ministers all too often ignored. Although a handful of evangelical clergymen like Crosse or Grimshaw might temporarily arrest this process, their stated aims of forging a truly comprehensive religious communion, in which the poor could participate, never got very far. Indeed, the heavy-handed tactics toward which their objectives impelled them alienated many in all social groups. Quite apart from the attitudes of particular ministers, the nature of the parochial system itself made it unresponsive to the economic and demographic changes taking place in protoindustrial society and impervious to the needs of the burgeoning masses. In the far-flung Bradford Parish, three small hinterland chapels and one downtown central church were expected to serve the needs of a population that had grown to 32,516 by 1811. Precisely because they were fixed reflections of the communities that had existed in the Middle Ages, these traditional church structures inevitably failed to provide an adequate focus for the new and more complex eighteenth-century forms of community.[21]

Alienated and ignored by official institutions, the common people looked back nostalgically to the older informal face of village culture that was closer to the normative values of their moral economy than the formal "community" of the church. Like the church, this unofficial plebeian community had its geography, physically focusing on an open space known as the "Turls." Located at the center of the downtown settlement where the Bradford City

[20] Lawson, *Progress in Pudsey*, 87.
[21] *PP* (1821, XI), 407–26.

Hall stands today, the Turls was generally conceded by property owners and local officials as a commons or bowling green. Located next to the old medieval marketplace and the pillory where transgressors were publicly called to account, the Turls was adjoined by two taverns known as the Bull's Head and Fighting Cocks, which respectively denoted the activities for which they were best known.[22] With its pivotal location and broad range of popular activities, the Turls had always symbolized the centrality of a plebeian counter-community which had habitually coexisted, albeit somewhat uneasily, alongside the official community of the vestry and church.

Despite their indecorous appearance, such "rough sports" and popular recreations had traditionally played an important role in the life of the community. However brutal, they represented a respite from the even harsher yoke of manual labor and were eagerly anticipated by weavers and agricultural workers alike. Pitting family against family, and village against village, they often reinforced the clanlike solidarities that had once formed the building blocks of all community life. However, in the eighteenth century, as they were stripped of their integrative functions, they tended to become meaningless exhibitions of debauchery on the part of a demoralized, lower class. Although, in contrast to their nineteenth-century successors, Bradford's eighteenth-century gentlemen-capitalists did not repress these popular recreations, generally regarding them as harmless pastimes through which a frustrated populace could let off steam, they personally shunned such violent and uncivilized activities in favor of an aristocratic culture of hunting and coursing, which, if no less bloody, was more polite.[23]

Given the detached quality of the eighteenth-century Anglican establishment and the isolated, demoralized character of popular sports, a case could be made that the vital center of the protoindustrial community was not the church or the commons but the tavern and inn. As a "serviceable and necessary institution not only supplying ease, comfort, and refreshment... but even giving birth to movements and organizations of a useful and indispensable character," the eighteenth-century inn absorbed many of the activities that had hitherto been housed in the church, the marketplace, or the open ground. As the century progressed, it began to seem that the hostelry

[22] Cudworth, *Round About Bradford*, 137; James, *History of Bradford*, 287; idem, *Continuations and Additions*, 8–9, 90; Lawson, *Progress in Pudsey*, 58–9. For a general study of the subject see Robert Malcolmson, *Popular Recreations in English Society, 1700–1850* (Cambridge, 1973).

[23] Malcolmson, *Popular Recreations*, 64–74; Lawson, *Progress in Pudsey*, 56–7. Local newspapers often published lists of individuals with hunting licenses.

might now provide the kind of flexible, dynamic type of public focus that a growing protoindustrial community required.[24]

Inns became cultural crossroads because they were, in the first instance, physical ones. As receiving stations for stagecoaches, news, and visitors, inns were the points where otherwise isolated communities linked up with the world outside. After the 1740s, when the first turnpike roads were constructed, the number and significance of Bradford's hostelries increased. The inn became an important focus for economic activity acting as a depot, a warehouse, and sometimes even a marketplace. Before the erection of the Piece Hall, Bradford's clothiers were obliged either to exhibit their goods at the White Lion or to vend them on the streets.[25]

However, it was as a social center that the inn became most indispensable. This remained true even into the early nineteenth century when magistrates like Ellis Cunliffe Lister and John Sturges held sittings at various local taverns, while weekly petty sessions were conducted at the New Inn in the town center. Village meetings were lubricated by the publican's cheer, and when Bradford's Improvement Commission was first established, it met alternately in five different inns.[26] Committees of all sorts also met in taverns. During the 1825 woolcombers strike, the masters set up their headquarters at the Sun Inn, whereas the workmen gathered in the Roebuck only 200 yards away. Around the turn of the century, Henry Ramsbotham, Edward Pease, and a handful of other capitalists were reported to meet at an inn to fix prices of worsted yarns for the coming quarter, whereas a somewhat less exclusive "oyster club" was formed "where the spinners, manufacturers, and gentry of the town gathered to enjoy oysters and cold punch and to discuss politics and the commercial news brought fortnightly by the Hamburgh Mail." Beyond its commercial role, the tavern served as a center for all kinds of conviviality, from ribald gatherings to serious literary discussion groups or musical performance societies.[27]

Yet if the inn facilitated the integration of the diverse activities that protoindustrial capitalism still permitted, it harbored the social differentiation of the diverse groups and strata that a market-driven society increasingly

[24] Alan Everitt, "The English Urban Inn, 1560–1760," *Perspectives in English Urban History* (London, 1973) 91–137; Scruton, *Pen and Pencil Pictures*, 164.

[25] William Cudworth, *Musical Reminiscences of Old Bradford* (Bradford, 1885), 6, 12; idem, *Bradford Corporation*, 22; Scruton, *Pen and Pencil*, 115.

[26] Before the advent of distinct commercial, literary, and political organizations, nearly all collective social activity took place beneath the innkeeper's roof. Brian Harrison, *Drink and Victorians* (London, 1971), 51–4; William Cudworth, *Histories of Bolton and Bowling* (Bradford, 1891), 214; idem, *Histories of Manningham, Heaton and Allerton* (Bradford, 1896), 149; idem, *Bradford Corporation*, 22.

[27] Cudworth, *Musical Reminiscences*, 612; idem, *Rambles Round Heaton*, 42; Firth, "Genesis," 439; James, *Continuations and Additions*, 95.

required. Tavern culture worked to sort people out as much as to combine them as different groups and activities tended to concentrate in different inns. The Church Steps became noted for its connection with the staple trade whereas the Sun became a social center for the Anglican notability.[28]

Inns were effective as social centers, as foci for collective life, precisely because, unlike the church and commons, they never sought to comprehend the entire community. They flourished under conditions in which increasing differences in religion, wealth, interest, and social status inclined people to separate themselves into cliques and clienteles. So heterogeneous and fragmented a conception of social relations might facilitate capitalist development, but how far was it consistent with an overarching community life? In particular, in a society like protoindustrial Bradford, increasingly divided between plebeians and elites, how long could the paradigm of a comprehensive community continue to serve as a viable integrative social ideal?

Protoindustrial capitalism and the paternalist ideal

To reconcile the ideal of community with the realities of economic inequality may have appeared to Bradford's eighteenth-century protoindustrialists to be a novel problem. Yet it was an old dilemma that had preoccupied other agrarian elites. One solution, long deemed effective, had been to forge a paternalist link between social superiors and subordinates wherein the former would guarantee the latters' basic needs and interests, expecting to be repaid by deference and acquiescence in his rule. Because paternalism involved the projection of a biological family relationship onto a larger, man-made social frame, it tended to work best in manorial or quasifeudal contexts where relations between masters and dependents remained intensely personal, and the community itself assumed the form of an extended household.

Bradford had never possessed this kind of hierarchical social structure, and in the eighteenth century, when substantial inequalities began to appear, they occurred within a capitalist, rather than a feudal, context. Here the relationship between plebeians and elites was not the bond between master and servant but the impersonal market-oriented connection between a social group of employers and the collective pool of laborers who they employed. Nevertheless, since most of Bradford's protoindustrialists were not simply capitalists, but would-be gentlemen who sought the trappings of an aristocratic lifestyle, they tended to find the paternalist ideal attractive in principle, however difficult it might be to sustain in practice. So long as he remained a small protoindustrial employer who trudged from cottage to cottage with

[28] Scruton, *Pen and Pencil*, 163–75.

his woolpacks and mule, it was natural to feel fatherly solicitousness toward poorer neighbors and dependent employees. Although market imperatives might necessitate bursts of intense and driving exploitation, "where there was little difference in the appearance or style of dwelling occupied by the master clothier or stuffmaker and the hands he employed," an atmosphere of easy fraternity was not hard to maintain.[29]

Obviously, if the small clothier changed into a large capitalist with hundreds of workers scattered over the countryside, the atmosphere of labor relations changed. Nevertheless, even successful capitalists might use the memory of their parvenu origins to cultivate a common touch. For a generation into the nineteenth century, Bradford continued to harbor its "manufacturers of the old school, men who [spoke] in dialect and [had] a disdain for gloves." Particularly in the more distant hinterland communities, the transition to mechanized production by a single large employer might enhance the scope for employer paternalism by creating a virtually self-contained factory village. Indeed, in a place like Idle, "where all the chief millowners are named Shaw," where "Ely Shaw is the name of one great manufacturer and Ely Shaw the name of a large number of his fourteen hundred hands," paternalism may have existed in more than a metaphorical sense.[30]

However, by the middle of the eighteenth century, it was already clear that this was the exception rather than the rule, for the rise of large firms combined with the proletarianization of the cottage work force to undermine the material foundations on which paternalistic labor relations might have been built. Ever more subject to the fluctuations of an unstable labor market, workers found themselves facing a new class of distant employers who had few incentives for wanting to protect traditional standards and relationships and every reason to take advantage of their superior bargaining position to reduce their labor costs. During the depression of the early 1770s, employers precipitously cut workers' wages throughout the industry by an average of 28 percent. Although wage levels partly recovered during the prosperous 1780s, during the 1790s and early 1800s, their purchasing power sank as food prices more than doubled in the space of twenty years. By 1819, the average real wage of local worsted weavers was only 66 percent of what it had been forty years before.[31]

[29] Cudworth, *Bolton and Bowling*, 250–1.
[30] Cudworth, *Bradford Corporation*, 36; idem, *Manningham, Heaton and Allerton*, 106–7; anon., "Yorkshire Life and Character."
[31] James, *History of the Worsted Manufacture in England*, (London, 1857), 281, 291, 329, 385. This calculation of real wages is based on the consumer price index contained in E. H. Phelps Brown and S. V. Hopkins, "Seven Centuries of the Price of Consumables

Hand in hand with declining wages went deteriorating labor relations as capitalists sought, or were driven by the behavior of competitors, to increase the pace of work. Given the dispersed character of cottage manufacturing and the difficulties employers faced in supervising work, the problem of worker autonomy became an increasing preoccupation of employers who grew more determined to regiment their work force and to gain more direct control over the labor process. For some, it was these imperatives of work discipline and labor organization, rather than technological improvement and change, that motivated them to centralize production by bringing workers under one roof. However, even within the framework of the putting-out system, enhanced surveillance was deemed necessary to combat worker indiscipline and to insure subordination to employer control.[32]

These concerns were first articulated in the 1760s through a vociferous campaign on the part of manufacturers against what they perceived as a widespread practice among cottage employees of regularly embezzling small quantities of wool. In 1764, an ad hoc association had been formed to investigate this practice, and in 1777, the employers obtained, at considerable effort and expense, a parliamentary statute known as the Worsted Act, which set up a national committee of employer representatives to investigate and prosecute worker malfeasance. Empowered with quasi-official governmental authority and authorized to hire eighteen full-time inspectors to do its work, this Worsted Committee inaugurated a new era in labor relations in which the close-knit bonds between the old clothiers and cottagers gave way to an atmosphere of antagonistic impersonality in which both sides presupposed the enmity of the other and sought to advance their own interests through the exertion of organized pressure.[33]

With 22 percent of its inspectors and 15 percent of its members, including such luminaries as John Hustler, George Kellet, and James Garnett, Bradford was a major focus of the Worsted Committee's activity from the start. Over the next fifty years, its presence served as a festering reminder that, although protoindustrial capitalists might prefer to envision their workers as childlike dependents nurtured under the protection of the employer's roof, they were more likely to treat them as thieving recalcitrants who had to be cajoled and punished to do their jobs.[34]

Indeed, the eighteenth-century capitalist, as E. P. Thompson has per-

Compared with Builders' Wage Rates," in E. M. Carus-Wilson, ed., *Essays in Economic History*, vol. 2 (London, 1962), 179–96.

[32] Sidney Pollard, *The Genesis of Modern Management* (London, 1965).

[33] James, *Worsted Manufacture*, 293–8.

[34] Ibid; Herbert Heaton, *The Yorkshire Woolens and Worsted Industry* (Oxford, 1920), 418–37.

ceptively recognized, "wished devotedly to have the best of the old world and the new," abdicating his unprofitable paternalist responsibilities while continuing to regard the worker "as an unfree man, a servant," who could be expected to remain deferential and submissive even toward a master who violated traditional standards and rights. Yet according to Thompson, at the very moment when paternalism for capitalists was becoming a patent contradiction, more privileged and detached landed gentry were increasingly able to benefit from the aura of authority with which paternalism endowed them, without having to undertake onerous responsibilities that would cost them very much.

Periodically emerging from the privacy of their country residences for "certain significant ritual (public) appearances" on the bench, at the assizes, for the hunt, the distribution of alms, and ceremonial feasts, the rentier-gentleman could indulge in highly visible gestures of generosity to exact "a return in deference quite disproportionate to the outlay."[35] In many of the villages around Bradford, great public events, such as the peace of 1815 or the coming of age of John Tempest of Tong Hall, provided occasions when the entire population might be feasted by the manorial lord. In Shipley, the Wainmans even celebrated elections, gathering their freeholders to roast oxen and then march in procession to cast their votes at York.[36]

Insofar as they remained merely capitalists, Bradford's protoindustrialists could, of course, not hope to imitate this deliberate paternalist "theatre of the great." Nevertheless, occasional instances were reported of masters feasting workmen to celebrate major anniversaries in the family or firm. Even among wealthy Dissenters like the Hustlers, *noblesse oblige* was extended to poorer members of their congregation, who were periodically invited to dine at the family estate.[37] Clearly, for such men who wanted to be regarded as gentlemen, it was important to cultivate a paternalist image, if not directly in their capacity as exploiters of labor, then indirectly as community leaders who felt concern for subordinate members' welfare.

However, translating such aspirations from the realm of symbolic gestures into everyday reality was easier said than done. Preoccupied with accumulating capital to establish the profitable businesses that would make their status and authority secure, such men failed to make commitments to community welfare when it conflicted with their own immediate private ends. Despite the dramatic increase in the size and numbers of local concentrations

---

[35] E. P. Thompson, "Patrician Society, Plebeian Culture," *Journal of Social History*, 7:4 (1974), 389–90; idem, "Eighteenth Century English Society: Class Struggle Without Class?" *Social History*, 3:2 (1978), 133–65.

[36] Cudworth, *Round About Bradford*, 284, 511; Henderson, *Northern Counties*, 11–52.

[37] Cudworth, *Manningham, Heaton and Allerton*, 101; J. Maffey, "On Some of the Decayed Families of Bradford," *BA*, o.s. 1 (1888), 26–32.

of wealth, very few charitable endowments were established in eighteenth-century Bradford, and those created tended to be small.[38]

Even more serious was the new elites' failure to adhere to traditional norms and practices concerning the responsibilities that the well-off owed to the poor. According to the values of the indigenous moral economy, charity was regarded as the poor man's right. Although strangers might be treated harshly, the very notion of a community implied a collective responsibility toward deserving natives whose needs and circumstances were well known. In the hinterland, a disabled villager like "blind Jimmy of Heaton" was a regular fixture and, although dependent "upon charity for subsistence," was "in no sense of the word a beggar." Even in Bradford itself, during the eighteenth century, although anonymous vagrants were likely to be run out of town, the native blind were organized into an informal fraternity known as "the waits" who, marching as a rag-tag musical band, were given a tacit license to beg.[39] During the cold Christmas season, the customary right to public begging was extended to poor widows and children who, dressed in fanciful costumes as "mummers," would go "a Thomasing" through the town for alms. Superstition had it that to turn them away unrequited would mean bad luck for the coming year. As they went wassailing, they sang carols that reminded those whose houses they visited that "we are not daily beggars that beg from door to door, But we are neighbours children whom you have seen before."[40]

Perhaps as long as pauperism was a matter of orphans, widows, the disabled, and the aged, it could be handled by such informal networks of reciprocity within the plebeian community itself. In the late eighteenth century, however, as trade depressions worsened, and workers' purchasing power declined, chronic poverty and unemployment swept through the entire community undermining the independence of the able-bodied as well. Unfortunately, it was at precisely such moments of maximum working-class necessity that Bradford's protoindustrial elites, themselves faced with collapsing markets and evaporating profits, were least able to provide the kind of assistance that their own paternalist aspirations required. Thus when villagers turned to the protoindustrialists who had profited handsomely from their labor during good times, they found that traditional notions of mutual aid and reciprocity were no longer being respected by the new notables who, though they called themselves gentlemen, remained capitalists at heart.

Insofar as any provision for structural poverty was made, it was distributed

---

[38] James, *History of Bradford*, 253–7; Mary Lister, "Old Bradford Charities," n.s. 12 (1982), 118–28; 3:1 (1985), 25–30.

[39] J. H. Turner, *Yorkshire Notes and Queries* (1888), 1:234; Scruton, *Pen and Pencil*, 249–50.

[40] Henderson, *Northern Counties*, 66–7; anon., *Yorkshire Magazine* (Bradford, 1872).

almost exclusively through the official mechanisms of the Poor Law, and the dramatic increase in relief expenditures from Bradford Township provides a quantitative, albeit imperfect, measure of how serious the problem had become. Whereas poor rates had been £392 in 1771, they jumped by 25 percent during the next two years, rising to £660 during the mideighties, and £2,394 by 1803. Thus while population grew by 85 percent between 1780 and 1810, Poor Law expenditures rose by 290 percent.[41] Shifting the burden of poor relief from wealthy capitalists to small property owners, often denying assistance to immigrants without legal settlements, and subjecting recipients to public stigma and disgrace, the old Poor Law was widely regarded as inappropriate for supporting those who had become destitute through no fault of their own. In 1799, when wartime inflation reached its peak, a bushel of wheat cost 17s., and the traditional local Poor Law seemed on the verge of breakdown. Despite soaring expenditures and a supplementary voluntary subscription relief fund, many cottagers were reported to be subsisting on a near starvation diet of barley, beans, and pea meal.[42]

Although the reduction of the once independent cottager to a state of near starvation under the impact of inflation, depression, and war was perhaps not the direct responsibility of the gentleman-capitalist, his refusal to intervene in the marketplace to insure adequate provision threw into sharp relief an abdication of paternalist responsibility that had been in the making for some time. Unwilling to shoulder the burdens of community protection that followed from his paternalist self-image, he could scarcely claim the continued deference and submission of a populace that gained no benefit from his rule.

It was precisely under the pressure of such emergencies that the community itself rose up to ensure its protection by enforcing the provisions of the moral economy that were increasingly being ignored by a paternalist elite. In 1783, when the magistrates failed, in the face of rising grain prices, to impose the traditional "assize of bread," "Riotous mobs . . . assembled in Bradford and the neighbouring market towns . . . seized all the corn and meal on which they could lay their hands, and exposed it for sale at their own price."[43] Sixteen years later, when conditions were even worse, similar scenes were again repeated, accompanied by intimations of something far worse. In 1801, a demonstration was held in nearby Bingley "to expose fraud

[41] James, *History of Bradford*, 407–8; idem, *Worsted Manufacture*, 279.
[42] H. J. Maltby, "The Early Volunteer Movement in Bradford," BA, n.s. 4 (1921); Firth, "Genesis," 73–7. A local physician, writing in 1825, also recalled a time "some years ago, and particularly when trade was bad, the lower class of people ate very little animal food, but lived principally on corn and potatoes." John Simpson, *The Journal of Dr. John Simpson of Bradford, 1825* (Bradford, 1981), 20.
[43] James, *History of Bradford*, 156.

and every species of Hereditary Government" and to ask how long the people would "suffer [them]selves to be imposed upon by a Majority of mercenary hirelings, Government pimps – corndealers – placemen – petitioners – paracites etc. and [be] Starving for Bread?"[44]

Although the magistrates did not then "seem to give much importance to any suppos'd Conspiracies or Combinations," evidence had accumulated a year later to suggest widespread popular involvement throughout the West Riding in a shadowy organization known as the United Englishmen, which was implicated in the insurrectionary conspiracies of Col. Marcus Despard. Faced with such facts, it was difficult for anxious elites to avoid the conclusion that the paternalist values and protective obligations that had seemed the very essence of the traditional gentlemanly ideal were, in the context of a capitalist society, less likely to legitimate authority and promote social stability than to inflate plebeian expectations and inflame popular unrest.[45]

From gentleman-capitalist elite to oligarchy: the traditional community falls apart

Given the logic of capitalist development, perhaps it was only to be expected that paternalism would be transformed into its opposite – that what had originally been designed as a social control mechanism would become a sanction for popular revolt. However, what made the crisis of 1799–1802 particularly dangerous was the absence of any alternative avenues, more compatible with the conditions of capitalist production, for creating a consensus between elites and plebeians and keeping the strains and tensions of an emergency situation from tearing the protoindustrial community apart.

For a time in the 1760s, it had appeared as if the underlying antagonisms among social groups, which the conservative ideals of paternalism could not bridge, might be transcended in a progressive campaign uniting all classes within the community around the cause of political liberty and reform. As inhabitants of a distant, unenfranchised, provincial manufacturing center, uninitiated into the metropolitan world of political corruption and intrigue, Bradfordians of all social stations were predisposed toward a "country" political ideology that was hostile to what it regarded as the arbitrary encroachments of a southern, aristocratically dominated state.

Consciousness of parasitism at the national level was heightened by the

---

[44] Quoted in E. P. Thompson, *The Making of the English Working Class* (New York, 1963), 474–5.

[45] J. R. Dinwiddy, "The Black Lamp in Yorkshire"; J. C. Baxter and F. K. Donnelly, "The Revolutionary Underground in the West Riding: Myth or Reality," *Past and Present*, 64 (1974).

local persistence of residual feudal privileges and monopolies that elicited widespread resentment because they were, at once, affronts to the plebeian spirit of communal autonomy and impediments to protoindustrialists' projects for economic growth. The "soke" rights, which entitled their holders, the Smythe family, to a percentage of all corn milled within Bradford, were widely regarded as legalized robbery that brought no advantages to the community. Even worse were the manorial rights, which entitled their absentee owner, the Marsdens, to a market monopoly, precluded the operation of free trade in provisioning, and thus retarded the development of adequate retailing facilities and civic amenities for several decades.[46]

For leading protoindustrialists like the Hustlers, whose improvement schemes were frequently obstructed by manorial powers, experience only confirmed the enlightenment dictum that economic freedom necessitated political liberty and that the rationalization of production and distribution would first require the rationalization of local government affairs. For plebeians who were, first and foremost, concerned with protecting what they regarded as their social and economic rights, these feudal remnants were obnoxious because they appeared as violations of the libertarian spirit of the traditional common law.

As much of the recent writing on this subject reminds us, there was a close connection within preindustrial English popular culture between material standards promised by the moral economy and the legal status of "freeborn Englishman" on which they were ultimately deemed to rest. Although tyranny might be the norm in other countries, reducing the common people to abject submission or violent revolt, Englishmen enjoyed the benefits of belonging to a constitutional community in which rulers were accountable to their subjects, authority was constrained within the limits of due process, and members were, at least theoretically, equal before the law.[47]

In fact, there is some evidence that during the 1760s, sentiments of this sort became widespread at all social levels. In local government, the self-governing vestry could be counterposed to manorial institutions with their stamp of servility, while in the realm of national politics, the Wilkesite movement became a lightning rod for open expressions of hostility to the evils of political tyranny, corruption, and oligarchical rule. In 1770, when Wilkes was released from prison, the town was "the scene of illumination and fireworks," and "Wilkes and Liberty" was seen in almost every window. Here, the language of liberty, at once endorsed by ancient custom, yet still

---

[46] William Cudworth, "The Bradford Soke," *BA*, o.s. 1 (1888); James, *Continuations and Additions*, 90–2.

[47] John Brewer, "The Wilkesites and the Law," in John Brewer and John Styles, eds., *An Ungovernable People* (London, 1980); Thompson, "Eighteenth Century English Society."

perceived as essential to gentleman-capitalists' plans for economic growth, became an ideological bridge between popular cultural traditions and the rationalist elite culture of protoindustrial development.[48]

Nevertheless, in the unfavorable economic climate of the early 1770s, when the bonds of paternalism began to come apart, the libertarian alliance also began to unravel as the equation of economic with political liberty on which it was grounded ceased to hold true. The first indication of serious conflict between the libertarian values of the plebeian community and the exercise of legal authority on behalf of capitalist elites came in 1769–70 when a group of magistrates and leading worsted manufacturers launched a campaign to suppress the practice of gold and silver coining and clipping, which had recently become widespread throughout the West Riding. According to John Styles, who has expertly reconstructed this episode, the Yorkshire "yellow trade," as it was called, received widespread support throughout the community because it provided a badly needed economic benefit in a region desperately short of specie and suffering a depression in its staple trade. Local people readily accepted diminished coins in transactions because it was the only way to obtain adequate means of exchange.[49]

The yellow trade itself came to constitute a lucrative business from which substantial portions of the community, particularly in nearby Halifax where it was centered, could realize at least modest pecuniary gain. Although counterfeiting was a skilled occupation, requiring careful organization and specialized tools, clipping was a simple task open to anyone in possession of a guinea, even workers, like woolcombers, whose shears gave them a perfect clipping tool. Hence, although the yellow trade was not defended on the basis of any customary sanction, it evoked widespread support and participation throughout the population because (notwithstanding its legal status as a capital offense) its deliberate flouting of an irresponsible government mint monopoly seemed to provide a vehicle for the community to fulfill its own needs.[50]

But one portion of the community did recognize the yellow trade as a threat. With their far-flung trading networks outside the region, the large capitalists found themselves losing money as they faced distant customers and suppliers who, unlike local tradesmen, either refused to accept, or demanded a discount on, obviously debased coins. Acting through the resident magistrate, Samuel Lister, himself a landowner who was their ally, Bradford's large protoindustrial capitalists used their manufacturers' association to fi-

---

[48] Firth, "Genesis," 73–7; James, *History of Bradford*, 155.

[49] John Styles, " 'Our Traitorous Money Makers' The Yorkshire Coiners and the Law, 1760–83," in Brewer and Styles, eds., *An Ungovernable People*.

[50] Ibid.

nance a vigorous investigation and prosecution of coiners and clippers in an attempt to root out the yellow trade. Given the stringent evidentiary standards required for conviction and the local community's widespread support of the trade, this campaign was a dismal failure, but it seems to have evoked a new determination in elite circles to tighten the reigns of public administration and order and to become more class conscious in their recourse to the law.[51]

In the year of the American Declaration of Independence, as plans were underway for the subjection of workers to the policing provisions of the Worsted Act, local elites also petitioned Parliament for a more effective weapon against small debtors through the establishment of the local Court of Requests. Placing justice directly in the hands of a commission of forty-eight notables and dispensing with common law procedures and jury trials, this court, whose "large discretionary powers," in the words of Blackstone, "create[d] a petty tyranny," which, at least in Bradford, resulted in sentences of several months imprisonment for even a few shillings debt.[52]

Although the Court of Requests and the campaign against the coiners were not, like the Worsted Act, directed exclusively against workers, all three signaled an unmistakable hardening of class attitudes, at least among the wealthiest gentleman-capitalist elites. In 1779, 437 Bradfordians signed Christopher Wyvill's petition advocating a reduction of government expenditures, "to reduce all exhorbitant emoluments; to rescind and abolish all sinecures, places, and unmerited pensions," but when he subsequently organized his Yorkshire Association as an extraparliamentary pressure group, the once progressive local notables were conspicuous by their absence.[53]

Only in the 1790s, however, did the full flowering of elite conservatism occur. By then, the original protoindustrialists had grown old and complacent while a new generation, accustomed to wealth and privilege, was coming of age. Less interested in pioneering new frontiers of social and economic development than in consolidating, amidst an era of great volatility, the economic assets they had already acquired, Bradford's gentleman-capitalists became increasingly beleaguered and oligarchical as they sought to hold back the tides of social and political transformation that were gathering ominously outside their gates. In 1792–3, these floodgates finally burst open as the

---

[51] Ibid.

[52] Wade Hustwick, "An Eighteenth Century Woolstapler," *Journal of the Bradford Textile Society* (Bradford 1956–7); James, *History of Bradford*, 156–7, 180; idem, *Worsted Manufacture*, 299–300; William Blackstone, *Commentaries on the Laws of England* (Philadelphia, 1902), 3:82.

[53] Herbert Butterfield, *George III, Lord North and the People, 1779–80* (New York, 1949), 204–7; E. C. Black, *The Association: British Extraparliamentary Political Organization, 1764–93* (Cambridge, Mass., 1963).

French Revolution, in its radical phase, suddenly became the symbol of all the atheistic, anarchistic horrors that were now associated with popular rule. Although Bradford had few if any Jacobins, frightened elites began to imagine them behind every corner, and the outbreak of war in 1793 simply added the flames of patriotism to the already burning counterrevolutionary fire.[54]

Almost overnight, local notables began to outdo one another in their denunciations of a once fashionable progressive creed. Evangelical Anglicans like William Atkinson, the church lecturer, used the anti-Jacobin hysteria to whip up a witch-hunt against Nonconformity, whose inherent spiritual egalitarianism, however papered over, raised the specter that "no civil magistrate can have any right authority, or power over the conscience and religion of men." "Here," he contemplated, "the savage brute democracy under the mask of religion. . . . Here too we see the first *general* principles of Dissenters and government completely at variance. . . . While the flame of Democracy and religious dissension was confined to the dissenting meeting houses, it might have been as brilliant, and as hot as you pleased for me." But now, in a world traumatized by revolt and anarchy, "the solemn obligation of an oath" roused men like Atkinson from their lethargy "and determined him to oppose this detestable hypocrisy, this political monster upon earth, democracy under the mask of enthusiasm."[55]

Not surprisingly, under these circumstances, the leading Nonconformists and Methodists, with wealth and reputations to protect, lost little time in proclaiming their loyalty and in identifying even more closely with the orthodox values and programs of the Anglican Tory elite.[56] Those who refused to conform, whether Anglicans or Dissenters, were isolated, ostracized, and eventually persecuted as menaces to the public peace. In 1792, the authorities swiftly moved to stamp out a "political Book Club," which had recently formed in town. A church and king mob held a public book burning in which an effigy of Paine followed *The Rights of Man* and *The Age of Reason* into the flames, while a group of local radicals were run out of town.[57] By

---

[54] James, *History of Bradford*, 155–6.

[55] William Atkinson, *A Letter in Answer to the Jacobin Priests of the West Riding*, (Bradford, 1802), 18, 81.

[56] According to one nineteenth-century antiquarian, the Nonconformist Rev. William Vint of Airedale College, who had hitherto been among the "friends of human liberty . . . felt a keen disappointment in the catastrophe of the French Revolution. . . . That awful experiment [which] . . . frustrated the hopes of mankind solely because religion did not guide it." Turner, *Nonconformity in Idle*, 69.

[57] Thompson, *English Working Class*, 142; James, *History of Bradford*, 156. Unlike many of the official Nonconformists, the liberal Anglican Rev. Baldwyn had the temerity to stand against this reactionary tide, writing scathing satirical pamphlets against Vicar Crosse and Lecturer Atkinson of the church. However, in 1795, Baldwyn went too far when he signed a petition criticizing Pitt's suspension of habeas corpus and attacked his handling

the late nineties, all of Bradford's leading Anglicans, most of the prominent Methodists, and many of the Quakers and Presbyterians had aligned themselves with the new Toryism, which was represented by the ideas of Burke and the policies of Pitt. Theirs was the hard-nosed, post-enlightenment creed of a capitalist, propertied establishment that was prepared to countenance repression, jingoism, obscurantism, and hysteria to ensure that property was made secure.[58]

In 1794, J. A. Busfield organized property owners into a corps of "volunteers." Although the volunteers never saw overseas service, at the turn of the century they were called out to protect the Court of Requests against the mob, to quell local bread riots, and to lay plans in the event of a fullscale revolt.[59] This dependence on the military to insure domestic order underlined the vulnerability of private property in a town that, for all its recent development and expansion, was still devoid of police. Indeed, elites had long been troubled by this deficiency. More than anything else, it had fueled their dissatisfaction with traditional local government structures and had informed their quest for more elitist administrative forms. As early as 1759, local gentlemen had formed a society to prevent crime, inaugurating a long tradition of privately financed voluntary policing associations, which culminated in the Society for the Prosecution of Felons established in 1815.[60]

During the nineties, when social unrest came to overshadow endemic criminality as the main focus of property owners' fears, law and order might

of the economic crisis and the war. As a result of this subversive activity, Baldwyn was excluded from the Bradford Coffee Room and a nearly successful attempt was made to remove him as head of the grammar school. W. Claridge, "Incidents in the Life of the Rev. Edward Baldwyn," *BA*, o.s. 1 (1888); Edward Baldwyn, *A Congratulatory Address to the Rev. John Crosse* (London, 1791).

Baldwyn's accusation that Bradford's ironmasters were profiteers who lined their pockets on an unjust, unwinnable, and costly war was perhaps resented most bitterly of all, not least because there was more than an element of truth in it. However, support for the government was not limited to any sectional interest, but was widely evidenced by the entire elite, even by most of the textile capitalists whose businesses were probably more damaged by the disruption of foreign trade than helped by the availability of government contracts. The war, especially during its early stage, was popular because it was cast as an ideological crusade against radicalism, an ironic position since, more than any other factor, it was the source of the heightened economic instability that fanned the flames of popular unrest. Charles Dodsworth, "The Low Moor Ironworks, Bradford," *Industrial Archaeology*, 8:2 (1971), 127–8; Claridge, "Baldwyn"; Firth, "Genesis," 290–304, 405–8.

[58] Edmund Burke, *Reflections on the Revolution in France* (New York, 1955).

[59] Maltby, "Volunteer Movement."

[60] James, *History of Bradford*, 155–7; "Minutes of Society for the Prosecution of Felons," (Bradford Archives, D.B. 6/44).

have seemed the province of the military, but this did not solve the problem of creating mechanisms for policing the community in more ordinary ways. The most obvious structure in which a system of local law enforcement could have been housed was the vestry, which had supervised local government hitherto. Nevertheless, given its links with the popular traditions of community and its susceptibility to democratic influence, it was clearly inappropriate as an agent for a new administrative order designed to serve the class interests of protoindustrial elites.

Much more promising was the model suggested by the Court of Requests and the Worsted Committee – semiprivate, oligarchical, appointive commissions that were, nevertheless, given statutory public powers by act of Parliament which permitted them to operate in certain specified areas outside the confines of the customary culture or common law. In 1803, as the crisis of public order deepened, a subscription of £500 was canvassed in local notable circles to establish, through the mechanism of an improvement act, a commission of this nature, authorized to lay rates on Bradford's inhabitants and invested with broad administrative, policing, and regulatory powers.[61]

Although the improvement act was initially opposed by the lord of the manor and some nearby landowners, who feared that it might infringe on their rights, it was widely supported by most of the leading local gentleman-capitalists, both Anglicans and Nonconformists, who, under the leadership of Samuel Hailstone, Edmund Peckover, Matthew Thompson, and John Hardy, nursed the bill through Parliament later in the year. After its passage, fifty-eight commissioners were appointed – essentially those who had paid to get it passed – and the right to co-opt new members was subject to a £1,000 property qualification invested in the commission itself.[62]

Although the commission was entrusted with a broad range of local governmental responsibilities, street scavenging, lighting, and water supply were all contracted out to private enterprise, and only policing was undertaken directly by the commissioners themselves. The immediate appointment of seven night watchmen, raised in 1827 to thirteen, suggests that law enforcement was the commissioners' top priority and, indeed, the only function they consistently performed. Although this minimalist approach to local government would ultimately be seen as inadequate for the industrial city that Bradford was soon to become, it played a significant part in preserving public order during the dangerous early years of the nineteenth century. By organizing cheap public service, however inadequately, by leaving development

[61] Cudworth, *Bradford Corporation*, 17–8; Firth, "Genesis," 80–90.
[62] Cudworth, *Bradford Corporation*, 17–20.

open to free-market forces, and by creating an infrastructure of public administration that would be shielded from plebeian interference, the commission gave protoindustrial capitalists the type of local government they wanted and helped to facilitate the urban-industrial revolution that lay ahead.[63]

Conclusion

With elites' abandonment of paternalism at the turn of the century and their drift to a conservative politics of oligarchy, the protoindustrial community finally died. Denied an official community by the abdication of elites, the plebeian impulse toward collectivism and mutuality was forced to look inward toward the creation of new working-class communities all their own. Briefly channeled into an abortive insurgency that sought to impose from below the moral economy that had been repudiated from above, by 1805, public order had been effectively restabilized and the impulse of popular radicalism, driven underground.

Stymied in its effort to find satisfactory expression, the plebeian community was driven back to its own inner resources in what Thompson terms a "chiliasm of despair." Here fragmentary elements of the old popular culture, now decisively repudiated by elites, resurfaced convulsively among a desperate and defeated multitude in bizarre, almost hysterical forms. After the turn of the century, the popular spirituality, which had always been latent in this hotbed of dissent, suddenly erupted in a series of millenarian outbursts that corresponded chronologically with political radicalisms' defeat. Manifesting itself in emotionally charged moments of eschatalogical expectation, new communities, drawing on the remnants of the plebeian culture, formed in Bradford around charismatic, self-proclaimed prophets like Joanna Southcott or her successor prophet Wroe.[64]

The Methodists, ever sensitive to unsatiated currents of popular spirituality, were able to sublimate much of this mass anxiety to serve their own more conventional ends. In 1805, there was a major revival as nine hundred applicants went on trial for Wesleyan membership. Although many became backsliders, by 1807, local Wesleyan membership had risen to 1,874 or about 10 percent of the adult population. "The doors of the Octagon Chapel," at the height of the revival, "for ten or twelve weeks were scarcely ever closed ... no sooner, in many instances, was the text announced, then the cries of persons in distress so interrupted the preacher, that the service

---

[63] Ibid., 49–73.
[64] Scruton, *Pen and Pencil*, 244–6; Thompson, *English Working Class*, 375–400.

of the Word was, at once, exchanged for one of general and earnest intercession."[65]

The deliberate remaking of the personality and the self-conscious community building that millenarianism or Methodism entailed was, in Thompson's view, simply a pathological obverse of the working-class consciousness raising, which had begun through the solidarities of popular radicalism, but which had been diverted inward when the political movement failed. In both cases, however, Thompson stressed the significance of workers creating new forms of community, which were not only exclusively plebeian in composition, but qualitatively reflective of both the positive and negative features of the workers' collectively shared class experience as a proletarianized and dispossessed social group.[66]

Although there is much truth in Thompson's overall interpretation, the case of Bradford suggests that his chronology of class formation may be a bit premature; for while Bradford, by the beginning of the nineteenth century, had ceased to be a paternalist community that linked the plebeian culture with the culture of elites, it had not yet fully become a class society in which capitalist relations constituted the dominant axis on which social groups would interact. Protoindustrial workers, although in some respects already proletarianized, still lived in their traditional communities and worked within the framework of the family economy in which they sometimes retained a residual subsistence cushion and generally still exercised control over the actual process of work. It might well be argued that, when they participated in Methodist or millenarian revivalism, combated starvation with *taxation populaire*, or even joined an underground revolutionary conspiracy, they were not so much exhibiting the first stirrings of class consciousness as demonstrating the power that values and forms of action characteristic of the traditional village community continued to exert over their lives. When they acted collectively, it was to reassert the paternalist moral economy rather than to transform it, and they organized less frequently as producers to combat the alienation of their labor than as consumers to regulate the exhorbitantly high price of food.[67]

A comparable situation existed with regard to elites. Inasmuch as they were capitalists, competitive pressures of the marketplace separated their

---

[65] J. N. Dickons, "Kirkgate Chapel, Bradford and its Associations with Methodism," *BA*, n.s. 5 (1933), 219–22; W. W. Stamp, *Historical Notices of Wesleyan Methodism in Bradford* (Bradford, 1841), 86; Thompson, *English Working Class*, 375–400.

[66] Karl Marx, *Early Writings* (New York, 1963), 43–4; Thompson, *English Working Class*, especially, 350–400.

[67] Some of these points have been cogently made by Craig Calhoun in *The Question of Class Struggle* (Chicago, 1982). Nevertheless, as Chapter 16 of this work argues, his overall critique goes too far, obscuring the extent to which Thompson's basic argument is correct.

interests from those of the workers, leading them to abandon the dictates of paternalism and to withdraw from plebeian community life. Yet inasmuch as they aspired to be gentlemen, they could not comprehend their social function explicitly in capitalist terms. In the end, they never devised an entirely new, nonaristocratic, legitimating ideology that would correspond to the actual conditions of their class rule. Unable either to make paternalism a reality or decisively to dispense with it as a governing ideal, they responded to what must have seemed an impossible situation with a cynical policy of social abdication and oligarchical withdrawal.

Yet if neither workers nor elites during the protoindustrial period thought or acted predominantly in capitalist-class terms, after 1810, as the era of war and counterrevolution drew to a close, Bradford was engulfed in an urban-industrial revolution that, by 1850, had created a society in which capitalism and class had become compelling and palpably visible realities that largely determined the way all social groups worked and lived.

3

The urban-industrial revolution: 1810–1850

Bradford's urban-industrial revolution took off just after 1810, when the stagnation of war began to give way to a sustained economic and demographic boom. Over the next forty years, the output of Bradford's worsted industry rose thirteen times, and the power capacity of its factories expanded twenty-seven-fold, while the population of the four townships that became Bradford Borough climbed 648 percent, from 16,012 to 103,778. By 1850, a regional, protoindustrial market town had been transformed into an international, industrial capitalist city, the eighth largest in Britain, serving as the global center of worsted production and exchange. No other city in the world at that time experienced so rapid an ascent.[1]

Hand in hand with this quantitative expansion went a qualitative transformation that destroyed the spatial structure and social relations of the traditional community and created a new urban environment in its place. Under protoindustrial conditions, economic and demographic growth had been absorbed within the prevailing framework of dispersed, rural settlement and handicraft, domestic patterns of work. Now, as growth accelerated, it broke through these traditional frameworks destroying the last remnants of precapitalist self-sufficiency, concentrating both people and industry together within an urban center and taking on a developmental life of its own.

That these decades were a period not merely of growth but of fundamental reorganization can be seen from a cursory glance at statistics. The output of the West Riding worsted industry increased eightfold during this period, but Bradford's share of the total rose even more rapidly, from 17 percent in 1810 to 26 percent in 1830 and by 1850 to an even higher, indeterminate amount. By 1838, Bradford contained 36 percent of the worsted factory horsepower in Yorkshire and 29 percent of the national total. If industry was becoming urbanized as it expanded, so was population. Whereas in 1811, the future borough of Bradford contained only 2 percent

---

[1] Theodore Koditschek, "Class Formation and the Bradford Bourgeoisie" (Princeton, Ph.D. dissertation, 1981), 113–14.

of the West Riding's population, its share of a population twice as large had risen to 8 percent in 1850.[2]

That urbanization should accompany full-scale industrialization is not particularly surprising. The adaptation of the steam engine provided a powerful, reliable, and mobile source of energy, which made possible the concentration of production in an urban center. Capitalists found this new option desirable because it promised them cheaper, readier supplies of fuel, raw materials, and human labor. Moreover, the centralization of markets, customers, and the component parts of the production process all together in a common location added to the economic attractions of the city. The bustling, competitive urban environment acted as a stimulus to innovation and ensured the widespread and rapid diffusion of new machinery and industrial techniques.[3]

If urbanization fostered industrial capitalism, industrial capitalism facilitated further urbanization, attracting an influx of newcomers in search of opportunity or remunerative employment. The concentration of population and the centralization of production were mutually reinforcing trends. Whatever their relationship in other times and places, in early-nineteenth-century Bradford, urbanization and industrialization were two sides of a single process: complementary manifestations of the logic of competitive capitalism, working itself out in the terms of a new productive infrastructure that had to be located in a new environmental space.[4]

---

[2] Calculated from information in John James, *History of the Worsted Manufactures in England* (London, 1857); idem, *History and Topography of Bradford* (Bradford, 1841), 267–99; idem, *Continuations and Additions to the History and Topography of Bradford* (Bradford, 1866), 219–46.

[3] Phyllis Deane, *The First Industrial Revolution* (Cambridge, 1965), 147–9.

[4] Of course, there is a more general theoretical sense in which urbanization and industrialization represent not complementary forces but divergent paradigms for comprehending the transformation to the modern world. In mainstream Western social theory, reliance on concepts like modernization, bureaucratization, structural differentiation, and anomie entails a conscious or unconscious decision to depict the transition to modern industrial society in essentially naturalistic urbanizing terms, as a shift from a small-scale, close-knit, custom bound *Gemeinschaft* to a mass, impersonal, market-oriented *Gesellschaft*. Here, there is a tendency to comprehend the overall development of social relations in terms that are fundamentally spatial and environmental. By contrast, Marxism, which focuses directly on the transformation of productive relations under capitalism, eschews recourse to mechanical or biological metaphors and offers a distinctively human, historical interpretation of the rise of industrial society as an ongoing dialectic between its inherent logic of economic accumulation and the contingent interactions of its constituent social groups. Although this book takes an approach that is basically more Marxist than urbanist, it acknowledges the inadequacy of reducing the environmental dimension of modernization to a mere byproduct of capitalist productive relationships. Instead, it recognizes a more

Economic and demographic growth: 1810–1825

If it was inevitable that the industrial revolution in worsted production would gravitate toward an urban center, Bradford was by no means predestined to assume this leading role. Compared with Halifax, the other major eighteenth-century West Riding worsted center, Bradford entered the race for industrial supremacy with several disadvantages. Larger and less isolated than eighteenth-century Bradford, Halifax was located on the Calder River and was thus part of an extensive navigational system. Moreover, its rich endowment of fast-flowing streams made it a more viable location for the early water mills, whereas its longer tradition as a mercantile center probably gave it the edge in capital formation.[5]

Yet because Bradford was initially more backward, its experience of proto-industrialization was, of necessity, more complete. As we have seen, the absence of a traditional mercantile class and the need for a canal to facilitate transport created profitable opportunities in the course of surmounting natural impediments. When combined with the opportunities for investment in iron founding, these activities made possible the creation of a more innovative and cohesive group of local capitalists, better able than their Halifax counterparts to make the transition to the new industrial processes and techniques.[6] By 1810, Bradford's worsted output had drawn even with that of Halifax; thereafter it took a substantial lead. By 1830, the output of worsted yarn from the Bradford district was 67 percent higher than from the Halifax district. Yet where only 45 percent of Halifax's production was concentrated in the town itself, 75 percent of Bradford's was, and the output of Bradford town outpaced that of Halifax by 176 percent.[7]

Bradford's urban-industrial revolution took place in two distinct phases. During the first phase (roughly the years between 1810 and 1825), a surge in local industrial development set the pace for an increase in the town's

complex historical process in which urbanization operates, at least partly independently, through a distinctive environmental logic of its own. Marx himself showed little recognition of the difficulty in reconciling these two processes. Engels came closer to grappling with the problem in *The Condition of the Working Class in England* (Moscow, 1973) and *The Housing Question* (New York, 1935). However, it has only been given explicit attention by Marxist geographers in recent years, most notably by Manuel Castells, *The Urban Question: A Marxist Approach* (Cambridge, Mass., 1977) and David Harvey, *The Urbanization of Capital: Studies in the History and Theory of Capitalist Urbanization* (Baltimore, 1985).

[5] Gary Firth, "The Genesis of the Industrial Revolution in Bradford," (Bradford, Ph.D. dissertation, 1975); E. M. Sigsworth, *Black Dyke Mills* (Liverpool, 1958), 22–3; Paul Mantoux, *The Industrial Revolution in the Eighteenth Century* (London, 1964), 66; J. Maffey, "On Some of the Decayed Families of Bradford," *BA*, o.s. 1 (1888), 28.

[6] Sigsworth, *Black Dyke*, 17–29.

[7] James, *Worsted Manufacture*, 430.

population and for an expansion of the urban settlement that followed in its wake. This initial wave of industrialization and urbanization was a belated expression of the transformational logic that the mechanization of worsted factory spinning and the onset of mass production had first initiated around the turn of the century. By obstructing foreign exports and fettering home demand, the Napoleonic and American wars effectively delayed the full impact of the new mode of production for a decade. Now, as the fighting started to wind down and foreign markets reopened – first on the continent after 1811, and then in America after 1813 – Bradford's fledgling factory industry received the stimulus it needed. Between 1810 and 1815, output rose 30 percent and the worsted industry quickly outpaced the now depressed iron trade as the most dynamic economic sector in the town. The ground was prepared for a massive, sustained boom in industrial development.[8]

Moreover, the savage postwar deflation, which devastated agriculture and caused recession in many other industries, scarcely harmed the worsted trade at all. As Figure 3-1 and Table 3-1 show, between 1815 and 1820, ten new factories were built in Bradford, more than doubling the output of worsted yarn. It was during this period that the bulk of the second generation of Bradford's capitalist elite abandoned protoindustry and converted to factory spinning.[9] Even after 1820, the trend continued. A brief recession in the early twenties was followed by another boom, which lasted until 1825. As Edward Baines remarked in his 1822 *Gazette:*

> No manufacturing town in England has perhaps suffered so little from depression of trade as Bradford. In war and peace it has been alike prosperous. It has indeed felt the vicissitudes of trade in common with other places, but the depression has generally been of short duration and it has been among the first to feel the vivifying effects of the return to prosperous times.[10]

Thus two years after the sharp 1825 depression, a full recovery had resumed. By 1830, wool consumption for Bradford Township was 618 percent of the 1810 level, while factory horsepower in the four townships of the future borough was up 718 percent. Bradford's industrial revolution had commenced.

The bulk of the wealth generated in this sustained boom went into the pockets of the handful of large textile capitalists who had pioneered the local

---

[8] Ibid, 369–70, 388–9, 409, 430.
[9] Men like John Wood, William Rouse, Christopher Waud, G. W. Addison, James Wade, Swithin Anderton, and Richard Margerison all joined Bradford's factory pioneers, Fawcett, Smith, Thompson, the Rands, and the Garnetts, during this period as the leading millowners of the early industrial age.
[10] Edward Baines, *West Riding Gazette* (Leeds, 1822), 147.

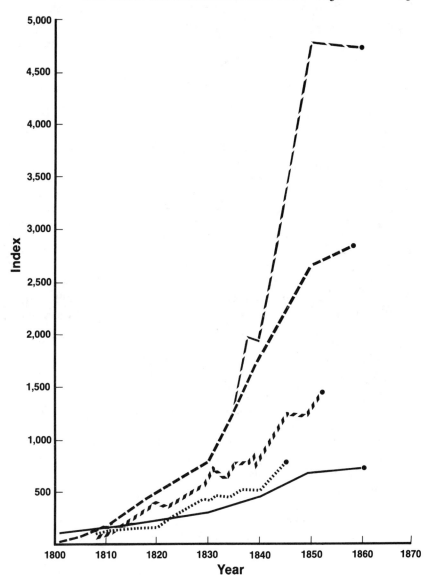

Key: ━━━━━━━━ , factory employment (Bradford Borough; 1835 = production index); ■■ ■■ ■■ ■■ , factory horsepower (Bradford Borough); ✹✹✹✹✹✹ , wool consumption (Bradford Township); ııııııııııı wool consumption (West Riding population); Bradford Borough Population ████ Compiled from sources cited in notes 2, 9, and 10, as well as pp. (1831, 18), 318, 804-5.

Figure 3–1. Comparative trends in worsted production. Index: 1810 = 100.

Table 3-1. *Factory building, Bradford Borough, 1800–41*

	Number built						
	1800–04	1805–09	1810–14	1815–19	1820–24	1825–29	1830–41
Bradford Township	2	2	2	6	6	1	20
Urban semiring	1	0	0	4	4	3	17
Borough total	3	2	2	10	10	4	37
Total horsepower added		120	130	288	168	156	334

Sources: John James, *History and Topography of Bradford* (Bradford, 1841), 225–6, 284; idem, *History of the Worsted Manufactures in England* (London, 1857), 606–11; Joshua Fawcett, *Rise and Progress of the Town of Bradford* (Bradford, 1859); *PP* (1834, xx), 70–207.

spinning industry. A number of them became extremely wealthy, selling yarn not only to local weavers, but to Scottish, German, and Russian handi-craftsmen too. This prosperity was reflected in the increasing size of factories. A study of insurance valuations taken from the entire region shows more than a threefold rise in the average value from £1,443 in 1800 to £5,527 in 1835.[11] Yet if the bulk of boom profits went to a handful of magnates, lesser benefits trickled down to a larger number of ordinary men. Enterprising individuals with a bit of capital who wished to take advantage of the almost constantly rising demand found opportunities as never before. The increasing scale of production made it harder to break into the world of the factory, but high profitability induced several local gentlemen such as E. C. Lister, hitherto unconnected to the staple trade, to construct mills, which they subdivided into rooms that were let to small manufacturers.[12] Moreover, as Dr. Hudson has demonstrated, even after mechanization took place, cir-culating capital continued to absorb 30 to 50 percent of the costs of man-ufacture, and large woolstaplers' continued willingness, at least before 1830, to provide several months credit on the sale of raw wool made it possible for relatively small men to continue setting up businesses at least as long as trade remained good.[13]

Finally, the extension of factory spinning in the town center dramatically

[11] D. T. Jenkins, *The West Riding Wool Textile Industry, 1770–1835: A Study of Fixed Capital Formation* (Edington, Wilts., 1975), 171–2; James, *Worsted Manufacture*, 491–2.
[12] Sigsworth, *Black Dyke*, 177.
[13] Pat Hudson, "The Genesis of Industrial Capital in the West Riding Wool Textile Industry c. 1770–1850," (York, D. Phil. dissertation, 1981), 226–61. For impressionistic evidence about the social consequences of the economic boom of the early 1820s see John Simpson, *The Journal of Dr. John Simpson of Bradford, 1825* (Bradford, 1981), 5–9, 17–20, 26, 30–6.

increased the demand for raw wool, the need for handloom weaving in the countryside, and thus, the opportunities for the petty capitalist to make a profit through these activities. The 1830 Bradford Directory listed only fifty-two full-fledged stuff firms but over four hundred small clothiers who attended the Bradford Piece Hall, almost twice as many as a half century earlier.[14]

Nor were opportunities entirely restricted to the capitalists. Accelerating production initially created an intense demand for labor, and wages in most textile occupations rose 20 to 80 percent above their admittedly abysmal wartime lows, while the price of provisions dropped by a third. At least until 1825, this heavy demand for labor benefited not only the largely young and female factory work force, but the adult male handicraftsmen as rising yarn output required more and more workers to process and fabricate it. The collapse of the East Anglian fancy trade and the wholesale migration of skilled occupations such as woolcombing to Yorkshire meant that artisanal opportunities around Bradford were increasing. Admittedly, the appearance of these trades in the industrial West Riding was a sign that they were being brought under capitalist control. For a time, however, they provided small weavers and farmers with opportunities for well-paid employment that had not existed before. In 1830, when the "golden age" of the handicraft worker had already come to an end, there were still several thousand woolcombers in Bradford itself together with the town's three thousand factory operatives and thirteen thousand hinterland handloom weavers within a radius of six miles.[15]

Bradford's industrial revolution created an extraordinary demand for people that far surpassed anything that the town's existing population, with its traditionally high indigenous fertility rates, was able to meet by natural increase. Fortunately, opportunities at all social levels proved effective in attracting a sufficient number of outsiders to meet the needs of the growing economy. In the decades after 1810, a wave of immigrants began to appear on Bradford's streets. Local biographical material bears frequent witness to the story of the young man (although women were statistically more common) who came to Bradford during these years, either with the promise of a specific job or with hopes that something would turn up. Parochial data on baptisms and burials combined with census statistics after 1801 make it possible to construct rough estimates of these demographic patterns even before the advent, in 1837, of civil registration of births and deaths. Table 3-2 reveals the close correspondence between the commencement of Bradford's urban-industrial revolution and the onset of migration into the parish.[16]

---

[14] William Cudworth, *Rambles Round Horton* (Bradford, 1886), 32; Firth, "Genesis," 451.

[15] William Scruton, "The Bradford Contest," *BA*, o.s. 1 (1888), 68; *PP* (1840, XXIII), 558. See also statement of handloom weaver in James, *Worsted Manufacture*, 479–80.

[16] Migration is calculated by subtracting the decennial surplus of births over deaths from the total population growth as recorded in the census. Of course, using parish registers,

Table 3-2. *Vital statistics and migration, Bradford Parish, 1761–1830*

Period	Baptisms	Burials	Surplus	Total growth	Immigrants
1761–70	2,865	2,329	536	—	—
1771–80	3,674	2,739[a]	935[a]	—	—
1781–90	4,565	3,182	1,383	—	—
1791–1800	5,921	3,146	2,775	—	—
1801–10	8,125	2,827	5,298	2,722	−2,576[a]
1811–20	10,299	2,817	7,482	20,438	+12,956[a]
1821–30	12,953	3,995	8,958	24,042	+15,048[a]

[a]Estimated figure

Source: Calculated from statistics presented in Gary Firth, "The Genesis of the Industrial Revolution in Bradford" (Bradford, Ph.D. dissertation, 1975), 137–8; *PP* (1831, XVIII), 318, 804.

At first, the dimensions of this migration were muted, at least by comparison with what was to come. Inferring maximum levels from the parish registers indicates that the migration component of total growth was, at most, 63 percent during each of the two census decades, from 1811 to 1830. In all likelihood, migration was considerably less than this. The Parish probably absorbed an average of about 1,000 newcomers per year during the 1810s and perhaps 1,200 annually during the twenties. Combined with a significant further increase in native fecundity, this immigrant influx generated a substantial local population increase. However, this population explosion was not distributed evenly throughout the large region that the Parish comprised. On the contrary, the protoindustrial pattern of dispersed rural settlement now gave way to a pattern of greater concentration in the urban core. This is reflected in the differential rates of demographic increase, which can be calculated for different parts of the region from the data presented in Table 3-3.

In the outer ring of nine townships, which belonged to Bradford Parish but which lay beyond the borders of the future borough, the population doubled between 1811 and 1831. In the inner ring of three borough town-

which record baptisms rather than births and burials rather than deaths, is a risky business. Not all of those born were baptized in the church, nor were the dead always buried there. This was particularly true in a community like Bradford with a large number of Dissenters. Nor can one assume that the discrepancies offset one another. Demographers generally regard the record of baptisms as less accurate than that of burials and have noted a general decline in the quality of registers in the early nineteenth century. Thus, parochial registration almost certainly understates the level of fertility and any inference about migration made from this source should be regarded as a maximum estimate.

Table 3-3. *Population of Bradford in the nineteenth century*

Year	Township	Borough	Parish
1780	4,506	8,525	—
1801	6,393	13,264	29,794
1811	7,767[a]	16,012	32,516
1821	13,064	26,309	52,954
1831	23,233	43,537	76,996
1841	34,560	66,715	105,257
1851	52,493[b]	103,778	155,579

[a]Total breakdown to 3,559 for East Bradford and 4,208 for West Bradford.
[b]Total breakdown to 29,931 for East Bradford and 22,562 for West Bradford.
Sources: Compiled from the published census reports. Until 1851 there were no population breakdowns between Bradford West (inner city) and Bradford East, the outlying, predominantly working-class portion of Bradford Township. The "Bradford Parish" coulumn is strictly accurate until 1841. In 1851, the Bradford Registration District was aggregated by the census compilers, and because this is a more logically constructed area, it has been used for 1851 onward although the Calverley and Pudsey subdistricts have been excluded because they were more properly in the orbit of Leeds rather than Bradford. In general, the main difference between the regional figures before and in 1851 is that, in 1851, the region includes the villages of Drighlington, Tong, Cleckheaton, and Wyke, which were certainly in the Bradford economic region, although they were not included in the old parish. The combined population of these places was 14,782 in 1851; thus, the true comparison with the 1841 region is 155,579 for 1851. However, in all districts there are slight changes in the areas reported between 1841 and 1851 (perhaps it is only that they were surveyed more carefully). See Theodore Koditschek, "Class Formation and the Bradford Bourgeoisie" (Princeton, Ph.D. dessertation, 1981), 121. These differences are inconsequential except in the case of the region and do not detract from the comparability of the population figures.

ships that surrounded the town of Bradford, the rate of population increase was 146 percent, while in Bradford township itself, the population quadrupled during these years. In 1801, when the first census was taken, these three areas already exhibited differences in population density, with 0.6 persons per acre in the outer parochial ring, 1.5 persons per acre in the borough inner semiring, and 3.8 persons per acre in Bradford Township itself. By 1831, the outer ring had an average of 1.4 persons per acre, the inner semiring 4.5 persons per acre, and the township 13.8 persons per acre.[17]

[17] The borough inner semiring includes Bowling, Horton, and Manningham townships. See Figure 4-1. Calculated from *PP* (1801, VI), 438–9; (1812, XI), 407–26; (1822, XV), 414; (1831, XVIII), 318.

Table 3-4. *Percentage of families chiefly occupied in trade or manufacture, 1811–31*

	Bradford Township	Inner borough semi-ring	Outer parish ring
1811	95	74	61
1821	97	81	86
1831	97	94	88

Sources: Calculated from *PP* (1801, VI), 438–9; (1812, XI), 407–26; (1822, XV), 414; (1831, XVIII), 318.

These differential patterns of demographic development were, of course, the consequences of the geographical differentiation of economic function that industrial capitalism brought in its wake. Factory spinning, the most rapidly developing economic sector, together with mercantile activity, urban provisioning, and the preparatory process of combing all concentrated in the urban center. Meanwhile, handloom weaving, garden farming, and coal and iron mining and founding expanded in the surrounding hinterland, creating several nodes of thicker settlement. Some of these nodes were overgrown farming and weaving villages, like Great Horton or Manningham. Others, like Bowling, were foci of iron and coal production whose site was determined by the location of mineral deposits.

As Table 3-4 indicates, rural population pressure, which had been building throughout the protoindustrial period and eroding the region's traditional agrarian base, finally exploded between 1811 and 1831, laying the foundations for a fully urban proletariat, effectively detached from access to the land. It is unfortunate that the existing census data do not permit a more detailed occupational analysis, yet it is evident from these crude figures that occupational specialization was becoming almost universal. The quasi-peasant household of the protoindustrial past was being stripped of its last vestige of economic independence as its members became dependent on paid employment and were integrated into factory work. Although the hinterland retained a rural appearance, it was losing its traditional protoindustrial autonomy as it became functionally subordinate to the needs of the urbanizing center. Where the town had once existed to serve the surrounding countryside, now the countryside was being subsumed within the economic orbit of the town.

As its population more than quadrupled, not only did the urban core come to dominate its hinterland economy, it began to encroach upon the hinterland space. This extension of the built-up area is displayed in Figure 4-1, in which the settlement areas shown in maps from 1802, 1834, and 1850 are superimposed upon one another. As the numbers of inhabitants thickened in the town center (West Bradford Township), rising from about four thousand in 1811 to something like eighteen thousand twenty years later, the size of the built-up area expanded simultaneously in two different ways. As it spread concentrically, it also stretched out radially in spokes of settlement that fanned out much farther from the center along the turnpike roads that fed the town. By 1834, the space of contiguous settlement had expanded from the original fifty acres to an area approximately six times as large.[18]

The urban core now encompassed virtually all of West Bradford and was spreading into part of East Bradford as well, whereas its radial spokes were protruding southwest into Little Horton, southeast into Bowling, where the coal and ironfields lay, and uphill in the north toward the village of Manningham. When Bradford was enfranchised in 1832, all four townships were rightly included to make a large borough of ten square miles. Although the bulk of this area remained technically rural, it was now inextricably linked to the life of the city that was germinating outward into the immediate hinterland.[19]

The passage of the Reform Bill and Bradford's enfranchisement as a parliamentary borough marked the beginning of a new era in the history of the town. The first phase of Bradford's urban-industrial revolution, which had made it a factory town with a population of 43,500, was now complete. The second phase, which would transform the factory town into an industrial city, was about to begin. The simple logic of economic ascent in which urban development and demographic expansion were automatic by-products of industrial growth was now to be replaced by a more complex developmental dynamic set in motion by the forces of economic disruption and reorganization and fraught with convulsive social effects.

The first indication that Bradford's urban-industrial revolution was entering upon a new and more problematic course came in 1825 when economic prosperity was interrupted by a bitter strike and deep depression. The optimism that Baines had articulated three years earlier about Bradford's ability to weather hard times was now put to a critical test.[20] On the whole, industrial Bradford emerged from this trauma more successfully than any of its neighbors, but the cost, both in the short term and in the long run, was high. Wages plummeted, profits dipped, and many small capitalists as well as a few large ones were forced into bankruptcy by falling prices and

[18] C. Richardson *A Geography of Bradford* (Bradford, 1976).
[19] *Leeds Mercury*, Aug. 13, 1831.
[20] Scruton, "Bradford Contest"; and Chapter 16.

declining demand. However, the town's leading gentleman-capitalists were able to forestall a full-scale collapse of confidence by putting their assets on the line. When the largest West Riding bank of Wentworth and Chaloner was forced into receivership by a run on deposits, only the Bradford branch (formerly Peckover & Co.) survived, because forty-two of the wealthiest local notables stood surety for £2,000,000.[21]

Although prosperity returned to Bradford's worsted industry in 1828, the age of easy profits was over. Thereafter, depressions became more frequent while competition grew increasingly stiff. This is not to say that the industry failed to expand. Between 1830 and 1850 Bradford Township doubled its consumption of raw wool while the factory capacity of the new borough increased fivefold, as the remaining production processes were brought within the factory gates.[22] Yet unlike the growth of the earlier period, the expansion of the 1830s and 1840s took place in an environment of economic dislocation, which had perilous consequences for the urbanizing process and had a decisive impact on the formation of social class. Whereas the first two decades of growth had permitted the benefits of industrial capitalism to be distributed widely throughout the region, in the 1830s and 1840s, there was a deepening divergence between the ways that the system was experienced by individuals depending on their place in the production process. This was an age of industrial concentration, reorganization, and renewed innovation. Those who became the agents of these forces secured the benefits that these forces had offered. But for those who could not adapt to change, the 1830s and 1840s would be remembered as a disastrous time.

Economic crisis and industrial reorganization: 1825–50

Although it took contemporaries some time to acknowledge it, the 1825 depression marked a turning point both in Bradford's development as an international worsted center and in the larger social history of the town. For the previous fifteen years, output had expanded exponentially as the spectacular labor savings attendant on the mechanization of spinning and the attachment of the flying shuttle to the handloom had extended the marketability of worsteds by cutting the price of piece goods approximately in half. However, after 1825, as this bounty was exhausted, it became clear that further growth would not be automatic and would require a major modernization and restructuring of Bradford's industrial base.

---

[21] *Bradford Old Bank, Centenary Souvenir*, (Bradford, 1903).

[22] James, *Worsted Manufacture*, 430, 450, 487, 489, 503, 510–13, 604, 611; *PP* (1837, XLV), 150–1; (1844, XXVII), 559; (1845, XXV), 431.

As we have seen, the fourteen years after 1811 had been a period of steadily mounting prosperity in which the volume of trade had accelerated within a mildly rhythmic framework of periodic slowdowns and renewed starts. In 1811–14, 1817–18, and 1820–4, there were spurts in demand followed by brief interruptions in 1815–16 and 1819.[23] However, in the two and a half decades that followed, the cycles began to oscillate with increasing volatility as the ratio of good to bad years declined. The severe depression of 1825–6 was followed by a buoyant market that lasted until 1829, a vigorous boom in 1832 and 1833, and more modest upturns in 1835 and 1836. These years of prosperity were interspersed with moderate recessions in 1830–1 and again in 1834.[24]

During the next twelve years, however, the cyclical swings became more violent, jeopardizing the stability of social and economic life. Between 1837 and 1849, depressions grew deeper and lasted longer while the short-lived booms became more feverish. Between 1837 and 1840, the entire economy experienced a profound crisis, until, in 1841, prosperity briefly returned. Then, between 1842 and 1844, the crisis returned and intensified only to be broken, in 1845, by an explosive boom. Finally, in late 1846, this boom went bust and was followed by a protracted economic collapse that was prolonged by the revolutions of 1848 and was brought to an end only in 1849, when a rising tide of more lasting prosperity set in.[25]

This economic environment of deepening crisis in Bradford, as in so many other contemporary English industrial towns, had a profound impact on the character of industrial capitalism during the 1830s and 1840s. It engendered constant disruption, forcing reorganization and speeding up changes that were already underway. John Foster, in his study of the Oldham cotton industry, has characterized this as an age of falling profit rates.[26] The Bradford evidence suggests, rather, an era of extreme volatility in which the rate of profit tended to fluctuate wildly from year to year and vary significantly from firm to firm. In part, this was simply a logical concomitant of violent oscillations in the cycle of trade. Dr. Hudson has collected profit rates from three unusually successful worsted firms during the 1840s, and the mean profit rate of this group, which was 19 percent during the boom of 1844, dropped to 4.6 percent two years later, shooting up to 33 percent in the boom of 1849. Nevertheless, a rising firm like John Fosters of Queensbury maintained a healthy profit of 15 percent in the 1846 depression, while a

[23] James, *Worsted Manufacture*, 354–428.
[24] Ibid., 428–78.
[25] Ibid., 478–519. For a general discussion of the violently cyclical character of British industrial capitalism during this period by a particularly perceptive businessman who experienced it first hand see Engels, *Condition of the Working Class*, 121–3.
[26] John Foster, *Class Struggles and the Industrial Revolution* (London, 1974), 80.

more marginal firm like Clough's (not in the sample) actually lost 12 percent of its capital value that year.[27]

Clearly, this was an era both of opportunity and danger for the capitalist. Long-term growth in this turbulent environment required wholesale industrial reorganization, the development of more attractive product lines, the discovery of cheaper raw-material inputs, and most importantly, a significant reduction in labor costs through a combination of further mechanization of the remaining parts of the production process and a lowering of the individual worker's wage. Bradford's success in pioneering these new innovations, which kept her on the worsted industry's entrepreneurial cutting edge, is attested by the increase, throughout the traumatic 1830–50 period, in horsepower capacity by 270 percent, while the complement of manufacturers increased from around 30 to 129. It was in these years that Bradford laid the foundations for its mid-Victorian prosperity, maintaining and consolidating dominance within the worsted industry as a whole. As a result, the town evolved from a mere hub of factory spinning to become a pioneer in novel yarns and fibers, a center for mechanization in weaving and combing, and an emporium for the finishing and distribution of manufactured goods.[28]

Although a few of the largest millowners of the older generation, men like J. G. Horsfall, William Rouse, or Christopher Waud, were able to make the transition to the new product lines and productive techniques, most of the capitalists who were in business in 1850 were men of a new generation, who had either not yet begun in 1830 or who were then so insubstantial as to leave no trace.[29] Indeed, by midcentury, only 32 percent of the 49 worsted firms that had been listed in Bradford's 1830 *Directory* were still operating, whereas only about 6 percent of the 293 worsted firms in the 1850 *Directory* had been in business two decades before.[30]

Reflecting on this proliferation of new and younger competitors, J. G. Horsfall wearily remarked that "scarce a week elapses in which there is not some addition to their numbers." Tested in the crucible of depression, these fledgling firms would be thinned out drastically as only the most efficient and best financed survived. An 1888 analysis of 227 firms that had existed in 1841 and had been started during the previous ten years showed that 64 percent failed at some point in the next forty-seven years, while 11 percent ceased operation as a result of retirement by owners, and only 25 percent

[27] Hudson, "Industrial Capital," 588.
[28] Sigsworth, *Black Dyke*, 1–68.
[29] In other cases, such as those of the Garnetts, the Illingworths, the Wades, and the Rands, their children successfully negotiated the shift.
[30] W. White, *Directory of Leeds and Clothing Districts* (Leeds, 1830), 250; James Ibbetson, *Directory of Bradford* (Bradford, 1850). See Appendix C, and Koditschek, "Class Formation," 133.

remained in business at the end.[31] An analysis of capitalist persistence reveals that the 1837–42 depression was a particularly dangerous period when many of the new firms found themselves tested by a spell of profitlessness only a few years after having been set up. Of the sixty-one Bradford spinners and manufacturers listed in the 1834 *Directory*, only 59 percent were in business eight years later, and only 35 percent of the original men or their descendants were listed in the same family firm. Thereafter, the intensity of competition scarcely diminished, as 62 percent of the ninety-five spinners and manufacturers listed in the 1842 *Directory* remained in business at midcentury, 54 percent in the same family firm.[32]

As these figures indicate, for all that depressions were drastic weeding-out experiences, not everyone was destroyed. For the few who were sufficiently ambitious, innovative, and fortunate, slumps provided an incentive to break into the new forms of enterprise that would lay the foundations for future success. Led by the great innovators, Titus Salt, Henry Forbes, S. C. Lister, Isaac Holden, Henry Ripley, and John Foster, who were followed by a raft of lesser but still successful men, this rising generation of entrepreneurial capitalists could feel themselves responsible for making Victorian Bradford what it eventually became.[33]

Their achievement was, in fact, all the more remarkable because it occurred as entry into the business became increasingly difficult for the small, underfinanced, first-generation parvenu. Technological change and industrial reorganization were fast eliminating the traditional clothier, that bulwark of small-scale enterprise that had been a stepping stone toward industrial capitalism for so many of the protoindustrial worsted men. In addition, there was a marked diminution in the role of the woolstapler, who had hitherto acted as a major source of credit for the small producer, often enabling him to finance the purchase of raw materials out of the expectation of final sales. Now, however, as markets became increasingly cutthroat, it was the manufacturer who might be expected to offer credit to his customers rather than obtaining it from someone else.[34] Finally, within the factory sector, there was a marked increase in the average size of firms, which was growing,

[31] *BO*, Apr. 10 1845.; J. H. Turner, "Some Old Bradford Firms" (Bradford Archives, D.B. 16/45).

[32] Calculated from information in *Pigot's Directory* (Manchester, 1834); W. White, *Directory of Leeds and Clothing Districts* (Leeds, 1842); Ibbetson, *Directory, 1850*.

[33] Among these lesser but still enormously successful men were Nathan Bentley, W. E. Forster, William Fison, John Priestman, Adolphus Tremel, John Glover, Henry Kershaw, James Drummond, Hudson Clough, Joseph Leach, William Smith, William Lythall, and Thomas and Isaac Dewhirst. Comparative statistics on the horsepower capacity, spindle capacity, and number of employees for forty-eight leading Bradford worsted firms between 1833 and 1851 is presented in Appendix C.

[34] Hudson, "Industrial Capital," 252–61; 352–72.

according to the factory statistics, much more rapidly than their number. Clearly, production was becoming concentrated within a proportionately narrower circle of business elites.[35]

Thus the rise of a new entrepreneurial generation, in spite of an economic environment basically hostile to the parvenu, was a consequence of these young capitalists' good fortune and ability to establish new forms of worsted enterprise that could pass the test of market contraction by maximizing opportunities for growth and innovation while minimizing the risks of overextension and loss. Most widely heralded among these new types of enterprise was the introduction of novel yarns and fabrics that could be produced more cheaply than the older plain worsteds or could tap mass markets that the latter could not reach. The most famous instance of this sort of innovation was Titus Salt's pioneering introduction of alpaca yarn. Almost overnight, alpaca became enormously popular, generating a whole new subindustry within the Bradford trade and underwriting Salt's meteoric rise to become the largest worsted capitalist of the mid-Victorian age.[36]

The success of alpaca induced Salt and several other ambitious young manufacturers, like John Foster and the Mitchell Brothers, to introduce other – then exotic – yarns such as mohair, which could be woven with worsted wool to create a new kind of fabric. However, the most important of the new fabrics that were devised at this time was what came to be known as the "mixed worsted." Mixed worsteds used cotton warps, which were woven together with worsted wefts, to create a lighter, more flexible and attractive design.[37] Like alpaca and mohair goods, they caught on because they corresponded to the more airy and decorative Victorian fashions that were just then coming into style. They met the demand for elegant, but relatively inexpensive mass-produced women's dress fabrics that arose with the emergence of a substantial body of middle-class female consumers throughout the Western world. Mixed worsteds were particularly desirable

---

[35] In 1838, in Bradford Parish, the average worsted factory firm employed 77 operatives and used 15.3 horsepower. By 1850, the average firm now employed 181 workers and used 22.1 horsepower. This expanding scale of production was even more marked among the new multiprocess firms. In Bradford Borough, in 1850, the average multiprocess firm employed 325 workers and used 41.6 horsepower. The largest firm in existence in 1834, Wood and Walker, employed only 527 workers. Fifteen years later, at the very least, sixteen firms and probably more had work forces larger than this. Among them was Wood and Walker, which then employed three thousand laborers, although they were overshadowed by larger firms such as Titus Salt's, which had not even been in business in 1834. See Appendix C and Robert Bulgarnie, *Titus Salt* (London, 1877), 36–104.

[36] Sigsworth, *Black Dyke*, 243–83; James, *Worsted Manufacture*, 452–69.

[37] R. M. Hartwell, "The Yorkshire Woolen and Worsted Industry, 1800–1850" (Oxford, D. Phil., 1955), 426; James, *Worsted Manufacture*, 470–6; Sigsworth, *Black Dyke*, 43–9.

because they capitalized on the declining cost of raw cotton in an age of rapidly escalating wool prices. By combining quality with cheapness in this way, the mixed worsted was perfectly designed to capture the widest and steadiest markets in an era of economic instability.[38] In 1838, many of the more forward-looking firms began to convert their looms to the new fabric, and by 1845, Christopher Waud, a leading manufacturer, estimated that three-quarters of all the pieces that Bradford produced were mixed-worsted designs. Thereafter, the cotton and worsted mixture became even more ubiquitous, and its popularity helped to ensure Bradford's industrial dominance throughout the mid-Victorian age.[39]

Hand in hand with the introduction of new and more attractive designs and fabrics went the rise to major proportions of the worsted finishing and merchandising sectors, which were necessary to realize the enhanced potential for marketability that the production of these product lines had opened up. As the search for new markets became all absorbing and as the entire industry shifted toward a more fashionable demand, the role of the stuff merchant and his close associate, the dyer, assumed greater importance in the overall structure of the trade. In 1822, there had been thirty-seven stuff merchants operating in Bradford. By 1853, their numbers had risen to 170, almost as many as manufacturers. Bradford, which had built its reputation as a center of spinning mills and steam engines, moved to consolidate its regional supremacy during the mid-Victorian period by supplementing its acknowledged status as a factory center with the new role of commercial capital, where the bulk of goods were inventoried, purchased, and shipped.[40]

Parallel to the emergence of Bradford's merchant community went the rise to major proportions of the export branch. The merchants who specialized in foreign exports grew more rapidly than the trade as a whole. In 1830, Bradford had 60 percent of the export stuff merchants, and by 1853 its share had increased to 92 percent. Like its manufacturers, Bradford's merchants grew more rapidly than their counterparts elsewhere and spe-

---

[38] James, *Worsted Manufacture*, 470–9; *BO*, Apr. 10, 1845.

[39] Sigsworth, *Black Dyke*, 62–8.

[40] Hartwell, "Woolen and Worsted," 379–410. Professor Sigsworth has documented this mercantile migration into Bradford by counting the number of worsted stuff merchants in different towns at different dates. In 1822, Bradford had only 14 percent of the total and the majority were located in Leeds, the traditional center of woolen commerce. However, during the 1820s and 1830s a new group of specialized merchants began migrating into the fast-growing town. In 1830, Bradford had 30 percent of all stuff merchants and its share rose to 42 percent in 1842. Then in the midforties, the wholesale transfer began to take place as the remaining holdouts moved their operations to Bradford. In 1853, 75 percent of all worsted stuff merchants were headquartered in the town. Only one of Bradford's seventy-five stuff merchant firms in business at midcentury had been listed in the city's Directory of 1830. Sigsworth, *Black Dyke*, 63–5.

cialized in the most advanced forms of economic activity while other places remained more conservative. These export firms, which traded over the entire globe, were almost all, of necessity, among the largest of the commercial houses. Their proprietors were themselves frequently foreigners, mainly Scots and German Jews, who were attracted by the lure of prospects in the growing town and added the most exotic element among Bradford's urban immigrants.[41]

Maintaining close touch with the needs of far-flung customers, these large export firms acted as clearing houses for the products of the entire worsted industry. Although the trade employed a small and heavily white-collar work force, as merchants became increasingly involved in sending out consignments and selling on credit, their trade, like manufacturing, became increasingly capital-intensive, and the most successful among them grew rich. In 1865, Jacob Behrens, one of the most successful, estimated that, whereas in the 1830s, the aggregate transactions of Bradford's commercial sector had amounted to a few hundred thousand pounds a year, by the 1860s, they had risen dramatically to an annual value of twenty millions.[42]

Like the parvenu manufacturer, the ascendant stuff merchant was an innovative and entrepreneurially minded capitalist who understood that the secret of success was to deal in volume with great flexibility at a discount price, always ready for shifts in fashion and direction of demand and always seeking to capture new suppliers and customers without becoming excessively entangled in the fragile web of overextended credit that gluts always reduced to shreds. Headquartered in large, ornate warehouses that dominated Bradford's mid-Victorian downtown, these new merchants with their detailed knowledge of worldwide economic conditions and consumer tastes were a far cry from the homely old protoindustrial clothier who had, little more than a generation earlier, been trading from his booth in the Bradford Piece Hall.

Traditionally associated with the business of the merchant, the finishing processes, especially dyeing, migrated into Bradford at about the same time. In 1822, there were only six dyers in the town. In 1850, there were fifteen, and in 1872 there were forty-one. But the importance of dyeing grew in more than numerical terms. As fashion became more sophisticated and competition more intense, the finishing processes loomed more critically in the chain of production. As in the mercantile sector, it was difficult to carry on the dyeing business in anything less than a large firm with substantial

---

[41] Koditschek, "Class Formation," 148; Hartwell, "Woolen and Worsted," 614. Among the leading Scots merchants were Robert Milligan, Henry Forbes, James Douglas, James Rennie, and James Law. Among the leading German Jews were Jacob Behrens, Martin Schlesinger, Charles Semon, and Martin Hertz.

[42] *BO*, Oct. 24, 1865.

capital assets. Indeed, by the middle of the century, the largest of the new dyers, Henry Ripley and Samuel Smith, had accumulated sufficient wealth and power to match that of almost any manufacturer or merchant.[43]

On the other side of the production process, increasing mechanization and rising output were generating a substantial local engineering and machine-making industry to meet the demands of the staple trade. In 1828, there were already 25 firms in this category, and by 1850, their numbers had risen to 150, now distributed within twenty-five different specialized trades. Here, in the very forefront of technical advance, the opportunities for small-scale enterprise and craft production persisted longer than in the worsted industry itself. However, a few of these machine-making firms began to look far beyond the local market and to produce on an increasingly international scale. With its handful of leading technical innovators, frequently protected by patent rights, and its supply of skilled, local mechanics, orders for machines came to Bradford from all parts of the industrial world and leading engineering capitalists, like Benjamin Berry, Samuel Hattersley, John Leeming, and John Ramsden, joined the new generation of nascent bourgeois elites.[44]

Industrial reorganization and the working class: 1825–50

As the foregoing analysis indicates, the ability of a new generation of entrepreneurial innovators to penetrate Bradford's primary industrial-capitalist infrastructure in an environment fundamentally unfavorable to the parvenu depended in large measure on their ability to expand their businesses in ways that would benefit the entire community, not only bringing profits to them as individuals, but opening up for others a host of lesser opportunities and jobs. Nevertheless, there is another side to the story of entrepreneurial triumph, which, though equally essential for the success of the new capitalists, not only failed to benefit most Bradfordians, but was undertaken largely at their expense.

In the past, the competitive superiority of the Yorkshire worsted industry had ultimately rested on its ability to reduce labor costs. During the first quarter of the nineteenth century, the region's initial advantages in this area were greatly magnified as the mechanization of yarn spinning permitted the replacement of dozens of hand spinners with the labor of a single operative tending a machine. Although by 1825, spinning had been almost entirely mechanized, mechanization had not yet affected either of the two remaining

---

[43] Koditschek, "Class Formation," 187.
[44] *Pigot's Directory* (London, 1828); Ibbetson, *Directory* (1850).

worsted production processes, weaving and combing, which were potentially convertible to automatic means. But since the power loom was already used in the cotton trade and a viable combing machine would soon be invented, it was inevitable that during the 1825–50 period, the same entrepreneurs who were pioneering new products and marketing strategies would attempt to realize the labor-saving potential that the full mechanization of the production process would permit.

No attempts were made to adapt the power loom to worsted weaving until the crisis of 1825. In sharp contrast to the case with spinning, in which the productivity gains of mechanization were immediate and immense, power weaving promised more modest labor savings over the cost of weaving by handloom. On the other hand, because manual weaving, unlike spinning, was performed not by low-paid women and children, but by better-paid and less easily exploited adult men, interest in the power loom mounted during the boom years of the early twenties as handicraft wages and worker intransigence rose.[45] Yet because of fears of violent opposition, worsted manufacturers were reluctant to follow the lead of the cotton capitalists until, in 1826, the combination of deep depression and the defeat of a bitter strike finally destroyed the weavers' trade organizations and broke their ability to resist. In that year, as employment levels plummeted and wages shrank by 24 percent, J. G. Horsfall inaugurated Bradford's first power-loom factory. Although the event was greeted by several days of popular rioting, his readiness to provide his mill with armed protection inspired other manufacturers to follow his example and, thereafter, the power loom rapidly spread.[46]

In truth, the workers had good reason to fear this development, not so much because the machine instantly jeopardized their jobs, but quite the contrary, because it undermined their competitive position while temporarily keeping their trade alive. Had the weavers possessed other employment possibilities they might simply have abandoned their doomed occupation and forced the capitalists to convert wholesale to machines. However, with their traditional agrarian subsistence economy now destroyed by three generations of high protoindustrial birthrates, they had been drawn during the postwar decade of mounting prosperity into dependence on the handloom weaving boom. Unable to find alternate employment in their villages, these weavers were forced to compete with one another for wages that were increasingly determined not by traditional standards or even subsistence requirements,

[45] James, *History of Bradford*, 168, 276; idem, *Worsted Manufacture*, 332–53.
[46] A. L. Bowley, "Statistics of Wages in the United Kingdom," *Journal of the Royal Statistical Society* (65, 1902), 104–6; W. Scruton, "The History of a Bradford Riot," *BA*, o.s. 1 (1888), 131–5; James, *Worsted Manufacture*, 400–16.

but by the lower costs of fabrication by machine.[47] In spite of the drop in
handloom wages by 50 to 70 percent in the post-1825 decade, a government
investigator estimated, in 1838, that there were still 14,000 weavers in the
Bradford district, 84 percent of whom lived in the rural hinterland.[48]

These men sought to compensate for falling incomes by working longer
hours, a strategy that inevitably resulted in overproduction, which exacerbated the labor glut. Under these conditions, many manufacturers found it
useful to maintain a handloom and power weaving mix for a time. Investment
in costly machinery could be kept to the minimum level of steady demand,
while inventories could be rapidly and inexpensively augmented by turning
to the expendable hand weavers when trade picked up. Nevertheless, by the
end of the thirties, when hand weaving wages had fallen to 8 to 12s. per
week, it was increasingly evident that this situation could not continue. When
a family of eight, containing three weavers in full employment, was reduced
to living on 12s. a week, it was obvious that they would simply have to
abandon their villages and move to the city, where at least wives and children
could find factory work.[49] As the manufacturers William Walker and William
Rand explained:

> The Factory System is fast superseding domestic employment... im-
> mense numbers of handloom weavers are brought into a pitiable con-
> dition of being unable to get work for themselves and at the same time
> of having their daughters employed in the factories for such long hours
> as are quite inconsistent with female strength and the performance of
> cottage duties.[50]

The handloom weaver, according to Richard Fawcett, was "of all classes
we have to do with the most orderly and steady." Like many other traditionally minded manufacturers, he regretted the economic revolution that
was undermining this bulwark of the traditional cottage economy and the
whole protoindustrial way of life. Nevertheless, after the depression of 1838,
the migration of weaving families into the city became irreversible as the
urban factory decisively supplanted the rural handloom.[51] By 1850, the transformation was complete as the work hitherto performed by thousands of

---

[47] Duncan Blythell, *The Handloom Weavers* (Cambridge, 1969); E. P. Thompson, *The Making of the English Working Class* (New York, 1963), 269–313.
[48] *PP* (1840, XXIII), 558, 564–82; Sigsworth, *Black Dyke*, 35, 138–52.
[49] *Report and Resolution of a Meeting of Deputies from the Handloom Weavers* (Bradford, 1835), 8.
[50] William Walker and William Rand, *A Letter to Sir James Graham on the Ten Hours Factory Question* (Bradford, 1841), 14.
[51] William Cudworth, *Condition of the Industrial Classes in Bradford* (Bradford, 1887), 45.

dispersed male weavers was now executed by 17,642 automatic looms tended by female and adolescent operatives in the urban downtown.[52]

Here, as elsewhere, it was the city of Bradford that maintained its position on worsted capitalism's economic cutting edge. With 60 percent of all the power looms in the West Riding (as compared with 46 percent of all the spindles), midcentury Bradford emerged as the hub of worsted factory weaving much as it had first triumphed as the center of factory spinning two decades before.[53]

By midcentury, it was obvious that Bradford's factory system, no less than the entrepreneurs who controlled it, had weathered the crisis years of the 1830s and 1840s in spectacular fashion as the entire trade was extended and transformed. It was almost as if, in the short space of less than a generation, Bradford and the worsted industry had merged into one. With a factory power capacity almost three times the 1834 level and employing more than three times as many hands, Bradford's industrial infrastructure at midcentury was augmented not only by its entrepreneurs' introduction of new products and cultivation of new markets, but by the mechanization of whole new sectors of the production process that had drawn much of the region's labor force away from the countryside and into the town.[54]

Demographic disequilibrium and urban growth

The double-edged process of social transformation, which appears from one angle as the urbanization of industry, from another as the industrialization of the town, can be glimpsed most dramatically from the demographic statistics in Table 3-3, which show that between 1830 and 1850, Bradford's population grew by 60,241 or 138 percent. Obviously, even if high urban-mortality rates had not limited natural increase to a minimum, a demographic expansion so enormous in such a short period of time could only have been the result of a massive wave of immigration. Indeed, the published census returns for 1851 report that, by then, 55 percent of the borough's inhabitants and 70 percent of its adults had been born elsewhere.[55]

---

[52] Koditschek, "Class Formation," 930–2.

[53] Mills that restricted themselves to spinning contained 29 percent of the horsepower and 21 percent of the factory workforce in Bradford Borough, while 16 percent of the horsepower and 24 percent of the workforce was now located in weaving mills. The bulk of production (55 percent of both horsepower and work force) was now concentrated in larger multiprocess factories that combined spinning and weaving in a single plant. Koditschek, "Class Formation," 930–2.

[54] Ibid., 105.

[55] Ibid., 80–1, 86, 89.

Since 64 percent of these newcomers were short-distance immigrants who had been born in other parts of Yorkshire, the demographic data seems to confirm the economic hypothesis that the bulk of them were displaced handloom weavers, mostly from the hinterland of Bradford, who were forced by collapsing opportunities in their villages to migrate to the expanding industrial town.[56] Similarly, demographic evidence further confirms the proposition that the vast bulk of this migration took place in the 1840s when the position of the rural weaver had become thoroughly impossible, while urban employment was rapidly, if somewhat erratically, opening up. Using a method described in note 57, an attempt has been made to compensate for the inadequacies of the registrar-general's early vital statistics and to assess the full magnitude of migration to Bradford in the decade before 1851. The estimates generated suggest that only 7,600 of the 37,000 population increment of this period can be attributed to natural increase and that 29,500, or 80 percent, must be attributed to an influx of immigrants. If these estimates are correct, 28 percent of Bradford's entire midcentury inhabitants and 52 percent of those who were immigrants must have arrived in the previous ten years.[57]

[56] Calculated from information in *PP* (1852–3, LXXXVIII), 2:737.
[57] Migration levels have been estimated by subtracting the component of population change attributable to natural increase (obtained by aggregating the balance of annual birth/death statistics for the decade from the *Annual Reports of the Registrar General*) from the decennial increment of population increase (obtained by calculating overall gain or loss of population between two censuses, for the same area) from the published census returns. Since general registration began only in the late thirties; 1841–51 is the first census decade for which satisfactory birth and death statistics can be obtained. To make matters worse, it was not until 1847 that the registrar-general broke the figures down below general aggregates for Bradford Parish. As a result, migration into the borough cannot be quantified at all until the 1850s. For the forties, there are figures (regarded by demographers as prone to inaccuracy) for the parish as a whole, but this defeats a large part of our purpose, since in-migration from the outer suburban ring to the city was a significant geographical component in migration as a whole. An effort has been made to compensate for this gap in the data through the construction of an estimate of the fertility/mortality experience of the borough during the forties when migration was at its highest pitch. This has been possible because (1) official registration statistics are available after 1847, and (2) the town clerk, W. H. Hudson, in *The Health of Bradford* (Bradford, 1859), gives a statement of annual mortality for the entire decade. It has been calculated that between 1852 and 1861 the number of deaths in the borough was 74.5 percent the number of births. Between 1847 and 1851, the percentage was similar (76.0 percent). Consequently, it has been assumed that this same basic birth/death ratio, which prevailed during the fifties and the last five years of the forties, prevailed during the first five years of the forties as well. Since the mortality/fertility relationship was unlikely to have been more favorable during the early forties than in the later years (if all literary evidence is to be believed) and may have been worse, the resulting estimates of migra-

This stream of three thousand average annual arrivals placed an enormous strain on the nascent urban-industrial infrastructure, which could hardly be expected to absorb them instantly or even to find them all remunerative work. To be sure, the opening up of ten thousand new factory jobs during this decade, mostly for women and adolescents, as well as a few thousand more for immigrant men, made the influx economically possible.[58] Nevertheless, it is difficult to avoid the conclusion that, unlike the earlier period when urban opportunities exceeded candidates to fill them, the number of new arrivals during the late 1830s and 1840s surpassed the aggregate of available opportunities as Bradford was inundated by a tide of desperate newcomers who were far less attracted by the pull of urban opportunity than expelled by the collapse of the traditional cottage economy in the protoindustrial villages from which they came.

During the boom years when employment levels expanded, the tide of new immigrants flowed at an even faster pace. In 1844, at the height of commercial prosperity, Rev. Fawcett estimated that they were arriving at a rate of a thousand per month.[59] Even more ominous, however, was the failure, during periods of contraction, of the influx of newcomers to wind down. This was particularly true during the 1846–8 depression, when an urban economy already overloaded with proletarianized weavers from the hinterland was again inundated by a new wave of rural immigrants, this time coming from famine-stricken Ireland, where dispossessed cottagers found themselves in even more desperate straits.

By 1851, 8.9 percent of Bradford's population and 16 percent of its immigrants were Irish born.[60] Although a few, mostly better-established worsted workers from the county of Mount Mellick had been trickling in since the 1830s, the overwhelming majority were destitute peasants who arrived in 1846–7, when Bradford could least afford to absorb them. That winter the potato blight became visible on local thoroughfares in the form of "crowds of poor creatures most of them hanging in rags [who] pour into the town from Ireland every day; and as they have no other means of subsistence, they immediately betake themselves to begging."[61]

Throughout the following spring, the wave of starving men and women showed no sign of abating. Respectable families reported first a dozen, then fifty or more such beggars on their doorsteps every day. Nine-tenths of

tion, dramatic as they are, may actually be understatements of the full extent of the phenomenon.

[58] Koditschek, "Class Formation," 105, 930–2; A. B. Reach, *The Yorkshire Textile Districts in 1849* (Blackburn, 1974).
[59] Fawcett, *Rise and Progress*, 8.
[60] C. Richardson, "The Irish in Victorian Bradford," *BA*, n.s. 9 (1975), 295–316.
[61] *BO*, Jan. 7, 1847.

these were estimated to be Irish, and when the stream of new arrivals diminished in November, it was followed by another wave of discharged railway workers from Lancashire.[62]

Displaced rural immigrants, who had moved to the city to escape unemployment and labor oversupply, now discovered that these scourges had migrated along with them, confronting them with greater extremity in their new home. The problem was most serious for the adult male breadwinners, whom the mechanization of weaving and the breakdown of the cottage economy had displaced. For a time, it appeared as though woolcombing (which was, unlike weaving, an urban handicraft) might be able to take up the employment slack. Yet as we shall see in Chapter 13, this trade quickly followed weaving down the path of industrial debasement and proved equally unable to provide a stable, long-term employment base.

Conclusion

By 1850, Bradford's urban-industrial revolution had transformed the face of social relations in the town. "When I was a little boy," recalled one anonymous inhabitant who had witnessed the transformation, "we all knew everybody, old and young, rich and poor, in the place." Now, he lamented, "I don't know a quarter of the streets there are for them to live on."[63] Yet the shift from a small-scale protoindustrial community to a large, impersonal industrial city involved more than simply an increase in scale. In creating, by midcentury, a city of immigrants drawn by capitalist development and tied to its fate, the urbanization of the worsted industry had brought to the surface the social contradictions and class bifurcations that had been only latent in the social relations of the protoindustrial age.

The experience of those who came to work in Bradford's factories was very different from that of those who came to build them and to extract profit from goods they produced. The same dynamic that brought wealth and achievement to successful parvenu capitalists, albeit after considerable entrepreneurial risk, also forced a mass of workers to leave their farming and weaving villages and to move to a city where poverty, squalor, and a sense of dispossession confronted them as an almost inevitable fate. For both social groups, these years of economic crisis and reorganization, when Bradford became a fully industrial city and the worsted industry took on its modern, urbanized form, represented a new and more overtly antagonistic stage in the dynamic of class relations involving the intensification of a

---

[62] Ibid., Nov. 26, 1846; Mar. 4, Nov. 4, 1847.
[63] Ibid., Oct. 11, 1855.

developmental dynamic that had been inherent in capitalist production from the start. Amidst the treacherous economic climate of this period, entrepreneurship was forced to become more creative, supplementing strategies of simple expansion with innovations that penetrated more deeply into the process of production and transmuted what had once been a rural handicraft industry into its fully mechanized urban-industrial form.

In 1805, a compilation of local property ratings, which suggests that half of the town's real property was held by 13 percent of its households, indicates that, even in the late protoindustrial period, a highly stratified social structure had evolved. However, not until the town became a city of 103,000 in which the combined assessment of the five largest ratepayers was equal to Bradford's entire ratable value forty-five years before, had a true class society finally emerged. Now, in 1850, half of all real urban property was concentrated in the hands of the top 8 percent of all ratepayers (sixteen hundred householders), while 21 percent was directly in the hands of the ninety-seven wealthiest individuals whose holdings were rated at over £150 per year.[64]

[64] Calculated from information in Cudworth, *Historical Notes on the Bradford Corporation* (Bradford, 1881), 27–33, and "Petitions for and against Incorporation," Bradford Archives, D.B. 69/2–3. For interpretation of this data see Koditschek, "Class Formation," 282–5, 347.

4

The development of the capitalist city: 1810–1850

In the preceding chapter we traced the material foundations of class formation in early-nineteenth-century Bradford by examining the mutually
reinforcing dynamic of demographic growth and economic expansion
through which the town's industrial revolution took place. Nevertheless, this
simple dialectic of population and industry constitutes only one dimension
of the historical process in which class relations were actually forged. If, in
one sense, the industrial city really was no more than an impersonal commodity marketplace, a giant agglomeration of people, capital, and instruments
of production that the requirements of capitalism had called up, in becoming
a center for capitalist enterprise, it also became a distinct social and economic
system in its own right that significantly affected its inhabitants' lives. The
city, however industrial, was not just a place which manufactured goods for
the outside world. Perhaps it could not, like its protoindustrial predecessor,
aspire to become a full human community with which its members would
completely identify. Nevertheless, as a physical environment in which a
growing number of people worked and lived, industrial Bradford did become
a locus for consumption generating an urban-service economy and social
structure that interacted with the primary economy and social structure of
capitalist manufacturing in a multitude of complex ways.

Although urban Bradford, considered as a center of internal consumption,
must be distinguished analytically from the primary structures of industrial
production housed within it, both systems shared the significant feature of
being free-market environments, essentially regulated by the laws of supply
and demand. The decline of the customary norms and communitarian institutions, that had opened the way for unrestrained industrial expansion
also ensured that the secondary service economy that it generated would
operate as a competitive private enterprise arena in which resources were
allocated by entrepreneurs to individual customers solely according to their
ability to pay.[1]

---

[1] Private enterprise as a mode of urban development has been analyzed most cogently by
the American historian Sam Bass Warner in *Private City: Philadelphia in Three Periods of*

Consequently, Bradford's privatized, free-market economy of the early nineteenth century was a mechanism for the distribution of goods and services that reinforced the class relationships generated through industrial production, translating widening differentials between profits and wages into concrete material form as divergences in housing, health, recreation, and diet. As the logic of industrial-capitalist development led to the creation of a large and impoverished proletariat, the quality of life for the majority deteriorated dramatically. By the forties, a decent, humane, and healthy environment had become difficult, if not impossible, for most Bradfordians to find.

Urbanization and the capitalist marketplace

Even with the best planning, most ardent public spirit, and amplest material resources, the attempt to build a viable urban environment in a generation for a population of 100,000 on the foundations of an overgrown medieval village would inevitably have entailed substantial ecological disruptions and strains. Yet early-nineteenth-century Bradford possessed no such advantages. With no collective institutions or effective regulatory authorities to guide the shape of the city, it developed in the most haphazard and anarchic way. The large and increasingly impoverished working-class majority, which could not afford proper provision of even the most essential goods and services, was largely left to fend for itself.

By the 1840s, half a century of virtually unrestrained private development had produced an environmental disaster that almost defies description.[2] The sky was permanently enveloped in a smoky fog that issued from the stacks of Bradford's hundred or so mills. The clear-running beck, where old men recalled trout fishing in their youth, had become a blocked, festering vat of chemical effluence. The canal was even worse, actually breaking out spontaneously into flames on occasion. Without public drainage, flood water was as common as drinking water was scarce. What passed for public thoroughfares could often scarcely be seen, much less traversed, through the piles of offal, dung, and otherwise indeterminate slush, though they could easily be discerned by their odor. Even those brave enough to venture out into the streets during the day were likely to turn back at night for fear of disappearing into some dark pothole or being attacked by the bands of vicious dogs that

its Growth (Philadelphia, 1968), and *The Urban Wilderness: A History of the American City*, (New York, 1972).
[2] See Georg Weerth *Vergessene Texte* (Koln, 1975), 231–7, for a perceptive, if somewhat overwrought attempt.

freely roamed the town. In the words of the Health of Towns commissioner, Bradford was "the dirtiest, worst regulated town in England."[3] "We have not infrequently heard it said," quipped the *Bradford Observer*, "that a great fire which would burn down all the buildings between Kirkgate, Ivegate, Bridge street, and Market street would be a public blessing."[4]

This environmental disaster was the result of a variety of different forces, some imposed by nature, others bequeathed by history, but all exacerbated by the mode of unregulated, free-market development by which Bradford's urban environment took shape. Both the steep-sloping topography of the downtown area and the construction of modern shops, houses, and factories on a foundation of narrow medieval streets contributed to Bradford's cramped, irregular, and dirty appearance, but their effect was intensified by the process of development itself, which took place without any central direction or control. The persistence of traditional village habits and practices in the new urban setting, such as throwing refuse out of windows or allowing pigs or even cows free run of the streets, constituted not only a constant nuisance, but a dangerous health hazard, whereas the expansion of settlement in the neighborhood of graveyards and slaughterhouses created further possibilities for the spread of epidemic disease. It was, however, the unwillingness of official bodies, such as the Improvement Commission, to confront these problems that ensured that Bradfordians would be perpetually surrounded by dirt and pollution, and that discomfort, uncleanliness, and recurrent illness would come to characterize the urban way of life.

Bradford's position at the floor of three valleys would have made drainage a challenge under any circumstances and one that only a concerted public response could effectively have met. The absence of any collective solution ensured that the downtown area was frequently transformed into a festering swamp of slush and sludge. In 1845, the Board of Surveyors admitted:

> There are no regulations for draining the town or district. The streets, courts or alleys are generally laid out without proper inclinations for the discharge of surface water. The majority of the streets are uneven, unpaved, and favorable to the retention of stagnant moisture and accumulations of refuse thrown from the houses. There are many stagnant pools contiguous to the houses.[5]

According to the Health of Towns investigator Joseph Ellison, since "everything which is done is done by private individuals, therefore, I am sorry to say there is no sewerage at all."[6] Indeed, the well-to-do might find their own means of refuse disposal and another investigator, James Smith, declared their streets to be generally in a respectable state, "but in most inferior and cross streets, chiefly inhabited by the working classes, the con-

[3] *PP* (1845, XVIII), 2:315.
[5] *PP* (1845, XVIII), 2:339.
[4] *BO*, Nov. 20, 1845.
[6] *BO*, Sep. 24, 1840; *PP* (1840, XI), 89.

dition is quite otherwise" as nonexistent or inadequate paving only made unsatisfactory drainage even worse.[7]

If blocked streets and surface pollution were serious health hazards and unsightly nuisances, blocked watercourses spelled near disaster for the town on several occasions of heavy rainfall. Here, too, paving and draining exacerbated the problem, and some parts of town were almost perpetually "nearly ankle deep in mud." The Health of Towns commissioner noted that the inadequacy of drainage was always felt most in working-class cellar dwellings and emphasized the connection between flooding and epidemic diseases among the poor and undernourished. However, nothing was done, and more floods occurred in June and August, 1838. Finally, property owners who had suffered severe damage called a public meeting to try to improve drainage, but floods continued as late as 1859, when there was one that was reported to have caused £40,000 in property damage.[8]

One of the most frequently cited causes of flooding was obstruction of the Bradford Beck. Proprietors thought nothing of building over it, creating stagnant pools that were dangerous sources of noxious waste. According to the Board of Surveyors, "On the sides of the stream there are a great many factories ... the soil, refuse and filth of which fall into the Beck." "In the summertime the water is low, and all this filth accumulates for weeks or months ... and emits a most offensive smell."[9]

However, the most serious form of pollution was the constant infusion of factory smoke into the atmosphere. As early as 1814, complaints were being voiced after the erection of Rands Mill. In 1831, a visitor exclaimed, "Never in my life did I see a more smoky place than Bradford," which made Halifax seem "one of the cleanest and most comely of manufacturing towns" by comparison. Thereafter, smoke pollution continued to worsen, but obviously nothing could be done to quell the stream of "black gold" on which Bradford's entire economy depended. The development of smoke consumption mechanisms made little impact on the industrialists' practices, and it was not until late in the century that the problem was seriously addressed.[10]

The prevailing view that public causeways and spaces were private property under a different name emboldened polluters and obstructors to act with abandon, with little fear of serious public censure, much less of official governmental restraint. Several attempts to promote even minimal street

---

[7] *Bradford Observer*, Mar. 1, 1838; June 19, 1840; *PP* (1845, XVIII), 2:315.
[8] John James, *History and Topography of Bradford* (Bradford, 1841), 162–3; William Cudworth, *Historical Notes on the Bradford Corporation* (Bradford, 1881), 142; *BO*, Feb. 8, Mar. 22, 1838; June 6, 1839; *PP* (1845, XVIII), 2:338–9.
[9] Cudworth, *Bradford Corporation*, 88.
[10] Ibid., 57; E. M. Sigsworth, *Black Dyke Mills* (Liverpool, 1958), 24; *BO*, Dec. 1, 1842; Feb. 23, 1843; Feb. 17, 1848.

improvements under the 1803 Watching and Lighting Act failed because the commissioners lacked the powers or the inclination to raise rates or make compulsory purchases. New streets were left to the whim of the private developer, and even the old streets under the jurisdiction of the commission were often treated as though they were the property of any private individual who had acquired a stake by habitually obstructing them.[11] The Board of Surveyors reported in 1845:

> About four months ago the Commissioners commenced an alteration in the causeway of one of the principal streets over which the public had passed during the memory of the oldest inhabitant. Nevertheless, the owners of the property adjoining drove off the workmen by main force, and the causeway has remained all winter in an unfinished state highly dangerous to the public.[12]

The ineffectiveness of the Improvement Commission meant that, outside the machinery of poor relief, which remained in the hands of the traditional vestry and township overseers until the implementation of the New Poor Law in 1837, Bradford possessed no viable local government at all. This situation was slightly alleviated, in 1843, when the Bradford Vestry elected a Board of Surveyors under the provisions of the 1835 Highways Act. But it was not until Bradford's incorporation as a municipal borough, in 1847, that the infrastructure of effective local government was laid. Before then and, in many respects, for a long time thereafter, essential public services either remained entirely unavailable or were provided only by privately owned joint-stock companies, which were organized on a profit-making basis and could offer their product only to the limited body of paying customers who could afford the going market rate.

The first joint-stock water company had been founded in 1740 and extended only once, in 1790. By the early nineteenth century, it was barely adequate even for the handful of relatively well-to-do families that could afford to subscribe. The rest of the population had to rely on street water hawkers, who sold three gallons for a penny. Even as late as 1834, provision was limited to one reservoir, which could supply one-third of the town one hour per day. The central tap was "at the caprice of an old woman who pleased herself whether she turned the water on or off." Most millowners and other wealthy people dug their own wells, and sometimes they sold their surplus water to others. In fact, a proposal for a system of public borings was rejected because it would have siphoned off too much of the water reserves that were needed by industry.[13]

[11] S. M. Gaskell, "Housing Estate Development, 1840–1918, with Particular Reference to the Pennine Towns," (Sheffield, Ph.D. dissertation, 1974), 3.

[12] *BO*, Apr. 7, May 5, May 26, 1836; Oct. 19, 1837; Nov. 20, 1845.

[13] Cudworth, *Bradford Corporation*, 72–3, 81; James, *History of Bradford*, 8.

However, the incentive for sinking private wells went deeper than just the ordinary domestic demands for water. One of the most serious dangers facing Bradfordians was that of fire, and public provision for fire fighting scarcely existed – in 1834 a single fireman with no alarm bells. The "parish engine" was already a museum piece. In 1839, the local paper, the *Bradford Observer*, speculated, "It might be of use in putting out a fire in a low cottage, provided the engine was placed under a waterfall, but if the water was to be lifted out of a well by means of an engine, ladders and a supply of pails would be more serviceable."[14] The largest millowners maintained their own private fire engines and water supplies, and these too could be hired by those who could afford it. An especially serious blaze on Market Street in 1838 was quenched only after three tries, when Wood and Walker's engine finally managed to put it out.[15]

As the town expanded during the second urban phase, the water crisis worsened dramatically. The water company did not have the resources to keep up with so rapidly growing a population. Moreover, the provision of water to the working class was not a profitable enough business to attract the requisite capital. By the thirties, the town was facing a constant water shortage, which was always worst in summer when the company was unable to live up even to its limited engagements. In 1834, a customer who was entitled to his daily hour of water complained that he received service only three times a week. Another, a year later, thought that the problem could be solved by the healthy competition of a rival waterworks company.[16]

Finally in 1837, after years of delay, three rival schemes were proposed for the establishment of a new waterworks. After some public discussion of their relative merits, a new joint-stock company was formed in 1839. Though the *Observer* expressed hopes that the company would not be organized on a monopolistic basis, its suggestions to mobilize the small capital of consumers, who were more likely to be interested in low rates than large profits, met with little response. Although £40,000 in shares of £20 was raised, the company remained under oligarchic control. Final implementation was further delayed until 1842 by economic depression and parliamentary obstruction. By then, the town had grown so large that the new company was insufficient to meet its needs.[17]

The early history of gas lighting followed the same pattern as the development of water supply. Illumination by gas was projected in 1821 with the formation of the Bradford Gaslight Company, which provided a small

---

[14] *BO*, June 26, 1834; June 27, 1839.   [15] *BO*, Jul. 12, 1838.

[16] *BO*, Nov. 24, 1834; Sep. 24, 1835; Oct. 19, 1837; Apr. 30, 1840.

[17] The directors were John Rand, Henry Leah, Richard Garnett, W. Holloway, John Aked, Robert Milligan, William Murgatroyd, William Walker, Martin Schlesinger, George Oxley, Robert Nicholson, and George Turner. *BO*, June 2, 1842. See also Cudworth, *Bradford Corporation*, 80–1; *BO*, Dec. 21, 1837; Apr. 19, 1838.

number of wealthy subscribers with what was then regarded as a luxury. Even so, for many years the company paid no dividends, and it was difficult to raise the necessary £15,000 capital to commence operations. Eventually the company expanded and began to offer some street illumination, but as long as it remained in private hands, cheap provision of gas service to the entire public remained out of the question.[18]

Indeed, the problems of water shortages and inadequate lighting continued until the water and gas companies were brought under municipal control in 1854 and 1871, respectively. "Water," the *Observer* confessed, "is a poor man's necessity of life as it is a rich man's luxury," but so long as private enterprise remained the means of supply, the poor man was unlikely to get what he needed. In the end, no one could "compel men to invest their capital in what they deem to be an ungainful speculation – nor when it has failed, can they make a bad speculation a good one."[19]

Problematic as it was to leave to private enterprise the provision of basic public services for the poor, it proved almost as difficult to organize any public projects requiring large infusions of social overhead capital through the free market, even when their benefits were directed exclusively toward the rich. By the twenties, it was already obvious that the protoindustrial transport infrastructure of canals and turnpike roads would be inadequate for the transport needs of the urban-industrial age. Even after two new turnpikes opened in 1825, London remained a 26-hour coach ride away, whereas nearby Leeds, which generated a traffic of three hundred passengers daily, was served by only two coaches per day. Moreover, with the slow and expensive system of arterial water transport overburdened by a growing quantity of heavy goods, local elites realized that it would be necessary to link up with the embryonic system of steam railways, if Bradford's urban-industrial revolution were to proceed.[20]

In 1830, a prospectus was issued for a railroad connection with Leeds at an estimated expense of £119,000. When this initial scheme fell through, it was followed by a stream of thirteen others, all equally abortive, between 1831 and 1844. By the early forties, as most of Britain's other major cities were linked to the proliferating network of national trunk lines, Bradford remained isolated.[21] Three factors appear to have accounted for this dangerously long delay. The first and least important was the exceptional dif-

---

[18] Cudworth, *Bradford Corporation*, 60–2; James, *History of Bradford*, 161.
[19] *BO*, Oct. 8, 1840.
[20] James, *History of Bradford*, 155; Gary Firth, "The Genesis of the Industrial Revolution in Bradford" (Bradford, Ph.D. dissertation, 1975), 215–17; *Memoir of Jacob Behrens* (London, n.d.), 37; *BO*, Oct. 22, 1835.
[21] J. R. Kellett, *The Impact of Railways on Victorian Cities* (London, 1969).

ficulty of cutting a line through the region's rugged terrain. The second, more serious, impediment was the opposition of local landowners whose property might be subject to compulsory purchase and who therefore obstructed all attempts to obtain a parliamentary act. However, the third and probably the most decisive factor was the difficulty in raising the requisite capital for what was bound to be a costly venture that might prove profitable only in the long run. Throughout the thirties and early forties, Bradford's existing capital resources were largely tied up in other basic investments, such as the mechanization of production or the construction of factories, warehouses, and housing stock. In spite of the obvious need for a railroad, there was little capital available locally, and outside investors were slow to get involved.[22]

Finally, in the midforties, this situation changed as a commercial boom brought windfall profits to many local capitalists, temporarily freeing money for more speculative investments. At the same time, the railway mania rapidly drew in the hitherto untapped resources of the smaller middle-class investor, both locally and nation-wide. The capital scarcity of earlier years suddenly gave way to a glut. "Inns and places of public resort were converted into share broking establishments," claimed one local commentator, and after the bubble finally burst, "great numbers of speculators were ruined in Bradford; well-to-do and prudent tradesmen became bankrupt and fled from their creditors."[23] In fact, so far from being bankrupted, leading capitalists like William Murgatroyed or the Rand brothers, who invested £320,000 in railroad stock, limited themselves to the sounder ventures whose modest but steady rates of return provided a useful alternative for the diversion of boom industrial earnings that could not profitably be plowed back into their firms.

Most importantly, however, this sudden aggregation of investment capital made it possible to connect Bradford, both eastward and westward, with the larger system of national routes. The first local line, providing a link with Leeds via Shipley, opened in 1846. It was financed by the Leeds-Bradford Railway Company under the guidance of George Hudson with a capital of £900,000. Two companies struggled for the rights to the second line to Manchester via Halifax, so construction was delayed. However, a compromise was worked out, and by 1850, service had commenced, stimulating the flow of cotton warps from Lancashire, which the new mixed worsteds required.[24]

[22] James, *History of Bradford*, 170; Firth, "Genesis," 218.

[23] John James, *Continuations and Additions to the History and Topography of Bradford* (Bradford, 1866), 105.

[24] J. T. Ward, "The West Riding Landowners and the Railroads," *Transport History* (1960), 4:251; John Marshall, *The Lancashire and Yorkshire Railway* (New York, 1969), 1:245–

Although Bradford's integration into Britain's railway infrastructure brightened the town's economic prospects, it did not resolve all problems of external transport and may have intensified internal bottlenecks as the thicker traffic engendered by the railroad simply exacerbated the congestion of cramped downtown streets.[25] With nine turnpikes, two railways, and a canal all dumping a steady flow of goods and people into the maze of lanes and alleys that privatistic property development had wrought, it became clear that without a systematic program of urban redevelopment, Bradford's transport revolution would never be complete. Yet the conscious redesign of the downtown district constituted a task that could never be undertaken by private enterprise. To divert valuable private property to unremunerative public purposes, to assume costs and risks of enormous magnitude, to risk offending vested interests that were multifarious and great, to devise integrated plans for mass transport and street improvement: such tasks required a degree of civic commitment and organization such as early industrial Bradford was unable to make.[26]

Intimately tied to the inadequacies of internal transportation – of which it was both consequence and further contributory cause – was the intense congestion and overcrowding of industry and population resulting from the extraordinary compression of Bradford's urban space. As Figure 4-1 indicates, the dramatic demographic increases of the 1830–50 period did not lead to a corresponding enlargement of the built-up settlement area. The expansion of settlement simply perpetuated the radial and concentric developmental pattern that had already been established during the initial urban development phase. The central core continued its expansion, growing beyond its original territory of West Bradford to encompass part of at least two of the three borough out-townships, whereas the radial spokes that spread outward along the transport routes thickened and engulfed the nearest nodes of hinterland settlement – Great Horton to the southwest, Bowling and Dudley Hill to the southeast, Manningham to the north, and Bradford Moor to the east, which endowed the borough out-townships with population densities by midcentury that approached urban levels for the first time (see Figure 4-1). Nevertheless, we must not forget, as Figure 4-1 demonstrates, that Bradford's actual built-up area at midcentury, in which four-fifths of the borough's 100,000 inhabitants lived, constituted no more than a single square mile.

7; *BO*, Oct. 2, 10, 17, Nov. 7, 1844; Feb. 6, 13, 27, May 8, Jul. 3, 7, Sep. 7, Nov. 25, 1845; June 25, July 18, 23, Aug. 27, Sep. 3, 1846.

[25] C. Richardson, *A Geography of Bradford* (Bradford, 1976), 58; *BO*, May 6, 1847. During the mid-Victorian period, the railroad transport network was expanded, and by the 1880s, Bradford was connected to the outside by sixteen different routes.

[26] Kellet, *Impact of Railways*, 311–18; *BO*, Feb. 23, 1863.

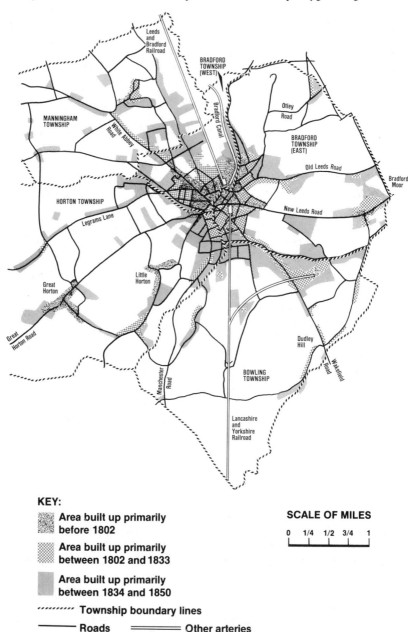

KEY:

Area built up primarily
before 1802

Area built up primarily
between 1802 and 1833

Area built up primarily
between 1834 and 1850

`········` Township boundary lines

Roads   Other arteries

SCALE OF MILES

0   1/4   1/2   3/4   1

Figure 4–1. The expansion of settlement in Bradford.
Compiled from John Johnson, *Map of the Township of Bradford* (1802); Kemp and
Sowerby, *Map of the Borough of Bradford* (1834); T. Dixon, *Map of Bradford* (1850);
and OS (1852).

Interspersed amidst mills and warehouses was a population of 80,000, or 125 persons per acre. "There is," complained one correspondent to the *Observer*, "a plethora of population out of all proportion with the means of its accommodation." "Naturally, it should surge healthily outwards." "As it is, it deepens and concentrates itself in most dangerous and insalubrious density."[27] Here, as in so many areas, it was the workers who suffered most. Too poor to provide a market for mass transport and too tired to countenance long suburban journeys to work, they were forced to remain within walking distance of the polluted industrial district downtown. Consigned to almost unimaginable levels of residential overcrowding by the inflated value of town-center property, these workers became the victims of slumlords who, in their turn, were obliged to cram their cheap cottages as closely together as they could (see Chapter 13).

Private enterprise in the urban economy

The dominance of Bradford's secondary-service economy by the same principles of privatistic free-market development that governed the primary industrial sphere had, from the perspective of the urban consumer, two far-reaching and decisive effects. In the first place, there was the inability of market incentives, unaided by civic planning and collective political will, to finance adequate public services with sufficient rapidity to meet the proliferating needs of the industrial town. This insured that, even for those who could afford them, the supply of consumer services and amenities would, in what was becoming the world's fastest-growing industrial city, lag dangerously behind the explosive pace of urban demand. The dynamic of industrial development, which forced a low-waged, dispossessed proletariat to migrate from the countryside to work in Bradford's newly constructed urban mills, also guaranteed that the overwhelming majority of them would not be able to pay for the consumer goods and services they desperately needed in their new home. Thus in the second place, the regulation of the secondary process of urban development entirely through entrepreneurial, market means caused the urban economy to act as a transmission belt through which the class inequalities generated in the capitalist relations of worsted production were translated into material deficiencies in housing, health, recreation and diet.

Yet if, as a system of consumer provision, Bradford's service economy reinforced underlying class divisions, insofar as it created a new group of petty

[27] *BO*, Apr. 10, 1845; Oct. 9, 1851.

Table 4-1. *Structure of firms in Bradford: number and percentage of firms by occupational type*

Occupational type	No. of firms in 1826	Percentage of total	No. of firms in 1850	Percentage of total	No. of firms in 1872	Percentage of total
Liberal professions	39	4.1	99	2.0	196	3.2
Minor professions	44	4.6	295	5.8	319	5.2
Distributive trades	394	41.0	2,670	52.9	3,437	55.6
Large producer	48	5.0	185	3.7	147	2.4
Small producer/ retailer	265	27.1	1,072	21.2	1,041	16.8
Service to worsted industry	25	2.6	150	3.0	140	2.3
Worsted industry	146	15.2	581	11.5	899	14.5
Total	961		5,052		6,179	
No. of trades listed	92		287		203	

Sources: Calculated on the basis of information in *Pigot's Directory* (London, 1828); James, Ibbetson, *Bradford Directory* (Bradford, 1850); and *Smith's Directory of Bradford* (Bradford, 1872).

producers and retailers, it had, at least potentially, a different social effect. Unlike the worsted industry, in which capital was becoming increasingly concentrated in the early nineteenth century and entrepreneurial opportunities were narrowing to a fortunate few, in the urban-service economy, capital tended to be dispersed among a large number of small-scale, family enterprises, and the opportunities that this opened up for the petty property holder more than compensated for those that industrial capitalism had closed off.

Table 4-1 shows that, as early as 1828 (if the small rural hinterland clothiers are excluded from the calculation), there were many more firms in the urban-service trades of food processing, retailing, construction, and small household craft production than in the worsted industry and its allied fields. To feed, clothe, house, and service a town population now approaching forty thousand were 152 grocers and shopkeepers, 72 butchers, 74 innkeepers, 30 tailors, 46 construction firms, and 675 other businesses distributed among specialized trades. During the second urban-industrial phase, as small-scale worsted production was undermined, the urban-service economy expanded even more dramatically, proliferating faster than the urban population itself. By 1850, there were 4,152 firms in 245 different urban-service occupations to meet the needs of a hundred thousand Bradfordians.[28]

Because the 1828 *Directory* excludes not only hinterland clothiers, but probably the smallest urban shopkeepers as well, it cannot be precisely compared with the more comprehensive 1850 *Directory*. Nevertheless, the basic growth trend is unmistakable and is confirmed by Dr. Elliott's calculation from the census occupational tables, which shows greater expansion in retailing and construction than in any other middle-class occupation between 1841 and 1851. As my own calculations from the 1850 *Directory* make clear, by midcentury, 82 percent of all private businesses in Bradford operated within the urban-service sector, whereas only 12 percent were within the primary staple trade.[29]

The proliferation of firms in Bradford's urban-service economy is striking in light of the concentration of the bulk of local capital and labor in the primary productive sphere. This suggests that, unlike the large-scale, factory dominated worsted industry, the town's urban-service economy was dominated by a multitude of small businessmen who formed the bulwark of the lower middle class. This point is confirmed by Table 4-2 which shows how the class basis of enterprise differed dramatically among the three basic economic sectors of the town.

Although the genteel and higher professional sector was bourgeois by definition, the social mix of proprietors in the primary and secondary urban occupational sectors was dependent upon the amount of capital that their different types of enterprise required and the levels of profit that prevailed within each. By midcentury, the worsted industry had become sufficiently capital intensive to ensure that most of its proprietors would be bourgeois. By contrast, the majority of proprietors in the urban-service sector stood lower in social scale.

Of course, this proliferation of urban-service entrepreneurs, which opened the way for the creation of a lower middle class, did not necessarily work to the advantage of the working-class consumer since the internal structure of the urban economy simply reflected the imprint of industrial capitalism with its dysfunctional pattern of consumer demand. Although Bradford had 175 beersellers in 1850, or one for every 593 inhabitants, the

---

[28] James Ibbetson, *Directory of Bradford* (Bradford, 1850).

[29] Ibid.; Adrian Elliott, "Social Structure in the mid-Nineteenth Century," in D. G. Wright and J. A. Jowitt, eds., *Victorian Bradford, Essays in Honour of Jack Reynolds* (Bradford, 1982), 110.

Table 4-2. *Social composition of middle-class business in Bradford: economic sector of enterprise by social status of proprietor*

	Percentage in bourgeoisie ($N = 1,259$)	Percentage in lower middle class ($N = 3,909$)
Genteel and higher professional sector ($N = 282$)	100	0
Primary industrial sector (worsted production) ($N = 732$)	61	39
Secondary urban service sector ($N = 4,152$)	14	86

Sources: This table summarizes the occupational composition of the Bradford bourgeoisie on the basis of an analysis of the 1851 bourgeois census population whose compilation is described in Appendix A. The figures for the entire middle class were obtained through an occupational analysis of all the householders in 1850, in Bradford's self-employed middle class who were listed in James, Ibbetson, *Directory* (Bradford, 1850) plus the rentiers obtained from the 1851 bourgeois census population. The occupational distribution of the lower middle class was obtained by subtracting the members of the 1851 bourgeois census population from the entire middle-class population in each occupational sector. It should be noted, as Appendix A explains in more detail, that all members of the genteel and higher liberal professions have been treated as bourgeois by definition.

town possessed only forty-seven doctors and dentists, or one for every 2,208.[30] Although such imbalances were inevitable in a working-class city where endemic poverty molded the shape of demand, they offer further evidence that the free-market economy failed to provide its working-class customers with the goods and services they most needed.

Yet however poorly it may have served the true interests of working-class consumers, the urban-service economy provided a critical opportunity for a host of shopkeepers, grocers, butchers, beersellers, and tailors to set up as petty entrepreneurs on their own. It is not exactly clear where this crowd of retailers came from, because their origins are nearly as obscure as those of the mass of laborers below them in the social scale. Many were probably recruited from the scores of rural hinterland clothiers and small-holding farmers, who were either being attracted by the prospect of new urban opportunities or were forced out of agriculture and domestic industry and into shopkeeping or comparable work in the town. The most marginal of

[30] Theodore Koditschek, "Class Formation and the Bradford Bourgeoisie" (Princeton, Ph.D. dissertation, 1981), 184.

the new urban retailers often rose from the ranks of weavers and rural cottagers who had accumulated small savings during periods of economic prosperity or had abandoned domestic manufacturing before the going got bad. John Wilson, for example, was a woolcomber and agricultural laborer who was able to start a small potato-bag-making business in the 1830s with £40 that his wife had saved.[31]

Sometimes it was a wife who would begin to keep shop part time when her husband lost his job or earned insufficient wages. If her business proved successful, he might take it over and open up a family shop on a full-time basis. Such families constituted the lowest and most vulnerable level of the urban lower middle class, able to remain independent only during boom periods, often sinking into the proletariat when trade declined.[32]

Nevertheless, if the urban-service economy had little to offer the proletariat, either as consumers or proprietors, for those with minimal property or family reserves to start out, it provided an outlet for enterprise and investment, facilitating the perpetuation of an independent petty propertied class. Hitherto dispersed throughout the countryside and integrated into the traditional economy of the region, the rapid growth of the industrial city and the proliferation of urban consumer demand drew or forced these small property owners into the city. By midcentury, 94 percent of Bradford's lower middle class made its living in urban-service trades.

Yet although Bradford's secondary-service economy provided the lower middle class with their main source of urban opportunity, it never became their exclusive preserve. As we have seen, the provision of some services, such as gas, water, and transport, required joint-stock companies, which were financed primarily by the investments of the established bourgeoisie. However, if the family firm prevailed, successful proprietors could aspire to the wealth and status of an urban elite. This was especially true in wholesaling, which tended to place a premium on large-scale operations, as is illustrated by such prominent firms as Tordoff and Sugden or David Harris Smith, which were rated, respectively, at £325 and £190 in 1845.[33] By

---

[31] Samuel Midgeley, *My Seventy Years' Musical Reminiscences* (London, n.d.) chap. 3; Joseph Wilson, *His Life and Work* (London, n.d.), 4–5.

[32] Joseph Barker, *History and Confessions of a Man* (Wortley, 1846), 84–5.

[33] The leading proprietors in some other service trades, such as wine and spirit merchants like John Middlebrook (rated at £189), R. B. Popellwell (£158), and John Lee (rated at £178 who died worth over £12,000 in 1848); and innkeepers like R. C. Fox (£250), William Wood (£244), Joseph Baxter (£157), and John Wade (£167); and Drapers like John McCroben and Henry Brown, could clearly hold their own with the smaller worsted manufacturers, although they could never hope to reach the levels of the leading magnates. Petitions for and against incorporation of Bradford (Bradford Archives, D.B. 69/2–3).

midcentury, the urban-service sector seems to have supplanted the worsted industry as the largest outlet of opportunity, even for the run-of-the-mill bourgeoisie. Among the 1,259 household heads in the 1851 bourgeois census population, whose compilation is discussed in Appendix A, only 35 percent were occupied in the primary productive sector, whereas 43 percent were engaged in secondary urban-service work, and 22 percent were liberal professionals or full-time rentiers.

As Tables 4-1 and 4-2 indicate, the liberal professions offered another alternative to men with the educational qualifications and capital to set up practice, permitting them to acquire bourgeois status without either the risks or rewards of entrepreneurship. At their best, professionals, especially clergymen, doctors, and writers of the generation who came of age in the thirties and forties, could play an important role as intellectuals for both liberal and Tory sectors of the urban bourgeoisie.[34] In most cases, however, the opportunities for such men, and for professionals in general, were limited by consumer demand. Those with the most money in early-nineteenth-century Bradford were the Anglican Tory gentlemen-capitalists, and the professionals who served their needs were among the wealthiest and most powerful men in town. Bankers like Charles Harris, who died worth over £80,000 in 1845, brokers like G. T. Lister and Thomas Dewhirst, solicitors like Samuel and Edward Hailstone, Richard Tolson (who died worth over £12,000), Greenwood Bentley, G. R. Mossman, and J. A. Busfield, and medical practitioners like Dr. Outhwaite, Dr. MacTurk, and Dr. Sharp were all among the fortunate few who moved in the exalted circles of local wealth and power. However, most of these men had been born into the local elite and would not have attained their position simply as diligent professionals.[35]

Marginal professionals, such as unlicensed medical practitioners and teachers, who served exclusively the needs of the poor, were much more numerous than the members of official liberal professions, but their incomes and status were often pathetic, and competition within their ranks was bitter and intense. Early-nineteenth-century Bradford was much less well served

[34] For two classic cases see F. G. Byles, *William Byles* (Weymouth, 1932); and Benjamin Godwin, "Autobiography" (Bradford Central Library, uncatalogued ms.).

[35] The influx and rise of a large new liberal generation of bourgeois entrepreneurs in the second quarter of the century provided new opportunities especially for lawyers, doctors, Nonconformist clergymen, and for newer professionals such as accountants and architects, but these opportunities were constrained by the financial and cultural limits of the middle class population that could afford to pay for their services. William Cudworth, "Old Bradford Lawyers," *BA*, o.s. 2 (1895), 65–71; John Maffey, "On some of the Decayed Families of Bradford," *BA*, o.s. 1 (1888), 26–32; *Ibbetson's Directory* (1850); *Registers of Wills, Yorkshire Archdiocese*, vols. 20–8 (Borthwick Institute of Historical Research).

by the professions than other towns its size, especially if they were older and more established or if their social structures were less radically bifurcated between rich and poor.[36]

The overall place of the professionals in midcentury Bradford is illustrated by Figure 4-2, which shows the distribution of property of individuals in several select occupations in 1845 for all property holders rated at £20 per annum or more. On the one hand, the manufacturers, stuff merchants, and woolstaplers in the primary productive sector displayed a wide spectrum of property holding, ranging from a residue of medium-sized and small manufacturers and merchants, with property rated below £100 or even £50 per year, to considerably wealthier men, whose fixed property was valued in the hundreds, in a few cases even in the thousands, of pounds per year. By contrast, the professionals and substantial retailers were more economically homogeneous, standing at the middle and lower wealth levels of the bourgeoisie and filling the borderline space within the social structure where it shaded off into the lower middle class.

By re-creating within the urban environment an intermediate stratum of small producers reminiscent of the rural pre- or protoindustrial age, Bradford's secondary-service economy contributed to the creation of a graduated social structure that might have blunted the stark antinomies between ascendant bourgeoisie and dispossessed workers that were generated in the town's primary industrial-capitalist sphere. By concentrating demand for the goods and services of new shopkeepers, artisans, and professionals in town, urban development reopened the middle ground of *petite bourgeoisie* and labor aristocrats that industrial capitalism had seemed to be closing off. Yet, so long as urbanization distributed these goods and services through the mechanism of the competitive marketplace, as a mode of consumption it worked to translate the inequalities generated by industrial capitalism into physical and environmental terms. At least before midcentury, the urban economy's primary role as a transmission mechanism for class differences overshadowed its role as an arena for petty entrepreneurship. Consequently, it could not realize its potential for facilitating the emergence of intermediate social groups, neither purely capitalist nor proletarian, which might come to serve as a bridge or buffer between the two.

Nowhere can this be seen more clearly than in the physical process of

[36] Koditschek, "Class Formation," 185–7; Elliott, "Social Structure," 103.

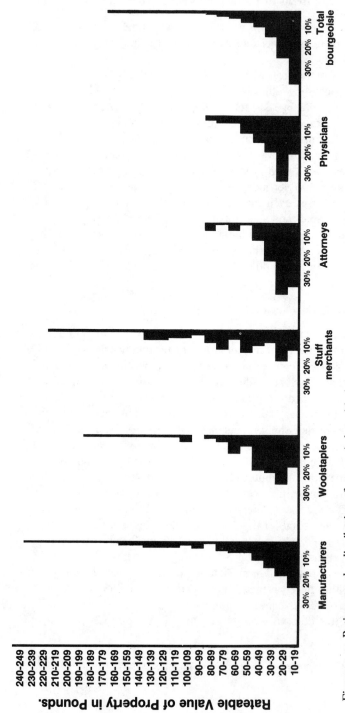

Figure 4-2. Rating sample: distribution of propertied wealth, by occupation.
These data are based on the declarations of signators on petitions for and against the municipal incorporation of the town. Because the issue was hotly contested and most men of property signed one or the other petition (sometimes both), the coverage of the data is fairly comprehensive, and though the accuracy of the declarations and their significance as a measure of individual wealth may be questioned in particular cases, the broad picture that emerges from the aggregate data is indisputable, revealing considerable differences in the property structure that characterized different occupational sectors of the bourgeoisie. Theodore Koditschek, "Class Formation and Bradford Bourgeoisie." (Princeton, Ph.D. dissertation, 1981), 902–26. Calculated from "Petitions for and against Incorporation" (Bradford Archives, D.B. 69/2–3).

construction through which the urban environment was actually built. As the largest sector of Bradford's service economy, employing 3,008 workers in 1851, the building trades and the developers who financed them constituted not only significant economic forces in their own right, but the most critical social agencies through which the logic of competitive capitalism was inscribed as a physical morphology – one that would literally shape the city for generations to come.[37] Here, in particular, the same economic forces that created new opportunity for the petty service entrepreneur were registering their most decisive impact in reinforcing the divisions between capital and labor with a new, ineluctable ecology of class.

The construction of the urban space

The construction of urban-industrial Bradford without any conscious regulation or planning, through a process almost entirely governed by impersonal market flows, was a product of the regional pattern of small freehold land tenure that had been inherited from the distant past. As we have seen, the gradual erosion of manorial authority, the absence of leaseholds or large properties, and the proliferation, at least throughout the lowlands, of a multitude of small farming and weaving freeholds created a property structure that harnessed the resources of the small investor for the task of urban development but also ensured that he would be guided mostly by the market incentives that enabled him to maximize his gain.[38] In sharp contrast to some nineteenth-century cities, such as Birmingham or London, where the presence of large landowners worked, even in the absence of civic regulation, to restrain market forces and develop properties in a coordinated way, the subdivision of Bradford Borough into 562 separate holdings, 84 percent of which were under fifteen acres in size, guaranteed a pattern dictated almost entirely by supply and demand.[39]

---

[37] *PP* (1852–3, LXXXVIII), 2:721.

[38] M. J. Mortimore, "Landownership and Urban Growth in Bradford and its Environs in the West Riding Conurbation, 1850–1950," *Transactions of the Institute of British Geographers*, 46 (1969). A late-nineteenth-century parliamentary enquiry confirmed that virtually all land within the borough was held in the form of relatively small fee-simple freeholds. Since property developers were invariably the owners, long-term building leases with restrictive covenants were virtually unknown, and attempts to introduce them proved extremely unpopular. *PP* (1887, XIII), 169.

[39] For the morphological consequences of different types of urban land tenure in nineteenth century England see H. J. Dyos, *Victorian Suburb* (Leicester, 1973); C. Chalklin, *The Provincial Towns of Georgian England* (London, 1974), 304–13; F. M. L. Thompson, *Hampstead: Building a Borough, 1650–1964* (London, 1974); and David Cannadine, *Lords and Landlords: The Aristocracy and the Towns, 1774–1967* (Leicester, 1980), 391–416.

Notwithstanding the explosive character of urbanization in Bradford and the town's extraordinary rate of demographic increase, its building trade proved remarkably successful in keeping pace with its inhabitants' housing needs. Whereas the average annual rate of increase in Bradford's housing stock had been 5.7 percent in the decade before 1811, it shot up to 6.9 percent per annum during the next ten years to match a 6.4 percent average annual population rise. This trend continued during the twenties, with both population and housing stock growing at about 6 percent per year. In these two decades, the number of houses standing in Bradford Borough almost tripled, rising from 3,812 to 8,630, and this does not even include the mills, shops, warehouses, and other structures that were built. Even in the thirties, this pattern continued as a 5.3 percent annual population increase was matched by a 5.5 percent annual rise in housing stock. Only in the demographic flood tide of the 1840s did a 6.3 percent annual rate of population growth overwhelm construction, which grew by an annual rate of only 3.6 percent.[40]

Because it mobilized the resources of a wide range of investors, from petty bourgeois property owners to wealthy capitalist rentiers, Bradford's freehold property structure stimulated the pace of urban construction, enabling it, even amidst an explosive economy, to keep virtually abreast of consumer needs. For local property owners of every description, urban landholding constituted a magnet that, at least before the railway boom of the 1840s, attracted the bulk of free capital not tied up in the staple trade. Given the ad hoc nature of free-market development, it is difficult to discern the social background of all these investors, but piecemeal evidence suggests that they fell into a few basic groups.

Most visible were the small protoindustrial landowners who had inherited property just beyond the existing boundary of settlement. Such individuals would find themselves under enormous pressure to develop as rising land values created the wherewithal to finance such activity, whereas nearby urban encroachments rendered their property useless for almost anything else. Wood's 1832 map, which names the plotowners who held undeveloped properties on what was then the immediate urban frontier, shows that owners, mostly a melange of local gentlemen, small farmers, and trustees of charities, responded to such incentives at differing rates. The result was a rather straggling, irregular pattern of construction on the edge of settlement, where open fields and isolated housing tracts were interspersed.[41]

---

[40] Calculated from *PP* (1801, VI), 438–9; (1812, XI) 413–14; (1822, XV), 414; (1831, XVIII), 318; (1844, XXVII), 222; (1852–3, LXXXVI), 214–15.

[41] "Wood's 1832 Plan of Bradford," in H. E. Wroot, "Bradford in 1832," *BA*, o.s. 3 (1912), 224–55.

Eventually, however, incentives for development proved irresistible, and owners who did not undertake this activity sold out to speculative developers who did. Although few of these men were real estate professionals, speculative building attracted individuals from every sphere of the local economy and every sector of the urban bourgeoisie. As downtown property values more than doubled in the early 1820s, the speculative spirit suddenly swept even the most staid and established elites.[42] Even more important was the appearance, in subsequent decades, of a new type of small investor who, in the words of Joseph Ellison, "may have a couple of thousand pounds and does not know what to do with it." Wishing "to lay it out so as to pay him the best percentage," he would take advantage of the prevailing small freehold urban property structure to "purchase a plot of ground, an acre and a half," building "as many houses...as he possibly can without reference to drainage or anything except that which will pay him a good percentage."[43]

This type of activity, while absorbing the energies of petit bourgeois slumlords, also constituted an outlet for larger rentier-capitalists who would, over the years, accumulate a number of parcels as they grew wealthier and as their commitment to industrial entrepreneurship decreased.[44] Even worsted manufacturers involved themselves in property development at least to the extent of purchasing the lot on which their factories were erected and throwing up a few dozen adjacent cottages on the space that remained after the construction of the mill.[45] Of course, a prime incentive to locate industry

[42] John Simpson, *The Journal of Dr. John Simpson of Bradford, 1825* (Bradford, 1981), 5, 26.

[43] *PP* (1840, XI), 89; (1842, XXVII), 199.

[44] With numerous small holdings all over town, the ironmaster Henry Leah appears to have been the most successful of these part-time developers, but Wood's 1832 map lists several others: the attorney Samuel Hailstone and the china merchant Charles Rhodes. Of the twenty-nine principal landowners in semirural Horton in the 1840s, six were gentlemen, three ironmasters, two farmers, and one a woolstapler. Occasionally, the developer can be inferred from the name of the development or the side streets within it, such as Thompson's buildings off Silsbridge Lane, Butterworth's buildings on Ivegate, Hustler's buildings on Bridge Street, Hustler Terrace in Barkerend, and Lister's row off of Bowling Back Lane. Compiled from "Wood's 1832 Plan"; William Cudworth, *Rambles Round Horton* (Bradford, 1886), 14; idem, *Bradford Corporation*, 154; and S. Wormald, *Reference to a Plan of the Township of Horton* (Leeds, 1840), which provides a comprehensive listing of the 1,817 plot parcels in Horton Township, with parcel sizes, descriptions of uses, and names of owners in 1839. See also Mortimore, "Landownership and Urban Growth"; Maffey, "Decayed Families"; *Ordnance Survey Map of Bradford* (1852) (five feet to the mile, in twelve sheets). Hereafter referred to as *OS* (1852).

[45] Among the early millowners, John Wood purchased seven acres to build housing for his workers whereas an 1821 ratebook noted Benjamin and Matthew Thompson as the owners of forty-seven cottages in Silsbridge Lane and Richard Fawcett as the proprietor of fourteen dwellings adjoining his Union Street Mill. Firth, "Genesis," 162; Gaskell, "Housing Estate Development," 41–73. The information in Wormald, *Plan of Horton*,

within the city was that it absolved the millowner of the obligation to house his work force and allowed him to leave all or part of the responsibilities for residential construction to other urban entrepreneurs. Since the capital needs and profit incentives of the staple trade necessitated the plowing back of industrial surpluses, most worsted capitalists kept building speculation to a minimum, although they knew that, if extra capital became available, property development and housing construction constituted an attractive way for it to be used.[46]

Finally, the widespread availability of modest-sized freeholds insured a role in property development, not only for the land speculator and rentier-investor, but for the building contractor too. Given the explosive demand for factories, cottages, and warehouses, it was inevitable that contracting and construction would become entrepreneurial outlets in their own right, and the proliferation of small masters undertaking small projects went hand in hand with the rise of a few general contractors and the reorganization of the bulk of the industry along large-scale lines.[47]

The 1851 census manuscript records twelve builders, five plasterers, one slater, and four timber merchants who either employed ten or more workers or kept domestic servants. Of these, only five firms employed more than twenty men. However, the widespread use of stone in local construction made master stonemasons and quarry owners the largest and wealthiest of Bradford's capitalist-builders. Twenty master masons fit the census criteria previously applied to the builders, and nine of these employed over twenty workers, in two cases, over fifty. This suggests that such men possessed a substantial capital base since stonemasons were highly skilled workers.[48]

An undated map, probably from the late nineteenth century, shows thirty-nine quarries in the vicinity of Bradford, mostly to the north and west of the town. Although many were not yet opened by midcentury, the 1851 census manuscript lists six quarrying firms having over ten employees. Impressionistic evidence suggests that at least two of these, John Jennings and Thackery & Cousen, were large businesses. However, the biggest contractor in early-nineteenth-century Bradford was undoubtedly Miles Moulson who specialized in constructing factories. His firm built many of the largest mills

suggests that millowners frequently owned their own factories and a few additional cottages or buildings, but only rarely owned the housing tracts in which the bulk of their workers lived.

[46] Ground plans contained in the OS (1852) reveal a pattern of close residential development emanating from Bradford's long and narrow mill district, which suggests at least some direct involvement by the millowners themselves.

[47] PP (1852–3, LXXXVIII), 2:721.

[48] Extracted from the census enumerators' manuscripts for Bradford, (HO, 107/2305–10).

in town, such as Waud's Brittania Mills, Garnett's Barkerend Mills, Drummond's Lumb Lane Mills, and much of Titus Salt's Saltaire.[49]

Although this successful mobilization of small or part-time development capital facilitated Bradford's extraordinarily rapid expansion, nothing contributed more to the town's environmental degeneration than the unrestrained right of these petty developers to do literally whatever they wanted on their uncoordinated jumble of small private plots. To be sure, all was not entirely chaos and anarchy as the market imposed its own ecological order of differential land values and locational imperatives. As Figure 4-3 indicates, these forces resulted in an embryonic pattern of functional differentiation whereby identifiable social groups and economic activities tended to concentrate in different parts of the town.

By midcentury, the ecology of the protoindustrial household, which had united businesses with residences and mixed the wealthy together with the poor, had been replaced by a complex morphology of zones in which the social classes were segregated and homes were separated from warehouses and factories, which were concentrated in specific parts of town. An 1848 survey reveals that 41 percent of Bradford Township's ratable property was devoted to nonresidential purposes, 27 percent to the worsted industry alone. By contrast, only 12 percent of the ratable value was for structures in which businesses and residences were combined.[50]

Warehouses and large shops had to be located downtown, near the canal and railway transport terminals and the major arterial turnpike roads. But the location of Bradford's factories was dictated by ecological considerations too. Congregated together in the low-lying town center, their need of outlets for industrial waste and sources of water for steam engines led them to spread in a narrow band along the Bradford and Bowling Becks, at the point where they passed through the urban valley. By 1850, this band of mills and foundries was 1.5 miles long, bulging out from the core in the north and west, and accentuating the radial dimension of Bradford's urban space.[51]

In addition to these geographical factors, economic forces, particularly the rapid inflation of downtown land values, affected the way property was used. For example, the plot on which the merchant Leo Schuster built his warehouse, for which he had paid 25s. per yard in 1836, was assessed at

[49] William Cudworth, *Worstedopolis* (Bradford, 1888), 5; *Bradford Portraits* (Bradford, 1892); anon., *Bradford, 1847–1947* (Bradford, 1947), 79.
[50] *BO*, June 22, 1848.
[51] C. Richardson, *A Geography of Bradford* (Bradford, 1976), 64, 85–7.

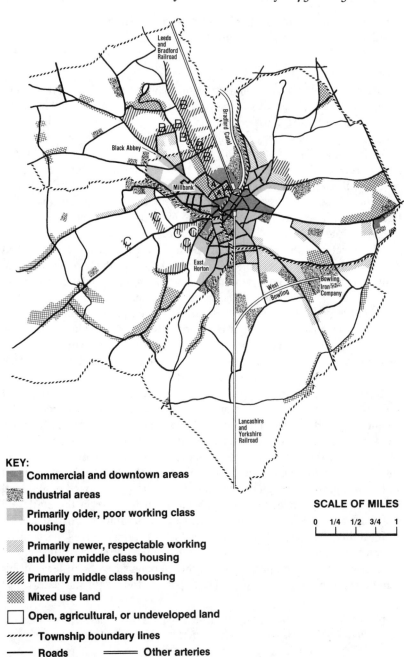

KEY:

▓ Commercial and downtown areas

▒ Industrial areas

▒ Primarily oider, poor working class housing

▒ Primarily newer, respectable working and lower middle class housing

▒ Primarily middle class housing

▒ Mixed use land

☐ Open, agricultural, or undeveloped land

••••••• Township boundary lines

━━━ Roads   ═══ Other arteries

Figure 4-3. Differentiation of land use in Bradford, 1850.
John Johnson, Map of the Township of Bradford (1802); Kemp and Sowerby, Map of the Borough of Bradford (1834); T. Dixon, Map of Bradford (1850); OS (1852).

£20 per yard three decades later.[52] To provide housing at rentals that tenants could afford, it was necessary to locate residences in the surrounding ring, where land was cheaper, and to limit respectable dwellings to the outlying regions of built-up settlement, which had the advantage of being less polluted and more attractive because they stood on higher ground. This left the noisy, smoky districts in the middle, on either side of the central commercial and industrial land, for the housing of the workers (see Figure 4-3).

By 1850, the bulk of these dwellings were concentrated in small patches of extraordinarily dense settlement. There, the dilemma of how to wring a profit out of housing working-class families with minimal resources in an area where land values were rising fast was solved by multiplying the number of tenants per acre as far as possible. Together, these areas covered only seventy acres, or barely one percent of the surface of the borough. But in this narrow space was concentrated a population of 22,158 at midcentury, or 21 percent of its inhabitants. The average density in these urban slums was 318 persons per acre, although some were much denser, and Mr. Richardson has noted one small plot, composed mainly of Irish immigrants, where the density surpassed 800 per acre.[53]

The worst of these slums had been constructed between 1810 and 1830 and by midcentury were in a state of advanced decrepitude. Built on the narrow crofts formerly cultivated by protoindustrial farmer-weavers, these lots – running perpendicular to the main public thoroughfares – each evolved into a hermetic slum neighborhood as it was filled with short rows of tiny back-to-back cottages divided only by miniature courts and alleys.[54] The smallest and most notorious of these slum districts was a 6.4-acre stretch known as Black Abbey along the west side of Westgate, where the density was 350 per acre. Rather larger, but equally bad was the Millbank district running from the beck up to Silsbridge Land and Longlands Street (see Figure 4-3). Here 7,559 people in 1,191 households were packed into 23.5 acres, which had to be shared with two chapels and graveyards, a timberyard, and five worsted mills. On the east side of town, the working-class slum areas were less clearly delineated, but Wapping, a piece of 7.8 acres to the northeast of the parish church, can be distinguished from the rest. Here population density reached 390 per acre. A similar situation prevailed on the south side of town, where the slum streets of East Horton shaded into

---

[52] William Cudworth, *Historical Notes on the Bradford Corporation* (Bradford, 1881), 153; *BO*, Nov. 26, 1863.

[53] Calculated from *OS* (1852), and HO, 107/2305–10; Richardson, *Geography*, 96.

[54] Friedrich Engels's classic description of working-class slums in Manchester might equally well have been applied to Bradford. See his *Condition of the Working Class in England* (Moscow, 1973), 63–113; *PP* (1840, XI); *PP* (1842, XXVII); *OS* (1852).

the slightly better working-class neighborhoods of West Bowling (see Figure 4-3).[55]

Of course, nothing contributed more to Bradford's environmental deterioration than this maze of unsightly and unsanitary slums. Yet so long as the proletariat could not afford decent accommodation and as long as the provision of their housing was left entirely to free enterprise, it was inevitable that these dens of pestilence and demoralization should constitute the characteristic environment in which most urban-industrial workers lived.

Conclusion: the rise of the private city and the decline of public life

As the foregoing shows, the invisible hand of competitive capitalism, not only in Bradford's industrial production process, but also in its secondary-service sphere, created a visible urban environment by midcentury very different from the protoindustrial village ecology that had prevailed little more than a generation before. Largely the spontaneous product of market forces, which had concentrated together an enormous agglomeration of anonymous people, buildings, mortar, and machines, this urban environment engulfed the traditional townscape over which it had proliferated, swallowing up those central, defining public spaces and activities that had for centuries given shape and focus to traditional community life.

The parish church, which had once towered above the community, was only one part of the industrial landscape, blending into the jumble of warehouses that lay below it and the clutter of terraces that rose above. After years of exposure to smoke and soot, its stone facade had progressively blackened to the same drab hue that it shared with every other building in town. Its once lofty spire was now overshadowed by the cluster of "dark, satanic" factory chimneys from which the offending pollution issued. Stately village streets like Kirkgate, which had once framed the church from which they radiated, were now humbled and lost amidst a crowd of buildings that spread out randomly in all directions.[56]

Urbanization also destroyed the old inn. It was already being stripped of most of its social functions before the stagecoach declined and the railway undercut its economic base. One commentator lamented:

---

[55] *OS* (1852); HO, 107/2,304–10.
[56] For church and chapel building see James, *History of Bradford*, 223–39; idem, *Continuations and Additions*, 183–97; William Scruton, *Pen and Pencil Pictures of Old Bradford* (Bradford, 1889), 39–46; L. Dawson, "The Earlier Daughter Churches of the Bradford Parish Church," *BA*, n.s. 3 (1912), 201–12; *BO*, Apr. 23, Oct. 1, 1835; Feb. 18, Nov. 3, 1836; Nov. 30, Dec. 14, 1837.

In times gone by, inns were places for listening to quaint stories, for discussing the questions of the day, for showing geniality towards your neighbors. . . . But now-a-days forsooth, the proprietors of these homes of "entertainment" are restless when talk is indulged in to any great extent, unless it is accompanied by a plentiful imbibition; and thus a restraint is placed upon their customers which, though it may lead to a more rapid consumption of drinkables, detracts from the comfort of the houses.[57]

Stripped of their role as centers for communal organization and activity, Bradford's inns shrank into sleeping and eating establishments or degenerated into the narcotic pathology of the dramhouse and beershop, where desperate, unemployed workers gathered to drown their hopelessness with the only opium of the people that really relieved their pain.[58]

As for the recreational commons, the other traditional communal space examined in Chapter 2, urbanization even more thoroughly undermined its function and sounded its death knell. As downtown property values soared, the Turls was divided up into lots and reincarnated as Tyrell Street, whereas other open spaces gradually followed suit. The most brutal popular sports, such as cockfighting and bull baiting, were suppressed. More harmless amusements and recreations were barely tolerated and consigned to more distant up-country moorlands.[59] By the 1830s, the web of plebeian culture that had survived protoindustrialization began to unravel as its threads of oral tradition became weakened and frayed. As old yarns died, in their final spinning they sometimes took a novel twist. Thus when a new generation of Hortonians were told the story of "fair 'Becca," they learned that she no longer haunted the neighborhood, having been "flayed away" by the whir of machinery at Cliffe Mills. As for the monstrous Guytrash, it too seems to have been subdued by urbanization for, "as it has never been heard of since the town was Incorporated, it is supposed to have become jealous of policemen, and so left the neighbourhood forever."[60]

Perhaps it was inevitable that the church and the medieval commons should cease to be the foci for an urban-industrial community or that their boundaries should no longer be defined by village meadows and streets. But in early-nineteenth-century Bradford, no alternative sites emerged to play a comparable role. In fact, the operation of the free enterprise urban economy

---

[57] One innkeeper with an eye for historical change altered the name of his establishment during the early years of the century from the The Horse and Jockey to The Beehive. Cudworth, *Bradford Corporation*, 36; James Burnley, *Phases of Bradford Life* (Bradford, 1871), 146.

[58] Koditschek, "Class Formation," 298, 398.

[59] Cudworth, *Bradford Corporation*, 6, 31, 46; Dixon, *Map of Bradford*, (1850).

[60] William Cudworth, *Rambles Round Horton* (Bradford, 1886), 172.

initially insured that Bradford would have few public buildings and spaces at all. By midcentury, the town's architectural foci, insofar as it had any, were the large factories and classical, colonnaded stuff warehouses that became the centerpieces of Bradford's new downtown.[61]

If little space was left for public uses that profited no one, little time was left for public displays and festivities out of which nothing useful was produced. As the routinized, utilitarian temporality of the marketplace replaced the periodicities of the sun and soil, activities that could not be productively

[61] *BO*, Oct. 6, Nov. 3, 1836; Feb. 8, June 14, 1838. Rouses's premises were sold for over £30,000 in 1847, *BO*, June 3, 1837. Of course, early-nineteenth-century Bradford was not entirely devoid of public buildings and amenities, but their construction was left to private charity and voluntary contributions which were very slow to materialize in a city whose economic elites were single-mindedly devoted to getting on or getting out – to the accumulation of capital which, if spent at all, would probably be spent somewhere else. Indeed, the few public buildings that were built under these circumstances were either, like the exchange rooms, not really public since they were constructed by elites largely to meet their own cultural needs and not to benefit the population at large, or like the infirmary, the courthouse, and the churches and chapels, to meet a public need which it was deemed extremely dangerous from the elite perspective to allow to go unfilled. Koditschek, "Class Formation," 415; Scruton, *Old Bradford*, 109–63.

Before the late twenties, Bradford had no secular, public buildings at all. The old manor hall was subdivided into shops and private offices, whereas the magistrates and Improvement Commission continued to meet in taverns. The town jail was a hole in the ground and the township workhouse was little more than a rambling shack, whereas the post office operated out of a succession of corner stores, as the part-time duties of postmaster were bought and sold between one small shopkeeper and the next. The only public institution that possessed its own building was the notorious and widely detested Court of Requests. See "The Bradford Mail over 300 Years," *BA*, n.s. 6 (1940), 170–9; Scruton, *Old Bradford*, 110–11.

In 1834, the construction of the courthouse for £6,000, raised by private subscription, gave the authorities at least a place to meet, but with the rise of social antagonisms and radical popular movements, which the latter increasingly restricted or suppressed, the courthouse, so far from being a focus for collective identity, became a symbol of the larger class oppression that urban-industrial capitalism seemed to have wrought. Although the opening of the Oddfellows Hall in 1837, the Temperance Hall in 1838, and the Mechanics Institute in 1840 did much to relieve the lack of large public auditoriums, these structures were all built by private voluntary associations and could serve as genuine public buildings only insofar as the societies that owned and operated them were themselves effective repositories of urban community identity and viable agencies of urban collective life. See David Ashforth, "The Poor Law in Bradford, c. 1834–1871" (Bradford, Ph.D. dissertation, 1979), 287–94; Scruton, *Old Bradford*, 111; Cudworth, *Bradford Corporation*, 72; *BO*, May 19, 1836.

In fact, it was only with the 1854 erection, at a cost of £35,000 raised by public subscription, of the truly ecumenical St. George's Hall that a genuine civic center finally became available. It was not until twenty years after that, with the opening of the £100,000 municipally financed town hall, that the city obtained a real architectural and communal center that was publicly operated and collectively owned.

harnessed were either suppressed or relegated to private domestic life. Now dismissed as "tomfoolery" inappropriate to "an enlightened age," the old tides, feasts, country fairs, and harvest suppers, traditionally occasions for the community to unite, were either abandoned or permitted by disdainful elites to degenerate into disruptive displays of plebeian debauchery, which only exacerbated urban pollution and refuse, and further clogged the narrow city streets.[62]

The elaborate septennial Bishop Blaize celebration, in honor of the woolcombers' patron saint, was last observed in Bradford in 1825, and the *Observer's* 1842 appraisal of its fate could have served as an explanation of the atrophy of other instances of ceremonial life. "Whether from the cupidity of our capitalists, the decline in our means to meet the expense, or the idea that such pageantry was a needless waste, unbecoming this enlightened age," the paper noted that, "of late years . . . the procession has been discontinued and the anniversary has had no celebration beyond a club dinner or a private party."[63]

This default of collective symbolism and ceremony, whether manifested spatially, in representational structures, or ritualistically, in time, attests to the demise of any sense of human community among a heavily immigrant urban population scarcely able to comprehend the environment its members inhabited in anything other than economic market terms. As in Charles Dickens's Coketown "you saw nothing . . . but what was severely workful," and an uninitiated visitor encountering industrial Bradford for the first time might well conclude that it was no more than a vast productive mechanism

---

[62] *BO*, Aug. 18, 1836; Aug. 5, 1852; Dec. 8, 1859.

[63] This tendency either to ignore or to "privatize" major public occasions, which would hitherto have been celebrated with elaborate civic ceremonial and pomp, can be seen in Bradford's reaction to the coronation of Queen Victoria in 1838. Initially, the *Observer,* in good Durkheimian fashion, had hoped for "a festival which fills the mind of a whole people with one idea, and their hearts with a common sentiment . . . and makes every man, however poor, feel himself a living part of a vast rejoicing community." *BO,* June 27, 1838.

However, in the tense political and economic climate of 1838, as workers took to the streets for very different ends, this sort of rhetorical affirmation of the urban community was wishful thinking of the wildest sort. A public meeting was called to consider what form the celebration ought to take, but no one could come up with any workable ideas. A suggestion that a congratulatory address be sent came to nothing because representatives of different political parties could not agree on the wording. The impossibility of feasting all the operatives in so large a town was pointed out. Finally, the manufacturer J. G. Horsfall expressed his relief at being spared a festival "that might only be remembered by the headaches the next morning." *BO,* June 7, July 5, 1838. Although, in the end, a hastily concocted public procession was drummed up, two years later, when the young queen married, no civic commemoration of any sort was organized, although "numerous private assemblies" of gentlemen were held. *BO,* Feb. 13, 1840.

of interchangeable parts, containing "several large streets all very like one another, and many small streets still more like one another, inhabited by people equally like one another, who all went in and out at the same hours."[64]

Yet, such a judgment would be superficial if only, as Dickens himself fully recognized, because people cannot live in this way. Even as a collective agglomeration of separate individuals, whom the pursuit of self-interest had concentrated together in one place, urban-industrial Bradford was spontaneously evolving its own insensate forms of social solidarity and its own unspoken framework for the development of collective identity within emerging social groups. Although these new forms of social identity and consciousness could rarely ground themselves in any overarching sense of urban community, they could, and did, form along the fault lines of capitalist class division and congeal in the form of mutually exclusive solidarities on the part of groups with radically divergent experiences of urban-industrial life.

This new class consciousness never entirely obliterated other forms of consciousness, nor did it achieve dominance in some automatic, predetermined way. Even within the urbanizing process itself, there were some counterpressures that worked to mitigate class polarizations by renewing the scope for small-scale economic activity within the urban-service sector. Nevertheless, before midcentury, these tendencies were always overshadowed by the urban market dynamic, which translated class disparities into consumption inequalities. Until these disparities and inequalities were addressed, there was no chance of realizing the latent potential within the urban environment for the creation of new forms of community in which class division and market competition might be tempered or channeled into more cohesive and cooperative social forms.

[64] Charles Dickens, *Hard Times* (London, 1969), 65. For a description of Bradford along these lines, see Georg Weerth, *Sämtliche Werke* (Berlin, 1956), III:165.

5

The industrial city and the traditional elite

The protoindustrial fusion of the gentleman with the capitalist, which the crisis of the early nineteenth century had strained, was sundered by Bradford's urban-industrial revolution. The contradiction between gentility and capitalism, which had been latent in the eighteenth century, became, by the 1830s and 1840s, open and irresolvable as local elites were forced to choose between the two. Capitalism had been initiated by their parents and grandparents, and it remained the source from which their own income was ultimately drawn. Yet in the new urban-industrial context, it seemed increasingly incompatible with their quest for elegance and refinement and the values on which their authority was based.

From active capitalists into rentiers

This contradiction between capitalist activity and the role of the gentleman was thrown into sharper relief by the subtle changes that took place within Bradford's economic and political establishment during the 1820s when the new elite generation came of age. Accustomed from birth to a life of luxury, these men were often more interested in enjoying what their parents or grandparents bequeathed them than in following the latter down an entrepreneurial path. At the very moment when Bradford's most explosive development opened new opportunities for parvenu competitors, their desire to consolidate already established positions made them cautious and conservative in their economic strategies. As Bradford expanded and threatened to engulf them, they grew more determined to keep it at arm's length.

The environmental deterioration that blighted the town when the pace of industrial development accelerated after 1825 made these second-generation gentleman-capitalists even more inclined to disdain entrepreneurship as an end in itself. "I am partial to a country life and rural sports & hate the bustle of a town, particularly the coarse rude bustle of a manufacturing town," the young physician John Simpson complained in his diary, as early as 1825. "Nothing would delight me more than to be able to retire into the country where I might live and act independently without being molested by anyone or subject to the cares and nonsense of the world."[1]

Although Simpson did not come from a capitalist family, as a gentleman-physician who moved in their circles he expressed attitudes that they shared – attitudes that suggest a deeper desire to abandon entrepreneurial involvement and to move into secondary or tertiary economic roles as professionals or as rentiers.[2] Simpson, for his part, saw a connection between the necessity that forced him to earn his living and the imperatives that motivated him to remain in town:

> I am very anxious to increase, if I could, my private income for then I should be able to live where I liked best. If from one source or other I had an income of three hundred pounds per annum independent of my profession I would leave Bradford and go to reside at Harrorgate or some place or other that better suited my ideas than this abominable manufacturing district.[3]

Simpson's desire to get out of Bradford was shared by many members of his generation. Some of the wealthiest and most prominent, like the manufacturer John Wood, who purchased a 3,000-acre Hampshire Estate, and the banker Charles Harris, who bought Fulford Grange outside of York, were able to do so in a particularly grand way.[4] However, many others who wished to retire found that this was easier said than done. Either because they lacked the financial resources or because those they possessed were tied up in industrial assets that could not be transferred, joining the rural squirearchy was not possible for most elites. Among the handful for whom it was, gentrification became possible only in the context of retirement, which necessarily entailed a diminution of all forms of active life. This was the case with both Harris and Wood, who remained in business until the age of sixty-one. In a family like the Horsfalls, where one brother, John Garnett, was willing to maintain the business, it was possible for others to retire much earlier. Two of his brothers moved to Bolton Royd, whereas his cousins Thomas Hill and Timothy, who purchased Hawksworth Hall in the 1820s, spent the next fifty years immersed in the pleasures of the hunt.[5]

Ironically, it was professionals, particularly physicians like Simpson, who had less difficulty pulling up their urban roots. Although they were less wealthy than the leading manufacturers, their professional practices did not

[1] John Simpson, *The Journal of Dr. John Simpson of Bradford, 1825* (Bradford, 1981), 6.
[2] Ibid.   [3] Ibid., 48.
[4] J. T. Ward, "Two Pioneers in Industrial Reform," *Journal of Bradford Textile Society* (Bradford, 1963–4), 33–51; idem, "Old and New Bradfordians in the Nineteenth Century," *Journal of Bradford Textile Society* (1964–5) 17–32; *BOB*, Apr. 21, 1906.
[5] *BOB*, Feb. 24, 1906; Simpson, *Journal*, 75.

tie them to the city and, in some cases, actually gave them an incentive to leave. Simpson was aware that a lucrative but undemanding practice, which would permit him to live out the gentlemanly role, was a luxury that he would never have in Bradford. "Bradford is a bad situation for a medical man, the bulk of the population being of the lowest description of people . . . Bradford will never be inhabited by Gentlemen and their families and those are the people to benefit a physician."[6]

As soon as he was able, Simpson moved to Harrogate, where he could find rich patients, a socially congenial environment, and even a modest country house. His example was soon followed by others, such as Willson Cryer, who left Bradford for Ilkley, and his friend John Outhwaite, who, in 1847, abandoned his long-standing medical and philanthropic activities in Bradford to follow Simpson to the Harrogate spas where he died twenty years later almost forgotten by the inhabitants of his native town.[7]

Although others may have shared this desire to leave the city, only a minority got the chance. Tied to Bradford and its development by the legacy of family investments, they could not liquidate their assets and move away. However, continued residence in the city by no means precluded abandoning entrepreneurship for the passive economic role of a rentier. A study of probate valuations for all Bradfordians who died between 1838 and 1857 leaving personal property worth £100 or more shows that most of these men and women at time of death were not receiving their income in profits but in dividends, interest, shares, and rents. Since most of these wealth holders belonged to the generation that was born in the last two decades of the eighteenth century, the data presented in Table 5-1 can be taken as a fair indicator of the occupational distribution at different economic levels of Bradford's second-generation traditional elites.[8]

As Table 5-1 indicates, although Bradford was a city in which virtually all wealth was derived from industrial production, only a minority of those who died with substantial property were, at time of death, involved in the staple trade. At every wealth level, the textile capitalists were overshadowed by individuals whose income came from other sources. Among the moderately wealthy (those who died leaving £100 to £999 personalty) tradesmen and small proprietors in the service sector formed a majority, with gentlemen and textile capitalists coming far behind. What is surprising, however, was

---

[6] Simpson, *Journal*, 30, 65.

[7] J. H. Bell, "Some Fragments of Medical History," *BA*, o.s. 1 (1888); Simpson, *Journal*, 6; *BO*, Feb. 20, 1868; *Calendar of Yorkshire Wills* (mss., Borthwick, Institute).

[8] *Calendar of Yorkshire Wills*, 20–29 (1838–57).

Table 5-1. *Socioeconomic structure of early-nineteenth-century elite: Occupational sector by personal wealth of all Bradfordians deceased between 1838 and 1857 with estates over £100.*

Percentage in specific occupation	Probate Values			
	£100–£999 (N = 473)	£1,000–£14,999 (N = 206)	£15,000+ (N = 27)	Total
Worsted manufacturing	7	15	30	10
Woolstapler or merchant	3	10	7	5
Total primary production	*10*	*25*	*37*	*15*
Traditional industry	1	3	7	1
Professions	5	18	4	9
Rentiers and gentlemen	12	26	52	18
Total genteel	*18*	*47*	*63*	*28*
Total urban-service sector	*54*	*24*	*0*	*43*
Total unknown	*18*	*4*	*0*	*14*

Source: Calculated from *Calendar of Yorkshire Wills* (1838–1857).

that at the higher levels of wealth, where the small proprietors of the service sector dwindled into insignificance, it was not the industrialists, but gentlemen and professionals who constituted the bulk of the group. This was particularly true among the wealthiest of Bradford's traditional elites, the twenty-seven individuals who possessed over £15,000 personalty at the time of their deaths. This group contained nearly twice as many rentiers as industrial capitalists, and almost two thirds of its members were either full- or part-time gentlemen whose incomes were derived less from profit than from secondary revenues such as interest, fees, and rents.[9]

Since real estate was excluded from the probate valuations, the data used in the compilation of Figure 5-1 underestimates the proportion of rentier property in the overall composition of wealth in the town. Nevertheless, even when personalty alone is considered, the predominance of gentlemen and the insignificance of industrial assets before midcentury is clear beyond all doubt.[10] Rentiers who died between 1838 and 1857 held £968,850 in personal wealth, more than twice as much as the worsted manufacturers, who

[9] Ibid. (1838–57).
[10] See W. D. Rubinstein, *Men of Property: the Very Wealthy in Britain Since the Industrial Revolution* (New Brunswick, 1981), 56–116; and John Vincent, *Pollbooks, How the Victorians Voted* (London, 1967), 34–42, for general discussions of this phenomenon.

held £417,050. Even the handful of men who limited themselves to industries like iron founding, coal mining, brewing, and transport succeeded in accumulating £221,800 in personal property, whereas wool merchants and professionals came a distant fourth and fifth with £169,450 and £152,700 in personalty, respectively. Taken as a whole, those in the genteel sector, although only 28 percent of the £100-plus wealth holders, monopolized 54 percent of the group's personal wealth. Although 43 percent of the group was in the service sector, these individuals held only 15 percent of its wealth, whereas those occupied in the primary productive sphere comprised 15 percent of the group's members and obtained only 25 percent of its wealth.[11]

This study of property holding among Bradford's second-generation elites at the time of their deaths suggests an inescapable conclusion – that the group witnessed, indeed that its members presided over, a transfer of surplus wealth from industrial production to derivative forms of property, such as land, buildings, government securities, and company shares. A drift toward rentier status, which had begun during the protoindustrial era, reached greater proportions among those elites who survived into the early industrial age. What is at issue is no longer occasional purchases of land, cottages, stocks, or bonds by industrialists with surpluses that their own businesses could not absorb. Rather, the data indicate a near abandonment of industrial entrepreneurship by the second generation as its assets were transferred from active enterprises into passive property forms.

This tendency for the second generation to give up entrepreneurship and to rely on coupon clipping was most noticeable among the iron founding dynasties such as the Hardys, the Wickhams, the Dawsons, and the Pollards, whose wealth enabled them to insert themselves painlessly into the regional gentry. By the 1830s, these men had joined the ranks of the established country families like the Lister-Kayes of Manningham, the Sharp-Powells of Horton, the Fields of Heaton, and the Tempests of Tong. Together these families formed a tiny, almost universally Tory, regional oligarchy that dominated public administration and law enforcement to midcentury by their virtual monopoly of the county bench.[12]

Among families with a background in textiles, this rentier metamorphosis was slower and, in some cases, less complete. For the wealthiest of the eighteenth-century textile capitalists, the transition could, of course, be made with ease. John Hustler's children, William and John, Jr., gradually abandoned their father's worsted operations and depended heavily on speculation in their Undercliffe suburban estate. By the third generation, John Hustler III had developed an un-Quaker-like taste for hunting and extravagant living,

[11] Calculated from *Calendar of Yorkshire Wills* (1838–57).
[12] William Cudworth, *Round About Bradford* (Bradford, 1876), 256–69, 509–17.

which dissipated much of the fortune that his grandfather had taken a lifetime to amass.[13]

Others, who began with less wealth than the Hustlers and who lacked the resources to purchase an estate, also employed modest and incremental speculations in urban property as a wedge to work their way out of entrepreneurship. A prime example of this type was Samuel Margerison, who shifted the family's resources from his father's successful textile business at the turn of the century to urban land and bank investments, dying worth £60,000 personalty in 1853.[14] In the case of John Bower of Middlethorpe Hall (£25,000 personalty), who owned farms in Bradford, Horton, Thornton, and Clayton, the inflation of urban land values figured prominently in the accumulation of wealth. Similarly, the former stuff merchant Joshua Mann seems to have found being a landlord so much more pleasant than being a capitalist that he retired to his Manningham townhouse to spend the rest of his days in a life of ease.[15]

Of course, abandoning the worsted industry did not necessarily entail leaving business altogether, as in the case of the Peckover-Harrises who went into banking.[16] After apprenticing in textiles, Matthew Thompson (1781–1847) followed the example of a brother who had married the daughter of a brewer and switched to the less intensely competitive drink trade. As Bradford's working class increased both in numbers and in level of intoxication, Thompson grew increasingly rich. This paved the way for his son, Sir Matthew (1820–91), to train as a barrister and to gain a reputation as one of the most able Tory politicians in town. Marrying his cousin and consolidating his fortune, young Matthew combined brewing with railway investments that brought him several company directorships, helped him finance two expensive parliamentary campaigns, and could hardly have been absent from the government's motivation in granting him a baronetcy in 1890.[17]

[13] John Maffey, "On Some of the Decayed Families of Bradford," *BA*, o.s. 1 (1888), 26–32; H. R. Hodgson, *The Society of Friends in Bradford* (Bradford, 1926), 48–53.

[14] John Hollings and Francis Duffield (who died worth £14,000 personalty in 1841) were also rentiers by the early nineteenth century whose ancestors had begun in the worsted trade. Other examples of the type were John Brogden (£25,000 personalty) and William Pearson (£10,000 personalty), who benefited greatly from the possession of choice town-center property. *Calendar of Yorkshire Wills*, 26–28 (1853).

[15] Simpson, *Journal*, 3, 75; *Calendar of Yorkshire Wills*, 20 (1838), 21 (1841), 22 (1843–5), 23 (1845–6), 26 (1852), 28 (1856); William Cudworth, *Histories of Bolton and Bowling* (Bradford, 1891); idem, *Histories of Manningham, Heaton, and Allerton* (Bradford, 1896); 16, 36–7, 61, 163, 181.

[16] Simpson, *Journal*, 78; Gary Firth, "The Genesis of the Industrial Revolution in Bradford" (Bradford, Ph.D. dissertation, 1975), 177–80; *Calendar of Yorkshire Wills*, 23 (1847), 24 (1848–9).

[17] *Calendar of Yorkshire Wills*, 23 (1847), 24 (1848–9); Cudworth, *Manningham, Heaton, and Allerton*, 95–8.

Thompson's reliance on professional training to lubricate his transition from capitalist to gentleman reflects a common pattern in nineteenth-century English society that was characteristic of other members of Bradford's original business elite. The liberal professions of medicine, the church, and, particularly, law had always provided an outlet for second-generation wealth holders to enter into genteel circles. This process had been at work even in the eighteenth century when men like John Hardy moved up from managerial work to professions that allowed them to live well with minimal effort and to intermingle with the cream of the local elites. Although many of early-nineteenth-century Bradford's doctors, lawyers, and clergymen were descendants of long-standing professional families, others like Rev. William Fawcett, whose father bought him the incumbency of Bierley, were children of manufacturers. Eager to translate their wealth into social prestige, they hoped to give their children a life of elegance and leisure that they had never been able to achieve for themselves.[18]

For the most part, their sons did not disappoint them. The wealthiest professionals within the nineteenth-century city were well known for their adeptness in re-creating the trappings of an aristocratic life without ever leaving Bradford. Samuel Hailstone, for example, after building up a successful legal practice, set himself up as an urban squire and rented Horton Hall. At one time, Bowling Hall was rented by Rev. Nicholas Heineken, a wealthy Unitarian minister connected by marriage to the Anglican Horsfalls. Other professionals such as the surgeon J. A. Illingworth, who died worth £14,000 personalty in 1848, also purchased land in the city and suburbs.[19] So widespread was the flight of the second-generation elite from the factory that, between the failure of some who had been manufacturers (Richard Smith, Robert Ramsbotham, and Richard Fawcett) and the abandonment of the worsted industry by most of the rest, the list of industrialists in 1850 contained only four firms that had been prominent in the industry before 1825, those of the Rouses, the Wauds, the Garnetts, and the Rands.[20]

These facts testify to the cultural attraction of gentility as an ideal that drew most of early-nineteenth-century Bradford's elites away from involvement in entrepreneurship and toward the role of rentier. Although, in most cases, this shift appears to have been a decision motivated by noneconomic factors, such as the desire to build status or political authority, there were also underlying structural forces that encouraged the drift of capital away

---

[18] Firth, "Genesis," 25–37; William Scruton, *The Fawcett Family* (Bradford, 1908).

[19] Simpson, *Diary*, 6; A. Cobden-Smith, *Historical Sketch of Chapel Lane Chapel* (Bradford, n.d.); *Calendar of Yorkshire Wills*, 27 (1854).

[20] See Appendix C, and also Scruton, *Fawcett*. Even those families who remained in industry tended to diversify their holdings. As we have seen, the Rands were reported in 1846 to have £300,000 in railway shares. J. T. Ward, "West Riding Landowners and the Railways," *Transport History*, 4 (1959–60), 242–51.

from manufacturing, where it was most productive, toward other forms of property, where, in monetary terms, it could sometimes be more profitable and was invariably more secure.

In the first place, the process of generational transition often required such a transfer of manufacturing assets to more easily disposable property forms. An examination of some forty-eight wills of wealthy Bradfordians who died between 1838 and 1857 reveals the difficulty of properly dividing a family estate when it was tied up in the form of machinery, materials, and mills. Unless there was a son willing and able to carry on the business, there was no alternative but to sell the property and invest the capital, at least temporarily, in shares or bonds. Since primogeniture was almost never practiced in these families, even when an heir existed to perpetuate the firm, the constraints of guaranteeing benefits for other family members or of reconstituting partnerships broken by death made it impossible to continue the business without an audit and settling of accounts.[21]

In some instances, this was unproblematic as at William Rouse's death in 1843 or Nathan Bentley's in 1848, when their mills and machinery were reconstituted as partnerships of their sons. However, William's brother John Rouse, who had died in 1838 worth £70,000 personalty, had to specify that his four-year partnership with his brother should continue to term before his share was liquidated to meet the claims of his heirs. When Richard Garnett (£16,000 personalty) died in 1849, his partners, a brother and a cousin, were forced to submit to an outside valuation of the business and were offered the option of purchasing his share in six annual installments, failing which the partnership would lapse and the property be sold. The Garnetts appear to have met these conditions, but before Richard's brother James died two years later (£30,000 personalty), he attached a similar codicil to his will.[22]

However, the most important motive for transferring one's assets out of industry and for desiring that one's beneficiaries be protected by receiving their inheritances in a different form was the disparity in early-nineteenth-century property laws. Although industrial property was subject to the rigors of free competition, other forms, like land, securities, and joint stock shares, were protected by the state. Of those special forms of property, land was the one most thoroughly privileged by legal safeguards and psychological attitudes. With national food requirements constantly expanding and legal protections like primogeniture, strict settlement, and the Corn Laws in place, ground rents were consistently cushioned, if not inflated, and large landholders perpetuated their proprietary monopoly to the point where, even as late as

[21] *Calendar of Yorkshire Wills* (1838–57).
[22] Ibid., 20 (1838), 22 (1843), 24 (1848–9), 25 (1849–50), 26 (1851), 26 (1852).

1880, less than 2 percent of the nation's families held over 75 percent of Britain's cultivable land. It is, therefore, not surprising that landholding, especially in the vicinity of (or within) a rapidly growing city, would appear to be a particularly desirable investment even from an economic point of view.[23]

The agricultural depression after 1815 did not diminish the attractiveness of land around Bradford, but it did lead to a growing interest in other forms of investment such as annuities, joint-stock companies, and guaranteed state bonds that were less protected by legal or de facto monopoly but that were also subject to regulation by the state. Particularly in a place like Bradford, where urban opportunities were opening up for transport and utility companies to serve the growing business and consumer needs of the town, investments of this sort might appear almost irresistible to someone looking for a safer return.[24]

Under the impetus of these incentives, combined with the awareness of the deepening cultural antagonism between entrepreneurship and the gentlemanly role, Bradford's early-nineteenth-century elites abandoned the former for the latter and evolved a set of cultural and political institutions and practices that seemed irrelevant to the problems of Bradford and unsuited to the needs of the staple industry that it housed.

The making of a conservative culture of gentility

As long as the role of the gentleman had been compatible with the activity of the capitalist, there seemed little contradiction between the good life of leisure and the imperatives of innovation and political progress. In eighteenth-century Bradford, local elites had seemed of a piece with the environment that they dominated. Their authority, though not always appreciated, had always been acknowledged by the poor no less than by the upwardly mobile who aspired to enter their ranks. Gentlemen were the natural leaders of a protoindustrial community, and it was to the ideal of gentility that Bradford's potential leaders aspired. Gentlemen, in their turn, could afford to appear flexible, progressive, and enlightened in their relationship with the larger community and exercise leadership in a positive and responsible way.

By the second quarter of the nineteenth century, the urban-industrial

[23] G. E. Mingay, *English Landed Society in the Eighteenth Century* (London, 1963), 26; F. M. L. Thompson, *English Landed Society in the Nineteenth Century* (London, 1963); John Bateman, *The Great Landowners of Great Britain and Ireland* (New York, 1971).
[24] See Chapter 4.

society not only required a different kind of leadership, but had become a place where no true gentleman could feel at home. As Simpson lamented:

> I am at a loss what to do for there is no kind of society here, every one being engaged in trade and thinking of nothing else. There are no pleasant rides, no pleasant walks, all being bustle, hurry and confusion. The lower orders of people are little removed above the brute creation being the rudest and most vulgar people under the sun.[25]

Although Simpson's chagrin at this absence of refinement might equally well have been felt by his counterparts a generation earlier, it would not have been expressed in such alienated and hostile language. Protoindustrial gentlemen often lamented that the claims of business constrained pleasure, but they never regarded the two as incompatible; nor, with their sense of status and political responsibility, would they so glibly and openly have dismissed the lower orders as "little removed above the brute creation," however much they may have occasionally feared this to be the case.[26]

By 1825, however, Simpson's attitude had become more characteristic of his circle, whose increasing drift toward rentier status combined with Bradford's industrial transformation to create a dissonance between its members' subjective interests as a privileged establishment and their objective position as a ruling elite. As we have seen, the withdrawal of this Tory establishment from participation in the wider society had begun during the counterrevolutionary era. It was intensified in the three decades after 1815 as the second- and third-generation elites abandoned entrepreneurial activity just as entrepreneurship emerged as the only form in which urban leadership could meaningfully be cast. Unable to inspire public confidence in the natural legitimacy of their rule, Bradford's Tory elites withdrew defensively into an oligarchical culture that invoked the traditional privileges of authority without embracing the social responsibilities that the latter entailed.

Because this new Tory establishment culture was intended to be inward looking and socially exclusive, it was, for the most part, private in character, centering around the dinner table, the library, the club room, the ballroom, and the hunting field. Between January and March of 1825 alone, Simpson records attending two public dinners, four formal parties or dances, one theater performance, three hunting expeditions, one six-day holiday during the assizes at York, and thirty-nine small dinner gatherings with friends. The frequency with which Simpson dined out was probably unusual because of his bachelor status and the peripatetic nature of his profession, but the

[25] Simpson, *Journal*, 11.
[26] See Chapter 3.

remainder of his busy social life seems characteristic of other members of his class.[27]

Such men were prepared to devote large quantities of money and energy toward replicating, under unsuitable circumstances, a rural and aristocratic style of life. The old halls and pseudovillas that dotted the urban hinterland were, for the wealthy, a way to preserve the illusion of rusticity and to protect themselves from the urban blight and utilitarian bustle that surrounded them on all sides.[28] Moreover, although it was not incompatible with domestic attachments, this culture of aristocratic imitation tended to be patriarchal in character, conjuring up the image of a vigorous, manly squire exercising lordship through his mastery of leisure and sport. Hunting and coursing formed part of the recreational regime, providing not only entertainment and exercise, but also an opportunity for the formation of lifelong friendships. Such was the basis for the comraderie between Simpson and E. C. Lister, a wealthy Manningham gentleman who stood considerably above him in the social scale. As Simpson explained:

> Mr. Lister keeps one of the best pack of harriers I know of, unless they are those of my friend Mr. Slingsby. He hunts generally in Wharfedale about Bolton Bridge but occasionally in the neighborhood of Bradford. I have hunted many a day with him, but did not get out once last season.[29]

Even a staid Anglican clergyman like Rev. Patrick Brontë saw no contradiction between his passion for blood sports and his clerical duties. Both helped him to cultivate a genteel, pseudoaristocratic image that his income could scarcely support.[30]

Of course, hunting was an expensive activity requiring equipment, animals, and tracts of open land, which were scarce in the vicinity of Bradford. For those like Simpson who could not support such a habit alone, banding together in a sporting club was an attractive option. In 1842, a local newspaper noted the annual meeting at Sir John Lister Kaye's estate of the Bradford Coursing Club with the prominent Tory manufacturer Cowling Ackroyd in the chair.[31]

After hunting, the most popular male recreation was eating well and getting drunk. Attitudes in local elite circles toward tippling, theater, and idle amusement remained lax in the early nineteenth century, and most of

---

[27] Simpson, *Journal*, 1–22.
[28] See especially William Scruton, *Pen and Pencil Pictures of Old Bradford* (Bradford, 1889); James Burnley, *West Riding Sketches* (London, 1875).
[29] Simpson, *Journal*, 38.
[30] John Lock and W. T. Dixon, *A Man of Sorrow, The Life Letters and Times of Rev. Patrick Brontë, 1777–1861* (London, 1965), 296.
[31] *BO*, Sep. 17, 1840; *Bradford Herald*, Jan. 2, 1842.

the subsequent open opposition to temperance and "teetotal fanaticism" came from members of this group. To be sure, persistent debauchery was frowned upon, but men like Simpson and his friends, or even Rev. Brontë, were not ashamed of an occasional drinking bout so long as their normal functioning was unimpaired. Certainly, the continuing importance of taverns in elite culture attests to the regularity with which conviviality was lubricated by drink.[32] Such behavior, which served no productive purpose, might seem out of place in the utilitarian urban-industrial milieu. Up to a point it might be borne as a badge of superiority by those privileged enough to have time to relax. However, with the formation of an unoccupied rentier class, it was inevitable that self-indulgence and debauchery would sometimes assume more pathological forms. There is some evidence that this problem increased during the 1830s and 1840s when the children of Bradford's second-generation elites grew to maturity, often with too much leisure time and too little sense of purpose. Such seems to have been the case with John Hustler, the high-living, gun-loving heir of his family fortune who died in 1849 of brain fever at the age of thirty-three.[33]

The case of Rev. Patrick Brontë's son, Branwell, who died of alcoholism and drug addiction in 1849, is better known. As a frustrated writer and gentleman of ease, Patrick projected his unrealized aspirations toward cultivation and gentility on his apparently literary and artistic son. Mixing in the fashionable circles of Bradford's high-class taverns, particularly the George, among aspiring artists, writers, and young dilettantes of independent means, Branwell drank in a heady bohemian atmosphere but failed to muster the seriousness of purpose and self-discipline necessary for creative success. Alternately indulged and hectored by his doting father, Branwell sank deeper into drink, debility, and debt while his sisters quietly penned their masterpieces in the seclusion of the Haworth parsonage parlor.[34]

The Brontë sisters were profoundly marked by their brother's tragedy, which provided the inspiration for one of Anne's novels, *The Tenant of Wildfell Hall*. Haunted by the social and self-destructive power of the debauched, aristocratic values and behavior to which she saw her brother succumb, Brontë wrote one of the first domestic feminist critiques of a dysfunctional elite male culture. In the context of a complex, interdependent, market-oriented society, the patriarchal parasitism that she acutely diagnosed inevitably led to personal and social disaster. Only the moralizing force of maternal authority could save Brontë's male characters from their degeneracy

---

[32] Lock and Dixon, *Man of Sorrow*; Simpson, *Journal*.
[33] Maffey, "Some Decayed Families."
[34] Lock and Dixon, *Man of Sorrow*, 276, 306, 402–16; Winifred Gérin, *Branwell Brontë* (London, 1961), 139–46.

by inculcating in them the self-discipline and responsibility that were necessary for the autonomous individual to function successfully in the new
capitalist world.[35]

Of course, the achievement of the Brontë sisters shows that there was
more to early-nineteenth-century Bradford's elite culture than hunting and
drinking – that it was a culture that also offered scope for literary and
intellectual cultivation in which women also could play a part. The Brontës
and their Bradford friends, such as the Firths and the Outhwaites, had
always spent a large part of their time reading, drawing, and attending
lectures on literary or scientific topics, and their behavior was not atypical
of their class. Even a man like Simpson spent much of his day reading books,
and as early as 1818 there was a sufficiently large clientele to support a
literary publication, the *Bradford Miscellany*. Modeled after the London literary reviews, the *Miscellany* resolved in its first issue that it would not stoop
to examine "the most striking among recent improvements in machinery."[36]

Intellectual avocations, scientific experiments, and antiquarian research
had always been outlets for the energies of the more serious among
Bradford's men of independent means. This trend continued in the early
nineteenth century and was particularly pronounced among the Tory professionals of Simpson's generation who enjoyed an income beyond what they
obtained in fees. Dr. Sharp was noted for his knowledge of science and Dr.
Mossman for his literary skill. Dr. Outhwaite served as director of the
subscription library, and the lawyer Samuel Hailstone was known as a bot-
anist and geologist, whereas his son Edward became an antiquarian and
built up one of the largest private libraries in the West Riding.[37] Leading
Quakers, like the Hustler brothers and their friend Benjamin Seebohm of
Horton Grange, often demonstrated strong interests in botany and established local mineral and plant collections. Even some of the Anglican manufacturers such as J. G. Horsfall shared these rather esoteric interests.[38]

Moreover, among the third generation of elites, youthful flirtation with
intellectual or artistic bohemianism did not necessarily lead to physical or
moral debility. Against the example of Branwell Brontë must be placed that
of Clayton Bentley (1809–52), son of the lawyer Greenwood Bentley. After
training locally in watercolors and landscapes, Bentley went to London where
he became a successful steel engraver specializing in magazine illustrations.
Others of his generation, like the Cousen or Geller brothers, sons of "re-

---

[35] Ann Brontë, *The Tenant of Wildfell Hall* (New York, 1969).
[36] Simpson, *Journal; Bradford Miscellany* (January 1818).
[37] William Cudworth, *Rambles Round Horton* (Bradford, 1886), 58–62; J. H. Bell, "Some
Fragments of Local Medical History," *BA*, o.s. 1 (1888).
[38] Hodgson, *Society of Friends*, 45–6; James Burnley, *West Riding Sketches* (London, 1875);
BO, Feb. 27, 1845.

spectable local trades[men]," embarked on artistic careers, although lack of local interest in their work led them to move away to the metropolis. Although these men might hope to earn money from their work, even the most talented took years to establish artistic reputations and often remained largely dependent on family support. Artistic training was also costly, especially in cases like that of young George Knowles, who combined it with a two year tour of Italy and France, where he took in a smattering of continental culture and studied the masterworks of European art.[39]

Although these literary, scientific, and artistic activities were more edifying than hunting or drinking, they were only slightly less alien to the character of early-nineteenth-century Bradford or to the mass of its new working population. Unlike the utilitarian mineralogical experiments of Rev. Joseph Dawson, the work of Bradford's nineteenth-century scientific and antiquarian dilettantes was divorced from the practical requirements of the local economy. Local artists concentrated on classical and rural themes or on portraits of local notables. Even the Brontës wrote with incomprehension of, if not unconcern for, the social and economic transformations that were taking place a few miles away. Culture, for such people, was a means of escape from, and resistance to, industrial capitalism, rather than a vehicle for integrating into it.[40]

The incapacity of Bradford's elites to address the needs of their environment is exemplified by the history of the town's attempts at a literary and philosophical society. The first effort to form such a society came in 1823 when Samuel Hailstone raised forty-two subscriptions of £50 each. Although the opposition of Henry Heap, the reactionary vicar, frightened many gentlemen away, fifteen years later, Dr. Sharp enlisted the aid of the new vicar, William Scoresby, himself a gentleman scholar and arctic explorer, in forming a society with a broader base of support.[41]

Had this literary and philosophical society succeeded in becoming representative of broad sectors of the urban population, it might have evolved into a genuine civic organization providing a vehicle for the exploration and diffusion of knowledge and a focus for the intellectual life of the town. However, an examination of the membership list between 1839 and 1841 demonstrates that the society remained an elite preserve. Of the 138 mem-

[39] Butler Wood, "Some Old Bradford Artists," *BA*, o. s. 2 (1895), 26–32; "Knowles Diary," (Bradford Archives, D.B. 37/1).

[40] See, for example, Emily Brontë, *Wuthering Heights* (Boston, 1956). Even Charlotte Brontë's *Shirley* (Oxford, 1981), in which Luddites and manufacturers play a major role, the characters are stereotyped and the working-class movement is trivialized and misunderstood.

[41] John James, *History and Topography of Bradford* (Bradford, 1841), 245–8; Scruton, *Old Bradford*, 91–2.

bers whose occupations were recorded, 17 percent were gentlemen, 30 percent were professionals, and 39 percent were connected with the staple trade. None of the members were workers and only 9 percent were in the retail and service activities that occupied most of the urban middle class. The governing committee and most of the membership read like a list of local Tory notables, interspersed with an occasional German or Nonconformist merchant or manufacturer.[42]

The exclusive, oligarchical character of the Bradford philosophical society was the consequence of several factors. The annual fee of half a guinea alone would have kept most workers and many of the insurgent bourgeoisie from joining, and the absence of lectures on practical subjects discouraged even informal participation. From the start, the society seemed less concerned with encouraging broad-based participation than with raising funds from its wealthy sponsors and with building up specimens and collections for its museum.[43] Its policy of limiting investigations to esoteric or noncontroversial subjects, during a period of intense intellectual ferment, so far from immunizing it from party or ideological divisions, insured that it would be associated with the disdainful attitude of privileged indifference characteristic of the Tory elite.

As we shall see, Bradford's bourgeois liberals and working-class radicals would meet their educational and intellectual needs through alternative institutions, which, openly acknowledging the realities of ideological conflict, would abandon the Olympian pose of the philosophical society as an illusory virtue that was only permissible to those with the luxury to appear disengaged. So dogged was its detachment from urban life and conflict that, by the mid-forties, even elites lost interest in the society's affairs. When it began construction of an elegant and expensive headquarters, elite contributions proved insufficient to meet the cost and the society collapsed in financial ruin.[44]

If the philosophical society failed to provide an institutional framework for the exclusive culture of Bradford's Tory elites, other, less remorselessly didactic institutions could encompass a wider range of their day-to-day interests and needs. The most important of these was the Bradford Exchange, opened in 1826, which offered a club room, a reading library, and dining, meeting, and ballroom facilities, and constituted a watered-down provincial imitation of the sophisticated milieu of a metropolitan club. Steep subscriptions, tight management, and a policy of refusing rental to undesirable groups kept ordinary Bradfordians out of the Exchange and it soon became a favorite

---

[42] Calculated from "Members of the Bradford Philosophical Society" (mss. Bradford Archives, D.B. 4/3/7).

[43] *BO*, Apr. 18, May 16, June 27, Aug. 29, 1839; Jan. 29, Mar. 5, 12, Apr. 9, Dec. 24, 1840.

[44] James, *History and Topography* 245–8.

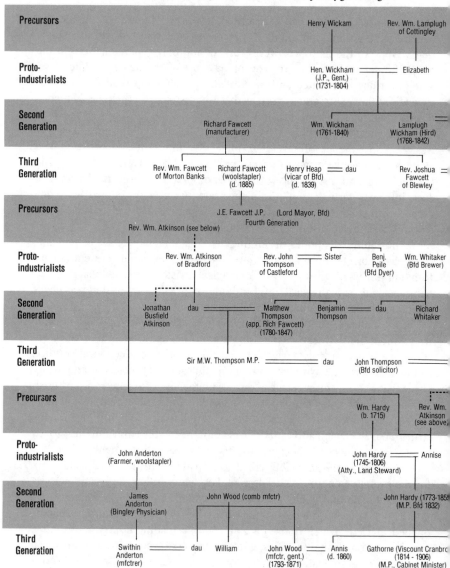

Key: ——— certain link; – – – – probable link; ═══ marriage.

Figure 5-1. Bradford Anglican Tory elites: kinship networks, 1750–1850.
This chart draws on information from a wide range of different sources, most notably
William Scruton, *Pen and Pencil Pictures of Old Bradford* (Bradford, 1889); William
Cudworth, *Round About Bradford* (Bradford, 1876); idem, *Rambles Round Horten*
(Bradford, 1886); idem, *Histories of Mannigham, Heaton and Allerton* (Bradford, 1896);
idem, *Histories of Bolton and Bowling* (Bradford, 1891); idem, *Historical Notes on the*

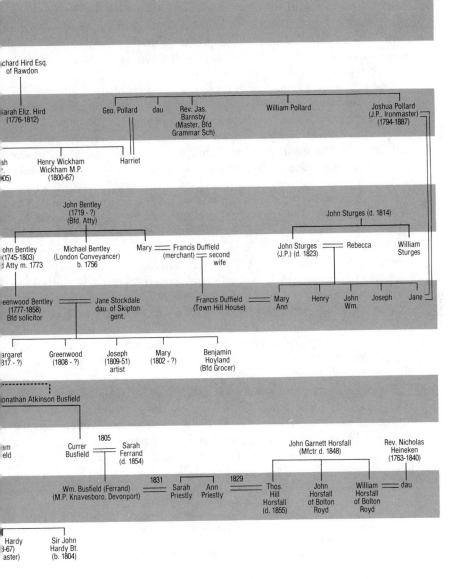

Bradford Corporation (Bradford, 1881); John James, *History and Topography of Bradford* (Bradford, 1841); idem, *Continuations and Additions to the History and Topography of Bradford* (Bradford, 1866); John Maffey, "On Some of the Decayed Families of Bradford," *Bradford Antiquary* o.s. 1, (1888), 26–32; and J. T. Ward, "Old and New Bradfordians in the Nineteenth Century," *Journal of Bradford Textile Society* (Bradford, 1964–5), 17–32.

elite refuge where gentlemen could meet and relax in the congenial company of a select group of friends.[45] The success of the Exchange led to the formation of a comparable, but more exclusive Bradford Club in the 1840s whose membership was limited to one hundred top notables, each paying a subscription of one guinea per year.[46]

One of the most important and popular activities of the Exchange was the periodic formal dress balls, which provided not only opportunities for high-class entertainment and displays of conspicuous consumption, but as Simpson noted, "the best places in the world for meeting [suitable] husbands and wives."[47] Not surprisingly, economic privilege and cultural exclusivity led to increasing endogamy among established elite families. This tendency to seek marriage partners from within the group can be seen in Figure 5-1, which shows how the core of Bradford's Anglican Tory notability was woven not only into a cultural collectivity, but into a tight-knit web of kinship as well.

Figure 5-1 shows that, as early as the closing years of the eighteenth century, a few of these elite unions were already being made. But such marriages took place only sporadically, and those that did rarely bridged the social gap between old county gentry and the scions of the newer protoindustrial elite. Only in the years between 1790 and 1820, as the second elite generation came of age, did endogamy reach full-scale proportions as the nexus of Bradford's establishment grew dense with a thicket of genealogical ties that brought nearly every leading local Anglican Tory family into some blood relationship with every other.

Bonds between families were extended and compounded, linking the Wickham/Hirds; the Fawcetts and the Pollards; the Pollards and the Sturgeses; the Sturgeses and the Duffield Bentleys; the Bentleys and the Whitaker Thompsons; the Thompsons and the Atkinsons; the Atkinsons, the Hardys, and the Woods; the Woods and the Andertons; the Atkinson Busfields, the Ferrands, and the Priestleys; the Priestleys and the Horsfalls, the

[45] Scruton, *Old Bradford*, 120–2; James, *History and Topography*, 252.

[46] "Membership List Bradford Club" (ms., Bradford Archives, D.B. 4/3/6).

[47] Simpson, *Journal*, 46. From the perspective of established elites, one of the most attractive features of these bachelors' balls was that they excluded, in the words of one correspondent to the local paper, "persons following any ... trade or business which might be considered objectionable to the aristocratic feelings of the bulk of their guests." Nevertheless, the writer acknowledged that such a rule caused difficulty "when it is considered that Bradford is really and truly nothing but a working place [where] all are *in essence*, shopkeepers or something not so respectable." In response to this dilemma, the correspondent could only express his outrage "that such men should have the audacity to sit in judgement on the respectability, and the eligibility to be admitted to the ball." *BO*, Feb. 10, 1842.

Blamires and the Cousens, as well as the Powells and the Sharp-Bridges. Among the town's leading Quakers, there was also a rash of intermarriages.[48]

What is notable about these intermarriages, especially those within the Tory network portrayed in Figure 5-1, is that they represent not only alliances between families in the same industry (although a number of matches between iron magnates or among worsted families like the Fawcetts and the Woods fall in this category), but social alliances between different occupational types and frequent fusions of second-generation protoindustrial heirs with the lineages of the rural squirearchy that had dominated the region in the distant past. A new amphibious elite was being created who, unable fully to abandon their urban-industrial origins, looked outward to the rural world of the old gentry. It was this fusion, the creation of a separate governing caste, that gave early-nineteenth-century Bradford's establishment its appearance of inaccessibility and fed the arguments by which its opponents would denounce it as a parasitic, unproductive oligarchy incapable of providing leadership for the town.

The making of an Anglican Tory political establishment

The ambivalence that Bradford's gentlemen-capitalists exhibited in their relations to the urban-industrial environment not only set the framework for a distinctive elite culture, but shaped political and ideological orientations too. As we have seen, the protoindustrialists had been drifting toward conservatism since the late eighteenth century, and the advent of social crisis at the turn of the nineteenth century only intensified the dimensions of this shift. With the explosive economic development of the 1810–50 period, elite conservatism gained an even deeper hold. By the 1820s, 1830s, and 1840s, it had become irreversible as the twin threats of an angry, impoverished proletariat and the challenge of a parvenu, entrepreneurial bourgeoisie led to a widespread sense within the oligarchy that urban-industrial development had spiraled out of control. Fearful of a collapse into social anarchy and beleaguered by a new wave of social and economic transformation, established elites began seeking ways of regulating and restraining the developmental process itself. So alienated were they becoming from their environment that they began to look to the rural agrarian aristocracy to protect them from the political forces and interests that were challenging them within their own world.

In 1826, when the Leeds manufacturer John Marshall stood as candidate

[48] For Quaker intermarriages see H. R. Hodgson, *The Society of Friends in Bradford* (Bradford, 1926).

for the West Riding, even the moderate *Bradford Courier* objected not only to his Whig principles as a candidate, but to the idea that someone of his background and experience should serve as M.P. "The representative of Yorkshire," the paper declared, "should... be a man whose habits and education have not been trammelled by the pursuit of wealth." The electors would demonstrate their own vulgarity if they were to choose, "the upstart flax spinner who thinks to emerge from the obscurity of Water Lane... and who imagines that it is the same thing to command the attention of Parliament as make an impression on a few gaping operatives in the Leeds Mechanics Institute."[49]

Nevertheless, established elites who disdained Marshall's person also had some reason to fear his philosophy and to see their political interests as best represented not by the liberal forces within their own environment, but by the protectionist bulwark of the landed elite. Even in the protoindustrial era, there had been a powerful protectionist strain among Bradford's clothiers and woodstaplers, who had organized to resist the efforts of woolgrowers to repeal the mercantilist prohibition on the export of raw wool. Using the machinery of the Worsted Committee, the West Riding capitalists, under William Hustler's leadership, had constituted a powerful lobby that repeatedly blocked all efforts to promote free trade in wool.[50] After the advent of industrialization, when growth was increasingly driven by foreign demand, the benefits of laissez-faire became more obvious. Nevertheless, the threat of foreign competition appeared sufficiently serious that some preferred the known advantages of industrial autarchy to the opportunities that would come with open international trade.

The rise of a new generation of entrepreneurial insurgents, totally dependent on foreign markets and increasingly drawn to the exotic fibers made from imported fleeces, rendered the triumph of laissez-faire sentiments inevitable, a triumph marked, in 1824, when industrialists allowed the repeal of the prohibition on raw-wool export in return for being permitted to import foreign wool duty free. Nevertheless, some old-school manufacturers like Richard Fawcett remained wary of this sort of laissez-faire trade-off and continued to support industrial protectionism even after the main source of danger had shifted from foreign competitors to a new breed of aggressive industrialists at home. Concentrating on the relatively stable domestic markets, which had once been serviced by the now defunct East Anglian trade, men like Fawcett and John Wood relied more heavily than their competitors

---

[49] *Bradford Courier*, June 8, 1826.
[50] James Bischoff, *Comprehensive History of Woolen and Worsted Manufacture* (London, 1842), 1:400–482.

on home-grown fleeces. In the intensification of competition and industrial reorganization that came with the hypercosmopolitanism of the 1830s, they saw not an opportunity, but a threat.[51]

More significantly, during the 1830s and 1840s when the claims of agriculture replaced those of industry as the centerpiece of the protectionist case, most Tory manufacturers continued to support the ideal of economic autarky, even as its advantages to the capitalist diminished while its benefits to the landlord increased. For established industrialists like Fawcett, endorsement of the Corn Laws was inspired less by unrealized ambitions to become a landowner than by a belief that industry itself had to rest on the foundations of agricultural prosperity if it were to develop in a balanced and healthy way. "I should be sorry to support any measure," he concluded, "that would be to the injury of the agriculturalist; for I am confident that in the same proportion the manufacturer would be injured.... The agriculturalists are our best customers.... Therefore, should they be so depressed as not to be able to purchase, the manufacturer must feel the consequence."[52]

Such arguments in support of agrarian protectionism should not be read as expressions of outright hostility toward industry but as reflections of a widespread desire within the establishment to promote a particular type of industrial development that would proceed in a controlled and gradual way. In a town like Bradford, unequivocal opposition to manufacturing was scarcely a viable position, even for those whose income was not derived from industry itself. Even rentiers or professionals like Dr. Outhwaite recognized that it was "to Trade" that "we all owe our fortunes, if not immediately, yet remotely."[53] For a manufacturer like Fawcett, advocacy of the Corn Laws would have been inconceivable if it had not been reconcilable with a certain vision of industrial life.

Agricultural protection, though not conceived as inherently inimical to industry, was, however, designed to inhibit the sort of explosive, unregulated industrial revolution that, in Bradford during the 1830s and 1840s, was actually taking place. Such development was deemed undesirable both because it concentrated production and poverty in squalid, jerry-built, uncontrollable urban centers, and because it rested on the tyranny of a global marketplace that left the producers, both capitalists and workers, at the mercy of impersonal forces. In the words of William Walker, another Tory manufacturer, "*Cheapness*, the great aim of the advocates of free trade has been

---

[51] Bischoff, *Woolen and Worsted*, 2:1–92; John James, *History of the Worsted Manufacture in England* (London, 1857), 396–7, 415–6. *Bradford Courier*, Nov. 9, 1826.
[52] *Bradford Courier*, Nov. 9, 1826.   [53] Ibid., Feb. 8, 1827.

realized...and in every branch of manufacturing industry to which the principles of free trade has been directly applied, prices, profits and wages have fallen in a greater or lesser degree."[54]

This pattern of hyperdevelopment was anathema to thoughtful conservatives like Walker who saw it as the surest road to social chaos, political anarchy, and economic ruin. The experience of Bradford during the 1830s and 1840s reinforced in the minds of these men a nostalgia for the quasi-rural and dispersed type of manufacture through which they or their families had risen. Economic innovation, which had at one time been warmly embraced, was regarded as a dangerous source of social instability now that it threatened to engulf them too. Fawcett, whose outlook had been formed during the era of wartime stagnation, was firmly convinced, in the 1840s, that the limits of industrial expansion had already been reached. Although he had been one of the pioneers of factory spinning in Bradford, he now worried about the dangers of overcompetition and tried to dissuade others from building more factories. Most significantly, he deeply regretted the spread of mechanization to other parts of the production process through which the domestic system would be undermined.[55] By the thirties, the Corn Laws and the perpetuation of aristocratic class rule seemed to offer the only hope for the regulation of spontaneous industrial expansion and the re-creation of the sort of stable order that was not incompatible with the gentlemanly ideal.

Moreover, the same conservatism and protectionism that conserved and protected the elite, could be cast ideologically as the conservation and protection of the larger traditional values, institutions, and reciprocal social relationships on which all social groups depended and the very fabric of society was deemed to rest. To Parson Bull, protectionism was desirable, not so much because it protected the landlord, but because it entailed

> a system that *distributed* the *dense* population of this country into rural districts – to cultivate the land which is not, I am sure, *half cultivated,* – and a system which would encourage manufactures on a *small* scale rather than a *large* one which would restore them to the cottage again.[56]

Yet such rosy visions of a stable community, led by a benevolent manufacturer and surrounded by a flock of happy industrial peasants who divided their time between the subsistence plot and cottage loom, had scarcely reflected the pattern of social relations that had prevailed during the bygone protoindustrial age. If industrial paternalism had fallen short even in this

---

[54] William Walker, *Free Trade, its Principles and Results* (London, 1858), 8.

[55] *PP* (1806, III), 185; Cudworth, *Bradford Corporation*, 37.

[56] *Proceedings of a Public Meeting of the People of Bradford on the Ten Hours Bill* (Bradford, 1833), 16.

traditional setting, how much more problematic would it become in the highly competitive environment of the industrial city?[57]

Even during the protoindustrial period, the community leadership of elites had been exercised not in their industrial capacity, but in their social capacity as gentlemen. Here the tendency for second-generation gentleman-capitalists to exchange the role of entrepreneurship for the status of rentier might have provided the foundations for the assumption, in the nineteenth century, of a more visible leadership role. Had the Tory oligarchs of early-nineteenth-century Bradford been able to identify with the problems and prospects of the burgeoning city, they might have been able to repulse the simultaneous challenges of disaffected workers and parvenu competitors, both of whom were coming to question the legitimacy of their status as a natural elite.

Conclusion: the crisis of Bradford's Old Regime

Bradford's new Watching and Lighting Commission, created by parliamentary act in 1803, might have provided an institutional framework for Bradford's establishment to evolve into an urban patriciate. Of course, as an institution founded in the crucible of counterrevolution, the commission, from the outset, had evoked little enthusiasm among the urban population as a whole. Nevertheless, as the only responsible and potentially powerful local government body, with the authority to raise revenue and pass bylaws, it might have evolved into a genuine focus for civic leadership. Indeed, its oligarchical character might have enhanced its capacity for civic leadership, providing opportunities to translate the protectionist predispositions of the Tory establishment into a concrete program of environmental regulation and public monopoly for limiting the explosive dynamic of free-market development, and controlling the pattern of urban growth.

Moving quickly, after establishing its police force, to consider more ambitious projects for the lighting, cleaning, and repair of town center streets, the commission initially exhibited a spirit of improvement that suggested that it might eventually assume such a role. Nevertheless, as the sad story recounted in the last chapter should demonstrate, the early promise of its plans to rationalize local administration evaporated in the face of the urban-industrial revolution, which quickly passed beyond its powers of control.[58]

Already in the late teens and early twenties, the commissioners were beginning to lose touch with urban life. Direct management of basic services

[57] See Chapters 2 and 15.
[58] See Chapter 4.

became too ambitious an undertaking as lighting and scavenging were contracted out to private "contractors [who] seemed to emulate each other in their inefficiency." More substantial improvements were, of course, left to private developers with the result that public services were virtually ignored.[59] Faced with increasing responsibilities and diminishing resources, the commissioners became trapped in a vicious cycle, as their poor performance cost them the confidence of those who might have empowered them and sanctioned the additional revenues that would have been required to assume a more active role.

By the late twenties, it was clear that the commission had lost control of the urbanizing process. With the defeat of an 1828 improvement bill, which would have increased its authority, the commission retreated to a marginal place in local history – a mere footnote in the epic story of Bradford's growth. Even police work, which the commissioners had always taken most seriously, lagged sadly behind the pace of urban growth. As late as 1827, there were only thirteen officers, ill qualified, poorly disciplined, and abysmally paid. A reorganization of the police force in 1831 was, like most of the commissioners' other reforms, too little and too late. As crime and civil disorder mounted during the tumultuous subsequent decade and a half, even wealthy and established property owners began to recognize that local government would have to be radically reformed.[60]

Behind the commissioners' abdication of local governmental responsibility lay the more fundamental default of urban leadership on the part of Bradford's established elites. This deeper failure is scarcely surprising, because their withdrawal from entrepreneurship tended to make them even more hostile toward the environment of the city than toward the industrial activity that it housed. The noise, the effluence, the fetid atmosphere, and most of all, urban Bradford's relentless ugliness were, if anything, greater affronts to their genteel pretensions than the acquisitiveness of the new entrepreneurs. The private culture of gentility, which shielded them from the ecological catastrophe that less-privileged Bradfordians were forced to face, underwrote an attitude of political irresponsibility whereby they gathered the rewards of political monopoly without taking up the tasks that local government faced.[61]

As Table 5-2 indicates, the pattern by which the Watching and Lighting Commission selected new members reveals an entirely inadequate accommodation to the process of urban change. To be sure, the original mixture of clothiers, manufacturers, ironmasters, gentlemen, large tradesmen, and

[59] Cudworth, *Bradford Corporation*, 48–64.
[60] Ibid., 48–69.
[61] Cudworth, *Bradford Corporation*, 91–3; Adrian Elliot, "The Establishment of Municipal Government in Bradford: 1837–57" (Bradford, Ph.D. dissertation, 1976), 77–8.

Table 5-2. *Occupational composition of Bradford Watching and Lighting Commission, 1803–47*

Occupational type	Original members 1803	New members	
		1804–33	1834–37
Gentlemen	4	4	1
Iron industry	3	1	1
Professional	5	15	5
Worsted industry	12	21	34
Other industry	2	6	5
Tradesmen	18	6	9
Unknown	14	9	5
Total	58	62	60

Sources: Compiled from information in William Cudworth, *Historical Notes on the Bradford Corporation* (Bradford, 1881), 19, 35–48; 91–2; *Baines' Directory*, (Leeds, 1822); *Baines' Leeds and Clothing Directory* (Leeds, 1830); *Baines' West Riding Directory* (Leeds, 1847); James Ibbetson, *Bradford Directory* (Bradford, 1850).

professionals had accurately reflected the composition of the early-nineteenth-century protoindustrial elite. However, in subsequent decades, as Bradford grew, the commission became increasingly unrepresentative and degenerated into a closed and aging Tory clique. As the original tradesmen dropped off, they were not replaced by others but were supplanted by the band of wealthy and powerful Anglican manufacturers and professionals who were coming to dominate every other public institution in town.

The co-optation of new recruits did not occur piecemeal, as vacancies opened up, but tended to cluster around certain dates. In 1813, seventeen new commissioners were recruited and another large contingent arrived in 1825. Notwithstanding these infusions, until 1834, the commissioners remained almost uniformly Anglican and Tory. As the thirties wore on, the commission made a few attempts to improve its image without altering its internal balance of power. Although thirty new commissioners were recruited in the course of this period, of the eighteen whose religious affiliation Dr. Elliot has been able to trace, only five were Nonconformists. Only in 1843, three years before the commission was abolished, did the oligarchy give way, incorporating eighteen new men, fourteen of whom were prominent liberal Dissenters. By then, however, it was too late for internal reform. Bradford's liberals were committed to abolishing the commission, joining it only to expedite this aim.[62]

[62] Cudworth, *Bradford Corporation*, 95–7; Elliot, "Municipal Government in Bradford," 103.

To these liberal, Nonconformist insurgents, it was inevitable that the Watching and Lighting Commission would provide inadequate leadership for an urban-industrial society since failure, they believed, was virtually implicit in the commission's self-selecting, oligarchical form. In one of its earliest issues, their organ, the *Bradford Observer*, speculated, "There is something about the atmosphere of the office that produces apathy," and Joseph Ellison further explained, "If a meeting is called there may be a half-dozen got together but the door must be locked to keep them in the room."[63]

In truth, these Tory notables seemed too ambivalent or hostile to the urban experience to take seriously the complex problems of administration and management that governing a rapidly growing city posed. The commission had attracted them as a source of patronage and authority, as a political vehicle to help close their ranks. With the advent of urbanization they lost all taste for the social responsibility that went with an office of public trust. With every decade the commissioners drifted farther away from the tasks at hand, ceasing deliberation for eight months in 1817 and virtually closing down business in the traumatic year of 1826.[64] In 1834, the *Observer* complained:

> If the present Commissioners consider that a proper discharge of their duties would interfere too much with their business or domestic arrangements, why do they not at once resign their appointments into the hands of persons who will interest themselves to promote the comfort and improvement of the town.[65]

As the *Observer* attempted to answer its own question in the course of the next decade, it began to see behind this individual dereliction of duty, a corruption of governmental power. Although quorums were normally difficult to muster, whenever jobs were to be distributed or contracts handed out, commissioners would suddenly appear from the woodwork to insure that they got their share. These abuses, according to the new liberal Nonconformists, were inherent defects of oligarchy in which there were no mechanisms for insuring the accountability of power. So far from acting in the interests of the community, closed institutions like the commission engendered in their members a natural disposition toward lethargy and a temptation to abuse positions of public trust to favor private interests or achieve personal gain.

As the problems of urbanization mounted after the 1820s, compounding those of industrial conflict and class, it became clear to the rest of Bradford's

---

[63] Ellison quoted in *PP* (1840, XI), 90; Elliott, "Municipal Government in Bradford," 74; *BO*, Sep. 25, 1834.

[64] Cudworth, *Bradford Corporation*, 54, 57, 64.

[65] *BO*, Sep. 11, 1834.

population that the Tory establishment had abdicated its right to rule. Their onetime protoindustrial community had been transformed into a major manufacturing city – the world center of worsted production and trade. The new conditions had also created a new kind of population that was less willing than its protoindustrial predecessor simply to defer to traditional authority and power. Inspired by different values, interests, and antipathies, this new, largely immigrant generation of Bradfordians began to look with increasing concern and urgency for an alternative to Tory, oligarchical rule.

With the rise of the new entrepreneurial insurgents in the late 1820s and 1830s, such an alternative finally arose. Forged in opposition to the bankrupt establishment, the entrepreneurs' incipient vision of free-market liberalism seemed, at first sight, a natural, almost inevitable, model for the ordering of the urban-industrial world. Indeed, one challenge for the new entrepreneurial liberalism was to vanquish its crumbling establishment antagonist on the favorable fields of political and ideological conflict. However, its real test would be its practical ability to confront the deep problems of competitive capitalism – proletarian poverty, urban decay, and class division – problems that had been rendered much more perilous and intractable by years of establishment disengagement and neglect.

PART II

The emergence of a liberal entrepreneurial society and the rise of an urban-industrial bourgeoisie: 1825–1850

6

The rising generation of urban entrepreneurs

Who would fill the leadership vacuum caused by the abdication of Bradford's traditional elites? The rapid growth of industrial production in the city, the dramatic expansion and concentration of its population, its alarming environmental deterioration, and its deepening divisions of capitalism and class all posed challenges that seemed to threaten its survival. If established elites and conservative values could not solve the problems that Bradford's dynamism posed, solutions had to be sought through an entirely new kind of urban leadership, derived from the industrial-capitalist experience itself.

With the rise of a new generation of entrepreneurial capitalists in the quarter century after 1825, the outlines of a novel approach to social leadership and hegemony began to emerge. Unlike traditional elites, who saw the urban-industrial revolution as a threat and a challenge, these new men unreservedly identified with the unrestrained economic and demographic dynamism that they both envisioned as a basis for general social progress and mobility and recognized as their own personal ticket to wealth and power. Who were these new entrepreneurial insurgents, and what was it about their distinctive experience of urban-industrial capitalism in Bradford that enabled them to elevate the conditions of their own achievement into a universal vision of social progress – to project their own lives as models for a community that would be organized by the marketplace and based on the voluntary commitment of its members to the individualist values of self-discipline and free choice?

Immigrants, insurgents, and entrepreneurs: a statistical profile

As Table 6-1 reveals, the urban bourgeoisie that emerged by midcentury (as measured through the 1851 bourgeois census population described in Appendix A) was largely comprised of a type of individual who had not existed a generation before. Seventy percent of the 1851 bourgeois householders were immigrants, 76 percent were under fifty years of age, and 55

Table 6-1. *1851 bourgeois census population: social composition by nativity and generation of household head (N = 1,259)*

	Percent old generation (born 1781–1800)	Percent young generation (born 1801–20)	Percent neither generation	Total
Percent born in Bradford	9	15	6	30
Percent born elsewhere in Yorkshire	9	28	8	45
Percent born elsewhere	4	17	4	25
Total	22	60	18	100

Source: Calculated from 1851 census mss. for Bradford (HO, 107/2305–10). See Appendix A.

percent were both. Natives over fifty, who had reached their prime before the 1830s, constituted a mere 9 percent of the bourgeois householders at midcentury.

Bradford's midcentury bourgeoisie, like the industrial city over which it presided, was something entirely new – historically unprecedented – a dominant class composed of young men and outsiders who had come to town to take advantage of the unique opportunities that industrialization made possible and who had the good fortune to reach their biological maturity at the moment when those opportunities were at their peak. The extent to which the experience of this new generation was embedded in the larger urban-industrial transformation is further reflected in a comparison of the occupational distribution of old-generation natives (born between 1781 and 1800) with the different occupational distribution that prevailed among immigrants and members of the younger generation.

It will be recalled that the study of probate valuations of traditional elites who died between 1837 and 1856 (presented in Chapter 5) revealed that 63 percent of the wealthiest men and women and 47 percent of the moderately wealthy were either rentiers or individuals whose incomes were obtained from genteel and professional sources. The fairly even occupational distribution that Table 6-2 reveals among the small group of old-generation natives within the 1851 bourgeoisie reflects the predominance of surviving gentlemen within their ranks. Although a third of the old-generation natives in 1851 were located in the genteel occupational sector, 81 percent of the younger generation, 78 percent of the bourgeois immigrants, and 81 percent of those who were both were actively occupied in the entrepreneurial sectors of Bradford's economy, particularly in those that were expanding most rapidly during the 1830s and 1840s – worsted merchandising and, to a lesser extent, manufacturing, as well as the wide open field of urban service and retail enterprise, where opportunities were greatest for young men of modest means.

By midcentury, entrepreneurship in Bradford had become a characteristic of individuals who were relatively young or who came from immigrant backgrounds, and it was the predominance of men of this type within the bourgeoisie as a whole that endowed it with its strong overall entrepreneurial edge. Whereas 12 percent of the old-generation natives identified themselves as rentiers to the census takers, only 4 percent of the younger generation, 6 percent of the immigrants, and 2 percent of the young-generation immigrants were identified this way.[1] By contrast, there were twice as many young worsted manufacturers, three times as many young dyers and machine makers, and six times as many young stuff merchants as old ones in 1851. The latter were not only overwhelmingly young, but overwhelmingly immigrant (86 percent) as well. Nearly half of the latter had been born outside of Yorkshire. Within the urban-service sector, men of the younger generation and immigrants also predominated, with 64 percent and 69 percent, respectively, and 46 percent for those who were both. Nevertheless, unlike the immigrants who became stuff merchants and manufacturers, the majority, 74 percent of those immigrants in the service trade, were individuals born in one of the nearby Yorkshire towns and villages who had come to Bradford to take advantage of the opportunities that economic development opened up.[2]

Of course, while youth, immigrant background, and entrepreneurial involvement tended to go together, 25 percent of the members of the younger bourgeois generation were not immigrants, 18 percent were not entrepreneurs, and 4 percent were neither. Similarly, 22 percent of all 1851 bourgeois immigrants were not entrepreneurs, and the same proportion were members of the older generation, whereas a substantial minority (29 percent) of the entrepreneurs were natives and 19 percent were members of the older generation.[3] To what extent, then, is it meaningful to treat younger-generation immigrant entrepreneurs as a well-defined group within the Bradford bourgeoisie – as having characteristics that tended to be mutually reinforcing even if they did not correspond in every case? Although only 4 percent of the 1851 bourgeois census population possessed none of these characteristics, only 36 percent exhibited all of them at once. Nevertheless, as Table 6-3 indicates, if each characteristic is taken separately, a majority or

[1] HO, 107/2305–10.
[2] Ibid.
[3] Ibid.

Table 6–2. *1851 Bourgeois census population: Occupational distribution of young immigrant and old, native household heads*

	Young generation (born 1801–20) (N = 751)	Immigrants (N = 886)	Young and immigrants (N = 560)	Old and natives (born 1781–1800) (N = 108)	Total (N = 1,259)
Percentage in stuff production	14	14	13	27	15
Percentage in stuff distribution	19	18	22	5	15
Total % in primary production	36	35	38	34	35
Total % in retail and urban service	46	42	44	37	43
Percent gentlemen	4	6	1	12	8
Percent professionals	12	15	15	10	13
Total % in genteel sector	18	22	18	29	22

Source: Calculated from 1851 census mss. for Bradford (HO, 107/2305–10). See Appendix A.

Table 6-3. *Bourgeois census population: relationship between occupation, nativity, and generation (N = 1,259)*

	Percent
Entrepreneurs (*N* = 982)	
Young and immigrant	47
Either young or immigrant, but not both	40
Natives and older generation	8
None of the above	5
Younger generation (*N* = 751)	
Entrepreneurs and immigrants	61
Either entrepreneurs or immigrants, but not both	35
Natives and gentlemen	4
None of the above	—
Immigrants (*N* = 886)	
Young and entrepreneurs	52
Either young or entrepreneurs, but not both	38
Older generation and gentlemen	7
None of the above	3

Source: Calculated from 1851 census manuscripts for Bradford (HO, 107/2305–10). See Appendix A.

near majority of those who exhibited it also exhibited both of the others, whereas only a tiny minority exhibited the opposite characteristic to those that were associated with it.

These separate results can, perhaps, be more easily comprehended if they are synthesized and summarized in the following way: Of the 1,211 households in the 1851 bourgeois census population who were immigrants, members of the younger generation or entrepreneurs, 38 percent exhibited all three characteristics together (14 percent would be expected in a random distribution), whereas 41 percent exhibited two of them but not the other (42 percent would be expected in a random distribution), and only 21 percent exhibited one alone (42 percent would be expected in a random distribution). Evidently there was a close correlation of these characteristics among the midcentury bourgeoisie. Although none of the characteristics were interchangeable, they tended to cluster within a group of individuals who possessed at least two of them and often all three.[4]

[4] Ibid.

The experience of social and geographical mobility

Like the majority of ordinary Bradfordians in 1850, but unlike the residual remnant of the town's established elite, the typical bourgeois was a young immigrant, ambitious and hard working, who had come to town within the previous thirty years to take advantage of the manifold new opportunities that urban-industrial development brought in its wake.[5] Yet for all the apparent similarity in their aspirations, it was evident that, after their arrival in town, the experience of the bourgeois-to-be diverged from that of the rest. For most ordinary Bradfordians, involvement in capitalist enterprise meant becoming trapped in a handful of menial occupations in which they would be condemned to deepening squalor and poverty and stripped of all meaningful control over their work. With over 40 percent of midcentury Bradford's adults in unskilled wage labor and another 25 percent in paid or unpaid domestic work, it is evident that, for most Bradfordians who were young and immigrants, the characteristic bourgeois linkage between geographical and social mobility had become, in the urban-industrial environment, radically disjoined.[6] What was it about this small minority among Bradford's early-nineteenth-century generation of immigrants that enabled them to take charge of the forces of industrial development that brought poverty and proletarianization to most? What was it in their backgrounds, their attitudes, or the resources at their disposal that might account for their striking and rapid success?

Unfortunately, neither the census manuscripts nor any other systematically quantifiable source offers much information on the social, as opposed to the geographical, backgrounds of individuals, and any relationship between the two must be based on impressionistic evidence gleaned from a number of specific cases. Nevertheless, geographical origins offer a few hints about social background, and comparing the 1851 bourgeois householders with the entire adult population, several preliminary conclusions emerge. Compared with the immigrants who became bourgeois, those who came to swell the ranks of the urban working class were, in terms of geographical origin, a more homogeneous group. Sixty-four percent of the town's adult immigrant population had been born in the Yorkshire hinterland surrounding Bradford, and another 16 percent were Irish born.[7] Although 64 percent of Bradford's

---

[5] Whereas 75 percent of the householders in Bradford's 1851 bourgeois census population were under fifty, 82 percent of the town's entire adult population was under this age. Whereas 71 percent of the bourgeois householders were immigrants, the same was true of 55 percent of the overall adult population of the town. *PP* (LXXXVIII, 1852–3), 2:737; HO, 107/2305–10.

[6] *PP* (LXXXVIII, 1852–3), 2:737.

[7] This further confirms what Chapter 3 has already indicated – that the bulk of Bradford's

bourgeois immigrants had also been born in Yorkshire, a substantial proportion came from other settings that tended to be rather more conducive to subsequent success. Unlike the small contingent of long-distance, working-class immigrants who were almost all Irish peasants, 35 percent of Bradford's midcentury bourgeois immigrants came from many distant locations, most notably from London and the Home Counties (6 percent), Lancashire and Cheshire (5 percent), Scotland (4.6 percent), and continental Europe (3 percent). Only 1.4 percent came from Ireland.[8]

Moreover, in contrast to the rural character of working-class migrants, 35 percent of the bourgeois immigrants had been born in some other city or town and possessed some previous experience of urban life. Finally, the presence of native-born teenage children in many bourgeois immigrant households indicates a longer period of family residence than was typical of working-class immigrants and suggests that those who successfully rose into the bourgeoisie arrived earlier, paced their arrival less directly in response to the vicissitudes of the trade cycle, and persisted within the city over several years.[9]

Several studies of nineteenth-century American cities have shown that an important factor in urban social mobility was the ability to remain in town for an extended period of time. In Bradford, too, there is good reason to believe that those immigrants who had originally been pulled by the lure of urban opportunity and who possessed or acquired financial reserves for interludes of recession had a long-term competitive advantage over those who had originally been pushed by rural poverty and who were subsequently obliged to move repeatedly from place to place.[10]

By the 1830s and 1840s, ambition, ability, initiative, and drive were necessary but not sufficient conditions for entrepreneurial success. In general, personal contacts and a modicum of capital were necessary for the would-be entrepreneur to begin. Nevertheless, if the typical young bourgeois immigrant came from a different social background than the typical recruit into the urban working class, the two still had, in important respects, more in common with each other than either had with the established Tory notables.

Despite variations in social origin from one case to the next, nearly all of

---

working-class immigrants were either Irish peasants fleeing famine in their homeland or weavers and agricultural laborers from nearby West Riding villages whose lives and livelihoods were being disrupted by intense competition and mechanization. *PP* (LXXXVIII, 1852–3), 2:737.

[8] Calculated from HO, 107/2305–10. See Theodore Koditschek, "Class Formation and the Bradford Bourgeoisie" (Princeton, Ph.D. dissertation, 1981), 83.

[9] HO, 107/2305–10.

[10] Michael Katz, *The People of Hamilton, Canada West* (Cambridge, Mass., 1975).

Bradford's new parvenu bourgeoisie came from relatively modest, often Nonconformist, family backgrounds with deep roots in the protoindustrial lower middle and skilled artisanal working class. From these humble origins some merely inched their way up to situations of comfort or affluence, whereas others were more spectacularly elevated to the heights of industrial wealth and power with annual profits in the thousands or even tens of thousands and control of work forces almost as large. If few began in rags and many never ended in riches, almost all experienced some degree of upward mobility. Universally, those who attained bourgeois status shared the experience of ending their lives at a socioeconomic level considerably higher than that at which they had begun.

The most dramatic instances of upward mobility often occurred among the long-distance immigrants who made up in ability, ambition, and enterprise what they lacked in inherited status or wealth. Robert Milligan (1785–1862), who became the town's first mayor and was acknowledged as the senior representative of the new entrepreneurial group, was the son of a small-scale Scottish Congregationalist farmer. He began his business career as a traveling draper before coming to Bradford where he founded one of the first and most successful stuff merchant houses in the town.[11] Milligan's junior partner, Henry Forbes (1794–1870), also a Congregationalist of Scottish ancestry, was the son of a tenant farmer from Easingwold. The other leading Scottish Nonconformist merchants who came a bit later, John Russell, James Rennie, George Tetley (1805–73), James Douglas, David Abercrombie, and James Law (1818–83), all seem to have come from petit bourgeois backgrounds.[12]

The leading German merchant, Jacob Behrens (1806–89), a Jew, began as a traveling cloth peddlar in the vicinity of Hamburg before coming to Bradford in 1838 to establish a successful stuff export house. Many of the other Jewish and Christian evangelical merchants from Germany who followed him, such as Charles Semon (1814–77) and J. A. Unna, seem to have come from similarly modest backgrounds.[13] Since the mercantile sector was the Bradford worsted trade's newest and most rapidly growing arena, it is

---

[11] *BO*, July 3, 1862; Oct. 18, 1870.
[12] *BOB*, Feb. 3, 1906.
[13] *Memoir of Jacob Behrens* (London, 1925); anon., *The Face of Worstedopolis* (Bradford, n.d), 27; A. R. Rollin, "The Jewish Contribution to the British Textile Industry: Builders of Bradford" *Transactions of the Jewish Historical Society of England*, vol. 17 (1953); Michael Pratt, "The Influence of the Germans on Bradford" (Typescript, Bradford Central Library, 1971); *BO*, June 8, 1881.

not surprising that 78 percent of the 104 stuff merchants in the bourgeois census population were members of the younger generation and 86 percent were immigrants, 46 percent from somewhere beyond Yorkshire.[14]

Among the 156 worsted manufacturers in the bourgeois census population, distributions were less dramatically skewed. Only 54 percent were members of the younger generation, while natives and short-distance migrants predominated with 37 and 50 percent, respectively.[15] Nevertheless, the backgrounds of the industrial capitalists were similar to those of the merchants. This was especially true of the small group of long-distance immigrants, among them men such as Isaac Holden (1807–97), the son of a failed Wesleyan farmer in Scotland who had ended his career as a pit manager in a small mine; James Drummond (1810–91), a Wesleyan Reformer from Northumberland who, like Holden, was obliged to work his own way up from employee status to junior partnership before finally becoming, after 1851, one of the largest millowners in the town;[16] and William Lythall, an orphan from Henley-on-Thames, who seems to have risen entirely through his own initiative. Even those who possessed somewhat more substantial early advantages, such as William Fison (1820–1900), who came from East Anglian Wesleyan yeoman stock; and his partner W. E. Forster (1818–86), the son of a Quaker missionary from Dorset, depended on their own resources to make their factory a success.[17]

What was true of the long-distance immigrants who became industrialists was equally true of the more numerous, short-distance migrants who came to Bradford to set up as urban manufacturers between 1825 and 1850. Although a smaller percentage of these men achieved spectacular success, almost all came from the same respectable, Nonconformist, lower-middle-class backgrounds. The most famous of these men, Sir Titus Salt (1803–76), is a good example of the type. Descended from a long line of Yorkshire Congregationalists, Titus's father, Daniel, began as a yeoman-farmer and clothier who later tried his hand at woolstapling in town.[18] John Priestman (1805–66), another prominent mid-Victorian millowner, came from a family of Quaker shopkeepers in Shelf, and the machine maker Benjamin Berry

---

[14] HO, 107/2,304–10.
[15] Ibid.
[16] Anon., *Fortunes Made in Business* (London, 1884), 1:7–9; *BO*, Dec. 22, 1891.
[17] Although Forster was descended on his mother's side from a wealthy and prominent Quaker family of bankers, the Burtons, his own father was unable to provide him with much assistance, and the firm of Forster and Fison was established in 1842 largely on the basis of borrowed capital. T. W. Reid, *Life of Rt. Hon. W. E. Forster* (London, 1884), 1:75–9; *BO*, Feb. 18, 1868; *BOB*, June 9, 1906.
[18] Robert Balgarnie, *Sir Titus Salt* (London, 1877), 1–83.

(1786–1868), another Congregationalist, seems to have come from a similar background in Leeds.[19] Short-distance immigrants, like these men from rural Nonconformist lower-middle- or working-class backgrounds who aspired to enter the urban stuff trade, were likely to go into the manufacturing sector, although a few, like Nathaniel Briggs (?–1880), or Henry Mitchell (1824–98), the son of a rural manufacturer of yeoman ancestry, joined their counterparts from more distant locations, becoming stuff merchants after their arrival in town.[20]

Among the 36 percent of midcentury Bradford's bourgeois industrialists who were natives of the town, there were some with links to the traditional establishment who had inherited substantial wealth before embarking on their entrepreneurial careers. Men like William Walker (1803–67), Christopher Waud (1806–66), Swithin Anderton (?–1860), Cowling Ackroyd, William Rouse (1809–68), or the brothers John (1793–1873) and William (?–1868) Rand, were all children and/or junior partners of older Tory manufacturers who had accumulated their initial fortunes earlier.[21] One of the new generation of native manufacturers, Samuel Cunliffe Lister (1815–1906, later Lord Masham), was a younger son from a leading squirearchy family who voluntarily abandoned his privileged status to cast his lot with the rising entrepreneurial tide. To meet the challenges of the 1830s and 1840s, they had to adopt the same practices and techniques employed by their parvenu competitors.[22]

This pattern was even more striking among those native second-generation Victorian manufacturers who came from Nonconformist families. Although their parents or grandparents had founded the firms a generation

---

[19] Alice Priestman, *Recollections of Henry Brady Priestman* (Bradford, 1918), 1–10; *BO*, Jan. 23, 1868. James Bottomley (1816–88), who founded Victoria Mills in nearby Low Moor, was yet another Congregationalist who took pride in "humble origins." Descendants of small-weaving masters from the hinterland village of Shelf, he and his brothers began their fancy goods business by employing handloom weavers before mechanizing and expanding operations in the 1840s. Henry Priestley, a Baptist millowner from the village of Thornton, exhibited a similar pattern in his entrepreneurial career, getting his start through traditional handicraft manufacturing and consolidating his works in a modern factory at about the same time. Another Thorntonian, the Congregationalist Nathan Drake, who began his life as a millworker, eventually was able to open a business of his own, ending his entrepreneurial career as proprietor of the extensive Westbrook Mills, where he pioneered the manufacture of worsted coatings. *BO*, June 20, 1888; Sep. 19, 1892; *BOB*, Oct. 27, 1906.

[20] W. J. Heaton, *Bradford's First Freeman, Sir Henry Mitchell* (London, 1913); anon., *Memorial of Arthur Briggs* (London, 1893), 1–11; *BO*, Mar. 27, 1866; June 20, 1888, Apr. 28, 1898.

[21] J. T. Ward, "Old and New Bradfordians in the Nineteenth Century," *Journal of Bradford Textile Society* (Bradford, 1964–5), 17–32.

[22] Anon., *Lord Masham, The Story of a Great Career* (Bradford, 1906).

or two earlier, it was only with the onset of the Victorian age that the full potential of the business was achieved. Such was the situation of the Garnetts, an old Congregationalist family of protoindustrialists who had pioneered factory production in the town. However, not until the accession of the second generation, represented by the brothers Richard (1793–1848) and James (1795–1850) in the decade of the forties, did profits begin dramatically to increase, enabling the brothers to leave £16,000 and £30,000, respectively, at their untimely deaths around the middle of the century.[23] The Ripleys of Bowling were a native Congregationalist family, similar to the Garnetts, who had built a small dyeworks in 1807 that remained a small-scale seasonal enterprise for the next twenty-five years. However, in 1833, with the accession of Henry Ripley (1814–82) to management, the fortunes of the firm began to take off. Over the next fifty years, he built it into one of Bradford's largest and most profitable industrial plants, which dominated late-nineteenth-century Bowling much as the then ailing Bowling Iron Company had done two generations before.[24]

Like the Garnetts and the Ripleys, the Baptist Illingworth family got their entrepreneurial start in the early nineteenth century with a partnership between the brothers Daniel (1792–1854) and Miles (1788–1869). Although they were fairly successful, it was only after the midforties, when Daniel's sons Alfred (1827–1907) and Henry (1829–95) took over, that the full potential of the business was realized as it rose, after the opening of Providence Mills in 1838 and the larger Whetley Mills in 1865, to become one of the largest manufacturing establishments in town.[25] These successful second-generation manufacturers, who adjusted to the new entrepreneurship of the mid-Victorian age, are exceptional cases that underscore the unique and critically important place of the younger generation in Bradford's urban and industrial development. In fact, the majority of native-born industrialists in Victorian Bradford were not second-generation men, but came from exactly the lower-middle-class parvenu family backgrounds that characterized the bulk of the immigrant entrepreneurs. In a few cases, such as that of Thomas Ambler, an individual's rise to industrial proprietorship was eased by a managerial spell in one of the existing large-scale concerns. However, in most cases, the native entrepreneurs of this rising generation, like their immigrant counterparts, had to make it on their own.[26]

[23] *BOB*, May 19, 1906; *Calendar of Yorkshire Wills*, (mss. Borthwick Institute), 24 (1848–9); 25 (1849–50).
[24] William Cudworth, *Historical Notes on the Bradford Corporation* (Bradford, 1881), 164; idem., *Histories of Bolton and Bowling* (Bradford, 1891), 244–9; *BO*, Oct. 20, 1868.
[25] *BO*, Apr. 5, 1869; *BOB*, June 5, 1907; anon., *The Century's Progress: Yorkshire Industry and Commerce* (London, 1893), 65.
[26] *BO*, Nov. 28, 1889.

The Mitchell brothers of Bowling (Abraham, Joshua, and Joseph), descendants of an old local Wesleyan clothier family, display origins that are almost identical to those of their counterparts who had come from outside the town. The same pattern occurs again and again. Jeremiah Ambler (1800–76), the founder of Midland Mills, was the son of a Manningham yeoman-farmer, whereas William Ramsden (1821–90), the founder of Cliff Mills in Horton, was the son of a timber merchant. John Ramsden (1800–66), his obituary noted, began his career with "few early advantages" and acquired his business as a heald and slay maker as well as his position on the aldermanic bench by applying himself "with energy and perseverance" to improving his situation.[27]

Of course, as the 1851 census material indicates, worsted manufacturers formed, at most, a substantial minority within the midcentury Bradford bourgeoisie. What of the 43 percent, both immigrant and native, who achieved bourgeois status not by entrepreneurship in the sphere of industrial production, but by becoming retailers and businessmen in the urban-service trades?[28] Although these men were more numerous, only a small minority of them became as wealthy as the average manufacturer, and if the origins of the latter tended to be relatively modest, the origins of the former tended to be more humble still.

Naturally, detailed biographical information on such people is hard to come by. However, the evidence available strongly suggests that they frequently emerged from a lower level of the same respectable, Nonconformist lower middle and skilled working class that had fed the ranks of the new industrialists. Because most of these men had come from backgrounds that offered them few resources, and a substantial proportion were children of manual laborers, their rise to positions of mid-Victorian bourgeois comfort was, in its way, no less spectacular than the rise of the parvenu industrialists to positions of enormous wealth and power. This can be seen in the case of John Wood (1802–77), a Bradford teacher, shopkeeper, and freelance writer who compiled the first full city directory in 1845. Although his achievements seem relatively modest, they must be judged against his background in an impoverished Congregationalist handloom-weaving family from Allerton, which had been forced to send him to work in a factory at the age of six.[29]

The career of Joseph Farrar (1805–78), the son of a bankrupt Halifax

---

[27] Wade Hustwick, "The Mitchell Family of Bowling," *Journal of Bradford Textile Society* (Bradford, 1961–2); *BO*, Nov. 11, 1866; Aug. 31, 1891.

[28] HO, 107/2305–10.

[29] John Wood, *Autobiography* (Bradford, 1877), 4–22.

grocer, was even more striking. After coming to Bradford and working for Robert Milligan, Farrar made a name for himself through liberal political and voluntary work, whereas his marriage to the daughter of a local hatter soon brought him the inheritance of a downtown shop. This he built up into a thriving business, which, together with a sideline insurance agency, brought him sufficient income to launch a long and successful second career as a leading figure in municipal politics.[30] James Green (1787–1858), the son of "poor but respectable" laborers from Bingley, came to Bradford to set up as a cabinetmaker and joined the Wesleyans at the age of twenty-five. He extended his operations to construction, holding many positions in local government before he died.[31] William German (1810–90), who came to Bradford in 1831, was another immigrant from the town of Carlisle who built up a basketmaking business that he used to support liberal political involvements in his adopted town.[32]

Like these men, most of the other service entrepreneurs who set up in Bradford were immigrants, often from nearby villages and towns. However, 26 percent were natives of Bradford who had been able to acquire a small piece of urban property and build up a business that brought them success. Most of the forty-seven innkeepers in the bourgeois census population came from this sort of background, as did a certain proportion of retailers in the other trades.[33] Typical of this type, although unusual in the scale of his achievement, was the Congregationalist draper, Henry Brown (?–1878). He inherited a tiny downtown shop from his parents and together with his brother-in-law, Thomas Muff, built it up to meet the needs of an increasingly sophisticated urban market, ultimately transforming the business into Bradford's first department store.[34] Another way in which urbanization could benefit industrious natives, even from humble backgrounds, can be seen in the careers of John Clark, a Methodist laborer who was able to buy a small shop after marrying the cousin of a leading manufacturer, or George Ackroyd (1819–1901), a penniless orphan who was given a junior clerkship in the

---

[30] Joseph Farrar, *Autobiography* (Bradford, 1889), 21–38.

[31] *BO*, Nov. 4, 1858.

[32] *BO*, Apr. 15, 1890. A more exotic case along similar lines was that of Antonio Fattorini (1797–1859), a native of Lombardy, who came to the West Riding as a traveling peddlar after being exiled for revolutionary activity at home. Following the concentration of his customers in Bradford in the 1820s, he bought a small jeweler's shop, which was so successful that he soon added additional branches, becoming the largest jeweler in the West Riding by the time of his death. Patrick Beaver, *A Pedlar's Legacy, The Origins and History of Empire Stores, 1831–81* (Bradford, 1981), 16–38.

[33] *PP* (LXXXVIII, 1852–3), 2:737; HO, 107/2305–10.

[34] Anon., *The Bromuff Story* (Bradford, 1964).

Bradford Bank and worked his way up to managing director by the time he retired.[35]

Although Ackroyd was a typical among professionals in Bradford, they were also affected by urbanization and the immigrant influx. By midcentury, the clique of gentleman-professionals encompassed only a tiny minority of those then practicing, and of the 169 professionals encountered in 1851, 60 percent were under fifty, and 80 percent were immigrants.[36] To be sure, the upper reaches of the law and banking were still dominated by the same old Tory dynasties – the Harrises, the Bentleys, the Laycocks, the Mossmans, and the Hailstones – who had been dominant a generation before. However, they were now joined by a wave of younger competitors, such as John Clegg, J. R. Wagstaff, Richard Ridehalgh, John Rawson, and Benjamin Terry, to name only the most prominent, who were often very similar in background and experience to their age cohorts among the new entrepreneurs.[37]

This challenge of new men was more pronounced among the human-service professions that catered to the new population of the town: doctors, clergymen, teachers, journalists, and architects. Of course, the new immigrants who swelled these professions never became as wealthy as many of their entrepreneurial counterparts, and the high cost of professional training often prevented entry for those whose parents possessed insufficient means.[38] Nevertheless, the new professionals, both in background and experience, had much in common with the other members of the emergent bourgeois generation. This was certainly the case with several of the new generation of physicians such as Dr. Macturk (1795–1872) and Dr. Thomas Beaumont (1795–1859), who came to Bradford in 1824 and 1822, respectively, and were both active in the foundation and operation of the Bradford Infirmary. Beaumont, the son of a Leicester Wesleyan minister, took an active role in investigating public health problems, proposing sanitary reforms, and in agitating political support for their implementation.[39]

Public roles of this sort came more naturally to the town's new Nonconformist clergymen, Benjamin Godwin (1785–1871), Jonathan Glyde (1808–54), Arthur Miall, Daniel Fraser (1820–1902), Joseph Chown, and the Anglican evangelical G. S. Bull (1799–1865). Serving as ministers of key con-

---

[35] John Clark, "History and Annals of Bradford: Family Book of Reference" (mss., Bradford Central Library), 1–10, 35; *BO*, June 11, 1901.

[36] *PP* (LXXXVIII, 1852–3), 2:737; HO, 107/2,304–10.

[37] Cudworth, *Bradford Corporation*, 105–6; James Ibbetson, *Directory of Bradford* (Bradford, 1850).

[38] See Chapter 5.

[39] J. H. Bell, "Some Fragments of Local Medical History," *BA*, o.s. 1 (1888).

gregations, these men rapidly rose to prominence as community leaders and organic intellectuals for the emergent bourgeoisie.[40] The same was true of lay figures such as the journalists William Byles (1807–91), editor of the *Bradford Observer*, and James Hanson, editor of the more radical *Bradford Review*, as well as the writer John James (1811–67) and even architects like F. W. Delaney and Henry Lockwood (1811–78), who literally drew much of the future shape of the town.[41] Although many of these men came from solidly middle-class backgrounds, their move to Bradford was invariably accompanied by a significant rise in social position and often by an addition to their income as well. Bull and Beaumont were the sons of Leicestershire ministers, and Fraser, Miall, Glyde, and Byles were the sons of merchants in Glasgow, Portsmouth, Exeter, and Henley, respectively. This was even truer of the professionals, like Godwin and James, who had worked their way up from the poverty of early working-class upbringings to the comfort and eminence of their future roles.[42]

Conclusion

It should be evident from the foregoing analysis that the rise of a new bourgeois generation in Bradford, which arrived in the 1820s, 1830s, and 1840s and reached its maturity during the mid-Victorian years, was more than the simple biological renewal of a preexisting established capitalist elite. As young men who were generally immigrants, Nonconformists, and frequently children of relatively humble and obscure working- or lower-middle-class parents, the new bourgeoisie constituted not merely a new elite generation, but an entirely distinctive social group. In all but a very small minority of cases, these men bore no family relation to the traditional Anglican Tory establishment whose members monopolized the traditional cultural and political institutions of the town.

What is significant is not just that these men came from different backgrounds, but that they were themselves intensely conscious of the fact. Instead of seeking quietly to assimilate into the existing oligarchy, they gloried

---

[40] Benjamin Godwin, "Autobiography" (mss. Bradford Central Library); Arthur Miall, *The Life of Edward Miall* (London, 1884); J. C. Gill, *The Ten Hours Parson* (London, 1959); G. W. Conder, *Memoirs and Remains of Rev. Jonathan Glyde* (London, 1858); Lucy Fraser, *Memoirs of Daniel Fraser* (Bradford, 1905); J. P. Chown, *Sermons, with a Brief Sketch of his Life* (Bradford, 1875).

[41] *Bradford Telegraph and Argus*, Apr. 7, 1867; *BO*, May 5, 1864; July 23, 1878; F. G. Byles, *William Byles* (Weymouth, 1932).

[42] *Bradford Telegraph and Argus*, Apr. 7 1867; *BO*, Oct. 20, 1859; Byles, *William Byles*, 24–128; Conder, *Jonathan Glyde*, 54–188; Fraser, *Daniel Fraser*.

in their distinctiveness as self-made men. So far from trying to forget his working-class roots, the Baptist minister William Steadman "looked back on the obscurity of his origin and the necessities of his parents, not with feelings of mortified pride but with emotions of adoring gratitude ... he felt an evident pleasure in telling the story of his early days, persuaded that it abundantly illustrated the wisdom and goodness of his heavenly Father."[43]

Marked off at the outset by their origins and backgrounds from the town's traditional gentleman-capitalist elite, these largely Nonconformist, upwardly mobile, entrepreneurially minded insurgents could not help but come into conflict with the Anglican Tory establishment given their radically different experience of the urban-industrial revolution that was transforming the town. Riding the crest of this economic and demographic revolution during the quarter century after 1825, they fully identified with the vast social and economic changes that alienated the aging established notables and made the latter feel like strangers in their own native town. By contrast, urban-industrial Bradford constituted an environment in which the entrepreneurially minded parvenu immigrant could feel entirely at home. As the framework within which they underwent their own transition from youth to adulthood and the vehicle through which they experienced self-realization and success, Bradford's urban-industrial revolution seemed to them the very source of identity, not to mention the material foundation on which they built their personal incomes and careers.

This striking parallel between the expansion of Bradford and its staple trade and the rise of the bourgeois insurgents who came to dominate it was forcefully articulated in the obituary of the town's first mayor, Robert Milligan, whose life became a symbol for his generation and class. "Like him, Bradford has grown from a comparatively insignificant place into a large and wealthy town. ... It has grown by the same virtues that made its first representative a wealthy man."[44]

Bradford's development from economic adolescence to urban-industrial maturity seemed so intertwined with the careers of men like Milligan that their individual lives could serve as metaphors for the development of the city whose history was assimilated to their own. As an immigrant, a Nonconformist, an entrepreneurial capitalist, and a relatively lowborn parvenu, Milligan was everything that the native Anglican gentleman-capitalist was not. Not surprisingly, it was his virtues and qualities rather than theirs that appeared most functional in the sort of environment that Bradford was becoming, both for the achievement of individual success and fulfillment, and for the creation of a viable and prosperous urban community too. "Whilst

43 Thomas Steadman, *Memoir of Rev. William Steadman* (London, 1838), 9.
44 *BO*, July 3, 1862.

attaining to wealth and influence and reputation," the obituary continued,
"Robert Milligan probably contributed more than any other man of his time
to the material prosperity of the town of Bradford."

> Like the shrewd Scotsman that he was, he had a keen eye for business
> on his own account, and he had the wit to look a little further than his
> contemporaries into the commercial future and possibilities of the town
> of his adoption. Trained up from youth in habits of industry and econ-
> omy...he grew with his circumstances. As a citizen he performed his
> duties with the same degree of conscientiousness that had won him
> such success in his own affairs.[45]

It was inevitable that the entrepreneurial triumph of men like Milligan
would pose a fundamental challenge, not only to the social and economic
ascendancy of Bradford's Tory establishment, but to their cultural and political power as well. In the eyes of a traditional gentleman like Dr. Simpson
they might well seem "a disputatious, ignorant, lowlived set of people,"
whose "actions and sentiments [were] not accordant with the character of
true English Gentility." Yet even Dr. Simpson was compelled to admit that,
"the only reason...why they so abound in this place is, that the people are
in general a lowlived, ignorant, illiterate, brutal set."[46]

Here was a raw and upstart generation that fitted Bradford almost as
perfectly as Bradford fitted them. They considered themselves predestined
to assume the mantle of local leadership, evolving new institutions and values
that were suited to the environment in which they lived.

[45] *BOB*, Feb. 3, 1906.
[46] John Simpson, *The Journal of Dr. John Simpson of Bradford, 1825* (Bradford, 1981), 19.

7

The making of the self-made man

Nowhere is nineteenth-century sensibility more alien to our severely antih-eroic contemporary mind-set than in its characteristic image of the human personality: the self-made man. Although this image may still strike chords in the dreams that fuel contemporary popular culture, to most intellectuals it seems puerile or at best naive. Certainly it is easy enough to dismiss the rags-to-riches story as an illusion – an ideological fantasy that might offer false hopes to the downtrodden but that bore little relation to the actual facts of social mobility at the time.[1] However, the perception of the historian's subjects are also a part of their historical reality, and no ideology can simply be written off as false. Ideologies are, indeed, partial illusions that have real social meaning because they are able to feed on important truths, which, abstracted from their actual historical context, come to assume fantastic forms.[2]

Although the myth of the self-made man did not fit the reality of most nineteenth-century Bradfordians, it was in many ways an accurate reflection of the experience of the town's rising bourgeoisie. As we have seen, signif-icant achievement and upward mobility, if rarely of the spectacular rags-to-riches sort, was the characteristic experience of most individuals in this category and formed the basis of their collective consciousness. In this sense, the elevation of the self-made man to the status of an ideological hero was simply the outcome of the bourgeois social, economic, and political triumph that had taken place during the preceding twenty-five years. Having risen to positions of wealth and authority, it was only natural that these men should project their self-image on the larger urban canvas and offer their own careers in a form duly idealized as general models for social integration and success. For a world vision so inherently heroic, biography was the most appropriate medium for conveying ideology as general values were reified in a narrative recounting of the individual life process through which the self had con-sciously been made.

---

[1] Herbert Gutman, *Work, Culture and Society in Industrializing America* (New York, 1966), 211–33; Stephen Thernstrom, *Poverty and Progress* (Cambridge, 1964).

[2] Karl Marx, *The German Ideology* (New York, 1947); Karl Mannheim, *Ideology and Utopia* (New York, 1936).

Although many biographical works of this sort were produced in Victorian Bradford and the genre came to dominate the literature and even journalism of the age, the most sustained and searching expression of this bourgeois self-consciousness came from the pen of Samuel Smiles, whose books sold more copies than any other living author at the time. A radical journalist from nearby Leeds, Smiles was himself a member of the rising bourgeois generation who articulated many of the values of his Bradford counterparts, some of whom he counted among his friends. Smiles's gospels of success are familiar enough, but their central argument is frequently confused with the cruder rags-to-riches mythology that forms the theme for most of Horatio Alger's novels.[3]

Of course, like Alger's, Smiles's message was that merit and enterprise would receive their reward. But unlike Alger, he did not envision this primarily in material terms. Although Alger was willing to acknowledge that blind chance or fortune sometimes played a role in worldly achievement, Smiles's more philosophical conception of success saw it as a product of individual character and choice. What primarily interested Smiles was the process of self-development through which the successful individual's identity was consciously shaped. Although this experience of self-help and self-cultivation might lead to worldly fame or fortune, these were by-products of a process whose real reward lay in the sense of personal fulfillment that came with the realization of one's human capacities and powers.[4]

Smiles's belief that wealth was, at best, a sign of inner virtue, at worst a temptation that it would have to overcome, reflected a deep distrust of affluence among those of Bradford's new entrepreneurial bourgeoisie who were most adept at accumulating riches but profoundly ambivalent about enjoying them. The eulogy that was applied to Richard Garnett could have been applied to most of his class and generation: "He did not love money but he loved success."[5] Obviously this secular gospel, with its insistence on the link between self-sacrifice and reward, revealed its deep religious roots in the Christian drama of self-abnegation and divine redemption, particularly in its characteristically Calvinist form. In fact, by bringing the logic of the self-made man from the ideal world of the Christian heaven to the industrial-capitalist world of earth, Smiles made explicit a certain secularizing strain that had always been implicit in the Calvinist preoccupation with worldly signs. Worldly achievement was to be understood as a mark of God's favor,

---

[3] Samuel Smiles, *Autobiography* (London, 1905); Asa Briggs, *Victorian People* (London, 1954), 124–47; R. J. Morris, "Samuel Smiles and the Genesis of Self-Help: the Retreat to a Petit Bourgeois Utopia," *Historical Journal*, 24 (1981).

[4] Samuel Smiles, *Character* (New York, 1871); idem, *Self-Help* (London, 1925).

[5] Jonathan Glyde, *Sermon Preached at Horton Lane Chapel on the Death of James Garnett Esq.* (Bradford, 1850), 29.

worldly failure a prelude to a more permanent perdition. The vicissitudes of human fortune could be justified and explained by reference to the working of a mysterious but inexorable godly plan.

The efforts of Smiles and his contemporaries to rebuild this argument on purely secular foundations, without any explicit references to God, raised to the surface a certain heretical humanist strain that some puritan theologians had feared to be latent in radical Protestantism from the start.[6] Virtue, which had once been the emblem of salvation, now, in the human logic of self-help, had to be taken as its own reward. Thus without ever abandoning the Christian virtues of the self-denying martyr, Smiles's new secular self-made man simultaneously assumed some of the more aggrandizing virtues of the classical hero who unapologetically sought his fulfillment in the world.

The tension between self-realization and self-denial in this secularized puritanism – the attempt to justify the former in the latter's terms – reflected an ambiguity in the experience of the new entrepreneurial generation that at least partly derived from its character as a transitional parvenu group. Born in relatively humble circumstances but bound for wealth and power, the new entrepreneurial bourgeoisie aspired to positions of dominance and mastery but discovered that these could only be obtained by subservience to external imperatives and submission to an endless round of dull routine. This was the real dilemma of the self-made man – an inner paradox that makes him at once both actual and mythical – an ideological illusion engendered by historical fact.

Bradford's new entrepreneurs were, in fact, upwardly mobile, but their ascent as individuals occurred in a social and historical context that fostered the qualities of abstemious independence that they needed to achieve success. And even when they appeared most fully self-reliant, when they no longer had anyone to help them but themselves, so far from being the true masters of their destiny, they became more completely implicated with the impersonal forces that dictated the specific form in which their self-realization occurred.

Childhood and family background

Bradford's aspiring bourgeoisie could never have succeeded without some existing family resources to aid them in their struggle for success. As we have seen, by the 1830s, the capital requirements for successful entrepreneurship in industry were rising rapidly. During the thirties, forties, and early fifties, they were not, as yet, so high as to preclude entry for bold and

[6] Christopher Hill, *The World Turned Upside Down* (New York, 1972).

innovative parvenus, but economies of scale and rising costs of fixed capital were creating a situation in which access to several thousand pounds was an essential precondition for establishing a new factory firm.[7] Although the field was more open in the service sector, here too there was a correlation between the size of one's initial investment and the chances that the business would succeed.[8]

Although not all the members of the new bourgeoisie were able to obtain capital or credit directly from their families, inability to do so was a serious impediment. The dearth of banks and other lending institutions and the difficulty of accumulating capital through salaried work meant that even those with the most formidable abilities and best luck would have to delay entrepreneurship until their late thirties or forties unless relatives were able to ease their path. Those, like Titus Salt, W. E. Forster, Henry Ripley, Henry Forbes, William Fison, and J. V. Godwin, who achieved success at a relatively early age, did so only because their families provided them with capital or helped them to obtain it on favorable terms.[9]

Although monetary aid was important in early capital formation, family assistance could take a variety of other forms. Successful older brothers sometimes helped their siblings by taking them into partnership until they were able to set up businesses of their own.[10] The familial structure of enterprise survived the rise of a new generation of individualists and the changes in industrial organization that they made. An analysis of the city's 1845 *Directory* shows that, although 66 percent of all worsted firms were individually owned, another 23 percent were family partnerships. Partnerships between people not related by kinship were a rarity outside the staple industry and only a small minority within it. Only among stuff merchants who required larger reserves of working capital did they play a significant part, constituting 23 percent of all firms. Among factory capitalists, they constituted a mere 12 percent of all enterprises and only 6 percent of the smaller stuff manufacturing firms.[11]

Of course, worsted entrepreneurship was financed as much by credit as by capital, and here, family connections could play an even more critical role in providing direct loans or collateral, and in securing the contacts and character references that impersonal creditors would require. Moreover, in

---

[7] See Chapter 4.
[8] Ibid.
[9] Robert Balgarnie, *Sir Titus Salt* (London, 1877); T. W. Reid, *Life of the Right Honourable William Edward Forster* (London, 1888), 1:77–9; William Cudworth, *Histories of Bolton and Bowling* (Bradford, 1891), 244–9; *BO*, Oct. 18, 1870; Benjamin Godwin, "Autobiography" (mss. Bradford Central Library), 486–91, 528–9, 725–6.
[10] *BOB*, Mar. 3, 1906.
[11] James Ibbetson, *Directory of Bradford* (Bradford, 1845).

an age that lacked bureaucratic methods for recruiting personnel or evaluating ability, success in finding jobs, managers, and reliable customers depended on the personal knowledge that family networks could most effectively engender.[12] Nevertheless, even more than the family's capacity to provide material resources was its role as an agency of socialization. Indeed, the less it could offer in financial assistance, the more it had to concentrate on fostering ambition and resourcefulness in its children, animating them to accumulate their own stores of inner strength.

Here, religion played a critical part. As we have seen, the new men generally came from lower-middle-class Nonconformist families, which may have endowed them with only modest material means, but which determinedly inculcated from the earliest age in their children a sense of religious seriousness that set them apart.[13] "Dwelling in the seclusion of a village, at the time much cut off from the centers of population," the humble, Scottish, East Anglian, or rural Yorkshire congregations, from which most of the new entrepreneurs came, "nursed their piety and their prejudices.... In those early days," a local minister recollected, "there was a widespread religious feeling, deep rooted in the hearts of the people.... There was scarcely a house where religion was not ostensibly upheld and the Sabbath observed with puritanical strictness."[14] In these tight-knit enclaves of puritanical Nonconformity, the Protestant ethic of moral individualism was reinforced by the cohesive power of community to generate that attitude of worldly asceticism from which Weber contended a spirit of capitalism would arise.[15]

A host of local diaries, biographies, and memoirs attest to the importance of evangelical religion in the future entrepreneurs' lives. The fanatical conviction of Joseph Barker's father that children should not be permitted to

[12] Of course, the most common cases were those in which children inherited businesses directly from their fathers or obtained jobs through parental influence. However, more distant relations, particularly uncles, could be enlisted for career advancement by many young men. Isaac Holden employed several of his nephews as managers although he claimed to give them no preference over others on his staff. The solicitor H. F. Killick was recruited to Bradford by his uncle, the manufacturer William Fison. Alfred and John Priestman were induced to come to town by their uncle John, who had, himself, migrated a generation before. In a few cases, such as that of Thomas Priestley, nephews were taken on as partners by distant relatives who were impressed by their performance as employees in the firm. *Bradford Portraits* (Bradford, 1892); Alice Priestman, *Recollections of Henry Brady Priestman* (Bradford, 1918), 93–120; Holden Papers (mss. Bradford University Library) IA, I. Holden – J. Craven, Nov. ?, 1852; 3B, J. Holden – I. Holden, Aug. 2, 1864.

[13] A. D. Gilbert, *Religion and Society in Industrial England* (London, 1976), 60–3.

[14] Anon., *Memorial of Rev. James Gregory* (Leeds, 1876), 8.

[15] Max Weber, *The Protestant Ethic and the Spirit of Capitalism* (New York, 1958); Balgarnie, *Salt*, 10; J. H. Turner, *Nonconformity in Idle: with the History of Airedale College* (Bradford, 1876), 9–44.

play and that they should regularly be flogged to subdue their sinful spirits undoubtedly made his childhood more than usually dismal. But the early sense of guilt and introspective tendencies that Barker exhibited were common themes in the biographies of others who came from similar families.[16] The restraint under which young Jonas Sugden was placed by his parents, who "prohibited his attendance at feasts fairs and worldly amusements," isolated the boy from playmates and turned him into a lonely, unhappy, brooding child. Sugden, Benjamin Godwin, and W. E. Forster took parental anxieties over the state of their souls very much to heart from the time they were children and tried hard to conjure up the sort of religious feelings that they knew they were expected to have.[17]

That this heavy dose of puritanism in childhood had the ultimate effect of developing, rather than crushing, their wills was the result of a more complex interplay of influences from within the family environment that, to some extent, mitigated the psychological terror of an implacable patriarchal God. In a striking number of cases, Bradford's rising generation of self-made men experienced their actual biological father as someone less formidable than the angry deity they had been raised to fear. In the first place, almost all of them became more successful than their fathers. In part, this was the consequence of the greater range of opportunities that opened up in their generation. But in some cases, there is evidence that the father had a less forceful personality and was unwilling to exert authority over his son.

Isaac Holden's father lost status when he failed as a farmer and was forced to hire himself out as a manual laborer at a wage that could not support his family.[18] After he died, when Isaac was nineteen, the boy found a father figure in his employer and teacher John Kennedy. But in his twenties, the young man asserted his independence, and it was Kennedy who began to defer to his talented pupil, remarking at one point, "You have overshot your old preceptor who is little disposed to teach those who are better informed than himself."[19] A similar pattern appears in other cases. It was young Titus Salt who convinced his father that they should start a worsted partnership, and customers quickly learned that it was the son who was the brains behind the firm. When Titus took the risks that made his fortune, he did so in disregard of his father's cautious advice. By the time he was a teenager, Henry Ripley was managing his family's dyeworks. Several other

---

[16] Joseph Barker, *The History and Confessions of a Man* (Wortley, 1846), 79–85.

[17] Godwin, "Autobiography," 25–36; Reid, *Life of Forster*, 1:21; R. S. Hardy, *Commerce and Christianity, Memorial of Jonas Sugden* (London, 1857), 31.

[18] *Fortunes Made in Business* (London, 1884), 1:7–11; Elizabeth Jennings, "Sir Isaac Holden (1807–97), 'The First Comber in Europe'" (Bradford, Ph.D. dissertation, 1982), 1–3.

[19] Holden Papers, (mss. Brotherton Library, B.A. 5/9), J. Kennedy – I. Holden, Apr. 5, 1835.

cases are recorded where joint father and son partnerships began through the initiative of the latter.[20]

Although these fathers were not necessarily weak, they could not serve as role models for their more gifted, aggressive, or ambitious sons, who were forced beyond the level of oedipal conflict to forge identities all their own.[21] W. E. Forster found his father "trying to [Forster] by his almost morbid timidity, his want of decision, and his devotion to ideas with which his son could not have much sympathy." But instead of fighting with his father, Forster simply paid lip service to filial obedience while pursuing his own interests and going his own way.[22] Benjamin Godwin's father, an octogenarian adventurer who died in poverty when the boy was twelve, was even less able to serve as an authoritative example. In another case, an ambitious young Wesleyan with an unconverted and perhaps alcoholic father did not hesitate to upbraid his parent. "Yesterday evening," his diary noted, "took the opportunity to speak to my father as closely as I could on the error of his ways and commended myself to his conscience."[23] The absence of strong fathers in these cases may have heightened the sense of rootlessness that sons experienced in the course of their youth, but it also left them with a feeling of power and independence, which, when tempered by the disciplines of religion and morality, would stand them in good stead for future struggles.

If paternal influence and authority on many of the men destined to become bourgeois tended to be weak, then maternal authority and influence upon them seems to have been strong. Mary Ryan has noted a shift from paternal to maternal authority within the nineteenth-century family, which led to the creation of a more moral and "feminized" male personality that she associates with the self-made man.[24] Certainly all of Bradford's self-made men on whom evidence survives exhibited close and intense relationships with their mothers that had an unmistakable impact on their development as mature adults. In almost every case, the moral training and religious education of the child was the responsibility of the mother. In Godwin's case, the premature death of an elderly and irresolute father insured the paramountcy of the maternal role. But in many other cases where the father was physically present, the domestic environment was suffused by a moral influence exuded by his wife. Titus Salt, William Byles, Jacob Behrens, and others were raised

[20] Balgarnie, *Titus Salt*, 46–7, 68; in one case, Robert Shackleton, a working-class boy, actually started the business on his own, taking in his father and brothers as partners after it had begun to pay a profit. *Bradford Telegraph and Argus*, Nov. 28, 1913.

[21] Erik Erikson, *Young Man Luther* (New York, 1958), 156–7.

[22] Reid, *Forster*, 1:48.

[23] Quoted in *Bradford Telegraph and Argus*, Oct. 10, 1933.

[24] Mary Ryan, *Cradle of the Middle Class* (Cambridge, 1981).

by mothers who envisioned religion as a private domestic affair from which even their husbands were partly excluded.[25]

Although maternal influence was most important within the home, in a few cases it was also exerted on a wider plane to give the son precisely that example of self-culture and enterprise that the father was unable or unwilling to provide. From his youth, W. E. Forster was accustomed to being surrounded by confident Quaker women, not only his mother, who made an independent career as a preacher and philanthropist, but his spinster aunts, who were respected amateur scholars and social investigators.[26] In some cases, strong mothers who had themselves made unsatisfactory marriages could compensate for the failure of their husbands by concentrating their energies on a promising son, who might redeem them from their degradation and shame. This was certainly the situation in the family of young Joseph Farrar, whose mother's contacts with the Milligan family got him his first job and his entry into the inner circle of Bradford's new Nonconformist elite. Yet this identification with her son's career was, in part, a response to her husband's bankruptcy and to frustrations built up over many years. As Farrar explained, "My father made but little as a businessman and was greatly indebted to my mother for the position he occupied, she by her industry sustaining my father's failing fortunes at all times, for his indiscretion was such as to amount to folly."[27]

Comparable instances may have been widespread, albeit in less extreme form. The fathers of Isaac Holden and Titus Salt were hard-working and industrious individuals, but through no fault of their own, they seem to have gotten trapped by the economic dislocations of the war and postwar eras. The spectacular success of their sons may have been inspired, at least in part, by the force of frustrated conjugal hopes deferred into maternal expectations.[28]

Education and character

The families of Bradford's rising bourgeois generation provided their children with material assistance and, even more importantly, with the religious

[25] Balgarnie, *Salt*, 17; F. G. Byles, *William Byles* (Weymouth, 1932), 15–23; Godwin, "Autobiography," 10–56; *Sir Jacob Behrens, 1806–1889* (London, n.d.), 3–4.

[26] Reid, *Forster*, 1:19–21, 28–9.

[27] Joseph Farrar, *Autobiography* (Bradford, 1889), 20.

[28] Joseph Wilson, *Life and Work* (London, n.d.), 4. I am indebted to LeeAnn Whites whose unpublished analysis of the character formation of the American industrialist Andrew Carnegie led me to investigate the links between paternal failure, maternal ambition, and subsequent entrepreneurial success in Bradford.

and psychological reinforcement that was conducive to success. Beyond this point, however, the self-made man was on his own. The absence of any institutional cushion beyond the family to ease a young man on his way in this new world can be seen in the minuscule amount of formal education that most of the new bourgeoisie were able to obtain. Even a man like W. E. Forster, whose parents were comfortably endowed and who placed an unusually high value on education, felt that their son should leave school when he turned seventeen. Others, whose parents were not as well off or less obliging, were forced to end their schooldays even earlier. Joseph Farrar's education ceased at the age of fifteen, when his father went bankrupt; and Isaac Holden was forced to begin work at eleven, when his father's farm failed. Thomas Taylor, the son of Bradford's Congregationalist minister, had to choose a career when he turned fourteen, whereas Jacob Behrens was forced to interrupt his education at thirteen to begin a mercantile apprenticeship.[29]

Since there was no systematic provision for public education in early-nineteenth-century England, men and women from truly indigent families would obtain little tutelage. In fact, several members of the new entrepreneurial generation, such as the auctioneer William Haigh, the dyer Henry Heaton, or the manufacturer Jonas Whiteley, had literally no formal schooling. Others like Charles Rhodes, who, "by his indomitable courage and perseverance raised himself from the lowest poverty to a station of influence and comparative independence," were assisted by the most minimal level of instruction.[30] The quality of schools that these men attended, however briefly, was uneven. With the deterioration of the Bradford Grammar School in the early nineteenth century, even elite Anglican families were hard pressed to find good local schools for their sons. For immigrants, Nonconformists, and children of the lower middle class, the situation was worse. At the elementary level, the proliferation of small one-room schools and self-styled academies before the spread of denominational day schools in the 1840s resulted in a wide range in the quality of instruction. Many of these tiny "schools" were supplements to an illiterate widow's income. In the Bradford region, there was only a handful of higher-quality establishments with trained instructors. Many of the small schools were useless, and some parents, such as Joseph

---

[29] W. S. Matthews, *Memoirs and Select Remains of Rev. Thomas Rawson Taylor* (London, 1836), 7; *Holden-Illingworth Letters* (Bradford, 1927), 768; *Jacob Behrens*, 24; Farrar, *Autobiography*, 20–2.

[30] *BO*, July 30, 1863; see *Bradford Portraits*. Of the eighty notables surveyed in this prosopographical collection (most born between 1810 and 1840), at least fifteen had little or no formal instruction at all, whereas only twenty-four individuals were reported to have attended some kind of secondary school.

Farrar's, simply shifted their children from one incompetent teacher to another.[31]

In early-nineteenth-century Bradford, the only secondary education outside the grammar school was provided by the tiny Independent and Baptist Colleges at Idle and Horton, respectively, and at Joseph Hinchcliffe's Academy in Horton House, which educated most of the young bourgeois natives who obtained any secondary schooling. Hinchcliffe's curriculum was mainly commercial, but since he was a classical scholar, he was prepared to instruct children in Latin and Greek if their parents desired. Of course, university education was in theory available, not only in Oxford and Cambridge, but in London and Edinburgh, where, unlike the ancient universities, Dissenters could matriculate. In practice, however, except for those planning to become doctors, few of the new men were in a position to attend.[32] By the middle of the century, the situation was improving as many of the entrepreneurs had children of their own. Still, as late as 1851, only 50 percent of the coresiding male children under sixteen in the bourgeois census population were listed as being in school, whereas 35 percent were employed at work. Although elementary education for bourgeois children had now become all but universal, secondary schooling was still a rarity. Among those between sixteen and nineteen years of age, 90 percent were already working.[33]

"The printing office was my school," said William Byles, who at least had the benefit of a year at Henley Grammar School before beginning his apprenticeship at the age of fourteen. He reflected the attitudes and experiences of most members of his class and generation when he wrote in his newspaper, "It is not in schools solely or primarily that the mind is educated and the character formed." "The great rough world after all, is the best schoolhouse."[34] If Byles appeared to be making the best of a bad situation, Samuel Smiles elaborated his point in a more positive and sophisticated way:

> Work is one of the best educators of a practical character, it evokes and disciplines obedience, self-control, attention, application, and perseverance; giving a man deftness and skill in his special calling, and aptitude and dexterity in dealing with the affairs of ordinary life.... Schools, academies, and colleges, give but the merest beginnings of

---

[31] Even a future intellectual like Benjamin Godwin failed to learn to write in his first elementary school. Godwin, "Autobiography," 23; William Scruton, *Pen and Pencil Pictures of Old Bradford* (Bradford, 1889), 80.

[32] "Joseph Hinchcliffe, Schoolmaster," BA, o.s. 2 (1895).

[33] *PP*, (LXXXVIII, 1852–3), 2:737; HO, 107/2305–10.

[34] *BO*, Mar. 4, 1847; *The Bradfordian*, Jan. 1, 1862, 18; Byles, *Byles*, 10.

culture in comparison with it. Far more influential is the life-education daily given in our homes, in the streets, behind counters, in workshops.[35]

Some members of Bradford's emergent bourgeoisie such as Titus Salt and J. V. Godwin obtained their training through a formal apprenticeship, and although this was most common among would-be stuff merchants, it was a possible route of entry into other trades as well. However, most members of the new bourgeois generation learned their jobs in more informal ways. Those who were waiting to start their own businesses and could find someone willing to take them on might work for a short time, usually sampling the duties of several departments, to obtain a broad sense of the trade as a whole. Those who came with fewer resources and personal contacts might have to be content with long spells of paid employment either as a skilled laborer or in a managerial capacity.[36] Almost all agreed that a formal classical education, especially for those above the age of sixteen, was not only unnecessary, but undesirable. "To bring men from the loom, the plough, the shop, or the counting house, unaccustomed to habits of study," explained Isaac Holden, "and to put before them Latin, Greek, and Hebrew...is simply an absurdity."[37]

In contrast to traditional Bradford's gentlemen-capitalists who made a fetish of acquiring at least a patina of cultivation, the new bourgeois adopted a severely practical conception of learning and devalued the acquisition of a broad humanistic culture or the development of critical intellectual skills. Erudition was often distrusted on utilitarian as well as ethical grounds. According to Smiles, "Such facilities (Universities) may as often be a hindrance as a help to individual culture of the highest kind....Wisdom and understanding can only become the possession of individual men by traveling the old road of observation, attention, perseverance, and industry."[38]

Although attitudes of this sort sometimes became little more than masks for antiintellectualism, more often they reflected the desire for a different sort of education, one more thoroughly integrated into the process of self-development, actuated by the individual's inner capacity for initiative, and directed toward his immediate practical needs. If this devalued education from one perspective, from another it elevated what was traditionally a mere rite of passage into a lifelong mission pervading the whole personality. In one sense, this bourgeois glorification of self-education was simply a virtue made of necessity, but in another, it was a genuine reflection of the parvenu's fundamental attitude toward life, his belief that the individual could not

---

[35] Samuel Smiles, *Character* (New York, 1971), 51, 97; idem, *Self-Help*, 7.

[36] Holden papers (mss. Brotherton and Bradford University Libraries); Balgarnie, *Salt*, 37–8; Reid, *Forster*, 1:54.

[37] Holden Papers (mss., Bradford University Library), 1B.

[38] Smiles, *Self-Help*, 384.

merely be a passive recipient of experience but must strive to become an active agent participating in the creation of himself. The very ordeal of surmounting the difficulties inherent in this process of self-creation, however painful they might appear at the time, would, in retrospect, be recognized as a salutary experience contributing to one's capacity for mastery and control.[39]

This autodidact tradition would eventually take on a public face in Bradford when, with the advent of the Mechanics Institute, it became part of the bourgeois program for urban reform. But when it began, with the arrival of the new generation of entrepreneurs in the 1810s and 1820s, it was essentially a private experience that each individual had to work out for himself.[40] When young Isaac Holden was forced to leave school in 1817, he continued his quest for knowledge alone in the evenings after work. Deciding that he wanted to become a teacher, he drew up a reading list of several hundred titles on a wide variety of literary, theological, and scientific subjects.[41] Smiles particularly recommended that a young man study arithmetic, not only because it was a necessary business skill, but because "it teaches him method, accuracy, values, proportions, and relations." Jacob Behrens, who kept starting new subjects all his life, took up mathematics at the age of fifty-two, keeping a notebook of his progress from simple algebra to advanced calculus, whereas W. E. Forster found time in between business, politics, and social investigations to tackle complex mathematical puzzles.[42]

---

[39] Thomas Steadman, *Memoir of Rev. William Steadman* (London, 1838), 12.

[40] See Chapter 11.

[41] Holden/Bradford, 1B, "Booklist." As he wrote in his *Journal* at the age of seventeen, "I thought that I would read some other than books of divinity but I now find that variety is more pleasant therefore I have taken out Wood on mosaic creation." Holden/Bradford, 1B, "Journal."

[42] Reid, *Forster;* anon, *Jacob Behrens*, 47; Smiles, *Character*, 64. Though Forster and Behrens were atypical in their open commitment to rationalism, most other bourgeois of their generation also exhibited an identification with positive science that coexisted uneasily with the old theological orthodoxies that they also continued to believe. In fact, the naive worship of scientific truth and progress that reduced all questions about the physical and social world to a calculus of mechanical, chemical, or political economic laws was not so much an alternative or substitute for dogmatic religion as its emanation and extension in an increasingly industrial-capitalist society from the realm of theological abstraction to the concrete realities of the secular world. Like so many imperfectly educated men who find themselves faced with difficult choices, Bradford's new bourgeois were all too ready to turn what Matthew Arnold attacked as the defect of philistinism into a pragmatic virtue as singlemindedness, elevating their half-baked beliefs and principles into articles of faith and immutable laws. Matthew Arnold, *Culture and Anarchy* (New York, 1924), 72–108. Arnold was married to Forster's sister, and he probably was thinking of some of the Bradford capitalists with whom he was, at least indirectly, familiar, when he wrote his famous critique.

So far from withering in the crucible of worldly experience, the puritan mentality was

The determination to seek knowledge through life experience and the conviction that experience interpreted through a proper ideology was the soundest basis for the attainment of knowledge was most thoroughly summed up by the concept of "character," which became at once both a shorthand for all the parvenu virtues and an explanation for the success of those who embodied them. "Character," according to Smiles, "is formed by a variety of minute circumstances more or less under the regulation and control of the individual ... [it] exhibits itself in conduct, guided and inspired by principle, integrity and practical wisdom." Here was a whole new definition of individualism, a systematic social philosophy rooted in the self. "In its highest form it is the individual will acting energetically under the influence of religion, morality and reason."[43] It was thus both the precondition for and product of self-development. As the embodiment of individual virtue it was socially desirable because of the example that it set for others:

> Energy of will – self-originating force – is the soul of every great character. Where it is, there is life, where it is not, there is faintness, helplessness, and despondency.... The energetic leader of noble spirit not only wins a way for himself but carries others with him. His every act has a personal significance, indicating vigor, independence, and self-reliance, and unconsciously commands respect, admiration and homage.[44]

Here, Smiles offers a new type of humanistic hero in which the classical virtues of charisma, creativity, and will are tempered by the Christian virtues of humility, sacrifice, and devotion to duty, translated into secular terms. "The abiding sense of duty is the very crown of character ... Duty is not a sentiment but a principle pervading the life; and it exhibits itself in conduct and in acts which are mainly determined by man's conscience and free will."[45]

simply resurrected in the form of a dogmatic liberalism whose central tenets were treated as sacrosanct in the same sense as predestination or original sin. The essentially religious character of this approach to comprehending experience was unwittingly revealed by Joseph Wilson's biographer in his description of the dominating, almost demonic, role played by ideological faith in the construction of his supposedly scientific world view:

> These views [temperance, vegetarianism, and political liberalism] are not fads but convictions. He did not take them up, they took possession of him.... Exacting scientific study at the beginning of his career brought him conviction. Experience in varying circumstances and on a vast scale deepened his conviction and observation reinforced it; and if you could move the mountain you could not now change Mr. Wilson's mind or his manner of living on any of these things.

H. J. Taylor, "Foreword," in Wilson, *Life and Work*.

[43] Smiles, *Character*, 23.

[44] Ibid.

[45] Ibid., 195.

Like all heroic figures, the self-made man of character towers above the multitude of those who remain inferior, but his is a hierarchy not of rank, but of merit, and the nobility of character remains fundamentally democratic and open to all who are worthy of it. Yet if character is an attribute that cannot be monopolized, its universality remains a matter of potential, not of actual fact. In the real world, it remains a scarce resource that when accumulated can be offered as the moral collateral through which social and even financial credit could be obtained: "Character is property. It is the noblest of possessions. It is an estate in the general good-will and respect of men; and they who invest in it, though they may not become rich in this world's goods...will find their reward in esteem and reputation fairly won."[46]

The ambiguities of this new bourgeois ideology of character reflect the transitional nature of the experience of that class. Despite his populist identification with the common man from whose ranks he arose, the parvenu was nonetheless concerned to establish conditions for the formation of a legitimate elite. With its implicit critique of the old elite of privilege, the concept of character became double edged, justifying a new elite of merit that would stand on firmer ground. Those who failed its competitive test of membership could not complain of arbitrary exclusion. In the eyes of the successful new bourgeois who saw himself as the embodiment of character, such individuals had only themselves to blame.

Anxiety and anomie

If the ideology of character provided retrospective justification for the new bourgeoisie after its triumph, it offered only limited guidance and sustenance for individual members at an earlier stage before success had been achieved. Largely freed from traditional restraints, the young immigrant could, indeed, see the opportunities that might allow him to reach his goal. After his arrival in Bradford in 1822, the new Baptist minister Rev. Benjamin Godwin realized that, "A new field of action was opened to me affording larger scope than any in which I had hitherto moved."[47] The town was a hive of activity filled with others equally determined to get ahead:

> In the principal thoroughfares...might be seen, especially on a market day, rolling along and scattering the mud or dust around them, carts, waggons, and drays, laden to the utmost of the horses' power with coals, stones, lime, timber, ironwork, stuff pieces, and huge piles of wool;...

[46] Ibid., 18.
[47] Godwin, "Autobiography," 367.

All whom I met in the streets seemed to have an air of business and determination about them.[48]

Yet at this point in a man like Godwin's career, when success was still a distant hope, this vibrant urban setting could also appear as a frightening environment in which the individual could easily lose direction and be swallowed up. Upon his arrival, Godwin experienced an initial sense of disorientation that must have been more widespread:

> In all the precincts of the town, the roughness of almost all classes seemed to me, on coming from the South, very strange, to have stones or mud thrown at you by little ragamuffins who lived on the roadside was no uncommon thing. . . . In addition to these things, the language, especially of the working classes and the villagers, and the tones of speaking seemed very uncouth. I was often quite at a loss as to their meaning. . . . I found that I was in a new social element altogether, where all was activity, energy, determination, independence, with not a little that was plain, rough, and stern, but that with these qualities were combined much of hospitality, generosity and sincerity.[49]

As Godwin and his contemporaries were aware, to navigate in so unstructured an environment was to subject oneself to enormous risks, to take a gamble that was not merely economic, but psychological too. Not surprisingly, he confessed that, "Though conscious of the right motives . . . I felt no little anxiety respecting the results."[50] This nagging sense of anxiety that Godwin and others experienced, the constant threat of failure and the danger of sinking into a void, could only be combated by husbanding all one's material and psychological resources, vigilantly grasping at each opportunity, and avoiding every temptation along the way. The ambition that brought these men to town could easily lead to disastrous results. As Rev. J. P. Chown wrote a generation later, to "sever them from the associations of a pious home," even in the name of "commendable enterprise, and diligent desire to do well for themselves in all that is right and praiseworthy" was to thrust temptations before young men who had not yet reached maturity and who desperately needed religion to guide them on their path.[51]

Clearly, the puritan moral and religious legacy that these men had inherited from their families would be critical in guiding them along the rocky road to worldly success. In fact, the salvation-centered psychology of Nonconformist Calvinism in which most of these individuals had been raised, proved perfectly suited to their existential dilemma as young, anxiety-ridden immigrant pilgrims making their progress in an uncertain competitive, urban-

---

[48] Ibid., 364.
[49] Ibid.
[50] Ibid., 367.
[51] J. P. Chown, *Sermons, with a Brief Sketch of his Life* (Bradford, 1875), 44–6.

industrial world. The man who aspired to make himself could find a reflection of his inner loneliness in the private divinity of the Protestant creed. Its spiritual claim of salvation or damnation at the hands of an unknowable God was an apt metaphor for his own sense of perpetual suspension between a worldly success or material failure that depended on the action of impersonal forces beyond his conscious control.[52] The merchant Henry Mitchell was only abstracting from his own experience when he imagined an atomistic, free-enterprise heaven that, unlike earth, could never be socialized. On judgment day it was each man for himself.[53]

To be sure, a religious sensibility so radically egocentric was more likely to intensify than to assuage feelings of anxiety, but at least it provided a cultural vehicle through which anomie could openly be expressed. More to the point, the puritan ethic of worldly asceticism, although it offered no illusions of comfort or fantasies of assurance, promised a real solution to distress. The idea that mankind was enjoined to the service of God, not through mystical contemplation, but through disciplined, purposive, worldly work was accepted by every Nonconformist Protestant sect. Even the Methodists, who had abandoned the Calvinist predestinarianism that Baptists and Congregationalists continued to embrace, saw sobriety, diligence, and industry as visible signs that the individual who exhibited them stood in God's grace.[54] "If the fruit of the spirit be not evidenced in the life and conversation," argued a local Wesleyan class-leader's book, "there is no proof of his indwelling." The leader was admonished to make his members "deeply sensible that a lawful occupation, properly managed, is no hinderance at all to religion."[55]

As a devout Wesleyan, Isaac Holden shared these views, which he expressed to his somewhat more skeptical wife:

> I do not see why we should not live a truly Christian life even amidst the busiest concerns of the world. We may pursue its active duties and enjoy the privileges and pleasures pertaining to our rank and circumstances in the world and yet serve Christ. It is not necessary to go out of the world to be his servants. That is an old and superstitious idea.[56]

By the time Holden wrote this, success had made him somewhat complacent, for he neglected a point of which, in his youth, he had been painfully aware. It was not enough for worldly activity to be compatible with God's service, it had to *be* the godly service itself, conducted not to obtain "privileges and

---

[52] Weber, *Protestant Ethic,* 53.

[53] W. J. Heaton, *Bradford's First Freeman: Sir Henry Mitchell* (London, 1913), 49.

[54] Weber, *Protestant Ethic,* 139–4.

[55] E. P. Thompson, *The Making of the English Working Class* (New York, 1963), 369; Holden/ Bradford, 54, "Methodist Class Book."

[56] *Holden–Illingworth,* I. Holden – S. Holden, Aug. 24, 1853.

pleasures," but to harness one's spirit to a yoke of self-discipline and a regime of perpetual self-denying toil. For the young Holden and many others like him, anxiety could not be assuaged. The dangers of rootlessness and of falling into the material or moral abyss were all too real. However, with God's help they might successfully be resisted by the repression of wayward instincts and by a commitment to disciplined labor and rigid self-control.[57] Self-renunciation in the name of self-fulfillment: This was to be the fate of the self-made man. His irony, which the Protestant ethic so wonderfully captured, was that, to realize his goal of self-cultivation, he would have to subordinate his will to some ulterior purpose. His energy, his labor, his very personality would have to be sublimated to the demands of some arbitrary calling that came as a mysterious voice from beyond.

Careers and callings

To find a career that could also be a calling, a form of worldly work that could be sanctified as a godly service – this was a task that most ambitious young Nonconformists who came to Bradford could scarcely avoid. Of course, not all were equally troubled by this dilemma; the language of worldly asceticism spoke more powerfully to some than it did to others. Those who inherited a position or a family business might find the quest for divine favor to be less relevant to their predicament. But to those who had to make their own way and bear responsibility for success or failure, the selection of a vocation could be a moment of almost unbearable anxiety, relieved only by the anticipation of some providential sign that one had chosen correctly and found a redemptive calling through which the grace of God would shine.

But wither did the hand of providence lead? The equation of the Protestant ethic with the spirit of capitalism, so obvious in retrospect, was by no means self-evident at the time; for a striking number of the earnest young men who ended up as successful entrepreneurs in Victorian Bradford had not originally intended to become capitalists at all. As a youth, Titus Salt had hoped to become a physician, whereas both W. E. Forster and the merchant J. V. Godwin had aspired to legal careers. However, their parents could not afford to pay for the requisite training, so the young men entered the worsted trade.[58] Even Isaac Holden hoped to become a minister or

---

57　Stephen Marcus, *The Other Victorians* (New York, 1964); G. J. Barker-Benfield, "The Spermatic Economy: A Nineteenth Century View of Sexuality," *Feminist Studies*, 1:1 (1972).

58　Reid, *Forster*, 1:36–8; Godwin, "Autobiography," 528–9; in the case of Salt, failure to pursue medical training was the result not only of parental impecuniousness, but also of providential signs that he might be unsuited to the calling. Balgarnie, *Salt*, 29–30.

schoolteacher, and it was only after several frustrating years of self-doubt and career stagnation that he concluded that his talents might be put to better use in a business career.[59]

The superiority of entrepreneurship over other possible callings, particularly in the professions, was by no means obvious when these men were in their youths. Neither self-interest nor some larger aspirations to social usefulness pointed unequivocally in the direction of the worsted trade. Before the 1830s, its economic horizons were shrouded in uncertainty in a world where business suffered from low status and financial insecurity.[60] Even in a backwater like the West Riding, the professions might appear to offer not only greater security and perhaps higher incomes, but also more status and self-esteem for those who could afford to join them. Professional work could be more easily seen as an act of service to God or the community than private enterprise in business for oneself. In particular, the ministry seemed a natural choice for many serious-minded and hardworking young men. Ministerial work was intellectually stimulating, it carried high status within the community, and provided a modest but respectable income. Moreover, the cost of training was less prohibitive than in the case of other professions since a theological education could be picked up cheaply at one of the small local denominational colleges. Finally, of course, what more conspicuous way could there be of serving God than to preach his gospel?[61]

Yet to the self-denying Calvinist mind, the attractiveness of a ministerial career was itself sufficient grounds for suspicion. Benjamin Godwin, Isaac Holden, John Wood, and Thomas Taylor experienced the same dilemma on this score. Wood was ready to begin his training when he "began to be of the opinion that the encomiums which had been heaped upon me by some of my friends had a tendency to encourage my feelings of vanity and pride." "I therefore gave up all thoughts of ever becoming a minister."[62] Wood, like Holden and others, could justify his secular calling in religious terms more easily than those earlier desires for a ministerial career, which had seemed tainted by selfish motives. Moreover, as the new generation of entrepreneurs was to show, the character of entrepreneurship in Bradford was itself changing. This change was being recognized by perceptive Nonconformist theologians like the radical Congregationalist minister Edward Miall, who distinguished the older type of capitalism, which seemed largely speculative and immoral, from the new type of industry, which, when con-

---

[59] Holden/Bradford/Brotherton.

[60] Edward Miall, *The British Churches in Relation to the British People* (London, 1849), 311–17.

[61] W. J. Reader, *Professional Men* (London, 1966), 1–42; Lucy Fraser, *Memoir of Daniel Fraser* (Bradford, 1905), 36–120; Godwin, "Autobiography," xxvii–xxxii.

[62] John Wood, *Autobiography* (Bradford, 1877), 18–20; Godwin, "Autobiography," 164.

ducted in a properly Christian spirit, was more conducive to "temperance, benevolence, forbearance [and] meekness" than any other occupation, including his own.[63] Indeed, nothing was more likely to facilitate that subtle blend of self-sacrificing obedience with self-realizing command essential to the development of Christian virtue as economic enterprise directed toward rational and productive ends:

> It accustoms us to subordination – for "method" as is proverbial "is the soul of business" [yet] it raises us to posts of responsibility and government.... It places our earthly lot so far within our own reach as to hold out an almost certain reward for diligence and frugality – and yet its issues are so far beyond our individual control ... as to throw us most sensibly upon the over ruling providence of God.[64]

Through its role in promoting commerce, peace, and prosperity throughout the world, mass production could be viewed as a missionary agent propagating to the most backward and benighted continents the spiritual gospel of Christian love:

> Trade multiplies our relations with our fellow men.... It creates countless grades of mutual dependence and necessitates mutual trust in all its stages.... I can scarcely conceive of a high cultivation of spiritual life in this world ... save by means and arrangements partaking very closely of the nature of trade.[65]

If the new entrepreneurship could be glorified as a means of serving God, its role as a vehicle for upward mobility was becoming even clearer. By the late 1830s, it was evident that the young man who hoped to rise in Bradford would be most likely to do so by going into business either in the primary worsted industrial sector or, alternatively, in the secondary urban-service economy. When the members of the new bourgeois generation chose their careers, 36 percent of them went into worsted enterprises, whereas 46 percent went into urban-service trades and only 13 percent became professionals.[66] That this decision to opt for an entrepreneurial career could help resolve anxieties and religious doubts can be seen from an examination of several cases in which the postadolescent search for a calling was experienced as a much deeper crisis of identity that was resolved only through subsequent achievement in the world.

As a young man of nineteen in the throes of deciding among teaching, the ministry, and an entrepreneurial career, Isaac Holden experienced a

---

[63] Miall, *British Churches*, 294.
[64] Ibid., 296.
[65] Ibid., 296–7.
[66] See Table 6–2.

religious crisis in which he articulated his feelings of self-doubt in terms of his relationship to God: "O how much I lament over my baseness. It is indeed a mercy that I am spared. Alas, I feel little heavenly soundness... I feel that I have been very inattentive to and very unconscious about the Eternal welfare of my dear friends.... I have also been awfully inattentive to my own."[67] Yet two months later he wrote in his *Journal*, "I have this morning had a blessed time in communion with my God. I have been, for some time, under a cloud, but glory to his name I can now say; now I have found the ground whereon my soul's anchor may remain."[68]

These rapid emotional oscillations are uncharacteristic of the mature Holden. After his decision five years later that God had, in fact, called him to go into business, he appears psychologically to have settled down. By 1835, his old teacher John Kennedy was able to congratulate him: "You have now, my dear Isaac, all that the world can afford to make you happy. Health, affluence, honour, and what is no less valuable as an element of happiness than these, an employment suited to your talents and sufficient to engage most of your energies."[69] For his part, Isaac, though by no means a superstitious man, was ready to see the guiding hand of divine providence behind his subsequent business success. In 1849, he explained to his unhappy wife why it was necessary to pull up roots and open a factory in France: "Providence, I believe, has called me to be here. As a man of business I enter into the most inviting openings that Providence places before me, and there remain with contented mind, till providence again directs my path into a course more desirable."[70]

Holden's brother-in-law, Jonas Sugden, experienced a similar postadolescent identity crisis in which he too was tortured by an acute preoccupation with his spiritual unworthiness.

> I have now lived almost twenty-two years, upwards of five of which I have professed to be a follower of Jesus Christ. But I see the whole abounds with defects, shortcomings, breaches of promise, and neglect of taking up the cross; yea, sin has been attached to the whole of my conduct.... O Lord, when shall I be delivered from my lowness and become wholly devoted to thee?[71]

Doubtful of his abilities and in need of clearly defined goals, young Sugden made a covenant with God to help him expand a small business inheritance. "Thou knowest Lord, that without thy aid I can do nothing;

[67] Holden/Bradford, 1B, *Journal*, Mar. 10, 1826.
[68] Ibid., May 8, 1826.
[69] Holden/Brotherton, B. A. 5/9, J. Kennedy – I. Holden, Apr. 7, 1835.
[70] Holden/Bradford, 22, I. Holden – S. Holden, Jan. 10, 1851.
[71] Jonas Sugden, "Journal," in Hardy, *Commerce and Christianity*, 57.

but by thee strengthening me I can do everything."[72] As his factory grew more profitable and as he put his system of worker discipline into effect, Sugden felt that he had truly been called to his labor and felt duty bound to reinvest the bulk of his profits in ways that would further redound to the glory of God. "There was no selfishness in his earnest heart," his biographer insisted, as "it was for others rather than himself that he undertook his formidable task. . . . The vision before him was not that of mansion, equipage, and rank: but of prosperous brothers and happy sisters . . . of a whole neighborhood, through every one of its classes and constituents, moral in character, comfortable in its homes, and hallowed in its religious principles."[73] Personal success was thus transmuted into providential destiny as Sugden's apparently selfless determination to help others seemed to sanctify the calling by which he would help himself:

> The rise of Mr. Sugden was not the effect of chance. . . . It was the result of deep thought, a settled plan, and invincible determination. He saw that in the free constitution of this country, the recent improvements in machinery, the enterprise of the age, and the openings for trade that are appearing in every part of the world, an opportunity was presented to the manufacturers of Britain without an equal at any other period.[74]

If Holden and Sugden, after wrestling with temptation, took the risks of entrepreneurship and received their rewards, Thomas Taylor, the son of Bradford's Congregationalist minister, was unable to resolve his quest for a godly and fulfilling career in so straightforward a way. Like Holden, and many others of his class and generation, he was initially attracted to the ministry but feared that his motives might be impure. At the age of fifteen, he was apprenticed to a merchant, but finding the work unrewarding, he left two years later to take up printing.[75] However, it was not long before a dramatic conversion experience made him conclude that his original goal of the pulpit had been the correct choice after all: "I am now convinced it is not mere vanity, disaffection with my present situation or seeking after more ease or worldly fame that drives me on. Rather, I want to lead others down the righteous path."[76]

However, this resolve did not put an end to young Taylor's religious anxieties, which grew only more intense in the following years. He continued to call himself "the vilest of sinners," though his only sins seem to have been nocturnal thoughts, perhaps impulses to masturbate: "Last night I felt

[72] Sugden, "Journal," 57.
[73] Hardy, *Commerce and Christianity*, 186.
[74] Ibid.
[75] W. S. Matthews, *Memoirs and Select Remains of Thomas Rawson Taylor* (London, 1836), 8–9.
[76] Ibid., 9, 20.

the power of sin rising most malignantly within me and striving to lead me from God."[77] His obsessive fear of damnation soon began to manifest itself as masochism and necrophilia. Young Taylor both dreaded and longed to sink into nothingness. As he wrote several verses entitled "Communion with the Dead," he castigated himself, writing, "I know I must be purged from my dross, and if this can only be done by the refining fire, let the furnace be heated seven times hotter than its wont."[78] A serious illness was simply grist for his self-flagellation: "I think this affliction has been sent also that I may be better able to preach about afflictions."[79] Though Taylor, too, might eventually have shed his guilt and discovered his identity, he did not appear to be headed that way at the age of twenty-eight when, racked by physical weakness and emotional exhaustion, he sank into his premature grave.

Perhaps there was no connection between Taylor's psychological and physical demise and his failure to answer the call of entrepreneurial capitalism. However, men like Holden and Sugden as well as many others among mid-Victorian Bradford's industrial magnates saw an intimate connection between their personal success and their readiness to follow the dictates of production and accumulation and to subordinate themselves to the logic of impersonal market forces that were beyond their control. Their success in "making themselves" was a social triumph, but it was purchased at a certain psychological cost. It was their irony that the act of self-creation was also an act of self-denial, a subordination of all their energy, creativity, talent, and skill to the pursuit of an end that came from outside them and operated according to laws all its own. The sense of having violated some inner integrity to assume an entrepreneurial identity, which came as a call from beyond, was usually repressed in the rush of daily living or rationalized through the self-sacrificing ethic of the puritan creed. However, some, like W. E. Forster, who were unusually self-conscious, felt an undercurrent of dissatisfaction even as they began to rise in the world. To Forster, "the majority of those around him were too deeply immersed in the pursuit of wealth." Yet for all that Bradford seemed "a decidedly uncongenial atmosphere," it was one that he and many others like him had chosen to enter and had determined to master and make their own.[80]

[77] Ibid., 25, 37.
[78] Ibid. 78.
[79] Ibid.
[80] Reid, *Forster*, 1:82.

8

The life of the self-denying entrepreneur

To become an entrepreneur in nineteenth-century Bradford was to subject oneself to the dictates of external imperatives – to subordinate oneself to a powerful transforming force that exacted a heavy price in hard work and self-denial, without any assurance of success. For the young parvenu without substantial initial capital, competition imposed a regime of abstinence and austerity for the mere chance that an uncertain reward might be reaped.

Abstinence and opportunity

Those who began with least had to work hardest, often delaying aspirations toward independent proprietorship by starting as an employee of someone else. As late as 1851, 15 percent of the bourgeois householders at work in the worsted industry were not independent proprietors, but salaried employees.[1] The most obvious way for such men to accumulate capital was to save as much as possible from the salaries they received. However, in most cases, this was a slow and ultimately futile endeavor. In mid-nineteenth-century Bradford, the typical salary of a junior clerk was somewhere between £50 and £100 per year. At best, such men could hope, like William Drummond, to get a job in "a respectable mercantile or manufacturing establishment where I could expect progressive advancement" and to be "not fastidious as to the salary for the first year."[2]

Although talented managers were rare and men who proved their worth could receive substantial raises – sometimes even a percentage of profit was paid out – they rarely earned enough to accumulate sufficient capital to set up on their own. Joseph Wilson began working for the Rands at the age of twenty at an annual salary of £60. Thirty-five years later, when his income

[1] 1851 bourgeois census population (HO, 107/2305–10). See Appendix A.
[2] Holden Papers in Brotherton Library, University of Leeds (hereafter referred to as Holden/Brotherton), B.A. 5/6.

had risen to £500, he was ready to start his own business, but by then he was on the verge of old age.[3] Isaac Holden, who was more impatient, began working for the Townends in 1830 at a salary of £100, which rose to 6 percent of the profits (or about £500 per annum) by the time he quit fifteen years later. The £2,300 he saved from this and other sources left the business he established so underfinanced that it almost went bankrupt after one year.[4] Even for employees of large firms, like Henry Forbes, William Walker, and Wilson Sutcliffe, who eventually became partners in their firms, the terms of partnership varied widely. Only very rarely, when the senior partner had no sons or business heirs of his own, could an employee hope to take over the firm.[5]

Although owning a business was generally more lucrative than working for someone else, small firms in the staple trade and the urban-service sector sometimes brought in less than a skilled manager could expect to earn. Although the entrepreneur had more control over his expenditures, there were enormous incentives for plowing back profit into the firm to make it the kind of enterprise on which long-term prosperity could be based. Consequently, the parvenu, whether salaried or self-employed, was obliged to adopt a long regime of personal austerity.

To maximize their investment in the accumulation process, entrepreneurs strove to keep their living expenses to a minimum. A bachelor could live frugally by going into lodgings and by avoiding frivolous or unnecessary expenses. Aspiring young men like Jacob Behrens and W. E. Forster saved a great deal by spending years as lodgers in the homes of respectable widows.[6] As late as 1851, almost 10 percent of the householders in the bourgeois census population (mostly those headed by women) took in one or more lodgers of whom 65 percent were either bourgeois or petit bourgeois by occupation. Similarly, 8 percent of the bourgeois census households contained nephews, nieces, or cousins of the householder, 57 percent of whom were old enough to be employed.[7]

Money could also be saved by restricting one's expenditures to necessities alone. Since these men generally spent almost all their time working and distrusted idleness and entertainment, this was not difficult to do. The theater

---

[3] Joseph Wilson, *His Life and Work*, (London, n.d.), 16, 21.

[4] Elizabeth Jennings, "Sir Isaac Holden, (1807–97)" (Bradford Ph.D. dissertation, 1982), 33–45; Holden/Brotherton, B.A. 5/6.

[5] William Cudworth, *Histories of Bolton and Bowling* (Bradford, 1891); J. T. Ward, "Two Pioneers of Industrial Reform," *Journal of Bradford Textile Society* (Bradford, 1963–4), 35–51; *BO*, Oct. 18, 1870.

[6] Anon., *Sir Jacob Behrens* (London, n.d.), 38; T. Wemyss Reid, *The Life of the Right Honourable William Edward Forster* (London, 1888), 1:77.

[7] Calculated from HO, 107/2305–10. See Appendix A.

was off limits to orthodox Dissenters, and even novel reading was widely regarded as a potentially debilitating diversion from the serious business of productive life.[8] In contrast to the traditional gentleman-capitalist, the rising entrepreneur conceived of recreation in utilitarian terms, as those activities that were physically necessary to re-create one's capacity for work. By definition, it was limited to such purposive activities as self-education, physical exercise, and voluntary public or religious work.[9]

Even minor indulgences were only permitted when rationalized as means to some practical end. When Titus Salt saved up his first £1,000, he rewarded himself with the luxury of a gold watch.[10] The absence of play or spontaneous amusement from this entrepreneurial regimen made it possible to live on a very low budget and to devote almost all of one's waking hours to work. Up to a point, an ambitious young man could make up for lack of capital through increased labor. The salaried employee could improve his marketability by establishing a reputation for diligence, whereas the struggling self-employed businessman might keep himself on the cutting edge by working just a little harder than his competitors.[11] Entrepreneurs who also acted as day-to-day managers had to work at least as long as their employees, which generally meant a ten- to twelve-hour day. In his early years as an industrialist, S. C. Lister regularly kept his factory open from 6:30 in the morning to 7:30 at night.[12] If, like Holden or Salt, he wished to experiment with machinery, pursue private customers, or examine accounts, he could work up to fourteen or fifteen hours.[13]

To keep to such a routine, not only in the early years of a business, but for two or three decades, might well seem a pointless sacrificing of human spontaneity and youth. However, Bradford's rising entrepreneurs were not entirely mistaken in their belief that they could not afford to relax. Even after a firm had become established, its future was not automatically secure. Especially in the volatile conditions of the 1830s and 1840s, the specter of failure cast an omnipresent pall over entrepreneurial prospects. Bankruptcy, as Peronnet Thompson argued, was the Malthusianism of the middle class, the natural law that kept their numbers from expanding beyond the capacity of the economy to absorb them: "Bankruptcy is the check to the indefinite multiplication of traders as the evils arising from a diminished food are the

---

[8] Benjamin Godwin, "Autobiography" (mss., Bradford Central Library), 392; F. C. Byles, *William Byles* (Weymouth, 1932), 64–8.

[9] Peter Bailey, *Leisure and Class in Victorian England* (London, 1978), 56–77.

[10] Robert Balgarnie, *Sir Titus Salt* (London, 1877), 49.

[11] Reid, *Life of Forster*, 1:54.

[12] Anon., *Lord Masham, The Story of a Great Career* (Bradford, 1906), chap. 5.

[13] Anon., *Isaac Holden: From Draw Boy to M.P.* (Keighley, 1892), 11.

check to that of the inferior classes of labourers. Both take place when they do in consequence of a limitation of commerce."[14]

However, where unemployed and impoverished workers helped one another to get by, in the bourgeois community, the bankrupt risked becoming a social leper as the mere fact of business failure was treated as a moral stain.[15] Bankruptcy not only led to financial loss, but threatened scandal, proletarianization, and descent into poverty. In some cases, it actually led to imprisonment and, in most cases, to ostracism or, at best, a condescending sympathy from former colleagues who remained afloat. Before midcentury, no one was too well connected or established to be immune from fear of bankruptcy, and even thereafter, the fear would resurface during cyclical crises when demand and credit grew suddenly tight.[16]

Bankruptcies were most common among the small retailers of the urban-service sector, and with each commercial depression, as consumer incomes dropped and poor rates soared, a procession of lower-middle-class shopkeepers filed their way into bankruptcy court. However, the depressions also brought a wave of bankruptcies in the industrial-capitalist sector where the repercussions were much more serious. Once again, it was the cyclical periods of depression when the problem became most acute. Between 1837 and 1841 alone, thirty-one firms in the factory district around Thornton Road were forced to call in their creditors and wind up affairs.[17]

In fact, most entrepreneurs had at least one bout with near insolvency at some point in their career. Isaac Holden came to the brink of bankruptcy in the trade depression of 1848. Few young capitalists had more initial advantages than J. V. Godwin, yet it took him nearly a decade to find his feet. In 1840, his father noted, "John has been working energetically and with much business talent since his apprenticeship and has done little besides increasing the business considerably and getting it in order." It was not until the boom of 1844 that his father, somewhat prematurely, dared to express relief: "I had the satisfaction of knowing that after years of almost unrequited toil he was succeeding in business."[18] Even the spectacularly successful firms

---

[14] T. Perronet Thompson, *Exercises, Political and Other* (London, 1842), 4:523.

[15] *BO*, Mar. 5, May 28, Dec. 31, 1857; Jan. 14, 1858.

[16] William Byles must have touched a raw memory in many of his listeners when he reviewed this phenomenon from the retrospective comfort of 1866. "They saw men struggling and toiling," he recollected, "eating the bread of carefulness that they might acquire riches, and yet, after many years of severe labour many of them succumbing under the pressure of adverse circumstances and in a worse plight than when they began their career."*BO*, Jan. 6, 1842, May 31, 1866.

[17] *BO*, Jan. 27, 1842; Mar. 19, 1846.

[18] Godwin, "Autobiography," 569, 691.

like Lister's, Salt's, and John Foster's Black Dyke Mills were not out of danger, since profits tended to fluctuate wildly from year to year and an overrapid commitment to capital investment might leave even the strongest dangerously exposed. This appears to have happened to S. C. Lister, whose worsted empire nearly unraveled during the credit crisis of 1857.[19]

Such near failures left deep scars, and even the most successful of Bradford's entrepreneurs were hesitant to change their approach even after their fortunes had been made. For nearly his entire life, Isaac Holden suffered from a sense of insecurity. Even in 1859, when he was making profits of over £30,000 per year, he warned his eldest and entirely respectable son, Angus, "It is astonishing how the best business may be the means of sinking a fortune, and that soon, by mismanagement."[20]

It was this fear, half rational and half conditioned, of losing everything in a moment of weakness that kept these men with their noses to the grindstone for so long after they might have chosen to relax. Afraid of sinking into the economic abyss, their work provided them with an anchor for their personalities and led many of them to neglect other interests and pursuits. In contrast to the traditional gentleman-capitalist, who subordinated accumulation to his quest for gentility, the entrepreneurial capitalist of the 1830s and 1840s subordinated himself to the accumulation process as an end in itself. Capitalism, which had once been a mere economic underpinning in Bradford, changed under his auspices into a revolutionary, transforming force. Nevertheless, those who directed its accumulation process were not social leaders, but in the words of the local poet Ben Preston, "a race of moles that burrowed in the earth and needed not the sunshine of amusement: a generation that was forever hungering and thirsting, scraping and saving – on weekdays saving money, and on Sundays striving and hoping in the very insanity of avarice to save even their own joyless, worthless, miserable souls."[21]

Marriage and family formation

That preoccupation with the affairs of business could be carried too far was acknowledged even among the new bourgeoisie. In 1846, at Horton Lane Chapel, Rev. Glyde warned a congregation filled with upwardly mobile young capitalists "of the man who denying himself the pleasures in which others

[19] E. M. Sigsworth, *Black Dyke Mills* (Liverpool, 1958), 220; Jennings, "Isaac Holden," 87; *BO*, Dec. 17, 1857.

[20] *Holden-Illingworth Letters* (Bradford, 1927), 258.

[21] Ben Preston, "Sarah and t' Playgoers," *Yorkshireman's Comic Annual* (cutting, Bradford Central Library).

innocently indulge and suffering the social affections to die within his bosom, devotes himself to labor and anxiety, for no purpose, and spends life in poverty, only that he may die rich."[22] Although the necessary counterpoint to productive labor could not be expected to come from the struggling young entrepreneur himself, marrying and raising a family was one way to create a space in life relatively free from the imperatives of the market. As Rev. Godwin pointed out when he feared that his son John was too absorbed in business,

> Your necessarily occupied time and the multiplicity of business endanger the due remembrance of what relates to our highest and most permanent interests, and, you have no "help meet" no one when you retire from the warehouse to whisper in your ear thoughts of holier and better things, to encourage you in domestic devotions, but you are left a prey to all the solitudes of business from the morning light to the evening shade, if not on your solitary pillow.[23]

As if this were not enough, Mrs. Hanson, the wife of a local journalist and teacher, even wrote a poem entitled "To a Bachelor," in which she encouraged him to "picture the pleasure, contentment and peace comprised in home of *your own* / A sacred enclosure, a region of bliss Enjoyed by its inmates alone. / See the wife ever aiming the love to increase which won her young heart to be yours. / Possessing attractions that never can cease, – the virtue which always allures."[24]

As these quotes indicate, the job of creating a domestic space, of providing for the human needs of reproduction and comfort, was the special work of women just as productive labor was the work of men. To some extent, this had always been the case, but the separation of production from the household that industrial capitalism engendered, with its reconstitution of productive activity as a separate and autonomous sphere governed by competitive laws, meant that the functions of reproduction, which had previously been integrated (albeit in a subordinate position) into the traditional patriarchal household, now also had to be reconstituted as a separate sphere with its own distinct logic that stood under the management and control of the wife.[25]

These two developments, the separation of domesticity from production and the transfer of the wife from productive labor under paternal supervision

---

[22] Jonathan Glyde, *A Sermon Preached at Horton Lane Chapel* (Bradford, 1846), 5–6.
[23] Benjamin Godwin to J. V. Godwin, Nov. 20, 1843, in Godwin, "Autobiography"; J. A. Banks, *Prosperity and Parenthood* (London, 1954), 69.
[24] Mrs. James Hanson, *Poems and Tales of Social Life* (Bradford, 1868), 201.
[25] Barbara Welter, "The Cult of True Womanhood," *American Quarterly*, 78 (1966). For Britain, this process has now been traced masterfully by Leonore Davidoff and Catherine Hall in *Family Fortunes, Men and Women of the English Middle Class, 1780–1850* (Chicago, 1987), which appeared when this book was in the editorial stage.

to a new role as quasi-autonomous domestic manager, were, for the bourgeoisie, largely completed by the middle of the century. The 1851 census manuscripts reveal that the bourgeois domestic economy had achieved autonomy in all but a few cases, although a great deal of overlap between household and workplace remained among Bradford's lower middle class, and the proletariat scarcely possessed any viable domestic space at all.

Only 6.6 percent of the 1851 bourgeois census households contained live-in employees, and these were almost all concentrated in a few specific occupations such as stuff merchants. Not surprisingly, virtually no bourgeois wives (only 2 percent) worked outside the home. Although many wives clearly played a critical behind-the-scenes economic role that the census does not record, only 4 percent were listed as working for their husbands and, in 67 percent of these cases, there were three or more children living at home, at least one of whom was old enough to run the household.[26] In the lower middle class, particularly among the families of shopkeepers, it was quite common for wives to work in the family business. Yet among the higher bourgeoisie, the domestic economy under the wife's direction had, by mid-century, been almost entirely separated from the sphere of production in which she rarely played a direct part.[27]

Supporting a separate domestic establishment was a relatively expensive proposition that necessarily drew into the sphere of immediate consumption resources that might otherwise have been accumulated as capital. Setting up a household was generally reckoned to require about 80 percent of a year's income. Then, more money was needed to maintain it and still more to raise children.[28] A small family could live modestly on £200 per annum and could survive for £100. However, even these sums were beyond the reach of many parvenus before their mid or late twenties, and the desire to save often induced them to postpone marriage until they were even older.[29]

[26] Theodore Koditschek, "Class Formation and the Bradford Bourgeoisie; 1750–1870" (Princeton, Ph.D. dissertation, 1981), 6, 593.

[27] Hall and Davidoff find a broadly similar pattern in their studies of Birmingham, Essex, and Suffolk, *Family Fortunes*, 272–315, 357–75, although they see a slower process and lay greater emphasis on the hidden contribution of women to family enterprises. In part, this is a product of their focus on regions that were less economically dynamic than industrializing Bradford. Nevertheless, their sensitive exploration of the latter subject suggests a level of hidden involvement that my own analysis has not captured, and their work on this point should be consulted as a supplement to the present book. As the *Bradford Observer* noted, even when wives were not formally involved in the family business, prudence counseled that a wise husband would keep her informed about the general state of his affairs, *BO*, Nov. 11, 1858.

[28] Though a bourgeois family in Bradford could get by on considerably less than the £300–500 minimum that London guidebooks suggested, most young men had difficulty obtaining amounts that were a good deal less. Banks, *Prosperity and Parenthood*, 44–5.

[29] *BO*, Nov. 29, 1855.

Though the dangers of improvident marriage were often exaggerated, the necessity of keeping up appearances while maintaining a large family on an insufficient income was one of the leading causes of bankruptcy among smaller businessmen. The draper H. F. Newell, for example, became insolvent in 1855 after his £100 profits failed to cover his £569 household expenses. A year later, a grocer spent £763 and went bankrupt when his profits fell to £392.[30]

Under these circumstances, it is not surprising that many ambitious young men were wary of marriage until they felt that their positions were secure. Jacob Behrens was so worried about financial solvency that, to his mother's horror, he delayed marrying until the age of thirty-eight. By this standard, Titus Salt, Henry Mitchell, and Arthur Briggs were comparative youngsters when they married at the age of twenty-seven. William Byles tied the knot when he was thirty, and although his domestic economy was "never cheap and nasty," his son recalled, "There were times when Ashfield housekeeping had to be economical."[31]

When men, daunted by such prospects, decided to wait, it was up to women, who could acquire authority only through the creation of a domestic economy, to soften prospective partners with a vision of the charms of domestic life. Domestic responsibilities could sometimes serve even more powerfully than individual ambition as a timely prod in the struggle to succeed. In another story, Mrs. Hanson's bachelor, "conscious of many cares," was reconciled to facing them by the knowledge that he could share them with a loving wife:

> He knew that there was an incessant demand on his purse for the means of supplying food, clothes, and other necessaries... great as were his anxieties and deep as were the responsibilities connected with this active and youthful group, Ned felt that they were each and all precious to his heart, and that for their welfare he could joyfully continue, and if need be redouble his cares and toils.[32]

Even if the young entrepreneur agreed with Ned that it was time to marry, he might discover an appropriate partner was hard to find. Unlike the town's traditional elites, the new bourgeoisie was a class in transition and lacked established social networks for initiating courtship. As upstarts they were excluded from the fancy-dress bachelors balls, which, in any case, they would probably have eschewed as frivolous. However, there were few alternative social opportunities for meeting eligible members of the opposite sex from the same social level as themselves. Consequently, it was left to the family,

[30] *BO,* Jul. 30, 1855.

[31] Anon., *Sir Jacob Behrens,* 42; Byles, *William Byles,* 67; Balgarnie, *Salt,* 55–7; W. J. Heaton, *Bradford's First Freeman: Sir Henry Mitchell* (London, 1913), chap. 6; Anon., *Memorial of Arthur Briggs* (Bradford, 1893), 13.

[32] Hanson, *Poems and Tales,* 66–88.

Table 8–1. *Bourgeois census population: birthplace of husband by birthplace of wife in households headed by married couples* (N = 986)

	Percentage of husbands born in Bradford	Percentage of husbands born elsewhere in Yorkshire	Percentage of husbands born elsewhere	Subtotal
Percentage of wives born in Bradford	16	11	3	30
Percentage of wives born elsewhere in Yorkshire	11	28	8	47
Percentage of wives born elsewhere	3	6	14	23
Subtotal	30	45	25	100

Source: Calculated from 1851 census mss. for Bradford (HO, 107/2305–10). See Appendix A.

the religious congregation, and one's own initiative to find an acceptable spouse.

With only these resources, the overwhelming majority of Bradford's new male bourgeoisie sought wives outside of town (Table 8-1). It is not surprising that 79 percent of all married immigrants among them had wives who were born elsewhere. However, it is striking that 47 percent of the married natives also had immigrant wives. Many of these matches were made through family connections, and it was not uncommon, as in the case of the Holdens and Illingworths, for several members of two families to intermarry. Some people were even driven to marry their own distant relations. William Byles's daughter, for example, married her cousin and Joseph Farrar noted seven cross-cousin marriages within his own extended clan.[33] Denominational connections were another channel through which spouses could be obtained from a distance. Both William Byles and Titus Salt found their wives in this manner. In Salt's case, the courtship was abetted by his frequent business travels. Indeed, the Congregationalist farmer from Grimsby, whose daughter Titus married, betrothed three of his daughters to Bradford entrepreneurs.[34]

[33] Joseph Farrar, *Autobiography* (Bradford, 1889), 19; Byles, *William Byles*, 79.
[34] Byles, *William Byles*, 29–30, 52; Balgarnie, *Salt*, 55–7.

However, for many men, finding a wife, like so much else, depended primarily on their own initiative. Samuel Midgeley met his wife at a rehearsal of their village choral society, whereas Joseph Wilson met his, even more casually, at a plot day party at his cousin's house.[35] Some young men, like Joseph Farrar, exhibited still greater resourcefulness. As a shop employee, he eyed attractive female customers until he found one whom his mates assured him was fair game. He then contrived to meet her several times apparently by accident, once even following her to chapel in order to walk her home. After only a few such meetings he made his proposal to her, which ultimately was accepted. Two and a half years later they were married.[36]

Of course, the absence of rigid rules governing courtship and marriage, although creating obstacles that had to be surmounted, also engendered a freedom of individual choice that was impossible in aristocratic circles in which dynastic considerations were paramount. Although daughters still required parental approval, the actual choice of a partner was invariably in their hands. In the case of young men, already well into adulthood and financially independent, parents were generally notified and often consulted, but they rarely exercised or expected any right to veto.[37] Unlike the offspring of Bradford's gentlemen-capitalists, most of the new men were free to envision marriage as a personal rather than a family matter and often justified their choice of partner on romantic grounds. This was evidently the case with Benjamin Godwin who regarded his wife as "the name of a powerful spell" that "operated on me like an enchantment." Indeed, "the sight of a shoe that she had worn has to me been like a pilgrim."[38] Others, like Joseph Wilson, expressed their attachment in more prosaic terms: "When I was thinking of my own life companion my chief desire was that she should be a good girl: it didn't matter what her occupation was if she were only good ... she was of a good family, had not a sweetheart and her whole love would be centered on me." What is more, Wilson's parents "didn't think I could do better.... The matter was settled: She was a grand girl, a good girl with a passionate love for me – a real helpmeet."[39]

As Wilson's comments indicate, Bradford's upwardly mobile parvenus generally looked for wives who could help and support them in their careers,

---

[35] Samuel Midgley, *My Seventy Years Musical Memories, 1860–1930* (London, n.d.), 61–5; Joseph Wilson, *His Life and Work* (London, n.d.), 10.

[36] Farrar, *Autobiography*, 19.

[37] See Lawrence Stone, *The Family, Sex and Marriage, in England 1500–1800* (New York, 1979), 181–215; John Gillis, *For Better, For Worse, British Marriages, 1600 to the Present* (Oxford, 1985), 37, 119.

[38] Godwin, "Autobiography," 132.

[39] Wilson, *Life and Work*, 10.

who possessed feminized versions of the same qualities of character and industriousness that they valued in themselves. That mythical figure, the idle Victorian lady, was not much in evidence in Bradford, and local guide books warned women against developing "this sickly, sentimental sort of feeling that is frightened by a sudden rap at the door... or a rough looking fellow in the street."[40] To manage households with limited budgets, wives had to be hardheaded and hardworking. They were expected to keep busy raising children, doing needlework, and either directing servants or undertaking domestic chores themselves.[41]

Although it was not uncommon for these upwardly mobile young men to receive some financial benefit from their marriage, this was not uniformly the case. Those who married after they were already financially established were more likely to choose wives from better-off families and to make formal marriage settlements in which property would be consolidated or exchanged.[42] Such was the case with Isaac Holden who used his second wife's marriage settlement to bolster his credit rating, and to a lesser extent, with Joseph Farrar who was taken on by his father-in-law and eventually inherited the family shop. However, there is no reason to believe that either of these men married primarily for money, which did not, in any case, provide them with anything more than a wider range of opportunities that were up to them to turn to account.[43]

Underconsumption and the domestic economy

Engagement and courtship brought new desires and aspirations to the emergent bourgeoisie that could not always be easily reconciled with abstinence and the requirements of capital accumulation. The fulfillment of sexual appetites and emotional attachments, the desire to beget heirs, to-

[40] A. McKechnie, *The Right Sort of Stuff to Make a Woman* (Bingley, n.d.), 6.

[41] *BO*, Nov. 11, 1858, June 6, 1869; Godwin, "Autobiography," 220–31; Holden Mss. (Bradford University Library, 2), Sugden – S. Holden, June 12, 1859. McKechnie, *Right Sort of Stuff*. See also Davidoff and Hall, *Family Fortunes*, 380–8.

[42] Davidoff and Hall lay heavy emphasis on this process in one of the best and most original chapters of *Family Fortunes*, esp. 205–22. Here again, their emphasis reflects their focus on a provincial middle class that was more established and less wholeheartedly entrepreneurial than that of early-nineteenth-century Bradford. Later, when the children of Bradford's original parvenus married during the mid-Victorian period, their behavior was much closer to that which Davidoff and Hall describe.

[43] William Cudworth, *Historical Notes on the Bradford Corporation* (Bradford, 1881), 194; *Bradford Portraits* (Bradford, 1892); Farrar, *Autobiography*, 40–3; *Arthur Briggs*, 11; J. W. Turner, "Some Old Bradford Firms" (mss., Bradford Archives, D.B. 16/45).

gether with the prospect that a wife might help raise some money, or at least could help save some through domestic management, all contributed toward a deepening resolve that matrimony ought not to be indefinitely delayed. If incomes or profits did not rise with sufficient rapidity, the young man would be forced to marry under circumstances that could create serious budgetary strain.

When Isaac Holden obtained his position as bookkeeper with the Townends, though his salary was only £100, he felt secure enough about his future prospects to decide that marriage could not wait. As he informed the parents of his fiancee, "Kind providence after several changes and as many successes has placed me in proper circumstances.... I believe our wish is mutual that you would give your parental consent to our union."[44] Although Isaac encountered no opposition, William Byles faced a more difficult job of convincing his future father-in-law that an income of £150 to £200 was sufficient to support a wife. Joseph Wilson, whose early prospects were even dimmer, recalled, "I had only £80 at the time I was married and my employer thought that I was very brave to commence married life on such a small income."[45]

The only solution to this problem was to apply the same stringent habits of economy and austerity that these men had learned as bachelors to the ordering of their married households. Extreme abstinence was, of course, greatest among those, like struggling professionals and small-scale retailers, whose incomes were low.[46] However, even some of the most successful of the new entrepreneurs maintained plain households long after they might have become more indulgent. As late as 1865, Isaac Holden was moved to admit, "I still punish myself by my unconquerable desire to effect economies. How foolish it is to do so when one has enough to get through the world more easily."[47]

The birth of children, particularly when they came in rapid succession – more rapidly than incomes were able to rise – further increased the strains on the family budget and made household economy even more compelling than before. By 1851, 85 percent of Bradford's bourgeois nuclear families had children living with them, 44 percent with two or three. The mean age of household heads in those families with one or two coresiding children (34.6 years), or even of those with three or more (41.6 years), suggests that,

---

[44] Holden Mss. (Brotherton Library, B.A. 5/5, I. Holden – Mr. & Mrs. A. Love.

[45] Wilson, *Life and Work*, 10; Byles, *William Byles*, 29–31.

[46] Rev. Godwin, for example, had to support his entire family plus two parents while he was trying to finance his son's education. His only income was his £220 annual ministers salary. Godwin, "Autobiography," 490.

[47] *Holden-Illingworth Letters*, I. Holden – S. Holden, Oct. 3, 1865.

in most cases, maximum earning power was reached only after the children were already leaving.[48] In addition, the acute local shortage of decent middle-class housing was another problem that raised the cost of living in Bradford. As one harried house hunter lamented in 1851,

> I have traversed at least fifty or sixty miles [within Bradford] in search of a cottage whose rental shall lie between the limits of £7 and £14 per annum, and the search has been utterly futile...you may assail the proprietor of a house with the most rhetorical supplications; you may distract him with all the ingenuities of persuasion and fail.[49]

Bourgeois residential aspirations, at least before midcentury, were motivated, on the one hand, by the need to live as plainly as possible and, on the other hand, by the desire to get away from the low-lying city, which had become fouled by factories and working-class slums.[50] In 1851, only 7 percent of the bourgeois census householders lived in the downtown district amidst mills, warehouses, and the working class. At the same time, only a tiny minority moved out to a villa in the countryside, beyond the built-up area of town. Analysis of Bradford's electoral register for 1846 reveals that only 5 percent of the 1,966 £10 borough property holders resided beyond the boundaries of the borough, whereas an examination of the residential geography of the 1851 bourgeois census households indicates that 80 percent of those who lived within the borough resided in the built-up parts of town.[51]

There were several reasons why most bourgeois families remained close to the city. The absence of adequate rail connections before midcentury made retirement from daily work almost a precondition for moving beyond the borough and delayed the construction of garden suburbs on its outer edge. The desire for economy and plain living was an equally compelling reason that kept many within the crowded urban environment even after they might have been able to leave. Except for the tiny minority who remained in the industrial districts, mostly millowners determined to live by their works, Bradford's midcentury bourgeois families were congregated in three different types of neighborhoods. Eighteen percent of the 1851 bourgeois householders were scattered amidst the generally working-class and lower-middle-class neighborhoods that circled the downtown business district in the east, the south, and the southwest (see Fig. 4-3). Although these districts were considerably superior to the inner-city slum areas, they were still relatively

---

[48] Koditschek, "Bradford Bourgeoisie," 593.

[49] *BO*, Oct. 9, 1851.

[50] *BO*, Feb. 19, 1857.

[51] *Register of Electors for the Borough of Bradford*, (Bradford, 1846); 1851 bourgeois census population, HO, 107/2305–10.

marginal neighborhoods in the central town basin where smoke pollution and urban decay could not always be escaped.[52]

Another 15 percent of the bourgeois householders lived in the rows of townhouses that lined the streets north of Kirkgate, just above the center of the town (area A in Fig. 4-3). Although close to the downtown district, this neighborhood stood at an elevation, with larger, more regular, and attractive buildings designed for a respectable clientele. Its proximity to the downtown business and factory district made it desirable for stuff merchants, professionals, and substantial retailers.[53] However, the largest group of Bradford's 1851 bourgeois householders (40 percent) lived in two quasi-suburban residential districts that rose along the hillsides above the central town basin below. These two districts had been built almost entirely within the previous ten years. The Ordnance Survey Map prepared in 1849 shows small bourgeois housing developments of a block or two interspersed with open plots to be developed within the next ten years. These neighborhoods were primitive prototypes for the much more opulent villa suburbs that would spread like wildfire during the mid and late Victorian age.[54]

The first of these original suburban clusters to the north (see area B in Fig. 4-3), housed 24 percent of the bourgeoisie at midcentury. Although the street names Spring Gardens, Belgrave Place, Bellevue Place, Park Street, Victoria Street, Arcadia Street, Hanover Square, and Southfield Square speak of the developers' environmental aspirations, in reality, they contained tracts of comfortable but modest row houses with six to ten rooms apiece. On the west side of town, sloping uphill into Horton, arose a smaller cluster of residential neighborhoods (area C in Fig. 4-3) housing 16 percent of the midcentury bourgeois householders. These were similar to the ones in the north, although a few of the streets in this area such as Ashgrove and Summerseat Place contained expensive, detached houses on larger lots.[55]

The 1851 census was taken at a moment of transition when the first stirrings of a vast wave of bourgeois suburbanization were beginning to make themselves felt. By the 1880s, these spreading suburbs would etch the sloping high grounds of the borough with lines of elegant, detached villa estates. During the ten or twenty years before midcentury, the bourgeois desire to escape industrial pollution and inner-city decay took a less extravagant and

[52] Ordnance Survey (OS), *Map of Bradford; 6"-mile*, (London, 1850); 1851 bourgeois census population, HO, 107/2305–10.
[53] *OS, Map of Bradford;* 1851 bourgeois census population, HO, 107/2,304–10.
[54] John Hart, *Block Plan of Bradford* (Bradford, 1861); Milnes and French, *Map of Bradford Center* (Bradford, 1876); William Byles, *Plan of the Town and Environs of Bradford* (Bradford, 1887); *OS, Map of Bradford;* 1851 bourgeois census population, HO, 107/2,304–10.
[55] *OS, Map of Bradford;* 1851 bourgeois census population, HO, 107/2304–10.

more purely functional form as the first middle-class housing developments were opened on the bottom edges of the hillsides, rarely more than a half mile from the center of town.[56]

Nowhere was the early bourgeois commitment to abstinence and domestic austerity more evident than in attitudes toward keeping servants. Throughout much of nineteenth-century England, especially in the South, servantholding was regarded as a middle-class necessity. In Bradford, it was treated as a luxury that respectable, and even prosperous, families – such as one mill-owner with over 600 employees at work – might do without. Even at mid-century, excluding innkeepers whose servants were productive laborers, only 1,108 families, or about 5 percent of all families in town, kept live-in domestics. Only 336 families kept more than one servant whereas only a minuscule 114 kept more than two.[57]

Few families in lower-middle-class occupations kept any servants, and the practice was by no means universal, even among the industrialists, professionals, and large retail businessmen. Although servantholding was one of the criteria for inclusion in the 1851 bourgeois census population, over 12 percent of the group actually kept no servants but were included because they met other criteria for selection (see Appendix A). Keeping three or more domestics was very rare, even at the highest income levels, except among the few remaining scions of traditional genteel elites. "Bradford folks," the Observer noted, "understand the old adage that 'with one servant the work is well done; with two, only half done; but with three, not done at all.' "[58]

One reason why servantholding was so rare in Bradford was the widespread availability of factory employment for the pool of unmarried women from whom domestics were drawn. Whereas domestics in 1851 constituted 13.8 percent of the national work force, in Bradford they comprised a mere 3.3 percent. This resulted in a perpetual shortage of hired domestic labor, created more unpaid work for the bourgeois housewife, and raised the level of wages that servants could demand.[59] As the Observer, in 1859, pointed out: "Mills and manufactures are in every part draining away female labor from

[56] Kemp and Sowerby, Map of Borough of Bradford (Bradford, 1834); Thomas Dixon, Map of Bradford (Bradford, 1850); OS, Map of Bradford; Milnes and French, Map of Bradford Center; Byles, Town and Environs of Bradford.
[57] Calculated from HO, 107/2305–11. See Appendix A.
[58] Ibid. Quote from BO, Feb. 20, 1845.
[59] Calculated from PP (LXXXV, 1852–3).

domestic circles... the old institution with more than a dash of feudalism about it... is nearly extinct and ladies may grumble about it as they please."[60]

J. A. Banks argues that each servant cost a family at least £25 per year, and the figure was probably higher in Bradford. Petitions circulated in 1845 provided information on the total ratable fixed property valuations of 390 of the householders in the 1851 bourgeois census population, and an analysis of this rating-linked sample shows a clear relationship between wealth, as measured by propertyholding, and consumption as measured by the keeping of servants. Among the 60 percent of householders with property valued between £15 and £49 per year, 77 percent kept less than two household servants whereas only 23 percent kept two or more. However, among that small elite (9 percent of the householders in the sample) who held fixed property valued at over £200 per year, the relationship was completely reversed. Only 24 percent kept one or no servants whereas 76 percent kept two or more. Among those with property valued between £50 and £199 per annum, 56 percent kept one or no servants whereas 44 percent kept two or more.[61]

Wealth, however, was not the only factor that governed the level of abstinence that families typically maintained. As Table 8-2 indicates, conspicuous underconsumption was more characteristic of those in entrepreneurial occupations than of those in the professions or of rentiers. To some extent, these occupational differentials in servantholding can be explained as indirect manifestations of differentials in wealth: The retailers in the service sector displayed the lowest levels of domestic consumption largely because they were among the least affluent members of the bourgeoisie. However, a closer examination reveals some important differences between the occupational rank order in terms of consumption as well as in terms of propertied wealth. Although only moderately wealthy property holders, Bradford's professionals were, by far, the most conspicuously consumption-oriented occupational group. By contrast, the worsted manufacturers, though the wealthiest Bradfordians, exhibited levels of domestic consumption (with an average of only 1.3 servants per household) that were well below the mean for the entire bourgeoisie.

As Table 8-2 indicates, the degree of conspicuous underconsumption typical of any given bourgeois occupation tended to vary with its proximity to industrial entrepreneurship. Although those in the professional and genteel sector displayed the highest levels of servantholding relative to low levels of wealth, those in the primary productive sector displayed low levels of

---

[60] *BO*, Sep. 15, 1859.

[61] Petitions For and Against Incorporation of Bradford (mss., Bradford Archives, D.B. 69/ 2–3); 1851 bourgeois census population, HO, 107/2305–10.

Table 8-2. *1851 bourgeois census population and 1845 rating population: servantholding and mean property rating by occupational sector of household heads*

	1851 bourgeois census population				1845 rating population	
	Percent holding <2 servants	Percent holding 2 + servants	Mean number of servants	N	Mean ratable value of property (£)	N
Primary production sector	70	30	1.3	438	£92	532
Urban-service sector	83	17	1.2	532	£35	855
Genteel and professional sector	64	36	1.5	280	£48	283
Total	73	27	1.5	1,250	£55	1,670

Sources: Calculated from 1851 census mss. for Bradford (HO, 107/2305–10); Petitions for and against incorporation of Bradford (mss., Bradford Central Library, D.B. 69/2–3). See Appendix A.

Table 8-3. *1851 bourgeois census population and 1845 rating population: servantholding by select occupations of household heads*

	Percent holding <2 servants	Percent holding 2 + servants	Mean number of servants	N	Mean ratable value of property (£)	N
Rentiers	71	29	1.5	113	£80	34
Professionals	64	36	1.5	169	£28	137
Worsted manufacturers	71	29	1.3	165	£170	171
Stuff merchants and dyers	42	48	2.2	90	£77	78

Sources: Calculated from 1851 census mss. for Bradford (HO, 107/2305–10); petitions for and against incorporation of Bradford (mss., Bradford Central Library, D.B. 69/2–3). See Appendix A.

servantholding relative to the highest levels of wealth. Those occupied in the urban-service sector, the most marginal group within the bourgeoisie, exhibited relatively low levels of both.

However, this inverse relationship, which generally held between consumption on the one hand and productivity on the other, breaks down in a number of specific cases (see Table 8-3). The rentiers, for instance, were by no means the most conspicuous consumers. Clearly, the presence of a large number of relatively penurious widows and spinsters in this statistical category tended to bring its servantholding averages down. Stuff merchants, who stood next to the industrialists in the spectrum of entrepreneurship were, by contrast, considerably less abstinent than the latter, although they were considerably less wealthy too. These specific occupational peculiarities notwithstanding, the statistics reveal a generally close connection between entrepreneurship and domestic abstinence. Even as late as the middle of the century, when entrepreneurial incomes were beginning to rise dramatically, the habits of austerity to which entrepreneurs had grown accustomed proved difficult to abandon or break.

Women in the domestic economy

Bradford's public capitalist economy of production and its private domestic economy of consumption were not simply separate, albeit interdependent, social units in competition for the same resources of family wealth. They were also the embodiments of a sexual division of labor from which bourgeois gender relations would evolve during the Victorian age. The supremacy of men, which had hitherto rested on their patriarchal authority within the family, was now coming to depend in a more structured and less personal sense on the precedence that their sphere of capitalist production and market relations obtained over the female sphere of domestic consumption, which required production to exist at all.[62]

However, in contrast to traditional patriarchal society, the new bourgeois woman was, though still subordinate, acknowledged as the mistress of her sphere. The home had become "the woman's domain – her kingdom where she exercises entire control."[63] Her softening influence helped to relieve her husband of his obsession with abstinence and work by providing a space within the family in which the cares of a competitive world could be kept at bay. Her activities in setting up the home and rearing the children were

---

[62] LeeAnn Whites, "Southern Ladies and Millhands: The Domestic Economy and Class Politics; Augusta, Georgia, 1870–90" (University of California, Irvine, Ph.D. dissertation, 1982), 1–27.
[63] Samuel Smiles, *Character* (New York, 1871), 47.

not inherently less valuable or rewarding than those of her husband and provided at least some measure of compensation for the loss of opportunities for public expression that were now regarded as inconsistent with her private, gendered role.[64]

In the protoindustrial community, women of the lower middle and working classes – the social levels from which most of the new bourgeois women came – had been well integrated into productive life. Women engaged in spinning and sometimes weaving or dairy farming, as well as shopkeeping, and certain "feminine" crafts.[65] Women worked beside their husbands in different occupations, and a survey of Bradford wills from the 1830s and 1840s shows that it was still quite common for petty retailers and tradesmen to bequeath their businesses to widows who managed them independently after their husband's death. Ibbetson's 1850 *Directory* listed 128 small female run businesses which represented nearly all of Bradford's milliners and bonnet makers, 45 percent of the teachers in town, 13 percent of the innkeepers and beersellers, and 11 percent of the grocers and shopkeepers.[66]

Women who came from such backgrounds but married upwardly mobile bourgeois men found that they had entered a different world in which most of the traditional opportunities for female independence were closed off. If they were to find sources of satisfaction and achievement, these would have to be sought in their roles as housewives. In this capacity, they could certainly understand their husbands' commitment to austerity and justly pride themselves on their ability to make the most of the meager household budgets within which they were obliged to work. However, the male bourgeois propensity toward underconsumption often did cause resentment when it was accompanied by a devaluation of domesticity, a neglect of family life, and an impervious, total immersion in the world of work.

To be sure, some bourgeois men, like Jacob Behrens and William Byles, seem to have been genuinely attached to their domestic connections and were willing to save significant amounts of energy and time for their wives.[67] However, in other cases, long hours of hard work left many bourgeois men exhausted and indifferent to their families.[68] In the case of Isaac Holden,

---

[64] Byles, "William Byles," 64–71; *Sir Jacob Behrens*, 42.

[65] Ivy Pinchbeck, *Women Workers and the Industrial Revolution, 1750–1850* (London, 1930), 7–27; Joan Scott and Louise Tilly, *Women, Work and Family* (New York, 1978).

[66] James Ibbetson, *Directory of Bradford* (Bradford, 1850); "Yorkshire Wills, 1837–1856" (mss., Borthwick Institute).

[67] Byles, *William Byles*, 69–70; anon. *Sir Jacob Behrens*, 42.

[68] Though not denying the existence of this phenomenon, Davidoff and Hall, *Family Fortunes*, 107–18, 162–7, 270, emphasize the genuine attachment of most bourgeois men to their families and contend that, under the influence of evangelical Christianity, many embraced the domestic ideology almost as fervently as their wives. Here, their work displays a certain static quality that lumps together different phases of family development

whose obsession with his work took precedence over everything else, the consequence was an almost constant undercurrent of smoldering antagonism between a husband insistent on the primacy of entrepreneurship and a wife who wished to see the claims of domesticity receive their due.[69]

Isaac's attitudes were revealed very early in the course of his first marriage when he was so absorbed with business that he scarcely noticed his wife. Once when she was away visiting her parents her husband remarked, "My head is so full of business that I forget often that I am solitary." Still Isaac was not entirely unresponsive to his wife's needs, for he once abandoned the idea of renting a particular mill because the house that was attached "daunts my wife, wives as you know hold domestic comfort sacred, and she is excusable on that score."[70]

After Mrs. Holden's sudden death in 1847, Isaac, with his career about to take off, found himself saddled with four small children and hastened to look for a second wife. Unlike his first wife, who came, like himself, from a poor Scottish family, Sarah Sugden, the woman whom Isaac found to replace her, was the daughter of a small worsted manufacturer and the sister of Jonas Sugden, who, as we have seen, built up the business. Sarah appears to have been attracted to her husband and was not averse to domestic frugality. Her management of his household would enable him to cut costs. "Mr. Holden has left the management of the house entirely to servants & whatever has been wanted has not been refused so that the expense has been great."[71]

Although linked by common values and Wesleyan chapel involvements, Isaac's interest in the match was colored by his family responsibilities and career aspirations, and although there is no reason to question the truth of his retrospective judgment, its tone appears to protest a bit too much: "I married you not for your money, neither did I marry you that you might

and does not differentiate between occupational groups. In Bradford, the "feminization" of bourgeois men by wives and daughters was primarily a phenomenon of the post-1850 second generation. Such traces as may be found in the first half of the century were generally mixed with quite different paternalistic impulses derived from the culture of the traditional gentleman-capitalist elite. For most parvenus, at least during the 1830s and 1840s, the imperatives of entrepreneurship were too demanding to permit much identification with the virtues of consumption within the domestic realm. For men like Holden, the dictates of evangelical Protestantism led them not back into the family, but ever more relentlessly into the productive world of work. See also Theodore Koditschek, "The Triumph of Domesticity and the Making of Middle Class Culture," *Contemporary Sociology*, 18:2 (1989), 178–81.

[69] Holden Papers in Bradford University Library (hereafter referred to as Holden/Bradford), Box 21, 22, 52.

[70] Jennings, "Isaac Holden," 18, 32.

[71] *Holden-Illingworth Letters*, 141.

make *little or great encomiums in my domestic establishment.* I married you because I loved and *respected* you and your family, because I wished to make you more happy and too feel myself *more happy in doing so.'*[72] Preoccupied with getting his new factory in order, Isaac was eager to be married as quickly as possible. "I am sorry I shall have so little time just then our Business being so heavy and demanding so much of my personal attention so that if I could arrange to get married on the Wednesday I should like it better but say Friday at the latest."[73] When snags developed, Isaac began "to feel a sort of youthful fidgetiness to have the affair closed," and relied on his fiancee's "sympathy in endeavoring to indulge" him.[74] Sarah found her future husband's singleminded absorption in his business disturbing and was not above enlisting the aid of religion in her attempts to capture his full attention. In a letter she reminded him of "the awful danger there is of being too much entangled with the world. I think my greatest wish is that you and I may get more of God. Make ourselves more familiar with each other in spiritual things, with a godly jealousy watch over each other."[75]

Isaac, who regarded his career as a godly calling, remained unmoved by his wife's "old and superstitious" appeal.[76] Indeed, his decision, in the midst of the depression of 1848, that providence had called him to accept a partnership with S. C. Lister, which required him to abandon his English markets and move his family and factory to France, was the spark that ignited domestic antagonism and threatened to tear his marriage apart. Although Sarah knew of Isaac's plans before the marriage, it is clear that she envisioned, at most, a short-term arrangement and was disheartened at the prospect of leaving her country and her family for very long.

The conflict between Isaac and Sarah revolved around the definition of domesticity and its proper relation to the productive sphere. To Isaac, "home" was merely an appendage to entrepreneurship that followed him around wherever his business went. To Sarah, the world of domesticity was an autonomous space with its own independent activities and inviolable needs. It encompassed not only her husband's household, but a whole constellation of family, friends, and female networks, which she could not bear to leave behind. The letters that passed between Sarah and her sisters reveal dense lines of feminine activity – bazaars, meetings, sewing circles, charitable work, and chapel gossip – which rounded out the daily drudgery of household chores and domestic management and brought charm to an otherwise dull routine. Bored and isolated in a foreign country, surrounded by people whose

[72] Holden/Bradford, 22, I. Holden – S. Holden, Jan. 10, 1851.
[73] Ibid., 52, I. Holden – S. Sugden, Mar. 14, 1850.
[74] Ibid., 52, I. Holden – S. Sugden, July 30, 1850.
[75] Ibid., 21, S. Holden – I. Holden, Dec. 4, 1850.
[76] *Holden-Illingworth Letters*, I. Holden – S. Holden, Aug. 24, 1853.

language she did not understand, Sarah felt frustrated by her marital predicament. On the one hand, it was her duty to serve her husband and to sacrifice her desires at the altar of his career. On the other hand, it was her right and responsibility as a woman to insist that the logic of accumulation be placed in proper perspective and subordinated to the higher claims of religion and life.

Sarah's rather unsatisfactory solution to her dilemma was to insist on making frequent trips back home. Her decision to prolong her Christmas visit in 1850 provoked her husband's sarcastic response: "However great my pleasure may be in hearing of your felicity at a distance, it would be a still greater pleasure to enjoy your presence at home."[77] Feeling threatened by Sarah's challenge to his masculine authority, Isaac lit into her for some minor household request about which she had written: "I *shall feel* on my return *much grieved if it is not done.*" To Isaac, such language, which might appropriately be addressed to a wayward servant, was hardly proper when directed at the master of the house. An angry assertion of his male prerogative was the only reply he saw fit to make:

> I cannot think you mean you will be grieved at me as it cannot in that sense be an expression *suitable* for a *good wife* to address to her *Husband*.
> ...Between husband and wife the language and manner dictated by a gentle and tender affection is always the best, and especially submission by a wife to a husbands judgement combined with affectionate counsel is most influential with a *manly* husband.[78]

Sarah's reply has not survived, but apparently she stood her ground and it was not she, but her "manly" husband, who was the first to back down. Realizing that the future of their relationship had been placed in jeopardy, Isaac responded in a less hostile, but more manipulative way. Her letter had made him "sad and pensive," perplexed "how to respond to you and how to act."

> You seem to be so much happier with Brothers and among your old friends than with me, that as I love you and above all things wish you happiness, I think whether it is not my duty to allow you to remain and enjoy yourself while I pine away in solitary blessedness for your sake ...that your *married* life should be one of *sorrow* I do not understand and your expression of such a feeling gives me the most intense pain. Surely you do not attribute the fault to me. I think I have never shown you anything contrary to true affection.[79]

Having won her point, Sarah agreed to return home, a decision that her husband was certain would "be greatly contributive to my domestic comfort

---

[77] Holden/Bradford, 22, I. Holden – S. Holden, Jan. 4, 1851.
[78] Ibid.
[79] Ibid., Jan. 10, 1851.

and peace of mind." He was "longing to see you & I do hope we shall both be much happier, better and more loving than ever."[80] After this, Isaac reconciled himself to his wife's periodic absences, whereas she resigned herself to the prospect that it would be a long time before her husband would leave France. In the end, Sarah's wish was finally fulfilled by the Cobden–Chevalier treaty of 1860, which induced her husband, now a wealthy man, to leave his French works in the hands of a manager and to return to Bradford to open a new mill with his sons. For Sarah, he built an expensive mansion on the outskirts of town.[81]

Conclusion

Sarah Holden's dilemma did not make her a particularly attractive person. Her letters and those of other members of the family suggest a rather sanctimonious, long-suffering Victorian matron, whose willingness to sacrifice for the needs of others resulted in snappish bouts of ill humor and a morbid preoccupation with illness and death. Nevertheless, she and many other bourgeois wives, often in the face of overwhelming male opposition, were beginning to stake out and defend an autonomous, domestic space built upon the material substructure of capitalist production but operating according to its own laws. To the logic of production, with its abstract demands for abstinence and accumulation, this domestic consciousness of bourgeois women replied with the concrete claims of human reproduction. So long as the needs of accumulation remained paramount in Bradford, this "male" logic of production held primacy over the "female" logic of consumption, attenuating the scope for family life.

And yet this domestic world of home and family contained the germ of an alternative social vision that, in the period after midcentury, would serve not only to justify the private activities of women, but to round out the competitive capitalist universe created by men. Absorbed in their personal dramas of success and salvation, men like Holden were, in some ways, ill equipped to confront the problems of gaining mastery over their world. As they struggled to assert their hegemony over the industrial community and to translate their personal values and principles into universal, ideological terms, they found that capitalism, as a system of social relations, generated problems that capitalism, as an engine of production, could not resolve. Here they could not help but benefit from their own domestic experiences, which contained an implicit model, at once authoritarian and consensual, of

---

[80] Ibid., Jan. 17, 1851.
[81] *Holden-Illingworth Letters*, 240–740; Holden/Brotherton, 2, 4, 41.

human relations in a social world. Initially, the domestic, familial experience might be taken for granted or relegated to the insignificance of the private realm. Nevertheless, as they sought to humanize the industrial environment that their enterprise had fashioned, Bradford's new generation of capitalists would eventually find themselves applying, to the world of the factory and the marketplace, ideals and imperatives that many of them had first encountered in domestic values and aspirations articulated by their wives.

9

The promise of a liberal entrepreneurial society

The view of human life that sees it as an emanation of labor, so eloquently articulated in the 1840s by the young socialist Karl Marx, was actually derived from the experience of entrepreneurial capitalists, like those of Bradford, whose purposive activity had fashioned a new environment in steam, in spindles, in smoke, and in stone. To such men, their own life and that of the society around them really appeared as though it was their conscious creation, and the language of work provided an effective vehicle, not only for expressing their own self-understanding, but for comprehending society as a whole.[1]

Yet for most Bradfordians, work was not a redemptive calling. It was an external constraint that might engage the labor of their bodies but from which their inner personalities were estranged. At midcentury, industrial entrepreneurs constituted only a tiny minority of Bradford's adult population, of whom about 55 percent were wage laborers and 25 percent were house-wives at home. Even if small retailers and businessmen are included among them, entrepreneurs comprised no more than 20 percent of Bradford's adults. Industrialists, the real shapers of the growing city, accounted for only a tiny fraction of the total populace and remained a minority even within the bourgeoisie. Their unique propensity to conceive life from the standpoint of labor was thus an aberration that other Bradfordians could not whole-heartedly share.[2]

As the entrepreneurs rose during the 1830s and 1840s, the task of building and managing individual enterprises began to merge with a larger, if more inchoate, mission to assert their collective hegemony as a class. Increasingly sensitive to their exposed position as a small minority in an extremely diverse society whose other members did not share their experiences, they began to question the glib assumption that the mass of ordinary Bradfordians would spontaneously embrace entrepreneurial values or world views. To cast society in one's own self-image, to see Bradford as the self-made man writ large,

[1] Karl Marx, *Economic and Philosophical Manuscripts of 1844* (New York, 1964), 106–19.
[2] *PP* (LXXXV, 1852–3), 2:720–5.

proved an inadequate strategy for forging an ideological consensus around capitalist values amidst a population that rarely fit the entrepreneurial mold. Precisely because the individualist philosophy of character so powerfully reflected the entrepreneurial experience, it could not, by itself, encompass the very different experience of workers, of women, and of the petit bourgeoisie.

Achieving entrepreneurial hegemony, convincing all of Bradford's inhabitants that labor really ought to be the essence of their lives, required a more comprehensive ideological enterprise. The values that the self-made man embodied had to be set into a new type of liberal voluntaristic culture, meaningful to all inhabitants of the urban-industrial milieu. To secure the allegiance of all social groups to the industrial-capitalist society and to legitimize the entrepreneur as its natural elite, it was necessary to demonstrate that the principles of productive labor, free-market exchange, and individualist voluntarism were not just individual but also social principles bringing order and progress to the community as a whole. The forces that were making entrepreneurs rich and powerful had to be portrayed as universally beneficial, demonstrating to all Bradfordians that they would become happy and prosperous only insofar as the entrepreneur could become powerful and rich.

As we have seen, many of these new men were already predisposed toward this sort of hegemonic thinking by their religious tendency to find the meaning of personal choices and behavior in the predestined operation of God's providential plan. Now as a larger physical and social environment actually crystallized out of the private initiatives that divine agency had empowered, their spiritual impulses toward self-justification got urgent reinforcement from a secular imperative to justify their dominance within a dynamic and destabilized urban-industrial world.

Entrepreneurial labor and the productive society

Before the 1830s in Bradford, the assumption that private profit brought public prosperity would have seemed deeply problematic. In the expanding industrial-capitalist environment of the next two decades, it began to make more sense. Under pre- or protoindustrial conditions, capitalism had coexisted with more traditional modes of production, particularly domestic handicrafts, which restricted the full competitive development of its dominant industrial form. As long as capital operated within this economic environment, where the forces of production could not be transformed, maximum profits came not from manufacturing enterprises that produced new products, but from commercial businesses that distributed existing ones along relatively stationary lines.[3]

As long as bargaining, speculation, monopoly, and intrigue could generate higher profits than innovation, production, and hard work, capitalist entrepreneurship could not be regarded as an entirely honorable activity through which nobility could be achieved. Traditional capitalism, like that of protoindustrial Bradford, was a way of making money, but it offered no blueprint for organizing society nor mechanism for advancing its collective welfare. The town's previous economic elite had justified their supremacy not on the basis of their economic position as capitalists, but on their social role as aspiring gentlemen. The material wealth generated by capitalism could only bring social authority when it was used to underwrite paternalism or purchase leisure and culture, creating that stance of Olympian detachment that was the traditional hallmark of wise and benevolent rule.[4]

As we have seen, by the 1820s in Bradford, the relevance of this equation between leisure and authority was being called into question, while capitalism was beginning to offer a new ethical foundation on which new forms of authority might rest. The intensification of competition, the extension of markets, and the spread of mechanization to all manufacturing processes, which characterized the quarter century after 1825, were all symptomatic of the transfer of the locus of profit from commercial manipulations of temporary market imbalances to industrial enterprises systematically geared to maximizing the rate of surplus value within the production process itself. Commercial expansion began to follow, rather than to precede, industrial development.[5]

Of course, this trend had begun with the mechanization of spinning a quarter century earlier, but it was only in the second quarter of the nineteenth century that its full impact was felt. Moreover, spinning and weaving were derivative processes that involved the transfer of existing technology to the worsted sector rather than the pioneering of novel manufacturing forms. Only with the new entrepreneurship of the 1830s and 1840s did the revolutionary character of industrial capitalism become entirely apparent in Bradford. At that point, attention focused on the innovators who were bringing this transformation about.[6]

Titus Salt has been seen as the prototype of the self-made man. The most striking feature of his career, his ability, in volatile economic conditions,

---

[3] Karl Marx, *Capital* (Moscow, 1954), 1:145–72.
[4] Max Weber, *The Protestant Ethic and the Spirit of Capitalism* (New York, 1958); Edward Miall, *The British Churches in Relation to the British People* (London, 1849).
[5] See Chapter 3.
[6] E. M. Sigsworth, *Black Dyke Mills* (Liverpool, 1958), 30–71.

to build an enormously successful business from a very modest start, was displayed by many others on a lesser scale. Salt began his career in his early twenties, while working in his father's small woolstapling firm. Dissatisfied with a routine business, he employed his growing familiarity with different fibers to imagine the possibility of entirely new yarns and fabrics that might create new vistas for the Bradford textile industry while making him a wealthy man. On impulse, he bought a consignment of Donskoi wool in 1834, and after finding that no Bradford spinner was interested in taking it, he purchased a mill and manufactured it himself. Soon the new yarn became so popular that within a few years Titus had five mills.[7] His greatest triumph, however, came in 1836, when, in Liverpool, he bought three hundred pounds of alpaca, which was widely regarded as a useless waste. Salt adapted his machinery to spin the fiber and an entirely new range of worsted products was brought into being. So popular were alpaca fabrics that, within a few years, two million pounds of fleece were being imported annually and Salt, together with the few entrepreneurs who joined him, had become enormously rich.[8]

Salt's triumph prefigured a new type of entrepreneurship, one no longer content with maintaining existing forms of production but constantly seeking new products and processes to open untapped markets. Such a strategy was often the only way that a parvenu could compete in the volatile trade of the thirties and forties and survive the years of recession when other marginal producers collapsed. This same readiness to make risky innovations in the hope of high returns can also be seen in the career of Henry Ripley. His advances in the chemistry of dyeing were the most important factor in facilitating the proliferation of mixed-worsted fabrics that became the mainstay of Bradford's textile industry for a generation to come.[9] Emboldened by Salt's initial triumph with alpaca, Ripley enlisted the aid of the merchant Robert Milligan (who became his father-in-law in 1836) to develop a new mode of dyeing animal and vegetable fibers together so that it would finally become economically feasible to use cotton warps and worsted wefts in a single fabric. The result was not only enormous wealth for both Milligan and Ripley, but the opening of a new era for the entire industry. Diversified product lines bringing skyrocketing profits, previously limited to the few firms that pioneered exotic fibers like mohair and alpaca, were now the goal of dozens of more ordinary manufacturers, albeit on a smaller scale. The

---

[7] Robert Balgarnie, *Titus Salt* (London, 1877), 61–78; Jack Reynolds, *The Great Paternalist* (London, 1983).

[8] Balgarnie, *Salt*, 61–78.

[9] Sigsworth, *Black Dyke*, 43–55.

ensuing revolution in production enriched the entrepreneurs who pioneered it and brought prosperity to the rest of the community with new products, new wealth, and new jobs.[10]

However, the innovation that had the greatest impact on worsted production and on the entire industrial structure of the town was the woolcombing machine, which was reputed to do the work of a hundred hand combers at a fraction of the original cost. Perfected in the late 1840s, the automatic woolcomb was designed to replicate a process unique to the worsted industry involving a set of motions so delicate and complex as to have defied satisfactory mechanization for over fifty years. Because experimentation was extremely costly and time consuming, prospective inventors had to take enormous risks with no guarantee of success.[11] Work undertaken in the thirties and forties by five different individuals proceeded simultaneously on several fronts. When, by midcentury, a cost-effective machine was finally produced, it combined the achievements of all five, but only two of them, Isaac Holden and S. C. Lister, reaped the windfall profits that machine woolcombing initially brought.[12]

Though they combined their resources in an uneasy partnership, Lister's and Holden's very different backgrounds and experiences resulted in important divergences in approach. An arch-Nonconformist from a humble social background, Holden was typical of his generation and class in acknowledging the critical importance of competitive superiority for industrial success. His partner, the son of an Anglican Tory squire, was from a much more comfortable and privileged background. Unlike Holden, Lister had no difficulty financing his woolcombing experiments, and his family's resources allowed him to buy the patents of poorer inventors, giving him the edge in synthesizing a complete machine.[13] The de facto monopoly that success finally brought him was an advantage he thought he could enjoy indefinitely through the protection of his patents and through industrial secrecy. He reminded Holden early on in their partnership, "Your Keeping exclusive possession of your trade will depend as much upon your keeping your machines secret as upon the patent. . . . The best protection is the *inability* of anyone to imitate you."[14]

---

[10] John James, *History of the Worsted Manufacture in England* (London, 1857), 579; Sigsworth, *Black Dyke*, 43–9; *BO*, Apr. 10, 1845.

[11] David Landes, *The Unbound Prometheus* (Cambridge, 1969), 212; Sigsworth, *Black Dyke*, 38–43.

[12] *Fortunes Made in Business* (London, 1910), 1:3–86; James, *Worsted Manufacture*, 562–84.

[13] S. C. Lister, *Lord Masham's Inventions* (Bradford, 1905), 8–46; *BO*, Apr. 19, 1855.

[14] Holden Mss., (mss. Bradford University Library, cse. 58, S. C. Lister – I. Holden, Sep. 25, 1841), hereafter referred to as Holden/Bradford. See *BO*, Apr. 19, 1855 for an attack by another manufacturer on Lister's autocratic and monopolistic tendencies.

Not believing, as did Lister, that an entrepreneur could remain shielded indefinitely from the rigors of competition, Holden maintained a more market-oriented approach. His success was a consequence not only of technical skill and ingenuity, but also of a talent for sensing exactly when to get into or out of a particular product line. His aim was not jealously to guard his gains, which he saw as futile, but continually to exploit new opportunities. As he reassured his banker during a difficult spell, "I have always struggled hard to make my business pay by accommodating it to the demands of the time."[15] Even Lister, for all his dreams of permanent monopoly, ultimately behaved according to the rules of the new entrepreneurial game. Instead of resting on his laurels, during the 1850s and 1860s, he invested virtually his entire woolcombing fortune (£360,000) in developing an even more complex mechanism to recycle silk waste, spin it, and weave it like ordinary silk. This success enabled him to build his gargantuan Manningham Mills in 1871, the largest textile factory in its time. It also permitted him eventually to retire to the countryside as Bradford's first industrial millionaire.[16]

Although these innovations in technology, in marketing, in materials, and in management may not seem very impressive by twentieth-century standards, they represented a fundamental transformation in the industry of their time. In each case, they brought great wealth to the entrepreneur who introduced them, and together they opened a new era for the worsted industry, profoundly altering the character of its products and dramatically expanding the dimensions of its trade. Moreover, what made Salt, Ripley, Milligan, Holden, and even Lister for most of his career, so different from the older generation of worsted businessmen was their disinterest in donning the mantle of the gentleman and their willingness to identify unreservedly with their entrepreneurial roles. Instead of retiring to live lives of leisure, they remained in business long after their fortunes were made because they saw themselves not merely as capitalists reaping personal profit, but as public benefactors performing socially useful roles.

For bourgeois ideologues like Samuel Smiles, this convergence of private profit with social productivity sufficed to justify the rewards of the entrepreneur, which could be portrayed not merely as incidents of ownership, but as the earned fruits of his activity as an inventor or engineer. Having risen "to celebrity mostly by their habits of observation, their powers of discrimination, their constant self-improvements, and their patient industry,"

---

[15] Holden/Bradford, 58, I. Holden – S. Laycock, Feb. 4, 1848.
[16] *Fortunes Made in Business*, 1:47–86; Lister, *Lord Masham's Inventions*, 46–86.

entrepreneurs were not only capitalists, but a specially heroic species of laborer, the natural aristocrats of the world of work.[17]

However, in contrast to the hereditary aristocrats who had hitherto ruled in the precapitalist world, these heroes of the new urban-industrial order embodied a nobility not of birth, but of merit, having been raised by the unerring judgment of the marketplace in which their competitive superiority was proved. In the inverted humanism of this productive society, the essence of civilization no longer appeared in the leisure of its cultural or political masters, but in the "genius and labor" of those most adept at fabricating it in the material sense. In the past, insistence on aesthetic, intellectual, or civic perfection as the ultimate in human ideals had sanctioned, at least implicitly, the privileges of an aristocratic minority whose special position had been justified as a necessary condition for the pursuit of higher ends. Now, however, as the increasing productivity of industrial capitalism raised the possibility of a future where leisure and cultivation might be open to all, the true social leader, ideologues like Smiles insisted, was the man who "set in motion some of the greatest industries" whereby "daily life" for the mass of ordinary people "has been rendered in all respects more easy as well as more enjoyable."[18]

Here was a whole new conception of social hegemony in which entrepreneurial virtues could be portrayed not only as morally or spiritually advantageous in the individual search for salvation or self-help, but as collectively beneficial to the community at large. In the past, economic activity had been denigrated as a source of corruption, a realm of disorder and brute necessity that higher virtues had to transcend or tame. Now, refracted through the lens of entrepreneurship, it emerged triumphantly as the very font of all virtue, refining and improving the individual's character, while laying the foundation for a future of freedom in which the social goods, hitherto restricted to a tiny minority, could be extended universally throughout the world. Corruption, in the new scheme, was not a consequence of capitalism, but an anachronistic by-product of aristocratic entrenchment, the inevitable result of selfish efforts to monopolize social resources that rightfully belonged to all.[19]

[17] Samuel Smiles, *Lives of the Engineers* (London, 1874), 1:xvii.
[18] Samuel Smiles, *Self Help* (London, 1925), 34.
[19] Adam Smith, *The Wealth of Nations* (New York, 1937), 3–16, 314–32; Elie Halévy, *The Growth of Philosophical Radicalism* (London, 1972), 153–312; A. N. de Condorcet, *Sketch for a Historical Picture of the Progress of the Human Mind* (London, 1955). Even in eighteenth-century Britain, as J. G. A. Pocock demonstrates in *The Machiavellian Moment: Florentine Political Thought and the Atlantic Republican Tradition* (Princeton, 1975), 401–505, virtue was widely regarded as an agrarian, aristocratic attribute, whereas credit and commerce were perceived as inherently corrupting activities. Even those well aware of

Most Bradfordians were probably not so utopian as to believe that industrial capitalism would ever entirely master the forces of nature that had hitherto dominated men. Nevertheless, amidst the entrepreneurial advances of the 1830s and 1840s, a more circumspect version of this progressive optimism began to make considerable sense. More to the point, as the larger social significance of entrepreneurship became obvious, it grew increasingly difficult for inhabitants of the industrial city to regard traditional gentlemen as legitimate elites. Indeed, analyzed in the terms of the entrepreneurial critique, aristocratic forms of hegemony based on privilege or monopoly often appeared as little more than fraudulent ruses through which a narrow clique of parasitic idlers expropriated the wealth of those who had produced it, without providing any social benefit in return. Whether this parasitism was imposed through naked force or upheld more subtly through ideological mystifications, it was recognized as being morally unjust and increasingly dangerous to the long-term welfare of the society that allowed it to prevail.[20]

Ultimately, it might prove unwise even for the greedy aristocrat, who might kill the goose that laid his golden eggs. To divert social resources away from productive employment in wages and profits was to sacrifice the future interests of the entire society for the temporary pleasure of a priviledged few. When the social surplus was expropriated through rents, sinecures, and government bonds, it was less likely to be reinvested in productive enterprises. Instead of increasing the wealth of the community, it would be frittered away in the wasteful, conspicuous consumption of elites.[21]

---

their material benefits often feared the latter as sources of uncertainty and disorder, harbingers of cultural extravagance and effeminacy, which only a strong dose of austere and manly virtue could keep in check. In nineteenth-century Bradford, however, this kind of thinking was increasingly hard to sustain. Commerce and credit, now subordinated to a larger system of industrial productivity, seemed to engender not disorder and degeneracy but precisely the sort of abstemious self-control and worldly potency that the concept of "virtue" had classically entailed. Here, as capitalism itself emerged as the font of virtue, "corruption" became associated with the aristocracy – as the natural recourse of any oligarchy (whether agrarian or mercantile) whose position depended on artificial privileges rather than on its members' ability to compete in the world. For a critique of Pocock that argues for the currency of liberal and even quasi-entrepreneurial categories of thought in the eighteenth century, see Isaac Kramnick, "Republican Revisionism Revised," *American Historical Review*, 87:3, (1982); and idem., "Eighteenth Century Science and Radical Social Theory: The Case of Joseph Priestley's Scientific Liberalism," *Journal of British Studies*, 25:1 (1986).

[20] T. Perronet Thompson, *Exercises, Political and Other* (London, 1842), 1:4–5, 226, 367; 4:226, 367.

[21] Thompson, *Exercises*, 1:207; 4:480–1, 498, 500–508. Arguments of this sort assumed particularly somber tones when they were cast in the theoretical framework of Ricardian economics that saw economic development as a natural process of decline to some eventual profitless, low-wage, stationary state. Under these circumstances, only the most

Though it was located far from the heartlands of the rural aristocracy, Bradford was well within the reach of the English Old Regime. Legal monopolies and the investment practices of aristocratic elites transferred wealth from productive industry to landownership or other passive rentier forms. As rising industrial productivity caused rent rolls to fatten while profits and wages stagnated or declined, antiaristocratic sentiment deepened, and entrepreneurs concluded that the control they exercised within their own enterprises would never be entirely secure until it had been extended into a larger capitalist hegemony in which the full possibilities of urban-industrial development could be realized. Government, in both Britain and Bradford, could no longer safely be left to the established elites. To clear the path for entrepreneurship, the society and polity, scarcely less than the economy, would have to be recast in an entrepreneurial mold.

Of course, not all of Bradford's rising entrepreneurs had the vision or self-confidence to break completely with previously accepted political ideologies and social values, and the critique of aristocratic parasitism was not embraced by all. In the aftermath of the French Revolution, embryonic versions of anti-aristocratic radicalism had been abandoned by most middle-class people, as fears of social upheaval overshadowed resentment of corrupt elites.[22] Nevertheless, by the 1830s and 1840s, when the new entrepreneurial generation had appeared and the memory of Jacobin outrages had dimmed, a new wave of bourgeois radicalism began to swell. Grounded not only in the principles of political economy, but also in the puritan traditions of Nonconformity and the personal values of the small producers from whose ranks most entrepreneurs came, these new impulses toward social and political insurgency were simply the natural responses of a generation of capitalists whose experience had shown them both the possibility and necessity of reforming society in the same terms that they had formed their enterprises and themselves.

As in many other places, the critical watershed in Bradford was the 1828–35 period when the surging currents of religious and political transformation made radicalism again respectable and drew young, hitherto quiescent, en-

---

heroic infusions of entrepreneurial innovation to increase the productive power of industry could forestall the stagnation that lay ahead. That this natural economic monopoly enjoyed by the landlord was reinforced by artificial, legally imposed monopolies was a testament not only to aristocratic rapacity but to the folly of the entire community that impotently acquiesced in this collective self-abuse. David Ricardo, *The Principles of Political Economy and Taxation* (London, 1960), 33–45, 64–76, 263–71; Maxine Berg, *The Machinery Question and the Making of Political Economy* (Cambridge, 1980), 43–74.

[22] E. P. Thompson, *The Making of the English Working Class* (New York, 1963), 718–32.

trepreneurial upstarts into the leadership of a popular movement that would pit the broad masses of productive citizens against the privileges of a narrow, parasitic elite. Radical social reconstruction in rationalist, utilitarian, laissez-faire terms, which, in 1789, Burke had dismissed as the utopian fantasy of "philosophical theologians," was now more formidably reasserted as the practical program of a new generation of ascendant entrepreneurs.[23]

The vision of a productive society that united the reformers of this period promised to elevate the entrepreneurial philosophy of character from an individual self-help strategy into a universal social and political program for advancing the public good. In a world still under the heel of aristocratic tyranny, the central line of fissure within society was the inherent political antagonism between parasites and producers, not the economic competition or class divisions that might incidentally arise within the productive community itself.[24] Whereas the former was envisioned as a fundamental and ultimately irreconcilable opposition between progressive and reactionary modes of social organization, the latter was portrayed as a mere functional distinction between interrelated groupings, each of which had its proper role to play. "The distinction of capitalist and labourer," explained the *Observer*,

> is a natural and not an artificial one – that is, it arises spontaneously by the natural working of the social elements and is not consequent on arbitrary and one-sided class legislation. Every day men are passing from the class of labourers to that of capitalists by mere force of industry and integrity or of mechanical skill and commercial tact. There are no laws of caste as in India which fix a man's lot to a particular occupation forever as by an irreversible decree of fate.[25]

Unlike the traditional cultural and political authority of the gentleman, the rule of the entrepreneur in the productive society could scarcely be questioned since it was depicted as flowing naturally from the competitive environment itself. The entrepreneur was simply the man who had proven himself to be the ideal citizen of the working world. His success was not an unearned windfall, but the consequence of his own motivation and resources, which the impersonal forces of the market had rewarded for being most consistent with their own inexorable laws. Whatever inequalities existed among producers were the result of individual differences in character and ability. This natural selection within the productive community was welcomed as an instrument of progress, ensuring a better future for all. "Dif-

---

[23] Edmund Burke, *Reflections on the Revolution in France* (New York, 1955); Benjamin Godwin, "Autobiography" (uncatalogued mss. Bradford Central Library), 494–528; see Chapter 12.
[24] John Wade, *History of the Middle and Working Classes* (London, 1833).
[25] *BO*, May 28, 1840.

ference of talents is a great good," argued the stuff merchant Abraham Mitchell. "Without a diversity of gifts the world would stand still."[26]

In particular, liberal ideologues argued, the downtrodden workers, so far from having cause to resent their entrepreneurial superiors, had a special interest in enlisting under the entrepreneurial banner to force the corrupt aristocracy to give way, for it was only the entrepreneur who possessed the ability to organize an alternative social order in which the needs of the producers would become paramount. At the same time, many of the new entrepreneurs understood that, if they expected workers to defer to their authority, it would have to be an authority that they had legitimately earned. Ultimately, even the entrepreneurs' profits and control of the production process had to be justified by their ongoing contributions to the world of work. For some, any profitable employment of capital under competitive conditions constituted such a contribution since it would, by definition, tend to increase productivity or, at least, the aggregate level of social wealth. But others, like Isaac Holden, insisted on a more direct connection between the monetary rewards of the capitalist and the socially useful work he performed. When he inadvertently invented what later came to be known as the lucifer match, Holden declined to take out a patent because, he said, "I thought it was so small a matter and it cost me so little labour." However, after he had spent £50,000 and the best years of his life perfecting his woolcombing machine, he felt fully entitled to his reward.[27]

Yet this assimilation of entrepreneurial capital to productive labor did not represent a logically necessary connection, but a historically contingent one, rooted as it was in an early stage of industrial-capitalist development when entrepreneurship remained personalized, embodied in a succession of heroic individuals and embedded within a larger social and political environment in which an entrenched aristocracy still ruled. To justify capital in terms of labor or to fuse them in the heat of an antiestablishment campaign were, at best, momentary ways of conjuring up an alliance that could be achieved permanently only insofar as the emerging realities of urban-industrial capitalism actually underwrote the social consensus on which it was based. Without the cult of a self-made innovator to inspire popular emulation or the specter of a parasitic aristocracy to arouse popular ire, could the entrepreneurial vision really carry conviction within a larger population like that

---

[26] Abraham Mitchell, *Parable of the Talents by a Bradford Merchant* (Bradford, 1887).

[27] *Fortunes Made in Business*, 1:19. Recognizing that "capital is the conserved result of labour," Smiles, in an argument that surely revealed more than he intended, associated it not with property, but with thrift. "The capitalist is merely the man who does not spend all that is earned by work. He is a man prepared to forego present satisfaction for the hope of future reward." Quoted in Asa Briggs, *Victorian People* (Chicago, 1955), 128.

of nineteenth-century Bradford, which encompassed so many nonentrepreneurial groups?

In fact, this entrepreneurial vision proved inherently unstable and the union between labor and capital that it abstractly posited threatened to dissolve into contradiction when extended in practice from the entrepreneurs who embodied it to the rest of the urban middle and working class. Up to a point, other middle-class property owners could readily identify with the entrepreneurial paradigm and regard themselves as performing socially useful work. Nevertheless, as professionals or petit bourgeois shopkeepers and businessmen, their activity as producers lacked the epic quality of a Milligan, a Ripley, a Holden, or a Salt. Although they recognized their dependence on the prosperity of industry, their distance from its entrepreneurial inner core gave them distinctive interests and anxieties of their own. In fact, most middle- and lower-middle-class people, including many of the more marginal manufacturers, feared sinking into the impoverished proletariat far more than they dreamed of spectacular entrepreneurial success. As petty property owners, they, unlike the workers, had something to lose, and an ideology that exalted labor and productivity even at the expense of established property rights was likely to make them extremely uneasy. Perhaps they, scarcely less than the elite establishment, might be threatened by the constant upheavals and revolutions in production that unrestrained entrepreneurial competition seemed to bring. If they should find their own hard won security jeopardized by the relentless onrush of social transformation, perhaps they would reject the entrepreneurial vision in favor of a conservative status quo alliance with the established elite.[28]

If most middle-class people were likely to opt for the privileges of property over the power of productivity should the entrepreneurial synthesis between them appear to fail, propertyless workers were naturally predisposed the other way around. Indeed, workers were extremely eager to exalt the value of labor, but their experience of urban-industrial development might well

---

[28] A. J. Mayer, "The Lower Middle Class as Historical Problem," *Journal of Modern History*, 47:3 (1975); Geoffrey Crossick, ed., *The Lower Middle Class in Britain* (London, 1977), 11–59. Radical bourgeois ideologues of the 1830s and 1840s like Smiles, Richard Cobden, and Perronet Thompson feared that the bulk of the middle class might lack the requisite courage and independence to embrace the new values of progress and productivity and would abdicate its natural leadership role. As Thompson noted, middle-class people after the passage of the Reform Bill, having themselves obtained the vote, were no longer interested in agitating for full-scale democratic reform. They were, he complained, "all busy nursing existing evils in hopes that one son will get a commission in the army another in the customs." Nevertheless, he still hoped that they "will perhaps come to their senses at some time and compare the value of the mess of pottage for which they sell themselves with the value of what they abandon in return." *Exercises*, 1:225.

lead them to question whether capital really constituted its highest form.[29] Such a view might make instinctive sense against the background of small-scale farming, artisanal craft production, and even protoindustry in which a master and a skilled worker had shared control of the labor process and worked together in relative harmony. Most of Bradford's new industrialists had come from such backgrounds and saw their subsequent careers as dramatic confirmation that capitalist profit and productive work were naturally combined. What they failed to recognize was that their own personal fusion of working capital and directive labor had the effect of transforming the production process so as to insure that, for the new industrial proletariat, labor would permanently be separated from control.[30]

In the very act of performing his role of raising productivity, the entrepreneur separated the fulfilling labor of management that he henceforth monopolized from repetitive task execution that became the workers' lot, for raising the productivity of labor required mechanization and subdivision of function. Work was taken out of the small artisanal shop or cottage household and reconstituted in a large, often multiprocess factory employing hundreds, even thousands of anonymous drones, most performing a single specialized operation under external managerial control. Hence, it was precisely when the capitalist became an active worker that his supervisory function opposed itself most completely to the self-interests of his employees. Indeed, his sense of personal fulfillment and, to a great extent, the monetary profit he received depended on his ability to work against those he hired, organizing their labor as efficiently as possible and augmenting their powers to create an alien product that only further enhanced his powers over them.[31]

Nowhere did this contradiction arise more ominously than over the question of mechanization, which demonstrated irrefutably that it was precisely when entrepreneurial virtues were most in evidence that the greatest challenge to working-class interests was certain to take place. The entrepreneur's status as agent of the general welfare rested, first and foremost as we have seen, on his ability to serve successfully as an industrial innovator, implementing new productive and labor-saving techniques. Yet nothing threatened workers more directly than such innovations, especially when they took the form of new machines.[32] Invariably, as we have seen, the introduction of machinery into the worsted production process spelled rapidly declining

---

[29] Thomas Hodgskin, *Labour Defended against the Claims of Capital* (London, 1825); William Thompson, *Labour Rewarded: The Claims of Labour and Capital Conciliated* (London, 1827); J. F. C. Bray, *Labours Wrongs and Labours Remedies* (London, 1839).

[30] See Chapter 7.

[31] See Chapters 3 and 15. Andrew Ure, *The Philosophy of Manufactures* (London, 1835); Marx, *Capital*, 1:312–5.

[32] Berg, *Machinery Question*, 43–74, 131, 339.

wages and ultimately unemployment for the artisans whose labor was directly superseded. Worse still, their families and larger class interests were scarcely compensated by their subsequent replacement with a smaller complement of less-skilled and lower-paid, machine-tending operatives, whose labor was almost entirely under direct entrepreneurial control. Whatever its immediate benefit to the consumer or even long-term advantage to society at large, mechanization under capitalist auspices clearly would not render the daily life of the laborer "in all respects more easy as well as more enjoyable."[33]

Bradford's new entrepreneurs were not entirely unaware of this dark side to their self-professedly noble work. When Isaac Holden began the experiments that led to his combing machine, his old teacher John Kennedy admonished him to consider all the "numerous and complicated results both immediate and remote." He trusted "that personal gain is not to your heart a motive sufficiently strong to counter the claims of Christian philanthropy" and hoped "that at no remote period [it will] be productive of such good to society at large as could more than compensate for the immediate evil occasioned to those whom its introduction might deprive of bread."[34] Whatever doubts Holden may have had were apparently laid to rest by Lord Brougham's pamphlet on the machinery question. There is no further reference to the issue in his extant papers. Certainly he did not stop his woolcombing experiments nor, given his entrepreneurial self-image, could he have allowed himself to be detained by moral qualms about the very activities that were the source of his virtue.

Nevertheless, the problem would not go away. Entrepreneurs like Holden, though they might repress the realization, dimly perceived that "productivity" was an explosive concept as likely to lead, at least in the minds of others, to fundamental questions about the utility of private property as to sanction their own vision of permanent entrepreneurial rule. As long as the productive society remained, in reality, a capitalist society, productivity would have potentially divisive social consequences and could never wholly serve as an integrative ideal to unite all social groups within the industrial city. To forge an ongoing progressive consensus that would sanction the accession of capitalist hegemony and recast the world in entrepreneurial terms, it was necessary to look beyond the troubled concept of productivity to find another ideological construct that could be more effectively universalized. To remove from the spotlight those aspects of the capitalist experience that recalled the divisions of social antagonism and economic class, it was necessary to shift the ideological focus from the arena of productivity where the individual entrepreneur had sought his legitimacy to the arena of exchange where the

---

[33] See Chapters 3 and 15.
[34] *Holden-Illingworth Letters* (Bradford, 1927), J. Kennedy – I. Holden, Apr. 7, 1835.

larger hegemony of capitalism as a system of social relations seemed almost tautologically assured. If the factory, the capitalist's original realm of freedom, turned out to be a regime of servitude for everyone else, in the market, freedom was, by definition, an attribute that was meaningful only insofar as it belonged to all. If the entrepreneur could never entirely realize his hegemony as a productive agent in the world of work, he might, therefore, alternatively seek it as the bearer of progress and freedom within the realm of market exchange.

Market freedom and the progressive society

Of course, the entrepreneurial vision of the marketplace presupposed an expansive industrial foundation, and its ideal of freedom of exchange supplemented, rather than supplanted, the underlying ideal of a productive society. It represented not so much an alternative world view as a different ideological emphasis, and is often encountered in the same arguments and texts in which the entrepreneurial vision was set out. Indeed, the theory of market freedom was employed to reach exactly the same conclusions as the experientially grounded ideal of entrepreneurial labor. It simply worked at a higher level of abstraction, in language designed to appeal more seductively to a wider cross section of the urban population.

Unlike the freedom of the factory, the freedom of the marketplace did not exist for the capitalist alone. The right to hold property and the freedom to exchange it were widely regarded as natural rights, possessed by everyone independently of personal background or class position. The bourgeois or lower-middle-class retailer or professional to whom the factory appeared a mysterious institution could recognize the industrialist as a fellow property owner participating in the wider economic community through market exchange. Even the worker was believed to hold a minimal property in his ability to work. Selling it in the labor market at a competitive price he also entered the realm of exchange.[35] Indeed, all Bradfordians were embedded in market relations, and the language of exchange provided a common mode of discourse accessible to all. The very physical structure of the urban environment, assembled through an impersonal dynamic of supply and demand, could be seen as a giant marketplace of people and resources in which individuals sought to maximize their opportunities and limit their losses with the property and abilities at their command.[36]

[35] John Locke, *Of Civil Government: Second Treatise* (Chicago, 1955), 21–40; Marx, *Capital*, 1:172.

[36] See Chapter 4.

What made the market an ideal centerpiece for an ideology of universal progress was that it was not just a vehicle for the maximization of individual returns. As the most efficient mechanism for the distribution of goods and services in a manner conducive to economic growth, its social utility far outweighed its potential as an instrument of self-interest. Like an invisible hand, the market mechanism fulfilled the larger interests of the community through the action of a multitude of individuals who each sought only to maximize his private gains. According to Adam Smith, only the free flows of market supply and demand could insure that productive activity would be directed with maximum efficiency to the provision of actual human needs. Moreover, only with the widening of market demand could the division of labor generate economies of scale, raising the productivity of labor to the point at which the wealth of society would be increased.[37]

In this more explicitly theoretical, rationalist approach, market competition would guarantee what entrepreneurial initiative had only promised and often, in practice, had failed to provide. Behind the moral heroism of the innovator now lay the impersonal laws of the marketplace, which, by forcing all participants to compete with one another, would elevate the imperative to increase productivity from an exceptional achievement into a compulsory social norm.[38] However, the market mechanism could only play its role of social improvement and equilibration when it was permitted to operate freely, without restraint. If certain participants possessed special advantages or monopolies, this would distort the spontaneous balance of supply and demand forces, and impede the course of equitable distribution and material advance. Even intervention by genuinely neutral governmental authorities would sap the self-reliance of market participants and discourage the most talented and socially useful from developing their full powers. Where the state was ruled by an aristocratic oligarchy, such artificial intervention was a clever ruse by which the vested interest groups lined their pockets and defrauded the public in the guise of a higher good.[39] In this theory of market freedom, the old aristocracy was clearly being hauled back into court. Now, however, the bill of indictment would contain some additional charges. Already convicted of parasitism and immorality, the aristocracy would now be charged by liberal ideologues with irrationality, obscurantism, and a propensity toward violence, which simply provided an additional list of reasons why "the people" should rise up to end its corrupt rule.

During the late twenties and early thirties, when this antiaristocratic insurgency first gathered force, Bradford's aspiring entrepreneurs and their

---

[37] Smith, *The Wealth of Nations*, 3–21; Halévy, *Philosophical Radicalism*, 89–120.

[38] Weber, *Protestant Ethic*, 54–5.

[39] Smith, *Wealth of Nations*, 398–439.

fellow reformers turned to more experienced ideological spokesmen who helped them formulate a multidimensional vision of social freedom and progress, a vision whose richness and complexity unfolded as it was articulated through a critique of the economic monopolies that harmed their interests and the political, religious, and intellectual monopolies that propped economic privilege up. For the restless, young, provincial insurgents who were just beginning to explore their possibilities and powers, nothing more eloquently voiced their own inchoate sentiments than Col. Perronet Thompson's *Corn Law Catechism*, which quickly went through five editions after its publication in 1828. Thompson, who would later be elected as Bradford's M.P., was, in addition, the editor, proprietor, and primary writer of the influential Benthamite *Westminster Review*.[40]

Although Thompson's whole purpose was to demonstrate that the Corn Laws were but one part of a larger monopolistic system, he and his readers singled them out as a symbol of the entire complex because of the laws' key role in protecting the market in grain, that most basic of all commodities, whose price level regulated the distribution of economic resources throughout the whole society. According to Thompson, the system of agricultural tariffs, by artificially inflating the price of bread, diminished the purchasing power of the laborer and increased the capitalists' production costs. Worse still, by excluding the products of foreign agriculture, the Corn Laws dealt a further blow to industrial development by providing foreigners with a powerful incentive to close their own markets to British manufactured goods. The result not only distorted the natural flow of market forces in favor of a bloated and inefficient domestic agriculture, but fettered the development of productive industry, particularly in the most competitive export trades. Although this diminished entrepreneurial opportunities, in the end, it was the worker who suffered the most. "There are, " Thompson contended, "thousands of capitalists waiting to give him employment and millions of men waiting to give him food in return for his labour, and it is the pleasure of the agriculturalist that they shall not."[41]

Nevertheless, the greatest travesty of this corrupt and illogical system lay not in the damage it inflicted on any particular interests, but in its injury to the overall engine of progress, to the spontaneous distribution of resources in a global marketplace in the manner most conducive to economic efficiency and growth. "Whenever," according to Thompson, "anything is taken from one man and given to another under the pretense of protection to trade, an equal amount is virtually thrown into the sea in addition to the robbery of

---

[40] L. G. Johnson, *General T. Perronet Thompson* (London, 1957), 125–38, 142–58; Joseph Hamburger, *James Mill and the Art of Revolution* (New Haven, 1963), 48–111.

[41] Thompson, *Exercises*, 4:508.

the individual."[42] Such a visible affront to the general interest could be perpetuated on an ongoing basis only because society was not the true master of its fate. Thus agrarian economic monopoly pointed back to the aristocratic political monopoly by which it was sustained. The Corn Laws, according to Thompson, were no more than a logical corollary of the constitutional system whereby landlords dominated both houses of Parliament while a town like Bradford was not represented at all. At best, "each class is to have a representative, or it may be two or three; *and those who live upon the public are to have the rest.*"[43] "No one," he continued, "would endure such nonsense in a joint-stock company and there is no more reason for enduring it anywhere else." The great public corporation would only be well governed when it was forced to become accountable to popular rule.

Thompson's breezy equation of popular with efficient government, his glib assumption that liberal entrepreneurial authority and the sovereignty of market exchange would be endorsed by the democratization of political power, may seem, from hindsight, extraordinarily naive. He was, however, at least partly cognizant of the danger that the populace might repudiate liberal entrepreneurial leadership, but his position was predicated on the conviction that, if they did so, it would be because they had been corrupted by aristocratic deception and certainly not because it was genuinely in their interests to act in this way. Indeed, it was precisely because aristocratic rule was so patently illegitimate, its violation of natural law so transparent and complete, that it could be perpetuated only by a system of ideological obfuscation that kept the masses in the dark. Here was the most vicious consequence of aristocratic monopoly, that it necessitated an atmosphere of intellectual ignorance and moral degradation to prevent the masses from recognizing their true interests and demanding their rights. Reinforcing popular superstitions, stirring up atavistic hatreds, and playing on irrational anxieties and fears, the rule of aristocratic elites and their ideological agents in the clerical establishments created an environment in which the independence of public opinion and the integrity of rational discourse was constantly in danger of being undermined.[44]

In the last resort, there remained the feudal traditions of force and violence, which a threatened oligarchy could always invoke, endangering the liberty of other nations and repressing all criticism and opposition at home. Thompson was one of the first to point out the close connection between domestic reaction and militarism abroad. "War," he noted, "is self-defence against reform: and however just and necessary this may be, it is acknowl-

---

[42] Ibid., 4:498.
[43] Ibid., 1:223.
[44] Ibid., 4:517.

edged to be better to carry it on in a foreign territory than in your own."[45] By contrast, free trade was the most certain recipe for domestic harmony and international peace. As Thompson's young understudy Richard Cobden, himself a rising manufacturer, explained, "It unites, by the strongest motives of which our nature is susceptible, two remote communities, rendering the interest of one the only true policy of the other and making each equally anxious for the prosperity and happiness of both."[46]

The free market, as these comments indicate, was not simply seen as an instrument for the distribution of material commodities. It was exalted as a mechanism for harmonizing all interests, spreading moral values, and diffusing ideas. In contrast to the corrupt reign of aristocratic monopolism, a society governed by free-market principles could no more tolerate intellectual censorship or political repression than it could sanction restrictions in the economic realm. Voluntary popular education, concentrating on the truths of political economy and the virtues of Christianity and fostering self-reliance and self-respect, was indispensable to a free society. Only a people accustomed to rational argument would be capable of discerning its real self-interest and rejecting demagoguery, whether from the right or the left.[47]

This theme was taken up by Dissenting ministers such as Edward Miall, the brother of a local Congregationalist pastor, who would also later be elected as a Bradford M.P. As a national leader of the campaign against Anglican and Tory interference in mass education, Miall emphasized the need for popular enlightenment. "To inspire a universal taste for knowledge ... and, above all, to encourage that mental independence without which cultivated faculties even of the highest order are but tools for prejudice to work with" was a precondition for liberal capitalist rule. Only when "popular education and good government [were] so intimately associated as to become well nigh identical," Miall concluded, could the future of freedom and progress be insured.[48]

Knowledge, the local Congregationalist minister Walter Scott insisted, "was never given to any to be hoarded or monopolized or confined to any grade or class of society, but to be diffused as widely as possible."[49] Even ideas that were considered shocking or dangerous must be tolerated and controverted openly, not persecuted or tacitly suppressed: "To attempt to seal the mouth, or stifle the voice of an opponent is not the way to convert him. Intolerance and bigotry, far from exterminating or suppressing errors,

[45] Ibid., 1:286.
[46] Richard Cobden, *Political Writings* (London, 1886), 225.
[47] T. Perronet Thompson, *Audi Alteram Partem* (London, 1859), 6–7.
[48] Edward Miall, *Nonconformist Sketchbook* (London, 1867), 89.
[49] J. Ackworth, *Speech at the Inauguration of the Bradford Mechanics Institute* (Bradford, 1837), 7.

are its fastest friends, and best patrons. They may make hypocrites and liars, but they can never produce disciples."[50] It was for such reasons that Rev. Godwin agreed to debate Bradford's Socialists and atheists. He gave a series of lectures on the subject that were much more popular and effective than those of the vicar, who simply denounced the infidels out of hand. According to Miall, all arguments about religion, even the most blasphemous, had their uses, if they called attention to abuses and stimulated reforms.[51]

Although it would be utopian to expect completely free access to knowledge regarding technical innovations, voluntary schools like the mechanics institutes and the natural effects of open competition would insure that improvements, even if they began as private property, would eventually be diffused or superseded by others throughout the industrial world. Here, the advent of industrial exhibitions, where potential customers gathered to see goods competitively displayed, created strong incentives to abandon or at least limit industrial secrecy and to reap the benefits that openly advertising new products and processes brought.[52]

Clearly, in this expanded entrepreneurial ideology, the competitive market was increasingly viewed not just as an economic engine of productivity, but as a social and political agent of moral progress in the fullest sense. To implement the beneficent laws of the market, to eliminate monopoly not only in economics, but in government, religion, and knowledge too, would insure the happiness and improvement of the whole world. Thus the simple doctrine of free-market competition would form the ideological lynchpin of a universal philosophy of liberty in whose terms it seemed self-evident that the private pursuit of individual interest would, at least within the framework of an urban-industrial society, be the only effectual way to promote the collective good.

Voluntary association and the cohesive society

This vision of market freedom as the lynchpin of a progressive society had a logical grandeur and simplicity that appealed to a population desperately trying to extract some sense of higher purpose from the chaos of urban-industrial life. However, as a universal principle of social and political organization, it suffered from a fatal flaw that any Bradfordian could instantly

---

[50] Ackworth, *Speech*, 17.

[51] Benjamin Godwin, *The Philosophy of Atheism Examined and Compared With Christianity* (Bradford, 1853); anon. *An Examination of the Arguments for the Existence of A Deity: An Answer to Dr. Godwin's Philosophy of Atheism Examined* (London, 1853); William Scoresby, *Lectures on Socialism* (Bradford, 1840); Miall, *British Churches*, 46.

[52] *Holden-Illingworth Letters*, A. Holden – I. Holden, Sep. 16, 1862, 345.

recognize from personal experience; for the free market operated as a so-
cialising agency only at the level of theoretical abstraction, as an impersonal
mechanism or an invisible hand. In practice, it simply crystallized the individual's sense of isolation in a volatile environment by forcing him to
internalize its impersonal imperatives and to accept their logic as his own.[53]
The problem lay on two related fronts. First, nineteenth-century Bradford
was not just a market society of equal individuals, but also a capitalist society
of unequal participants in a mode of production that structured their access
to exchangeable resources along class lines. Consequently, the market, instead of being purely an abstract instrument for the realization of freedom
and equality, was, more immediately, the mechanism by which external
compulsions and inequalities were manifested in material form.[54]

Second, there were some values that simply did not translate into the
language of the market and some benefits that competition, no matter how
open and extensive, could never bring. Though the market could help some
individuals to realize their ambitions, it offered no integrative social focus
with which they could collectively identify, for at its best, the market was a
culturally atomizing force. Its radically individualistic mode of competition
produced a sense of outer anomie and inner loneliness that would, but for
the biological bonds of family, have led to an almost entirely asocial world.[55]
Even the entrepreneurs who had done well for themselves in the market
might, at times, feel the need for something more. Without turning their
backs on the benefits that market freedom brought them, these men and
their families sought alternative sources of social cohesion that were still
consistent with competitive individualism, but which derived from a collective, human source. To integrate individuals into a larger community without
obstructing their ability to maximize their interests and develop their powers
– this was the central challenge of an entrepreneurial order that aspired to
be more than just a mode of producing and distributing commodities. To
become a general engine of cultural progress, bringing social stability without
economic stagnation or intellectual retreat, it would be necessary to create
a whole network of voluntary associations in which distinctively liberal, entrepreneurial forms of sociability could arise.[56]

[53] Marx, *Capital*, 1:76–87.
[54] See Chapter 4.
[55] Emile Durkheim, *Suicide* (Glencoe, 1951), 169–70, 246–58; idem. *The Division of Labor
in Society* (Glencoe, 1933), 253–7; Louis Wirth, *On Cities and Social Life* (Chicago, 1964),
60–83. The problem was, perhaps, best diagnosed by one anonymous correspondent to
the local paper who, in 1837, complained that "a keen, grasping, inordinate lust for gain
pervades all classes, uprooting the germ of sympathy in its infant development. No moral
project even arrives at its end or very few...in the absorbing pursuit of wealth all
intermediate considerations are sacrificed." *BO*, Feb. 9, 1837.
[56] Though the significance of associational voluntarism as the ideal means of providing
social cohesion in an individualistic market society has not been much examined in the

Like the market, the voluntary association was an institution founded on freedom of choice. Like the market, it was based on a covenant, formal or tacit, between individuals to work jointly for a common object. However, whereas the market threw people into competition with one another, the voluntary association brought them together and taught them the benefits of cooperation and solidarity, if only as means to the achievement of fundamentally individual ends. Of course, voluntary associations were nothing new in nineteenth-century Bradford, having long played an important role in the town's religious and secular life. However, in the past, they had always been supplementary agencies augmenting the primary integrative institutions of church and state. Voluntary associations had assisted these established institutions or, alternatively, had offered partial escapes from their power, but had never challenged their status as embodiments of the community as a whole.

However, in the context of the urban-industrial revolution, there emerged, first in the religious and then in the secular sphere, a new type of voluntary association aiming not merely to supplement traditional institutions, but to supplant them. Voluntarism would become the central organizing principle of society and would replace the monopolist cultural and political establishments with a free market in competing associational agencies, among which each individual could and must choose. Through this spontaneous proliferation of voluntary associations, it was hoped the market mechanism that had regulated Bradford's urban and industrial development could be forged into a cultural and political instrument that would, without any sacrifice of freedom, reconcile individual interests and social needs."Nothing," the *Observer* argued in 1868, "more vividly marks our civilization than the multiplication of separate societies and agencies religious, charitable, political, economical, educational, professional, friendly, recreative, and what not."[57] It seemed logical, perhaps inevitable, that, within a dynamic industrial city, established institutions should give way to a plurality of alternatives based on individual choice and sustained by the free flows of market demand. Legal privileges and monopolies could, at most, slow down this apparently spontaneous evolutionary process.

The new culture of associational voluntarism differed greatly from the traditional culture it was replacing in inner content as well as outward form. Whereas traditional culture had been proscriptive, grounded in the certainty of a higher authority that endowed participants with enduring values and identities, the culture of voluntarism was ethically neutral, obliging individ-

historiography of nineteenth-century Britain, it constitutes a key theme in Tocqueville's analysis of democracy in the nineteenth-century United States. Alexis de Tocqueville, *Democracy in America* (New York, 1966), 481–501.

[57] *BO*, Oct. 5, 1868.

uals to formulate values and identities for themselves. Whereas traditional institutions appeared to emanate from God or from nature, voluntary associations were manifestly human creations, aggregates of otherwise autonomous individuals who had banded together to fulfill a common need.[58] Unlike traditional culture, voluntarism could not absolve the individual of responsibility for self-definition. So far from shaping him, he shaped it, creating specific associations to achieve particular purposes with others who shared the same goals. Consequently, voluntarism did not so much resolve the problem of urban anomie as reconstitute it in a less dangerous form. In association, the individual obtained succor in facing the traumas of personal success or failure and support in finding his identity and organizing his life. But ultimately, he confronted these dilemmas alone. The group could only reinforce values and behavior patterns to which its members were already committed in their hearts.

For the self-made man who found his identity in experience, for the self-denying entrepreneur who found his calling in a career, associational voluntarism provided a perfect means for uniting with others to develop himself. His preoccupations with spiritual salvation and secular self-help, two sides of a single coin, served as animating principles around which he and, to some extent, also his wife and children, could unite with like-minded fellows to build a thick web of associational life. But what of other sectors of the urban-industrial population whose experience did not necessarily lead to such concerns? Could they find some meaningful anchor amidst the diversity of this associational culture, or would its very fluidity and lack of focus only reinforce their sense of disorientation, reminding them that they lacked the fixity of purpose or stability of position from which to exercise their freedom of choice? The *Observer* expressed its sympathy with such individuals when it considered the pitfalls of a voluntarist culture. "The many-sidedness of our social life," the paper lamented, "repels the most active and capacious mind that would grasp it all.... A man feels lonely in his helplessness and ignorance in the midst of these multifarious organizations and instrumentalities."[59] While the editor recognized that "the increasing density of population doubtless affords greater facility for concentrated action," he also feared that it "increases and intensifies the evil influences which are peculiar to large towns and cities."[60]

To provide an antidote to these ever worsening "evil influences" on the increasingly "helpless" and "ignorant" urban-industrial working class, Brad-

[58] Max Weber, *Economy and Society* (Los Angeles, 1978), 1:24, 29, 30, 63–74, 82–6; Ferdinand Toennies, *Community and Society* (Ann Arbor, Michigan, 1957).
[59] *BO*, Oct. 5, 1868.
[60] *BO*, June 23, 1853.

ford's ascendant bourgeoisie turned with mounting hope and expectation to their own "multifarious organizations and instrumentalities" of religious salvation and secular self-help. Through a culture of voluntarism, the bourgeoisie would finally attempt to achieve that social consensus around its values and authority that neither the work of production nor the free flows of the market had, in themselves, been able to create. More than the factory and even the marketplace, the voluntary association was framed as an institution for crossing class lines. Its purpose was given by its bourgeois founders, but its mission was to compete in the cultural marketplace, catering to the masses and converting lost souls.

Unlike traditional institutions, which either ranked their members in an immutable hierarchy or reduced them to anonymity, the voluntary association reflected social relationships in flux. It was, in the words of Rev. J. R. Campbell, a dynamic, constantly growing organism based on "the diversity of function and harmony of working in the members [which] reveals its general health and vigor." Although based on the ideal of equal opportunity, it operated on the competitive assumption that not all of its members would prove equally successful. Hence it was "a fraternity which is not equality and which is most beautiful in the absence of equality."[61]

The primary aim of these new voluntary associations was to create such a fraternity of intrinsically unequal members, each of whom was to be socially and culturally integrated at whatever level his or her ambition and ability would allow. Through these associations the entrepreneurial bourgeoisie sought to demonstrate in practice what it had hitherto only asserted as an ideal, that its own class values could be extended to the rest of the urban-industrial population who would embrace them as providing the most favorable climate both for individual and for general social advance. Commenced in the first quarter of the nineteenth century, this associational nexus came of age in the volatile decades of the 1830s and 1840s when it provided the framework for a systematic bourgeois culture and politics that sought to achieve hegemony over Bradford's restive working class. Although not succeeding in causing most workers to acquiesce in bourgeois leadership, the culture of voluntarism that emerged in this period set the stage for a much more effective kind of bourgeois hegemony during the mid-Victorian period when a network of more genuinely inclusive voluntary associations did underwrite the kind of social consensus in which entrepreneurial capitalism could prosper and prevail.

[61] J. R. Campbell, *Lessons in Social Science from the Life of our Blessed Saviour* (Bradford, 1859), 8.

10

The culture of voluntarism:
religious association

The triumph of Bradford's new culture of voluntarism can be seen most clearly in the sphere of religion. The decades of the urban-industrial revolution were also a period of dramatic and precipitous decline for the established church and of expansion for the voluntary Nonconformist sects. If religion reflects the character of society, providing a reified image of its members' collective life, this should come as no surprise. Given the anomic, market-oriented character of the society that was emerging in early-nineteenth-century Bradford and the intensely individualistic, salvation-centered preoccupations of many of its successful elites, it was only natural that so many diverse, autonomous, and competing forms of worship should proliferate within the town.[1]

The triumph of Nonconformist voluntarism

The full extent of the Nonconformist triumph in Bradford was revealed by the 1851 religious census, which showed that only 23 percent of all morning worshippers on census Sunday (March 1) chose to attend Bradford's established churches. By contrast, almost 60 percent worshiped in forty-one different Nonconformist chapels (Table 10-1).[2]

Of course, the Anglican church's hold on the population had always been tenuous. Even before the nineteenth century, the majority of the community had attended only infrequently. A minority, by no means insignificant, had openly identified with the Presbyterian or Quaker denominations of Old Dissent. Still, the parish was the fundamental political unit and its church served as the most official community symbol. However, by midcentury, as Bradford became a city of 100,000, this had ceased to be true. Although the church retained some of its political monopoly and Anglicanism remained an official religion, the religious census revealed that only 4,719 men, women,

[1] Emile Durkheim, *The Elementary Forms of the Religious Life* (London, 1957), 415–47.
[2] *PP* (LXXXIX, 1852–3), cclii–cclxxii.

Table 10-1. *1851 religious census: accommodation and attendance by denomination*

Denomination	Available sittings as % total ($N = 32,287$)	Attendance at morning service as % total ($N = 20,438$)
Anglican	31.1	23.1
Presbyterian	3.5	2.7
Quaker	3.1	0.8
Independent	11.1	12.3
Baptist	10.6	12.8
Wesleyan	21.9	17.4
Primitive Methodist	6.1	4.2
Other Methodist	9.4	9.2
Catholic	1.2	15.8
Other	2.1	1.7

Source: PP (LXXXIX, 1852–3), cclii–cclxxii.

and children, 4.6 percent of the urban population, showed up at Anglican morning service on March 1, 1851.[3]

The precipitous decline of Bradford's Anglican church from official emblem of the traditional community to an enclave of economic and political privilege was a consequence of the process of urban-industrial development in the town. The very advantages that the national church enjoyed, which made it so appropriate for a stable, hierarchical, rural world, insured that it would be unable to adapt to the conditions that now confronted it. Its extensive property and patronage, its close ties with the landed elite and the state, its territorial system of parochial organization – all bulwarks of the church's power and authority – put it at a disadvantage in the mobile environment of industrial Bradford, where population, wealth, and centers of power were constantly shifting in response to market forces.[4]

Frozen into a preindustrial pattern of social geography, Bradford's parochial and clerical authorities were unable to respond to the influx of population that was turning an overgrown village into a major city. An enormous, far-flung parish of fifty-three square miles made sense in an era of scattered settlement, but by 1851, it encompassed a population of 170,361. Although some efforts had been made to construct new churches, the difficulty of

---

[3] Of all the towns and cities in England, only in Preston was the performance of Anglicanism more dismal. Ibid.

[4] A. D. Gilbert, *Religion and Society in Industrial England* (London, 1976), 3–20.

freeing resources tied up in ecclesiastical patronage as well as the closefist-edness and indifference of local Anglican elites meant that such activity was too little and too late.[5] Before 1815, when Christ Church was constructed, the parish church was the only Anglican place of worship in town. Another twenty-one years elapsed before a third urban church was built. Thereafter, between 1840 and 1850, five additional churches were hastily built, but since they were located in what were then the suburbs, they were primarily for the benefit of the middle classes.[6] As late as 1858, 78,232 souls, the vast bulk of Bradford's population, were still under the jurisdiction of the old parish church. With his staff of four underpaid curates and his extensive parochial administrative responsibilities, even the most talented and hard-working vicar could provide little spiritual sustenance for such a flock. More-over, since the fourteen hundred pews were legally appropriated by local elites, this population had at its disposal only two hundred makeshift seats in the aisles.[7]

The failure of the Anglican church to provide accommodation for the growing population was serious enough. More serious still was its failure to attract even those for whom it had room. The tepid theology of early-nineteenth-century Anglicanism – the ignorance, venality, and reactionary politics of all too many of its beneficed clergymen – were not likely to appeal to the intelligent and industrious people that the urban environment tended to attract. As Dr. Simpson lamented in 1825, "The present clergy of the established Church are doing great harm to their own cause and are be-coming every day more unpopular."[8] In particular, Rev. Henry Heap, who was vicar of Bradford from 1816 to 1839, was, by all accounts, an incom-petent timeserver who let many opportunities for improvement slip by. Ac-cording to Simpson, in addition to not being "a man of sufficient talent for the situation he holds," Heap was "very vain and jealous of popularity so that he always takes care to have a curate worse, if possible, than himself."[9] Even the advent of able clergymen in the 1830s and 1840s, such as George Bull, the curate of Bierley (1826–39) or William Scoresby, the energetic vicar who reorganized parochial administration between 1839 and 1847, at best slowed down the rate of Anglican decline.[10] Such individuals could not

---

[5] *PP* (IX, 1857–8), 417.

[6] John James, *History and Topography of Bradford* (Bradford, 1841), 221–3.

[7] *PP* (IX, 1857–8), 417.

[8] John Simpson, *The Journal of Dr. John Simpson of Bradford, 1825* (Bradford, 1982), 38.

[9] Simpson, *Journal*, 38.

[10] J. C. Gill, *The Ten Hours Parson* (London, 1959); idem, *Parson Bull of Byerley* (London, 1973); Tom and Cordelia Stamp, *William Scoresby, Arctic Explorer* (Whitby, 1975). In 1843, an attempt to subdivide the parish into more viable units foundered on a conflict

reverse forces that were structural in nature, and their aggressive programs of church defense generated as much antagonism as extra support. The full measure of the Anglican failure can be seen in the 1851 census: Less than half of Bradford's available church sittings were occupied, as 95 percent of the population simply stayed away.[11]

The cultural and spiritual void left by the failure of Anglicanism in early-nineteenth-century Bradford was not left entirely unfilled. With 22,261 sittings and 12,491 attenders in Bradford's Dissenting chapels, the Nonconformists, on census Sunday morning, outnumbered the Anglicans by a margin of three to one. Although this left many people still untouched by any organized religion, insofar as there was a dominant form of worship in midcentury Bradford, it was the voluntary Nonconformist and not the established Anglican form. Indeed, the census statistics revealed that, by 1851, Bradford had become the most intensely Nonconformist town in England.[12]

This explosion of sects was clearly connected with the urban-industrial revolution that was transforming social relations in town. The link between economic and demographic expansion and the rise of the voluntary Nonconformist sects can be seen in the data in Table 10-2, which compares the timing of church and chapel construction. The number of chapels in Bradford began to increase significantly only after urbanization commenced, and the rate of increase accelerated during the 1820s when the second phase of urbanization began. Sixty percent of Bradford's pre-1850 chapels were constructed during the 1820s and 1830s as the bulk of the aspiring new immigrants arrived.

What makes this Nonconformist explosion particularly impressive was that it was concentrated almost entirely in three denominations, the Baptists, the Congregationalists, and the various Methodist connections that had, with the exception of the Wesleyan Methodists, scarcely even existed before urbanization began. By contrast, the Old Dissenting sects, the Quakers and the Presbyterians, who had constituted the core of Nonconformity in protoindustrial Bradford, were largely unresponsive to the urban age. Neither opened any new chapels throughout the period, and the 1851 census enumerated congregations not much larger than they had been a century earlier.[13]

---

of authority between Scoresby and the ecclesiastical commissioners and ultimately led to his resignation in 1844. *BO*, June 1, 1843; Feb. 15, 1844; Jan. 23, Mar. 6, 1845.

[11] *PP* (LXXXIX, 1852–3), cclii–cclxxii.

[12] Ibid.

[13] Like the Anglican Church, Bradford's old Dissenting denominations were becoming narrow oligarchies of wealthy, established, protoindustrial families whose experiences were increasingly out of touch with the urban-industrial environment in which they lived.

Table 10-2. *Church and chapel building in Bradford: 1800–80, by decade*

	Number of churches built	Number of Methodist chapels built	Number of other chapels built	Total number of places of worship built
Before 1800	2	1	4	7
1800–9	0	0	0	0
1810–19	1	2	0	3
1820–9	0	9	2	11
1830–9	2	8	5	15
1840–9	4	5	3	12
1850–9	1	4	6	11
1860–9	9	4	3	16
1870–9	16	19	13	48

Sources: Compiled from a variety of sources, notably from John James, *History and Topography of Bradford* (Bradford, 1841), 222–37; idem, *Continuations and Additions to the History of Bradford* (Bradford, 1866), 176–97; and the 1851 Religious Census Manuscripts (HO, 127/499). See also Theodore Koditschek, "Class Formation and the Bradford Bourgeoisie, 1750–1870" (Princeton, Ph.D. dissertation, 1981), 499, footnote 15.

However, Baptists, Congregationalists, and Methodists proliferated with astounding rapidity in Bradford between 1810 and 1850, growing from virtual insignificance at the turn of the century to encompass thirty-seven chapels with 11,419 morning worshipers representing 56 percent of all attenders in 1851.[14] This expansion depended on the recruitment of new members, a process which took place in two very different ways. On the one hand, growth resulted from the arrival of immigrants who brought their Nonconformist identities with them. On the other hand, it also came from the conversion of godless or nominally Anglican individuals who were encountered within the town.

Although the Dissenting denominations relied on both types of expansion, the Baptists and the Congregationalists increased primarily as a result of the former, whereas the Methodist denominations proved to be most adept at the task of evangelical conversion, seeking to bring as many as possible of the uprooted masses under the aegis of the godly way.[15]

The denominations that stood at the heart of the voluntaristic system,

A. Cobden-Smith, *Historical Sketch of Chapel Lane Chapel* (Bradford, n.d.); H. R. Hodgson, *The Society of Friends in Bradford* (Bradford, 1926).

[14] *PP* (LXXXIX, 1852–3), cclii–cclxxii.

[15] Gilbert, *Religion and Society*, 51–68. W. R. Ward, *Religion and Society in England, 1790–1850* (New York, 1973), 71.

whose liberal organization and hyper-Calvinist theology were best suited to the needs of the entrepreneurial bourgeoisie, were the Baptists and the Congregationalists. The history of these two denominations, from their humble beginnings around the turn of the century to their dramatic rise in numbers, wealth, and social standing in the two and a half decades after 1825, closely mirrors the careers of their leading members.[16] Most of Bradford's early Congregationalists and Baptists had been poor, but their sects' individualistic and salvation-centered orientation tended to select the most enterprising and self-directed of the new Bradfordians, many of whom were destined for success. The arrival of such individuals in increasing numbers after 1820 caused a growth spurt in the development and prosperity of these two denominations. By the midcentury religious census, the two chapels had multiplied to nine with 4,637 attenders between them.[17]

During these years, the Baptists, particularly at Westgate and Sion Chapels, nurtured such future luminaries as the manufacturers Alfred and Daniel Illingworth, Thomas Dewhirst, William Whitehead, Jonathan Thornton, and Briggs Priestley; the merchants William Murgatroyd, Thomas Aked, John Godwin, and Arthur Briggs; as well as the builder J. A. Illingworth; the iron founder John Cole; and John Morley, the proprietor of a large pawnbroking chain.[18] At Horton Lane Congregationalist Chapel, an even more stellar cast of rising entrepreneurs took shape. A burial register from the 1840s shows that, even among the 221 individuals who died during this decade, 42 percent were bourgeois whereas another 20 percent were lower middle class. Only 28 percent were skilled workers and 10 percent unskilled.[19] A list of pewholders complied a few years earlier shows that the active part of the congregation was now even more uniformly bourgeois. Filled with names like Daniel and Titus Salt, John and Richard Garnett, Henry Forbes, Samuel Smith, James Rennie, and William Byles, it reads almost like a register of Bradford's mid-Victorian notability-to-be. Spawning four of Bradford's first five mayors, a large majority of its early aldermen and municipal justices as well as the editor of the *Bradford Observer*, this "Cathedral of Nonconformity," as it came to be known, served as a training ground where much of mid-Victorian Bradford's civic leadership was forged.[20]

[16] William Cudworth, *Horton Lane Chapel, Old Time Reminiscences* (Bradford, 1893); anon., *The Centenary: A History of the First Baptist Church in Bradford* (London, 1853).

[17] *PP* (LXXXIX, 1852–3), cclii–cclxxii.

[18] *First Baptist Church*, 31, 48; anon., *The Centenary Souvenir: Sion Baptist Chapel, 1824–1924* (Bradford, 1924); anon., *Westgate Baptist Chapel: List of Members* (Bradford, 1867); Benjamin Godwin, "Autobiography" (mss., Bradford Central Library), 554.

[19] Compiled from "Horton Lane Gravesites" (mss., Bradford Archives, 57D76/2).

[20] Other names on the list of pewholders include James and Thomas Hammond, John Russell, Robert Monies, John Tordoff, Robert Pullen, George Rogers, William Marten,

Nevertheless, the success of the Baptists and Congregationalists in attracting the most promising of the new bourgeoisie was marred by an equally striking failure to incorporate more than minuscule elements of other social groups. In fact, the Calvinist focus on an inner-directed spiritual elite fostered a disdain for the sinful multitudes who, nevertheless, constituted the majority of the population in town. However, what gave the Baptists and Congregationalists the luxury of ignoring the masses was the activity of the evangelical Methodist denominations, which were more responsive to popular needs. With 6,294 worshippers on census Sunday morning or 31 percent of all religious attenders, the Methodists were the largest single denomination, 33 percent larger than the Anglican church. Although five different Methodist connexions were represented in Bradford at midcentury, 56 percent of all Methodists were still in the parent Wesleyan body from which the others had originally broken away.[21]

Although Wesleyan membership, as measured in Table 10-3, was, as in every denomination, disproportionately middle class, the Wesleyans were more successful than the Baptists or Congregationalists in attracting a substantial number of people from the skilled working and lower middle class.[22] The secret of the Wesleyans' success, both in attracting large numbers and in drawing from a broad social range, lay in their emphasis on the conversion experience, which fostered a special commitment to evangelical outreach. This conscious decision to seek out sinners rather than to serve a spiritual

William Wyrill, George Haigh, and Thomas Buck. Not included in the list but also prominent members of the congregation were the dyers George and Henry Ripley, the machine maker Benjamin Berry, and the merchants Robert Milligan, Edward Kenion, and James Law. William Cudworth, *Historical Notes on the Bradford Corporation* (Bradford, 1881), 112–37, 227; idem, *Horton Lane Chapel*. After the 1830s, the new Baptist and Congregationalist chapels built in the suburbs were almost all primarily middle class from the outset, *BO*, Dec. 21. 1867.

[21] *PP* (LXXXIX, 1852–3), cclii–cclxxii.

[22] Nevertheless, despite their larger scale and broader social base, Bradford's Wesleyan congregations also nurtured the same type of upwardly mobile, entrepreneurial aspirant who was more characteristic among the Baptists and Congregationalists. Indeed, a substantial number of Bradford's new generation of industrial capitalists – such as Issac Holden, James Drummond, Benjamin Illingworth, Lodge Calvert, Thomas Dewhirst, John Rhodes, Edward Onions, and Thomas, Francis, and John Mitchell – worked their way up in the Wesleyan ranks. The same was true of the leading stuff merchants William Peel, Isaac Naylor, Henry Mitchell, and John Broadbent; the retailers Abraham Brumfitt, James Bottomley, and Thomas Milner; as well as the druggist Joseph Roper, the surgeon William Beaumont, and the builder George Smith. J. N. Dickons, "Kirkgate Chapel, Bradford, and its Associations with Methodism," *BA*, n.s. 5 (1933), 68–97, 205–24; J. N. Dickons and R. Poole, *Kirkgate Chapel, Bradford* (Bradford, 1911); Anon., *Eastbrook Chapel, 1825; Centenary Souvenir*, (Bradford, 1925); "Manningham Methodist Circuit Reports, 1884–93," (Federer mss., Bradford Archives, 194.1/197).

Table 10-3. *Kirkgate Wesleyan Chapel: social class of deceased members over 18 years of age at death, 1815–54*

Period of death	Percentage of semiskilled workers	Percentage of skilled workers	Percentage of lower middle class	Percentage of bourgeoisie	N
1815–34	29	27	30	14	160
1835–44	26	32	29	13	161
1845–54	26	23	40	11	172

Source: Compiled from "Kirkgate Chapel Grave Books, 1815–37; 1837–55" (mss., Bradford Archives, 57D76/2).

elite led to a very different style of religiosity that was more spontaneous and emotional than that of other Dissenters but also more disciplined and centrally controlled. Where the Baptists and Congregationalists combined open and democratic forms of ecclesiastical organization with the rigorous theology of a spiritual elect, the Wesleyans combined a flexible and egalitarian theology that offered hope to the ungodly with an authoritarian organization that would help the spiritually weak to remain within the fold.[23]

As Table 10-3 shows, during the protoindustrial era, 56 percent of all Wesleyans in Kirkgate Chapel had been artisans or members of the working class. In fact, during the 1800–10 decade of economic crisis, Methodism had undergone an immense revival, and membership had shot up by 43 percent. During the next twenty years, there was a lull in recruitment, punctuated by a spurt that took place in 1824. However, with the return of hard times in the 1830s and 1840s, membership once again began to increase. During the thirties, the Bradford Circuit added over one thousand members, and in 1835, it was divided in two. Then in 1844, there was another major revival when membership shot up by 23 percent to 4,800.[24]

Although Table 10-3 indicates that the proportion of working-class Wesleyans was gradually diminishing as urbanization proceeded, by midcentury, workers still accounted for about half of all members in Kirkgate Chapel according to death records. Moreover, any diminution in working-class Wesleyan participation was more than compensated by the rise of the breakaway Primitive Methodists who attracted 867 morning worshippers in 1851, as well as 1,785 in the afternoon and evening.[25]

The attack on the Anglican establishment

The practical success of Bradford's Nonconformists in undermining the Anglican religious monopoly made the church's privileges seem even more galling, since they were perpetuated in opposition to the clear verdict of popular choice. Like the entrepreneur in the realm of production, or the liberal reformer in the state, Bradford's Dissenters believed that they had proven their competitive superiority in the crucible of the market, yet they remained subordinated to a corrupt establishment that they were expected to subsidize as it kept them down.

This more aggressive Nonconformist posture first surfaced during the

[23] E. P. Thompson, *The Making of the English Working Class* (New York, 1963), 355–64; Bernard Semmel, *The Methodist Revolution* (New York, 1973).
[24] William W. Stamp, *Historical Notices of Wesleyan Methodism in Bradford* (Bradford, 1841), 85; James, *Continuations and Additions*, 195; *BO*, Aug. 30, 1838.
[25] *PP* (LXXXIX, 1852–3), cclii–cclxxii.

struggles over the Test and Corporation Acts in 1828–9, when Dissenters, no longer content with their second-class status, began to sense their potential power.[26] To a man like Godwin, though he expected not "the least benefit personally" from the repeal of these measures, their abolition made him feel like a full citizen for the first time in his life. "It seemed to have thrown off a burden," he remembered decades later, "to have got rid of something which impeded the free action of my limbs. A mark of degradation was taken off the body to which I belonged ... [and] I felt that truth and righteousness were gaining ground, that liberal principles were advancing & that Britain had raised herself to a moral elevation among the nations of Europe greater than any she had previously occupied."[27]

Basking in their newfound freedom and moral elevation, Bradford's young Nonconformist immigrants, especially the Baptists and Congregationalists among them, took advantage of the prevailing momentum to mount a full-scale attack on the obligatory church rates. In 1834, a petition calling for their abolition was signed by 5,500 Bradfordians. Then in 1835, two Quaker millowners refused to pay their rate and the town's leading liberals called for mass attendance at the annual church vestry to prevent the laying of a rate in the following year. Intending to use the procedural democracy of the vestry to defeat its oligarchical function, the liberal Dissenters brought out a large crowd who voted the rate down. For the next four years, the same tactic was repeated until the controversy entered a new and more acrimonious phase.[28]

In 1837, the "friends of the Church of England" called a meeting at which Anglican millowners spoke up in defense of the establishment. John Rand saw the merits of religious voluntarism but "would have this voluntary principle to come in aid of a certain and permanent endowed system, and not that it should supplant that system." J. G. Horsfall agreed that "no country can be happy which does not maintain an established religion," for this was "the great bond of social union" around which an entire people could unite.[29] In 1839, the Anglican reaction intensified after the appointment of the aggressive new vicar, William Scoresby, who was determined that the church rate would not die. For the next two years, the rate was again defeated, but in 1841, when a Tory political revival was in full swing, the frustrated Scoresby obtained ecclesiastical permission to levy the tax in spite of the ratepayers' votes. Several leading Dissenters refused to pay on principle, and when distress seizures against their property were made, liberal

[26] G. I. T. Machin, *Politics and the Churches in Great Britain, 1832 to 1868* (Oxford, 1972), 1–27; Ward, *Religion and Society*, 105–292.
[27] Goodwin, "Autobiography," 466.
[28] *BO*, Feb. 27, May 8, 15, Sept. 30, 1834; Mar. 5, July 2, 9, 1835.
[29] Anon., *Church or No Church* (Bradford, 1837); *BO*, May 25, 1837.

opinion in the town was outraged and the Nonconformist leaders vowed to fight back. At the next vestry meeting they elected a Congregationalist churchwarden, the printer John Dale. After this, local Anglican officials ceased trying to extract further church rates.[30]

Having won their battle over the church rates, Bradford's leading Dissenters were now ready to take aim at the very notion of an established church. As early as 1841, the Congregationalist minister Walter Scott established the Voluntary Church Society whose object was the abolition of tithes and "the complete separation of church and state."[31] In 1847, Edward Miall and the merchant Henry Forbes called a meeting to set up a Bradford branch of the Anti-State Church Association that would agitate for the disestablishment of Anglicanism much as the Anti-Corn Law League had fought for the repeal of economic protectionism. Over the next few years, support for disestablishment grew, and it remained a central issue in local politics for the next twenty-five years.[32]

Nonconformist radicals like Edward Miall hoped to mobilize the same popular resentment of aristocratic monopoly that had inspired the struggle for reform and free trade to the anticlerical struggle for religious disestablishment. Unlike France, where anticlericalism was the battle cry of secular radicals, in England, it was advocated in the name of true religion itself. To Miall, state monopolies in religion were even more egregious than their counterparts in politics or trade precisely because they represented a defilement of the most holy institution by men pursuing sordid, worldly ends. "The truth is," Miall protested, "I cannot recognize civil establishments of Christianity as organizations for the extension of Christ's Kingdom in any sense." "They are not churches – they are merely political arrangements for the real, or ostensible attainment of spiritual objects.... They are not an association but an aggregation merely for the bond of union is only nominal."[33]

The essence of Protestantism, in this view, was the recognition that Christ's Kingdom was the kingdom of love, the realm where the tyranny of the Old Testament gave way to the freedom of the New. "We are called unto liberty." "The spirit breathed into us by christianity is not a spirit of bondage ... our obedience is to be in the nature of a free will offering."[34] If government and the marketplace were properly the realms of freedom,

---

[30] *BO*, July 7, 14, 1836; Apr. 13, 1837; Nov. 22, 29, 1838; Nov. 21, 28, 1839; Mar. 24, 1842; Adrian Elliott, "The Establishment of Municipal Government in Bradford, 1837–1857," (Bradford, Ph.D. dissertation, 1976), 66–9.

[31] Walter Scott, *The Objects of the Voluntary Church Society Stated* (Bradford, 1841), 7.

[32] *BO*, Oct. 7, Nov. 4, 1847; Jan. 20, Feb. 24, Mar. 23, 1848.

[33] Edward Miall, *The British Churches in Relation to the British People* (London, 1849), 361.

[34] Ibid., 88.

then how much more so was Christianity, the source from which all freedom derived. The gospel could only effectively be preached by men and women who freely believed in it and genuine religious communion was possible only among those who voluntarily chose to participate. At heart, Christianity was a religion of individuals grounded in a private relationship between themselves and their God. Hence the true church was but a voluntary association founded to help its members in achieving life's most important end. It followed that state monopolies were more than simply wasteful vanities, abuses of power, or insults to the simple dignity of faith. Much worse, they were profanations of divine ordinance, which turned Christianity to fundamentally un-Christian ends.[35]

To turn Christianity into a compulsory monopoly was to strip it of its moral appeal, to deny that Christ's teachings were actually practicable, and to bring religion into contempt among the more intelligent portion of the population. To Miall, spiritual apathy and the spread of godlessness and immorality among the workers were evils to be laid directly at the doorstep of the establishment whose corruption and cynicism gave the gospel a bad name.[36] Shielded from the full rigors of religious competition, its devotional agencies, when not deliberately vicious, were inefficient and hopelessly weak. Its clergy, in spite of their expensive university educations, were often ignorant and temperamentally unsuited to their work, relying on ritual and empty ceremonies as a substitute for serious preaching or pastoral care.[37] So long as this system was officially sanctioned and subsidized, lay enthusiasm could never be stirred. Among the respectable, church-going middle class, a trancelike mechanical approach to religion would set in while the workers, "identifying Christianity with the nationally authorized exhibition of it and taught to regard the Church Establishment as sanctioning and abetting the oppression which crushes them to earth, [would find] their natural distaste for the solemnities of religion ... irritated into a malignant hatred."[38]

According to this radical Nonconformist diagnosis, true religion could never fully perform its socially integrative role so long as the established church remained in place. To build a new moral and cultural consensus around the values of voluntarism, Dissenters would not only have to proselytize the masses, but enlist them in a populist political campaign to end the unfair system of religious protection that prevented the earthly realm of Christian freedom from coming into its own.

---

[35] Ibid., 364.
[36] Ibid., 211–25.
[37] Ibid., 365–9.
[38] Ibid., 379.

Congregationalism as a way of life

Not all Dissenters went as far as Miall in envisioning wholesale church disestablishment as a necessary condition for the triumph of Christian liberty, but even those who were less radical recognized theirs as a fundamentally different kind of religiosity than the worship of the established church. These differences between church and chapel and the ascendancy of the latter were immediately obvious in architectural terms. Whereas the parish church had once towered over the community, binding its parishioners through an entity greater than themselves, Bradford's string of early-nineteenth-century chapels were plain to the point of anonymity. The vaulting Gothic edifice of the national establishment, with its ornate altar and raised pulpit, communicated the awe and mystery of its Holy Communion and the clerical majesty of its officiating priest.[39] In striking contrast, the Nonconformist chapels blended into the general atmosphere of undifferentiated urban blight. The puritan aesthetics of their congregations and the limited financial resources of their early years led to a design that placed a premium on outward physical ugliness as a guarantee of inner moral purity and strength. Even the most substantial of the early chapels, Westgate, Horton Lane, Sion, and Eastbrook, appear in surviving sketches as boxy, prosaic, and purely functional buildings, whereas the smaller chapels of the poorest congregations were little more than glorified shacks. These utilitarian structures were deliberate expressions of their members' business-like, no-nonsense, spiritual approach.[40]

Inside, the rituals that bound congregants in mutuality were not, as among Anglicans, passive acknowledgments of a community bequeathed by history and sanctified by God, but conscious acts of voluntary commitment to a set of beliefs and practices that were derived from the character of the individual himself. To attend the parish church had been to ratify a public birthright; to join a Nonconformist congregation was to make a personal choice. Needless to say, this form of religious worship placed a great responsibility on the shoulders of the believer while giving him a wide berth to pursue his own course. Participation in the life of the congregation offered no easy or automatic solution to the problem of salvation, which remained a private matter between the individual and his maker. Consequently, congregants often displayed a certain reticence about publicly professing their faith. Often, those who were slowest to step forward turned out to be the most truly devout. At Salem Baptist Chapel, members were constantly withdrawing

---

[39] James, *History of Bradford*, 87–237.

[40] The original Baptist College at Horton was described by its classical tutor as "like a little old fashioned warehouse or worsted mill." Godwin, "Autobiography," 359; William Scruton, *Old Bradford Views* (Bradford, 1897).

themselves temporarily from communion when they feared they might be unworthy of grace. Many Congregationalists, including Titus Salt, though regular chapel goers their entire lives, did not make a public communication of faith until they were old and approaching death.[41] No one doubted that Robert Milligan was anything but a true believer, but "of his own feelings on religious matters of a personal kind he spoke sparingly."[42]

Nevertheless, there was a danger that this privatistic religion, if carried too far, could undermine the spirit of brotherhood that was the essence of the Christian creed. The Baptist Rev. J. P. Chown was well aware "that private worship has its unspeakable advantages." Yet he warned his congregants at Sion Chapel not to use private piety as an excuse for neglecting public worship. "You are to seek for it, not merely for yourselves personally, but [for] encouraging and cheering one another." Public worship, though not the source of absolution, was the framework of Christian fellowship in which "the richest spiritual man amongst you will gather wisdom and grace from the kind Christian service of the poorest and unworthiest." By relieving the believer's sense of inner loneliness with the reinforcement of a human collectivity, "public worship, when rightly and spiritually attended to will give a blessing that no other kind of worship can impart."[43]

This goal of mutual aid in pursuit of personal justification can be seen in the spiritual and social covenant drawn up by the aspiring self-made men and women who, "being desirous for our mutual edification and the advancement of our saviour's cause to work together in the fellowship of the gospel," had originally founded Sion Chapel in 1824. Contracting together to form a congregation they vowed "to consider this society and place as our family and home, as long as divine providence shall continue our lives and our residence in this neighborhood."[44]

Those denominations that consistently followed the logic of voluntarism organized themselves similarly along congregationalist lines. Like its members, the congregation was an autonomous entity with its own ministers, officers, and legal trustees. As Rev. Godwin of Sion Chapel explained:

> I believed . . . that every separate individual Church was an independent community possessing solely and entirely the right of managing their own concerns in every respect, subject to the control and interference

---

[41] Robert Balgarnie, *Sir Titus Salt* (London, 1877), 76.

[42] *BO*, July 10, 1862. In the case of Arthur Briggs, his minister contended that "his characteristic sensitiveness and reserve long withheld him from pledging himself by vows to which he felt his courage and consistency might prove unequal." *Memorial of Arthur Briggs* (Bradford, 1893), 19–20.

[43] J. P. Chown, *Sermons, with a Brief Sketch of his Life* (Bradford, 1875), 16, 18, 22.

[44] Anon., *Sion Jubilee Chapel; The Church Covenant with Historical Notes* (Bradford, 1883), 6,7.

of no authority but that of Christ; that this community was a little republic, a pure democracy, in which every individual had equal rank and equal power conducting their affairs by means of officers (pastor and deacons) of their own selection who might be displaced at any time by the will of the Church.[45]

To the aspiring parvenus who established these congregations, the "little republic" of religious association gave them their first experience of collective action outside the family as well as a primary model that they would draw on implicitly when devising more secular and complex organizational forms. Preoccupation with salvation drove them to religion, but the dilemma of salvation was connected with the problems of life. Thus the new religious associations became bourgeois workshops in which solutions to these problems could be explored and implemented on a modest scale. The "pure democracy" of the self-governing congregation was an environment that gave them the personal autonomy they demanded while providing them with a genuinely social arena in which capacities for cooperation and leadership could be developed. Any religious agency, Rev. Fairbairn argued at the Horton Lane Chapel Centenary, must "test its worth by the kind and quality of the men that it makes."

> The church that creates the best citizens is the best and noblest national church.... Our Churches [Congregationalist], by their very constitutions qualify men for good citizenship; for they are in their nature religious brotherhoods where the highest principles are discussed and applied to various problems, events, and difficulties of a small yet complex society.[46]

A glance at the Horton Lane membership list demonstrates that this was no mere idle boast. The miniature democracy of the Nonconformist congregation was, after the family, the first and most important school of character, providing the aspiring young bourgeois with a perfect environment for cultivating qualities of public leadership and for formulating egalitarian modes of social interaction based on the voluntary flows of individual choice. Of course, chapel involvements were also important for business reputations. Contacts and friendships made in common worship could often lead to valuable partnerships or lucrative deals. The image of probity, rectitude, and solidity of character that active participation in a chapel like Horton Lane automatically conveyed was itself a valuable commodity whose worth could be measured in monetary no less than spiritual terms. In an environment relatively devoid of established family connections and status hierarchies, it was inevitable that chapel involvement would play a large, sometimes over-

[45] Godwin, "Autobiography," 622.
[46] Anon., *Horton Lane Chapel Centenary Memorial* (Bradford, 1883), 44.

whelming part in the establishment of reputations of creditworthiness and trust.[47]

Nevertheless, although the material benefits of membership in a high-status chapel were obvious, for many, the formal display of respectability was genuinely less important than the personal opportunity to develop a social practice that would help prepare them for larger social and political roles. Congregational work and governance, which absorbed enormous quantities of time and energy, was eagerly undertaken by even the busiest entrepreneurs who would have been unwilling to make comparable commitments in any other sphere outside remunerative work. Almost immediately after his arrival in Bradford, William Byles joined the congregation at Horton Lane, and according to his biographer, "become at once a very active member of the Church; a deacon, a superintendent of branch school, a trustee of chapel."[48]

The office of deacon was a position of great power and responsibility, and congregations generally elected their most prominent and successful members to serve in this role. Trusteeship was another extremely important position since the trustees represented the congregation as a legal entity and were responsible for its financial well-being. Trusteeship generally devolved upon the wealthiest congregants, who usually regarded it as an honor that they could not turn down.[49] In addition to the burdens of chapel management, successful members were expected to make financial donations in proportion to their ability to give. This was generally treated not as a substitute for personal involvement, but as a supplement that would be offered as a matter of course. Subscription lists for major projects were frequently published, and they were meant to read like socioeconomic maps. Contributions that seemed unjustifiably niggardly were likely to be the subject of open remark and the guilty parties would suffer an unspoken loss of status that must have outweighed any benefit of savings even in purely calculated terms.[50]

Just how powerfully such pressures could operate on a given individual, especially when he was a parvenu who had to demonstrate largess, can be

---

[47] For a discussion of this question see Lenore Davidoff and Catherine Hall, *Family Fortunes, Men and Women of the English Middle Class, 1780–1850* (Chicago, 1987), 99–106.

[48] F. G. Byles, *William Byles* (Weymouth, 1932), 55.

[49] Thus, in 1828, Horton Lane named the worsted capitalists Richard and James Garnett, George Haigh, John Russell, and three others as trustees, and eleven years later when a new crop of their members had made good, Henry Forbes, Robert Monies, Edward and Henry Ripley, John McCroben, William Milnes, James Rennie, and Alex Robertson were added to the list. Cudworth, *Horton Lane Chapel*.

[50] Dickons and Poole, *Kirkgate Chapel*, 42; *BO*, Apr. 10, 1856; May 15, 1862. See also Balgarnie, *Salt*, 50–1.

seen from the case of William Whitaker who gradually rose up from a humble working-class background to a junior partnership in the leading stuff firm of Milligan and Forbes. In fact, Whitaker's success turned out, in part, to have been a consequence of his prominence in Wesleyan Methodist circles, which made others regard him as a man of character, entirely worthy of business trust. However, to maintain this image, Whitaker had to make large and frequent financial contributions that he was, in actuality, unable to afford. In the end, this proved to be his undoing since it led him deeply into debt. When finally forced into bankruptcy in 1860, his position became evident and led to public humiliation and disgrace.[51]

Of course, Nonconformist theology did not limit lay leadership to secular matters of church administration but placed a premium on active participation in collective worship itself. Devout Congregationalists could be chosen as prayer leaders who served as guides for smaller groups, whereas the Methodists, with their offices of local preacher and class leader, carried this institutionalization of lay religious authority to its logical end.[52] Although the lines of spiritual authority within the congregation did not necessarily mirror worldly distinctions, upwardly mobile entrepreneurs were unusually prominent within the ranks of lay leadership that took responsibility for the spiritual oversight of the flock. Many of the prominent Wesleyan industrialists, such as Isaac Holden, Jonas Sugden, and the merchant Henry Mitchell, served as class leaders throughout most of their careers. Although lay preaching was somewhat rarer for such men, the prominent physician and sanitary reformer William Beaumont got his introduction to public speaking and public affairs through his work as a local preacher and Wesleyan circuit official.[53]

Nevertheless, the place where lay agency achieved its fullest expression was in extracongregational activities that propagated religious values and dogmas to the unconverted in ways that would have been both unnecessary and inappropriate within the congregation itself. The first and foremost of these religious auxiliaries were the Sunday schools, which absorbed large amounts of time, energy, and sometimes money from leading laymen.[54] Other

[51] *BO*, Apr. 4, June 13, 1861; Sep. 4, 1862.
[52] Cudworth, *Horton Lane Chapel*; Anon., *Eastbrook Chapel*, 22, 24, 31–3; "Methodist Class Leaders Meeting Book" (mss., Bradford Archives, D. B. 19/10), 16.
[53] *BO*, Oct. 20 1859; W. J. Heaton, *Bradford's First Freeman: Sir Henry Mitchell* (London, 1913), 36–48; R. Spence Hardy, *Commerce and Christianity* (London, 1857), 45–7.
[54] Documented instances of this are so numerous that a few particularly striking examples will have to suffice. Richard Fawcett not only helped put Bradford's Methodist Sunday schools on a stable footing, but provided a warehouse in which classes could meet. Later he built a schoolroom, which he let at a very modest rent. "Early Bradford Sunday Schools" (cutting, Bradford Archives, D. B., 35/16 #10). While struggling to build up their business during the 1820s and 1830s, the Garnett brothers reorganized Horton

spinoff associational agencies ostensibly designed for evangelical ends followed the establishment of Sunday schools: bible or tract societies to spread the word among the urban masses, and missionary societies to reach the heathens abroad. Although such associations were intended as active instruments of outreach, in most denominations they quickly settled into relatively dull routines of fund-raising, becoming cultural and political outlets in which ambitious young men and sometimes women could develop skills of political organization such as holding meetings and elections, managing collections, and writing reports.[55]

Especially important in this regard were the charitable associations connected with almost every denomination. In some cases, such as that of the Quakers, the Westgate Baptists, and the Methodists, these societies were originally designed to provide assistance to aged and impoverished members of the congregation itself. However, as the general problem of urban poverty worsened during the thirties and forties, they were forced to look beyond their own boundaries, devising investigative techniques for distinguishing between deserving and undeserving paupers and raising funds for the distribution of food, clothing, and blankets to all deemed to fall within the former group.[56]

Lane's Sunday schools and served as superintendents and librarians for several years. The school secretary was Robert Milligan, and one of the teachers was young Titus Salt. James Garnett was so absorbed by his Sunday school activities that he continued taking classes long after becoming one of the leading manufacturers in town. As for Salt, whose entrepreneurial success was also accompanied by a promotion to school superintendent, "his connection with Horton Lane Sunday school," according to his biographer, "was of great benefit to himself . . . [it] diverted his thoughts and sympathies once a week into other channels, leading away from self and business, Godwards. . . . In trying to teach others, he was himself taught, and in being associated with a band of christian workers, he formed friendships that conduced to the growth of his true manhood." *BOB*, Feb. 3, May 19, 1906; "Early Bradford Sunday Schools"; Balgarnie, *Salt*, 40–1; *BO*, June 13, 1850.

Among the Baptists, John Brogden and Miles Illingworth were singled out for their unusually active work. Though not all of the young parvenus could devote the time and energy necessary for Sunday school activity, few considered such work to be beneath their dignity. Joseph Wilson, who himself began Sunday school at the age of six, later became both a teacher and a superintendent and recalled that the time spent involved in this sphere "was the happiest time of my life . . . I never did more good nor saw more result of service." Joseph Wilson, *His Life and Work* (London, n.d.), 4.

55 James Garnett, who served as a treasurer of the London Missionary Society, even made valuable social and business contacts through such denominational work. *The British and Foreign Bible Society in Bradford, 1811–1961* (Bradford, 1961); *BO*, June 13, 1850; *Bradford Herald*, June 23, 1842.

56 *BO*, Mar. 9, 1843; *Bradford Herald*, Jan. 27, 1842; *First Baptist Church*, 68. During the great depressions of 1839, 1842, and 1848, when rampant unemployment caused widespread destitution and the whole social fabric threatened to come unglued, these

If the scope for democratic participation that religious congregationalism offered was important for Bradford's emergent male bourgeoisie, it was even more important for bourgeois women who had no alternate outlets for public expression. Because of its close connection with charity and education, which were themselves associated with women's private domestic sphere, the religious arena had always provided a special if subordinate place for women. Moreover, as bourgeois men became more and more successful, less preoccupied with the problems of identity and salvation, and more deeply enmeshed in secular life, religion was increasingly left to women who, in turn, increasingly identified their interests with its own.[57]

The exact place of women in congregational religion varied greatly from one denomination to the next. Although almost universally excluded from chapel governance, they were, among some groups, particularly the Quakers and the Primitive Methodists, accepted as men's spiritual equals, if not superiors, and frequently held positions of power and responsibility as lay preachers and class leaders within the sect. In other denominations, such public roles were generally closed to women, but each sect had its auxiliary women's organization that involved itself in missionary and charitable work.[58] As we have seen, such activities were extremely important to Sarah Holden and constituted the major reason for her reluctance to follow her husband to France. The constant round of bazaars, teas, sewing circles, Dorcas Society gatherings, prayer meetings, and charitable visitations which filled her spare time provided a central focus for her own identity that she could not bear to give up. As she wrote to her husband in 1850:

> I was at Bro' Jonas' on Friday evening enjoying the company of class leaders & Local Preachers, of Oakworth Society. ... The conversation was mostly on theology and closed with singing & prayer. Several said it had been the most interesting meeting they had attended. How much my dear did I wish you had been there to have joined in and enjoyed the company.[59]

ongoing, chapel-based charitable associations served as prototypes for massive interdenominational emergency efforts in which all the bourgeois sects and parties briefly rallied together to raise sufficient funds to keep hunger from turning into outright starvation and to counter the threat of total working-class revolt. David Ashforth "The Poor Law in Bradford, c. 1831–71" (Bradford, Ph.D. dissertation, 1979), 272–94; *BO*, June 1, 1837; Dec. 19, 1839; Jan. 2, 1840; May 18, 1848; Dec. 24, 1856. See Chapter 24.

[57] Ann Douglas, *The Feminization of American Culture* (New York, 1978).

[58] Stamp, *Wesleyan Methodism in Bradford*, chap. 4; Hodgson, *Society of Friends*, 46; Joseph Wilson, *The Great Horton Primitive Methodist Church* (Bradford, n.d.), 49–50, 78–9. Olive Anderson, "Women Preachers in mid-Victorian Britain: Some Reflections on Feminism, Popular Religion, and Social Change," *Historical Journal*, 11 (1969).

[59] Holden Papers (mss., Bradford University Library, 21), S. Holden – I. Holden, Dec. 4, 31, 1850.

Perhaps the single most important outlet for women's public involvement in religion came from Sunday school teaching in which women played a role as significant as that of men. It was accepted that girls ought to be taught by women, and with the expansion of the Sunday-school movement in Bradford, there were, by 1840, 1,492 volunteer teachers, 47 percent of whom were women.[60]

The wide scope that Congregationalism offered for lay participation on the part of its members, both men and women, was a reflection of the spiritual egalitarianism that radical Protestant theology imposed. In these autonomous priesthoods of all believers, the distinction between clergy and laity was not an intrinsic division between different orders but a functional differentiation between alternate roles. Ministers who were, in many cases, elected by their congregations, possessed no special prerogatives, and their influence over the flocks that employed them depended entirely on the personal authority that, as individuals, they possessed. This often led to a tense and confused relationship in which opportunities for conflict appeared without end. Ministers were expected to provide spiritual guidance and cultural leadership but could do so only in terms that were acceptable to a group of independent and often obstreperous laymen. For theological as well as practical reasons, ministers were well advised to devalue their own professionalism while exalting lay agency, and this put them in an exposed position for which they themselves were partly to blame.

Even the most diligent and competent ministers periodically sparked rebellions when they took positions or actions of which prominent laymen disapproved. Thus Rev. Godwin's rather feeble attempts in the 1830s to wean his congregants at Sion Chapel from the old fire-and-brimstone Calvinism led to years of incessant struggle that was resolved only by his eventual resignation under threat of being removed from his post.[61] Later on, ministers complained more frequently about the opposite problem. Congregations were no longer sufficiently serious about religion; they wanted everything sugar coated and predigested so that it could effortlessly be absorbed.[62]

Clerical incomes were always inadequate, usually offered grudgingly, and sometimes not promptly paid. In the early years of the century, Dissenting ministers were sometimes forced to supplement their living by secular employment. Although this phenomenon was rare, after the 1820s, ministers were carefully scrutinized by increasingly rich and powerful congregants, who often treated them "with as much indecency and rudeness as though they were domestic servants."[63] Sermons and ministerial autobiographies,

---

[60] James, *History of Bradford*, 263–5.
[61] Godwin, *Autobiography*, 621; John Clark, *History and Annals of Bradford* (Typescript, Bradford Central Library), 2:151.
[62] *Census of Public Worship in Bradford* (Bradford, 1882), 40.
[63] Isaac Mann, *Memoirs of Rev. William Crabtree* (London, 1815), 70.

amidst the obligatory litanies of devotion and self-sacrifice, frequently betray a sense of insecurity about their authors' positions and a latent fear of and hostility toward recalcitrant congregations. Overworked and underpaid, despised for their powerlessness while suspected of tyrannical designs, Nonconformist ministers were in an impossible position. That their jobs were so eagerly sought after is a testament to the paucity of alternatives for would-be intellectuals in places like early-nineteenth-century Bradford.

Nevertheless, in spite of these inherent difficulties, relations between ministers and congregants were sometimes quite good. This was certainly the case with Rev. Thomas Taylor, minister of Horton Lane Chapel between 1808 and 1835, who, according to the published centenary commemorative, "was greatly honoured in molding the character of many who might literally be called the Makers of Bradford," for example, "the names of Garnett, Milligan, and Salt."[64] In truth, these rising entrepreneurial insurgents needed organic intellectuals to guide them as individuals and to voice their class ideologies at least as much as the intellectuals needed them. "Who," asked Rev. Godwin rhetorically, reminiscing about his own indispensable role, "would have been daring enough to head a movement for the first time which would incur the determined opposition of those who had hitherto assumed a kind of leadership in the town, the Manns and the Horsfalls, and the Rands and Dr. Outhwaite?"[65] In light of his work in organizing a local antislavery movement and in catalyzing a local parliamentary reform campaign, the question hardly needed to be answered. So useful was Godwin regarded in local, liberal, Nonconformist circles that, when he resigned his pastorate, a subscription was briefly canvassed to try to keep him in town.[66]

The dilemma of these sectarian ministers reflects a deeper problem of voluntary religious organization that severely limited the Nonconformists' ability to expand by congregational methods alone, for the internal cohesion and stability of congregations, as well as their place in the larger constellation of urban cultural life, depended entirely on the power, resources, and status of their members, who constituted the only basis of organization and authority on which Congregationalism could rest. Unlike the established church, Bradford's new chapels had no institutional foundation apart from that provided by the members they attracted. Denominations like the Baptists and Congregationalists were successful because they spawned and attracted successful men. Hence the chapels were caught in a self-reinforcing process whereby their competitive value as spiritual agencies was enhanced by the worldly success of their members,

[64] *BO*, May 21, 1882.
[65] Godwin, "Autobiography," 524.
[66] *BO*, Sep. 8, Oct. 6, 13, 1836.

which made other aspirants more eager to join. As the original congregations at Horton Lane and Westgate became emblems of successful integration into the urban-industrial setting, they received a flood of new applicants and were able to maintain or even raise the standards for admission. At Horton Lane, Rev. Glyde noted the fact that overcrowding "prevented the reception of many desireous of joining us" and left no incentive "to increase the congregation by drawing hither the ignorant and depraved." The "possession of . . . a discipline which gently but firmly repels those who are evidently unfit for the Communion of Saints" may well have made the communion "more sacred, more tender and more spiritual," but it contradicted the imperative to evangelical outreach, the primary task of religious voluntarism in the growing town.[67]

If congregationalism could promote the development of urban religion only up to the preexisting level of market demand, it was thwarted even at this level of accomplishment by limitations inherent in congregational organization itself; for denominations could only expand by mitosis, when existing congregations sent out members from the nucleus to seek others to join them in an independent congregation of their own.[68] Just as every believer within the congregation was the equal of every other, every congregation within the denomination was equal with and autonomous from every other, as all were engaged in open competition to attract participants and provide what spiritual assistance they could. These methods of denominational organization, in which spiritual unity depended on voluntary cohesion among a host of competing and self-governing congregations, provided a rather fragile and tenuous institutional framework for the structuring of public worship in the town. Something else was obviously needed if urban religion was to be more than the province of an elite minority. Not surprisingly, those denominations like the Methodists, who expanded most rapidly and drew membership from a range of different social groups, were successful largely insofar as they departed from strict congregationalist practice and embraced more authoritarian organizational forms.

---

[67] Jonathan Glyde, *A Sermon Preached at Horton Lane Chapel* (Bradford, 1846), 10.

[68] Thus, in 1824, Sion Baptist Chapel came into existence when twenty-two members of the original Chapel at Westgate raised £1,000, whereas Sion itself, in 1862, dismissed 110 members to create Hallfield Chapel. In the meantime, a Zoar Chapel was created in 1844. Similarly, thirty-seven Congregationalists at Horton Lane raised £5,000 in 1834 to found Salem Chapel, which was built in Wibsey, while in 1853 these two together dismissed fifty-nine members to form Greenfield Chapel. Finally, in 1839, College Chapel was established in Manningham to even out Congregationalist coverage in the town. *Sion Jubilee Chapel,* 9,10; *BO,* Oct. 29, 1863; *BO,* Oct. 3, 1844; anon., *Salem Chapel Centenary* (Bradford, 1936); anon., *Greenfield Congregational Church, Jubilee Souvenir* (Bradford, 1911); Lucy Fraser, ed., *Memoirs of Daniel Fraser* (London, 1905), 54.

Congregationalism in the framework of urban religion

Unlike Baptists and Congregationalists, the Methodists possessed institutional structures and hierarchies that existed independent of their members and that were designed to help guide individual believers along the godly path. Congregations did not exist as autonomous entities but were organized in a connexional network that was largely under clerical control. Hence both individual Methodists and the congregations they belonged to were subject to a variety of external disciplines, ostensibly designed to promote the godly way of life. This authoritarian element was justified by the Methodists' peculiar mission, which was not simply to serve the godly, but to convert the sinners who had proven unable to internalize religious values by themselves. Initially attracted by the overwrought emotionalism of the camp meeting or evangelical revival, the convert would then be subjected to the test of Methodist discipline before being permanently included in the ranks of the upright.[69]

It was this system of chiliasm followed by control that had attracted so many working people to Methodism in the first place, and it facilitated the retention of a certain proportion permanently within its denominational fold. During the early years of the century, the Methodists had been most successful in attracting members from all social ranks. However, with the demographic onslaught of the 1830s and 1840s and the emergence of a massive urban working class, the character of Methodism began to change. It became clear that there existed a large and growing sector of urban society that even the most ardent evangelicalism could not reach. Moreover, the social composition of Methodism itself was changing as working-class participation dwindled among the Wesleyans and, as Table 10-2 indicates, the denomination became increasingly dominated by the lower middle class. Apparently, Wesleyanism was performing much the same function for Bradford's shopkeepers and small businessmen that the Baptists and Congregationalists were performing for the industrial entrepreneurs.[70]

As these men and women became modestly successful and grew more comfortable with urban religious life, it was almost inevitable that they too would begin to resent the clerical despotism that characterized Wesleyan religious practice at the time. Similar responses were also, for different reasons, exhibited by working-class believers who objected to being subordinated to a bourgeois-dominated connexional hierarchy as they became increasingly conscious of their separate interests as a class. Thus by the late 1830s and 1840s, the logic of Congregationalism began to infect even the

---

[69] Thompson, *English Working Class*, 368–71; R. F. Wearmouth, *Methodism and the Common People of the Eighteenth Century* (London, 1945), 189–268.
[70] See Table 10-2.

Methodists in spite of valiant attempts on the part of the denominational hierarchy to uphold central authority and to keep it out.

Congregationalism invaded urban Methodism as a result of a series of traumatic denominational splits. The undercurrent of resentment against the Wesleyan Conference oligarchy periodically erupted in full-scale movements of rebellion that resulted in whole congregations or groups within them breaking away. By 1851, 44 percent of Bradford's Methodists were outside the original Wesleyan Order in four different splinter sects.[71] Despite wide variations in social composition, all these Methodist breakaways shared a desire for more congregational autonomy and for a greater lay authority within the church. In 1851, the Wesleyan reformers explained, "The service conducted in this place is on account of the tyrannical proceedings of the Wesleyan Preacher in the Bradford West Circuit in expelling members, leaders and preachers, simply because they were anxious to have certain popish innovations expunged from our Wesleyan Church polity."[72]

Although these new connexions retained some of the traditional Methodist structures, they were all more decentralized than their Wesleyan parent, and when members wished to push reform still farther, a second split might subsequently ensue. The increasing prosperity and self-assurance of Bradford's Methodist population as well as the goad of competition from the breakaway sects forced even the orthodox Wesleyans to liberalize their practices and to bring themselves into closer alignment with mainstream Dissent. Successful Methodist industrialists of the rising generation, such as Isaac Holden, were instrumental in this process since they, like their counterparts in the other denominations, tended to identify openly as Nonconformists and used their power and influence to push Wesleyanism away from its traditionally Tory predisposition and toward an alliance with the radical Miallite wing of dissent. Though Wesleyanism remained politically divided, there was a noticeable movement in the 1840s away from the old Tory connexional traditions toward a more left-leaning membership fully integrated into the liberal fold.[73]

The experience of the Methodists suggests that the logic of Congregationalism – with its frank recognition that religion in the urban-industrial environment would have to adapt to the prevailing, competitive, voluntaristic market forms – was not only appropriate for an elite minority, but essential for all religious bodies that hoped to attract any urban social constituency away from godless apathy or the lure of other sectarian groups. Nothing illustrates this Congregationalist imperative more clearly than the stance that

---

[71] *PP* LXXXIX (1852–3), cclii–cclxxii.

[72] *HO*, 127/499.

[73] Ward, *Religion and Society*, 135–76; D. A. Gowland, *Methodist Secessions, The Origins of ree Methodism in Three Lancashire Towns* (Manchester, 1979).

local Anglicanism itself eventually adopted in response to the aggressive competition of dissent. As we have seen, the church's initial reaction to the Nonconformist challenge was simply to ignore the problem in hopes that it would go away. However, by the mid-1830s, it was becoming clear that, if Anglicanism were to survive as a viable religion, it would have to adopt at least some of the new evangelical and congregational methods that its competitors were employing with such positive results. The change began with the arrival of a new generation of clergymen like Parson Bull and Vicar Scoresby who were acutely conscious of the dimensions of the problem and willing to initiate substantial reforms. Abandoning the fiction that the church was a comprehensive communion, they began, in practice if not in theory, to behave as though it were a competitive denomination, taking steps to satisfy the needs of regular congregants while simultaneously seeking to broaden its evangelical base.[74] As Rev. Godwin put it rather condescendingly in describing the new breed of evangelical priests,

> They appear to be adopting all the modes of usefulness which Dissenters have long employed. Their conversation on the topic while it delighted me almost made me smile, while they were so warmly interested in the apparently new discoveries which had been so long familiar to their nonconforming friends ... how greatly is the Church of England indebted to the Dissenters for its improvements, both for the example of voluntary and energetic zeal – and for the reaction which they have produced in the National Church.[75]

The congregational religious culture that Godwin and his fellow Nonconformists pioneered did leave the entire bourgeoisie in their debt, for religious voluntarism was perfectly suited to the psychological and social needs of a parvenu elite that knew exactly where it was headed and sought new cultural forms for enlisting the masses to reach the same goal. The "little republic" of congregational voluntarism necessarily constituted the subliminal kernel out of which their larger social and political superstructures would grow. But could the same institutions that served entrepreneurial needs and catered to a bourgeois clientele also integrate the rest of the urban population into the same liberal, capitalist, cultural frame?

Congregationalism and the urban-industrial worker

To those who hoped that the new nexus of religious voluntarism would provide a means of integrating Bradford's emergent working class, the 1851 religious census came as a terrible blow. With 80 percent of the population

---

[74] Gill, *Ten Hours Parson*, 1–11; Gilbert, *Religion and Society*, 138–43.
[75] Godwin, "Autobiography," 746.

staying away from morning service on census Sunday and about 72 percent not attending at all, the figures were a dismal confirmation of what a committee to investigate the moral condition of the town had already, in 1849, begun to suspect, that "a large proportion of our inhabitants are neither connected with any of our congregations nor in the habit of attending divine worship, but are opposed or indifferent to the religion of Christ, and in too many cases, grossly ignorant and immoral."[76]

Since it may be assumed that most middle-class people, who constituted about 20 percent of Bradford's midcentury population, attended some religious service, it is unlikely that more than 15 to 20 percent of the town's working class attended any at all. Moreover, since the attendance figures were inflated by the inclusion of Sunday school children who came involuntarily and by Irish Catholics (16 percent of the morning attenders) who were almost uniformly working class, the proportion of active working-class Protestants must have been minuscule, probably about 5 to 10 percent of all working-class adults.[77] This grim picture was reconfirmed two years later when the Bradford Town Mission provided documentary evidence to support its "deep and painful sense of the immorality and irreligion which pervaded the masses of our fellow townsmen." Out of 310 working-class cottages visited, 62 were Catholic, and "out of the remaining 248 only 1 profess Protestant religion and 25 regularly attend to the means of Grace."[78]

The most comforting explanation of working-class nonattendance was the insufficiency of places of worship to accommodate them. It is true that, if every Bradfordian had tried to attend morning service, only about a third of them would have found room. But since virtually every denomination held three Sunday services, theoretically almost everyone could physically have attended at least one. In fact, the levels of religious accommodation were not noticeably lower than in other industrial cities and, if that provided by the Anglicans was inadequate, this was compensated by a substantial number of Catholic and Nonconformist sittings, far more extensive than in many larger, older, and wealthier towns. The intense activism of Bradford dissent probably prevented working-class attendances from being even lower, as low, for example, as in Sheffield, which had few Irish, or Preston and Oldham, where the Nonconformist presence was not as great.[79]

Indeed, the vast majority of Bradford's workers did not avoid church or chapel because there was no room for them, but because the religious culture

[76] *PP* (LXXXIX, 1852–3), cclii–cclxxii; *BO,* Mar. 7, 1850.
[77] *PP* (LXXXIX, 1852–3), cclii–cclxxii.
[78] *BO,* Mar. 24, 1853.
[79] Theodore Koditschek, "Class Formation and the Bradford Bourgeoisie" (Princeton, Ph.D. dissertation, 1981), 436–7.

of the mainstream denominations was alien to their experiences and needs. To be sure, there was a very different kind of Christianity, based on the preaching of spiritual equality and the exaltation of the humble and meek, that was deeply engrained in traditional working-class culture. For a small and extremely articulate working-class minority who were radicalized within the framework of rationalism or Owenite socialism, the uncongenial character of official Christianity did lead to a total rejection of religion. However, the vast majority, even among the radicals, remained deeply religious and found, in their own distinctive reading of Christianity, ample ammunition with which to attack the false morality of the rich.[80]

What alienated most workers was not Christianity, but the egocentric, salvation-centered, neo-Calvinist version of it that dominated the theology and culture of the mainstream sects. To the rising generation of entrepreneurial insurgents, this sort of religion grew organically out of the experience of life. To most workers, it was apt to seem incomprehensible or, worse, a cruel and hypocritical rationalization of exploitation that, under the mask of pseudospiritual egalitarianism, sought to keep the downtrodden in their subordinate place. This latter view was expressed quite forcefully by a nearby weaver in a long and sarcastic anticlerical poem. In his eyes, it was precisely those aspects of bourgeois religion the new entrepreneurs most valued that seemed most fraudulent and absurd. The intense competition between different denominations so characteristic of the new urban-entrepreneurial world was not, as bourgeois Nonconformists claimed, a source of religious purification but something that looked more like "the parsons' . . . right useful plan":

> To keep up as many strange sects as they can;
> For, if they can get them all waged in a war,
> They'll part with their money more freely by far.

> For now, as they value all sects in these days,
> According to what sums of cash they can raise,
> It serves as a matter of triumph and boast,
> For two sects to strive and see which can raise most.[81]

What most infuriated this worker was not the corruption or indifference of the old Anglican establishment, but the canting aggressiveness of the new

---

[80] The best studies of this phenomenon are James Obelkevich, *Religion and Rural Society: South Lindsey, 1825–75* (Oxford, 1976), and Deborah Valenze, *Prophetic Sons and Daughters, Female Preaching and Popular Religion in Industrial England* (Princeton, 1985). See also, K. S. Inglis, *Churches and the Working Classes in Victorian England* (London, 1963), and Owen Chadwick, *The Secularization of the European Mind in the Nineteenth Century* (Cambridge, 1975), 88–106.

[81] Anon., *The Weaver's Complaint* (Keighley, 1834), 12.

Nonconformists whose evangelical gospel of the marketplace had only led to a monstrous inversion of Christian values, replacing the religion that comforted the poor and downtrodden with a religion that glorified the successful and rich:

> And now men of wealth may with pleasure behold
> A new-fashioned doctrine preached up in God's fold,
> Exhibiting scripture in such a kind light
> As always to make them appear in the right.
>
> And though the notion was held, long ago,
> That no man can serve God and Mammon also,
> Our doctrine now proves the reverse is the case,
> And that hunting gold is the way to gain grace.
>
> For no fellow-feeling or brotherly love,
> Is requisite now a true Christian to prove;
> But gain is the business, and self is the creed,
> By which saints, at this day, to heaven proceed.[82]

This self-righteous nonsense would be bad enough if it were only an exercise in bourgeois vanity. But its real and more sinister purpose was to keep the impoverished workers enslaved. Within this Nonconformist spiritual democracy, capitalists could find only evidences of grace. By contrast, their working-class brethren who were less materially successful would have to

> Learn to regard those continual attacks,
> Which poverty makes on your bellies and backs,
> As so many ills which the flesh must endure
> To work for your soul some particular cure.[83]

Indeed, so far from being the worker's oppressor, his capitalist coreligionist, by subjecting him to hard unremunerative labor, would turn out to be his greatest spiritual ally:

> For he, worthy man, through a brotherly care,
> Lest plenty should prove to your souls as a snare,
> Takes this friendly method to cut off, in time,
> That which might produce a temptation to crime.
>
> And when he had screwed your industry so hard,
> That hunger and rags are its only reward,

---

[82] Ibid., 31.
[83] Ibid., 24.

Rejoice that you have, in their place, a supply
of that food and raiment which comes from on high.

When covered with rags, which are laid on your backs,
By means of low wages, dear victuals and tax,
Accept them with joy since your souls have access
To heavenly wardrobes of pure righteousness.[84]

Doubtless, this weaver's complaint represented an extreme opinion, or perhaps only an unusually perceptive critique. But the nonparticipation of all but a tiny minority of workers in organized religion suggests that many others shared, if only subconsciously, at least some of his views. Trapped in exploitative and insecure jobs that scarcely provided them with a living income much less with any chance of rising in the world, most workers could not seek their spiritual self-realization through active callings in the world of work.[85] Surrounded by filth, disease, and urban squalor, there was little in the self-denying culture of bourgeois religion to enrich their already constricted lives, and they were apt to feel no love for the distant capricious deity who could senselessly predestine them to so miserable a fate. In short, it was the underlying character of their class experiences, diametrically opposite that of the rising bourgeoisie, that made it impossible for all but a few of Bradford's workers to take communion with their worldly masters as spiritual equals and effectively unite in the same congregational groups.

The difficulty of maintaining a sense of spiritual community among social groups whose worldly destinies had begun to diverge can be seen most clearly in the case of the Horton Lane, Westgate, and Sion congregations in which the impact of social bifurcation was first felt. During their early years around the turn of the century, these chapels had been fairly homogeneous, composed of relatively poor but aspiring artisans and petit bourgeois. When Rev. William Steadman came to a Westgate Baptist Chapel teetering on the edge of bankruptcy in 1805, he found that "the congregation at Bradford is in general plain, and most of the members of the church poor."[86] However, soon thereafter, the congregation was reported to include "several wealthy members inclined towards liberality with their money."[87] With the worldly rise of Bradford's Baptist and Congregationalist entrepreneurial elect in the 1830s and 1840s, the whole atmosphere of their congregations was transformed. The first signs that the serpent of class conflict had entered Sion

---

[84] Ibid., 25.
[85] Ibid., 7.
[86] Thomas Steadman, *Memoir of Rev. William Steadman* (London, 1838), 229.
[87] Anon., *Centenary: A History* 48.

Chapel's Elysium came during the great strike of 1825, when working-class members began to realize that the upwardly mobile fellow congregants who now employed them might not, after all, be their brothers in Christ. As Rev. Godwin complained: "Ministers were obliged in their preaching to be fastidiously careful of any language which might be construed as an attack on the Union. The members who were workingmen had scarce any charity towards their fellow members who were masters."[88]

When forced to take sides, it was clear that Godwin's sympathies, not to mention his income, lay with the capitalists. A deacon pulled him aside and told him that his allegiances were causing many to stay away from services. Though tempers eventually cooled after the strike failed, the old cross-class solidarity at Sion Chapel could never be revived. Gradually, as the successful bourgeois congregants became rich, their domination of associational life made the more plebeian component feel more and more uncomfortable. As its members died out or left the fold, the old plebeian element was not replenished. In 1829, Rev. Godwin detected an undercurrent of discontent among his working-class charges who felt that they were being relegated to the position of second-class citizens in the "little republic" of Sion Chapel. "The Poorer part of the Church and Congregation it was almost impossible to satisfy and when once an individual had become a member he seemed to think he had a claim on regular and frequent visits."[89]

Yet despite his heavy schedule and the overwork of which he constantly complained, he found the time to cultivate deep and personal friendships with several of the rising Nonconformist worsted men, such as Robert Milligan to whom his son was apprenticed, William Murgatroyd, and Thomas Aked, about whom he said, "I had been as a father or as a brother – I was more intimate with him than with any other member of the Church – he was warm, zealous, energetic. In all his plans, and hopes, and feelings, I gave him my warmest sympathies."[90]

By the midthirties, Godwin's refusal to support the cause of factory reform, despite the leading role he had taken in the suffrage and antislavery movements, convinced any who still had doubts that Sion had become a thoroughly bourgeois chapel as had Westgate and Horton Lane, whose membership was now over 60 percent middle class. Thus when Rev. Glyde, Horton Lane's minister during the 1840s, asked his congregants to "sit down, rich and poor together, and listen to Moses and Jesus with simplicity of heart and exchange some sentiments with each other," he was expressing

---

[88] Benjamin Godwin, "Autobiography" (mss., Bradford Central Library), 400–1.
[89] Ibid., 486.
[90] Ibid., 491.

hopes that, under the circumstances, he could scarcely have expected to be fulfilled.[91]

To Nonconformist radicals like Edward Miall, this bourgeoisification of congregations was a disturbing development that undermined their vision of a popular, progressive movement uniting productive workers and capitalists against the power of entrenched, political, and spiritual elites. Yet by the 1840s, even he was obliged to confess that "British Christianity is essentially the Christianity developed by a middle class soil." As such, he worried that "its vitality is becoming impaired." Falling "into a routine of devotional exercises. . . . It puts orthodoxy in place of reverence for truth and substitutes pecuniary subscriptions for active personal exertion. . . . It builds up interests instead of grappling with evils."[92]

To those bourgeoise unconcerned about the failure of Nonconformity to grapple with evils or to enlist workers in the activist cause, there remained a strong consciousness of dissent's marked failure, particularly the failure of the Methodist denominations to inculcate values of work discipline and respectability into an increasingly unregenerate working class. By the 1830s and 1840s, many of the same tendencies toward bourgeoisification first evident among the Baptists and Congregationalists were being manifested in Wesleyan congregations too. Problems often surfaced over the question of pew rents, which were seen by poorer members not only as an economic hardship, but as an introduction of invidious social distinctions into the service of public worship itself. Although some bourgeois Wesleyans like Henry Mitchell agreed, pew rents remained popular among most middle-class worshippers because they promoted a sense of congregational stability and made chapel seem like an extension of home.[93] As the chronicler of Eastbrook Chapel explained, "Whole families were woven into its spiritual texture. . . . The pews were so exclusive that they quickly acquired the names of the families which used them . . . whenever a youth married into the family of another pew holder, he joined the pew of his mother's family."[94]

Of course, Bradford's Methodists never lost touch with the urban-working-class population as thoroughly as the Baptists and Congregationalists did. Even during the crisis years of the 1840s, workers constituted just under half of the membership of Kirkgate Wesleyan Chapel, while their participation in other chapels and in at least two of the breakaway Methodist connexions was undoubtedly even greater. Indeed, there is a large literature about the impact of Methodism on working-class consciousness and its role

[91] G. W. Condor, *Memoir and Remains of Rev. Jonathan Glyde* (London, 1858), 337.
[92] Arthur Miall, *Life of Edward Miall* (London, 1884), chap. 10.
[93] W. J. Heaton, *Bradford's First Freeman: Sir Henry Mitchell* (London, 1913), 40–8.
[94] Anon., *Eastbrook Chapel: Centenary Souvenir* (Bradford, 1925), 52.

in preventing revolution or in channeling proletarian activism toward respectable and reformist ends.[95]

Taking a different approach to the problem of working-class Methodism, particularly of the orthodox Wesleyan variety, E. P. Thompson has treated it as a "chiliasm of despair," which did not so much preempt radical action as follow parasitically in the wake of its defeat. Following the line of analysis initiated by our weaver, Thompson portrayed Wesleyanism as a form of "psychic exploitation" in which men and women who found themselves oppressed and defeated, without hope of realizing themselves in the world, were lured by the promise of religious consolation into positively embracing their lot of poverty and hard labor as a necessary prelude to glory after death. Working-class Wesleyanism was but "the desolate inner landscape of utilitarianism" by which "the character-structure of the rebellious pre-industrial labourer or artisan was violently recast into the submissive industrial worker" through the "transforming power of Christ's cross."[96]

Of course, Thompson is well aware that Wesleyanism constitutes only one chapter in the story of working-class Methodism, and his critics have pointed out that even the Wesleyan experience was less monolithic and debilitating than his analysis allows.[97] Nevertheless, the evidence from Bradford suggests that there is still some validity in Thompson's view. Certainly, the three major Wesleyan revivals in early-nineteenth-century Bradford, 1806, 1824, and 1844, all came at moments of working-class political defeat.[98] Moreover, the diary of one local working-class Methodist, Samuel Gill, suggests that he did take his religion as a sort of opiate to sweeten life's otherwise bitter pill. "This morning," he wrote, "while my hands were engaged with work, my heart was in heaven." Gill's God seems to have been some kind of glorified capitalist, for when he felt satisfied with his religious state, he exclaimed, "My Lord is a good master he pays me good wages." When Gill's actual employer raised his wages, he dutifully ascribed this boon to "the providence of God," but when he was thrown out of work he consoled

---

[95] The classic statement of this view is Elie Halévy, *England in 1815* (London, 1949), 387–485. It is further assessed in E. J. Hobsbawm, *Labouring Men* (London, 1964), 23–33; Bernard Semmel, "Introduction," in Elie Halévy, *The Birth of Methodism in England* (Chicago, 1971); Gertrude Himmelfarb, *Victorian Minds* (Gloucester, Mass., 1975), 292–9; and R. F. Wearmouth, *Methodism and the Common People in the Eighteenth Century* (London, 1945); and idem, *Methodism and Working Class Movements of England, 1800–1850* (London, 1937).

[96] E. P. Thompson, *The Making of the English Working Class* (New York, 1963), 354–70.

[97] R. M. Hartwell and R. Currie, "The Making of the English Working Class?" *Economic History Review*, 18:3(1965); Semmel, *Methodist Revolution*, 197–8; Valenze, *Prophetic Sons and Daughters*, 5–11.

[98] Stamp, *Wesleyan Methodism in Bradford*, 85; Dickons, "Kirkgate Chapel," 218.

himself saying, "But by-and-by, if I am faithful I shall receive a crown of glory that will never fade away." When Gill's workmates asked him why he always talked and thought of nothing but heaven, he replied, "Where the treasure is, there will the heart be also."[99]

As this interaction between Gill and his workmates indicates, the real problem with seeing Methodism as an opium of the masses is not that it did not serve such a function for some individuals, but that, except perhaps momentarily at the peaks of revivalism, its hold on the working-class majority was simply too tenuous to perform any function at all. Moreover, as Thompson himself reminds us, there was another, much more positive tradition of working-class Methodism that was enacted primarily outside of the Wesleyan fold in the breakaway connexions, especially the Primitive Methodists who were attracting more and more of Bradford's Methodists as the 1830s and 1840s wore on.[100]

With 1,980 attenders on census Sunday morning and 952 members officially on the books, the Primitive Methodists were the largest of the breakaway connexions and were unique in attracting a membership that was uniformly working and lower middle class.[101] Primitive Methodism first appeared in Bradford in the 1820s, brought by a series of traveling preachers whose Methodist credentials raised them only a cut above the self-appointed ranters who combed the manufacturing districts during these years.[102] The sect caught on most firmly in the outlying township of Great Horton, where much of the old protoindustrial village cohesion still prevailed. As the older denominations found themselves becalmed in respectability during the 1830s and 1840s, the Primitive Methodists continued to ride the waves of revivalism and retained a distinctively plebeian tone. Since "the Society consisted of very poor members," it experienced difficulties unknown to the bourgeois sects in constructing a chapel. Unable to afford a contractor, the members all pitched in to do the excavation work by hand.[103]

The fortunes of this congregation continued to fluctuate with the employment cycle, and before the middle of the century, it went through a series of extremely hard years. Still, in spite of these difficulties, the Great Horton Primitive Methodists constituted an extraordinarily cohesive sect.

[99] Samuel Gill, "The Blameless Christian," (cutting, Bradford Central Library).
[100] Thompson, *English Working Class*, 391–2. This theme has been developed most insightfully, especially with reference to working-class women, by Valenze, *Prophetic Sons and Daughters*.
[101] *PP* (LXXXIX, 1852–3), cclii–cclxxii; *General Minutes of the Primitive Wesleyan Connexion Conference*, (1850).
[102] H. B. Kendall, *History of the Primitive Methodist Church* (London, 1919), 12–63; J. F. C. Harrison, *The Second Coming* (London, 1979), 135–60.
[103] Wilson, *Great Horton Primitive Methodist*, 12.

Indeed, their sense of community was much greater than was typical of the bourgeois congregations, as religion became for them not just a matter of worship, but a pattern of concrete mutual aid. Almost all the members lived together in the same neighborhood, and an extraordinary number of their children intermarried. By midcentury, the congregation had virtually evolved from a voluntary association into an extended family.[104]

For the semirural weavers, combers, and other workers in Great Horton who were undergoing the pressures of proletarianization, the religious community acted as a defensive shield against the rigors of unrestrained capitalism. Blending the organic solidarities of the traditional community with new urban-capitalist voluntary associational forms, they combined in a distinctly working-class way. Unlike the bourgeois denominations, they constituted not simply a spiritual community, but a total human community that tried, as far as possible, to become self-contained.[105]

The behavior patterns of temperance and frugality that this community instilled in its members represented not so much an imitation of bourgeois values as the working out of a logic of collective self-help.[106] Nevertheless, the very success of this proletarian version of associational collectivism ultimately worked to undermine its class base. The defensive solidarity that protected members during times of trouble also opened the way for greater individual mobility when prosperity appeared. Thus in the more benign economic climate of the 1850s and 1860s, a number of working-class Primitive Methodists, especially those of the second generation, were able to leave their class, becoming teachers, shopkeepers, innkeepers, and in a few cases, even small manufacturers.[107]

The experience of the Great Horton Primitive Methodists suggests that the bourgeois models of associational voluntarism could, at least under certain circumstances, be adapted to working-class conditions and needs. Here, where the impulse for religious association was not imposed from the outside by bourgeois reformers but arose spontaneously from within the working-class community itself, it could create a genuine sense of fellowship by eschewing the salvation-centered obsessions of theological individualism and by concentrating on a practical program of mutual aid. However, the Great

---

[104] This conclusion is based on the author's tracing of Congregational intermarriages reported in Wilson, *Great Horton Primitive Methodist;* and anon., *One Hundred Years of Primitive Methodism in Great Horton* (Bradford, 1924).

[105] William Cudworth, *Rambles Round Horton* (Bradford, 1886), 23–37.

[106] Although the Primitive Methodists, as a denomination, remained ostensibly apolitical throughout the 1830s and 1840s, many members became deeply involved in the Chartist movement, even on the militant "physical" force side. Ibid.

[107] Wilson, *Great Horton Primitive Methodist*, 73–6; idem, *His Life and Work*, 9; and anon., *Primitive Methodism in Great Horton.*

Horton Primitive Methodists were atypical of Bradford's workers, for the position from which they had started was relatively privileged. Even when poor, most seem to have been relatively established protoindustrial villagers who either owned their own tools or had access to a small plot of land. In the downtown factory districts, working-class Congregationalism of the sort that succeeded in Great Horton proved virtually impossible to sustain. This can be seen from the history of the Prospect Street Baptist Chapel, which made a valiant but ultimately futile attempt to become established.

This congregation was founded in 1832. Four years later, it built a small chapel in the heart of the notorious slum district around Silsbridge Lane. As General rather than Particular Baptists, they were unconnected with the bourgeois Baptists, and their membership was thoroughly working class. Although this outpost of piety in the midst of degradation somehow managed to scrape by, a study of its minute books has shown that many of its members had a harder time. Out of 403 individuals admitted during these years, 30 percent were either expelled or forced to withdraw. Most of the expulsions were for backsliding, fornication, drunkenness, or other forms of immorality. A few people were ambiguously charged with "being ashamed of God" or "unfit for Christian Fellowship," whereas a few others like Nancy Silson "acknowledged herself destitute of piety" and voluntarily withdrew. Wholesale expulsions of this sort did not take place in the bourgeois chapels. The rate at the Westgate congregation during the same period was a mere 7.2 percent.[108]

Given the conditions of working-class slum life during the 1830s and 1840s, these backsliders and casual attenders scarcely need to be explained. What rational purpose could the Calvinist ideals of work discipline, deferred gratification, and individual initiative serve in the lives of people as fully proletarianized and demoralized as those in the neighborhood of Silsbridge Lane? Certainly, no group within urban society had a greater need to establish a viable community, but the constant, losing war against immorality, which this congregation and its members fought, indicates that community was impossible on the foundations that evangelical Nonconformity laid down.

To workers, who knew that good behavior and hard work did not necessarily pay off, disciplines that seemed so desirable to the upwardly mobile parvenu might well appear as unnecessary gestures of self-abuse. Joseph Lawson's recollections of the working-class chapel and chapel-goer during the 1830s undoubtedly reflect a much more widespread impression on the part of the majority of workers who stayed away:

---

[108] C. J. Ratcliffe, "Who were the Prospect Street Baptists?" (typescript, Bradford Central Library). For conditions in Silsbridge Lane see James Burnley, *Phases of Bradford Life* (Bradford, 1871), 134–68.

Many who went to chapel did not seem to like it, and were pleased when service was over. They did not appear to be as happy as those who stayed away. Our impression was that those who attended chapels did so because they dared not stay away, for fear of future consequences. They talked about this being a "poor miserable world" a "waste howling wilderness," a "vale of tears," and looked as if religion had more thorns and briars than roses in its path, and that their way was harder than that of the transgressor.... Religion was seldom said to be better for this life, apart from any promise of future rewards after death. It seemed to have no object of present utility, and there was no idea of making earth a Paradise; only of escaping some very hot place after death, and receiving a golden crown.[109]

To make earth a paradise, or at least a halfway livable place, Bradford's workers would not find sectarian Nonconformity to be of much help. Its individualistic, salvation-centered brand of spirituality neither generated the kind of community they needed nor facilitated the creation of a viable associational life. A few workers remained within the bourgeois denominations, and a few others formed working-class congregations of their own. For the vast majority, however, the solution lay entirely outside the religious sphere, in the formation of openly secular associations, self-consciously designed to confront the actual problems of urban-industrial existence.

The Sunday school movement and the working-class child

Although organized religion in Bradford was primarily a middle-class phenomenon that encompassed only a miniscule proportion of the town's workers, there was one sphere in which religious voluntarism did have a significant impact on working-class life; for the 1851 religious census, which reveals adult workers' widespread nonattendance, also indicates that the great majority of them sent their children to Sunday schools.[110] Bradford's first Sunday schools had been established by Anglican elites with Methodist assistance in the late eighteenth and early nineteenth centuries as an antidote to the popular restiveness of that crisis-ridden age. In 1808, 1810, and 1814,

---

[109] Joseph Lawson, *Letters to the Young on Progress in Pudsey* (Stanningley, 1887), 89.
[110] This inverse relationship between adult working-class church- or chapel-going and Sunday school attendance by working-class children was not unique to Bradford. Professor Laqueur has shown that it was a common feature of almost every nineteenth-century industrial city in England, which led him to conclude that "in certain urban areas, particularly in the north, Sunday Schools replaced church or chapel as the focus of working-class religious life." Thomas Laqueur, *Religion and Respectability* (New Haven, 1976), 59.

Table 10-4. *The development of Sunday schools in Bradford*

	Number of schools	Number of scholars on books	Percentage of children aged 5–14
1835	24	7,796	60–75
1851	59	16,077	71
1860	76	29,233	131

Sources: Compiled from statistics in *PP* (XLIII, 1835), 1152–4; (xl, 1852–3), CLXXXVI; *The State of Popular Education in England* (London, 1861), 2:192.

schools were set up by the Wesleyans, the Congregationalists, and the Baptists, respectively, as the new Nonconformity made its entry into the Sunday school field. Thereafter, there was a lull until the twenties when a new wave of Sunday school expansion began, this time with the Dissenters, especially the Wesleyans, taking the lead.[111]

As fast as Bradford's population grew during the next twenty-five years, the Sunday schools grew at an even faster pace. By 1843, according to Edward Baines, there were eighty-eight Sunday schools in the Bradford region with 4,854 teachers and 19,550 pupils enrolled. Moreover, if Baines's statistics are to be believed, those attending Nonconformist Sunday schools now outnumbered those in church schools almost four to one.[112] A more reliable set of statistics for Bradford Borough compiled from various parliamentary returns is compared, in Table 10-4, with the age-specific population statistics to estimate the proportion of children whom Bradford's Sunday school movement touched. By 1835, there were already enough scholars listed on the Sunday school books to account for 60 to 75 percent of all children between the ages of five and fourteen. Since Professor Laqueur's statistics from Stockport suggest an average enrollment of less than three years, it may be inferred that by the end of the thirties, virtually all working-class children must have attended Sunday school at some point in their lives.[113] As the parliamentary investigator J. Winder lamented a year later: "No other schools call out anything approaching to the zeal and general interest lavished on these. With the Dissenters generally they are far more

[111] "Early Bradford Sunday Schools" (cuttings, Bradford Archives, D. B. 35/16, no. 10).
[112] Educational Services Committee, Bradford Corporation, *Education in Bradford, 1870–1970*, (Bradford, 1970) 40–1.
[113] Indeed, the figures for later years are so high as to appear suspicious, since by 1860, there seem to have been more Sunday school attenders than there were children in the town.

popular than day schools and absorb, I cannot but think, an amount of energy and attention disproportionate to their real value, great as it may be."[114]

It is easy to understand why religious denominations put such a "disproportionate" amount of "energy and attention" into their Sunday schools, even at the expense of other types of evangelical work; for their failure voluntarily to convert the working-class adult to their values and spiritual identity naturally led them to refocus their energies on the more malleable working-class child. In 1858, Rev. Chown openly admitted that evangelicalism had to be aimed primarily at children since, "if we allow the time of youth to pass by, the work is the much harder and less likely to be done. ... It is confessedly and avowedly the young who are the hope of the church and the world."[115]

What is less easy to understand is why working people would expose their children to religious organizations in which they would not participate themselves. Several reasons can be adduced. For many families, Sunday was the only day when husbands and wives could be together. Given the cramped, overcrowded conditions of working-class living, it is not unreasonable to think that they might want some time alone. In addition, working people were not necessarily averse to exposing their children to modest doses of the values of work discipline and respectability that were so patently preconditions for, if not guarantees of, urban-industrial success.[116]

However, the most important reason for Sunday school attendance was that most workers wanted to educate their children and could do so in no other way. A group of Sunday school teachers themselves "lamented any necessity to instruct children of the Productive Classes in the mere rudiments of reading on the Lord's Day, but that under present circumstances, it is not possible for a very considerable part of those who are engaged in factory labour and occupation, to acquire the most scanty portion of literary information on the weekday."[117] Given the ineffectiveness of the educational clauses of the Factory Act long after their passage in 1833, putting children in a day school meant forfeiting their wages from work. This was a sacrifice that most working-class families were either unable or unwilling to make. The Sunday schools, being voluntarily staffed and run, were (unlike the day schools) entirely free and did not, therefore, place an unacceptable strain on the extremely tight working-class family budgets of the day.[118]

Professor Laqueur has expertly shown how the task of drawing and re-

[114] J. S. Winder, "Report on Bradford and Rochdale," in *The State of Popular Education in England* (London, 1861), 2:192–3.
[115] J. P. Chown, *Fraternal Responsibility* (London, 1858), 9, 14.
[116] Laqueur, *Religion and Respectability*, 147–78.
[117] "Petition to House of Commons," Mar. 7, 1836 (mss., Bradford Archives, D .B. 27).
[118] Ibid.

taining the allegiance of the urban working classes forced the Sunday schools to take a more liberal and secular direction and blunted the patronizing, authoritarian strain that had been a central part of their original bourgeois design.[119] However, the evidence from Bradford suggests that he goes too far when he calls the Sunday school a "generally democratic institution," which "was a part of and not an imposition on to," the working-class community that it served. Certainly, Sunday schools did draw upon an extraordinary reserve of lay enthusiasm and spawned a cadre of volunteer teachers so large as to almost certainly have encompassed segments of the lower middle and respectable working classes.[120] However, in Bradford, the Sunday schools always remained closely tied to the denominations that sponsored them, and though they were generally managed by laymen, most ministers also played an active role, advising the directors and catechizing the pupils. Moreover, the laymen who held real power in the Sunday schools were not the teachers, but the governing or management boards, which were invariably limited to the most prominent and respected members of the congregation. Among the Anglicans, all subscribers of over £21 automatically became directors, whereas lists of the governors of Union Street, Horton Lane, and Westgate Nonconformist Sunday schools show that management boards were almost entirely bourgeois.[121]

Furthermore, the very assumption on which the Sunday schools operated, whether implicit or openly expressed, was that most working-class parents were incapable of properly rearing their own children to become respectable citizens, and thus outside agencies had to intervene. To Parson Bull, the Sunday schools were "an indication of national degradation" that visibly revealed "a great deficiency of useful knowledge and of true religion in the great mass of the people.... Were it not so," Bull continued, "every cottage would be a Sunday school and every parent the Sunday School Teacher." He thought, "the great *aim* of all who are engaged in Sunday schools, should be to effect their abolition – that is to say, to rear up a future race of parents whose children would not require them."[122] Bull even publicly indulged in a fantasy of the Sunday school child carrying his teacher's values home to his parents and through the example of "dutiful, gentle, orderly, and affectionate behaviour" softening "the heart of even a sabbath-breaking, public-house haunting parent."[123]

Of all bourgeois commentators, the "ten hours parson" was the one most

---

[119] Laqueur, *Religion and Respectability*, 187–243.
[120] Ibid., xi,xii.
[121] "Early Bradford Sunday Schools"; William Scoresby, *Records of the Bradford Parochial Schools, 1840–6* (Bradford, 1846), 33–40.
[122] G. S. Bull, *Laying the First Stone of a New Schoolroom* (Bradford, 1837), 2.
[123] G. S. Bull, *Beneficial Results of Sunday Schools* (Birmingham, 1854), 163.

likely to have given workers the benefit of the doubt, yet he made clear that the function of Sunday schools was not only to internalize respectable values such as "honesty, carefulness, diligence, and strict conscientiousness," but submissiveness and "humble behavior" too.[124] Vicar Scoresby told his Sunday school teachers to impress upon their children "the evil nature of their hearts."[125] Unlike adult believers, these Sunday school children constituted a captive audience for whom this harsh religious language of sin and damnation was not a spontaneous psychological response to actual conditions but an externally imposed, authoritarian discipline to which they had no choice but to submit.

Nonconformists, especially the Baptists and Congregationalists, were more willing than the Wesleyans or Anglicans to permit working-class desires for secular instruction to impinge on their own religious agenda. Still, there were important limits as to what any Christian Sunday school was prepared to teach. The fact that local Owenite Socialists and Chartists both ultimately established their own radical nonsectarian Sunday schools indicates that the more articulate and self-conscious among the workers were not satisfied with the product offered by any of the denominations.[126] Of course, it matters little what the purveyors of the Sunday schools intended, since working people took what they wanted from the experience – a smattering of reading, writing, and arithmetic, and sometimes a commitment to a temperate, respectable way of life – and simply ignored or forgot the rest.[127] It was a widely acknowledged if lamented fact that few Sunday scholars continued their religious associations after they became consenting adults. Of the thousands of children who passed through Sion Baptist Sunday school between 1848 and 1868, only about four hundred subsequently joined the congregation.[128] If the Sunday school experience failed to inculcate working-class religion, it did little to instill working-class docility either. In 1839, at the height of Chartism, Parson Bull preached a sermon specially aimed at the radicals. Looking over his audience he could "recognize many who had been Sunday Scholars of the late Rev. Mr. Crosse, many of his own Sunday Scholars, and many who had been Sunday Scholars at other places." He could only regret that they had all turned infidel and joined a movement tainted with the spirit of disloyalty and violence.[129]

If institutions like the Sunday school are to be seen as bourgeois class instruments, as hegemonic weapons of social control, such facts must be

---

[124] Ibid.
[125] Scoresby, *Parochial Schools*, 39.
[126] Laqueur, *Religion and Respectability*, 125–46.
[127] Ibid., 95–145. *Northern Star*, Oct. 19, 26, 1839.
[128] J. P. Chown, *A Twenty Years' Review* (Bradford, 1868), 6, 7.
[129] *BO*, Aug. 8, 1839.

taken into account; for while this may have been one of the objectives of the religious institutions that organized them, in reality they had to operate within an often resistant working-class community that possessed its own cultural values and readily ignored bourgeois condescension when its sense of self-respect was offended. Nevertheless, if we remember this proviso, there is no reason, as Gareth Stedman Jones and F. M. L. Thompson have recently suggested, to abandon the concept of social control.[130]

Such a notion would, of course, be almost entirely inappropriate with regard to the egalitarian Congregational religion based on a fraternal priesthood of all believers, which was embodied in the bourgeois voluntary associational ideal. However, after the 1820s and 1830s in Bradford the associations actually organized around these principles increasingly failed to bridge the class divide. Most became almost entirely bourgeois or lower middle class in social composition, whereas the handful that still concentrated on the workers succeeded only insofar as they made this their primary preoccupation and adapted to a social and economic environment that was fundamentally alien to the bourgeois world. When institutions like the Sunday schools or the secular associations soon to be examined were more successful in crossing class barriers, this was because they broke, in fundamental ways, with the Congregational model and organized themselves along more authoritarian lines. Although built upon voluntary associational foundations they successfully operated as transclass agencies only insofar as they abandoned the egalitarian tradition and replaced the fraternal democracy of the autonomous congregation with a two-tiered structure that divided participants into the bourgeois or protobourgeois reformers and directors, and the passive objects (usually workers) deemed to be in need of reform. Such organizations might be more or less effective in attracting working-class involvement, and they might be more or less responsive to proletarian problems and needs. In all cases, however, they represented a sharp departure, in practice, from the voluntary spiritual associations on which a whole urban-industrial culture was supposed to have been built.

---

[130] F. M. L. Thompson, "Social Control in Victorian Britain," *Economic History Review,* n.s., 24:2 (1981); Gareth Stedman Jones, *Languages of Class* (Cambridge, 1983), 76–88.

11

The culture of voluntarism:
secular association

The psychological yearning for spiritual salvation was, among other things, a metaphor for the pursuit of secular self-help. Preoccupation with justification in heaven usually signaled anxiety about prospects for achievement on earth. Thus it was probably inevitable that Bradford's bourgeois culture of religious voluntarism would spawn a complementary secular associational culture that was explicitly aimed at worldly ends. Like the religious culture on which it was founded, this secular culture developed in accordance with two distinct but related goals. On the one hand, the voluntary associations that comprised it were designed as vehicles to meet the social and political needs of the emerging bourgeoisie. On the other hand, they sought to create a much more universal framework for the social and political integration around liberal, entrepreneurial values and aspirations which would encompass all of urban Bradford's diverse social groups.

From spiritual salvation to secular self-help

The foundations of the new secular voluntarist culture were laid within the religious associations themselves, for the congregational structure of the new Nonconformity harbored deep if unacknowledged secularizing tendencies that threatened to undermine the sacredotal foundations of sectarianism and transform the marketplace of competitive spiritualities into a primarily secular, cultural bazaar. Such tendencies were scarcely avoidable since they flowed from radical Protestantism's central aim: the reduction of the collective realm of the sacred to egocentric, salvation-centered terms.[1] This left religiosity too dependent on the psychology of the believer, who became, however unconsciously, the master of his subjective God. The disenchantment of the mystery of communion and the exultation of lay agency over clerical control tended to turn, especially within an urban, capitalist environment, public worship into a rational and individual act. Given the worldly

[1] Martin Luther, *Selections from his Writings* (New York, 1961), 42–85.

preoccupations of the parvenu bourgeois who made up these congregations, it is not surprising that the religious life of the city would generate a series of utilitarian spin-offs whose calendar of secular events and activities would come to overshadow religion's devotional core.[2]

In the associational auxiliaries considered in the last chapter, Sunday schools, missionary societies, and charitable and women's clubs, members sought to discharge their obligations toward evangelical outreach in a manner that would reinforce the internal cohesion of their congregational core. Yet beneath these highly visible evangelical associations lay a dense and often informal substratum of religiously affiliated networks that aimed not so much at converting the heathen as at enhancing the quality of internal congregational life. By the 1830s, new chapel-based associations, improvement clubs, miniature educational institutes, temperance societies, and building or provident clubs had emerged to guide aspiring young members and to help them keep to the straight and narrow path.[3]

Such coteries could form the basis for lifelong friendships and serve as intellectual workshops in which the new ideology of bourgeois liberalism could be hammered out. Rev. Godwin described one such regular gathering, exceptional only for the stature of its participants and the significance of its outcome:

> A few of the leading Dissenters of the town formed an "Amicable Book Society".... We met quarterly at each others houses, and very agreeable such season's were. The topics which usually engaged our attention were not only literary or theological, but anything which related to the religious or civil interests of the town, and of Noncomformists in particular. It became a bond of union and the means of a profitable exchange of thoughts and feelings. It was in these meetings that the *Bradford Observer*, was originated.[4]

This tendency for a secular culture to develop under the cover of religion and for religion to devolve into a culture of daily life was reinforced by the fact that, at least in the beginning, religion was the only available institutional framework within which a culture of respectability could germinate and flower. "Concentration about one's religious home," recalled one who was then a

---

[2] Owen Chadwick, *The Secularization of the European Mind in the Nineteenth Century* (Cambridge, 1975).

[3] William Cudworth, *Horton Lane Chapel: Old Time Reminiscences* (Bradford, 1893); anon., *Salem Congregational Church, Centenary, 1836–1936*, (Bradford, 1936); anon., *One Hundred Years of Primitive Methodism in Great Horton* (Bradford, 1924); anon., *The Centenary: The First Baptist Church in Bradford* (London, 1853); *BO*, Oct. 29, 1835; Apr. 14, 1859; *PP*, (1852, V), 41–2, (1874, XXIII), 2:206.

[4] Benjamin Godwin, "Autobiography" (mss. Bradford Central Library), 573.

youngster, "was more common and sustained than it is now; partly because there were fewer competing attractions." Without "tram-cars to spirit folks from one quarter of town to another...they stayed at home more....Not only was the chapel the social center for the flock, it was a more vital and aggressive force than it is today."[5]

Chapels like Horton Lane became social centers for their members because they, above all other institutions, were best suited to the sort of rational, respectable culture that the emerging bourgeoisie sought. Voluntarily joining a congregation was a choice in more than just a religious sense. It was also an act of substitution whereby traditional forms of leisure, which were deemed inherently brutalizing – feasts, fairs, taverns for plebeians, or even the more dignified aristocratic hunt – could be exchanged for a new set of leisure and recreational activities that were edifying and improving – teas, anniversaries, love feasts, outings, and charity bazaars, which not only turned amusements to productive purposes, but also shifted their focus from the sort of violence and debauchery characteristic of the culture of unattached young men to a set of decorous, family-oriented activities in which women and children would not hesitate to take part.[6]

Not surprisingly, this new, rationalistic approach to leisure quickly spread beyond the religious base of the Nonconformist congregation and began to assume explicitly secular forms. The result was a whole culture of rational recreation that channeled impulses that had hitherto fed debauchery and idleness into quite demanding and often remorselessly didactic activities and forms. From the outset, the paucity of formal educational opportunities for many of the new bourgeois aspirants and their natural preoccupation with self-improvement inclined them to direct what little leisure they had at their disposal into activities that would build character and increase knowledge. A whole host of informal discussion clubs and study groups in every district in town sprang up to meet this demand. The Bradford Moor Juvenile Improvement Society, the Stott Hill Mutual Improvement Society, the Bradford Literary and Debating Society, and the Bradford Essay and Discussion

---

[5] F. G. Byles, *William Byles* (Weymouth, 1932), 104.

[6] Not all aspects of this chapel culture were novel since prohibitions on dancing and debauchery, long common among Dissenters, had forced them to develop alternative culture forms. Some of the most popular activities like choral music were, in fact, inheritances from the rural chapels of the protoindustrial era, where "it was the practice every Sunday evening to hold a prayer meeting at the Minister's house, and chiefly owing to the excellent singing these were invariably well attended." John Wood, *Autobiography* (Bradford, 1877), 11. Because it became an important part of urban culture, music constituted one link between the popular culture of village dissent and the new world of urban voluntarism. However, in the context of the capitalist city, the spontaneous conviviality of a religious community gave way to a more studied, self-conscious approach.

Society were unusual only in being noted by the press.[7] Dozens, perhaps hundreds, of comparable groups met alongside them, such as Thomas R. Taylor's discussion circle in which a group of young men got together on a regular basis to read and criticize each other's essays. Typically, such groups would meet weekly, although one that was organized in the village of Pudsey met every morning from 5:00 to 6:00 and several evenings a week after work got out.[8]

Although this culture of self-improvement concentrated on the mind, it did not entirely neglect the body. To replace the violence of traditional recreations, a series of disciplined individual and team efforts were organized in which a premium was placed not only on physical skill and coordination, but on attitudes of sportsmanship and moral self-control. Thus in 1836, the Bradford Cricket Club was established as an antidote to the cock fighting, bear baiting, and pugilistic contests that had hitherto prevailed.[9] Every year, at Whitsuntide, a struggle between the old and new recreations would be joined as the new urban religious and secular associations scheduled a whole series of counterattractions to lure young people away from traditional games and debauches. As the *Observer* noted during Whit week in 1849, "Formerly wrestling matches, gingling matches, [and] foot races were the order of the day... we now have club feasts, school festivals, temperance galas, cheap trips all of which the young generation enjoy with as much zest as their fathers enjoyed the conservative sports of their day."[10]

Not content simply to reform the traditional agrarian calendar and to suppress most of its fairs and feasts, the new recreational culture strove, after the opening of the railroad in 1846, to create a distinctly urban "bank" holiday in late August, when businesses would close and special excursion trains to London, Liverpool, or Scarborough would be scheduled. At first, before midcentury, most of the vacationers were families traveling first or second class. However, by the fifties, when cheap fares were instituted, these respectable holidays were gradually enjoyed by more and more workers as well.[11]

Secular associations were formed, not only to meet the new Bradfordians' needs for knowledge and recreation, but also as a response to shared interests and experiences. Because the region had long possessed strong musical

---

[7] William Cudworth, *Round About Bradford* (Bradford, 1876), 128; *BO*, Feb. 5, Apr. 12, Oct. 13, 1835; Feb. 2, 1837; May 2, 1839; May 1, 1845.

[8] W. S. Matthews, *Memoirs and Select Remains of Rev. Thomas Rawson Taylor* (London, 1836), 10; Joseph Lawson, *Letters to the Young on Progress in Pudsey* (Stanningley, 1883), 63.

[9] John James, *History and Topography of Bradford* (Bradford, 1841), 278; *BO*, Mar. 28, 1939; Nov. 28, 1844.

[10] *BO*, May 31, 1849.

[11] *BO*, Aug. 27, Sep. 3, Oct. 1, 1846.

traditions, it was in this area that secular voluntarism developed first. In 1821, the Bradford Musical Friendly Society (later to become the Bradford Choral Society) was founded as a union of all the most interested and talented amateur singers and musicians from each of the denominations. Nine years later, a rival and, apparently, more "Tory" Philharmonic Society was established to offer public subscription concerts. In 1845, the Gentleman's Glee Club was formed and in 1856, the largest and most spectacular of these organizations, the Bradford Festival Choral Society, was begun. When they rehearsed their musical harmonies, these middle- and lower-middle-class amateur performers (as they themselves occasionally recognized) were also practicing the skills of social harmonization that the new associational culture generally required.[12]

Among those ascendant bourgeois who were long-distance immigrants, ethnic associations could perform a similar role – serving as cures for the loneliness of the alien and antidotes to the experience of urban anomie. In 1836, a local Caledonian Society was established and its chairman, Robert Milligan, told his fellow native Scots, "Age and accidental differences of wealth and education are lost sight of in a general fraternity while they furnish a spur to industry and good conduct that cannot fail to be productive of the happiest consequences."[13]

The Bradford Germans also had their ethnic associations. As the merchant Jacob Behrens explained, "A number of us are now congregated in this thriving town, and, though our paths do not all run alike ... and our worldly interests be at variance, still we are united by ties of language, by bonds of early association and by homely feelings, which neither time nor space can alienate or destroy."[14] Among their other contributions, these German merchants brought a more sophisticated taste in music to the community, and in the midforties, a group of them formed themselves into a *Liedertafel* and reorganized the subscription Philharmonic concerts to take account of the latest continental tastes.[15]

After the middle of the century, these secular improvement associations would again expand, both in number and in range of activity, as the growth of bourgeois and lower-middle-class leisure sparked interest in more esoteric forms of self-cultivation. In 1853, fifteen professionals and businessmen founded the Bradford Chess Club whose membership increased over the years. By 1860, a Microscopical Society was in existence, and like the Chess Club, it held public demonstrations and soirees. In 1863, the Bradford Field

[12] William Cudworth, *Musical Reminiscences of Bradford* (Bradford, 1885), 5–9, 12, 38–42; G. F. Sewell, *A History of the Bradford Festival Choral Society, 1856–1906* (Bradford, 1907).
[13] *BO*, Jan. 14, 1836; Feb. 2, 1837.
[14] *BO*, Jan. 13, 1859.
[15] Cudworth, *Musical Reminiscences*, 42.

Naturalist Society was organized and planned its first annual trip to Baildon. As the century wore on, this club expanded, and its activities provided a means of combining weekend recreation and instruction for many bourgeois families in town.[16]

The proliferation of all these middle-class associations in Bradford, organized around the principles of rational recreation and self-help, betokened the development of a rich participatory culture well attuned to the demands of urban-industrial success. And yet, at least before the middle of the century, this culture remained in social character almost entirely bourgeois. Of course, secular associations that appealed directly to the worldly concerns and interests of the populace had a greater chance of eliciting the involvement of workers than the religious associations in which assurance of salvation set the underlying framework for the pursuit of self-help. Yet no less than religious evangelicalism, any secular evangelicalism that sought to convert the unregenerate masses to the liberal entrepreneurial vision of urban-industrial life had to come to terms with the realities of class division and the difficulties of organizing bourgeoisie and workers together within any common associational frame. It was to address this difficulty during the critical decades of the 1830s and 1840s, when workers seemed most alienated from respectable habits and values and the imperatives of integrating appeared most great, that two remarkable voluntary associations, the Bradford Temperance Society and Mechanics Institute, were formed. Although neither succeeded in its objective of becoming the lynchpin of a universal social consensus and both remained restricted to a relatively narrow working-class elite, each made significant inroads into the capitalist class barrier that religious associations had found almost impossible to penetrate.

The temperance movement

In protoindustrial Bradford, drink had been an integral part of community life. Given the prevailing belief that beer was necessary to provide strength for work, home brewing loomed large within the cottage economy, whereas the inn played a critical role not only as a social institution, but as an economic and political center too.[17] With industrialization, however, the cottage economy began to collapse, and with urbanization, the multiple functions hitherto

[16] C. H. Leach, *History of the Bradford Chess Club* (Bradford, 1853); *BO*, Oct. 11, 1860; May 21, 1863; *Bradford Telegraph and Argus*, Sep. 19, 1913.
[17] See Chapter 2.

performed by the inn were spun off to other activities and institutions. We have already seen this process at work with the transfer of business from public inns and piece halls to private warehouses and factories – a process intensified by the emergence of the railroad, which undermined the inns' role in travel and transport as well.[18]

However, with the rise of the privatized bourgeois family and the proliferation of chapels, churches, and voluntary associations, which either possessed or aspired to meeting places of their own, a similar process can be seen in the cultural realm. Although inns continued to proliferate in absolute numbers, their relative significance diminished with urbanization. Where there was one for every 580 Bradfordians in 1828, by 1851, there was one for every 961.[19] As social and economic elites ceased to depend on the tavern, the Nonconformist, entrepreneurial goal of a culture of sobriety grounded in the values of work discipline and self-help became, at least for their own class, a realistic possibility. However, for most workers, this new culture of sobriety continued to run counter to the natural environmental influences of their world.

Given the squalor of most working-class dwellings, the poverty of domestic life, as well as the deadening impact of long hours of mechanical labor, it is hardly surprising that most workers, or at least most male workers, found drinking with their mates in a comfortable setting the most desirable way to spend their short periods of leisure. However, the decline not only of drink in the home, but also of the older sort of public tavern around which the traditional culture had revolved together with the growing separation of classes, meant that this new urban, proletarian culture of consolation needed separate drinking establishments of its own.[20]

The rise of distinctively working-class pubs in Bradford, as in so many other places, was facilitated by the Beer Act of 1830, which enabled small retailers to open up beershops without going through the restrictive and expensive licensing procedure that was necessary for general taverns and inns. During the two decades of "free trade in beer," there was a veritable explosion of beershops in Bradford. A host of tiny beersellers proliferated much more rapidly than any other type of retailer in town. By 1850, Bradford had 175 beershops, or one for every 593 inhabitants. Twenty-two years later, their number had risen to 327, which was almost three times the number of inns in the town.[21]

That there was a difference between the decorous culture of the traditional

---

[18] See Chapter 4.
[19] *Pigot's Directory* (London, 1828); James Ibbetson, *Directory of Bradford* (Bradford, 1850).
[20] Brian Harrison, *Drink and the Victorians* (London, 1971), 83–6.
[21] *Smith's Directory of Bradford* (London, 1872); Ibbetson, *Directory of Bradford*.

tavern and the the demoralized culture of the low working-class beershop was something about which Bradford's first police chief had no doubt. In 1849, he claimed, "in almost every beershop within the Borough amusements which are not allowed or tolerated by licensed victuallers are instituted."[22] Several years later, the beerhouse scene was described more colorfully by a local writer, James Burnley, to whom the clientele seemed "such a medley of humanity as cannot be seen together under any other circumstances.... Respectability there is not in any shape," he lamented, "but all the seven cardinal sins... and a great many additional ones," were represented by "a group of thick-throated men... [who] garnish their conversation with numerous allusions to each other's eyes and limbs, and speak as if in a ferment for a deadly quarrel." Among them, "many volatile sons of Erin dodge about in the crowd and add to the noise with their endless loquacity," often accompanied by their wives and sweethearts, "strong agricultural looking females who seem quite competent to hold their own in a family quarrel." For the rest, the crowd was a mix of "cabmen, navvies, tradesmen on the high road to bankruptcy, seedy clerks, and millworkers in Saturday night dress."[23]

Even if we discount Burnley's bourgeois prejudices, it is impossible to doubt the overall accuracy of the picture he paints. Scarcely a weekly session of the borough court passed when one or more "disorderly beerhouse keepers," could not be found among a crowd of shoplifters, pickpockets, gamblers, vagrants, and prostitutes in the dock. Even if the beerhouse was not, as many bourgeois observers imagined, simply a center for these other criminal activities, there can be no doubt but that it was the source of a great deal of

---

[22] In the same year, the Town Council passed a resolution supporting a parliamentary bill that would suppress the beershops. *BO*, Mar. 22, May 24, 1849.

[23] James Burnley, *Phases of Bradford Life* (Bradford, 1871), 147–9. Many beershops had singing rooms attached where bawdy songs were performed as drinks were served by waitresses "of jaded appearance." The largest of these shaded off into prototypical music halls or full-scale dancing parlors, which were, in their way, just as far removed from elegant upper-class ballrooms as the beerhouse was from the traditional inn. "From the fashionable ball-room as I have described it to the common dancing saloon, as I am about to describe it," wrote Burnley, "is a descent such as to an outsider would seem impossible in the society of a civilized community; the contrast is as great as, in point of ethnology, is apparent between the intelligent European and the Savage of a remote tribe in the interior of Africa. The low dancing-room is a fit, and perhaps an inseparable adjunct to the dramshop. The same individuals frequent both places to a considerable extent." After screwing up his courage to go inside, Burnley found the usual debauchery with subtle insinuations of something worse. "There is abandon enough in all conscience, but not a hint of grace; there is plenty of vigor but no accompanying sense of propriety ... The girls are, I should think, all factory operatives," he continued, and "have a bold unflinching look, which in some instances amount to callousness; and the sensuality of their demeanour is painful to contemplate." Burnley, *Bradford Life*, 163–5.

public drunkenness, domestic violence, illness, and financial waste on the part of Bradford's working class. To Burnley, after the closing of the beer-shops, nocturnal Bradford evoked nothing so much as the carnage of a battlefield after a great encounter had been fought and lost. Looking over the sorry scene, he saw "people lying about in doorways and causeways so far gone in intoxication as to be quite beyond the power of striking a po-liceman or (as most of the bold drunkards prefer) going home and beating their hungry wives."[24]

Obviously, so long as such a situation persisted, the working class could never be brought fully to embrace the values of work discipline and rational recreation that were not only necessary for the proper functioning of an industrial society, but from the perspective of the bourgeoisie, eminently desirable for the individual who wished to get ahead. Temperance was not so much a final goal as a precondition that would be necessary if the positive bourgeois message of spiritual salvation or secular self-help were to have any chance of reaching its working-class mark.

The Bradford Temperance Society, the first of its kind in England or Wales, was founded in February 1830 by the Scottish-born stuff merchant Henry Forbes, who got the idea on a business trip back home.[25] From the start, the essentially bourgeois, Nonconformist character of the organization was evident in its base of financial support. In 1832, at least 45 percent of the society's income came from subscribers, most of whom were prominent Nonconformists in the town. The governing board had a similar social composition, for it included such parvenu Dissenting capitalists as Thomas Aked, Miles Illingworth, Benjamin Seebohm, John McCroben, William Murgatroyd and David Harris Smith, in addition to Forbes. Since the An-glican ministers G. S. Bull and William Morgan, as well as the industrialists John and William Rand, were also included, temperance was more than just a secular translation of Nonconformist evangelicalism. However, since many Anglicans suspected the movement of infidel, or at the very least, of dem-ocratic, leveling tendencies, they kept their distance. Contemporaries rec-ognized that temperance was, in large measure, a liberal, Nonconformist preserve.[26]

Certainly, the temperance diagnosis of urban capitalism reveals some striking parallels with the liberal, Nonconformist world view. Since the whole temperance position was grounded in the assumption that drink was not a symptom, but the primary evil in itself, temperance implied a moral rather

[24] Burnley, *Bradford Life*, 105.
[25] George Field, *Historical Survey of the Bradford Temperance Society* (Bradford, 1897), 4; Harrison, *Drink and the Victorians*, 104–5; *BO*, Mar. 31, 1836.
[26] Field, *Bradford Temperance Society*, 5; Bradford Temperance Society, *Annual Report* (Brad-ford, 1832).

than a materialist critique that focused, not on the inequities of a competitive society, but on the inadequacies of the individual who could not successfully compete.[27] Drunkenness, like sin, was a moral failing whose solution lay in the hands of the individual. By attributing the poverty and misery of working-class life almost entirely to a demonology of drink, temperance, like neo-Calvinist Nonconformity, can be seen, in part, as the ideological self-justification of the successful. However, what made temperance particularly attractive to the Nonconformist mental frame was its diagnosis of urban social pathology as a disease inherited from the preindustrial past; for drunkenness was regarded as a reactionary atavism; the legacy of popular ignorance and brutality that the reign of aristocratic privilege and corruption had left in its wake. To visualize the evils of industrial capitalism through the lens of temperance was to see not exploitation or poverty, but a pattern of degenerative barbarism whose proper antidote was not class militancy but precisely the sort of enlightened, purposive, individualist mentality that industrial capitalism both generated and required. The initial dislocations of urbanization, with its loosening of traditional bonds and restraints, might well temporarily increase the dangers of demoralization and debauchery, but they also provided the requisite freedom that the virtuous individual would need for self-reform.

It was to facilitate such a voluntarily chosen commitment to temperate, respectable behavior, especially among members of the working class, that the Temperance Society was founded.[28] The bourgeois leadership would set an example that the working-class membership could follow and extend. By its first anniversary, the Bradford society had 580 members, and three years later, enrollments had risen to 1,400. By the end of the decade, there were 2,500 members, or about 6 percent of all adults in the town. As these figures indicate, the Temperance Society, even at the height of its popularity, was far from encompassing the bulk of the urban working class. Still, its membership indicates that it was more successful than any religious denomination, including the Wesleyans, in drawing a broad base of working-class support.[29] In part, this was because the Temperance Society, unlike the Wesleyans, although remaining firmly under bourgeois governance, was willing to become increasingly plebeian in orientation as it grew more and more sensitive to its members' needs. By 1848, the society had become largely self-financing as the proportion of income obtained from subscribers dropped to 22 percent; almost all the rest was obtained from proceeds of lectures, galas, and other activities supported by the members themselves.[30]

---

[27] Harrison, *Drink and the Victorians*, 354–9.
[28] Ibid., 179–95.
[29] *BO*, Dec. 24, 1835; Mar. 13, 1837.
[30] Bradford Temperance Society, *Annual Report* (Bradford, 1848), 7.

The increasing significance of the working-class element in temperance caused the society to focus more seriously on active outreach work. A special missionary was hired in 1831, and the members themselves, at a later date, sponsored outdoor meetings and cottage visitations "into the neighbourhoods most pregnant with vice, where they sought out the habitations which have been rendered desolate by intemperate habits."[31] As the *Annual Report* noted in 1848; "This mode of advocacy has been found to be more effective than any other, for during the last three months upwards of 400 signators to the teetotal pledge have been obtained, many of whom were in the most abject position through drunkenness, but who now have become sober characters."[32] Even more spectacular were the periodic visits of the temperance campaigner Father Matthew to Bradford's Irish slums, which can only be described as charismatic secular revivals:

> The rush about the carriage was tremendous, so anxious were the crowd to catch a glimpse of the great man … a public meeting was held in the vacant ground behind the Temperance Hall, which was attended by from two to three thousand persons. Father Matthew spoke from a waggon. He then administered the pledge, both in English and in Irish, to a great many persons who repeated after him. After this, he descended into the crowd, and spent nearly two hours administering the pledge to others who took it kneeling.[33]

However, like other evangelicals such as the Methodists, Bradford's temperance workers found that it was easier to attract adherents than to keep them successfully within the fold. Once again, in deference to the needs of its working-class clientele, the leaders of the Temperance Society warily adopted the total abstinence pledge, giving up not only spirits, but all alcoholic drinks. To most bourgeois, this seemed an unnecessary excess that smacked of fanaticism. However, for working-class members who were closer to the concrete dangers of demoralization and backsliding, even the smallest temptation might prove fatal to an individual who lived in the midst of a culture of intoxication and depended entirely on his willpower to resist.[34]

Consequently, what really determined the success of the movement in holding onto its adherents was not the form of the pledge, but its ability to provide alternative activities that would enable its members to find amusement and sociability without succumbing to the debilitation of drink. As one local temperance advocate put the problem:

> When urging the claims of Temperance I have met with the following objection more frequently than any other: "If I am a teetotaler, I cannot go to the public house and where shall I find society and amusement?"

[31] Ibid., 6.
[32] Ibid., 7.
[33] Quoted in Field, *Bradford Temperance Society*, 16.
[34] *BO*, Jul. 7, 14, 1836.

> Now it cannot be denied that there is some force in this remark. In
> Bradford, scarcely any place can be found where, after the labours of
> the day, the artizan or shopkeeper can resort to enjoy a little relaxation
> and amusement.[35]

What really made temperance more successful than evangelical Protestantism
in attracting a working-class clientele was that temperance, with its overtly
secular orientation, was able to generate a whole series of cultural counterattractions that represented a viable and, in many ways, a superior alternative
to the dominant proletarian culture of drink.

From the start, the society sponsored a round of teas, anniversaries, and
festivals at Whitsun and Easter to serve as antidotes to the beershop and
the traditional wake. In 1835, a giant regional temperance fair was organized
in the nearby village of Wilsden, and the event was repeated the following
year, when festivities lasted for two full days.[36] At the same time, independent
temperance entrepreneurs began to open coffee houses, temperance hotels,
reading rooms, and working men's clubs that catered to the newly sober
clientele.[37] The most impressive achievement of the movement, however,
was the erection in 1837, of the Temperance Hall, the first of its kind in
the entire country. Built at a cost of £1,400, £900 of which was raised in
£1 shares, the Temperance Hall was, until 1853, the closest thing that
Bradford possessed to a large, centrally located public building. Providing
not only a club room for society members, but a large meeting hall, it quickly
became a center for other social and political groups.[38]

Clearly, Bradford's teetotalers were no isolated minority. They quickly
moved to the core of the town's self-help culture and drew a broad spectrum
of support into the temperance cause. Even groups and individuals who
found teetotal arguments less than compelling, recognized the value of the
movement in providing a means of self-acculturation to industrial values and
behavior for many who might otherwise be unable to adjust.[39] Gradually,
the temperance idea began to percolate through the entire web of Bradford's
associational culture, providing a diagnosis of social pathology and the rudimentary materials for devising a cure. Chapel auxiliaries were, in some
cases, founded, and even a church temperance society was started at a later
date.[40]

---

[35] *BO*, Feb. 28, 1839.
[36] *BO*, Apr. 23, 1835; Apr. 21, 1836; Dec. 12, 1844; Field, *Bradford Temperance Society*, 7.
[37] The 1850 *Directory* listed thirteen separate temperance establishments. Ibbetson, *Directory of Bradford* (Bradford, 1850).
[38] Peggy Raistrick, "The Bradford Temperance Movement" (typescript, Bradford Central Library), 28; Field, *Bradford Temperance Society*, 9–11; *BO*, Jan. 6, 1842.
[39] Godwin, "Autobiography," 525–8; *BO*, Jul. 7, 1836.
[40] Raistrick, "Bradford Temperance Movement," 23.

In 1834, the Youth Temperance Society was established that held popular Whitsun celebrations and attracted a membership of 2,000 by 1840. The Bands of Hope brought the temperance movement into the Sunday schools as children increasingly became a central focus of teetotal work. After 1840, the Bands of Hope had an annual parade that became a major event in the civic calendar when thousands of orderly Sunday school children thronged downtown streets under the supervision of their teachers while multitudes of adults gathered to watch.[41] Even some of the friendly societies became infiltrated by temperance principles, and in 1838, the first Rechabite society was organized in Bradford, while in 1840, the Oddfellows themselves opened a teetotal lodge.[42] The movement even made its mark on the conduct of local politics, canvassing 709 electors in 1841 and getting 532 of them to oppose the use of public houses by candidates in political campaigns.[43]

Although this temperance culture never became a fully dominant culture, at least not for most members of Bradford's working class, it did become a powerful instrument of social consensus for those who participated in it. Infusing a multitude of diverse associations with its object, the temperance movement united members from a range of different social groups around a common diagnosis of the ills of society and a clear-cut prescription for effecting their cure. Yet because the secular culture of temperance was so successful in touching base with diverse elements in the urban-industrial population, it was also prone to register the strains and conflicts that were creating divisions in the larger society.

The major development that reveals this inner conflict was a split that took place within the movement in 1838, when a group of militant working-class temperance reformers broke away from the mainstream Temperance Society, ostensibly over the form of the pledge. Regarding any form of moderation as "a white robed demon" that would lure its unsuspecting victim into "a posture so demure," these thoroughly plebeian temperance extremists insisted on the most rigid commitment to teetotalism as a precondition for participation in their movement.[44] Reconstituting themselves under the name of the Long-Pledged Teetotal Association, they committed themselves even more firmly than before to evangelicalism among the fallen and to mutual reinforcement within their own ranks.[45]

Pursuing the goals of the Temperance Society in a more radical and intensive way, the Long-Pledged Teetotalers developed their own set of countercultural attractions, such as annual Whitsun galas, Sunday schools,

[41] Field, *Bradford Temperance Society*, 15; *BO*, May 25, 1843.
[42] *BO*, Apr. 4, 1839; Jan. 2, 1840.
[43] Harrison, *Drink and the Victorians*, 345.
[44] Raistrick, "Bradford Temperance Movement," 17.
[45] *BO*, June 20, 1844; Apr. 10, June 27, 1845.

a reading room, library, educational institute, and discussion groups in which teetotalers could gather. Fully alive to the domestic consequences of intemperance and the interest of women in the temperance goal, the Long-Pledged Teetotalers spawned the Female Temperance Society, which, unlike the mainstream society, gave women a more active and public role.[46] Finally, when they found themselves excluded from existing meeting places, the Long-Pledged Teetotalers scraped together enough money to purchase a rather seedy structure called Southgate Hall for £208 in 1846. Located in the heart of the Millbank slum district, this Teetotal Hall was, unlike the establishment model, designed as a missionary outpost within the dens of sin. By 1844, the Bradford Teetotal Society had recruited 1,588 members.[47]

Notwithstanding the vigor of their temperance proselytizing, the Long-Pledged Teetotalers evoked a storm of disapproval and occasional outright opposition from more respectable, bourgeois quarters both within the movement and without. In part, this antagonism came from local ministers who regarded the radical teetotalers as cryptoinfidels who were substituting total abstinence for God. The parallels between the aims and organization of temperance and religion had always been obvious and engendered a certain unease on both sides.[48] At first, ministers were inclined to look on temperance reformers as much needed allies in the uphill battle against urban irreligion and sin. Yet because the objects of the two were so similar, the potential for conflict was very great. Even ministers who were staunch defenders of temperance, such as J. P. Chown, insisted that total abstinence must be seen as a plain between the city of drunkenness and the mountain of faith. "The plain is not the mountain," Chown reminded his listeners, but "every one who would go from the city to the mountain, must pass over it."[49] For its part, the Temperance Society had made it clear that "In attempting to exterminate the vice of Intemperance as a great national sin, the Society would desire to rest their hopes of final success not on mere human agency, but on the countenance and blessing of Him, who alone can crown their efforts with the desired result."[50]

What worried ministers about the Long-Pledged Teetotalers was their fear that the latter were neglecting this proviso and were acting as though

<hr />

[46] BO, Apr. 31, Dec. 17, 1846; BOB, Dec. 7, 1907; Raistrick, "Bradford Temperance Movement," 55–63.

[47] Joseph Wilson, His Life and Work (London, n.d.), 49–57; BO, June 27, 1844; Mar. 26, Oct. 6, 1846; Mar. 11, 1858.

[48] Harrison, Drink and the Victorians, 179–95; BO, Jul. 7, 1836.

[49] J. P. Chown, "The City, the Plain, and the Mountain," in The Temperance Pulpit (Glasgow, 1859).

[50] Bradford Temperance Society, Annual Report (1832).

total abstinence was an alternative rather than a supplement to God. According to Rev. James Bromley, the teetotal pledge was a blasphemy on the Bible, a document in which intoxicating beverages play a leading part. The teetotal practice of teaching secular subjects in their Sunday schools also did not endear them to many clergymen.[51] Even among groups like the Primitive Methodists, teetotalers like Joseph Wilson were suspected of infidelism by their fellow congregants. However, this sectarian quibbling over theological niceties, the instinctive response of the radical Nonconformist mind, was not the primary reason for elite hostility toward what the militant teetotalers were trying to do. Their most serious objection to the Long-Pledged Teetotalers Association was that its working- and lower-middle-class members would not subordinate themselves to bourgeois authority, and were prepared to make alliances with radical political groups.[52]

Unlike the Temperance Society, the Bradford teetotalers insisted on maintaining democratic forms of governance through which working-class members could control their own affairs. It was probably for this reason that leading bourgeois figures like John Rand, E. C. Lister, and Titus Salt refused to participate in the opening of Teetotal Hall. John Priestman, who agreed to speak, took the occasion to chastize the teetotalers on their choice of "one of their committee."[53] What was particularly unpalatable about the teetotalers uncompromising sense of independence was their readiness to use it to ally themselves, at least tacitly, with the radical Chartist working-class politics of the day. The very timing of the original teetotal break in 1838 can hardly have been an accident, for this was the great year of Chartist expansion and a time when class tensions in Bradford were rising to unprecedented heights. This was certainly the view of the mainstream temperance leadership, which attacked the teetotalers for politicizing the movement and importing what seemed to be a "new and dangerous doctrine" similar to the "teetotal chartism" that cropped up in other places. It was this unholy alliance of "chartists, socialists, and catholics" under the banner of temperance that most frightened the mainstream leaders, and they were determined to do what they could to put the new movement down.[54]

Although these fears of teetotal political involvement may have been exaggerated, they were basically close to the mark. The Long-Pledged Teetotaler Association never hesitated to rent their hall to the Chartists when the latter could not find any other place in which to meet. Later,

[51] Raistrick, "Bradford Temperance Movement."
[52] See R. J. Morris, "Organization and Aims of the Principal Secular Voluntary Organizations of the Leeds Middle Class, 1830–51," (Oxford, D.Phil. dissertation, 1970).
[53] Raistrick, "Bradford Temperance Movement," 60; *BO*, Dec. 17, 1846.
[54] Raistrick, "Bradford Temperance Movement," 14–16.

when the teetotalers, burdened with debt, were forced to sell their property, it was to the Secularist Society that they passed it on.[55] In some cases, the links between teetotalism and political radicalism were much more direct, as in the case of John Bates, a Chartist factory worker who was drawn by his political beliefs to become a temperance activist, convinced that total abstinence, no less than parliamentary democracy, constituted a way of "do[ing] something to right the wrongs of the working classes."[56]

However, with the gradual easing of class antagonisms in the late 1840s, radical temperance advocates and the mainstream temperance movement began, once again, to explore their common ground. By the 1850s, the two groups reestablished a modus vivendi, and although the wounds of division took some time to heal, a decade later, the Bradford movement had reconverged in the United Temperance Society. In nearby Queensbury, John Bates had not only joined the mainstream temperance society, but in 1854, became the organization's secretary, a post he continued to hold for the next forty years.[57]

The Mechanics Institute

If temperance provided a powerful diagnosis of urban dysfunction cast entirely in liberal individualist terms, the Mechanics Institute was to serve as the foundation of the self-help superstructure that would be built upon the ground that temperance had cleared. Indeed, it would be difficult to overestimate the importance of the Mechanics Institute in the minds of its bourgeois founders, not only as a vehicle for their own autodidacticism, but as the primary instrument through which entrepreneurial values and useful knowledge could be diffused to the urban working class.[58]

The Bradford Mechanics Institute was founded in February 1832 by a group of aspiring young Nonconformists, the schoolteachers William Clough and John Lamb, the linen draper Daniel Hainsworth, and the lawyer John Reid Wagstaff. This group was led by the hatter Joseph Farrar, who was twenty-six years old at the time. Excluded by the prohibitive costs of subscription from the Philosophical Society and the proprietary library frequented by established elites, these parvenus found themselves "greatly

---

[55] Wilson, *His Life and Work*, 49–50; *BO*, Mar. 11, 1858.
[56] John Bates, *A Sketch of His Life* (Queensbury, 1895).
[57] Raistrick, "Bradford Temperance Movement," 36–8; Field, *Bradford Temperance Society*, 18; Bates, *Sketch of His Life*.
[58] J. F. C. Harrison, *Learning and Living, 1790–1960* (London, 1960).

hampered in their individual attempts to improve their minds."[59] The Mechanics Institute was to provide a library and classes through which ambitious young men like themselves, as well as those who possessed even fewer advantages, could obtain the practical scientific and technical training that they would need to improve themselves. With its emphasis on useful knowledge, the Mechanics Institute would be a populist alternative to the intellectual monopoly hitherto maintained by the established Anglican, Tory elite.

Nevertheless, the Mechanics Institute's populism was tempered from the start by the recognition of its organizers that it would have to be accepted as a legitimate and respectable educational and cultural institution, at least by the rising Nonconformist entrepreneurs. Without financial assistance from such individuals or support from the Dissenting clergymen of the town, the Mechanics Institute could not hope to survive. This was particularly well understood by the new institute's founders since their efforts had been presaged in 1825, when a group of free thinkers under the leadership of Squire Farrer and Christopher Wilkinson had attempted to organize a mechanics institute along truly radical and populist lines.[60]

Adopting a radically democratic constitution, the original institute's rules stipulated that artisans would always form a majority of the governing committee, which would be elected annually by a ballot of all the members. In addition, workers too poor to join the institute as members could use its facilities upon payment of a 4s. annual fee. The radical cast of this institute's leadership and the proletarian orientation of its rules horrified the leading Tory gentlemen of Bradford, who, after recognizing its true character, steadfastly refused to give their sanction or support.[61] With the outbreak of the Great Worsted Strike a few months after the institute's founding, its radical class basis became even more obvious as its leaders were driven by events to offer their organization as an antidote, not only to ignorance, irrationality, and political reaction, but to poverty, exploitation, and economic inequality too. Not surprisingly, the failure of the strike and the onset of deep depression in the winter of 1825/6 caused the underfinanced institute to collapse.[62]

The memory of this first mechanics institute rankled in the minds of Bradford's elites who were, at first, wary of Joseph Farrar's proposal seven years later to form a new adult school along more ideologically acceptable lines. Even the rising Nonconformist ministers and bourgeois laymen, though not as hostile as the Anglican elite, were initially skeptical and waited for assurances that the institute's range of intellectual enquiry would not stray

---

[59] Charles Federer, "Bradford Mechanics Institute," in L. A. Fraser ed., *Memoirs of Daniel Fraser* (London, 1905); Joseph Farrar, *Autobiography* (Bradford, 1889), 44–6.
[60] Harrison, *Learning and Living*, 61.
[61] *Rules of Bradford Mechanics Institute* (Bradford, 1825).
[62] See Chapter 16.

beyond Christian orthodoxy and classical political economy before offering their active support.[63]

Eager to get the institute underway, Farrar and his co-workers quickly agreed to a preamble to the constitution that was worded in the following way:

> The designation of this Institute shall be "The Bradford Mechanics Institute," or Society for the Acquisition of Useful Knowledge, and although this Institute does not profess to assume the character of a Religious Society, yet it fully recognizes the Divine authority of the Holy Scriptures and the important truths of Christianity as recorded therein ... further, that all subjects immediately connected with controversial theology, or party politics, shall also be wholly inadmissible.[64]

At this point, perceptive and progressive Nonconformist leaders like Benjamin Godwin addressed their lay and clerical colleagues with arguments along the following lines:

> You see gentlemen, it is no longer a question whether an institution of this kind shall be formed in this growing town but it is principally under what direction and influence it shall move – you fear that its tendencies will be towards Skepticism in religion and ultra-democracy in politics – come then and unite yourselves with it, give it your patronage and aid, take your share in its direction as the best possible way of preventing the evils which you fear.[65]

It was not long before the other then leading Nonconformists, John Hustler, Benjamin Seebohm, Robert Milligan, Charles and Henry Harris, Dr. Thomas Beaumont, as well as Rev. Steadman and Rev. T. R. Taylor, followed Rev. Godwin's advice and agreed to put down their names as officers and directors of the new organization. A few prominent Anglicans such as Samuel Hailstone and E. C. Lister joined them, but most of the rest of the establishment remained aloof, unconvinced of the desirability of educating the plebeian masses and deeply suspicious of the parvenu Nonconformists who were to do the job.[66] Donations of £110 were raised from the sponsors, and a set of rules was carefully drawn up. Prospective candidates could join only after being nominated by existing members and approved by the directorate. Members were divided into two categories depending on whether or not they paid an entrance fee. All members paid an annual subscription of 10s., which was steep, but not absolutely prohibitive for a well-paid operative. For this the member or subscriber was entitled to all the benefits that the institute offered as well as the right to elect officers and directors

---

[63] Farrar, *Autobiography*, 46; Federer, "Mechanics Institute," 225–6.
[64] Federer, "Mechanics Institute," 227.
[65] Godwin, "Autobiography," 537.
[66] Ibid., 536–8; Federer, "Mechanics Institute," 228–9.

at the annual meeting. Although the new institute did not offer a cheap 4s. nonvoting membership like the first venture, persons under the age of twenty-one were admitted at 6s. per year.[67]

Notwithstanding the care registered in its constitution and the higher level of its minimum fee, this new Mechanics Institute, no less than the first, was intended not simply as a vehicle for the self-education of its middle-class originators, but as an agency for the diffusion of their rationalistic culture to the urban working class. This evangelical sense of purpose was evident in the speeches of its bourgeois leaders that were made at the inauguration of their new headquarters in 1837. The Congregationalist Rev. Walter Scott hoped that the institute might "reclaim some idlers, or drunkards" and "convert them into industrious, sober, respectable, happy members of society... [enabling them] to perform their social duties of every kind, more punctually, and better in every respect, than the ignorant and vicious possibly can." "Instruct them," averred the Baptist Rev. Ackworth, "and they will be sensible that to the conservation of personal freedom and private property, all the elegances and comforts... of life... are referable; and that themselves, therefore, are as deeply interested in the maintenance of order, and the enforcement of law as any other class."[68]

Nevertheless, if the Mechanics Institute were to be more than just a mouthpiece for propaganda, it would have to show how work discipline and political economy could provide vehicles for working-class upward mobility by opening up new opportunities for the most enterprising among them and improving the quality of life for all. To develop the technical skills of the most able and ambitious members of society and to channel their energies toward constructive ends would, as Rev. Scott shrewdly noted, turn frustrated and potentially dangerous individuals into useful citizens and contented men:

> Many who might have... been the Galileos, the Bacons, the Miltons, or Newtons of their country and generation, were only the most clever mechanics or tradesmen of the lowest order... the most noisy and arrogant pothouse politicians, or perhaps the ringleaders in vice, the greatest pests or nuisances of the village or street in which they lived and died.[69]

In the nineteenth century, Rev. Ackworth argued, these undiscovered Galileos or Newtons might not only become scientists or philosophers, but entrepreneurs whose practical ingenuity could advance the material welfare

---

[67] *Rules of Bradford Mechanics Institute* (Bradford 1845); J. V. Godwin, "The Bradford Mechanics Institute," in *Transactions: National Association for the Promotion of Social Science: 1859* (London, 1860), 340.

[68] James Ackworth, *Speech at Inauguration as President of Bradford Mechanics Institute* (Bradford, 1837), 9, 24–5.

[69] Ibid., 5–6.

of all: "Who can tell but that some happy thought, suggesting itself to the mind of a hitherto obscure member of a Mechanics' Institute, may pave the way to results, far surpassing in splendour and usefulness, those which the genius of a Watt, a Bolton, or an Arkwright has achieved."[70]

Although Rev. Scott did not imagine that the Mechanics Institute by itself would be "the great means of regenerating the world, and of raising all operatives, & mechanics, & labourers to the intellectual elevation of philosophers and scholars," he believed it could unite the community by facilitating material prosperity and by creating a new moral and intellectual consensus of all educated people around the values of reason and respectability: "The bonds by which society is united will thus be multiplied and strengthened. The spirit of love and harmony will be more effectually diffused throughout the whole social body, And thus the peace and prosperity of the community will be secured."[71] Education, as Rev. Ackworth pointed out, helps to bridge social divisions, not only by opening the way for upward mobility, but by providing a common language of discourse transcending, if not eliminating, class lines: "The cultivation of a genuine fellow feeling, is one of the surest and most direct means of felicity, not only to others, but also to the individual himself... lead[ing] him to regard other members of his race, not as rivals or foes but as friends and brethren."[72]

In the course of teaching the truths of market freedom and the values of entrepreneurial labor, the Mechanics Institute, perhaps more self-consciously than any other voluntary association, would impart that sense of common purpose among its members that the market society could not generate on its own. Participants would be drawn in by self-interest, but providence, according to Rev. Scott, would turn this to social use by making the institute "a kind of rallying point, a centre of attraction" that would absorb the energies of all social classes and "contribute to the permanence of society," both through its direct educational work and through the associational culture that it would promote.[73]

To achieve these aims, the Mechanics Institute did three different things: It established a library, promoted a series of public lectures, and developed a program of classes. The institute was most successful in the first of these areas, as it addressed a clear-cut bourgeois and lower-middle-class intellectual need. Book purchases absorbed 69 percent of the first year's budget, and by 1837, when there were 562 members, the library consisted of 2,249 volumes and had an average weekly circulation of about 365. Since the rules

---

[70] Ibid., 20.
[71] Ibid., 8.
[72] Ibid., 22.
[73] Ibid., 10.

specified that no member could have more than one book at a time, these figures show that virtually all of the institute's members borrowed a new volume almost every week. Already, Bradford's institute library was much larger than the older and wealthier libraries of York and Leeds. Clearly, a great deal of energy had been expended in amassing a substantial collection of scientific, technical, and other improving literature primarily for the benefit of bourgeois and lower-middle-class members, who expected their money's worth from the subscriptions they had paid.[74]

Although the library was aimed at a select group, the lectures were intended to acquaint a wide audience with the institute's other offerings and aims. Serious without being esoteric, they were pitched at a popular level without degenerating into superficial displays. The initial program was cautious: a handful of lectures on geography, geology, electricity, mechanics, chemistry, astronomy, physiology, grammar, and social economy, most of which were given by local men like Rev. Godwin or by speakers recruited from other institutes nearby.[75]

However, by the midforties, the institute had dramatically expanded its lecture program to offer not only the usual topics but special subjects that were somewhat less didactic, such as "Shakespearian Characters," the "Philosophy of Labour," and the "Influence of Women," which actually was delivered by a woman, Clara Lucas Balfour. Nevertheless, in spite of this variety and though they were free to all comers, there is evidence that the lectures were not reaching very far beyond a small group of habitual attenders. Attempts to draw in outsiders usually failed, as in 1840, when the Lecture Committee hoped "that on no future occasion will such important and interesting Lectures have to be addressed to such thin audiences." In 1846, even popular topics drew only two to three hundred listeners.[76]

At the core of the institute's outreach efforts were the evening remedial classes for young men and women who had enjoyed little or no formal education as children. Although access to a substantial library and to lectures on scientific and theoretical topics dramatically improved the intellectual climate for Bradford's middle class, these classes aimed to serve the more basic needs of the town's workers. In 1833, a basic class in writing and arithmetic was organized, and about thirty people signed up. These numbers gradually rose to about a hundred by the middle of the century. Although most of those attending the course were skilled workers, together with a smattering from the lower middle class, it attracted only a tiny minority even

[74] Bradford Mechanics Institute, *Annual Report* (Bradford, 1833); Federer, "Mechanics Institute," 234–5, 241–2, 244–5.
[75] Federer, "Mechanics Institute," 233–40.
[76] Bradford Mechanics Institute, *Annual Report* (1841); (1847).

Table 11-1. *Bradford Mechanics Institute, 1842: social composition of writing and arithmetic class*

	Unskilled worker	Skilled worker	Lower middle class	Middle class	Unknown
Father's occupation 1842	6	8	3	3	6
Student's occupation 1842	5	18	3	0	0
Student's occupation 1859	1	0	16	9	0

Source: Compiled from J. V. Godwin, "The Bradford Mechanics Institute," *Transactions: National Association for the Promotion of Social Science: 1859* (London, 1860), 343.

from this latter group.[77] A study of the class of 1842 both reveals the social background of its members and allows for as an assessment of their upward mobility in subsequent years.

Table 11-1 reveals the overwhelmingly artisanal character of the student body and shows that its members advanced modestly (by one step in the social scale) over the next seventeen years. Most of the men in the class started out as warehousemen and rose with maturity to positions as salesmen, small retailers, or salaried clerks. To what extent their success was due to Mechanics Institute training and how far it simply represented the normal pattern of a successful career is impossible to gauge. Clearly, even in remedial education where its services were aimed most explicitly at a plebeian clientele, the Mechanics Institute attracted only a tiny minority of workers, usually of a specially privileged sort.

This conclusion is reinforced by membership statistics that show that the social base of the institute always remained much narrower than that of the temperance organizations, which attracted five to ten times as many adherents. Gradually rising from 352 when the institute first opened, membership fluctuated slightly with the trade cycle until 1847 when it reached 937. Thereafter, it leveled off, rising only about twelve hundred by 1859.[78] In that year, J. V. Godwin claimed that 65 percent of the members were mechanics, laborers, and warehousemen.[79] Instead of educating the masses, the institute was catering to a few hundred among the upper reaches of a class numbering in the tens of thousands.

The institute's leadership was aware of this situation and, despite their

[77] Idem, *Annual Reports*, (1833–52).
[78] Ibid.
[79] Godwin, "Bradford Mechanics Institute," 342.

propensity for self-congratulation, confessed in the 1844 *Annual Report* that "the working population of Bradford are not fully aware of the great advantages afforded nor of the small pecuniary sacrifices by which these may be secured."[80] In reality, the annual 10s. subscription was far from a "small pecuniary sacrifice," even for workers earning 20 to 30s. per week. Moreover, restricting applicants to those sponsored by existing members and then subjecting them to public scrutiny in every case must have further dampened recruitment efforts. Finally, the explicit exclusion of all atheists, socialists, and radical Paineites from active participation in an age when the most energetic, intelligent, and independent workers were joining these groups, further impeded the recruitment of those most interested in improving their minds.[81]

The problem was one of authority. As in the temperance movement, the institute's bourgeois founders hoped to attract working-class participation, but only in a subordinate capacity. They were unwilling to address the radical working-class agenda or share power with independent representatives of those whom they sought to reform. Although formally democratic, the structure of the Mechanics Institute precluded any internal challenge to bourgeois authority or interests by those whose needs the institute was allegedly designed to serve most. This can be seen in the leadership's decision to devote almost all of the institute's income for the first fifteen years first to acquiring a library collection and then to financing elaborate headquarters, which cost over £3,000 to build. These projects not only deflected energies away from working-class educational needs, but also kept the institute's solvency dependent on regular donations from Bradford's leading Nonconformist capitalists. During the critical years between 1837 and 1842, when workers all over Bradford were organizing and demanding their rights, the Mechanics Institute was worrying about increasing its building fund, buttering up its wealthy patrons, and sponsoring art shows and natural history exhibits to raise additional cash.[82]

The most vital and popular activity in working-class adult education during this period took place not under the auspices of the Mechanics Institute but through a series of smaller and often short-lived grass-roots associations formed and run by working men themselves. Some of these were consciously intended as secularist alternatives to the orthodox institute, whose structure they mimicked. The library catalogue of the Bradford Secular Improvement Society, for example, reads like a list of the authors the Mechanics Institute

[80] Bradford Mechanics Institute, *Annual Report* (1844).
[81] *Rules of Bradford Mechanics Institute* (Bradford, 1845).
[82] Farrar, *Autobiography*, 47–51; Federer, "Mechanics Institute," 239–48.

banned: Paine, Volney, Voltaire, Coombe, Owen, Cobbett, and Bray. Other institutions, like M. de St. Hilaire's People's Educational Institute, were private ventures run, usually marginally, along profitmaking lines.[83]

The most important of these grass-roots associations were those connected with the town's two major radical political groups, the Chartists and the Owenite socialists. In 1839, the Chartists established a program of Sunday instruction, and in 1842, established a library. In the latter year the socialists bought a hall in which lectures on political and educational topics were frequently held.[84] Finally, in 1849, the *Observer* referred to the existence of a "democratic schoolroom," although it provided no details of its character or purpose.[85]

The proliferation of associations for working-class adult education helps to explain why the Bradford Mechanics Institute avoided the debilitating internal conflicts that wracked its counterparts in places like Leeds.[86] However, this inner peace was purchased at the cost of an intellectual rigidity and social exclusiveness that belied the purpose for which the institute had been formed. After 1845, with the return of prosperity, several changes were made to try to lure workers back to the institute. The rules were liberalized slightly, and women were admitted as members, albeit as subordinate ones. In 1849, all members became eligible for election as officers and directors, and several respectable artisans, who had long been active in the institute's day-to-day work, were finally included on its governing board. Even the old Paineite Squire Farrer was given a position. By 1850, the *Annual Report* was calling on Bradford's workers to "bestir themselves" and to "embrace with due alacrity the opportunities here supplied for the acquisition of valuable knowledge and mental culture." With the onset of the mid-Victorian calm, the bourgeoisie, in a new spirit of ecumenicism, encouraged workers "to come forward and assist in the management of the Institute."[87]

Yet although working-class participation probably increased after 1850, the image of the Mechanics Institute became even more firmly bourgeois.[88] When the governing board was expanded during the late forties and early fifties, much more striking than the co-optation of a handful of workingmen was the wholesale inclusion of most of the newly successful Nonconformists

[83] *Rules of Bradford Secular Improvement Society* (Bradford, n.d.); *BO*, Sep. 20, 1849.
[84] *Northern Star*, Oct. 26, 1839; *BO*, Jul. 28, 1842; Feb. 2, 16, 1843; Brian Simon, *The Two Nations and the Educational Structure, 1780–1870* (London, 1974), 246.
[85] *BO*, June 21, 1849.
[86] Morris, "Voluntary Organizations of Leeds," 263–87.
[87] Bradford Mechanics Institute, *Annual Report* (1850); Godwin, "Bradford Mechanics Institute," 342–3; Federer, "Mechanics Institute," 256–7.
[88] Barnett Blake, "The Mechanics Institutes of Yorkshire," in *Transactions: Association for Social Science*, 335.

such as Nathaniel Briggs, W. E. Forster, J. V. Godwin, William Lythall, James Law, Edward Kenion, Mark Glover, Samuel Smith, Henry Brown, Henry Forbes, and Titus Salt. Their inclusion was connected with a fundraising drive netting £753 from thirty-two bourgeois subscribers to clear the building debt. It is not surprising that, during that year, six aldermen and two councillors sat on the governing board.[89]

The increasingly bourgeois and lower-middle-class character of the Mechanics Institute was reflected not only in its leadership, but in the direction that its curriculum took. Instead of offering more elementary classes, the institute developed special subjects catering to those capable of more advanced work. The first such classes, in French and grammar, were offered in 1835. Geometry was added in 1839 and drawing and mutual improvement in 1841. By the end of the forties, this advanced curriculum had expanded to include German, chemistry, history, composition, and music.[90]

Although these classes did attract some working-class graduates of writing and arithmetic, their popularity was greatest among young men from bourgeois or lower-middle-class backgrounds who hoped, by building upon the elementary education they had obtained in childhood, to further their careers. By the forties, the most popular of the advanced courses was drawing, which appealed to those who desired basic training in textile design. This newfound entrepreneurial concern with aesthetics was the consequence of the new products of the 1830s and 1840s – alpaca, mohair, and the mixed-cotton worsteds. The Bradford industry was now in competition with elegant French handicrafts and had to "assume more and more the character of a fancy trade."[91] Concerned with developing a pool of artistically literate managers and designers, eleven leading stuff merchants subscribed nearly £40 to apply to the government for a local school of design. Similarly, the firms that employed sophisticated dyeing techniques needed supervisory workers with some knowledge of chemistry, and ten industrialists subscribed £25 so that the institute could buy equipment for a lab.[92]

By the late forties, the Mechanics Institute was granting successful "graduates" certificates of proficiency in specialized subjects, with prizes awarded for superior work. Yet as important as it was in training middle-class men to meet the increasingly technical requirements of work, the institute may well have been equally important to middle-class women seeking education outside the home. The admission of women and the periodic appearance of female lecturers was followed by the establishment of special women's classes

---

[89] Bradford Mechanics Institute, *Annual Report* (1850); Federer, "Mechanics Institute," 257.

[90] Bradford Mechanics Institute, *Annual Reports*, (1834–52).

[91] Ibid., *Annual Report*, (1847).

[92] Ibid.

centering around domestic science. The introduction of some of the same subjects taught to young men made some uneasy, and the institute justified its educational work with women by asserting that such training would not unsex women, but would actually make them better household managers and wives.[93]

Bourgeois and lower-middle-class women were quick to take advantage of these opportunities. Many gravitated toward subjects such as drawing, which developed an acceptably feminine skill that went beyond the drudgery of domestic routine.[94] Still, educational opportunities for women were much more limited than those for men, and bourgeois women could only lament that, "the progress of female education cannot but be slow and difficult until it shall be based on a truer estimate of woman's powers and on a recognition of her equal claim with man to the full exercise and unhindered application of her faculties."[95]

The temperance movement and the Mechanics Institute, taken together, demonstrate the extent to which the bourgeois culture of associational voluntarism could really be extended to encompass the urban working class; for, unlike the religious congregations of Nonconformist Protestantism, which excluded or ignored the bulk of nineteenth-century Bradford's proletariat, these secular associations were specifically designed to address working-class problems and needs. With their aims firmly rooted in the dilemmas of material experience, the Temperance Society and Mechanics Institute offered an approach to working-class self-improvement that eschewed the metaphor of spiritual salvation in order to attract a group of people who had little prima facie basis for seeing themselves as members of a providential elect. Yet as they cast bourgeois values in terms meaningful to industrial workers, these new associations also worked to restate the bourgeois Nonconformist diagnosis of working-class dysfunction in what amounted to little more than a secularized version of the individualistic moralizing terms in which neo-Calvinism would have it framed.

Because they bridged the gap between bourgeois philosophy and working-class experience in a way that voluntaristic religion had not, these secular self-help associations did succeed in drawing at least a minority of workers to acquiesce in the bourgeois leadership that ran them and to embrace the entrepreneurial self-help values they purveyed. Nevertheless, the failure of

[93] J. S. Howson, "Schools for Girls of the Middle Class," in *Transactions: Association for Social Science*, 308.

[94] Butler Wood, "James Lobeley, A Bradford Artist," *BA*, (o.s., 3).

[95] Fanny Hertz, "Mechanics Institutes for Working Women," in *Transactions: Association for Social Sciences*, 348.

temperance and adult education to become mass movements on which a universal social consensus could be built underscores the difficulties of transcending the deeply rooted class divisions that industrial-capitalist development had left in its wake. Particularly during the 1830s and 1840s, the crisis decades when the new associations took shape, their history disclosed the limits of the entrepreneurial vision of consensus and the impossibility of forging any genuine fraternity between classes whose social experiences so radically diverged. As individuals, a minority of workers might join the Temperance Society or Mechanics Institute and find in them effective vehicles for personal self-help, but, in themselves, neither abstinence nor autodidacticism could ever constitute a viable reforming program around which to organize a working-class program of collective improvement; for even when they regarded these goals as desirable, most workers recognized that they represented only part of the solution and were best pursued, not through acquiescence in bourgeois-run causes and organizations, but by the creation of their own independent associations that would recast the very essence of the self-help program into a distinctively proletarian set of terms.

12

The politics of liberalism

If the history of religious voluntarism in Bradford disclosed the difficulty of transcending class divisions through voluntary associations, the history of the more genuinely popular temperance and adult education movements brought a far more disturbing revelation: To catalyze workers' aspirations for secular self-improvement was not necessarily to attach them to the framework of bourgeois voluntarism and the values of individualist moral reform. On the contrary, at least during the late thirties and forties, the example of the Temperance Society and Mechanics Institute seemed only to stimulate the formation of militant, autonomous, self-help associations that advanced a distinctively working-class agenda and operated under the control of the workers themselves. This same tendency was manifested even more dramatically by bourgeois voluntarism in the political realm, for here, the liberal entrepreneurial effort to arouse the workers and to enlist them in a bourgeois antiaristocratic campaign probably contributed more than any other factor to opening the way for independent working-class initiatives that would eventually be turned against the entrepreneurial bourgeoisie.

Inevitably, the antiestablishment thrust of bourgeois voluntarism forced it into the political realm. So long as religious, political, and economic privileges persisted, their ill effects could not be ignored. If nothing else, the imperative to free up the cultural marketplace in which they aspired to operate compelled voluntary associations, which might have been otherwise apolitical, to confront the established bastions of power. Yet for Bradford's rising entrepreneurial insurgents, politics could never become an end in itself. Their libertarian distaste for illegitimate authority encouraged them, at least initially, to conceptualize political action negatively, less as an instrument of hegemony than as a weapon of attack. So long as government remained under aristocratic domination, it was a fortress that had to be stormed and sacked. But what bourgeois liberals might do once they commanded the citadel was far less clear.[1] "The truth is," averred the *Observer*,

---

[1] In 1835, the *Observer* insisted that "in proportion as it is necessary to have recourse to the system of coercion . . . there is something wrong or defective in the subject or in the way in which it is treated. . . . In heaven," the paper continued, "the voluntary system

320

"that legislation generally, has been only a barometer marking the progress of the national mind and character – the offspring, not the parent of improvement. The resources within a man's self, are of infinitely more value as regards his personal condition . . . than any which just and equal legislation can bestow upon him."[2]

For such men, immersed in their parvenu mentality, it was exceedingly difficult to develop an indigenous civic vision or to achieve any positive understanding of how constructively to wield power. With their Lockean vision of government as a voluntary association and their "nightwatchman" conception of the state, politics was understood through the economic lens of entrepreneurship and the familiar voluntaristic cultural forms.[3]

Thus the bourgeois liberal model of political organization came less from the elitist world of Westminster than from the provincial religious and cultural associations that the new bourgeois liberals themselves had formed. For such men, political liberalism was but an integral component of a larger entrepreneurial voluntarist worldview. The Liberal party, as they conceived it, was a special kind of voluntary association, designed to agitate for an end to corruption and tyranny so as to secure the political foundations of liberty on which the chapels and self-help societies would subsequently build.[4] Like these voluntary associations on which it was modeled, political liberalism confronted a two-fold task – it had to serve as a vehicle to promote the interests and authority of the new bourgeoisie, but it also had to secure the allegiance of the working masses who would endorse the legitimacy of industrial-capitalist leadership and affirm the universality of the entrepreneurial creed.

Within the conceptual framework of the antiaristocratic insurgency, it seemed perfectly natural to unite downtrodden workers and aspiring bourgeois together within a single political party around the banner of a common campaign. However, this strategy presupposed that both groups would find the outside threat of aristocratic domination so dangerous that the fissures of class division within the industrial-capitalist environment would appear insignificant by contrast. Hence the fate of liberalism as a popular movement in Bradford depended largely on the ability of the entrepreneurial liberals to focus working-class hostility on the evils of oligarchy, convincing workers to see their suffering as the product of political privilege rather than exploitation in the economic realm.

exists and works in perfection and is the spring of all the order and all the happiness which prevail there." *BO*, May 28, 1835.

[2] *BO*, May 28, 1840.

[3] John Locke, *Two Treatises on Government* (Cambridge, 1960).

[4] John Vincent, *The Formation of the British Liberal Party, 1857–68* (London, 1966), 30–2.

The rise of a Liberal party in Bradford: 1829–37

In the late 1820s and early 1830s in Bradford, liberalism, as a broad-based popular political movement, came closest to realizing these aims. Before then there had scarcely been any liberal organization at all. With the early-nineteenth century magistracy, vestry, and Watching and Lighting Commission all under Anglican Tory control, there was no institutional basis for political heterodoxy in the town. An undercurrent of antigovernment sentiment among the West Riding freeholders had brought victory to Lord Milton in the 1807 county election, and a mild Whiggism occasionally resurfaced from time to time.[5] Yet until the arrival of the first wave of the new immigrant, entrepreneurial, Nonconformist generation in the middle to late 1820s, such a movement would have been inconceivable.[6]

The first dent in this monolithic establishment was made when the young, recently arrived Baptist Rev. Godwin stirred the somnolent political atmosphere by attacking the system of colonial slavery. Contending that "the history of Britain is that of a perpetual struggle for civil and religious liberty," he concluded that "the slavery of our colonies is a mockery of all law, a contempt of all right, and a stigma of reproach on the British Constitution, to which it is in the highest degree repugnant."[7] Joined by the Congregationalist merchant Henry Forbes and the Wesleyan physician Thomas Beaumont, Godwin began to proselytize the town. Although the antislavery movement did not directly challenge the local establishment, and although it received the official blessing of the vicar and roused a few Anglican evangelicals like Rev. G. S. Bull and Richard Oastler to join the attack, most local notables remained aloof, distrusting a rhetoric whose defense of black liberties called more general attention to "the rights and attributes of man."[8]

Although Godwin argued "that the advocates of slavery are not fit persons to be entrusted with the liberties of Englishmen," even for most liberals, slavery remained a distant and abstract evil. If liberalism was to be sustained and made popular, outrage against the slaveholder would have to be redirected against those who shackled liberty at home.[9] Links between West Indian slaveowners and the English aristocracy were tentatively established in 1825, when the prominent radical Henry Brougham won the West Riding parliamentary election on a platform that joined the antislavery issue with a

---

[5] Gary Firth, "The Genesis of the Industrial Revolution in Bradford, 1760–1830" (Bradford, Ph.D. dissertation, 1974), 105–7.
[6] Benjamin Godwin, "Autobiography," (mss., Bradford Central Library), 523–4.
[7] Benjamin Godwin, *Lectures on British Colonial Slavery* (London, 1830), 2, 104.
[8] Idem, *Paper Presented to the General Anti-Slavery Convention* (n.d.), 4; *Leeds Mercury*, Mar. 13, May 1, 1830; Apr. 6, 13, May 18, Jul. 20, 1833.
[9] Godwin, "Autobiography," 491–525.

call for religious liberty and economic free trade. Yet it was not until the end of the decade that opposition to slavery in America gave birth to a full-scale movement for domestic reform. In 1829, Catholic emancipation and the partial enfranchisement of Dissenters made the first breach in the walls of political monopoly, opening the way for wider constitutional change. Emboldened by these half measures of religious liberalization, men like Godwin began to enlarge their demands, insisting that, like slaves, Bradfordians suffered under milder forms of bondage, which also deprived them of legitimate human rights.[10]

As the fifth-largest unrepresented town in England, Bradford stood to benefit from almost any scheme of parliamentary reform. When it became clear that the winds of change were blowing, "many of the millowners and the commercial men in general, as well as some of the younger men of the Town," according to Godwin, "entered warmly into the reform question." Where hitherto "tory influence had been predominant among the more respectable or wealthier classes ... and among the workpeople no strong political bias was general, [now] society became agitated ... and employers and the employed caught the mighty excitement."[11]

Unlike the antislavery movement, this new campaign for domestic reform posed an immediate threat to Bradford's Anglican Tories, who feared that elections under a broadened franchise would spell the end of their unquestioned monopoly of local government and public affairs. When Godwin and his friends held public meetings in 1831, circulating a petition that obtained 4,700 signatures, he "became the object of dislike to all the fiercer tories." As tempers rose, "the high church and tory inhabitants became, as the losing party, exceedingly bitter and scarcely anything could gain attention but the proposed reform."[12]

The establishment's fear of this burgeoning reform movement further intensified as it went beyond merely articulating entrepreneurial interests to demand the enfranchisement of the working class. For Godwin, such a broad "representation of the people ... constituted the strength and wealth and the whole value of any country whatever," and political democracy was the only foundation on which a general reform program could reliably be built.[13] To mobilize industrial workers who had never before involved themselves in party politics, the Bradford Political Union was organized in which future working-class leaders like Peter Bussey stood on the same platforms and sat on the same committees as future leaders of the new bourgeoisie. To

[10] Ibid.; D. G. Wright, "Politics and Opinion in Nineteenth Century Bradford," (Leeds, Ph.D. dissertation, 1966), 92–100.
[11] Godwin, "Autobiography," 523.
[12] Ibid., 528, 540; *Leeds Mercury*, Mar. 19, 1831.
[13] *Leeds Mercury*, Feb. 26, 1831.

celebrate their unity, a monster rally for manhood suffrage was held in the hinterland on Hartshead Moor. Here, ten to fifteen thousand from Bradford alone gathered to demand a democratic franchise and to attack the evils of corruption, monopoly, and oligarchical control.[14] Decades later, Rev. Godwin vividly recalled this stirring scene:

> In Bradford, all the carriages and vehicles of every kind from the chariot to the cart and wagon were put in requisition. Processions of horsemen, open carriages, gigs, and pedestrians were formed, and with banners flying and bands of music playing, they marched in order out of the town. ... As we moved on, the whole road from Bradford to Wakefield seemed swarming with population, glowing with bright orange color in the forms of ribbons, cockades, and flags with appropriate mottoes of all kinds and sizes... All was peaceable, but everything was ripe for a revolution.[15]

Of course, Bradford's reformers got neither revolution nor manhood suffrage, but the right, under a £10 borough franchise, to send two representatives to Parliament. As a result of this property qualification, Bradford's first electoral register consisted of only 1,137 voters, or about 12 percent of the adult males in town. The £10 restriction had been explicitly designed to exclude most workers and to split the reform coalition in two. But in cities like Bradford with low property valuations, the franchise did not exactly mirror class divisions as much of the lower middle class remained disenfranchised too. Clearly, the political drama that would be enacted among the new electors would involve a much narrower social cast of actors than that from which the original impetus for reform had emerged.[16]

Immediately it became evident that, in so restricted an electorate, the Tory establishment would retain an upper hand. Wisely resisting an impulse to select a candidate from among the diehard defenders of the Old Regime, their first choice, the prominent notable John Hardy, was returned without opposition. Although the other Tory George Banks was unsuccessful, E. C. Lister, the local Whig gentleman who defeated him, was a moderate who seems to have satisfied both sides.[17] Understandably, the young radicals who had struggled for more representative government were disaffected, and even moderates like Lister publicly regretted that the Reform Act did not extend the franchise to the lower classes.[18] To maximize their influence, the leading Dissenters caucused to coordinate strategy for the future. In Brad-

[14] Ibid., Apr. 28, 1831; May 12, 1832.
[15] Godwin, "Autobiography," 541.
[16] D. G. Wright, "A Radical Borough, Parliamentary Politics in Bradford, 1832–41," *Northern History*, 4 (1969).
[17] Wright, "Politics and Opinion," 108–10; *Leeds Mercury*, Dec. 24, 1831; Aug. 30, 1832.
[18] *Leeds Mercury*, Oct. 8, 1831.

ford, as elsewhere, popular dissatisfaction with the £10 franchise was reflected in the continued activity of the Political Union through the general election of 1835. However, Bradford's union was distinguished by the continued involvement of liberals right up to the very end.[19]

In 1834, to further publicize the liberal message and to express the need for more extensive reforms, a group of ninety shareholders, led by Robert Milligan, James Garnett, Henry Forbes, Thomas Aked, Samuel Laycock, Miles Illingworth, John Rawson, and Benjamin Godwin, founded the *Bradford Observer*.[20] William Byles, a young writer for the *Athenaeum*, was selected as editor and informed of the perspective the proprietors had in mind: "As in most manufacturing districts the bulk of property and influence is in the hands of enterprising tradesmen. A liberal feeling prevails – persons are not honoured merely for *having a title* – or despised for being *tradesmen* or *dissenters*."[21]

Although the *Observer* was clearly a partisan undertaking, it wished not only to preach to the converted, but to speak for the entire town. According to Godwin, although the paper "should support what are generally termed liberal principles," it "should not be conducted in the spirit of party either political or religious." In the absence of any other local paper, the *Observer*, if it appeared sufficiently ecumenical, might gain unchallenged influence over local opinion. Because he was "perfectly aware that our old friends the Tories can never hope to have a journal of their own in Bradford," Byles was willing to "offer them an opportunity of lucubrating on their favorite topics." More importantly, he wished to speak to the workers and to "show that the real interests of the employer and the employed are identical."[22]

As champion of progress, the *Observer* gave notice in its opening prospectus that it would press, both locally and nationally, for another round of constitutional reform. More frequent parliaments, an end to tithes and church rates, abolition of the pension list, municipal reform, the repeal of the Corn Laws, and cautious extension of the franchise were among its initial list of demands.[23] The paper believed that these measures were the way of the future and that the triumph of liberalism, both in Bradford and in Britain, could not long be delayed: "The hopes of the Tories are baseless. They may bluster and foam: they may even get into office and govern madly for a limited term: but they cannot turn back the ocean tide of popular feeling

[19] Ibid., Mar. 2, 1833.
[20] Godwin, "Autobiography," 573–5.
[21] W. Copley to W. Byles, *Byles Papers* (uncataloged mss., Bradford Archives).
[22] *BO*, Feb. 1, 1834, Feb. 5, 1835; D. M. Jones, "The Liberal Press and the Rise of Labour, with Particular Reference to Leeds and Bradford" (Leeds, Ph.D. dissertation, 1973).
[23] *BO*, Feb. 6, 1834.

– consequently, they cannot succeed in perpetuating either their principles of their power."[24]

Yet as this bold prediction was being issued, the tide of popular anti-aristocratic feeling on which it was riding showed signs of drying up. Indeed, the alliance between workers and bourgeois liberals had been problematic from the start; for although the ideal of democracy appealed to the workers, they resented the insensitivity of the *Observer* and its patrons to the effects of economic inequality. Not sharing the liberals' attraction to the principle of market freedom and fearing the suffering that unfettered competition could bring, most workers were deeply skeptical of liberalism's economic ideology even when subscribing to its political creed.

The *Observer*, for all its claims to representing the whole community, had great difficulty attracting readers outside the middle class. Just months after the paper was inaugurated, a correspondent reported that it was popularly regarded as an "enemy of the working class." Two years later, a major reduction of the newspaper duty resulted in no substantial increase in its weekly circulation, which remained about eight hundred, rising only to eighteen hundred during the next decade and a half. This at best kept pace with Bradford's rapid population expansion and suggests that the paper was read regularly by about only a fifth of Bradford's adults. By 1838, even Byles admitted that the paper was getting "little or no support" from those who opposed its laissez-faire positions.[25]

These weaknesses in the liberal–working-class alliance were, as we shall see, exploited by Tory radicals who sought to wean the workers away from political liberalism by promising economic protection and regulation of the factories. As spokesmen for the entrepreneurial interest, the liberals strenuously objected to any such restriction of free competition but were discomfited by the realization that conservatives, too, could appeal to populism and that working-class leaders like Bussey, who had been allies in the struggle for political emancipation, were now joining with their archenemies to demand a factory act. Still, they could find some comfort in the realization that workers would never entirely abandon the liberal alliance so long as liberals, unlike the Tories, endorsed the political enfranchisement of the working class.[26]

The *Observer* seems to have recognized from the outset that, if workers were to remain loyal to liberalism, then liberals must work toward getting them the vote. Although the paper balked at any immediate grant of universal suffrage, it reiterated its support for democracy in principle, adding that the

[24] *BO*, July 17, 1834.
[25] *PP* (XVII, 1851), 545–57; *BO*, June 5, 1834.
[26] *BO*, Nov. 3, 1836; May 3, 1838. See Chapter 5.

people must first be educated before they could be entrusted with full political rights.[27] The general election of January 1835 gave Bradford's liberals an opportunity to demonstrate their strength. Their progressive alliance would be called upon to show its numbers, and their predictions that Toryism had ceased to be viable would be put to the test. Determined that the Tory incumbent Hardy should be defeated and replaced with a candidate unmistakably their own, the liberals drafted a prominent radical Dissenter from Manchester, George Hadfield. Hadfield ran on a platform of free trade, religious disestablishment, and electoral reform and made a special effort to attract working-class support. Yet in an electorate within which Nonconformists remained a minority and workers were hardly represented at all, such a militant liberal seemed, in the words of one local conservative, not only "an entire stranger to the town and country, [but a man] of sentiments totally subversive of the constitution." When election day came, Hadfield, despite his overwhelming majority among a throng of 10,000 at the hustings, trailed Hardy 392 to 611 in the poll.[28]

Liberalism and bourgeois politics

The results of the 1835 election came as a shock to men like Byles and Godwin. Liberalism had failed, not only in achieving political hegemony, but in mustering a bare majority of voters from all sectors of the urban bourgeoisie. As pollbooks from the entire period consistently indicated, radical liberalism's main base of support lay in the generation of immigrant entrepreneurs who rose to prominence in the decades after 1825. This conclusion is reinforced by the results of a survey in which the present author sought to trace the political identities of the 1,259 households in the 1851 bourgeois census population.[29] By midcentury, when this group had become fully dominant, liberals constituted 54 percent of the 677 householders whose political identities could be traced.[30] Moreover, internal analysis shows a

---

[27] *BO*, June 5, 1834; Feb. 12, 1835.
[28] *BO*, Nov. 20, 27, Dec. 4, 11, 24, 1834; Jan. 1, 8, 15, 1835; Wright, "Politics and Opinion," 129–33; *Pollbook* (Bradford, 1835).
[29] The bourgeois census population is compiled on the basis of information in HO 1037/2305–10. See Appendix A for a discussion of the method.
[30] Most of the information on political affiliation used to compile this politics-linked sample (a subset of the bourgeois census population) was obtained from the *Pollbook* (Bradford, 1847), from the general election of that year. This pollbook, which records 1,789 votes out of a total electorate of 2,083, affords a particularly good litmus test of bourgeois political identity for two reasons. First, it was chronologically close enough to the 1851 census to make record linkage a realistic possibility. Second, the election itself was hotly contested between four candidates, and voting broke down almost entirely along party

Table 12-1. *Bourgeois politics-linked sample: politics by occupational sector of household head*

	Genteel occupational sector (N = 154)	Urban-service sector (N = 294)	Worsted and related sector (N = 234)
Percent Liberal	36	54	67
Percent Tory	64	46	33

Note: χ^2 = 35.8; p = .001.
Source: Calculated on the basis of the politics-linked sample. See note 30 of Chap. 12 and Appendix A for a discussion of the sources on which the politics-linked sample is based.

statistically significant correlation between political affiliation and the underlying social structural dichotomies in terms of occupation, nativity, and generational position, which Chapter 6 established in its examination of the formation of the urban bourgeoisie.

As Table 12-1 demonstrates, those who had chosen entrepreneurial occupations in the worsted industry were disproportionately liberal, whereas those in the genteel and professional sectors were overwhelmingly Tory. Tables 12-2 and 12-3 show a similar if less striking statistical relationship between politics and both generation and nativity within the urban bourgeoi-

lines, with only a mere 8 percent of the electors' splitting their votes between the two moderates in each camp (William Busfield, Whig, and Henry Wickham Wickham, moderate Tory). Conversely, 92 percent voted a straight party ticket, either Busfield and the liberal radical Perronet Thompson, or Wickham and the ideological Tory Gathorne Hardy. This high level of polarization and absence of centrist ticket splitting is itself a powerful testament to the intensity of political party identification among the midcentury bourgeoisie.

Unfortunately, the arduous work of record linkage between the 1847 *Pollbook* and the census manuscripts did not produce as many firm identifications as had been anticipated (see Appendix A). Thus the records of the next seriously contested election were also consulted, *Pollbook* (Bradford, 1859). This was a three way contest that enabled electors to vote either for the liberal radical Titus Salt, or the conservative Alfred Harris. A few additional firm linkages were made in this way. Finally, in a few instances, where linkages were suggested by the *Pollbook* data but were not conclusive, the "Petitions for and against Incorporation of Bradford" (Bradford Archives, D.B. 69/2,3) were used to try to establish firm identifications. This seemed justifiable since Adrian Elliott, in "The Establishment of Municipal Government in Bradford, 1837–57" (Bradford, Ph.D. dissertation, 1976), has demonstrated that most of the signators to the petition favoring incorporation were political liberals, while most of the signators to the petition opposed to incorporation were political conservatives. In the few instances in which more than one elector (and/or petition signator) was encountered in a given household, only the political affiliation of the household head was recorded. In only two instances did such a coresident elector vote differently than this household head.

Table 12-2. *Bourgeois politics-linked sample: politics by generation of household head*

	Older generation (N = 182)	Younger generation (N = 417)	Total sample (N = 682)
Percent Liberal	45	59	54
Percent Tory	55	41	46

Note: $\chi^2 = 35.8$; $p = .001$.
Source: Calculated on the basis of the politics-linked sample. See note 30 of Chap. 12 and Appendix A for a discussion of the sources on which the politics-linked sample is based.

Table 12-3. *Bourgeois politics-linked sample: politics by birthplace of household head*

	Born in Bradford (N = 219)	Born elsewhere in Yorkshire (N = 308)	Born elsewhere (N = 155)
Percent Liberal	47	54	65
Percent Tory	53	46	35

Note: $\chi^2 = 9.2$; $p = .02$.
Source: Calculated on the basis of the politics-linked sample. See note 30 of Chap. 12 and Appendix A for a discussion of the sources on which the politics-linked sample is based.

sie. Those members of the younger generation who had come of age during the last twenty years, were more liberal than the overall bourgeois population, whereas the majority of the remaining old generation were Tory. Similarly, immigrants, especially those who came from a distance, were prone toward liberalism, whereas natives were predominantly conservative. Relative youth, immigrant origins, and involvement in worsted entrepreneurship clearly predisposed people toward voting liberal. Among the 112 individuals in the sample who were all three, 71 percent recorded liberal votes. Of the twenty-two individuals who were older-generation natives in genteel or professional occupations, 73 percent were Tories.

This analysis confirms the conclusion amply documented through qualitative evidence that the ascendancy of political liberalism within the bourgeois electorate was, in large measure, a function of the ascent of the liberal generation of immigrant entrepreneurs. In the early 1830s when these men were arriving, political power was in the hands of older, more established, and conservative natives. By the late 1840s, however, the bourgeoisie had

Table 12-4. *Bourgeois politics-linked sample: political identity by nativity, occupation, and generation*

	Young and immigrant and entrepreneurs	Young or immigrant or entrepreneurs	Old or native or genteel	Old and native and genteel
Percentage of Liberals who were (N = 371)	22	94	49	2
Percentage of Tories who were (N = 311)	10	88	67	5

Source: Calculated on the basis of the politics-linked sample. See note 30 of Chap. 12 and Appendix A for a discussion of the sources on which the politics-linked sample is based.

become predominantly liberal as the majority of its members now belonged to "liberal" social groups.

Nevertheless, it would be a mistake simply to equate the triumph of bourgeois liberalism in Bradford with the numerical dominance of an inherently liberal bourgeois subgroup. After all, young, immigrant, Nonconformist, worsted entrepreneurs always remained a minority even in their own class. As Table 12-4 demonstrates, the status of liberalism as the dominant form of bourgeois politics depended on its ability to attract the allegiance of the vast middle-class majority, who might possess one or two of these characteristics, but whose overall social profile was mixed. Ninety-four percent of Bradford's midcentury bourgeois liberals were either immigrants, worsted entrepreneurs, or members of the younger generation, but less than a quarter of them were all three at once. Similarly, the residual strength of electoral conservatism derived less from its tiny base among the old, established, native, genteel elites, than from among older immigrants, young people who were natives, professionals, or urban-service proprietors, as well as many Anglicans of diverse ages, occupations, and places of birth.[31]

Even the links between religious Nonconformity and political liberalism (which cannot be measured statistically) were problematic and incomplete until the midforties when the traditionally Tory Wesleyan Conference leadership shifted its political allegiance to the Liberal party, bringing along

[31] J. A. Jowitt, "Dissenters, Voluntaryism and Liberal Unity: The 1847 Election," in J. A. Jowitt and R. K. S. Taylor, eds., *Nineteenth Century Bradford Elections* (Bradford, 1979); Wright, "Radical Borough"; A. J. Mayer, "The Lower Middle Class as Historical Problem," *Journal of Modern History*, 47:3, (1975); G. Crossick, "Introduction," in Geoffrey Crossick, ed., *The Lower Middle Class in Britain* (London, 1977).

many of the Methodist rank and file. Clearly, Anglicans, Wesleyans, West Riding natives, tradesmen, professionals, and small proprietors of every type constituted a vast "swing" group within the electorate, which was, during the early thirties, often politically quiescent or predisposed to defer to the leadership of the Tory establishment that had traditionally governed both the nation and the town.[32]

By midcentury, the majority of these voters had been converted to liberalism, but in 1835, as the election results showed, many were wary of a yet untested, still insurgent political movement that emphasized its radical populist aims. Clearly, the short-term goal of winning elections in a narrow electorate of cautious property owners was coming in conflict with the long-term objective of forging a progressive alliance that would make liberalism attractive to the urban working class. Liberals, a chastened *Observer* acknowledged, would have to pay more attention to the details of registering and wooing electors. For this purpose, a new party organization was needed, which, instead of mounting popular campaigns and mass agitations, would concentrate on the detailed work of fund-raising, canvassing, and facilitating backroom political compromise.

Thus after the 1835 election, when the Bradford Political Union collapsed, it was replaced by the Reform Society, whose aim was not so much to arouse the people as "to promote by all legal and constitutional means the return of truly liberal members for this Borough ... by carefully watching the formation of the official lists of voters and the proceedings of the Barristers Court."[33] At the same time, a separate nonelectors society was organized to isolate radical working-class issues, like suffrage extension and repeal of the Stamp Act, from the Liberal party mainstream. To attract bourgeois Anglicans and political moderates, the *Observer* and the Reform Society leaders rejected demands that they again nominate a radical candidate for the next election, choosing instead William Busfield, another local Whig gentleman who was very much like the incumbent Lister.[34]

When the election was called for July 1837, the *Observer* contended that "a fairer prospect for success could not be desired. ... The reformers have the game in their hands if they will only play judiciously" by adhering to the new strategy of electoral centrism and keeping the radical working-class and Nonconformist agendas under wraps. By the end of polling day, the results showed that this gamble had paid off. The Tory incumbent Hardy and his running mate were sent packing; the combined ticket of Lister and Busfield drew 63 percent of all the votes cast. "Hail to the honest and independent

---

[32] Wright, "Politics and Opinion," 289–307; Jowitt, "1847 Election."
[33] *BO*, Apr. 4, 11, 1835.
[34] *BO*, June 29, 1837.

electors of Bradford," vaunted the *Observer*. "You have shown that the Reform Bill with all its faults has some worth."[35]

The crisis of liberalism and the politics of class: 1837–42

As it turned out, this liberal victory had come at an enormous cost, for the overtures that the party was making toward political moderates and conservatives seriously damaged its original dream of a radical working-class alliance. Seeking to mollify the majority of the existing voters, the *Observer* indicated that the further enfranchisement of even a narrow working-class elite was no longer a high priority. Although the paper still believed that the electorate might profitably be widened, there were "more positive evils than a limited suffrage to contend with."[36] The suffrage question was now impeding the achievement of other liberal goals, such as free trade, efficient government, and abolition of the church rates, which were critical for the entrepreneurial bourgeoisie. The party would do well, the paper hinted, to drop the demand for electoral reform. Because the nomination of Busfield was a blow to the radical Nonconformists as well as to the workers, the simultaneous immersion of most party leaders in the church-rates controversy suggests a conscious trade-off facilitating the pursuit of religious radicalism in another arena where it would not jeopardize prospects for electoral success.[37]

With the workers, however, no such compromise was entertained. Increasingly upset at seeing the nonelectors treated as second-class citizens, Peter Bussey lambasted the Reform Society for its "indifference to the people's rights." In 1836, he formed the independent Radical Association, which brought the prominent Irish orator Feargus O'Connor to Bradford to agitate for universal suffrage and an unstamped press. The imprisonment that year of the radical bookseller James Ibbetson for selling the *Twopenny Dispatch* to an undercover agent and the indifference of the liberal leaders to his plight further inflamed the workers and intensified their sense of isolation from the party mainstream.[38]

Even those within the working-class movement most committed to the liberal alliance now admitted that it was falling apart. John Jackson, this faction's spokesman, had always deferred to the liberal leadership, endorsing its principles of political economy and gradualist strategy for political change. But when the official liberals abandoned the workers, even he felt betrayed.

[35] July 13, 27, 1837.
[36] July 13, 1837.
[37] Jowitt, "1847 Election."
[38] *BO*, Apr. 11, Dec. 24, 1835; Jan. 21, Feb. 4, 11, Nov. 10, 24, 1836.

Joining forces with the Radical Association, he protested the present "mock system of representation," and urged the workers to field a candidate of their own. Although in 1837, when the electors actually went to the poll, Bussey had to appear at the hustings without a candidate, he made it clear that the "10,000 working men who have grievances" and were in attendance would not endorse the liberal victory with the traditional show of hands.[39]

This declaration of working-class independence was particularly ominous to bourgeois elites of both parties because of the social and economic climate in which it was made. As 1837 was a year of increasing depression, unemployment, and working-class desperation, political radicalism was thus becoming a luxury that neither bourgeois party could afford. Even the young liberal entrepreneurs, who still prided themselves on having risen from the ranks, now had to face an alienated and hostile proletariat, which might well direct its fiercest feelings of resentment, not against the privileges of a distant aristocracy, but toward the young entrepreneurs' own recently acquired wealth and power.

Thus the liberals' repudiation of working-class radicalism, which had begun two years earlier as an electoral tactic, now assumed a compelling logic of its own. Even those who still advocated democracy in principle had to doubt its feasibility as long as society remained destabilized. Electoral centrism, which had originally induced liberals to abandon the workers and accommodate themselves to the mainstream, was now powerfully reinforced by social and economic crisis in which the political differences between the bourgeois parties were overshadowed by their common interests as property owners to insure that social order was maintained.

This estrangement between liberal and popular politics was graphically demonstrated by the antagonisms that erupted in 1837 in connection with the implementation of the New Poor Law. This law, which promised to facilitate cheap efficient government, to free up labor markets, and to wean the pauper from his demoralizing dependence on the state represented precisely the sort of rationalistic antiprotectionist measure that fitted the liberal worldview like a glove. During the economic downturn of 1834, when the law reached the statute book, the *Observer* cautioned that it not be used to break up families or to penalize the temporarily unemployed. However, amidst the prosperity of 1836, the paper was certain that "19/20ths are found to be paupers by choice or in consequence of their own follies and vices."[40] A year later, the editors responded with enthusiasm when they learned that the government planned to establish the Bradford Poor Law Union and organize elections for Bradford's Board of Guardians. Such a

[39] *BO*, June 29, 1837.
[40] *BO*, Apr. 24, May 1, 1834; Aug. 11, 1836.

board would provide an important focus for alternative forms of local government, taking poor relief away from the Anglican vestry and placing it under secular ratepayer control.

Since election rules allowed wealthy property owners multiple votes and distributed 63 percent of the guardians' seats to the union out-townships, which contained only 37 percent of the population, the board fell far short of being a fully democratic institution. Nevertheless, its franchise was much wider than the parliamentary franchise. When the first election, in 1837, gave liberals 81 percent of the seats, party leaders began to hope the board of guardians might provide an institutional framework for that universal consensus for progress that had eluded them in the sphere of parliamentary politics.[41] However, this liberal triumph in the board of guardians, even more than the parliamentary victory later in the year, had a diametrically opposite effect. Far from inaugurating a new era of civic harmony and liberal ascendancy, it became a lightning rod for violent class hostility that quickly reduced the Liberal party to discredit and defeat.

Given the deepening depression gripping the local economy in 1837, the New Poor Law, with its threat of subjecting the unemployed to the degradation of the workhouse and its promise to eliminate all outdoor relief, could scarcely have been implemented at a worse moment. Claiming that the law was "unconstitutional" and "denying the right of the Poor to live," Bradford's working-class radicals saw it as the ultimate example of the sort of brutal class legislation that the 1832 bourgeois electorate had wrought. With its administrative subordination to a body of London bureaucrats, its ratepayers franchise truncated by the disproportionate power of wealthy property owners, and the disenfranchisement of the many small occupiers who were now defaulting on their rates, the Board of Guardians easily appeared less democratic than the corrupt vestry had been.[42]

In May, an anti-Poor Law rally, which drew a crowd of 100,000 from all over the region, was held on the traditional radical meeting ground of Hartshead Moor. Leading bourgeois liberals, now entrenched as guardians and committed to the New Poor Law, expressed unequivocal disapproval. "We know of no terms too strong to deprecate the opposition now attempted," declared the *Observer*. "In most cases, it arises from ignorance of the principles and tendencies of the Bill." The law, concluded the paper, was simply an inevitable concomitant of progress, which only fools or reactionaries would resist.[43]

---

[41] *BO*, Sep. 15, 1837; Mar. 2, 1837; Mar. 29, 1838; David Ashforth, "The Poor Law in Bradford, c. 1834–1871" (Bradford, Ph.D., dissertation, 1979), 85; *PP* (1841), 2:386.
[42] *BO*, Jan. 26, Feb. 2, 9, 16, 1837.
[43] John Knott, *Popular Opposition to the 1834 Poor Law* (New York, 1985), 103–4; *BO*, Feb. 2, May 11, 18, 1837.

In October, tensions peaked when the government, after failing to implement the Poor Law in Huddersfield, made Bradford, where upper-class opinion was more favorable, the testing ground for its general introduction throughout the industrial North. Assistant Commissioner Power came from London to supervise the Bradford Guardians as they nervously discharged their responsibilities as executors of the law. Whatever their reservations about the timing, the liberal guardians were committed to their task. "You might as well try to stop the Ganges," warned E. C. Lister, "as to prevent this bill being carried into effect."[44]

The workers, however, denied this inevitability. As the guardians met, an angry crowd of six thousand gathered, demanding admission. Although unable to gain entry into the courthouse, the mob attacked and nearly trampled the London bureaucrat after the meeting broke up. When this scene was repeated two weeks later, the hussars were summoned and the Riot Act was read. The ensuing two-hour battle between mob and soldiery resulted in multiple injuries but, miraculously, no deaths.[45]

"The presumption of three hundred people not one third of them ratepayers," charged the irate *Observer*, "to represent public opinion [and] . . . to dictate to the Guardians . . . is an insult to them and derogatory to the dignity which ought to invest the office." Yet to many workers, the dignity of the office had already been besmirched by the guardians, who had used their authority to enforce a law that the majority of their constituents hated and feared. In the 1839 election, the ratepayers responded by throwing these liberal guardians out. The Tories who replaced them were able to dominate the Bradford Poor Law Board without serious opposition for the next seven years. Even the greatest liberal entrepreneurs like Robert Milligan, Titus Salt, Daniel Illingworth, and Henry Forbes, were summarily removed from their posts.[46]

The popular repudiation of liberalism that resulted from the 1837 Poor Law crisis hardened a year later with the emergence of Chartism, which dominated working-class consciousness for the next decade. Against the backdrop of protracted economic crisis and class conflict, Chartism gave Bradford's workers a sustained political voice that linked capitalist exploitation with oligarchical corruption and remained independent of either party of the bourgeoisie.[47] Although bourgeois liberals might dismiss the factory or anti-Poor Law campaigns as convulsive reactions to hunger and poverty that

[44] *BO*, Nov. 2, 1837.
[45] *BO*, Jan. 19, Nov. 30, Dec. 7, 1837.
[46] Ashforth, "Poor Law," 96–109.
[47] Ibid.

outside agitators exploited to serve their own end, Chartism, with its program of universal suffrage, challenged liberalism in the most fundamental ways. This was not only because the new movement was long lived and well organized, but because it questioned the liberal's very anthenticity, demanding the immediate enactment of the kind of progressive democracy that liberalism itself had already theoretically proclaimed. "When they had attended Whig meetings," one worker sarcastically taunted, "Mr. Byles had called them gentlemen, but when they had meetings of their own, Mr. Byles called them 'the shirtless, shoeless, penniless portion of the community.' "[48]

If Byles and other liberals condemned the Chartist program "as at once absurd, dogmatical, and unjust," it must be not on grounds of principle, but because the Chartists were unworthy of the goals they advocated. Embarrassed by the existence of these working-class radicals who flung liberal principles back in their face, the *Observer* was reduced to ad hominem attacks that dismissed them as hypocrites who "arrogate to themselves the title of champions of liberty [while] attempting to exercise the worst species of tyranny, threatening not only loss of custom but even loss of life to those who dare to differ from them in opinion."[49]

What most alarmed the liberals about Chartism was that it had transformed universal suffrage from a lofty abstraction into the lynchpin of a concrete social and economic program through which the workers could seek a set of independent class objectives that would inevitably conflict with the interests of the entrepreneurial bourgeoisie. In 1839 events suggested that a society grounded in the sanctity of private property could not long stand if the propertyless majority were invested with political power. By midsummer a frightened magistrate reported to the Home Office that "the peaceably disposed Inhabitants of Bradford in consequence of the frequent and unexpected Meetings of numerous assemblies of people who listen to and are excited by Violent harangues of evil disposed and Revolutionary speakers are in the utmost alarm, and without the protection of a Military Force they are persuaded beyond all doubt that some violent outrage will

---

[48] *BO*, Feb. 14, 1839. For comparable developments in Birmingham and Oldham see respectively, Trygve Tholfsen, "The Chartist Crisis in Birmingham," *International Review of Social History*, 3 (1958), and D. S. Gadian, "Class Consciousness in Oldham and other North-West Industrial Towns 1830–1850,"*Historical Journal*, 21:1 (1978).

[49] *BO*, Oct. 25, 1838; Jul. 18, 1839. Not surprisingly, this bourgeois liberal hostility toward independent worker initiatives that advanced class interests in opposition to those of the capitalist bourgeoisie surfaced most bitterly in relation to trade unions. "So long as combinations exist," the *Observer* expostulated, "marked by their present principles and practices, it will form an unanswerable argument against a claim to the extension of the political franchise to the people." *BO*, Feb. 22, 1838.

take place, and that neither the life nor property of the middle or upper classes of whatever political opinion is at all safe."[50]

By threatening class warfare the Chartists destroyed the consensual foundations of the liberal creed. Faced with a potential assault on their hard-won property by those whom they had once sought as political allies, Bradford's liberal entrepreneurs could no longer evade the truth that the preservation of order mattered more to them than the promotion of social progress. "The whole commercial and social framework of Great Britain," declared a frightened *Observer*, "is built upon private faith and public order. ... [Dissolve these and] the whole edifice crumbles into ruins." Having now acquired, with great effort, a piece of this edifice, it was they, even more than the aristocrats, who now stood to lose from a proletarian revolution that "would annihilate the authority of the civil magistrate ... [and] would be a carnival for villains of every kind and degree."[51]

Yet abandoning political progressivism and populist outreach proved counterproductive, even in narrow electoral terms, for, in posing as the defender of order, liberals contradicted their own ideology. Their creed presupposed the presence of a fundamentally stable social environment in which a progressive consensus would spontaneously arise. If this assumption of stability proved false, then the task of maintaining social order was better left to conservatives whose authority had always rested on the traditional values and hierarchical institutions that liberals had hitherto attacked. Having built their reputations as friends of the people, men like Byles inspired little confidence on the right when they attacked their former left-wing allies.

This lesson, that liberalism could not lead the charge of reaction and was endangered by conditions of economic crisis and political unrest, was demonstrated in the 1841 parliamentary elections when the growing conservatism of Bradford's Liberal Party played right into the Tories' hands. In the general election, the Whig–Liberal team of Busfield and Lister (with William Lister now replacing his ailing father Ellis) once again faced the Tory Hardy. This time, however, Hardy topped the poll, and the incumbent Busfield was defeated.[52] This trend continued several months later, when a by-election caused by young Lister's sudden death pitted Busfield against a Tory import, William Wilberforce, the son of the famous evangelical of that name. Busfield fought hard to regain his seat and won, though by a margin of only four votes. Wilberforce's robust showing strongly suggested not only a disen-

[50] Quoted in Dorothy Thompson, ed., *The Early Chartists* (London, 1971), 208; *BO*, Aug. 1, 1839.

[51] Joseph Hamburger, *James Mill and the Art of Revolution* (New Haven, 1963); *BO*, Nov. 8, 1838.

[52] *Pollbook* (Bradford, 1841).

chantment with liberalism among the electorate, but a moderate Whig difficulty in holding even a single parliamentary seat.[53]

Local historians have attributed these high Tory vote counts largely to working-class hostility to liberalism and to the Chartists' determination to expel the Whigs. Although this was undoubtedly a factor, working-class influence on the £10 electorate was limited to that fairly small group of neighborhood shopkeepers who depended on proletarian patronage and were substantial enough to qualify for the parliamentary vote. Moreover, by 1841, the Chartists were more interested in running their own candidate than in using the Tories to attack the Whigs. Over 15 percent of those who had voted liberal in 1837 now either switched sides or simply stayed away. The only explanation is that a substantial number of moderate (probably largely Anglican) property owners had concluded that liberalism did not work.[54]

Hence instead of generating the promised progressive consensus, the liberals, since their victories in 1837, had presided, both nationally and locally, over mounting economic dislocation and political strife. Now as social stabilization and political reaction replaced reform and social change as the primary concerns of the bourgeoisie as a class, liberalism lost credit and struggled to survive through a pale imitation of traditional conservatism. Bourgeois liberalism had failed to find a place for the workers, the foremost of its self-appointed ideological tasks. Chartism showed that they could not be integrated into the new urban-industrial politics without a major challenge to bourgeois class power. Yet if liberalism could not become a party for the workers, how long would it remain the party of the bourgeoisie?

The fate of the liberal political consensus

If the events of 1835–38 had taught Bradford's liberals the necessity of paying heed to conservative bourgeois opinion, those of 1838–41 taught that this did not absolve the party of its populist mission toward the working class. In the urban-industrial crises of this era, it became evident that the social consensus that the liberal coalition had presupposed had disintegrated into a bitter contest of parties and an even more ominous conflict between classes. Until liberals could restore the optimistic, consensual climate of progress on which their claims to legitimacy had been based, the party would continue to lose elections and make no headway in converting the urban-

---

[53] Wright, "Politics and Opinion," 229–46.
[54] Ibid., 235; Jowitt and Taylor, eds., *Bradford Elections*, 3.

industrial population to the its entrepreneurial, voluntarist ideals. In the heat
of its struggles with the Chartists, the *Observer* admitted:

> We know and deeply lament that there is a feud between the middle
> and working classes and that it does not altogether originate in the
> exclusion of the latter from political power, but principally on what we
> conscientiously believe to be erroneous ideas of their relative interests
> as capitalists and labourers.[55]

This class struggle, although it manifested itself in the political arena,
had a fundamentally economic source. So long as Bradford's workers could
not reasonably subsist due to low wages and unemployment, they would not
accept their role in the capitalist system, much less embrace the liberal
entrepreneurial creed. While depression and exploitation left them increasingly preoccupied with questions of economic security, they might well perceive the greatest immediate threat to their welfare, not in the hidebound
reaction of the Tory establishment, but in the unrestrained competition
imposed by the new bourgeoisie.

Yet the same forces of dislocation that devastated working-class living
standards often cut almost as deeply into the profits of the entrepreneur.
Since economic crisis harmed both social classes, finding an antidote to it
offered a goal around which they could potentially reunite. Reasserting the
common interests of all industrial producers against the socially dysfunctional
privileges of the monopolist aristocracy, once again, seemed to provide a
means of transcending capitalist class divisions and restoring the liberal vision
of harmony. To wean workers from their belligerent class consciousness
during periods of depression and to return them to the liberal fold, it was
even more necessary than in periods of prosperity to portray the poverty and
exploitation that appeared to emanate from the workings of the competitive
marketplace as, in fact, the consequence of illegitimate monopolies enjoyed
by entrenched elites.

By the late thirties, the *Observer* had begun to argue that it was not the
low or fluctuating level of wages, but the artificially high price of bread that
was primarily responsible for the workers' poverty. Criticism of the landowners' "bread tax" had always been a powerful liberal weapon in the
antiaristocratic arsenal, as in 1829, when Col. Thompson's *Corn Law Catechism* had helped mobilize a broad-based reform campaign. In 1837, the
Observer reintroduced this question, seeking again to make it the foundation
of a popular antiprotectionist crusade. In February, the paper called on the
workers in particular to take up this issue, since the vitality that free trade

[55] *BO,* Apr. 11, 1839.

would infuse into the industrial economy would benefit them even more than the capitalists.[56]

Yet over the next two years as the depression deepened and the Chartist movement spread, the behavior of Bradford's workers amply indicates that they saw themselves less as cheated consumers than as proletarianized producers who stood to gain little from mere freedom of trade. Forging a popular movement around this issue would require greater initiative from the bourgeoisie. In January 1839, an Anti-Corn Law lecturer exhorted "the mercantile men of Bradford to co-operate heart and hand with the men of Manchester, Glasgow, and Birmingham, etc. in the momentous struggle with the landed interest that is about to commence." The next week, the *Observer* berated its subscribers for having taken so long to agitate the cause. However, by the end of the month, it could rejoice that the question had "been taken up with spirit" and that a local branch of the Anti–Corn Law League had been formed. The paper explained a few months later that free trade had become much more than a morally desirable object. In the context of a devastating depression, it had become a sheer economic necessity, without which manufacturing communities like Bradford might not survive.[57]

In its first year, the Anti–Corn Law League held several public meetings at which Robert Milligan and James Garnett were selected as local delegates to attend a national conference in London. In 1840, the league held a series of anti-Corn Law banquets whose "glory and moral greatness" left the *Observer* at a loss for words. Although the league used similar agitational tactics to the Chartists, it remained firmly under bourgeois control. The leagues' coffers, unlike those of the Chartists, were quickly and lavishly filled by a handful of wealthy liberal subscribers who donated £2,768 in one year alone. In June 1840, 112 millowners circulated a petition that drew nine thousand signatures from their employees.[58]

Yet spontaneous worker response to the anti-Corn Law League was lukewarm at best. Most workers disapproved of the Corn Laws. But only a few like John Jackson were willing to give the league public support. Most working-class radicals were actively hostile, since they perceived the league as a popular front deliberately concocted by the liberals to divert proletarian agitation away from the People's Charter and to channel it into a movement that was bourgeois controlled. Most distressing to the workers was the league's insistence that the free-trade issue be kept completely separate from any demands for suffrage reform. Jackson himself dropped plans for an

---

[56] *BO*, Feb. 9, 1837; Apr. 10, 1838.
[57] *BO*, Jan. 3, Mar. 1, 1839.
[58] *BO*, Feb. 14, Apr. 25, 1839; Jan. 2, 16, 30, Mar. 26, June 25, 1840.

Operatives' Anti–Corn Law Association because the bourgeois leaders would not endorse a wider franchise.[59]

The league and Chartism remained rival movements, and anti–Corn Law meetings were invaded by bands of angry Chartists who sought to turn them into independent demonstrations of working-class power. To repeal the Corn Laws before obtaining universal suffrage would, the radicals argued, provide the capitalists with a perfect opportunity to lower workers' wages and increase their own profits at society's expense. By 1840, the league had done nothing to diminish most workers' attachment to Chartism and, by openly attempting to create a rival movement, may actually have exacerbated class tensions in Bradford.[60]

After their defeat in the 1841 election, however, the liberal leaders determined to make a change. The persistence of state agricultural protectionism had shown, even before their electoral debacle, that, unless aristocratic hegemony were dislodged in Westminster, liberal power at the local level would always remain insecure. As long as a Whig ministry had remained in office, Bradford's liberals had hesitated to jeopardize their compromise with moderate landowners by giving full voice to their criticisms of the aristocracy. However, after 1841, with an openly Tory ministry in power, local party leaders felt free to make a move to the left. Centrism had revealed its political bankruptcy when it resulted in a humiliating electoral defeat. The Reform Bill had not, after all, given enough power to bourgeois liberals and had preserved, in the name of caution and gradualism, too many vestiges of the old regime.

In a major shift of editorial position, the *Observer* now explained: "The more intelligent among the middle classes have made the discovery that the union of the two classes is indispensable to the carrying of those legislative measures so essential to their interests. With this conviction had come another ... that the working class had been pursuing a noble object."[61] If the bourgeoisie needed the workers to pursue its own class interests, it could not dictate the terms of their alliance unilaterally. It would have to compromise and implicitly acknowledge that the workers had class interests of their own. To do this, the relationship between free trade and democracy would have to be rethought. "Right or wrong, politic or impolitic, the questions of Corn Law repeal and the extension of the suffrage have become mixed together ... the difficult point is to what length may or ought or must the Repealers go in making advances to the Chartists."[62]

[59] *BO*, Jan. 2, June 25, 1840.
[60] *BO*, Feb. 7, 14, 1839; Lucy Brown, "The Chartists and the Anti-Corn Law League," in Asa Briggs, ed., *Chartist Studies* (London, 1959), 342–71.
[61] *BO*, Mar. 10, 1842.
[62] *BO*, Feb. 17, 1842.

Although a section of the Liberal party began to follow the *Observer*'s lead, there was, at first, no unanimity on this question. If the liberal–working-class alliance were reconstituted, argued W. E. Forster, who hoped that it would,

> it will be because the working classes believe the middle classes sympathize with them. The feeling in favor of universal suffrage ... is a resolute, long-held determination by a large body of the operatives, and they will not rest till they get some great concession; and considering the very large proportion they bear here toward the other classes, they demand great tact in management.[63]

After 1841, a large group of bourgeois liberals began actively to court radical working-class leaders and to seek a common ground. William Byles wrote:

> All the aberrations of the Chartists ... [have not] been able to shake the faith of such men in the ultimate union of the franchised liberals with the unenfranchised multitudes for the purpose of carrying out a large measure of governmental reform. We are not sanguine enough to believe that the middle and working classes have all of a sudden become cordially united. This is an event which still lies a good way into the future. [However] they have talked over their common wants and common wrongs, they have found that the enemy of one is the enemy of both, and that neither is able to cope with this enemy single handed.[64]

This new spirit of collaboration led to the formation of the Bradford United Reform Club, in September 1841, "to promote the union of the largest possible number of Reformers for the accomplishment of all practicable Reforms." In contrast to the original Reform Society, this new body was intended to be more than a liberal political machine. It aimed to become an out-reach voluntary association, like the Mechanics Institute or the Temperance Society, which would unite the classes in a common politics of antiaristocratic progressivism with the techniques of self-improvement and the culture of mutual aid.[65]

---

[63] T. W. Reid, *The Life of the Right Honorable William Edward Forster* (London, 1888), 1:127.

[64] *BO*, Feb. 24, 1842.

[65] Bradford United Reform Club, *Annual Report* (Bradford, 1842); Wright, "Politics and Opinion," 246–9. Indeed, the most prescient advocates of this new liberal strategy of negotiated class alliance, like Samuel Smiles who sought a similar fusion of working-class Chartists with bourgeois free traders in Leeds, recognized that even the mechanics institutes constituted an insufficiently democratic organizational model for such a venture in genuine class collaboration. Speaking before the Bradford United Reform Club in February 1842, Smiles criticized the mechanics institutes for excessive reliance on bourgeois direction and patronage, which, in his view, accounted for their failure to win the allegiance of the mass of ordinary working men. See Alexander Tyrell, "Class Consciousness in Early Victorian Britain: Samuel Smiles, Leeds Politics, and the Self-Help Creed," *Journal of British Studies*, 9:2 (1970), 119.

Selecting parliamentary candidates and winning elections was only one of the United Reform Club's aims. Ultimately it hoped "to promote the great principles of *freedom* for which all classes are struggling and the triumph of which will be ensured by *mutual concession and cooperation*." The club would not only canvass the electors but would circulate "sound political information by means of lectures, public meetings and the establishment of a reading room [to promote] the establishment of a purer and healthier political faith among the people [and] produce the most satisfactory practical benefits."[66]

Like the Mechanics Institute and the Temperance Society, the United Reform Club was initiated and largely financed by leading representatives of the entrepreneurial bourgeoisie.[67] Ordinary members' subscriptions of 10s. per annum brought in approximately £150 during the first year, and this was supplemented by an additional £100 donated by nine of the wealthiest liberal elites.[68] Despite its overwhelmingly bourgeois leadership, the Reform Club drew in some of the better-off workers and the petite bourgeoisie. Although the club never attracted more than five hundred members, 39 percent of them were skilled workers. 32 percent were lower middle class, and 24 percent were solidly bourgeois. Unskilled laborers constituted less than 5 percent.[69]

To preserve this relatively broad if not large popular base, the Reform Club immediately began to make conciliatory gestures toward the organized working class. Although the executive initially recommended supporting household suffrage, pressure from the rank and file led them to advocate that the vote be extended to all adult men. The club "hail[ed] with satisfaction the exertions of the anti–Corn Law League, [and] cordially invite[d] them to come out unanimously and aid in gaining for the people that political power which will at once and forever destroy the aristocratic domination by which this country has been reduced to its present indescribably distressed condition."[70] Most significantly, the committee made plans to participate

---

[66] Bradford United Reform Club, *Minutes*, Sep. 24, 1841 (mss., Bradford Archives D.B. 4/1).

[67] With officers like Henry Forbes, Titus Salt, Joshua Lupton, William German, and J. V. Godwin, authority within the new organization was concentrated in the same small clique of entrepreneurial parvenus who had dominated Bradford liberalism since the Reform Bill days. A few moderate working-class leaders such as John Jackson, Christopher Wilkinson, and Samuel Marten were included on the Board of Directors, but they were vastly outnumbered by the likes of William Byles, Henry Brown, Nathaniel Briggs, James Bottomley, Joseph Farrar, Edward Kenion, Joseph Illingworth, and John Dale, who ran so many of the other voluntary associations in town.

[68] Bradford United Reform Club, *Annual Report* (Bradford, 1843).

[69] Bradford United Reform Club, *List of Members* (mss., Bradford Archives. D.B. 4/1).

[70] Bradford United Reform Club, *Minutes*, July 20, 1842.

that December in a national Complete Suffrage Conference that was being organized by a group of radical Birmingham Corn Law repealers under the leadership of Joseph Sturge. Aiming to create a political alliance between bourgeois radicals and moderate working-class Chartists, the Complete Suffrage movement was a larger manifestation of the same impulses toward progressive reform that had generated the local United Reform Club.[71]

Despite such conciliatory gestures, the Reform Club never won more than a tiny minority of Bradford's workers away from their uncompromising Chartist stance. By the end of 1842, despite the Reform Club's promising beginning, class relations between liberals and workers had deteriorated almost as far as in 1839, for both were years of deep economic crisis, which put the political viability of the liberal–working-class alliance to an essentially impossible test.

In the beginning of 1842, bourgeois liberals were in a truculent mood. Excluded from political office both locally and nationally, they seemed inspired by a spirit of dispossession that they had not felt for a decade. In this mood of anger and increasing desperation, they now faced the prospect of an economic catastrophe following inexorably from the protracted depression of trade. Cornered by circumstances, it was the bourgeois liberals, now even more than the Chartists, who raised the specter of popular violence and revolution if the entrenched aristocracy did not peaceably give way. "Are the middle classes still haunted," the *Observer* queried, "by fears of the destruction of property? . . . Is not their property wasting like snow in the sun?"[72]

An anti-Corn Law petition circulated in February easily obtained nineteen thousand signatures in the town. Yet the government made it clear that popular sentiment would not move them, and the liberals, like the Chartists before them, concluded that petitioning was not enough. Throughout the spring, the *Observer* was full of vague threats and forebodings of the possible consequences if the Tories did not concede to reform. Ironically, now Chartist leaders like O'Connor urged caution, forecasting a great struggle between landowners and capitalists from which the workers would do well to remain aloof.[73]

However, the workers, the worst victims of the economic crisis, found neutrality a luxury they could not afford. Amidst increasing poverty and unemployment, a series of wage reductions in early August sparked them to take to the streets. Today, it is impossible to determine whether these

---

[71] *BO*, Mar. 24, 31, Apr. 28, May 5, 12, 19, 1842.

[72] *BO*, July 7, 1842.

[73] Wright, "Politics and Opinion," 246; *BO*, Feb. 10, March 3, 24, May 19, July 28, Sep. 22, 29, 1842.

wage cuts were motivated strictly by market conditions or whether, as the Tories contended, they constituted a deliberate conspiracy by the liberal entrepreneurs to curtail production without incurring layoffs, goading the workers to abandon work in hopes that this would spark a revolt that would bring down the government and play, politically, into the hands of the league.[74]

What is clear is that, by August 9, there were ten to twelve thousand strikers marching through Bradford, pulling out the plugs of the factory boilers and bringing industrial production to a halt. As one witness recalled several decades later,

> I well remember the savage appearance of a huge crowd of men as they marched from Horton to Bradford.... They came pouring down the wide road in thousands, taking up its whole breadth – a gaunt, famished looking desperate multitude, armed with huge bludgeons, flails, pitchforks and pikes, many without coats and hats, and hundreds upon hundreds with their clothes in rags and tatters. Many of the older men looked foot sore and weary, but the great multitude were men in the prime of life, full of wild excitement. As they marched they thundered out to a grand old tune a stirring melody, of which this was the opening stanza:
> Men of England, ye are slaves, Though ye "rule" the roaring waves. Though ye shout from Sea to Sea Britons everywhere are free.[75]

Not satisfied to echo the liberal demand for repeal of the Corn Laws, these men sought to free themselves from their condition of wage slavery by vowing to stay away from work until the People's Charter was made law. It took a full week and sixty-one arrests in Bradford to reopen the mills and restore public order.[76] Frightened by this conflagration, which spread far beyond their control, the liberal leaders toned down their belligerent language in the *Observer* and counseled tactical retreat: "The existing order of things ... is still too firm to be overthrown by such a *coup de main*. A strong physical force Government holds the reins of power; and rather than accede to the political demands of the 'turn-outs' the Government will deluge England with blood."[77]

Once the outbreak actually occurred, Chartist agitators swallowed their skepticism and rushed to take the lead, directing the strikers to revolt not only against the Tory aristocrats, but against the "grasping avaricious ty-

[74] G. N. Kitson Clark, "Hunger and Politics in 1842," *Journal of Modern History*, 25 (1953); *Bradford Herald*, Aug. 25, 1842.
[75] Frank Peel, *The Risings of the Luddites, Chartists and Plug Drawers* (New York, 1968), 338–9.
[76] Peel, *Risings of Luddites*, 332–3, BO, Aug. 11, 18, 25, 1842.
[77] BO, Aug. 25, 1842.

rants," the capitalists, "whose counting house was their church, their desks their altar, their ready reckoner their prayer book, and money their God."[78] In early September, a chastened *Observer* wrote:

> The middle classes have a delicate game to play at Present. The middle classes are a peace loving class: they hate all riots and rioters; and are ready, as we have seen, to unite with the aristocracy to put down all disturbances.... They may not, as a class be greatly in love with complete suffrage nor with chartism ... but we shall suppose they are Corn Law repealers. But whether [*sic*] do they think that the governing aristocracy hate chartism or Corn Law repeal the more?[79]

Once again, bourgeois liberals opted for a safe, conservative coalition of property owners when a radical alliance with the workers began to threaten their capitalist interests as a class. As the aftershocks of the summer plug plot disaster reverberated throughout the autumn and winter, the foundations of the Complete Suffrage alliance crumbled. The failure of the national conference in Birmingham was presaged by a struggle between Chartists and bourgeois liberals in Bradford over the composition of the local delegation. The final breakup of the Birmingham Conference, because of bourgeois resistance to the symbolism of the People's Charter and working-class refusal to give it up, was just one manifestation of the deep-rooted antagonisms dividing the classes and preventing them from pursuing any common political aims.[80]

Conclusion

In its elegy for the Birmingham experiment, the *Observer* tersely commented that the time had not been ripe. A week later, a Chartist correspondent insisted that Complete Suffrage had failed because "the middle class are jealous of the industrious portion of society having political power," not necessarily even because they feared revolution, "but because they wish to retain a power independent of the honest operative."[81] So long as the crises of industrial capitalism forced Bradford's liberal bourgeoisie into this position, radical populist political movements like the Reform Club could be no more successful in uniting alienated workers and bourgeois liberals than the cultural self-help associations on which they were modeled.

As we have seen, the infrastructure of competitive voluntary associations that these bourgeois liberals were forging during the 1830s and 1840s, in

---

[78] *BO*, Aug. 18, 1842.
[79] *BO*, Sep. 8, 1842.
[80] Dorothy Thompson, *The Chartists* (New York, 1984), 260–7; *BO*, Dec. 15, 1842.
[81] *BO*, Jan. 5, 12, 1843.

religion, in temperance, in education, and in politics, did very accurately reflect their own experience of Bradford's new urban-industrial capitalist world. However, their effort to transform this network of bourgeois voluntarism into a universal culture that would unite all social groups under entrepreneurial leadership around the principles of market freedom and individual self-help was, under the circumstances, bound to fail.

This was, indeed, a sobering and frightening conclusion which Bradford's rising entrepreneurial liberals, for as long as possible, tried to repress or deny. As E. J. Hobsbawm has perceptively noted, "the fortresses of aristocratic privilege, superstition, and corruption, which still had to be razed to allow free enterprise to introduce its millennium, also still protected them against the sight of the uncertainties and problems which lay beyond their walls."[82] Yet when the crises and conflicts of the late 1830s and 1840s finally thrust these problems and uncertainties inescapably into view, these bourgeois liberals could no longer avoid the obvious fact that their supposedly universalistic campaigns of aristocratic demolition were being repudiated by workers who responded with apathy to the entrepreneurial ideal of individual self and social reform or, more alarmingly, showed signs of appropriating liberal forms of voluntary association to their own independent and increasingly antientrepreneurial aims. When this happened, Bradford's rising generation of parvenu capitalists found themselves, no less than the rest of the urban-industrial population, confronting an entirely new and different social agenda that was set not by the consensual political aspirations of entrepreneurial liberalism, but by the divisive economic realities of proletarianization and class.

[82] E. J. Hobsbawm, *Industry and Empire* (London, 1968), 84.

PART III

The crisis of proletarianization and the stabilization of the urban-industrial world: 1825–1850

13

The process of proletarianization

During the second quarter of the nineteenth century, as the young, largely immigrant, and liberal generation of entrepreneurial parvenus arrived in Bradford to seek their freedom and to pursue their success, a new working class also emerged within the city whose members experienced the same urban-industrial capitalist environment in a profoundly different and more alienating way. The very forces that brought opportunity and advancement to the new entrepreneurs subjected their working-class counterparts to a process of proletarianization that dispossessed them of material and communal resources that they regarded as a birthright, irrevocably blighted their physical habitat, and in the worst instances, deprived them of the barest minimal subsistence that they and their families needed to live.

In Bradford, as in Britain generally, this process of proletarianization began as a gradual development whose roots went back to the medieval liberation of labor from feudal servility and which did not reach its final culmination until the mid-nineteenth century when this "free" labor became effectively mobile and detached from any residual access to the means of production or the land. Protoindustrialization in the eighteenth century had been both a sign that this process was already in motion and an impetus that led to its further intensification.[1]

Nevertheless, even in 1815, in Bradford, the process of proletarianization

---

[1] Robert Brenner, "Agrarian Class Structure and Economic Development in Pre-Industrial Europe," *Past and Present* 70 (1976), 30–75; E. P. Thompson, "Patrician Society, Plebeian Culture," *Journal of Social History*, 7:4 (1974), 383–405; and Peter Kriedte, Hans Medick, and Jurgen Schlumbohm, *Industrialization before Industrialization: Rural Industry in the Genesis of Capitalism* (Cambridge, 1981). Although there has been no full historical study of the process of proletarianization in Britain, Friedrich Engels, *The Condition of the Working Class in England* (Moscow, 1973); Karl Polanyi, *The Great Transformation* (Boston, 1944); E. P. Thompson, *The Making of the English Working Class* (New York, 1963); and John Foster, *Class Struggle and the Industrial Revolution: Early English Capitalism in Three Towns* (London, 1974), each provide classic, albeit partial and controversial, accounts. This chapter is heavily indebted to all of them. Another relevant work, Richard Price, *Labour in British Society* (London, 1986), appeared while this book was in the editorial stage, as did Ira Katznelson and Aristide Zolberg, eds., *Working Class Formation: Nineteenth Century Patterns in Western Europe and the United States* (Princeton, 1986), which provides useful comparisons with proletarianization in Germany, France, and the United States.

remained fundamentally incomplete. As long as the bulk of the population was dispersed in small rural farming and weaving villages where families continued to work together as productive units, even when they were employed by putting-out masters, they were able to retain some minimal autonomy and practical control over their work. No doubt the powerful market forces that increasingly pressed them, speeding up the pace and intensity of their labor and depriving them of recourse to subsistence agriculture, rendered their autonomy somewhat illusory. Still, as long as semirural working-class families continued to own their own tools, or possessed a pig and garden plot, they could preserve some cushion against the worst rigors of depression and price inflation such as occurred during the wartime crisis decades.[2]

At the climax of this crisis, in 1799–1800, when the sudden convergence of poor harvests with commercial depression was compounded by an environment of wartime inflation and heavy taxation of consumable goods, working-class subsistence was more seriously endangered than would ever be the case during the subsequent industrial era. But when the immediate threat of starvation receded a few years later, economic trends during the 1810s and early 1820s seemed to indicate that the working-class domestic economy had suffered little permanent damage. Its revival for a brief Indian summer during the decade-long postwar deflationary boom underlines the essentially conjunctural character of the *fin de siècle* crisis whose main causes, war, crop failure, and government extravagance, were largely extraneous to the emerging industrial-capitalist system itself.[3]

By contrast, the working-class crisis, which began after 1825 and lasted for the next twenty-five years, constituted a much more complex, structural transformation involving a succession of distinct yet interrelated assaults on traditional working-class ways of life. Unlike its forerunner during the protoindustrial period, the 1825–50 crisis was systemic because its specific manifestations, however apparently multifarious, were the products of a single process – the maturation of cosmopolitan industrial capitalism in the Bradford worsted trade during these years. Taken individually, these manifestations of industrial crisis were less devastating than the subsistence crisis that darkened the worst of the wartime years. Taken together, however, they proved far more significant in bringing full-scale proletarianization.[4]

By midcentury, Bradford's protoindustrial environment had been obliterated, and the proletarianization of its textile work force was substantially

---

[2] See Chapter 2.
[3] Ibid.
[4] This problem deserves far more scholarly attention than it has received. For two classic contributions that shed at least indirect light on it, see Engels, *Condition of the Working Class*, and E. J. Hobsbawm, *Labouring Men* (London, 1964), 64–125.

complete. A class once dispersed in cottages throughout the countryside was now huddled together in a city of 103,000. By 1850, manufacturing, having long since abandoned the arena of cottage handicrafts, was uniformly concentrated in about ninety factories, foundries, and engineering works located downtown. As a result of this industrial concentration, 76 percent of Bradford's 32,856 worsted workers were now employed by the 129 largest firms.[5] The experiences of industrialization and urbanization, which had facilitated rapid capital accumulation for a few, spelled dispossession and proletarianization for most workers. As they lost control over the process of production, they were forced to abandon the subsistence cushion that semirural domestic manufacturing had once allowed. In sharp contrast to the entrepreneurial bourgeoisie that migrated alongside them, their participation as autonomous actors in the marketplace entailed a loss of independence as producers who, stripped of traditional, communal, or paternalist protections, now retained only ownership of their capacity to work.[6]

Thus the 1825–50 crisis period, so critical in the class formation of the entrepreneurial bourgeoisie, constituted an even more critical moment in the long process of proletarianization out of which a modern industrial working class was born. Animated by the momentous social transformations that they experienced in their own particular way, the generation of workers who lived through this period responded to the challenge of urban-industrial capitalism in a manner quite different from that which liberal voluntarism prophesied.

The decline of the handicraft worker

The decline of the traditional worsted handicraft industries, which had been the bulwark of manufacturing employment in Bradford-dale, was the dominating experience of the generation of workers who came of age in the second quarter of the nineteenth century. Often dismissed by economic historians as a mere footnote to the main drama of the Industrial Revolution in which the foundations of future progress and prosperity were being laid, the story of the decline of the textile handicraftsman must stand at the center of any account of class formation; for his traumas were not merely the unfortunate by-products of economic modernization, they were the inexorable outcome of a logic of capitalist development that undermined and

---

[5] C. Richardson, *A Geography of Bradford* (Bradford, 1976), 64; *PP* (1852–3, LXXXVIII), 722, 724.
[6] Karl Marx, *Capital* (Moscow, 1954), 1:667–724.

subjected to technological obsolescence, during the 1825–50 period, a social group it had called into existence a generation before (Fig. 13-1).[7]

Chapter 3 has already examined the first phase of this process, the transformation of hand to powerloom weaving. Having created a subsistence crisis in the protoindustrial hinterland for a decade and a half after 1824, this transformation effected a wholesale reshuffling of the region's industrial work force during the 1838–45 period, as tens of thousands of weavers and their families were forced to leave their native villages for Bradford's urban downtown. Upon their arrival in the industrial city, a large proportion of these ex-weavers found work as woolcombers, an urban handicraft whose workers at least doubled, perhaps tripled in the course of these years (see Table 13-1).

Nevertheless, it soon became evident that woolcombing would not provide a stable, alternative artisanal employment to compensate for the weavers' demise. Although the combers were heirs to a long and glorious corporate craft legacy, it proved difficult to graft such traditions onto the new industrial landscape. Very quickly, the trade began to exhibit the same telltale signs of overcompetition, sweating, and breakdown of apprenticeship that had been plaguing handloom weaving for some time. From the start, the Bradford combers, for all their aspirations to autonomy, found themselves almost entirely dependent on the small group of large spinning capitalists, who constituted the only market for their "top." Then, although combers occasionally worked in their own houses, unlike the weavers, theirs was an occupation in which other family members only occasionally participated. Increasingly, they labored together in small shops of four or five male workers that began to spring up around the factories in Bradford's urban downtown.[8]

Most importantly, however, woolcombing, which had traditionally been regarded as a skilled occupation, was, at least after the defeat of a major strike in 1825, a job that was increasingly open to all comers and subject to the degradation of a sweated trade. In truth, the comber's work required little skill and few instruments. The ease with which his ranks were penetrated by immigrant interlopers indicates that his craft privileges were rapidly becoming more apparent than real.[9] In the commercial upswing of the late twenties, the dramatic increase in demand for combing workers brought wage levels up. During the boom of the midthirties, a comber in full work could expect to earn 14 to 18s. per week. Nevertheless, this was considerably less than the weaver, in his

[7] Thompson, *English Working Class*, 269–313.
[8] E. M., Sigsworth, "An Episode in Woolcombing," *Journal of the Bradford Textile Society* (Bradford, 1956–7), 113–25; A. B. Reach, *Manchester and the Textile Districts in 1849* (Blackburn, 1974), 19; Jonathan Smith, "The Strike of 1825," in D. G. Wright and J. A. Jowitt, eds., *Victorian Bradford* (Bradford, 1982), 63–80.
[9] See Chapter 16.

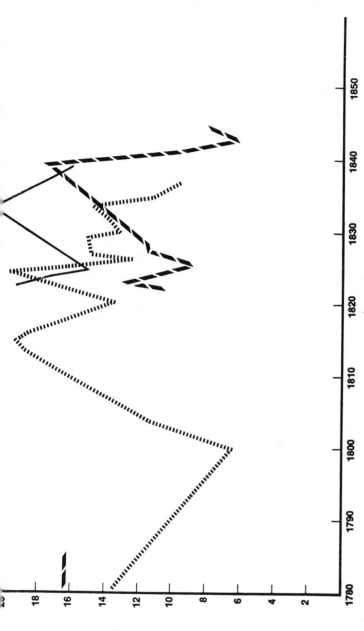

Wages in shillings

2 — 4 — 6 — 8 — 10 — 12 — 14 — 16 — 18 —

1780 1790 1800 1810 1820 1830 1840 1850

Key: ·········· handloom weavers; ◄—► handcombers; ——— factory overlookers.

Figure 13-1. Real wages of selected occupations, in 1850 shillings.
Compiled from A. L. Bowley, "Statistics of Wages in United Kingdom," *Journal of Royal Statistical Society*, 65 (1902), 104–6, 113; and John James, *History of the Worsted Manufacture in England* (London, 1857), 400–16. Real wages have been calculated using the classic price index contained in E. H. Phelps Brown and S. V. Hopkins, "Seven Centuries of the Prices of Consumables, Compared with Builders' Wage-Rates," in E. M. Carus Wilson, ed., *Essays in Economic History* (New York, 1966), 2: 179–96. In recent years several other price indexes have been proposed as superior for calculating real wages. However, because these are both less complete and, in some instances, mutually contradictory, the older Phelps Brown/Hopkins index has been retained here.

Table 13-1. *Approximate distribution of entire worsted work force in Bradford,*
1838–61

	1838	1845	1850–1	1854	1861
Handloom weavers	14,000[a]	?	—	—	—
Hand combers	4,000[b]	10,000–15,000[b]	7,989[b]	2,577	—
Factory operatives			24,872		
Adults	4,954	—		—	16,303
Children	7,502	—		—	7,889
Total	30,000[a]	—	32,861	—	24,192

Note: All figures are for Bradford Borough except where indicated.
[a]Includes Bradford hinterland.
[b]Estimate.
Sources: Compiled and calculated from the data in *PP* (1851, XXIII), 62–3; (1852–3, LXXXVIII), 2:720–32; (1862, LIII), 722–8; *BO*, Feb. 23, Mar. 9, 1854; E. M. Sigsworth, "An Episode in Woolcombing," *Journal of the Bradford Textile Society* (Bradford, 1956–7), 113–25; and John James, *History of the Worsted Manufacturers in England* (London, 1857).

prime, had formerly commanded and usually necessitated supplementary labor by wives or children. With the onset of protracted depression in the late 1830s and the demographic pressure that a floodtide of dispossessed rural weavers brought, the wages and working conditions of the combers precipitiously deteriorated.[10] By 1840, according to the combers' leaders, "homes, which were not many years ago the abodes of comfort and domestic enjoyment, have now in consequence of frequent reductions in our wages...become the dwelling places of misery and receptacles of wretchedness.... Wives," they continued, "who once were well clothed, comfortable and happy, are now miserable and clothed in rags. Our children, the pledges of our mutual love and conjugal affection, are squalid in their appearance with scarcely a rag to screen them from the bitter winter's blast."[11]

During the 1840s, their plight continued to worsen. At middecade, the original tide of impoverished weavers and agricultural laborers from the immediate hinterland was augmented by another stream of longer-distance immigrants from Leicestershire, Devonshire, and most dramatically, from Ireland. By midcentury, 87 percent of the woolcombers in the districts examined through the manuscript census were immigrants, 41 percent of

[10] John James, *History of the Worsted Manufacture in England* (London, 1857), 441; A. L. Bowley, "Statistics of Wages in the United Kingdom," *Journal of the Royal Statistical Society* 65 (1902), 104; William Cudworth, *Condition of the Industrial Classes in Bradford* (Bradford, 1887), 45–7.

[11] Quoted in James Burnley, *The History of Wool and Woolcombing* (London, 1889), 176–7.

whom were from Ireland. Woolcombing, which had once been a highly exclusive occupation, had degenerated, in the words of one workers' spokesman, into "a sort of common reservoir of all the poverty of England and Ireland," whose members were "constantly receiving new competitors... poorer than themselves."[12]

Of course, the plight of the woolcomber was greatly exacerbated by the dearth of alternate employment outlets for adult men. In 1851, the other major industries, ironfounding and mining, accounted for only 7 percent of the town's male work force. Urban-service occupations, although expanding during the 1840s, were growing much more slowly than the tide of candidates for jobs. In 1851, service trades absorbed 30 percent of the male work force, of which 10.6 percent were artisanal craft producers and 8.4 percent were in the construction trade. The factories themselves employed only a small minority, well under 10 percent before midcentury.[13] Since these more remunerative forms of male employment were generally monopolized by natives or long-time residents, recent immigrants had no choice but to turn to a debased trade like woolcombing or, if they possessed the strength and stamina, to seek the heaviest kinds of unskilled work.[14]

Not surprisingly, the entry of these desperate newcomers into woolcombing caused wage rates to drop precipitously. By the midforties, they had reached a rock bottom of 7 to 9s., for those who were fortunate enough to be fully employed.[15] Of course, declining piece wages only forced the combers to try to work longer hours, up to sixteen or seventeen per day. This exacerbated the problem of overproduction and further eroded the individual earnings of each. Moreover, because the new entrants had been pushed by rural poverty more often than they had been attracted by urban opportunity, their arrival in Bradford often coincided with commercial depressions during which the local economy was least able to absorb them. At such times, most combers, whether immigrant or native, were either entirely without employment or earning no more than a few shillings a week.[16] Cheap, but quality, worsteds, the battering ram with which Bradford's industrial capitalists were opening up new markets all over the world, constituted an advantage that, at least during the 1840s, was achieved primarily at the woolcombers' expense.[17]

[12] Calculated from information in HO, 107/2,308. See Appendix B and Chapter 3. George White quoted in *BO*, Apr. 10, 1846.
[13] Calculated from *PP* (1852–3, LXXXVIII), 2: 720–3.
[14] Cudworth, *Industrial Classes*, 31–50.
[15] James, *Worsted Manufactures*, 548; Reach, *Textile Districts*, 19; Cudworth, *Industrial Classes*, 47–8; *BO*, Nov. 6, 1845; *PP* (1844, XXVII), 226–7.
[16] Bowley, "Wages," 104–6; *BO*, Aug. 27, 1840.
[17] Karl Marx and Friedrich Engels, *The Communist Manifesto* (New York, 1932), 13.

As working conditions deteriorated, combing became not only increasingly unremunerative, but increasingly hazardous as well. As poverty forced combers to labor in tiny, ill-ventilated workshops in which the family of one might also sleep, they fell prey to a host of occupational diseases. The charcoal required to heat the combs generated noxious fumes that were not properly dissipated in heated rooms that were habitually over 85 degrees. One woolcomber, "a gaunt, sickly-looking man," explained that "he had often to brush away the fibres as they gathered round his lips, but he knew he breathed some of 'em." His wife said that his work often made him sick and that "he knew it wasn't wholesome but what could he do?"[18]

Unlike the mechanization of weaving, the mechanization of combing was not so much a cause as a consequence of the combers' distress. Indeed, the wages of handcombers dropped so precipitously during the 1840s as to have possibly delayed the development of a fully effective power comb. However, by 1846, as a torrent of freshly arrived famine victims converged on the labor market during one of the worst episodes of depressed trade, better established Englishmen abandoned, in rapidly growing numbers, what had obviously now become a dying trade. Thus when viable combing machines were perfected in the late 1840s, they were quickly adopted by the leading worsted capitalists. The hand combers, who had numbered over ten thousand a few years earlier, dwindled even in the boom of the 1849–52 period. By the midfifties, they had entirely disappeared.[19]

In sharp contrast to their predecessors' laments over the gradual passing of the handloom weaver, the new entrepreneurs of the thirties and forties viewed the rapid extirpation of the comber with relief. Highly politicized and organized in militant trade unions, the combers had constituted a large and fundamentally unassimilable occupation that belied the liberal image of an industrial community in which capitalist progress and prosperity trickled down to all.[20] If the rural weavers had been the bulwark of protoindustrial stability, enabling the traditional community to survive, the combers represented the failure of the new urban-industrial market environment that now emerged to take its place. Not only was the combing machine much more efficient than the hand producer, but it promised to eliminate, or drive out of town, a social element that the bourgeoisie regarded as inherently subversive–inimical to the establishment of a viable urban-entrepreneurial way of life. Although their experience contradicted the values of bourgeois liberalism, the combers had hitherto been necessary for capitalist production.

[18] Reach, *Textile Districts*, 20.
[19] Sigsworth, "Episode in Woolcombing."
[20] See Chapter 18.

Now the machine would make them superfluous and lay the foundations for a more stable urban-industrial community.

In 1854, a detailed survey of the hand combers found only 2,577 left in town. The situation of these men was truly pathetic, especially considering that 70 percent were married with families to support. Only 27 percent were fully employed, 40 percent were partially employed, and 33 percent were totally unemployed. Those who had to support dependents reported average weekly household incomes of less than 2s. per head.[21] Little is known of the fate of those who had left the trade. A small proportion were hired to operate the new combing machinery, while some others were absorbed into the better-paid textile or urban-service craft occupations that were expanding as a consequence of the mid-Victorian boom. Most, however, either died off slowly in squalid poverty or were compelled to leave the town. Some of the displaced combers went to new expanding cities like Middlesborough, while others emigrated to the United States or to the Canadian and Australian colonies in hopes of finding a better life. In 1854, a committee was formed to help at least some of these woolcomber emigrants, and a few hundred were provided with modest financial aid.[22]

Seventy-six percent of the combers in the 1854 survey were between the ages of thirty and fifty, men of the same generation as the successful new industrial entrepreneurs. As contemporaries, both groups had migrated together into the urban-industrial environment. Yet their experience in the years after their arrival could scarcely have been more disjunct. Although they both inhabited the same physical space, the social, psychological, and cultural universes that they lived in were becoming increasingly worlds apart.

The rise of the factory system

Side by side with the decline of the handicraft worker in Bradford went the rise of the new factory system from a supplement to traditional forms of

[21] *BO*, Jan. 26, Feb. 2, 9, 16, 23, Mar. 2, 9, 1854.
[22] Sigsworth, "Episode in Woolcombing." One working-class newspaper, however, remained unimpressed by the benevolent impulse behind this scheme:

> The woolcombers are convicted of the crime of poverty and are duly sentenced to transportation ... to us, who regard human beings as a primary consideration, goods as a very secondary one, and machinery as a mere means for the convenience of human beings, it is not such an obvious truism that men must content to be ruined and exiled because a new invention enables the few to make larger profits and to dispense with the living machine.

BO, Aug. 9, 1852.

manufacturing to the dominant mode of production in town. In 1833, with only 3,627 workers and 1,308 horsepower, Bradford's factories were largely confined to spinning, but by 1850, with 24,872 workers operating 3,187 horsepower, they had become the locus for virtually all manufacturing in a city that had now become the true center of the international worsted trade.[23]

As we have seen, this vast expansion of factory employment did, in some respects, come to provide an alternate source of working-class jobs and income. Up to a point, it could compensate for the loss of earnings attendant upon the decline of the traditional handicraft trades. Those who believe that early industrialization improved the workers' living standard often point to the factory to buttress their case. Factory work is portrayed as the way of the future, sowing the seeds of greater working-class prosperity and paving the way for full integration into urban-industrial life. In fact, wage statistics, at first glance, do seem to demonstrate that factory work was substantially better paying than most traditional handicraft work.[24] Adult males in Bradford's factories who, in 1833, took in an average wage of 23s. 6d. per week, earned almost as much as many skilled workers and far more than the multitude of combers and weavers who formed the bulk of the male working class. Yet at that time, there were only 170 of them in Bradford, a mere 6 percent of the factory work force in town. Consequently, there is an air of unreality to most discussions of the factory proletarian that assume the existence of an adult male subject when, in fact, she was much more likely to have been a young child, a teenage girl, or increasingly, an adult woman too.[25]

Heavy reliance on child and female labor by the factories tells much about the nature of the new industrial labor process and its incompatibility with the character of the proletarianized male artisan. Millowners argued that the work of tending machinery, especially spinning machines, called for a measure of quickness and manual dexterity that young children and, to a lesser degree, women uniquely possessed. However, when pressed, other motives were often admitted and were clearly in evidence even when not openly avowed.[26]

In the first place, children, who, in 1833, earned an average of 4s. 6d.

[23] PP (1834, XX), 97–121; (1850, XXIII), 512, 609.
[24] The fullest expositions of this "optimist" view of the workers' standard of living can be found in F. A. Hayeck, ed., Capitalism and the Historians (Chicago, 1954); R. M. Hartwell's contributions to A. J. Taylor, ed., The Standard of Living in Britain during the Industrial Revolution (London, 1975); M. W. Flinn, "Trends in Real Wages, 1750–1850," Economic History Review, 27 (1974); and most recently, and most unequivocally, P. H. Lindert and J. G. Williamson, "English Workers' Living Standards During the Industrial Revolution: A New Look," Economic History Review, 36 (1983).
[25] Calculated from information in HO, 107/2,308; and PP (1834, XX), 97–121.
[26] Andrew Ure, The Philosophy of Manufactures (London, 1835).

per week in Bradford's factories, and adult women, who earned an average of 9s. 2d., provided a vast reservoir of cheap labor from which millowners could make profits in intensely competitive conditions by driving their labor costs unprecedentedly low. This overwhelming reliance on cheap child and female labor meant that, despite the illusion of high wages for adult men, the average weekly cost per worker to a factory master in 1833 was a mere 6.8s., and this for a seventy- to eighty-hour work week.[27]

In the second place, rural-born adult male workers from agricultural or artisanal backgrounds were generally unable to adapt to the routines and disciplines of ordinary factory labor, regulated not by the independent action of the worker, but by the impersonal pace and operation of the steam-powered machine. Children and women were regarded as more docile. Lacking the traditions and expectations of independent craftsmanship and long accustomed to a dependent status within the household, it was widely thought that they could be subordinated more satisfactorily to mindless and alienated forms of factory labor than stubborn, intractable, and undisciplined men. The demand of factory work for strict punctuality, the persistent lengthening of the working day, and the omnipresent supervision of the overlooker were all more readily enforced on women and children than on men.[28]

As Table 13-2 indicates, children constituted the majority of Bradford's industrial workers during the factory system's unregulated early days. The long hours to which they were forcibly subjected, often fourteen or more per day, were held to be particularly dangerous for children, who lacked the concentration and stamina to apply themselves incessantly with only two or three short breaks. The carelessness and exhaustion that resulted from such intense exploitation increased the rate of industrial accidents. These, indeed, were all too frequent around unfenced machinery that often lacked even the most elementary safety devices.[29]

Excessive heat and poor ventilation made the factory a breeding ground for chronic illness, whereas the habitual bodily motions required by the action of machinery caused permanent deformations in young eyes and limbs. Moreover, child labor gave too much authority to the overlooker, who could easily abuse his defenseless charges when the pressure of employer expectations made it clear that his job was to get results. Finally, there was an increasingly widespread belief that children, even from the most humble social backgrounds, were entitled to a better fate than virtual enslavement in a factory that provided poor training for becoming an adult.[30]

---

[27] Calculated from *PP* (1834, XX), 97–121.
[28] Thompson, *English Working Class*; Marx, *Capital*, 1:173–294.
[29] *PP* (1833, XXI), 22–3; (1834, XX), 97–121.
[30] *PP* (1833, XXI), 22–3; William Dodd, *The Factory System* (London, 1842), 34–56; Cudworth, *Industrial Classes*, 9–10.

Table 13-2. *Age and gender composition of worsted factory work force*

	1833 Bradford (%) (N = 3,627)	1838 United Kingdom (%) (N = 31,628)	1845 Yorkshire factory district (%) (N = 48,097)	1850 United Kingdom (%) (N = 79,737)
Children under 13	39	14	15	12
Children 13–17	29	46	31	33[a]
Women 18+	26	30[a]	42	36[a]
Men 18+	6	10	12	19[a]

[a]Estimate.

Sources: Calculated and compiled from *PP* (1834, XX), 97–121; (1845, XXV), 51–3; (1850, XXIII), 62–5; (1854–5, XV), 344; (1857, III), 1:76; (1868, XIV), 11–17; and John James, *History of the Worsted Manufactures in England* (London, 1857), 445, 487.

Although few would deny the general force of this argument, recent research into the cotton mills of Lancashire indicates the presence of certain mitigating features that tempered the extremity of the new industrial labor process and made possible the re-creation, within the walls of the factory, of at least some elements of more traditional patterns of work. In particular, the reliance on mule spinning during the initial period of mechanization, together with the early capitalists' lack of managerial initiative and expertise, entailed the employment of a class of relatively privileged male operatives who not only commanded relatively high wages and a significant degree of autonomy, but also subcontracted for most of the ordinary child and female operatives who assisted them in their work.[31] Although the latest studies cast doubt on Professor Smelser's striking claim that this system of sub-contracting made it possible, at least before the advent of larger mules in the 1820s, to re-create, within the walls of the factory, traditional familial structures of work, it is clear that the unusual arrangements that prevailed in Lancashire did soften the impact of proletarianization in even the most advanced forms of textile factory work.[32]

Nevertheless, in Bradford's worsted mills, where the mule had generally been bypassed by the less physically exhausting technology of throstle spinning, no male elite developed among the factory operatives. Indeed, except for a few supervisors, adult men were rarely hired by the early factory masters. Without a class of privileged workers to act as a buffer between management

[31] W. H. Lazonick, "Industrial Relations and Technical Change: The Case of the Self-Acting Mule," *Cambridge Journal of Economics*, 3 (1979); and, more broadly, Raphael Samuel, "The Workshop of the World: Hand Power and Steam Technology in Mid-Victorian Britain," *History Workshop Journal*, 3 (1977); Jonathan Zeitlin, "Social Theory and the History of Work," *Social History*, 8:3 (1983); and Charles Sabel and Jonathan Zeitlin, "Historical Alternatives to Mass Production: Politics, Markets and Technology in Nineteenth Century Industrialization," *Past and Present*, 108 (1985). Drawing on such instances of incomplete proletarianization, William Reddy has even gone so far as to contend that "no market for labor was ever created." By treating free-enterprise capitalism as an ideological "market culture" rather than an actual productive system, Reddy argues that it "created not a competitive labor market but a wide variety of distortions in the distribution of labor," bringing profits to entrepreneurs "not by increasing productivity, but by the adroit playing off of various categories of laborers against one another." *The Rise of Market Culture: The Textile Trade and French Society, 1750–1900* (Cambridge, 1984), 4, 9. Without minimizing the significance of the phenomena that Reddy points to, his attempt to deny the systemic reality of nineteenth-century capitalism simply because it fell short of an abstract ideal surely leads to even greater distortions and oversimplifications than the crude story of laissez-faire triumph that he so determinedly attacks.

[32] Neil Smelser, *Social Change in the Industrial Revolution* (Chicago, 1959), 185–93; M. M. Edwards and R. Lloyd Jones, "N. J. Smelser and the Cotton Factory Family: A Reassessment," in N. B. Harte and K. G. Ponting, eds., *Textile History and Economic History* (Manchester, 1973); Michael Anderson, "Sociological History and the Working Class Family: Smelser Revisited," *Social History*, 6 (1976).

and labor, Bradford's capitalists exercised much more direct control over the factory work process in which subcontracting was virtually unknown.[33] With the mechanization of weaving and combing during the thirties and forties, this radically routinized form of labor was further extended, thus making the fully proletarianized, homogenous, operative machine minder the paradigm for the textile work force as a whole.[34]

Of course, the advent of child labor legislation after 1833 did improve factory working conditions. Thereafter, the prohibition on employment for children under nine and the limitation of those under thirteen to eight hours per day gradually resulted in the hiring of more adolescents and adult females who remained legally unprotected until the 1847 Factory Act[35] (see Table

---

[33] James, *Worsted Manufacture*, 347, 548. For the differences between mule and throstle spinning and the implications for the labor process, see Julia de L. Mann, "The Textile Industry," in Charles Singer, E. J. Holmyard, A. R. Hall, and T. I. Williams, eds., *A History of Technology: The Industrial Revolution, 1750–1850*, (Oxford, 1958), 4:291; and Ure, *Philosophy of Manufactures*, 290, 331, 362, 366–8. In 1856, W. E. Forster also testified that subcontracting was not generally practiced anywhere in the worsted industry. *PP* (1856, XIII), 111, 113. As for the question of family labor, although it may have been practiced in the early, rural water mills, in the urban steam factories there is no evidence that it was ever the norm. Certainly, by 1851, among the 209 households headed by males whose wives and/or children were employed in factory work, in our working-class census population, in 89 percent of all cases, fathers or husbands were employed outside the factory. Indeed, only in a mere ten instances was there any evidence even to suggest the existence of a family working as a unit within the factory's walls. Calculated from information in HO, 107/2,308. Clearly, Bradford's worsted industrial economy gave little scope for the perpetuation of family-based production as it transferred and concentrated the authority hitherto exercised by a multitude of plebeian family patriarchs into the entrepreneurial capitalist's hands.

[34] Marx, *Capital*, 1: 351–475.

[35] Smelser, *Social Change*, 294; Derek Fraser, *The Evolution of the British Welfare State* (London, 1973), 21–2. In 1833, adolescents and women had each constituted only about a quarter of the factory work force. Thereafter, the proportion of adolescents quickly rose to a maximum of 46 percent in 1839 and then declined as adolescents were replaced by adult women who constituted 42 percent of the factory operatives in 1845. Of the worsted factory workers encountered in our 1851 census manuscripts population, 40 percent were adult women, 37 percent were adolescents, and only 10 percent were children under the age of thirteen. Calculated from *PP* (1834, XX), 97–121; (1845, XXV), 51–3; (1854–5, XV), 344; and HO, 107/2,308. During this period there was also a slight increase in the proportion of adult men, which rose from about 6 percent of all factory workers to somewhere between 13 and 19 percent by midcentury. This strongly indicates that, in sharp contrast to Lancashire, where the male mule spinners formed a separate "aristocratic" operative caste, in the early thirties, Bradford mills employed men only in supervisory capacities. Although the increased numbers brought male participation levels in the factory work force close to the levels that prevailed across the Pennines, most of these additional men were not specially privileged laborers but, except for a small minority of overlookers, were ordinary operatives who were hired to do the same kind of work as women and adolescents at only slightly higher rates of pay. For com-

13-2). Since women were paid somewhat more than young children (7 to 12s. for spinners and 10s. for power weavers and combers), this tendency toward feminization within the work force not only blunted the impact of the worst abuses of child exploitation, but also elevated the average operative wage.[36]

Perhaps for young, unmarried women fresh from the countryside, the chance to make comparatively high wages by working in the factory seemed like a desirable opportunity. Nevertheless, after a few years of routinized labor, when the young factory girl began to search for a husband and a home, matters looked different. From the domestic perspective of the would-be housewife, the advent of wage labor in the factory for women was inextricably connected with the proletarianization of the male handicraftsman she replaced. From the collective perspective of the working-class family, these two developments appeared less as complementary processes than as opposite sides of the same class trauma that individual laborers may have undergone separately in the workplace, but that the family unit experienced as a whole.

Proletarianization and the working-class family

Echoing the atomistic, entrepreneurial assumptions of nineteenth-century liberalism, most modern economic and even labor historians have treated workers as a collection of individuals, largely ignoring the significance of the family as a basic unit of working-class identity and life. Indeed, the implicit aim of the industrial-capitalist transformation was to penetrate traditional collectivities like the family, drawing their constituent members into a free-labor market that would supply those individuals specifically suited to employer demand. A glance at the age and gender structure of Bradford's midcentury population – disproportionately female and young – reveals the extent to which this market-created society distorted the natural biological norm.[37]

In part, this was a result of the overrepresentation of marginalized immigrants, particularly of young women and widows, who comprised 13 percent of the household heads in our 1851 working-class population. The industrial city was clearly becoming a magnet for "unattached" females throughout the region who were well suited to the new urban employments

---

parisons with the Lancashire cotton industry, see Frances Collier, *The Family Economy of the Working Classes in the Cotton Industry, 1784–1833* (New York, 1968), 54–92.

[36] Bowley, "Wages," 104, 105, 108; James, *Worsted Manufactures*, 445, 478.

[37] *PP* (1852–3, LXXXVIII), 2:672, 677; Theodore Koditschek "Class Formation and the Bradford Bourgeoisie" (Princeton, Ph.D. dissertation, 1981), 77–9.

and unable to function alone in the protoindustrial countryside.[38] Nevertheless, given the scale and pace of Bradford's urban-industrial revolution, an adequate work force could be assembled only by mobilizing the labor of the intact families in which the majority of the region's workers were contained. For the town to attract laborers on a permanent basis who would produce the next generation of their class, it would have to create a place, not only for economically desirable workers, but for the working-class family as a social institution that could perform the necessary nurturing and integrative roles.[39]

Moreover, the family was not only required by capital, but demanded by the workers themselves as they experienced with even greater intensity the traumas and uncertainties of urban-industrial living that had made the family so important to the new entrepreneurial bourgeoisie. Hence, although the proletarian family lacked the space afforded to its bourgeois counterpart and was more constrained by the market forces in which it was enmeshed, it loomed even larger in the lives of its members, who desperately clung to it as their primary source of protection and relief.[40]

Of the 524 households in the five working-class districts studied intensively through the 1851 census manuscripts, 72 percent contained intact nuclear families whereas only 6 percent consisted of entirely unrelated individuals possessing no apparent kinship bonds.[41] The family, then, was both the basic unit of working-class consumption and the fundamental repository of proletarian identity and life. Because it was the primary arena in which the contradictions between the economic imperatives and social needs of capitalism were framed, fashioned, and ultimately played out, it constitutes the first arena in which the full impact of proletarianization was felt.

In the traditional protoindustrial setting, the family had not only lived together, but usually worked together, ideally under the supervision of an adult male head. By contrast, in the urban-industrial environment that had emerged by midcentury, the family had ceased to be a viable unit of work.

---

[38] Calculated from information in HO, 107/2,308.

[39] For a recent collection of essays on this subject see David Levine, ed., *Proletarianization and Family History* (Orlando, Fla., 1984), as well as his "Industrialization and the Proletarian Family in England," *Past and Present*, 107 (1985). For a telling study of a comparable process in the late-nineteenth-century southern United States, see LeeAnn Whites, "Family, Gender and Labor Militancy: Textile Workers in Nineteenth Century Augusta, Georgia" (unpublished paper).

[40] Michael Anderson, *Family Structure in Nineteenth Century Lancashire* (Cambridge, 1971), 160, 171.

[41] Calculated from information in HO, 107/2,308. See Appendix B for a discussion of the methodology employed in collecting and analyzing this data.

Now, workers were hired and remunerated as individuals with little reference to their family situation or domestic needs.[42] Under these circumstances, the family could survive as a unit of consumption only when its members pooled their individual earnings and only insofar as there existed a congruence between the biological imperatives of human reproduction and the urban employment opportunities available to them.

By examining the employment patterns of family members in the 1851 census manuscripts and adding up estimates of the wages each received, it is possible to assess the degree to which collective family incomes were or were not adequate to support the level of domestic expenditure dictated by a given family's consumption needs. For this purpose, the consumption standards formulated by Seebohm Rowntree in his 1901 study of working-class poverty in York have been adapted to our Bradford data to distinguish those families whose income was insufficient to obtain a minimal subsistence from those who were able to live in a modicum of comfort and from those who stood somewhere in between.[43]

Among the 480 working-class households examined, at least under the conditions of full employment that prevailed in 1851, 75 percent were able to meet the minimal requirements for subsistence whereas 25 percent were not. However, in only 30 percent of the families was a level of material comfort attainable upon which a lifestyle of real respectability could be based. The remaining 45 percent, who lived barely above the margin of subsistence, were unable to exorcise the specter of poverty that chronically crimped their always fragile existence and made them catastrophically vulnerable to changes of fortune such as illness, unemployment, or a downturn in trade.

As Tables 13-3 and 13-4 indicate, there was, in most cases, a clear relationship between the domestic standard of a given family and the occupational status of its head. A significant majority of the families living in comfort were headed by skilled workers outside the handicrafts, while it was only among such families headed by such individuals that a majority (57 percent) could live above the comfort line. By contrast, the vast majority of the families consigned to irremediable poverty were headed either by wool-combers (46 percent) or unskilled laborers (31 percent), whereas families headed by skilled men constituted a scant 8 percent. Although extreme

---

[42] See footnote 33, this chapter, for evidence that Bradford's worsted capitalists generally hired workers as individuals rather than as family groups.

[43] B. S. Rowntree, *Poverty: A Study of Town Life* (New York, 1971), 136–43. For a full discussion of the methods used in the present study, see Appendix B. For purposes of comparison, it may be noted that Foster, *Class Struggles*, 96, reports family poverty levels of about 20 percent in Oldham, 25 percent in South Shields, and 33 percent in Northampton for the same period. Anderson's *Family Structure*, 31, reports an overall 1851 poverty level of about 20 percent in Preston.

Table 13-3. 1851 working-class census population: occupation of household heads by domestic status of family

	Families headed by skilled workers (N = 158)	Families headed by semiskilled workers (N = 81)	Families headed by woolcombers (N = 143)	Families headed by unskilled workers (N = 98)	All families (N = 480)
Percentage in poverty	6	22	39	39	25
Percentage barely above subsistence	37	45	52	47	45
Percentage in comfort	57	33	9	14	30

Source: Calculated from information collected in HO, 107/2308. See Appendix B.

Table 13-4. *1851 working-class census population: domestic status of family by occupation of household head*

	Families in poverty (N = 121)	Families marginally above subsistence (N = 215)	Families in comfort (N = 144)	All families (N = 480)
Percent skilled household heads	8	27	62	33
Percent semiskilled household heads	15	17	19	17
Percent woolcomber household heads	46	35	9	30
Percent unskilled	31	21	10	20

Source: Calculated from information collected in HO, 107/2308. See Appendix B.

poverty was the province of woolcomber- and unskilled-laborer-headed households, the majority (61 percent) of the families in these occupational categories were, by means we will examine shortly, able to drag themselves marginally above the minimum poverty line. Nevertheless, the occupation and income of the adult male breadwinner had a critical, if not the definitive, impact on the collective living standards of the family as a whole.[44]

Structural poverty was, therefore, in the first instance, a function of Bradford's peculiar employment structure. Had the local economy provided well-paid jobs in sufficient numbers to meet the demand of adult male household heads, poverty would have vanished virtually overnight. However, because the trend ran in the opposite direction, transforming the skilled well-paid work of the male worsted handicrafts into the cheap factory labor of women and adolescents, there emerged a deepening contradiction between the economic structure of capitalist industry and the domestic imperatives of the working-class family.

Yet this sense that the factory system spelled a crisis in the family was a product only of its final stage. Before the collapse of traditional handicrafts, the factory wages of women and children had constituted a valuable supplement to the earnings of the male breadwinner. Under these circumstances, the factory had often been deemed tolerable, even beneficial, despite the impersonal oppressive quality of its labor process and its tendency to disrupt

[44] Charles Booth, *Life and Labours of the People of London: First Series: Poverty* (New York, 1902), 1:33–50; Rowntree, *Poverty*, 152–80.

older patterns of team work.[45] Only when the factory ceased to be a supplementary mode of production and emerged as the dominant, increasingly the only, productive form, did the earnings of women and children become transmuted into bulwarks of the beleaguered family wage.

At various points throughout the forties, especially during the worst depression years, the *Observer* noted that "the best remunerated portion of the working classes in the Bradford district are children and young women ...those most out of employ and worst paid are male adults." The paper was forced to the lamentable conclusion that "the main dependence of multitudes of working families is on their females."[46] Yet as one unemployed woolcomber bitterly exclaimed, "Our factories can never be supplied with women and children without their being co-existing husbands and fathers, and these surely have a moral right to employment in the same locality." In fact, female and child labor was an inadequate compensation for the lack of employment opportunities for breadwinning men. "If the wives and children are to support the men in idleness, such a state of things would be fraught with danger to the entire factory population and sow the seeds of depravity and popular disturbance."[47]

Yet in the economic structure that capitalism was imposing, this was, more and more, becoming the case; for our census data demonstrate that, in every type of working-class family, dependence on the earnings of children and women was increasing. Although married women showed some resistance to entering the work force, children and other dependents were almost invariably sent out to the factory as soon as possible. Their earnings of 4 to 10s., though certainly meager, were enough to defray the expense of child maintenance and to provide a small surplus for the family. With several children, this began to add up. Of course, children only became an economic asset after they had reached employable age. As child labor laws and unwritten moral standards began to edge this threshold upward, the period

---

[45] Smelser, *Social Change*, 184–93. Anderson, *Family Structure*, 111–19. Edwards and Jones, "Smelser and the Cotton Factory Family," and Anderson, "Smelser Revisited," have criticized Smelser's specific arguments about changes in family work patterns among Lancashire cotton operatives and his efforts to link these to the emergence of working-class protest movements. The former argues, in a manner similar to this book, that it was probably the general impact of migration from the countryside to the city more than specific changes in factory technology that led to destabilizing structural change. In any case, although Smelser's specific argumentation and chronology may be questionable and his Parsonian analytical framework is clearly suspect, his examination of the impact of capitalist productive transformations on family relationships, ideologies, and social roles represents a pioneering exploration of an extremely important subject that subsequent work has insufficiently pursued.

[46] *BO*, Jan. 27, 1842.

[47] *BO*, Feb. 9, 1854.

when children constituted an economic burden tended to grow. Hence a critical determinant of the living standard of a given working-class family was its particular balance between income-producing children who could be sent to the factory and those who remained a drain on family resources because they were too young to work.[48] As Table 13-5 demonstrates, the biological position of a family in the life cycle was even more decisive than the occupational status of its breadwinner in dictating whether the family would fall below the minimum subsistence line.

During the initial (or final) life cycle stages of a marriage (LCS 1), when a childless couple lived alone, it was not too difficult to meet expenditures, especially if the wife was prepared to work. The birth of a child (LCS 2) did increase family expenditures, but Table 13-5 suggests that it was a situation with which most families could cope. It was the five- to ten-year period when two or more young children were present but before any had reached an employable age (LCS 3) that constituted a time of acute economic danger that every working-class family in Bradford, to some degree, faced. Deprived not only of the income of children, but usually of that of the young mother who was under great pressure to stay at home, the family was reduced to dependence on the earnings of the adult male breadwinner at the very moment when family expenses mounted. Not surprisingly, Table 13-5 indicates that during this period, 68 percent of all working-class families and 90 percent of all those with unskilled or woolcomber heads were chronically forced below the minimum poverty line. For a time thereafter (LCS 4), when the eldest child became eligible for employment, conditions only slightly eased as 58 percent of the families headed by woolcombers or unskilled laborers remained below the poverty line. Of all the families in poverty in the population measured, 52 percent were in these two specific life cycle stages and 76 percent had young children under ten.[49]

This natural life cycle had a leveling impact, threatening nearly every working-class family in Bradford with structural impoverishment at this stage. When the breadwinner's earnings were declining or erratic, years of destitution were an almost inescapable fate. However, even the families of the skilled and well-remunerated found this period difficult. Twenty-nine percent of the families headed by skilled workers in our census sample found themselves reduced to poverty during LCS 3, and this accounted for 70 percent of all the households headed by skilled workers that were impoverished. More significantly, the proportion of their households that lived in comfort, 57 percent for the entire population, was only 25 percent for those in LCS 3. Through the universal impact of this phase in the life cycle, the

---

[48] See Anderson, *Family Structure*, 31.
[49] Compare with Anderson, *Family Structure*, 31–2; Foster, *Class Struggle*, 97–9.

Table 13-5. 1851 working-class population: life cycle stages by domestic status of family

	LCS 1[a] (N = 49)	LCS 2[b] (N = 45)	LCS 3[c] (N = 68)	LCS 4[d] (N = 45)	LCS 5[e] (N = 126)	LCS 6[f] (N = 116)	LCS 7[g] (N = 30)
Percentage of families in poverty	12	11	68	38	19	8	40
Percentage barely above subsistence	37	64	23	42	56	46	33
Percentage in comfort	51	25	9	20	25	46	27

[a]LCS 1 = married couple alone.
[b]LCS 2 = family with one child ten or under.
[c]LCS 3 = family with two or more children ten or under.
[d]LCS 4 = family with children ten or under plus one child over ten.
[e]LCS 5 = family with children ten or under plus two or more children over ten.
[f]LCS 6 = families with all children or relations over ten.
[g]LCS 7 = single individuals with no coresident family.
Source: Calculated from information collected in HO, 107/2308. See Appendix B.

contradictions of proletarianization were visibly expressed, revealing, for all to see, the incompatibility between the economic structure of capitalist industry and the imperatives of human reproduction and family life.

Yet if this middle stage of the life cycle underscored the tyranny of capitalism over the needs of the family, the same life cycle, in its later stages, reinforced the family's role as the most important institution in which workers protected themselves from the traumas of the marketplace by pooling their resources for collective relief. During LCS 5, as more children grew old enough to enter the work force, prospects for the entire family improved. Finally, for the families (LCS 6) containing coresident children, all of whom were over the age of ten, the same forces that had hitherto spelled economic dysfunction now afforded considerable relief.[50] According to Table 13-5, 92 percent of all the working-class families in this life cycle stage lived above the minimum poverty line whereas 46 percent passed beyond the threshold of comfort. Because they drew on a multitude of income sources, such families found themselves less dependent on the earning power of the breadwinner than any other family type. Indeed, in LCS 6, 86 percent of all the households headed by woolcombers or unskilled laborers were able to stay above the poverty line, whereas among the few households of this kind that lived in comfort, 60 percent were located in this life cycle stage.[51]

By pooling resources in this multiincome family in which most of the members were able to work, they could achieve a higher living standard collectively than any of them could have obtained alone. Individually, wages might be inadequate; together they began to add up. Parents obtained financial aid from their children, whereas children were spared the costly necessity of lodgings as long as they remained under the parental roof. The popularity of this arrangement is attested by the numbers, which reveal that 51 percent of all the working-class families in the 1851 census sample were LCS 5 and 6 families of this type. In many instances, children did not leave home immediately after they passed adolescence but continued to live with their parents as long as they remained single.

So effective was this multiincome family structure that it not only strengthened the nuclear family, but provided opportunities to enlist the force of wider kinship solidarity even beyond the nuclear core. Extended families accounted for 21 percent of all the working-class families in the census sample, although in LCS 5 and 6, which contained 83 percent of them, they accounted for 34 percent of the total. These figures suggest that this relatively

---

[50] Ibid.
[51] Calculated from information collected in HO, 107/2,308.

large, multiincome family could not only draw on extended kinship resources but could meet a variety of wider family needs. Perhaps most important were the possibilities for supporting aged or infirm parents or grandparents who were no longer able to fend for themselves. Such individuals were found in 6 percent of all working-class families, 71 percent of them in LCS 5 and 6. More common was a collateral arrangement whereby siblings continued coresiding even after one or more of them had formed their own family. These accounted for 8 percent of all working-class families in the census sample and 13 percent of those in LCS 5 and 6. Finally, the extended family could be used as an agency of social integration, as nieces, nephews, and cousins, usually from the countryside, were sheltered by relatives when they first came to town. Nevertheless, with such individuals in only 6 percent of all working-class households and 11 percent of those in LCS 5 and 6, the Bradford data suggest that other writers who have emphasized this phenomenon may have overestimated its significance.[52]

Clearly, families that could maximize the proportion of members who were employable could do a great deal to improve their collective living standards and to deepen the foundations of their domestic base. Nevertheless, even under conditions of full employment, a majority of these families still lived below the level of real comfort. Moreover, working-class efforts to maximize collective family incomes often succeeded only at a very high domestic cost.

These costs were most visible when not only children and dependents, but wives and domestic managers were sent out to waged work. Thirty-six percent of all married women in the 1851 working-class census population were listed as holding outside employment, and there was a clear correlation, at least when husbands' wages were inadequate, between the willingness of the wife to enter the work force and the ability of the family to keep above the poverty line. Among the woolcomber- or unskilled-laborer-headed households, which were most vulnerable, 42 percent remained in chronic poverty even when the wife took outside employment, but 57 percent were in poverty when she did not.[53] Inevitably, these families saw married women's employment as a trade-off in which greater prospects of economic security were being purchased at the expense of the housewife, whose extra burden

[52] Compare with Anderson, *Family Structure*, 43–56, 155–6; Foster, *Class Struggle*, 98; Alan Armstrong, *Stability and Change in an English County Town: A Social Study of York, 1801–51* (Cambridge, 1974), 188.

[53] Calculated from information collected in HO, 107/2,308. Compare with Anderson's finding for Preston of a 27 percent work force participation rate for married women. *Family Structure*, 73.

as wage laborer impeded her ability to perform her unpaid domestic role. Few working-class family strategies incurred greater bourgeois notice or hostility than this. As the Vicar William Scoresby argued: "No woman with a young family can possibly do justice to them whilst working abroad. Nay, no married woman can make her husband really comfortable and keep his home respectable while working herself as a factory operative."[54]

Of course, such judgments were oblivious to the realities of working-class poverty and failed to recognize that most married women worked out of necessity and not choice. Moreover, married women's employment provided, at best, a very crude measure of domestic inadequacy since domestic burdens varied considerably depending on a household's composition and size. Some households had no housewife, whereas in others, someone else performed her role. However, if we assume that any household with three or more members should have had a full-time homemaker, then the census data reveals that, in 37 percent of such cases, they did not.[55]

Of course, with a 31 percent poverty rate among the three-plus-member households that opted for the luxury of sound domestic management, as compared with the 16 percent among those that did not, it is not difficult to understand why so many working-class families rejected the advice of men like Scoresby and sent their primary homemaker out to work.[56] It is true, as bourgeois commentators occasionally argued, that the benefits to the family of a full-time housekeeper – better child care, greater cleanliness, more careful budgeting, the availability of homemade clothing and home-cooked food – represented not merely qualitative advantages, but services whose value could be calculated in monetary terms. Nevertheless, their conclusion that the disadvantages of married women's employment exceeded the value of her wage even in purely financial terms, though perhaps true at higher levels of consumption, did not hold for a working-class family on the margins of poverty that needed a wife's wages simply to eat and live.[57]

There can be no doubt that the prevalence of married women in Bradford's work force contributed much to preventing structural poverty from becoming even more widespread. That it also promoted domestic squalor, increased infant mortality, and exacerbated environmental decay is simply a

---

[54] William Scoresby, *American Factories and their Female Operatives* (London, 1845), 118.

[55] In a further 4 percent of the households with one homemaker, the presence of nine or more residents suggests the need for more. Calculated from information collected in HO, 107/2,308.

[56] Ibid.

[57] See discussion in Margaret Hewitt, *Wives and Mothers in Victorian Industry* (London, 1958); Standish Meacham, *A Life Apart; The English Working Class, 1890–1914* (Cambridge, Mass., 1977), 95–115.

measure of the price that industrial capitalism exacted from many working-class families in exchange for a sufficiency on which to live.[58]

Not only did the hyperexploitation of working-class women and children purchase family subsistence at great material cost. It also engendered a psychological challenge to traditional age and gender roles. As more family members spent longer hours away in the workplace, patterns of consumption and leisure began to follow the locus of production, gradually shifting away from the household and reestablishing themselves along gender and peer-group lines. Once the family ceased to work together and the wife and children became subjected to outside discipline and control, the patriarchal authority of the male *paterfamilias* seemed to be seriously jeopardized.

So, at least, thought many bourgeois commentators, and this moral and cultural aspect of the proletarian family crisis, much more than the economic trauma of structural poverty, became the focus of widespread contemporary concern. Even a radical like Friedrich Engels, who scarcely neglected the physical hardship that resulted when adult men were reduced to depending on the meager earnings of their wives and children, was particularly struck by the "reversal in the normal division of labor in the family" that this caused. By thus turning unemployable men "virtually into eunuchs," industrial capitalism undermined the paternal authority on which traditional social relations had stood.[59]

To conservatives, who deemed paternalism within the family to be the foundation of all social order, these challenges to traditional age and gender relationships were the occasion for considerable alarm. To Parson Bull, a system that removed women and adolescent girls from the kitchen to the factory was inimical to the most elementary requirements of domestic life. "Domestic duties," he insisted, "cannot be learned; all that is necessary to cottage economy and the character of a good housewife, it is nearly impossible to acquire."[60] To turn women into free economic agents as wage laborers was not only inconsistent with their primary function as homemakers, but tempted them to abandon the underlying "feminine" values of self-sacrifice upon which private domestic life would ultimately depend. Men might safely succumb to the values of individualism by seeking "perfect freedom" to pursue their own interests, but when women evidenced this kind of behav-

---

[58] LeeAnn Whites, "Southern Ladies and Millhands: Class Politics and the Domestic Economy; Augusta, Georgia, 1870–90" (Irvine, Ph.D. dissertation, 1982).

[59] Engels, *Condition of the Working Class*, 180–6. See also the discussion in Barbara Taylor, *Eve and the New Jerusalem, Socialism and Feminism in the Nineteenth Century* (New York, 1983), 111–14.

[60] *Letters and Speeches on Restricting the Hours of Children and Young Persons in Mills and Factories* (London, 1833), 18; Cudworth, *Industrial Classes*, 8–9.

ior, it was deemed "unfavorable to the formation of a delicate female character."[61]

Similarly, child labor, when systematically fostered by economic imperatives and sanctioned officially with the force of law, was thought to have a debilitating effect on the family, raising the specter of a new proletarian generation whose members, of both genders, would scorn every form of authority and would reject the claims of all social bonds:

> Parents of Bradford how say you? Do you consent that your little girls and boys when a day older than thirteen shall be held in the eyes of the law as independent of you? Is it for *your* comfort? Is it for their good? Will it mend their morals? Will it strengthen the bonds which hold society together? Oh worse than madness thus to strike at the very *root* of all social order and to spread the seed of anarchy and confusion all around.[62]

This exaggerated lamentation failed to recognize the resiliency of the working-class family in resisting the economic distortions that it faced. As we have seen, most working-class housewives continued to stay at home whenever economically feasible, and although cases could be found of adolescents abandoning their parents, the census data reveal many more instances in which they continued to live with and help support their families long after coming of age. Given the enduring power of custom and the powerful economic incentives to preserve traditional family forms, any tendencies within capitalism to undermine patriarchy had only a limited effect on the way working-class families actually functioned.[63]

However, there was another way in which the economic logic of capitalism penetrated the household that, if it did not dramatically strike at the heart of the nuclear family, blurred its boundaries in subtle ways; for kinship alone was inadequate to recruit an industrial work force and, lacking family connections, many young working-class immigrants were forced to lodge with strangers, at least for a few years. In 1846, a survey of 12,000 female workers in ninety-eight firms showed that 83 percent of these women were unmarried and approximately 10 percent were living in lodgings usually in the poorer sections of town. Our census survey of these areas suggests that lodging was even more widespread. Lodgers constituted 25 percent of all workers in the districts that were studied and well over 30 percent of all young adults.[64] "Oh," exclaimed an anxious Vicar Scoresby, "how many an

---

[61] *BO*, Jan. 14, 1847.

[62] *Proceedings of a Public Meeting of the People of Bradford on the Ten Hours Bill* (Bradford, 1833), 13.

[63] Anderson, *Family Structure*, 120–32, 160; Meacham, *A Life Apart*, 116–21.

[64] *BO*, Oct. 8, 1846; Jan. 14, 1847; and calculated from information in HO, 107/2,308.

amiable and interesting girl has come into this town of Bradford having the respect of all who knew her at home, falling into bad hands – a bad lodging house – has in a short time become a wretched depraved creature, ruined in body and soul."[65]

Yet if the vicar had investigated the matter more thoroughly, he might have saved his breath, for the lodgers in our census population were not usually concentrated in flophouses but were distributed among 178 residences, mostly otherwise normal working-class households that took in one or two lodgers to help make ends meet. In fact, 36 percent of all the working-class families in these districts took in lodgers, and 53 percent of all the lodgers lived in households that took in three or less. Only 25 percent lived in places that were primarily lodging establishments, housing six or more at once.[66] These results suggest that lodging, so far from dissolving family structures, reflected the primacy of familial social organization and was generally built on a nuclear family base. Nevertheless, as a relationship based on economic calculation, lodging also underscored the ways in which the whole family relationship depended not only on love and patriarchy, but on the economic self-interest of individual members.[67] For the family, taking lodgers was no act of charity, but one more strategy for raising its collective income. Yet in exacerbating overcrowding and further increasing the domestic responsibilities of the housewife lodging, as in the case of women's and children's employment, brought in cash at a substantial social and environmental cost.[68]

Thus the experience of the working-class family under the impact of proletarianization evoked a complex and multifaceted response. Although the logic of industrial capitalism transformed traditional familial structures and relationships almost beyond recognition, the urban working-class family not only survived, but emerged as the most important and universal welfare agency through which workers coped with their traumas. Scarred and distorted by the strains of proletarianization, the family became an arena for the formulation of new collective strategies as workers who found themselves individually vulnerable pooled resources to make ends meet. In practice, the results of these family strategies were mixed. They could be effective only at certain stages in the life cycle and often brought in income at a substantial domestic cost. Most importantly, however, their success also depended on a whole range of external circumstances that were entirely beyond any family's control. Death, illness, or sudden unanticipated expenses could wreak

---

[65] *BO*, June 24, 1847.

[66] Calculated from information in HO, 107/2,308.

[67] Compare with Anderson's findings for Preston, where 23 percent of all households took in lodgers. Anderson, *Family Structure*, 46.

[68] Foster, *Class Struggle*, 96–9.

havoc on the fragile domestic economy and send a family that had hitherto enjoyed subsistence, or even security, plunging below the poverty line.

In particular, the spells of unemployment that came during commercial recessions often destroyed any fragile foundations of prosperity that a family might have painstakingly built up. Because they are based on the circumstances of virtually full employment that prevailed throughout the 1851 census year, the measures of poverty considered heretofore indicate the lower limits of structural pauperization and provide no insight into the full extent of destitution during the worst depression years. Since depressions were becoming increasingly frequent and devastating as the international worsted market grew more volatile, extensive, and complex, it is safe to assume that, for most of the 1825–50 period, far fewer than 30 percent of Bradford's working-class families lived in comfort and far more than 25 percent sank beneath the poverty line. Exact numbers cannot be determined, but no account of proletarianization can afford to ignore these increasingly frequent and devastating periods, 1824–6, 1837–42, and 1846–49, when a majority of Bradford's workers and their families were temporarily reduced to the levels of destitution and degradation that the hapless handicraftsman endured as a permanent fate.

Primary poverty: the economic crisis of the capitalist trade cycle

Commercial recession had always haunted the region's worsted work force. But only in 1824 did the scourge of industrial overproduction replace that of agrarian harvest failure as the central component in an economic crisis that generated mass poverty locally for the next two years. A softening of foreign demand in the aftermath of a major strike left the worsted industry vulnerable. A series of dramatic bank failures then led to an implosion in production and trade. By 1826, wages and employment levels had plummeted, and the costs of poor relief had risen by 83 percent.[69] "A dreadful change," according to the *Bradford Courier*, "has been wrought as regards the working classes; one by one their little luxuries, their comforts, their necessities have been lopped off, until even bare subsistence has become the boon of charity."[70]

As devastating as this depression was, its sudden impact was, nevertheless, somewhat mitigated by the fact that it took place in an environment that was

[69] David Ashforth, "The Poor Law in Bradford, 1834–71" (Bradford, Ph.D. dissertation, 1979), 23.
[70] *Bradford Courier*, Apr. 13, 1826.

not yet fully urbanized and in which some vestiges of the cottage economy still remained. Its worst ravages, in fact, occurred not in the town center, but in outlying weaving villages such as Idle, where, in 1826, one-seventh of the population was on relief.[71] Although many of these weavers never recovered from the depression, other workers, particularly those drawn into the expanding occupations of the industrializing city, experienced the late twenties and midthirties as eras of relative opportunity. Between 1831 and 1833, this recovery was momentarily interrupted by a slump, which does not appear to have been particularly damaging except to the handloom weavers who were already under structural duress. Then, between 1834 and 1836, with the introduction of new products and processes, Bradford's industrial output spectacularly rose. Now the trade cycle seemed to be turning in the workers favor with its waves of urban development and economic growth. In 1835, the Bradford Savings Bank reported £40,000 on deposit in small accounts, £12,000 of which had come in during the previous year.[72] Yet the new employment possibilities that industrial Bradford afforded also lured the region's workers ever deeper into the proletarian nexus, deepening their dependence on the capitalist labor market as rural poverty and urban opportunity during the period of prosperity induced them to move their families into the town.

This dramatically increased the vulnerability of Bradford's workers in 1837, when worsted markets suddenly became dangerously glutted and a sharp economic downturn ensued. As in 1825, tight markets led to widespread unemployment and wage cuts, particularly in the textile handicrafts, in which the position of the worker was especially dire. However, unlike the depression of 1824–6, that which began in May 1837 marked the beginning of a protracted subsistence crisis that, as Chapter 3 indicated, dragged on through seven of the next eleven years.[73] As early as February 1838, the *Observer* reported, "Hundreds are literally pining for the means of subsistence . . . poverty, with its gaunt and haggard form, stalks along our streets and crosses our path . . . we may yet have to suffer the anguish and disgrace of men and women dying of starvation, unless something be done."[74]

The depressions of 1837–43 and 1847–9 differed from their predecessors not only in their depth and duration, but because they occurred in an urban rather than a rural setting, which made their worst consequences harder to escape. Between 1835 and 1839, the price of bread rose by 80 percent in

---

[71] Ashforth, "Poor Law in Bradford," 37.
[72] Cudworth, *Industrial Classes*, 37; P. H. J. H. Gosden, *Self-Help, Voluntary Associations in Nineteenth Century Britain* (London, 1973), 207–25.
[73] *BO*, May 25, June 1, 8, 15, 20, 1837.
[74] *BO*, Feb. 15, 1838.

Bradford, from 39s. 4d. to 70s. 8d. per quarter.[75] Since the majority of the town's workers were now recent immigrants from the countryside, they suddenly found themselves facing the twin traumas of unemployment and high food prices without the cushion of even the meagerest subsistence plot. Now, as depression struck them in the city, they found themselves to be completely vulnerable, without either the material or cultural resources of an established community to sustain them until prosperity returned. "They had come to the town from distant parts," Parson Bull explained, "because work was plentiful and, of course, until they had learnt their trade they did not earn much, and therefore, could not save: they were, many of them, frugal and industrious and some of them were truly religious young men."[76]

Given the enormity of the crisis that confronted them, it was doubtful whether either prayers or savings would have sufficed to see these workers through. Between 1838 and 1843, the labor market progressively tightened as the number of registered paupers and local Poor Law expenditures virtually doubled.[77] Although the handicraft workers were always first and worst affected, mass unemployment soon engulfed their wives and children in the dynamic factory sector, particularly in 1842 as slow markets and bulging inventories forced industrialists to cut production. In February 1842, 25 percent of the horsepower in Bradford Township was idle and only twenty-two of the thirty-six mills were operating full time. Ten mills were on short time and four had shut down.[78]

Not surprisingly, this distress within the town's staple industry spread to other sectors of the urban economy and drew other trades into the vortex of recession. Skilled crafts associated with textile production such as wool-sorting began to suffer high levels of unemployment whereas machinists were forced to accept wage cuts of 15 to 50 percent as a third of their number were thrown out of work. A deep slump in construction undermined the hitherto privileged status of masonry and building workers whereas belt-tightening among the rest of the urban population hurt the skilled artisans within the traditional consumer-goods crafts.[79] In the winter of 1841/2, when cyclical depression was compounded by winter cold and seasonal slack, it was estimated that two-fifths of Bradford's work force was without employment; as the *Observer* noted with alarm and dismay, "Skillful men formerly earning 24 to 30s. per week are now, in many cases, jobbing or breaking stones or dependent on their wives' and children's earnings."[80]

[75] Cudworth, *Industrial Classes*, 50.
[76] *BO*, June 1, 1837.
[77] Cudworth, *Industrial Classes*, 27; Ashforth, "Poor Law in Bradford," 158.
[78] *BO*, Feb. 3, 1842.
[79] *BO*, Jan. 27, 1842; Reach, *Textile Districts*.
[80] *BO*, Jan. 27, 1842.

Like the operation of the family cycle, the further blurring of distinctions between skilled and unskilled workers that the spread of unemployment and depression caused did much to foster a widespread sense of common griev-ance upon which classwide movements could arise. In such periods, all workers suffered together as the special skills and sectional privileges of the labor aristocracy were, at least temporarily, rendered useless by the great cataclysm that threatened to swallow everyone up. This sense that the crisis was becoming intolerable spread even beyond the working class. Faced with rising poor rates and dwindling customers, many small retailers were drawn up into its vortex too. As the *Observer* noted in July: "Amongst the most remarkable signs of the times are shopkeepers' meetings. The disease which has so long been preying upon the great body of the people has worked its way upwards and has now fairly laid hold of the middle classes."[81]

By the end of the summer, as the workers were closing down the factories, many small property owners were defaulting on their rates. Had depression persisted, there is no telling what might have happened. However, trade improved in the spring of 1843, and during the next two years, Bradford's staple industry grew more rapidly than at any other time in the history of the town. In September 1844, the *Observer* felt confident enough to edito-rialize on the "splendid appearance of the working classes in Bradford," remembering, as though it were ancient history, that "in 1842 every poor man's back was covered with rags."[82]

However, when this feverish boom was followed by the inevitable bust in early 1846, workers again lost their jobs in droves. In March the large firm of Rouse and Company suspended operations, and by April, fourteen hundred families were destitute. Although there was no further economic hemorrhaging, conditions did not improve during the rest of the year, and in early 1847, another deterioration occurred. In February, the number of registered paupers rose to 14,427, and poor rates climbed steadily upward to £40,000, or double the level of 1845. By December, most machinery was reported operating only two days per week, and 10 percent of the population received outdoor relief.[83] In the spring of 1848, the continental revolutions forestalled an expected trade improvement, and by May 18, worsted sales had virtually been reduced to a standstill. For the third consecutive year, hunger and unemployment haunted the urban-industrial working class. The factory inspector estimated that one-third of Bradford's machinery lay idle. Never within his recollection had "the state of the [worsted] manufacturing districts [been] so bad."[84]

---

[81] *BO*, July 7, 14, 1842.
[82] *BO*, Sep. 19, 1844; Mar. 19, 1846.
[83] *BO*, Jan. 15, Feb. 26, Mar. 5, 12, 1846; Nov. 18, 25, Dec. 2, 16, 1847.
[84] *BO*, Mar. 30, Apr. 13, May 18, June 22, 1848. Even as late as September 1848, fifteen

As in 1842, the collapse of the worsted trade resulted in a severe depression for the entire urban economy. This time, the problem was compounded by the presence of desperate Irish, who had recently escaped starvation in their native land. With nowhere to go and no hope of obtaining employment, these men and women were reduced to vagrancy, begging by day and sleeping on the street at night. Of course, vagrancy was scarcely a new problem in Bradford, and complaints of widespread begging had accompanied every depression, at least since 1839.[85] As long as rural poverty forced paupers out of the countryside, they would continue to arrive in the manufacturing towns whether or not there was work available. Indeed, some rural parishes appear to have been dumping their own paupers on the town.[86] By 1846–7, the combination of famine in Ireland and depression in Bradford led to scenes unlike any witnessed before. In November 1846, according to the *Observer:* "The town literally swarms with beggars at present, many of them evidently newly arrived from the sister isle. It is not uncommon in some parts of town to have a call from three dozen of them in one day."[87]

As with working-class distress in general, the problem of vagrancy manifested itself most dangerously during the cold winter months when lack of adequate food, heat, and shelter spelled illness and death for the victim and the threat of epidemic for the community at large. In 1848, a vagrant office was temporarily established to provide nightly accommodation and to isolate cases of smallpox and typhus before the disease could spread. However, because these quarters became so overcrowded, they may actually have disseminated the fever more widely.[88]

The appearance of these deep and increasingly frequent depressions, during an era of expanding labor supply, adversely affected the market position of the worker, undermining his bargaining position during the moment of crisis without fully restoring his situation when prosperity returned. Although wages and employment levels might quickly recover, general working conditions usually did not. Lengthening hours and speed-up were, indeed, the hallmarks of brief boom interludes, when capitalists scrambled to maximize profits and workers strove to dig themselves out of debt.[89] So far from being harbingers of freedom and autonomy, such interludes of full employment actually intensified exploitation and increased dependence on wage labor.

mills and fifteen warehouses with a rateable value of £11,853 were reported to be unoccupied. Cudworth, *Industrial Classes*, 28.

[85] *BO*, Sep. 19, 1839; June 16, 1842.

[86] *BO*, Feb. 17, 1848.

[87] *BO*, Nov. 26, 1846.

[88] Ashforth, "Poor Law in Bradford," 244–55.

[89] Karl Marx, *Early Writings* (New York, 1963), 73–5; *Capital*, 1: 579–80.

This intensified subordination of labor to capital, both in good years and in bad, was most alarmingly reflected in the rapid proliferation of "truck" forms of payment, which a parliamentary commission documented in 1841. Although partial or full payment of wages in goods had been common before 1815, industrialization, urbanization, and the spread of regional trade and banking seemed, initially, to be wiping it out. Several Bradford witnesses testified that, during the midthirties, the truck system had been all but unknown. Six years later, it had become widespread among the smaller manufacturers and not uncommon even among large ones.[90]

Since the amount of currency in circulation did not diminish and the number of shopkeepers and service entrepreneurs substantially increased, none of the traditional causes of truck payment can explain its revival during these years. All the commission witnesses agreed that the source of this trend was the new entrepreneurs' inordinate quest for profit and the deterioration in the competitive position of the urban working class. As Squire Autey explained, using grossly overvalued goods to pay their workers enabled manufacturers effectively to reduce real wages by 25 percent.[91] In addition, the capitalist could add the normal shopkeeper's profit to the surplus he extracted within production. Since goods could readily be obtained on credit, truck payment enabled the small but ambitious and undercapitalized businessmen to extend his operations almost at will. Indeed, during gluts, when manufacturers could not unload their products on the market, some reportedly paid their workers not only in food and clothing, but in the devalued worsted stuffs that they could not sell.[92]

Although such practices were illegal, they could be highly lucrative. They permitted struggling young entrepreneurs to keep their heads above water in the face of stiff competition, even during the worst depression years. Even though many capitalists disapproved of such practices, they were under enormous pressure to avoid being undersold by those who did. Under duress, even a large and respectable firm like Turner and Mitchell began to pay in goods.[93] Workers could not refuse employment under these conditions as long as work became increasingly "hardish to get.... There are hundreds without work," one operative explained to the committee, "and it is almost impossible for a man thrown out of work if he is once off, unless you have a friend to intercede for you."[94]

Employees did not need to be forced to accept their wages in kind. They simply understood that to insist on their legal right to money payment would

[90] PP (1842, IX), 1, 5, 27; Cudworth, *Industrial Classes*, 87–9.
[91] PP (1842, IX), 1.
[92] Ibid., 23–4.
[93] Ibid.
[94] Ibid., 24.

quickly leave them without a job. Anyone who made accusations against an employer would find himself blacklisted throughout the region. "I know what will cure this truck system," exclaimed one manufacturer who regretted its prevalence, "a good trade – a man, when he works for one master that pays in goods, he will soon leave him and go to a man where he could have money."[95] However, during the late thirties and forties, Bradford's workers did not have this choice. Faced with recurrent depressions, technological unemployment, and a supply of labor that was growing much faster than the pool of jobs, they were obliged to accept work wherever they could find it, at any wage, on any terms.

Secondary poverty: the environmental crisis of urban housing and health

The new forms of poverty and exploitation that proletarianization in the workplace had wrought were exacerbated by being experienced within an urban environment that lacked the mitigating features that had cushioned the full force of capitalist penetration in the protoindustrial countryside before 1815. As we have seen, the urban environment, in an almost un-mediated fashion, translated the class inequalities that industrial capitalism generated into material, consumption terms. Since urbanization developed without regulation, it transposed with remarkable accuracy the economic immiseration of the proletarianizing process, declining wages, labor inten-sification, and periodic unemployment into poor housing, domestic squalor, and unsanitary overcrowding as well as epidemic contagion and chronic ill health.

In the first place, working-class poverty obliged builders responding to market forces to construct extremely high-density housing, which crammed 21 percent of the town's poorest inhabitants into slum settlements that comprised only 1 percent of the borough's space.[96] The typical two-room (one up, one down) back-to-back cottages characteristic of these areas pro-moted extreme overcrowding even when occupied by a single family. Fre-quently, however, families of woolcombers or unskilled laborers who could not afford the 2 to 3s. weekly rental were forced to take lodgers or to dou-ble up.[97]

An 1845 survey of 81 woolcomber dwellings with 631 inhabitants showed how miserable conditions could be even in a relatively prosperous year. In

---

[95] Ibid., 26.
[96] *BO*, June 12, 1845.
[97] Cudworth, *Industrial Classes*, 57–8; Reach, *Textile Districts*.

one small patch of Millbank, thirty-three people shared seven beds, and in Thompson's buildings, the average bedroom of 17 × 15 feet housed eight residents in two beds. Although these are the worst cases, the average was hardly much better with 4.4 people per room and 3.6 to each bed.[98] The scenes inside these hovels were almost indescribable, although the report's compilers did their best. Investigators entering the Leys gave "a revolting description of the crowded state of the houses and sleeping apartments, and the mode in which both sexes lie huddled together, regardless of morality or decency." In Nicholson's buildings, "a man, his wife, and four children together with his mother lie on one bed." In the Club houses, a pregnant woman lay in the same room with various men, "exposed to their gaze." A dead child was laid in the same room.[99]

Although life in the slum cottages was grim enough, their inhabitants were better off than those who could afford only the cellar apartments underneath. These dark, damp holes, sometimes as much as ten feet below the surface, were inhabited chiefly by the families of woolcombers and recently settled Irish. To make matters worse, some combers worked in the room where their family ate and slept. Sixty-one such households were reported by the investigators containing 205 domestic workers, an average of 3.4 per household.[100]

Of course, not all workers were reduced to such squalor, and those who could afford to rent a whole cottage, even in the worst districts, were likely to find themselves considerably better off. Moreover, by the forties, more spacious terrace houses in newer, socially mixed residential neighborhoods (see Figure 4–3) were being constructed, permitting greater comfort and domestic amenity for those who could afford the 4 to 7s. weekly rental.[101] Nevertheless, the deepening troughs of depression and unemployment, combined with the life cycle's danger years, compelled even the most skilled and best paid workers to confront the possibility that increasing family size or unemployment might drive them back into the slums. Moreover, urban squalor, though ultimately caused by inadequate wages, became an ecological force in itself, exacerbating the environmental effects of proletarianization and extending them to everyone who had the misfortune to live downtown.

As we have seen, the demographic onslaught of the 1840s, which brought 37,063 new inhabitants during a period when only 5,100 new houses were

[98] *BO*, June 6, 1845; C. Richardson, "Irish Settlement in Mid-Nineteenth Century Bradford," *Yorkshire Bulletin of Social and Economic Research*, 20:1 (1968), 49.

[99] *BO*, June 12, 1845. For a description of working-class housing and interior furnishing during the 1830s, before mass poverty and overcrowding reached its peak, see Cudworth, *Industrial Classes*, 54–8.

[100] *BO*, June 12, 1845; Reach, *Textile Districts*.

[101] Engels, *Condition of Working Class*, 80; Cudworth, *Industrial Classes*, 58.

built, created, for the first time, a situation in which the supply of urban housing stock fell behind effective demand. As overall residential densities shot up from 5.1 per house in 1831 to 5.5 in 1851, all workers faced a housing shortage. With the rents inflated above market levels, everyone had to devote a disproportionate share of their income to housing. Taking in lodgers to compensate for overpriced housing only made overcrowding worse. Possessing little market incentive to keep up their properties, landlords often became willing accomplices in the process of urban decay. During depressions, the housing shortage was further magnified, as declining incomes forced families to huddle together. In 1842, notwithstanding the dearth of dwellings, one in ten was reported to be empty due to the eviction of tenants for nonpayment of rent.[102] According to the *Observer*, "hundreds of families have had their homes broken up, their means of comfort annihilated and their members scattered, as they are crowded together twenty or thirty persons in a house."[103]

Hence the threats to the stability of the working-class family initiated by its changing relationship to the labor market were reinforced by environmental conditions at home. Different categories of workers might bring home different wages with greater or lesser security in their jobs, but all too often, the houses to which they brought them were depressingly similar. This homogenizing impact of the urban environment imparted a significant uniformity to different workers' experience of urban life. By the forties, an ominous ecological dynamic was in motion, subjecting workers to substandard, overcrowded living and condemning them, as a consequence of inadequate public service and sanitation, to chronic sickness and premature death. Like most cities, Bradford was considerably less salubrious than the surrounding countryside, and even in 1830, a study had revealed that 59 percent of the town's population died before reaching the age of twenty, and 47 percent before the age of five.[104] However, even within the city, there were considerable differentials in life expectancy by social class. Calculations based on reports of mortality in Bradford between 1839 and 1841 showed that, although a professional or member of his family could expect to live to an average age of 39, and a member of a tradesman's family to 23, the average life expectancy of artisanal families was 18.4 and, of woolcombing families, 16.[105]

---

[102] *BO*, Jan. 27, 1842. In *Capital*, 1:619–21, Marx presents evidence from Bradford that indicates that the shortage of working-class housing continued to cause similar problems even in the more economically stable and prosperous 1860s.

[103] *BO*, Jan. 6, 1842.

[104] In rural Rutlandshire, the corresponding figures were 37.5 percent and 29 percent respectively. *PP* (1838, VIII), Appendix, 308–9.

[105] Cudworth, *Industrial Classes*, 64.

Although poor working conditions accounted for some of these differentials and virtually all manual occupations, woolcombing, woolsorting, and factory work were associated with particular workplace risks, the most important source of working-class mortality was domestic, the result of the endemic overcrowding and pollution at home. In fact, the disproportionately high levels of mortality among workers were only partly a consequence of adult ill health. Much more significant was the extraordinary death rate among working-class children, which, according to one estimate, claimed three-fourths by the age of twenty and two-thirds before the age of five.[106]

Every aspect of Bradford's urban slum environment contributed to the spread of both chronic and fatal working-class disease, particularly among infants, who were most vulnerable to infection and poisoning. The extreme overcrowding of tiny back-to-back cottages and their lack of window access to outside air prevented proper ventilation, especially during winter when families were preoccupied with conserving costly heat. Inadequate or tainted food, as well as inadequate child care when a mother returned to work too early, greatly exacerbated the underlying health hazards that working-class infants and young children faced.[107] Since so many working-class children began life at the danger point in the life cycle, their formative years were spent under conditions of environmental decay and economic privation that were extreme even by the generally low standards of their class.

For those who had to live in the downtown slums, pervasive industrial pollution made it impossible to escape the ill effects of fetid water and smoky air, even if sanitary regimens were practiced in the house. Particularly debilitating was the perpetually smoky atmosphere, which caused high rates of respiratory disorder and probably contributed more than other more tangible forms of pollution to chronic illness and premature death. Toxic wastes and contagion were also the products of once harmless practices and institutions that urban conditions had turned into public health threats. Traditional church and chapel graveyards inherited from the preindustrial era now became choked with rotting corpses that gave off noxious gases and bred typhus, malaria, and microorganisms that were the source of other diseases.[108] Slaughterhouses were another source of fever and toxic effluence, especially when carcasses were thrown into the beck or left out to decay.[109]

With the growth and increasing density of the inner-city population, the absence of public sewerage and the proliferation of unsanitary privies became another important threat to the public health. According to the 1845 wool-

---

[106] *BO*, Sep. 25, 1845.
[107] *PP* (1840, IX), 90; *BO*, Oct. 1, 8, 1840.
[108] *BO*, Jan. 2, Oct. 15, 1840; anon., *Bradford 1847–1947* (Bradford, n.d.), 24.
[109] *BO*, Nov. 12, 1840.

combers' survey, on a single slum block "there are two privies within six feet of the dwelling from whence the excrement overflows and sends forth an intolerable stench."[110] Since no one, before midcentury, possessed the authority to provide public sewerage, to regulate cemeteries or slaughterhouses, or even to force them to move out of town, the sanitary condition of the urban center continued to worsen with every year.

Weakened by overwork, hunger, smoke inhalation, and poor nutrition, and lacking access to proper medical care, it is not surprising that working people, especially working-class children, succumbed to a multitude of often fatal diseases. Indeed, for many contemporaries, it was the poor health and low life expectancy of working people, rather than their subordinate relationship to the means of production, that characterized their reality as an exploited class. Although the *Observer* could deny the antagonism between capital and labor, it could not ignore the biological discontinuity that divided the bourgeois from slumdwellers of all occupations, who experienced a very different kind of urban-industrial life:

> The life of this [working] class is only lingering death – for them there is no blessed buoyant childhood, no vigorous youth, no green old age. ...Both classes meet and mingle upon our streets, at our markets, in our churches and chapels; but they part – some of them to live in comfortable healthy houses; others in dens of pestilence."[111]

Conclusion

Historians of modern Britain have long confronted the paradox that the most serious social and political challenge to industrial capitalism came not during the subsistence crises of the Napoleonic era when even some optimists concede workers' living standards declined, but during the 1830s and 1840s when the wage of the average individual laborer, as even some pessimists now acknowledge, commenced a long and gradual increase.[112] Nowhere

[110] *PP* (1845, XVIII), Appendix, 2: 334–6; *BO*, Dec. 6, 1845; Oct. 4, 1849.

[111] *BO*, Sep. 25 1845.

[112] For the highlights of this debate about changes in the workers' standard of living during the industrial revolution, see J. L. Hammond and Barbara Hammond, *The Town Labourer, 1760–1832* (New York, 1967); idem, *The Skilled Labourer, 1760–1832* (New York, 1967); J. H. Clapham, *The Economic History of Modern Britain* (Cambridge, 1967), 1:539–602; Hayek, ed., *Capitalism and the Historians*; Taylor, ed., *Standard of Living*; Thompson, *English Working Class*, 189–349. The new, hyperoptimistic conclusions of Lindert and Williamson cited in note 24 of this chapter seem to have begun a new cycle of debate. See N. F. R. Crafts, "English Workers' Real Wages during the Industrial Revolution, Some Remaining Problems," and P. H. Lindert and J. G. Williamson, "English Workers' Real Wages: Reply to Crafts," both in *Journal of Economic History*, 45:1

does this paradox appear more clearly than in Bradford, where the essentially conjunctural crises of the late protoindustrial era, however devastating in their momentary impact, left the workers' traditional environment substantially intact. By contrast, the final stages of proletarianization amidst the dawning of the urban-industrial age irrevocably transformed the world of the worker and paved the way for the eventual appearance of a modern capitalist working class. The conjunctural crises characteristic of this era, however seemingly accidental, were really the products of deeper structures wherein the logic of industrial-capitalist development finally penetrated into the very heart of the workers' daily world. As each stage in the sequence of worsted manufacturing was successively taken out of the traditional handicraft sector and reconstituted in the urban factory, the emergence of a new mode of production entailed not only the application of steam power and the development of new machinery, but the search for novel forms of human labor that were appropriate to the altered conditions of production and which could be subordinated to industrial disciplines of work.[113]

The supply of laborers appropriate to these new forms of labor power was suddenly opened up by the collapse of the traditional cottage economy and by migration to the city, which broke down the working-class family as a viable unit of production and converted its constituent members into autonomous individuals who were henceforth to be integrated into a fully competitive urban labor market. At once separating the skilled adult male worker from the last vestiges of control over the production process while releasing the hitherto unpaid labor of his wife and children from the domestic duties of the protoindustrial cottage and applying it to the factory disciplines of the most technically advanced machines, this penetration of the family, like the splitting of the atom, unleashed explosive new productive powers that had hitherto lain dormant in the protoindustrial countryside. Now, in the new urban-industrial setting, they could be harnessed on an unprecedented scale.

For the worker, this dynamic of proletarianization, through which the productivity of his or her labor was dramatically increased, was experienced as a social and economic catastrophe that frequently brought a quantitative

---

(1985). For a more sustained critique, see R. S. Neale, *Writing Marxist History* (Oxford, 1985), 109–40. As this book was going to press, two further critiques have appeared, Joel Mokyr, "Is There Still Life in the Pessimist Case? Consumption During the Industrial Revolution, 1790–1850," *Journal of Economic History*, 48:1 (1988), and Charles Feinstein, "The Rise and Fall of the Williamson Curve," *Journal of Economic History*, 48:3 (1988), which suggest that Lindert and Williamson's hyperoptimistic conclusions about average working-class incomes before 1850 are probably not the last word on the subject.

[113] Marx, *Capital*, 206–84, 305–450, 486–96.

increase in poverty and exploitation and almost invariably entailed a pervasive qualitative sense of dispossession and loss. To be sure, the lure of freedom and comparatively high factory wages might momentarily seem appealing, especially to adolescents and unmarried women. But after a few years of mindless drudgery, the initial attraction was likely to fade. Seen from the perspective of the working-class breadwinner and the overall family wage, urbanization and industrialization represented a manifest decline. The mounting demand for the low-paid labor of women and children and the diminishing status of artisans in the textile handicraft trades compelled families to compensate for inadequate male earnings by drawing more heavily and urgently on the hitherto supplementary wages of unskilled or semiskilled adolescents and wives. The incongruence between the labor demands of capitalist industry and the domestic needs of the family as a group was most evident when the family was young – when it was saddled with more consumers than wage earners and depended most completely on the breadwinner's economic fate. Since every working-class family, even those whose breadwinners remained secure, inevitably passed through this life cycle stage, it tended to have a leveling and homogenizing effect. The life cycle itself acted as a social and economic transmitter through which the forces of proletarianization, which had their origins in the factory and the workshop, were converted into diminished standards of consumption and diffused throughout all sectors of the urban working class.

Of course, as the family grew older, the life cycle could be turned in its favor as more and more dependents were transformed into breadwinners to buttress the flagging contribution of an adult male household head. If the family maximized the opportunities for adolescent and female employment in the city, it was usually possible to obtain a subsistence as long as overall economic conditions remained good. Nevertheless, such opportunities could usually be taken advantage of only at considerable social, psychological, and environmental cost. To turn children and adolescents into premature laborers was to deprive them of education, recreation, moral development, and physical health. Similarly, the hyperexploitation of the working-class housewife, which jeopardized domestic comfort when she was sent off to work, represented a loss that, even when it could not be measured in money, adversely affected the material standard at which her family could live. Paradoxically, the very quest for material security could undermine the capacity of workers' families to produce the next generation of their class.

Most significantly, the distinctive character of the urban environment itself did much to translate even the most positive effects of proletarianization into negative material and environmental forms; for the prevalence of substandard housing and severe overcrowding, as well as the general spread of urban squalor and decay, dramatically added to the price that industrial capitalism exacted from the working-class family that sought to live within its available means. Although these evils were, in one sense, but physical manifestations of the exploitation to which Bradford's workers were subjected in the productive realm, no one who lived within the shadow of the downtown slum districts was free from the environmental degradation that characterized urban, proletarian life.

Perhaps by overworking low-paid, but readily employed wives and adolescents and by accepting the necessity of moving to a slum, the fully proletarianized family of the 1840s might obtain a higher monetary income than its rural protoindustrial counterpart of two decades before. However, when account is taken of the higher cost of living in the city as well as the greater insecurity and intensity of industrial work, the urban-proletarian family, even when it received a few extra shillings, was unlikely to find itself materially better off. Indeed, for those who migrated in the late 1830s, the loss of a subsistence cushion when food prices suddenly and dramatically increased must certainly have stimulated nostalgia for the countryside and fostered a belief that, in Bradford's new urban environment, more family members, even if they were lucky enough to be employable, would have to work much harder if even the most minimal living standards were to be maintained.[114]

While the cost of living stabilized somewhat during the 1840s, the trade cycle became even more volatile and, as our discussion of unemployment has indicated, the employment opportunities that proletarianization theoretically offered were, for much of the 1837–49 period, seriously curtailed in actual practice. The extreme fluctuations of the global commodity and trade cycles characteristic of the period, on which the new industrial mode of production was coming to depend, tended, in fact, to reduce the disposable incomes of industrial workers far below the level that official wage statistics suggest. Whatever their prospects during the intervening boom periods, many workers during the depressions of 1824–6, 1831–3, and even more between 1837–43 and 1846–9 found themselves reduced to a state of destitution reminiscent of the worst subsistence crises of the protoindustrial age. With their wholesale layoffs and wage or hour reductions spreading from the worsted industry to virtually every other trade, these depressions dramatically completed the process that the slow corrosion of the urban environment and the gradual, chronological operation of the family cycle had originally begun. At such moments, proletarianization was elevated from a transformation in

[114] Evidence on consumer prices compiled by N. F. R. Crafts, "Regional Price Variations in England in 1843: An Aspect of the Standard of Living Debate," *Explorations in Economic History*, 19:1 (1982), 62–3, suggests that the cost of living in northern industrial cities was about 15 percent higher than in the rural areas from which most of the new urban immigrants had come. See J. H. Treble, *Urban Poverty in Britain, 1830–1914* (London, 1979), to compare conditions in Bradford with urban poverty elsewhere.

the workplace to a general crisis that Bradford's workers experienced as a class.

When this happened, the viability of the whole urban-industrial capitalist system was called into question. The marketplace, which had so effectively organized the factors of production, spread chaos throughout the human community as wholesale poverty jeopardized the continued existence of the laborers whom capitalist production required. With a grim irony, the entrepreneurial promise of eternal progress and productivity evaporated in an orgy of overproduction in which the proliferation of an unmarketable surplus spelled destitution for the producing class. "Is it greatly to be wondered at," asked one querulous woolcomber, "that a man should be willing quietly to lie down and die of starvation in the midst of plenty of every description?" Newspaper reports in 1845–8 of woolcombers dying from malnutrition and of a poor sick woman eaten alive by rats show that such rhetoric was only a slightly exaggerated portrayal of what many experienced as an actual fact.[115] "Hundreds of us are now totally destitute," warned an unemployed woolcomber in 1847, yet the authorities had only seen fit to respond by swearing in special constables, refusing assistance, or proffering scant relief "with insulting language that no man of any spirit could tolerate."[116]

In the past, such disasters might have been tolerated fatalistically, as the inevitable products of some natural force. However, when they arose within the context of an industrial-capitalist civilization whose very legitimacy rested on its capacity to augment society's productive powers, the spread of poverty, exploitation, and misery were far more likely to sew the seeds of disaffection and revolt. The proliferation of want amidst a profusion of plenty, the spread of proletarian poverty beside accumulating capitalist wealth, betokened no inescapable scourge of nature. On the contrary, it stood as the mark of a flawed society that dispossessed the majority of its working members who labored to produce its goods.[117]

Here, in the specter of a proletarian movement to recover what capitalism had expropriated, horrified bourgeois liberals might glimpse an unanticipated manifestation of that insurgent alliance of productive citizens that had been foretold in their own entrepreneurial dream. As this dream was transformed into the nightmare that urban-industrial Bradford had become, they were forced to recognize that their universal values of freedom and opportunity had actually created a society that was even more unequal and divided than the hierarchical traditional order it had summarily replaced.

Uprooted and impoverished by the very market forces that were supposed

---

[115] *BO*, June 9, 16, 1842; Jan. 1, 1846; May 18, 1848.
[116] *BO*, May 27, 1847.
[117] *BO*, June 16, 1842; Dec. 24, 1846.

to bring them improvement, most workers rejected the ethos of competitive individualism upon which the new entrepreneurial edifice had been built. Unmoved by its egocentric preoccupation with salvation and its irrelevant quest for private self-help, most of them eschewed the bourgeois framework of cultural and political voluntarism that was supposed to integrate them into the new urban-industrial world. When men "might labour from Monday morning to Saturday night and scarcely be able to furnish themselves with the common necessities of life," it was infuriating to be told "to lay by for a rainy day" by the same sanctimonious capitalists who "were at the same time introducing machinery to rob them of their employment."[118] "When we leave off work," these victims of proletarianization lamented, "we are only fit for sleep or sensual indulgence, the only alternations our leisure knows.... We are sunken, debilitated, depressed," they continued, "unnerved for effort; incapable of virtue, unfit for anything which is calculated to be of any benefit to us at present or any future period." With "no power to rise above our circumstances or better our condition... no time to be wise, no leisure to be good," how could they make themselves into the self-reliant, autonomous individuals that the ideals of entrepreneurial liberalism required?[119]

[118] Quoted in Ashforth, "Poor Law in Bradford," 356. See also *BO*, Dec. 30, 1847, for a good example of the bourgeois attitude that elicited this sort of worker response.
[119] Quoted in Burnley, *Wool and Woolcombing*, 177–8.

14

From self-reliance to public relief: the bourgeois response to working-class poverty

When the Bradford bourgeoisie saw that proletarianized workers, instead of being junior partners in progress, were becoming impediments to the stabilization of the entrepreneurial world, their liberal ideology lost its celebratory tone. The dark prognoses about overpopulation and diminishing profit rates, which the "scientific" economists had long been issuing, suddenly registered in the minds of ordinary bourgeois liberals whose optimistic faith in the inevitability of progress gave way, in the face of social and economic crisis, to an alarmist mood of catastrophism that better suited the actual turn of events.[1] By the late thirties, the hope that workers might voluntarily embrace liberal individualist values was giving way to the fear that they had become so dehumanized as to have lost the capacity for values of any sort. Such fears, even when they were not explicitly articulated, were revealed by the language in which working-class modes of living were described:

> The scene was perfectly savage. The floor was earth, covered with splints of wood produced in match making. The articles of furniture were two. . . . A woman with skin so foul, that she might have passed for a negress, was squatted on the ground, and a litter, I cannot call them a group of children, burrowed about her. The woman could barely talk English: yet she must have been more than a dozen years in the country for the eldest boy, an urchin fully as old, told me he had been born in Lincolnshire. In a corner lay a litter of brown rags, the family bed.[2]

Here is a frightening new image of the worker who appears not as a challenge in the quest for perfectability, but as an irremediable danger to all civilized life. During the 1840s, the influx of destitute Irish activated long-standing ethnic prejudices and reinforced fears of class degradation with the

---

[1] Thomas Malthus, *An Essay on the Principles of Population* (London, 1914); David Ricardo, *The Principles of Political Economy and Taxation* (London, 1911).

[2] A. B. Reach, *The Yorkshire Textile Districts in 1849* (Blackburn, 1974), 18–19.

specter of an invading barbarian race. If the English worker still possessed some vestiges of order and morality, the Irish worker was believed to be completely uncivilized. An Irish family dinner was portrayed as an act of carnage in which domestic sociability played no part: "There is no sign of a plate, knife, or fork to be seen. . . . They simply pick the vegetables up in their fingers and eat them."[3]

Cultural backwardness and brutelike primitivism, so far from abolished by the triumph of capitalism, had penetrated to the heart of the industrial city. A new savagery was being nurtured within the temples of progress. One observer described his shocked reaction of mixed pity and revulsion on a visit to an Irish woolcomber's cellar room:

> I entered this horrid den and could not perceive any occupant owing to the darkness of the place, but in the course of a minute I heard a low moan, as of a person suffering from bodily pain. I advanced along the floor saturated with rain water from the door and recognized a female form laid on what it would be a shame to call a bed . . . on looking round more closely I beheld some wretched half-naked children huddled together.[4]

The language of this and the previous two passages denies its subjects the most basic human attributes. The "earthen floor" and "horrid den" with its "litter of brown rags" and "huddled," "burrowing," "half-naked children" describes the life of a human family in terms appropriate to a pack of hunted animals. The "female form" with her "low moan" lacks even the capacity for speech. Hidden away in their subterranean "darkness," these poor are the underside of industrial civilization, negating its promise of higher, freer forms of life. Spawned and then demoralized by capitalist society, they threaten its continuation as a viable social form.

So long as the scenes evoked in these descriptions remained hidden in the back alleys of Bradford's downtown slums, the message they conveyed about the redeemability of the worker could be repressed. However, wholesale subsistence crises at the depths of depression in 1838–43 and 1846–9 brought capitalism's contradictions to the surface, making plain that liberal voluntarism neither provided a true diagnosis of the workers' condition nor a real solution to their needs. At such moments the wonder was not that workers rejected liberal individualism and associational culture, but that they did not succumb to starvation or epidemic or bring down the capitalist edifice in a bloodbath of revolt. What the workers most required from the bourgeoisie was not spiritual and intellectual improvement, but the bare means of

---

[3] James Burnley, *Phases of Bradford Life* (Bradford, 1871), 27.
[4] *BO*, Oct. 6, 1845.

physical survival. Without this minimal cushion of subsistence, all the higher liberal goals of working-class advancement would be to no avail.

Since the liberal program of consensus through associational voluntarism presupposed that workers could provide for their own economic and environmental needs, the revelation that they could not called the entire voluntary system into doubt; for the tie that bound labor to capital was, in fact, one of dependence – compelling physical need. Workers needed, first and foremost, not cultural associations based on illusions of voluntarism and equality, but institutions of charity and public welfare based on a frank recognition of bourgeois wealth and power and of the social responsibilities that came in their wake. As the crisis of proletarianization deepened with its threats to social stability and public health, Bradford's bourgeois elite itself began to recognize that to make the new urban society stable and functional would require something more costly and substantial than an associational culture. It would require a welfare system to assist temporarily in economic crisis or medical emergency those unable to help themselves.

As discussed earlier, the most important institution to which needy workers instinctively turned was not bourgeois charity, but the working-class family, through which individuals with inadequate wages pooled their resources in a collective fund that was greater than the sum of its parts. Yet there were moments in both the trade and life cycles when the ability of the family to perform this function was seriously hampered or entirely cut off. With 25 percent of all working-class families below the minimal poverty level in a period of economic prosperity and perhaps double that proportion during a depression year, it was clear that Bradford's workers could not subsist on their earnings, and to avert wholesale starvation would require charitable assistance from elites.[5]

In the old Elizabethan Poor Law, traditional Bradford had possessed a rudimentary system of public assistance serving, at least minimally, the needs of its pre- and protoindustrial communities. Although the parish vestry had overall power of Poor Law administration, rates were collected and cases were processed in each township, individually, by overseers paid as public employees. Within this framework, relief of the destitute was financed on a small scale in relatively tight-knit communities in which ratepayers and recipients generally knew one another face to face. Individuals' rights to public assistance depended upon their acknowledged place in the community and upon their willingness to defer to its hierarchies and norms.[6]

Toward the end of the protoindustrial era, this community-oriented sys-

---

[5] See Chapter 13.
[6] See David Ashforth, "The Poor Law in Bradford, 1834–71," (Bradford, Ph.D. dissertation, 1979), 22–42.

tem of public assistance came under increasing strain. During the last quarter of the eighteenth century as poverty deepened and population grew, the poor rates doubled, straining to the limit the traditional community's ability to respond. After a brief respite in the early 1820s, the quickening pace of industrial expansion and the demographic concentration that urbanization brought had, by middecade, created a situation that the traditional Poor Law framework could no longer satisfactorily address. With the advent of migration and cyclical unemployment during the 1830s and 1840s, poverty in Bradford assumed an increasingly impersonal aspect.[7] As the rise and fall of pauperism became increasingly a function of structural and market forces, it became ever more difficult to distinguish between those who did and those who did not deserve relief; for neither the traditional dichotomy between the self-reliant and the feckless could be applied to a vast working population that was required by an industry that could only intermittently sustain it. Whether or not such people were morally deserving was irrelevant; the industrial economy and the urban social structure required a public welfare system to keep them alive.[8]

The voluntary relief committees

As the inability of Poor Law institutions to provide adequate relief became increasingly manifest, other, supplementary agencies of public welfare were formed. One particularly devastating aspect of the new form of poverty was its instability; it tended to fluctuate wildly according to market conditions, disallowing long-term solutions planned in advance. To avoid outright starvation at moments of crisis, the bourgeoisie instituted a series of large-scale voluntary charitable relief efforts that raised money by subscription from the wealthier classes to provide destitute working-class families with emergency assistance.[9]

The first of these campaigns came during the depression of 1825–6, when a group of notables under the vicar's leadership established a subscription fund and divided the town into nineteen districts appointing a "visitor" to

---

[7] Gary Firth, "The Genesis of the Industrial Revolution in Bradford, 1760–1830" (Bradford, Ph. D. dissertation, 1974), 73–7. For a discussion of general ideas about pauperism and working-class poverty during this period, see Gertrude Himmelfarb, *The Idea of Poverty, England in the Early Industrial Age* (New York, 1983), 3–144, and J. R. Poynter, *Society and Pauperism, English Ideas on Poor Relief, 1795–1834* (London, 1969).

[8] See Gareth Steadman Jones, *Outcast London* (New York, 1984), 241–61.

[9] See R. J. Morris, "The Organization and Aims of the Principal Secular Voluntary Organizations of the Leeds Middle Class, 1830–51" (Oxford, D. Phil. dissertation, 1970).

investigate cases in each. At first this scheme elicited hostility from capitalists like Richard Fawcett and Matthew Thompson who opposed giving charity to those who had been involved in the combers or weavers union or had participated in the 1825 strike. However, with the union's collapse this objection was mooted, and throughout 1826 and 1827, over £3,100 was raised to support anywhere from 1,000 to 2,700 families per week.[10]

Almost all of those involved in this initial relief effort were members of the Anglican Tory establishment. With the arrival of the new entrepreneurs over the next quarter century, larger and more frequent voluntary relief efforts were organized as the ravages of depression progressively worsened. When unemployment skyrocketed in the summer of 1837, a new committee was formed, and the town was divided into twenty-eight districts. This relief fund lasted only a month, but when another downturn in markets brought many of the poor to the verge of starvation, another committee was hastily formed. In late 1839, depression led to another subscription drive. By February 1840, the total expended over the previous three years was £4,165.[11]

No newspaper reports of comparable relief work appeared during the depression of 1842–3, and the entire burden of pauper relief appears to have been borne by the Poor Law authorities. However, in November, a volunteer-run soup kitchen for 600 families was opened, and between mid–1846 and 1848, the largest of the voluntary relief campaigns was mounted, raising £5,600 in two years and relieving up to 4,000 individuals per week. Although a number of important names were conspicuously absent, the list of subscribers included many of the new liberal entrepreneurs whose fortunes were made during the previous decade.[12]

In addition to temporarily easing the burden of the poor rate and providing emergency assistance to those who did not qualify for official relief, these voluntary committees served several important social functions. Proponents of voluntary charity argued that "when it is employed in relieving patient virtuous poverty [it] exerts a hallowing influence on donor and recipient, a result looked for in vain from official almsgiving."[13] Voluntary charity brought the poor not only material sustenance, but the knowledge that the wealthy had not forsaken them. When relief came as a gift rather than as a dole, it established an implicit social relation between those who gave and those who

[10] *Bradford Courier*, Nov. 24, 1825; Mar. 30, Apr. 6, May 18, 23, June 29, Jul. 6, 13, 1826.
[11] *BO*, June 1, 8, 15, Jul. 20, 27, 1837; Sep. 19, Dec. 12, 19, 1839; Jan. 2, 9, 16, 23, 30, Feb. 13, Apr. 23, 1840.
[12] *BO*, Nov. 10, 1842; Mar. 19, 26, Apr. 2, 9, 16, 23, 31, May 14, June 28, July 11, 18, 25, 1846; Jan. 21, 28, Feb. 4, 11, 18, 25, Mar. 11, 18, 25, Apr. 8, May. 27, June 3, Nov. 18, 25, Dec. 16, 30, 1847; Jan. 6, Apr. 27, May 25, June 1, July 6, 1848.
[13] *BO*, Mar. 22, 1855.

received. The latter would feel gratitude toward the former and acknowledge the benevolence of their rule.[14]

However, by bringing donors into an active relationship with their beneficiaries, voluntary charity benefited them as well. Even readiness to make a contribution could broaden the sentiments and soften the heart. Active involvement in the relief committee through fund raising, investigation, and distributing goods broadened the bourgeois participants' perceptions even more by thrusting them into direct contact with the poor. Often, these errands of mercy were all that drew well-to-do people into the working-class slums. Compiling and checking family incomes often provided committee members with their only real glimpse into how the other half lived.[15]

Unlike the Poor Law, voluntary charitable ventures were not bound by regulations or fixed procedures and were free to experiment with new approaches. By founding their relief policy on merit rather than eligibility, the voluntary committees sought to revive the distinction between deserving and undeserving cases (although, all too often, this distinction turned out to be arbitrary). To insure that beneficiaries would not squander what they were given, assistance was often proffered in food, such as oatmeal, soup, and potatoes, or other basic necessities, like blankets and clothes. Finally, unlike the Poor Law, the relief committees could often insist that their recipients perform useful (if unprofitable) public works. Men were sent to repair the roads or to clean, drain, or dredge the canal. One observer noted wryly that it was only during depressions that such public services were performed. Impoverished working-class women were also set to sewing, under the supervision of bourgeois wives and daughters, to make clothing that was redistributed to the poor.[16]

In general, the voluntary relief committees provided a much broader outlet for bourgeois women's energies than did the regular nexus of religious and secular associations. In contrast to many social activities, charity had always been regarded primarily as women's work. Although the relief committees were generally headed by bourgeois men responsible for raising subscriptions, the actual work of visitation and distribution was usually performed by women who, portraying themselves as the natural defenders of the family, sought alliance with or sponsorship of the working-class housewife in the privatized terms of their common domestic sphere.[17] From the bourgeois

---

[14] Jones, *Outcast London*, 241–61; *BO*, June 18, 1846.

[15] Kathleen Woodroofe, *From Charity to Social Work* (London, 1962), 29–32; *BO*, Jan. 2, 1840; Jan. 27, 1842; May 27, 1858.

[16] William Cudworth, *Historical Notes on the Bradford Corporation* (Bradford, 1881), 64; Ashforth, "Poor Law in Bradford," 274–5; *Bradford Courier*, Apr. 26, Aug. 24, 1826; *BO*, Mar. 9, 30, 1843; Apr. 16, 1846; July 6, 1848.

[17] *Bradford Courier*, Aug. 24, 1826; LeeAnn Whites, "Southern Ladies and Millhands: The

diagnosis of working-class poverty as rooted in collective moral failure and individual sin, bourgeois women worked to forge a transclass gender identity, which diagnosed poverty as a crisis of the family caused by the inadequate domestic training of working-class women and the intemperance, idleness, and habitual profligacy of too many working-class men.[18]

Despite their fleeting existence and ad hoc status, the emergency relief committees offered powerful possibilities for the reassertion of genuine bourgeois community leadership. By translating the liberal principle of voluntary action from a mere technique of cultural integration to a means of distributing resources, the relief committees reasserted the entrepreneurial ideology in a socially compelling way. The bourgeoisie had abandoned the tradition of paternalism with its assumptions about the inevitability of hierarchy and the permanent subordination of the working class. Now, the relief committees offered a pragmatic alternative based on the principles of voluntarism that could preserve the social equilibrium, which the market normally provided, during times when supply and demand were temporarily out of phase. Unfortunately, there were several reasons why, despite their promise, voluntary charities could not restore the progressive social and political alliance that the traumas of proletarianization had shattered.

First, the class relationship engendered by voluntary charity was very different from the egalitarian spirit of fraternity inspired by voluntary association. Recipients in the gift relationship were, by definition, supplicants. Although charity might inspire genuine feelings of gratitude, the deference it engendered could easily backfire in the face of bourgeois donors whose periodic gestures of openhandedness were not matched by any commitment to an ongoing protective, paternalist role.[19] The work of the relief committees was too transitory, too much concerned with emergency expedients, to penetrate deeply into the causes of working-class poverty or to cultivate much sympathy with working-class life. During depression, thousands of cases had to be dealt with at once, and personalized relationships had no time to form. In order for cases to be processed expeditiously, they were classified by procedures that might seem arbitrary and unfair. When dispensed superciliously, charity evoked not contentment but hostility. When those whom he perceived as responsible for his impoverishment demanded gratitude for giving him what seemed less than his natural right, the worker could feel more angry and insulted than if charity had never been proffered. One working-class leader condemned self-righteous benefactors who "subscribed

Domestic Economy and Class Politics; Augusta, 1870–90," (Irvine, Ph.D. dissertation, 1982), chap. 3; and idem, *Wives Mothers and Daughters: Gender and the Origins of the New South, Augusta, Georgia, 1860–1900* (forthcoming, Chapel Hill, N.C.).

[18] Margaret Hewitt, *Wives and Mothers in Victorian Industry* (London, 1958), 10–14.

[19] Marcel Mauss, *The Gift* (New York, 1967).

a sum of money and set the combers to work at the Beck in the mud and dirt by which several of them were killed, and this they called charity."[20]

However, the main problem with the voluntary relief committees was that they were never sufficiently successful for complaints such as this to become widespread. Although they provided emergency relief to thousands during the depths of depressions, at such moments tens of thousands stood in need. Bourgeois voluntary contributions did little to alleviate the overall problem of poverty, and the relief committees were always hopelessly underfinanced. Perpetually initiating new subscription drives, charities were often forced to rely on contributions from outside Bradford and sometimes were closed due to lack of funds.[21] A comparison of the expenditures of the voluntary committees with those of the Poor Law shows that, even at the worst moments of crisis, charitable contributions were usually less than 10 percent of the amount levied by rates.[22] Millowners in particular were frequently criticized for failing to contribute their fair share to relieving the unemployed from whose labor they derived their own profits. Yet given the intense competition among worsted entrepreneurs, especially during depression years when profits dropped precipitously, one can easily see why many fledgling industrialists offered only token assistance to those whom they had been forced to throw out of work.[23]

Before midcentury, voluntary charitable activity, in addition to relieving temporary destitution, limited its aims to treating disease. In 1825, the Bradford Infirmary with twenty-four beds and an outpatient clinic was opened to offer partially subsidized health care. Since disease, unlike poverty, could become contagious and might spread to the better-off, elites were particularly concerned about this issue, and this facility emerged at a relatively early date.[24] Designed specifically to confront a class phenomenon, the infirmary, like the voluntary relief committees, carefully steered clear of the intraelite religious and political antagonisms that not only accompanied but also fueled most other bourgeois voluntary associations in town. Although the infirmary was initiated by Anglican Tories like John Hustler and Richard Fawcett, and gentleman–physicians like Dr. Outhwaite, Dr. Simpson, and Dr. Mossman, in the early thirties, its governing board expanded to include many of the local Nonconformists who were now becoming increasingly prominent

[20] George White quoted in Ashforth, "Poor Law in Bradford," 280.
[21] BO, July 20, 1837; Dec. 19, 1839; Jan. 23, 1840; Apr. 31, June 11, 1846; June 3, Dec. 16, 1847.
[22] Bradford Courier, Mar. 30, 1826; Ashforth, "Poor Law in Bradford," 285.
[23] BO, Dec. 19, 1839; Jan. 6, 1842; May 27, June 3, 1847; Jan. 6, 1848.
[24] Anon., The Bradford Infirmary to 1880: A Sketch (Bradford, 1882).

and rich. In the early 1840s, with 325 regular subscribers and a few individuals willing to donate larger amounts, the infirmary raised £10,000 above annual operating costs to construct a new building, and by the midforties the institution was housing sixty inpatients and serving 3,000 to 4,000 outpatients per year.[25]

The infirmary was an important target for bourgeois charitable donations and a focal point for the local medical profession. However, it was even less effective at providing the mass health care necessitated by urbanization and industrialization than the voluntary soup kitchens had been at providing relief for mass destitution. Dr. Ashforth has estimated that, before 1850, even the outpatient dispensary never served more than 3 percent of Bradford's population. In part this was because the annual contributions of £700 to £1,700 were inadequate to provide treatments on a wider scale. However, to maintain even this level of service the Infirmary had to institute fees for examinations and medicine and even stiffer charges for surgery and accommodation, which effectively excluded all but the best-paid workers.[26] Given the environmental origins of disease and physical debility as well as their social roots in primary poverty, pollution, and residential overcrowding, it was inevitable that the infirmary would fail to meet the medical needs of the vast majority of the population, and especially of the old, the poor, the unemployed, and the disabled, whose problems were most severe.

Even on an emergency basis, voluntarism was inadequate to combat the poverty caused by urban-industrial development and its market fluctuations. More permanent and costly institutions like the infirmary, which focused on problems even more intractable and complex, were even less successful. Faced with a crisis so deeply rooted and far reaching as proletarianization, no local voluntary effort could hope to succeed. To tackle issues of this scope and complexity required intervention by the state, for only centralized, bureaucratic institutions that could mobilize the resources of the entire society could contend with problems whose scale was society-wide.

The New Poor Law

The various voluntary relief efforts mounted in Bradford were clearly no substitute for a Poor Law in providing for the welfare of the town. Somehow, the antiquated and inefficient Poor Law machinery would have to be overhauled and reorganized to make it more appropriate to the needs of the urban-industrial-capitalist milieu. The 1834 Poor Law reforms were fre-

[25] Ibid., 11, 14–15.
[26] Ashforth, "Poor Law," 289–92.

quently associated by contemporaries with Malthusianism and laissez-faire, yet from an administrative perspective, their most striking innovation was the establishment of a prototype for the centralized, bureaucratic welfare state, which has since come to dominate all modern capitalist societies. Certainly, the aims of the liberal Benthamite intellectuals who framed the New Poor Law, for all their commitment to economic free trade, were consistent not only with government intervention, but also with a more potent form of central state authority than had seriously been considered in Britain before.[27]

Benthamites recommended that the Poor Law be rationalized to make its operation more consistent and uniform, that its administration be reorganized on a systematic national basis and subjected to rule from above. Bureaucratic authority was to be protected from local interpretation or resistance by a set of neutral civil servants hired from a central office that would act outside of Parliament in the name of the state. Liberal Poor Law reformers like Edwin Chadwick intended not to weaken government, but, after the fashion of industrial capitalism, to streamline it, so that it could more efficiently and effectively pursue its appointed tasks.[28]

Nevertheless, the New Poor Law had not only to be consistent with the abstract principles of liberal rationalism. It had also to be palatable to the practical libertarianism of the grassroots bourgeoisie. Hence, its bureaucratic centralism was tempered by a provision for elective local boards of guardians, which would represent the taxpayers in executing the policies of the national commissioners. Moreover, neither commissioners nor guardians were to interfere with the spontaneous movements of the market; rather they were to liberate the exchange between labor and capital from the impediments that had hitherto prevented the supply of workers from flowing in the direction of employer demand. The reformers argued that the way to end poverty was not so much to relieve its symptoms as to free up the natural forces of economic expansion through whose operation it would spontaneously disappear.[29]

Hence, although the New Poor Law was a statist rather than a voluntarist measure, its aims were those of classical liberalism. With its plans to rationalize the national welfare system in the name of efficiency and its promise to make the worker more independent and competitive by weaning him from his dependence on charity, the New Poor Law seemed to offer a liberal

[27] Derek Fraser, "The English Poor Law and the Origins of the British Welfare State," in W. J. Mommsen, ed., *The Emergence of the Welfare State in Britain and Germany, 1850–1950* (London, 1981).

[28] Elie Halévy, *The Growth of Philosophical Liberalism* (London, 1972), 88–120.

[29] S. E. Finer, *The Life and Times of Edwin Chadwick* (London, 1952), 69–95.

bureaucratic solution to those problems of urban-industrial capitalism that voluntarism alone had been unable to solve.

However, in operation, the New Poor Law fell far short of these hopes. Although it was not the Malthusian disaster that many working-class leaders had feared, it offered no viable solutions to the new forms of poverty that had developed in urban-industrial Bradford. The failure of the administrative revolution undertaken by the Poor Law reformers resulted, in part, from the reluctance of Whig politicians to antagonize the many vested interests that benefited from the Old Poor Law. Yet although bureaucratic centralism failed partly because of administrative anachronisms from the Old Regime, many of the New Poor Law's most innovative features, such as the creation of regional Poor Law unions with elected boards of guardians, also facilitated the emergence of quasi-autonomous administrative centers that compromised the sovereignty of the bureaucrats in the center. Although the new unions were more uniform than the old ecclesiastical parishes and the largely middle-class guardians were generally more efficient than the old vestries had been, the new boards were often weighted toward traditional forms of authority and frequently retained local peculiarities long after the overall legal framework had been changed.[30]

Nowhere did this persistent localism manifest itself more significantly than in the retention of the ancient system of settlements, which required individuals to apply for relief in the locality where they had either been born or paid taxes for more than five years. Since most of Bradford's proletariat, and even more of the needy, were immigrants, many workers who required assistance were ineligible for relief under the law.[31] The Poor Law confronted the problem of unsettled paupers by sanctioning their removal to the union from which they originally came. However, such removals were costly and time consuming and were rarely initiated by the Bradford board. Some guardians considered it wrong to deport residents, who had contributed their labor to the local economy, the moment they became unemployed. Moreover, the town's leading capitalists wanted to retain the surplus labor, which kept wage rates down and which would be needed to permit expansion of employment when markets improved. Finally, shipping off paupers was a futile gesture, since little stopped them from returning whenever they chose.[32] In spite of several bold resolutions to institute a policy of wholesale removals, Bradford's Board of Guardians sent only a small minority of its unsettled paupers away. Some were relieved despite their official ineligibility, and by

[30] Fraser, "English Poor Law"; Anthony Brundage, *The Making of the New Poor Law; The Politics of Inquiry Enactment and Implementation, 1832–39* (New Brunswick, 1978).

[31] M. E. Rose, "Settlement Removal, and the New Poor Law," in Derek Fraser, ed., *The New Poor Law in the Nineteenth Century* (New York, 1976), 25–44.

[32] *BO*, Apr. 1, Aug. 12, 1847; Ashforth, "Poor Law in Bradford," 298–328.

the early forties, such individuals constituted a quarter of the union's relief rolls. The vast majority, however, were forced to depend on their families, private charity, or the doles of the voluntary relief committees. After these resources were exhausted, the only alternatives were to leave town or to starve. After 1846, the floodgates partially opened when settlement was re-defined more liberally, making one or two thousand more eligible for the rolls.[33]

The retention of the law of settlement was not the only concession to tradition and localism that impeded new approaches to urban-industrial poverty. Al-though ultimate authority over poor relief policy rested with the guardians and national commissioners, even after the 1834 reforms, the work of col-lecting rates and distributing relief remained in the hands of village-based township assessors and overseers. This constituted an entirely inadequate basis for a welfare system in a complex industrial age.[34]

Detailed evidence collected by Dr. David Ashforth shows that this fragmented subregional system of Poor Law administration made it im-possible for the authorities to respond effectively to the influx of impover-ished people from the hinterland to the city center during the second quarter of the nineteenth century. Relief expenditure for the entire Brad-ford Union in 1848 was four times the level of twenty-five years before. Yet whereas in 1824, the welfare burden had been distributed fairly evenly among townships within the parish, by 1848, the much greater burden was now borne almost singlehandedly by the central townships of Bradford and Horton, where most of the paupers now lived. In 1847–8 one-third of the union's paupers were now concentrated in Bradford Township.[35] As a result of this geographical inequality, Bradford's down-town ratepayers had to bear almost the entire burden of emergency relief, and a handful of overworked township officials had to process thousands of cases per week.[36]

Maldistribution of responsibility for poor relief stemmed not only from geographical imbalance, but also, and more importantly, from social inequity. By far the heaviest burden of subsidizing welfare payments fell upon the lower middle class. Here again, failure to reform the rating system meant that, outside the voluntary relief committees, most of the new wealth gen-erated by industrial development was not available for solving the social

[33] *BO*, Apr. 3, 1845, Feb. 12, 1846, Nov. 9, 1848; Ashforth, "Poor Law in Bradford," 298.
[34] Ashforth, "Poor Law in Bradford," 115–55.
[35] Ibid., 127.
[36] Ibid., 22–30, 119–30, 135–40.

problems that industrialization brought. Since the rates were levied exclusively on real property, those who held the bulk of their assets in liquid
capital were taxed at a much lower rate.[37] Most lower-middle-class shopkeepers and householders held the bulk of their property in real estate,
whereas wealthy Bradfordians, whether rentiers or industrialists, generally
held most of their fortunes in other, effectively tax-free forms. Shifting the
costs of working-class welfare away from the industrialist who incurred them
onto the backs of the petit bourgeoisie aided capital accumulation but also
contributed greatly to the fiscal unsoundness of the local relief system,
particularly during the depression years.[38]

When workers' purchasing power decreased as a result of poverty or
unemployment, shopkeepers were the first to feel the strain. In 1840, the
chairman of the Bradford Board of Guardians warned that many of the
ratepayers were not much better off than those they were relieving. In
July 1842, as expenditures soared and payments failed, the union was
barely able to meet its obligations. The authorities were forced to tax the
small ratepayer exactly when he was most vulnerable. In 1847, the woolcomber's leader George White pointed out that "it was a great shame to
put the burden [of poor relief] upon the struggling shopkeepers when the
rich who made their fortunes out of the labourers gave nothing."[39] Over-
taxation of the lower middle class, even when it did not lead to insolvency, stirred up undercurrents of political resentment and encouraged a
narrow-minded, penny-pinching attitude among the guardians that
stopped them from seeking creative solutions to poverty and cyclical unemployment. Weekly benefits were usually kept below 2s. per head and
were granted reluctantly by impotent Poor Law officials living in perpetual fear of a taxpayers' revolt.[40]

The ineligibility of a substantial portion of Bradford's poor and the grudg-
ing treatment given the remainder rendered the official Poor Law inadequate
as a source, not only of economic assistance, but also of potential health
care for the vast majority of the poor, who had access neither to private
physicians nor the infirmary. This failure was particularly significant because
of the close connection between poverty and disease. Because of the problem
of eligibility, the Poor Law medical system, at least before 1848, not only
serviced fewer cases than the infirmary, but also provided inferior care. Here
again, the already bad situation was worsened by the outmoded township
organizational structure, which left downtown medical officers hopelessly

[37] Ibid., 143–52.
[38] *BO*, June 24, 1834; July 30, 1835; Sep. 5, 1839; Jan. 23, 1845; Jan. 1, 1849.
[39] *Bradford Courier*, Aug. 3, 1826; *BO*, July 14, 1842; May, 27 1847, 1847; Ashforth, "Poor
Law in Bradford," 148–52.
[40] Ashforth, "Poor Law in Bradford," 161, 162.

overworked. Lax professional standards and low fees further reduced the quality of pauper medicine so that it often failed to meet even the most elementary health needs.[41]

"Less eligibility" and the provision of relief

Bradford's Poor Law guardians were hampered in formulating an effective response to the complex welfare problems of the late thirties and forties because of the New Poor Law's failure to modernize administrative anachronisms. Yet the one major innovation that the reformers did implement, the Malthusian principle of "less eligibility," had, by far, the most devastating effect. This principle specified that public assistance should be made so unattractive that anyone with the least personal resources would eschew official relief.[42]

To the Poor Law commissioners, such a policy followed from the logic of the 1834 Act. The increasingly meaningless distinction between deserving and undeserving would be abandoned (at least for Poor Law purposes), and the pauper would be induced to assume economic responsibility for himself. The commissioners believed that they could implement this policy departure through one simple, if rather draconian step. The authorities would cease all outdoor relief and supplementing of sub-subsistence wages. Public support would henceforth be offered only to those desperate enough to leave their families and communities and accept the stigma of incarceration in a workhouse where they would be treated as public wards.[43]

The threat to impose such a policy, when the Poor Law was implemented in 1837, sparked both a series of riots and an organized mass protest campaign. Moreover, the cyclical character of industrial employment, which made periodic depressions a built-in feature of the process of capitalist development, rendered the workhouse an utterly implausible solution to working-class poverty. If the market could not always provide workers with subsistence wages, then the Poor Law, unless its purpose was to starve them, could scarcely offer them less.[44]

[41] Nevertheless, it must be acknowledged that this system of pauper medicine, by which the authorities appointed physicians who were paid 4s. 6d. to 7s. 6d. per case, however inadequate it may have worked in practice, contributed, at least on paper, as a precursor for subsequent schemes of national health. Ashforth, "Poor Law," 196–213, 288–94; M. W. Flinn, "Medical Services under the New Poor Law," in Fraser, ed., New Poor Law, 45–66.

[42] Finer, Edwin Chadwick, 69–95.

[43] Derek Fraser, The Evolution of the British Welfare State (London, 1973), 45–50.

[44] Ashforth, "Poor Law in Bradford," 157–64.

Applied to the urban-industrial context, the principle of less eligibility had an Alice-in-Wonderland effect. A policy that purported to make the worker independent would reduce him to even greater dependency. Far from making the Poor Law cheaper and more efficient, honoring the threat to institutionalize every pauper in Bradford would have meant the collective rehousing, feeding, and clothing of tens of thousands of the poorest urban workers every time they had the misfortune to be unemployed.[45] Indeed, the fears of the Poor Law's critics turned out to be exaggerated only because their most extravagant claims – that the law would lead to the wholesale breakup of families and the transformation of the "free" proletariat into a class of state slaves – represented essentially an accurate diagnosis of the consequences of a policy that was unenforceable for precisely this reason.

Even if Bradford's liberal guardians had wished to undertake such an experiment, the violent outbreaks that accompanied their organizational meetings obliged them, at least temporarily, to desist. Henry Leah, the board's first chairman, became "convinced that the Poor Law Act could not be carried into force in this District and therefore he should attend no more meetings of the Guardians to risk his life."[46] With the advent of Tory dominance of local Poor Law administration after the liberals' defeat in 1839, prudent circumspection gave way to overt obstruction as the Bradford Board of Guardians began a smoldering controversy with the London commissioners, which represented both a practical reassertion of traditional relief policies and a principled defense of local rights. Although Bradford's Tory guardians were scarcely known for their generosity toward the poor, they bristled at the interference of an authoritarian bureaucracy and at the inhumanity and expense of the "workhouse test."[47]

No new workhouses were built in Bradford throughout the 1840s and notwithstanding numerous orders from London, virtually all paupers continued receiving outdoor relief. Only the elderly, the handicapped, orphans, lunatics, and incorrigible idlers were placed in custody, all of whom had to be institutionalized in any case. Nevertheless, if less eligibility could not be realized through the workhouse test, attempts were made to enforce it through a less drastic "labor test," which would require all able-bodied applicants to perform long hours of backbreaking toil.[48] Like the workhouse, the labor test became a subject of controversy. To avoid competition with

---

[45] J. Leesom, *The Cost of In-Maintenance, An Answer to the Report of A Committee of Guardians* (Bradford, 1869).

[46] Quoted in John Knott, *Popular Opposition to the Poor Law* (London, 1985), 171.

[47] *BO*, Apr. 24 1834, Feb. 23, 1837, Apr. 5, 26, 1838, June 15, July 20, 1848; Ashforth, "Poor Law in Bradford," 44–53.

[48] Ashforth, "Poor Law in Bradford," 165–76.

private employment, pauper labor had to be relatively unproductive and menial. Skilled workers, including the woolcombers, when forced by unemployment to claim public relief, resented being impressed into hard outdoor labor, which they found not only morally degrading, but injurious to their often delicate health.[49]

In reality, only a small proportion of Bradford's paupers were ever actually subjected to the labor test, in part because the guardians sometimes waived it, but largely because the vast majority of those on the relief rolls would never have been eligible. Indeed, the principle of less eligibility, with its individualistic focus, was almost entirely irrelevant to the forms of poverty, refracted through the family economy, that most of Bradford's workers actually faced. The assumed object of less eligibility, the autonomous adult male laborer who had to be goaded into economic independence, was largely a figment of the Poor Law commissioners' imagination and turned out to be quite different from the flesh and blood paupers whom the Bradford Board of Guardians relieved. According to Dr. Ashforth's evidence, of the thirteen thousand or so paupers on the Bradford union's books at the depths of the 1848 depression, only 10.5 percent were able-bodied men. Twenty-one percent were old or disabled, 17 percent were women, and 51 percent were children under the age of 16.[50]

The real function of public welfare in Bradford, which it spontaneously assumed, was not to make independent some illusory individual, but to protect the working-class family unit by giving supplementary assistance to dependent women and children whenever the death disability, unemployment, or diminished earning power of the male breadwinner jeopardized the family's economic capacity to survive. What was required of public relief was to provide a supplement to the family economy that would raise those who had lost, either temporarily or permanently, the ability to support themselves, at least to the level of bare subsistence.

Nevertheless, the London commissioners dogmatically insisted that the irrelevant principle of less eligibility be strictly applied. The essential functions of poor relief were either obscured or impeded, and the resulting welfare system was more muddled and inefficient than if its tasks had been squarely faced and understood. Because it was necessary to disguise family supplements as relief to destitute individuals, family members in marginal employment might actually be forced to quit their work so as to be eligible for benefits.[51] Although it was recognized that temporary subsidies of family

[49] BO, June 24, 1847; Ashforth, "Poor Law in Bradford," 177–83.
[50] Ashforth, "Poor Law in Bradford," 184–95.
[51] Guardian Samuel Cowling quoted in Ashforth, "Poor Law in Bradford," 176.

income, food, or rent might be necessary to keep a household together, such assistance was strictly prohibited, except occasionally for widows, for whom exceptions were sometimes made.[52]

The limits of public welfare within the Poor Law framework were revealed during the crisis of 1848 when the Bradford Board of Guardians briefly sought to confront the problem of working-class poverty more systematically. An 1846 change in the definition of settlement insured that, in subsequent crises, the majority of Bradford's indigent would become eligible for official relief. By 1848, the guardians' role had expanded, not only in the payment of doles, but also in the field of medical services, which expanded dramatically, if only temporarily, while the relief rolls grew.[53]

In the 1848 guardians' election, the advent of a liberal majority for the first time in nearly a decade insured that, as the scope of their activity widened, the spirit with which they approached it would radically change. Infused with a new concern about working-class welfare and a new municipal ethos (which will be explored in detail in Chapter 18), the liberals were determined that the problem of pauperism, which had brought them down in 1838, would never again be left to the Tories by default. Seeking to eliminate the administrative structure that left the urban Poor Law hostage to the beleaguered hinterland ratepayer and gave conservative interests a disproportionate weight, the new liberal guardians succeeded in having the original Poor Law Union divided and the Bradford authority made coterminous with the parliamentary and municipal boroughs and more closely congruent with the geography of the urban space.[54]

Freed from out-township dominance, the Bradford Board of Guardians could now apply more aggressive treatments to urban poverty by redoubling their efforts to relieve cyclical poverty while seeking antidotes to the chronic problem of structural unemployment in trades like woolcombing. A permanent solution to the woolcombers' plight, they argued, however costly it might be, would be both humane and judicious and would ultimately save the ratepayers money by removing a perpetual community charge. In the spring, the guardians joined forces with the voluntary relief committee to start a common fund to subsidize woolcomber emigration and resettlement, which would draw not only on private contributions, but on a £2000 grant

[52] J. H. Treble, *Urban Poverty in Britain, 1830–1914* (London, 1979), 97.
[53] Ashforth, "Poor Law in Bradford," 240–2, 326; *BO*, Feb. 17, Nov. 23, 1848; Feb. 1, 1849.
[54] Ashforth, "Poor Law in Bradford," 362–5; *BO*, Dec. 4, 1849.

from the rates. Several months later a similar public–private venture was projected to set up surplus woolcombers on agricultural allotments to be carved out of open space on Bradford moor.[55]

In both instances, however, the Central Poor Law Board ruled that it was illegal to use ratepayers' money for such purposes and forced the Board of Guardians to pull out. After this final triumph of dogma over necessity, the guardians ceased their efforts to treat urban-industrial poverty more humanely and creatively. Henceforth, all attempts to aid the woolcombers and to confront the problem of structural unemployment had to rely purely on private, voluntary means.[56]

Conclusion

Despite its ideologically novel appearance, the New Poor Law in Bradford was, in practice, not that different from the Old. The few innovations actually implemented rarely improved its performance and all too often made it even less appropriate to the urban-capitalist age. The emergence of an industrial proletariat had created a new set of public welfare problems that the bureaucratic Poor Law was no more successful in resolving than the voluntary relief committees had been. The administrative reforms envisioned by the proponents of the New Poor Law introduced an important new prototype on which a welfare state would later be built. The passage of national legislation to promote uniformity in Poor Law administration reflects an embryonic recognition that capitalist labor and commodity markets had made poverty a national problem requiring the active intervention of a centralized state. The idea that the administration of this state system was a task for a bureaucracy of professional civil servants, operating according to impersonal rules, also set important precedents.[57] Finally, the policies advocated by enlightened liberals during the subsistence crisis of 1848 to some extent foreshadowed future government programs, which would augment the usual patchwork of temporary expedients with more creative policies inspired by a dim understanding that poverty is a built-in consequence of capitalist development, necessitating permanent involvement by the state.

Nevertheless, these innovations in principle resulted in very little actual change; for the New Poor Law, in how it compromised with traditional practices, and even more, how it tried to reform them, resulted in an unrealistic, ineffective approach to poverty that forced tens of thousands of

[55] *BO*, Feb. 17, June 22, Nov. 30, 1848.
[56] *BO*, Jan. 1, 25, 1849; Feb. 2, 1854.
[57] Fraser, *British Welfare State*, 45–50, 85–7, 91–114.

working people to lose hope in the ideal of economic self-reliance and to live out their lives in misery and disgrace. The Poor Law, the voluntary relief committees, the working-class family, and the benefit society together provided sufficient resources for Bradford's urban proletariat to survive, at least marginally, during the late 1830s and 1840s; for, in spite of widespread exploitation, poverty, and periodic hunger, very few Bradfordians actually starved. The existing agencies of welfare, both public and private, could not resolve the contradictions of urban-industrial capitalism, but they could keep the system from total collapse.

Nevertheless, public welfare could be no more than a temporary expedient for an emergency situation. To attempt long-term solutions to the structural problems that the spread and intensification of proletarianization brought required deeper penetration into the nature of industrial capitalism than either the relief committees or the Poor Law could undertake. Indeed, with its utopian assimilation of the cause of human progress to the course of capitalist development and its blindness to contradictions arising between them, classical liberalism, whether voluntaristic or bureaucratic, lacked the conceptual tools for diagnosing the ills that urban-industrial society now faced. Only after entrepreneurial liberalism had been challenged by alternative approaches to capitalist crisis, advocated by traditional conservative and radical working-class groups, could its equation of productivity and progress be reformulated in a more plausible way.

15

Urban-industrial paternalism and the Tory radical revival

The social crisis of the 1830s and 1840s in Bradford placed traditional conservatives in a paradoxical position. On the one hand, the urban-industrial revolution had undermined their authority – eroding their capacity for economic and political leadership while destroying their cultural and environmental space. On the other hand, the failure of entrepreneurial liberalism to resolve the capitalist crisis of class lent a new relevance to the apparently discredited conservative program. So long as progress had seemed compatible with order and the market itself was viewed as a stabilizing force, the conservative project of paternalist protection could easily be dismissed as an obsolete myth. But when market freedom brought poverty instead of progress, the conservative values of order, hierarchy, and protection might well be reconsidered as potential answers to the problems that liberal individualism could not resolve. "The theory of universal non-interference," argued the Tory manufacturer William Walker, "so zealously advocated by some, is an impossibility . . . in continual collision with the practical facts."[1]

With the realization that Bradford's urban-industrial revolution posed not only a challenge to their own privileges and authority, but a material threat to the workers' physical welfare and life, Tory elites were emboldened to question the liberal equation of individual interest with social advancement and to insist that they, rather than their entrepreneurial antagonists, should rule. Amidst the mass poverty of 1842, they started their own newspaper, the *Bradford Herald,* to advance these claims. Editorializing against all the classic tenets on which the liberal *Observer*'s political position was built, the *Herald* attacked the nefarious system whereby "men are actuated by the spirit of unshackled covetousness" and permitted "to devote the lives of the working classes to their own unhallowed and unlimited gains." Bradford's "rich upstart, disaffected millowner[s] and merchant[s]," so far from being public benefactors, were a profoundly destructive group who, "finding it impossible to screw down their factory workers to a lower state of starvation," tried to

[1] William Walker, *Free Trade, Its Principles and Results* (London, 1858), 22.

414

deflect attention away from their own exploitation by "plac[ing] the guilt on the landowners."[2]

Although the *Herald* waxed eloquent about the iniquity of a system that paid "homage and respect to wealth irrespective of character" and that "made poverty a crime and treated the poor factory worker...as a mere machine," what was needed alongside this negative criticism was a positive program that could somehow translate nostalgia for preindustrial values into solutions appropriate for an urban-industrial age.[3] In fact, during the late 1820s and 1830s, there arose a new generation of Tory intellectuals who sought to transform conservatism into a social reform program for the stabilization of capitalism and the improvement of the welfare of the urban working class. Although these men spoke in the name of the Anglican Tory establishment, they had, both in personal style and social background, much more in common with the liberal entrepreneurial insurgents they attacked. Taking a leaf from their antagonists, they were determined to transform conservatism from a cynical defense of oligarchy into a popular ideology with universal appeal. Exalting the traditional values of deference and hierarchy, they also mounted an appeal to reason and self-interest, seeking to convince Bradfordians that what they needed was not the freedom of the competitive marketplace, but the stability that only paternalist protection could bring.

Tory radicals and the attack on liberalism

The most important of these new Tory Radicals, as they came to be known, was Richard Oastler (1789–1861) who became leader of the factory reform campaign. The son of a Leeds woolen clothier from Yorkshire yeoman ancestry, Oastler emerged from the same kind of lower-middle-class Methodist background that produced so many of Bradford's new entrepreneurs.[4] Apprenticed as an architect, he found employment as an estate steward in the West Riding hinterland. Although Oastler clearly relished the opportunities that his work afforded to play the role of a surrogate squire, he was no dyed-in-the-wool Tory during his youth. Quite the contrary, his earliest public involvements in Wesleyan evangelicalism, in the antislavery movement, and in organizing his employer's tenants to refuse to pay their tithes suggest affinities to the liberal Nonconformist creed.[5]

---

[2] *Bradford Herald*, Feb. 24, 1842.
[3] *Bradford Herald*, Feb. 10, Mar. 17, 1842.
[4] Cecil Driver, *Tory Radical, The Life of Richard Oastler* (New York, 1946), 13–16.
[5] Ibid., 17–35.

What turned Oastler decisively to the right was an invitation to investigate the condition of Bradford's factory children by the leading Anglican manufacturer John Wood. Horrified by what he saw, Oastler wrote a stirring letter to the liberal *Leeds Mercury*, appealing to his fellow advocates of negro emancipation to publicize the plight of their own wage slaves. To his astonishment, Oastler's appeal elicited not liberal assistance, but a series of harsh, vituperative attacks.[6] Stunned at the behavior of these friends of liberty, Oastler began turning his considerable polemical talents to unmasking the "canting oppressing capitalists" and "sleek, pious, Dissenters of Bradford" who would not extend the freedom they demanded for the black West Indian to the English children who worked in their mills. As he attacked the "brawling, praying, canting Dissenters...Messrs. Get-All, Keep-All, Grasp-All...Lie-Well, Swear-Well, Scratch-Em and Company," Oastler displayed the marks of a man who felt betrayed. These selfish, hypocritical, entrepreneurial upstarts who, "by means of cheating and lying had managed to scrape some thousands of pounds together," were brazen enough to proclaim, "We are the real benefactors of the poor – We are they who find them employment." Although they droned on endlessly about God and salvation, their behavior condemned them as "practical heathens" who worshipped only money and success.[7]

Although Oastler clearly relished this style of ad hominem vituperation, he also recognized that it was not enough merely to expose the hypocrisy of the Nonconformist industrialist. It would also be necessary to devise some realistic alternative to his liberal, individualist ideals, for Oastler knew firsthand that "the absurd notion that every individual in seeking his own aggrandizement must necessarily pursue the course which will benefit society" was a seductive, if dangerous, idea. To combat it, conservatives could not simply depend on ingrained habits of deference, but had openly to controvert the "cant" of "progress," demonstrating with the same logic and sophistication employed by liberals that "every step in this boasted progress leads backwards to the barbarism from which we sprang."[8]

Such concepts as "liberty," "progress," and "individualism" were, Oastler insisted, empty abstractions around which no real human relationships could form. Liberalism, so far from being a secular savior, was a monstrous illusion that brainwashed its victims with a fraudulent air of inevitability while wreaking havoc on every human reality that it touched:

[6] Ibid., 36–70.

[7] Richard Oastler, *A Letter to the Shareholders of the Bradford Observer* (Bradford, 1834), 13, 15.

[8] Richard Oastler, "Address to Meeting of Trade Delegates" (Bradford Archives, D.B. 27/17).

The Demon called *Liberalism* who is now stalking through the land scattering absolute want in the richest corn fields, and the deepest distress amongst the busy rattling of our looms assuming first one name and then another – March of Intellect, Political Economy, Free Trade, Liberal Principles, etc., but always destroying the peace of the cottage and the happiness of the Palace.[9]

With dismay Oastler watched these dogmas triumph economically and lamented even more bitterly as they were "adopted by every government as the foundation of all the new fangled *experimental* Acts that have recently disgraced our statute books and destroyed the value of labor.... What," he queried, "has been the result? Misery, wretchedness, destitution and despair accumulated in masses such as men had never before to study."[10]

Yet liberalism was not, as its prophets proclaimed it, an irresistable natural law. Like all "demons," it was, in reality, a delusion that its victims had allowed to be perpetrated on themselves. If the workers and traditional elites who were the losers in this experiment simply awoke to their common interests, they could join together to resist it, restabilizing the community in a conservative consensus in which the people would realize their true collective interests by subordinating themselves to benevolent paternalist elites. Unlike that of the liberals, the Oastlerite vision of consensus frankly acknowledged social inequality but insisted that hierarchy was perfectly acceptable to the lower orders so long as their needs were taken care of and their deference was duly earned.[11]

Oastler was joined in his quest for conservative renewal by several of Bradford's rising Anglican clergymen, particularly by the evangelical curate Rev. G. S. Bull. Like Oastler, Bull was troubled by the liberal image of society that placed impersonal laissez-faire "laws of nature" over actual human requirements and needs. As a clergyman, he particularly disliked what he perceived as an unconscious tendency toward atheism, not only among the new entrepreneurial voluntarists, but among the Dissenting ministers who articulated their creed. Bull marveled that men who called themselves Christians could defend child labor or the New Poor Law. He concluded that they had replaced the gospel's message of "love for thy neighbor" with an arrogant and materialistic worship of themselves. "Shall we pull down the altar of domestic piety," Bull queried, "and set up the golden calves of avarice and say 'these are thy Gods O' Israel'?"[12]

To abandon the dictates of Christian charity and community for the liberal

[9] Quoted in Driver, *Tory Radical*, 295.

[10] Oastler, "Address to Trade Delegates."

[11] Driver, *Tory Radical*, 292–306.

[12] J. C. Gill, *The Ten Hours Parson* (London, 1959); idem, *Parson Bull of Byerley* (London, 1973); G. S. Bull, *Public Meeting in Bradford on the Ten Hours Bill* (Bradford, 1833).

dogmas of market competition and individualist self-help was to invite not only divine retribution, but economic disaster with social suffering on an unprecedented scale:

> Trade may *fly* from place to place, and then the people must *fly* after it. And when they have flown till they can *fly* no longer, where are they to go – to the Parish? Oh No!...the national charity is to be abolished or nullified...the sacred right to have a subsistence from the land is to be denied to the poor.[13]

To the abstract "man" of liberal dogma, Bull, like Oastler, offered up the concrete case of the poor widow and the factory child. Like Oastler, he hoped that by publicizing their misfortunes he could goad both the old and the new industrial capitalists to rediscover that sense of paternal responsibility that was the hallmark of legitimate rule. To protect society from the dangers of chaos and perdition, to make the urban-industrial environmental socially stable and secure, a new social and political establishment would have to be constituted by a new kind of capitalist paternalism uniquely suited to the conditions of Bradford's urban-industrial world.

Industrial paternalism as a Tory radical ideal

Although Bradford's urban-industrial revolution undermined the material foundations of traditional paternalism, the Tory radicals were not entirely unrealistic in their hopes that industrial capitalism itself might harbor new forms of employer paternalism under which traditional relations of authority and deference might be revived. From the liberal egalitarian vantage of the marketplace, the industrial city appeared as an impersonal realm of competitive individualism in which customary hierarchies were out of place. Yet from the vantage of the factory where capitalist production was centered, social relations appeared in a different light. Here, beneath the surface of formal equality, a whole host of real hierarchies and inequalities were silently gestating and transforming the experience of the nascent industrial working class.[14]

Unlike the competitive marketplace, the factory was a structured social mechanism in which each actor was subject to supervision and authority in the performance of a set task. Here, freedom gave way to discipline as the requirements of mechanized production placed assistant, operative, over-

---

[13] Bull, *Public Meeting*.
[14] Patrick Joyce, *Work, Society, and Politics* (New Brunswick, 1980), xix, 50–89.

looker, and employer not as equal, autonomous competitors, but as links in a chain of coordination and command.[15]

As a society of ranks rather than an association of equals, the factory was closer to a feudal or bureaucratic military institution than to a voluntary association of the liberal ideal type. As in feudalism, authority and hierarchy were primarily instruments of dominance and exploitation used to extract an economic surplus from a mass of subordinate drones. Yet in both cases, domination and exploitation were not inconsistent with a modicum of paternal protection and sympathy. Like the feudal lord or slavemaster, the industrialist was motivated to care for his human machinery not only out of benevolence, but out of self-interest. Thus despite the decline of traditional modes of paternalism, there were reasons to think that the rise of the factory might provide material foundations for a new and more comprehensive paternalist regime.[16]

According to Tory radicals like Bull and Oastler, the paternalist role, once performed by the traditional gentleman, might now be assumed by the industrial capitalist who would find the task of supervising and protecting his workers beneficial, not only to the larger community, but to his own business success. Hence, the industrialist could make his claim to social and political hegemony, not as the impersonal bearer of abstract freedom in the marketplace, but through concrete leadership over working-class dependents that he exerted in the most immediate and personal way. To Vicar Scoresby, "no feeling" was more deserving of being cherished by the masters "than that of a kind, watchful, and strictly paternal consideration for their work-people. Every man and woman employed in a factory," he told a public meeting, "was a son or a daughter of the employer, so long as they were employed on his works." If capitalists would only acknowledge their paternal responsibilities, most of the social problems of industrialization would solve themselves. To perform on a large scale, the familial functions of nurture and protection might compensate for some of the failure of the working-class family itself. Under the guise of a watchful paternalist, poverty, exploitation, and environmental pollution, even if not entirely eliminated, would assume less dangerous, destabilizing forms. Most importantly, elites would regain the trust and affection of the masses, and harmonious class relations could be restored.[17]

Factory paternalism had long been practiced in the early, isolated, rural

---

[15] Karl Marx, *Capital*, 1 (Moscow, 1954); Andrew Ure, *The Philosophy of Manufactures* (London, 1835).

[16] David Roberts, *Paternalism in Early Victorian England* (New Brunswick, 1979), 22, 36, 171–83.

[17] William Scoresby, *American Factories and Their Female Operatives* (London, 1845), 106; *BO*, Nov. 13, 1845.

mills where it grew organically out of the technical requirements of industrial management. Here, where workers had to be recruited, housed, provisioned, and trained in the new disciplines of mechanized labor, the capitalist was obliged to be more than a mere employer. Necessity forced him to serve as the head of the factory community within which his workers both labored and lived.[18] Yet with the migration of industry to an urban setting, most of these supplementary management functions tended to disappear. The decision to locate in the city was often motivated by the capitalist's desire to limit relations with his workers to a cash basis, leaving the responsibility for recruiting, housing, feeding, training, and moralizing them to developers, shopkeepers, reformers, and the workers themselves. Could factory paternalism survive in the industrial city with its impersonal labor markets and large manufacturing plants? Could it become the basis for new forms of social hierarchy and collective responsibility that might grow out of the imperatives of capitalist production itself? Acting under the inspiration of Bull and Oastler, John Wood and a handful of other Anglican Tory manufacturers made a concerted effort in the late 1820s and 1830s to prove that it could.[19]

Wood's factory paternalist experiments cannot be separated from the problem of child labor since it was this problem that inspired his first ventures and always guided their subsequent shape. Of course, children were a particular species of worker and stood incontrovertibly in need of parental assistance and control. By taking child labor out of the cottage and putting it in the factory, especially if the work was not conducted under parental supervision, the capitalist had assumed obligations that were paternal in the most literal sense of the word.[20] "Can the child . . . brought up not under the eye of an affectionate and judicious parent but under the strap of an overlooker," asked Parson Bull, "be expected to become a loyal subject?" If capitalism had stripped the working-class family of its socializing functions, then the capitalist would have to take them up.[21]

As we have seen, Wood had always been sensitive to the practical and moral problems posed by child labor, and it was he who urged Oastler to draw public attention to them. As the largest millowner in Bradford after 1826, he felt guilty about his own role. As a businessman, he had to compete with other industrialists who worked young children thirteen or more hours per day. But as an evangelical Anglican who took the Bible seriously, in

---

[18] Sidney Pollard, *The Genesis of Modern Management* (London, 1965), 189–244.
[19] Roberts, *Paternalism in Victorian England*, 81.
[20] Neil Smelser, *Social Change in the Industrial Revolution* (Chicago, 1959), 184–205.
[21] G. S. Bull, *A Respectful and Faithful Appeal to the Inhabitants of Bradford* (London, 1832), 10.

every page he read, "My own condemnation."[22] Since Wood was compelled to employ young children, he resolved to make a virtue of this regretable necessity by improving their working conditions as much as he could, using his authority as their workday master to assume some responsibility for their general upbringing and welfare. Since Wood was more established than any of his competitors, he could more easily afford such *noblesse oblige*. He abolished all corporal punishments in his factory and introduced incentives by which industrious children could earn an extra copper per week. He expected his overlookers to treat their children kindly, and in 1833, he unilaterally reduced his working day to eleven hours.[23]

Most importantly, however, Wood built his factory children a school and hired a master and mistress to teach them moral values and the three Rs at his own expense. To insure that every child laborer spent at least two hours daily in school, he staggered their hours and hired an additional sixty hands. So proud was Wood of his educational experiments that he once called the schoolroom "the best room in my works." According to Lord Ashley, throughout the entire establishment, "Order, cleanliness, decency, comfort, reciprocal affections prevail." Five hundred children, he continued, "are receiving daily the benefits and blessings of a bringing-up in the fear and nurture of the Lord."[24]

Wood's paternalism in relation to his factory children (who constituted 84 percent of his workforce in 1832) increasingly began to color his attitudes toward all his workers and their families, even those who were mature adults. He made it a habit to visit long-standing employees when they were sick or disabled and invited them to dine with him at Horton Hall on Christmas day. More importantly, he set himself up as a resident squire in urban Horton by purchasing seven acres in the vicinity of his factory on which he built a series of working-class cottages and endowed and constructed an Anglican church. As curate, Wood hired Parson Bull, who was assisted by another Tory Radical, Matthew Balme, as schoolmaster.[25] Wood's logic in this costly and ambitious undertaking was explained by Rev. Bull himself:

> Mr. Wood has amassed considerable wealth in the trade of this town.
> He knows that without your hands that wealth could not have been

[22] Driver, *Tory Radical*, 41; J. T. Ward, "Two Pioneers in Industrial Reform," *Journal Of Bradford Textile Society* (Bradford, 1963–4), 33–51.

[23] *PP* (1833, XXI), 22; *BO*, May 15, 22, 1845; *BOB*, Apr. 21, 1906; J. T. Ward, "Matthew Balme, Factory Reformer," *BA*, n.s. 8 (1962), 218–28.

[24] *PP* (1833, XXI), 22; "The Factory System," *Blackwood's Edinburgh Magazine*, Apr. 18, 1833. Ashley quoted in Ward, "Two Pioneers," 45.

[25] John Clark, "History and Annals of Bradford, or Family Book of Reference" (typescript in Bradford Reference Library), 2:29, 35; Ward, "Two Pioneers," 33–51; *BOB*, Apr. 21, 1906.

created. He has thus been the means (as many other masters have) of locating a vast population in this town and neighbourhood, and he considers it his duty to God and to you, to provide you with a place where your children may be instructed, and to build you a sanctuary where, if you be so minded, you may assemble to worship your God."[26]

To such sentiments, Wood's workers seem to have responded in kind. "All seemed glad to see him," one later recalled, "as if it were felt and fully recognized that his was the grateful task to watch over them and promote their general good and that only one common interest existed between them."[27]

Wood's industrial-paternalist example was eagerly taken up by Bull and Oastler to convince other manufacturers to follow his lead. According to them, his experiments demonstrated that paternalism was more than just a morally satisfying gesture. It was a socially stabilizing policy that would restore habits of deference and tranquility to the working-class community and could even raise profits, at least in the long run. Short-term costs would be later recovered in the cultivation of a healthier, happier, and more productive work force, which would require less support from charity and poor relief.

Even before Wood enlisted Oastler in his campaign against child labor, he had spent five years trying to convince his fellow manufacturers that they ought voluntarily to limit the exploitation of young children, if only for reasons of enlightened self-interest. A few of the other second-generation, gentlemen–capitalist employers, such as Matthew Thompson and the brothers John and William Rand, did try to implement some of Wood's innovations and helped him canvass others to follow their lead.[28] However, the overwhelming majority of the other manufacturers, particularly those of the first generation, made no more than cosmetic adjustments because they put a priority on maximizing their immediate rate of return. Industrial paternalism was decisively repudiated, not only by Dissenters like Simeon Townend, but even by pillars of Bradford's Anglican Tory establishment, such as J. G. Horsfall, Thomas Hollings, and Swithin and John Anderton, all of whom were horrified by the prospect of a ten-hour limit on child labor or the obligation to subsidize their own factory schools.[29]

With the influx, over the next decade, of the new generation of Nonconformist insurgents, such sentiments became more militant and widespread. The intensification of competition in worsted markets and the insecurity of foreign demand dictated that the paternalist impulse be even more thoroughly

[26] G. S. Bull, *Laying the First Stone of A New School Room* (Bradford, 1837).

[27] Clark, "Annals of Bradford," 2:31.

[28] *BOB*, Apr. 21, 1906; Ward, "Two Pioneers"; William Cudworth, *The Ten Hours' Bill, Was it Passed by a Liberal or a Tory Government?* (Bradford, n.d.), 7.

[29] *PP* (1834, XX), 99–100, 105–6; Driver, *Tory Radical*, 52.

subordinated to the quest for profit and short-run success. For the parvenu liberals, this practical hostility to paternalism was reinforced and justified by the dictates of their theoretical creed. Uninspired by the paternalists' familialistic imagery and put off by the vision of a servile, dependent working class, they rejected all demands for special protection as interferences with market forces and as violations of the liberty of both masters and men. So unwilling were these liberals to treat their workers like children that they ignored the obvious fact that the vast majority of their workers were just that. Consequently they dismissed as an ideological regression what was, in fact, merely an incontrovertible biological need.[30]

For the parvenu preoccupied with capital accumulation amidst increasing competition, these biological needs of the working-class family might well seem like expensive luxuries that he could not afford. Moreover, competition itself introduced an almost irresistible imperative for all manufacturers to adopt the the lowest standards of labor management employed by those who treated their workers the worst. Even such staunch advocates of paternalism as Rand and Wood were compelled to temper their private schemes and special worker benefits and to behave more and more like everyone else.[31]

What made this lowest common denominator so truly abysmal was not only economic insecurity, but a psychological propensity exhibited by some parvenu industrialists to abuse newly acquired powers of domination and control. According to Parson Bull, "Such a power and influence is not infrequently placed . . . in the hands of men who have not profited by their own state of servitude, who have emerged from the ranks of labor not to show a clemency which they once so highly prized, but to exercise a tyranny against which they would have rebelled."[32] "It is to be feared," concluded the vicar in 1845, "that our master spinners and manufacturers *as a body* do by no means feel the responsibility in regard to the moral character and conduct of their hands which, on principles of Christian obligations, distinctly attach to them."[33]

Insofar as these "Christian obligations" for moral oversight might improve worker discipline or increase output, they were, of course, unhesitatingly embraced by millowners of all political creeds. Such was the case with the parvenu Dissenter Jonas Sugden who insisted that his employees attend Sunday worship and that anyone found drinking or gambling after hours be fired. Among most other employers, a less draconian system of

---

[30] John Fielden, *The Curse of the Factory System* (London, 1836).
[31] J. T. Ward, "Slavery in Yorkshire," *Journal of Bradford Textile Society* (Bradford, 1961–2), 41–52; idem, "Old and New Bradfordians in the Nineteenth Century," *Journal of Bradford Textile Society* (Bradford, 1964–5), 17–32.
[32] Bull, *Appeal to Inhabitants of Bradford*.
[33] Scoresby, *American Factories*, 103.

fines and penalties was implemented. Much rarer, at least before mid-century, were unremunerative acts of benevolence or any real evidence of entrepreneurial awareness of their workers' unrealized potentialities and unmet needs.[34]

Industrial paternalism in the Victorian city

After midcentury, employer attitudes, at least on the surface, did sometimes change. With the collapse of class militancy among the workers and the transformation of the entrepreneurial insurgents of the 1830s and 1840s into wealthy and established mid-Victorian elites, new possibilities for industrial paternalism seemed to open up. The first indication that the new conditions might bring a change in employer attitudes came during the economic upswing of 1849, when Titus Salt, suddenly finding himself awash in windfall profits, chartered a train one Saturday in August and treated all of his two thousand employees to a country excursion. As workers in other mills heard of this phenomenon, they requested a similar bounty from their masters, and over the next four weeks, at least twenty-one other Bradford millowners gave their fourteen thousand operatives and family members a Saturday holiday treat with trips to Skipton, Harrogate, Birkenhead, and Ripon.[35] "Two years ago," the *Observer* remembered, "employers were giving their £10, £50, and £100 to feed their unemployed workpeople; they are now giving their £100, £200, and £500 to feast them." "The effect of such entertainments," however apparently fleeting, was, the paper continued, "permanently good. . . . They tend to enlarge and refine the minds, and to cement the feelings of respect and attachment which must exist between the employer and his workpeople who participate in them."[36]

Such a widespread and spontaneous expression of employer generosity had been unprecedented in Bradford hitherto. In the past, a handful of the wealthier Tory millowners had treated all or part of their workers on rare public occasions, at the formers' weddings, anniversaries, or other family and firm events. Now the lead in these gestures of munificence was taken not by genteel conservatives like Thompson or Wood, but by the most successful of the new Nonconformist liberals, such as Salt, Illingworth, Garnett, Forster, and Smith, who had hitherto never treated their workers so openly solicitously.[37] Although the extravaganza of 1849 was never re-

---

[34] PP (1834, XX), 97–122; R. Spence Hardy, *Commerce and Christianity, Memorials of Jonas Sugden of Oakworth Hall* (London, 1857), 94–8; BO, June 3, 1858.

[35] BO, Aug. 23, Sep. 6, 13, 20, 27, Oct. 4, 11, 18, 1849.

[36] BO, Sep. 6, 1849.

[37] BO, Sep. 6, 13, 20, 27, Oct. 4, 11, 18, 1849.

peated, the tradition of factory feasts was continued by many industrialists, most often on special occasions such as openings, anniversaries, weddings, or industrial expositions and, in a few instances, as a regular annual event. To Robert Milligan, this represented a justifiable expense because of the wonders it worked on employee morale. At one point he joked, "If he meant to get rich, the more feasts he gave, the sooner he would be able to retire from business."[38]

The sight of masters and employees together on a weekend outing or sitting down at the dinner table in a transformed weaving shed conjured up the image, unmistakably familial, of a relationship transcending economic self-interest, suggesting bonds of a deeper and more permanent nature such as those between a father and his child. However, in practice, factory feasts were but ephemeral and symbolic affirmations of an industrial community that had little substance in ordinary workaday life. Only in a few exceptional instances were they really meant as preludes to a systematic commitment to build such a community in mortar and stone.

The first and most important of these mid-Victorian industrial-paternalist experiments was the model factory village that Titus Salt created five miles outside of Bradford in the bucolic valley he named Saltaire. In his recent study, Mr. Reynolds has demonstrated that Salt's decision to build his model community was the product of a mixture of Christian obligation, managerial imperative, and a desire for more effective social control. Reacting against the chaos of urban-industrial Bradford, Salt edged away from the uncompromising voluntarism of militant Nonconformity and began to pursue his functions and responsibilities as a successful industrialist in a quasi-paternalist mode.[39] A growing distaste for "that already overcrowded Borough" combined with a desire to consolidate his manufacturing operations, which had grown enormously during the 1830s and 1840s and were now dispersed among many combing workshops and four different mills, induced Salt to centralize operations in an entirely new factory village that would provide a healthier moral and physical environment for the workers while affording handsome profits for himself.[40]

In September 1853, on his fiftieth birthday, Salt celebrated the opening of his seven-acre spinning and weaving facility, then the largest in the world, with a gala dinner for 3,500, at which his intentions were publicly proclaimed: "to draw out around me...a population of well paid, contented, happy

---

[38] *BO*, Apr. 8, 1858. In 1863, at least twenty-two manufacturers again treated workers to celebrate the marriage of the Prince of Wales. However, on this occasion, most employers restricted the festivities to a relatively small skilled elite. *BO*, Mar. 12, 1863.

[39] Jack Reynolds, *The Great Paternalist* (London, 1983).

[40] *BO*, Sep. 22, 1853; Apr. 21, 1859; Reynolds, *Paternalist*, 70; Robert Balgarnie, *Sir Titus Salt* (London, 1877), 105–82.

operatives."[41] Over the next two decades, 815 model housing units were constructed for a population of 4,389, at a cost of £120 to £220 each. In contrast to the slum dwellings of downtown Bradford, these cottages, though small, were attractive, solidly constructed, well ventilated, and properly drained. In addition, they were provided with outhouses and hookups for utilities. By charging 2s. 4d. to 7s. 6d. per week to employees from piecers to overlookers, Salt was able, not only eventually to recover the costs of construction, but to obtain a 4 percent annual return.[42]

Churches, chapels, schools, public parks, and baths were also ultimately erected, and an institute to serve as a social and recreational center was built for £25,000 in 1871. Although Salt did not reside in his model community, he carefully supervised the activities and moral behavior of the workers who did, using his dual power as employer and landlord to enforce an atmosphere of Christian piety and temperance and to keep undesirable influences such as beershops out.[43] As Factory Inspector Redgrave correctly noted:

> Mr. Salt, in erecting an enormous pile of buildings, in filling them with modern machinery, and in providing habitations for the bulk of his workpeople, must be considered as so far performing no more than was necessary for the successful issue of a commercial enterprise: but it is the spirit in which all the separate parts have been conceived and the manner in which they have been executed, which extend beyond speculation and prove the benevolence and public spirit of the founder.[44]

Yet although inspiring effusive outpourings of praise and congratulation, Saltaire also evoked a degree of skepticism from the start. Bradfordians might well wonder if Salt was not simply abandoning the industrial city and its problems, evading his responsibilities as a municipal leader and ratepayer by decamping to a pristine, picturesque environment where a hothouse class harmony could be purchased on the cheap.[45] More and more it became evident that an isolated model community like Saltaire provided no real antidote to the problems of the industrial city. With its atypical conditions and unique advantages, it constituted an escape from, rather than a solution to, the problems of the urban-industrial milieu.

Few industrialists had either Salt's resources or incentives to create a

---

[41] *BO*, Sep. 22, 1853.
[42] Jack Reynolds, *Saltaire* (Bradford, 1980), 2.
[43] Reynolds, *Paternalist*, 256–325.
[44] *PP* (1854–5, XV), 337.
[45] Although overt criticism of Salt was rare, there were always some who suspected that his motives were more self-interested than philanthropic. Reynolds, *Paternalist*, 263–5, 281–6; *BO*, Apr. 21, 1859. This researcher encountered one explicit accusation of civic irresponsibility in Salt's move to the countryside. Unfortunately, the reference and citation have been lost.

self-sufficient industrial community. In Bradford, only W. E. Forster followed Salt's example by building a large factory in the countryside around Burley-in-Wharfedale, where he had chosen to reside. Such behavior, however noteworthy, represented a throwback to an earlier stage of manufacturing not characteristic of the industrial patterns of the Victorian age. No longer monopolized by a handful of pioneering magnates, industrial enterprise was now dispersed among dozens of ordinary, medium-sized firms. In this preeminent age of the industrial city, both population and enterprise tended to concentrate in large urban settings at a rate unmatched either before or since. No one would deny that the benefits of factory paternalism were at least partly attainable in a small-scale rural community where a wealthy industrial squire could rule, whether tyrannically or benevolently, with a vigilant, omnipresent eye. But it was highly doubtful whether such conditions could be re-created in the industrial city, where the anonymity of market relations held sway.

Although the question falls largely beyond the chronological scope of this study, it cannot be ignored because a school of revisionist historiography has recently arisen, arguing that paternalism, so far from being inimical to the Victorian urban-industrial environment, constituted one of the most important and effective ruling-class techniques for the preservation and restoration of social stability and for the consolidation of a new capitalist elite. According to David Roberts, it was precisely the "new and frightening problems" of these "urban and industrial revolutions" that not only "transformed paternalist ideas into a social theory," but "called for the more conscious practice of paternalism as a social remedy."[46] In a stimulating recent study, Dr. Patrick Joyce has gone even farther to argue for "the development of a far reaching employer paternalism" in the decades after 1850, not only in a handful of planned communities, but more broadly throughout the urban-industrial milieu. According to Joyce, industrial paternalism came to constitute a systematic mode of capitalist hegemony that provided much of "the mechanics of social stability and class domination" that underpinned the mid-Victorian consensus.[47]

Resting his case on what Dr. Martin Wiener has called the "gentrification of the industrialist," Joyce contends that "later nineteenth century society developed in such a way as to make localism and territory more rather than less significant." Focusing his attention on the urban setting, Joyce paradoxically concludes that "the ecology of the factory town," the persistence "of the English family firm," and the spread of conservatism among the

---

[46] Roberts, *Paternalism in Victorian England*, 22. See also D. C. Moore, *The Politics of Deference: A Study of the Mid-nineteenth Century Political System* (Hassocks, Sussex, 1976).

[47] Joyce, *Work, Society and Politics*.

employer class all "powerfully retarded the growth of impersonality, calculation, and class segregation that are so often and so simplistically supposed to have marked the development of factory life." In the face of this onslaught of employer benevolence, "the worker acquiesced in his own subordination," and the stabilization of mid-Victorian society was achieved not so much through the embourgeoisement of a labor aristocracy as through "the emergence of feelings sufficiently deep-rooted to be called deference" in the vast majority of ordinary factory hands.[48]

Although Joyce's arguments highlight the vigor and diversity of the paternalist impulse in the industrial setting, as a general explanation of bourgeois hegemony or mid-Victorian social stabilization his argument fails. Most of his evidence is drawn from the middle-sized Lancashire and Pennine factory communities such as Ashton, Blackburn, Bolton, and Staleybridge where, even after midcentury, a small clique of established industrial magnates dominated to an unusual degree. Even here, many of Joyce's conclusions about the power of employer territoriality rest on questionable inferences and debatable links. Proletarian neighborhood culture is equated with a "culture of the factory," which is, in turn, assumed to be an employer-inspired culture, initiated and supervised from above. Evidence about working-class religion and social life, which might have been interpreted through the lens of associational voluntarism and understood as indigenous manifestations of the working class, is enlisted in the paternalist argument as further evidence of employer power.[49]

Joyce is on strongest ground in his path-breaking studies of working-class voting, which clearly demonstrate that, in parliamentary elections, many operatives who lived and worked under the shadow of leading millowners consistently followed their employers' lead.[50] However, in the context of the mid-Victorian state and society, it is unwise to equate electoral deference with deference in other spheres. Given the restricted social basis of the franchise, it is not surprising that party politics in Westminster rarely confronted the basic issues of social and economic welfare in which workers were collectively interested as a class. "The political situation of electors," Professor Vincent reminds us, "did not in general involve capitalism, factory production, a propertyless proletariat, or personal conditions arising from the conditions of production." Even during the late thirties and forties, when militant workers were determined to change this state of affairs, class issues entered the party political arena only in distorted and attenuated form. Hence

---

[48]   Ibid., xiv, 90, 94.

[49]   Joyce, *Work, Society and Politics*.

[50]   Patrick Joyce, "The Factory Politics of Lancashire in the Later Nineteenth Century," *Historical Journal*, 18:3 (1975). See John Vincent, *The Formation of the British Liberal Party* (London, 1966), 112–52.

voting is a highly imperfect measure of consciousness, and mid-Victorian working-class deference at the hustings did not preclude the persistence of a fiercely independent spirit in trade unions, friendly societies, and neighborhood pubs.[51]

Most significantly, Joyce has trouble extending his claims about paternalism from factory towns that were dominated by a few millowners to larger industrial cities like Bradford in which capitalist wealth and power were more widely diffused.[52] Given the anomic character of the urban environment, it is difficult to imagine how meaningful personal relationships between masters and workpeople could ever have been established or maintained. By midcentury, even small factories had employees in the hundreds, composed largely of adolescents and young women who rarely stayed more than a few years. Frequent changes of proprietorship further limited the intimacy that was possible between workers and millowners.

Even in the more stable economic environment of the 1850s and 1860s, when the wave of bankruptcies, layoffs, and wage cuts that had characterized the previous two decades began to taper off, the atmosphere of class relations in the factory only marginally improved. The widespread tendency of most millowners to continue to blame accidents and abuses on misguided overlookers or the carelessness of the operatives suggests that they had only a limited knowledge of, or interest in, what actually went on day to day in their plant.[53] As for the life of the laborer after the work day had ended, "What wide and absorbing interests she has; a mother at home, a sick brother, a young baby, a dying father; herself diseased perhaps, or under great temptation, troubled in conscience or in deep sorrow. You take in her work and pay her wages," complained this anonymous critic of Bradford's employers. "Ah if you only knew her at home. What a world of interests which machinery is deaf to. But you are a machine to her and she to you. It is, indeed, the Iron Age."[54]

It was a rare capitalist who could (like Joseph Wilson) seriously claim, "My object and purpose when in business is to keep in mind the Sermon on the Mount." Even his gestures of special interest such as sending each of his 250 employees an individual birthday letter, though surely welcomed, seem a bit artificial and strained.[55] In any case, the intentions of individual employers, whether benevolent or exploitative, were less important in setting

---

[51] John Vincent, *Pollbooks: How the Victorians Voted* (Cambridge, 1967), 27.
[52] To Joyce, *Work, Society and Politics*, 26, Bradford is "the largest of the factory towns rather than the smallest of the industrial cities." An apt characterization of its transitional nature, this observation would have been more accurate the other way around.
[53] *Reports of Factory Inspectors.*
[54] *BO*, May 27, 1858.
[55] Joseph Wilson, *His Life and Work* (London, n.d.), 29–32.

the tone of factory relations than the structural forces that operated in an impersonal way. The level of social control that was normal in an isolated factory village was simply impossible to achieve within the city, whether the industrialist sought it or not. The mounting concern expressed by elites during the 1840s and 1850s over the deteriorating moral condition of the work force reflect bourgeois anxieties about the growing autonomy of the workers much more than changes in working-class behavior itself.[56]

The persistence of employer territoriality that Joyce emphasizes so heavily was little in evidence in Victorian Bradford. As in many other contemporary towns, the pattern of urban development was governed by the preponderance of the petit bourgeois builder and the primacy of the small-scale freehold plot. Outside certain parts of Bowling and Manningham, no working-class neighborhood was dominated by a single mill. This tendency for employer power and influence to be distributed through several medium-sized firms meant that the Saltaire model of a planned factory community was largely irrelevant to the circumstances in which the urban industrialist was placed. Even those few who might have had the resources to attempt such an experiment came to realize that there was not much chance it could succeed. Their search for hegemony over the industrial proletariat necessarily had to take entirely new forms. The old methods of traditional paternalism were simply irrelevant to the task at hand.[57]

The impossibility of paternalism under urban-industrial conditions can be seen in the failure of Bradford's Anglican Tory manufacturers to accumulate sufficient local influence and authority to play the role of industrial squires. With their hierarchical image of social relations and their attachment to traditional institutions and beliefs, such men were under far more ideological pressure than the liberals to expand their protective, paternalist roles. Moreover, in the established church, they possessed a potentially powerful instrument, which their Nonconformist counterparts lacked, for translating territorial and patriarchal authority into effective institutional terms. The parish had played a key role in organizing the traditional community and

---

[56] *BO*, Oct. 26, 1848; June 21, 28, Jul. 26, 1849.

[57] By contrast, in the hinterland villages surrounding Bradford, employer territoriality was more tenacious. In Low Moor, where the Low Moor Ironworks owned most of the land, class relations seem to have remained almost feudal well into the mid-Victorian age. When the resident owner, Charles Hardy, feasted all 3,600 company employees to celebrate the Prince of Wales's marriage in 1863, the workers proclaimed their loyalty in no uncertain terms: "Many of us have from our earliest childhood until now known no other masters and it would afford us much pleasure to think that our children after us should have the benefit of the same happy relation." *BO*, Mar. 21, 1863.

had, throughout the medieval and early modern periods, served as a bulwark of gentry rule. By building and endowing their own factory churches, the Anglican Tory manufacturer might have re-created a style of leadership that went beyond the specific functions of the workplace boss.

John Wood was particularly conscious of these possibilities, and church endowment constituted an important part of his overall paternalist scheme. Nevertheless, the results of Wood's experiments in this area did not encourage other industrialists to follow his lead. In his efforts to make his factory church a de facto parochial center, Wood encountered stiff opposition from Vicar Scoresby, who regarded all fees collected within the Bradford jurisdiction as his own ecclesiastical prerogative. According to Wood, this petty-minded, self-interested attitude "must virtually prevent the object I had in view, forbidding the minister the performance of one office and... in effect denying all others, depriving such district of the benefits of the parochial system, without which, in my humble opinion it avails but little to build churches."[58] Disillusioned with the prospects for Christian paternalism in the industrial city, Wood moved away in 1840 to an estate in Hampshire, where he could function more effectively as a true country squire. In disgust, he simply closed his factory church in Horton and sent his minister, Parson Bull, to Birmingham for a better job.[59]

After this debacle, no other Anglican manufacturer in Bradford ever again endowed his own personal church. Most could not have afforded to do so, but even among the few who could, the prospect of building a territorial chapel only to have it swallowed up in the anonymity of Bradford Parish cannot have been appealing. Moreover, in light of the religious apathy and cultural diversity of the urban work force, the elusive potential benefits of church endowment had to be set against the certainty of its enormous cost. St. John's Church, built in 1840, was funded wholesale by a wealthy outsider, and thereafter, all future churches constructed within Bradford Parish were financed through a combination of local subscriptions and large grants from the ecclesiastical commissioners or church building societies that drew in donations from wealthy Anglicans unconnected with the town.[60]

Although leading Anglicans, such as Charles Hardy, John Hollings, Samuel Laycock, J. G. Horsfall, Joseph Sturges, Joshua Mann, and William Rand, all made contributions of several hundred pounds over the years, no particular church bore the distinctive stamp of any single patron, and no donor achieved sufficient ascendancy over any minister or congregation to

---

[58] Ward, "Two Pioneers," 40.
[59] J. C. Gill, *The Ten Hours' Parson* (London, 1959), 191.
[60] John James, *History and Topography of Bradford* (Bradford, 1842), 223; idem, *Continuations and Additions to the History of Bradford* (Bradford, 1866), 184–6.

enforce his unilateral will. Sometimes this resulted in messy controversies. In one, between Rand and the rector of St. John's, whom he partly subsidized, squabbling spilled over into the pages of the press. Unwilling to increase his annual contributions, Rand was publicly berated by his irate minister as an irresponsible patron who was "fickle in his affections" and neglectful of professed commitments to support the church.[61]

The absence of dominant lay patrons in Bradford's churches further enhanced the authority of the vicar, elevating him into a subdiocesan administrator who, subject to the support of leading lay donors, coordinated clerical activities throughout the town. Gradually, whatever paternalist impulses remained among mid-Victorian Bradford's Anglican industrialists were channeled into collective projects, promoted by the professional clergy, and mediated by the institutional bureaucracy of the church.

If Bradford's Anglican Tory manufacturers abandoned urban paternalism, the liberal Nonconformists, who lacked their ideological predispositions, were even less inclined to become industrial squires. Although liberals might toy with the symbolism of factory feasts as a minor component of their consensual celebration of mid-Victorian equipoise, naked paternalism made them uneasy, and they continued to seek social harmony not through overt working-class deference or submission, but through voluntary acceptance of liberal values and entrepreneurial ideals. Although "the employer of labour," the *Observer* argued, had "responsibility beyond paying his workmen their wages," the paper remained convinced, "There is a considerable difference between the position of the country squire and that of the employers of labour in the towns."[62] Even Titus Salt did not see his model community so much as a paternalist venture as an effort to find a painless short cut to the original liberal goal of creating a self-reliant working class. No doubt it was illogical to pursue this voluntaristic object by patriarchal, even despotic, means, but this was a contradiction inherent in the liberal entrepreneurial vision, which Saltaire merely brought into sharp relief.[63]

This ambivalence and even hostility toward blatant paternalism was even more marked among other entrepreneurial parvenus, as evidenced by the behavior of Henry Ripley, the only one of Salt's contemporaries who even attempted to transport his vision of a planned factory community directly into the urban milieu. Amidst the renewed prosperity of the 1850s and 1860s, Ripley looked back nostalgically to the harmonious class relations that, he imagined, had prevailed before his time. Seeking to recover "a

---

[61] James, *History of Bradford*, 223; idem, *Continuations and Additions*, 184–6; *BO*, Nov. 9, 23, 1854.

[62] *BO*, Aug. 17, 1865.

[63] *BO*, Sep. 22, 1853.

certain sociability and freedom of intercourse which had since passed away," Ripley began to reach out to his employees not by projecting the image of an authoritarian patriarch, but by "making those with whom he came in contact feel that he was not merely their master but one of themselves, as far as it was possible for a master to be."[64]

As a prosperous dyer who had established himself in Bowling, Ripley was one of the few entrepreneurs who had acquired substantial tracts of urban land. In 1865, he built 300 cottages to sell on mortgage to his workers and overlookers through a special building society partly financed by himself. Although the idea was not to make the inhabitants of Ripleyville into permanent dependents of their employer, but independent homeowners in a model housing tract, considerable difficulty was experienced in attracting suitable candidates for purchase. The inflated value of urban property and high cost of construction made it virtually impossible to provide housing that was both decent and affordable. When it became clear that the model dwellings were beyond the means of the majority of workers, a less ambitious scheme was implemented, providing cheaper units only marginally superior to existing housing in other working-class districts. As these cottages were gradually bought up by the same small speculators and landlords who owned most working-class housing throughout the city, Ripleyville disappeared as a distinctive community and remained only a name on the map.[65]

The failure of these neopaternalist ventures and the unwillingness of most Victorian manufacturers to attempt even such schemes demonstrates the fundamental incompatibility between the original Tory radical ideal of factory paternalism and the basic structure of the urban-industrial milieu. Industrial paternalism was put on the social and political agenda in the early 1830s because the evils of child labor in the factory posed a threat to the viability of the urban working-class family. If the millowner would assume, the Tory paternalists argued, broad responsibility for the education and socialization of his youthful employees, he could legitimize his authority and mitigate the worst symptoms of urban poverty and class exploitation.

Naturally, most millowners were either unwilling or unable to assume the burden of regulating the work and subsidizing the education of their factory children. When the task was not accomplished spontaneously by benevolent capitalists, it had to be undertaken compulsorily by the state. Once this had happened, by the middle of the century, the campaign for industrial paternalism ran out of steam. A system that failed to meet even the most basic needs of children could hardly be expected to address satisfactorily the

---

[64] *BO*, Oct. 20, 1868.
[65] S. M. Gaskell, "Housing Estate Development, 1840–1918, with Particular Reference to the Pennine Towns" (Sheffield, Ph.D. dissertation, 1974), 102–4.

complex problems and possibilities of adults. Despite the familiaristic imagery of factory feasts and outings, the shift to a largely adolescent and adult factory work force effectively undercut paternalism as a significant industrial-capitalist managerial mode.

When carried beyond the walls of the factory, paternalism was, in the fully urbanized environment, an even less appropriate mode of social control. In an isolated rural factory village like Saltaire, it could function as a means of supervising and improving the work force although even here it had to be supplemented by less authoritarian means. In the industrial city, with its diverse population and multidimensional cultural possibilities, it was almost entirely out of place. However resentful workers may have been of their inability to achieve independence within the framework of liberal industrial capitalism, conservatives erred in thinking that the former rejected self-reliance as an ideal. Accustomed to scoring points with workers by attacking liberal hypocrisy, Vicar Scoresby badly misjudged his audience when he condemned "the spurious species of independency which would incline him [the worker] ... to act disrespectfully to those above him."[66] "The Bradford Operatives," warned the *Observer*,

> are generally speaking persons of advanced intelligence.... They are independent, acute, and self-relying.... You have not to arouse or awaken the Yorkshire factory labourer; he is thoroughly aroused and wide awake, nor will he be moved by sentimental addresses or appeals to traditional connexions. He has his brains and his fingers and those who want them must buy them, and he will sell them in the best existing market.[67]

Of course, the history of the mid-Victorian age of equipoise demonstrates that the urban worker could be integrated into industrial-capitalist society. However, such integration would not be extracted by fear, deferential habits, or the patriarchal mystifications of elites. It would take place voluntarily through the workings of the marketplace where self-interest and purposive rationality reigned. Moreover, when Bradford's workers finally acquiesced in the wage–labor relationship as the most realistic framework within which self-improvement could be obtained, their deference was not directed to some individual capitalist father figure, but to capitalism as an impersonal system and to the entrepreneurial bourgeoisie as a hegemonic class.

Tory radicals, workers, and the state

Although the Radical Tory revival that Bull and Oastler initiated failed to inaugurate a new urban-industrial paternalist age, it catalyzed a groundswell

---

[66] William Scoresby, *American Factories and their Female Operatives* (London, 1845), 102.
[67] *BO*, Sep. 8, 1853.

of independent working-class radicalism and laid some of the first foundations of the future welfare state. These results formed no part of the Tory Radicals' original aims, for Bull and Oastler remained, first and foremost, conservative traditionalists who simply assumed that the new urban-industrial order required the active leadership of indigenous elites. Nevertheless, the failure of Bradford's capitalists to perform their appointed role in the drama of paternalist revival compelled serious reformers to look beyond the myth of benevolence and to explore more innovative political solutions to capitalist crisis and more radical agencies of social transformation.[68]

In the face of conservative elite apathy and liberal entrepreneurial hostility to their admonitions about the necessity of voluntary factory reform, Bull and Oastler were compelled, almost from the outset, to advocate compulsory regulation by the state. This put them in an awkward position, for as conservatives, they were hostile toward strong central government and remained sentimentally attached to the tangle of local, traditional authorities that had been gradually accumulating for centuries within the framework of the English Old Regime. Nothing evoked in them a greater horror than the intrusive, centralizing forms of governmental intervention (such as the 1834 Poor Law) that characterized the legislative agenda of the post–1832 Whig liberal regime. To the Tory radicals, this embryonic, utilitarian, bureaucratic state was inconsistent with sacred values and time-honored rights. Under the cloak of political and economic liberty, it portended a new kind of capitalist class tyranny that would reduce freeborn Englishmen to the status of wage slaves.[69]

By contrast, men like Bull and Oastler were drawn to a more traditional vision of government, less rationalistic and more concerned with the social content of rule. The state, according to this older perspective, was not so much an impersonal apparatus for public administration as the institutional repository of moral authority that bound the constituent elements of society into an organic whole. Grounded in a corporatist vision of unity, such a state was inseparable from the hierarchically graded ranks and orders of civil society that made it up. As an ethical, as much as a regulatory body, this kind of state would necessarily subordinate the logic of efficiency to the dictates of morality, empowering local elites within stable communities at the expense of bureaucratic control from above.[70]

Although this traditional body politic had a secular existence, it was inconceivable without the transcendent bulwark of a religious establishment that could hallow its worldly institutions and aims. But if the state needed the church, Oastler argued, the church also could not perform its religious function of making "men in all their actions fully aware of their duties to

---

[68] Driver, *Tory Radical*, 49–190.
[69] Ibid., 191–268.
[70] Karl Marx, *Critique of Hegel's Philosophy of Right* (London, 1970), 131–2.

God and their neighbours" until it had thoroughly "Christianize[d] the State. ...All the great questions of the age," he continued, "are each and all directly within the province of Christianity and, consequently of a national Christian Church."[71]

In stark contrast to the voluntarism of the liberal Nonconformists, Oastler believed that Christian faith would conquer the heart of the private individual not when religion was divorced from government, but when, through the agency of a clerical establishment, the practical morality and teaching of the gospel became the basis for the political and social policy of the state. "I gather my politics from the Holy Scripture," he insisted, for "Christianity is part and parcel of the law... [it is] interwoven in our constitution." Thus, Oastler only needed to turn to the Bible to justify his conviction "that it is the first duty of government to protect the health and strength of the people and to see to it that health and strength shall always everywhere be used for the increase of the national wealth."[72] When government became merely instrumental or utilitarian, losing sight of these higher, spiritual ends, individuals would lose their sense of connection to a wider community and their capacity to be moved by ethical ideals. If Bradford's elites had abandoned their social responsibilities in a squalid search for economic gain, this was, at least in part, because they had rejected the moral authority of a politicized church and succumbed to the ethical nihilism inherent in the very notion of a secular state.

Yet just as the failure of voluntary paternalism had compelled the Tory radicals to turn to state compulsion, their reactionary, almost theocratic conception of government ultimately led them to turn from elites to the laboring masses to gain support for their social reform campaign. At the outset, Oastler had envisioned the factory question as a humanitarian issue. When his initial appeals to paternal benevolence fell on deaf ears, his first instinct was not to rouse dispossessed provincial workers, but to appeal to the politicians who ruled in Westminster. Only when this strategy got him nowhere did Oastler recognize the necessity of building a popular movement that could combat the ideological appeal of liberalism by advancing its own, even more universalistic claims.[73]

In fact, Oastler's turn to populism came at a critical moment, when popular liberalism was at its peak. To astute conservatives, the factory issue offered an irresistible opportunity to embarrass their increasingly formidable opponents, while generating their own political antidote to the liberal clamor for constitutional change. Nothing was better calculated to deflate the liberal entrepreneurs' self-image as providential vessels of the general good than

[71] Richard Oastler, *Convocation: The Church and the People* (London, 1860), 14.
[72] Ibid., 29.
[73] Driver, *Tory Radical*, 41–57; *Leeds Mercury*, Oct. 16, 1830.

to arouse the workers against the exploitation and cruelty that their factories practiced as a daily routine.[74] Well aware of its value in turning back the challenge to their social and economic authority that had been mounted by the new generation of entrepreneurial parvenus, leading establishment Tories like Wood, Walker, Rand, and Thompson provided Oastler's campaign with financial backing, Wood donating over £40,000 during the course of the decade.[75]

This focus on the factory was attractive to conservatives, not only because it turned workers against the insurgent liberals, but because it disclosed the most promising possibilities for established elites and exploited laborers to find a common social and political ground. Rampant, unchecked industrial development was a prospect that equally threatened both. Together they stood to gain from a slower, more stabilized pattern of socioeconomic development than entrepreneurial liberalism allowed.[76] By attacking the factory system, elites could demonstrate that conservatism was more than a cynical rationalization of their privileges – that it also advanced a social vision superior to that of the liberals, offering greater benefits to society as a whole.

Yet as good conservatives who identified with the establishment, Oastler and the Anglican Tories who joined him were wary of any alignment with popular radicalism and initially sought to keep the organized working-class movement at arm's length. Although freely acknowledging that, alongside the throne and the altar, the humble cottage constituted a pillar of the state, Oastler and his Tory backers responded nervously when the cottagers left their proper place as objects of benevolence and emerged as active agents of social and political change.[77]

Nevertheless, in sharp contrast to the political reform campaigns of the liberals, factory reform was an issue in which workers had an independent interest that grew directly out of their conditions of life. Their support could be harnessed by the Tories, but it did not have to be first conjured up. Long before Oastler discovered the factory question, trade unions had raised the issue, and his campaign became the catalyst by which a whole series of seething class grievances were openly voiced. Forming themselves into operative-run, short-time committees in the spring of 1831, Bradford's workers, under the inspiration of Oastler's rhetoric, began to articulate all the inchoate anticapitalist instincts that liberalism habitually tried to repress.[78]

At first, even Oastler was taken aback by this new development, and he

---

[74] Driver, *Tory Radical*, 100–117, 178–90; William Paul, *History of the Operative Conservative Societies* (Doncaster, 1845), 2.
[75] Ward, "Slavery in Yorkshire," 45.
[76] See Chapter 5.
[77] Driver, *Tory Radical*, 85–9.
[78] Ward, *Factory Movement*, 41; G. D. H. Cole, *Attempts at General Union* (London, 1953), 67–9.

reconciled himself to active working-class participation only after the strength and political color of the opposition became clear. In June, he received a deputation from the short-time committees, and after some discussion, a tacit compact was made "to work together totally irrespective of political or party considerations" to achieve a ten-hour limit on factory work. By 1832, the new movement had adopted all the now familiar liberal tactics of mass meetings, processions, and organizing committees. Petitions were circulated obtaining 12,000 signatures in Bradford, and in July 1833, a demonstration on Wibsey Moor was reported to have attracted a crowd of 100,000. In the same year, the Bradford Political Union, against the wishes of its liberal founders, registered support for the ten-hours cause.[79]

How the factory movement differed from its liberal counterparts was that it became more, rather than less, working class in character as its organization improved. Although Tory radicals placed greater reliance than the liberals on charismatic leadership, institutionally, the workers themselves assumed more and more control over the movement, as elites scrambled to follow their lead. Oastler himself was deeply influenced by his contact with the workers, and his role as popular spokesman led him and, to a lesser degree, Parson Bull to turn their visceral hostility toward liberalism into an increasingly systematic social and economic critique. The ideology that resulted from this encounter began to press the limits of Oastler's vision of a philanthropic Tory theocracy, momentarily stumbling onto the yet undiscovered vistas of a modern, redistributive welfare state.[80]

This shift from philanthropy to the borderlands of social democracy can be seen most clearly in the factory movement's change of focus from the limited desire to curb child labor to a wider determination to obtain a ten-hour day. Limiting the factory workday in this manner represented a much more radical intervention into the labor market, protecting not only children, but adults in both the factory and handicraft trades. The ten-hour limit was intended to diminish economic instability, to raise wages for all categories of labor, and to ease the position of marginal small masters too. According to the representatives of Bradford's handloom weavers, it would "prevent that severe competition amongst masters and manufacturers which has loaded their warehouses with an overabundant stock, glutted all the markets of the world, reduced the price of commodities, broken up or which threaten to break up all who do not trade upon abundant capital."[81]

"Without some equalization of employment," Parson Bull prophesied,

[79] Driver, *Tory Radical*, 88; Ward, *Factory Movement*, 32–106; Ward, "Slavery in Yorkshire," 45–7.

[80] Driver, *Tory Radical*, 81–139.

[81] "Petition of Inhabitants of Bradford to House of Commons" (Bradford Archives, D. B. 27/17).

"the small owner of machinery can get no profits and the honest operative no sufficient wages." By thus acting as a check on the anarchy of the trade cycle, factory reform would "bring the supply of manufactured goods more nearly equal to the profitable demand." Here again a ten-hours law would be a stabilizing influence, rendering the workers' class position less insecure. Moreover, "by employing more hands at better and more steady wages," it would "increase buyers and consumers in the home market," thus lessening the dependence of the entire industry on the violent ebbs and flows of international trade."[82]

Built upon the old Tory hostility toward liberal cosmopolitanism, these rudimentary underconsumptionist arguments began to take on an increasingly sophisticated, socialistic strain. Insofar as it remained compatible with the older Tory protectionist tradition, Oastler was able to support this new vision of social stabilization through economic autarky. "How erroneously we build our hopes," he argued, "when we flatter ourselves that prosperity has increased in proportion to our exports. . . . The very reverse is the fact, that increase being the consequence of our ability to consume at home."[83]

To liberal warnings that factory regulation would undermine the competitiveness of British manufactures, the Tory radicals argued that, even if true (which they did not believe), the alternative of a more diversified, self-sufficient domestic economy in which the sordid quest for profit maximization would be contained might be beneficial even in purely material terms.[84] A measure that eased cut-throat competition might also support proletarian purchasing power and would permit the beleaguered capitalist to forge a broader sense of his calling in which the imperatives toward economic innovation would be intermixed with a sense of obligation to those he employed: "Instead of constantly grovelling among the concerns of the factory, he would occasionally be enabled to cast an eye towards subjects more ennobling to his faculties and better calculated to advance his happiness. He would also have the satisfaction which a good conscience confers."[85]

According to William Walker and William Rand, the ten-hour measure would not only enable the operatives to educate their children, it might also ease the overcrowding and disease of the dense inner city by leaving them time to commute from the suburbs to work. Indeed, the Tory radicals hoped that government regulation would facilitate the relocation of factories back

[82] Bull, *Meeting on Ten Hours' Bill;* anon., *Report and Resolutions of a Meeting of Deputies from the Handloom Worsted Weavers* (Bradford, 1835); "Petition of Handloom Weavers and Employees of Bradford to the House of Commons" (Bradford Archives, D.B. 27/17).
[83] Oastler, *Address to Trades Delegates.*
[84] Driver, *Tory Radical,* 59–80.
[85] "Speech of Charles Walker" (Bradford Archives, D.B. 27/17).

to the countryside, or even a revival of some domestic handicrafts and a return of some urban-proletarian families back to the land.[86]

As the factory movement went beyond Oastler's initial Tory humanitarianism to the frontiers of an anticapitalist critique, it grew more intransigent, reacting with intensified hostility to the 1833 Whig Factory Regulation Act. This hostility has often been attributed to the radicals' jealousy of their opponents and their fear that the success of a half-measure would undercut the chances for more comprehensive reform.[87] Alternatively, it has been suggested that the short-time committees were using factory children as battering rams to fight adults' battles and that they rejected any limitation on child labor that did not also benefit adults.[88] Although there is some truth in both explanations, the movement's opposition to the Whig factory legislation was also deeply rooted in ideological grounds.

The explicit purpose of the 1833 act was to reconcile minimal regulation of the factories with the laissez-faire principles of the liberal creed. By declaring children under thirteen incapable of being economic free agents, it could legitimize government regulation of their labor without any interference in the competitive labor market for independent adults. Like the Poor Law, the Factory Act was a utilitarian measure designed to buttress the natural operations of the marketplace by separating out those who were necessarily dependent and placing them under the supervision of centralized bureaucratic rule. In fact, it was this aspect of the Factory Act, particularly its provisions for the creation of a professional inspectorate, that enraged Tory radicals like Oastler the most. Tyrannical intrusions by outside investigators would, he argued, be entirely unnecessary if the work force were not artificially classified into dependents and free agents by the arbitrary criterion of physical age. The ensuing thicket of bureaucratic paraphernalia, medical certificates, relay schedules, and educational clauses, could all have been avoided by the enforcement of a universal ten-hour day.[89]

But as the influence of their alliance with organized workers pushed the Tory radicals into an increasingly anticapitalist stance, their supporters among Bradford's Anglican Tory establishment began to edge away. Even more alarming than radicalism in theory was the adoption of new tactics of political militancy, which drew respectable figures like Bull and Oastler to applaud and even participate in confrontational activities. The defeat of Sadler's Ten Hours Bill in 1832 and the passage of an unacceptable alter-

---

[86] William Walker and William Rand, *A Letter Addressed to Sir James Graham on the Ten Hours Factory Question* (Bradford, 1841); *Bradford Herald*, Jan. 20, 1842.

[87] Driver, *Tory Radical*, 237–50; Ward, *Factory Movement*, 110–19; Smelser, *Social Change in the Industrial Revolution*, 2, 39–40.

[88] Oliver MacDonagh, *Early Victorian Government, 1830–70* (London, 1977), 42–54.

[89] Driver, *Tory Radical*, 237–50.

native in the following year generated widespread bitterness throughout the movement rank and file. Alienated by the intransigence of the post-Reform government, Bull and Oastler adopted a new tone of angry belligerence that seemed to belie their status as Christian gentlemen who spoke in the name of conservative elites. In 1834, Bull lost credibility in genteel circles when he attended a meeting of Bradford's socialists even though he had come to coax them back to the fold.[90] Two years later, when Oastler began to advocate strikes to obtain a ten-hours act, his old patron, John Wood, broke off relations as did several other establishment elites.[91]

However, what brought Tory radicalism to its point of crisis was the confrontation that erupted in 1837, when the authorities began implementing the New Poor Law. Repudiating the last vestige of traditional protection and embodying the ascendancy of the new liberal utilitarian creed, this action solidified, with the authority of the statute book, the same assault on the viability of the working-class family that the factory system had begun in the economic realm. "I will not submit to it," Oastler bluntly expostulated. "It is an act of TREASON against the constitution, against Christianity, against the State, and against the King as well as the Poor." The factory short-time committees were justified in organizing a campaign of Poor Law resistance because, he contended, "The two questions were . . . inseparably connected."[92]

Yet when Oastler joined workers in open defiance of the law, he pushed the limits of radicalism that could still remain Tory, and he lost the good will of his remaining supporters in the conservative camp. A few months later when the anti–Poor Law movement turned violent, he was even deserted by his erstwhile ally Parson Bull. Even Oastler was sobered by the autumn rioting, which tempered his own desire to seek social justice and reawakened his deepest impulses to see order maintained. By 1838, when the working-class radicals openly repudiated paternalism and embraced their own independent Chartist creed, Oastler warned that universal suffrage would bring only "universal confusion." At this point he too began to lose the support of the masses who turned to a new set of leaders of their own.[93]

With the rise of independent working-class Chartism and the departure of Richard Oastler from center stage, Tory radicalism effectively collapsed. First abandoned by the conservative elites who had initiated it, now rejected by the mass of the workers themselves, it became clear by the end of the

[90] *BO*, Feb. 27, Mar. 6, 20, 1834.
[91] Ward, "Slavery in Yorkshire," 49.
[92] *BO*, Mar. 9, 1837; G. S. Bull, *The Substance of a Lecture on the New Poor Law Act* (Bradford, 1834); Driver, *Tory Radical*, 334, 339.
[93] *BO*, Nov. 2, 1837; Driver, *Tory Radical*, 350–408; John Knott, *Popular Opposition to the Poor Law* (London, 1985), 163.

1830s that the crisis of urban-industrial capitalism in Bradford would never be resolved by a return to the past. Establishment Tories continued making half-hearted bids for working-class allegiance and played on popular anti-liberalism for tactical advantage in elections. Never again, though, would a mass, extraparliamentary movement be organized by conservative leaders along traditional lines.

The Bradford Operative Conservative Society, founded in 1837 and promoted just as the factory movement was winding down, was an attempt to institutionalize the spirit of that movement, whose failure showed how much the situation had changed. Organized by James Wade, a local Tory innkeeper and election agent, the society never attracted more than a few hundred members and never obtained even passive mass support. With a reading room and facilities for meeting and discussion, the society was clearly important in the lives of its members, providing them with their own associational culture and contributing much to the creation of a local Tory Party organization that could canvass and register conservative electors. However, this was a pale reflection of that brief moment in the early and mid-1830s when charismatic leaders like Bull and Oastler could rouse tens of thousands of workers with their vision of a stable, moral, and constitutional order based on the benevolence of paternal employers and the protection of a Christian state.[94]

Conclusion

Tory radicals like Bull and Oastler were among the first to face a dilemma that has haunted reflective conservatives ever since: how to defend an established order in an era of rapid social change. Under these circumstances, even a return to traditional values and practices constitutes a form of disruption and marks a breach with the status quo. When conservatism takes the form of radicalism, that which is to be conserved has already been lost. Conservatism, by nature, resists radicalization and belies universalization in explicitly ideological forms. Its legitimacy derives not from the revolutionary promise of totalizing abstractions, but from the concrete reality of specific social hierarchies and traditions, historically present at a particular time and place. As they root themselves in tradition and history, conservatives must find sustenance in some still living source. The yearning for order degenerates into reactionary nostalgia when it cannot draw upon vital wellsprings

---

[94] Paul, *Operative Conservative Societies*, 26–9.

of authority, breathing legitimacy into otherwise arbitrary hierarchies and giving stability definite meaning and shape.[95]

Unlike liberalism, which failed because its ideals and values were too narrowly rooted in the experience of a single class, Tory radicalism was doomed from the outset because it was fully acceptable to none. With its emphasis on the values of order, tradition, and community, it was, at root, a conservative doctrine primarily concerned with legitimating elites. Yet it was rejected by Bradford's mid-nineteenth-century industrial capitalists because the paternalist obligations to which it enjoined them were too onerous to bear in a competitive economic environment and proved largely irrelevant to the task of social stabilization in a dynamic, impersonal urban milieu.

Repudiated by the elites who were its natural beneficiaries, Tory radicalism was forced to rely on social institutions and agencies that were fundamentally inimical to its underlying aims. When industrialists did not voluntarily subscribe to his doctrine that "property has its responsibilities as well as its rights," Oastler was forced to turn to the state. Yet he knew that the bonds of community, if they were to be truly organic, had to arise spontaneously and could not be imposed by bureaucratic fiat. However, in the urban-industrial environment, his alternative vision of a paternalist theocracy was bound to fail. Paradoxically, his efforts on behalf of factory regulation contributed to the bureaucratic welfare state of the future, whose Benthamite prototype he hated and feared.

Oastler's turn to a fundamentally alien state administration as his instrument for social reform was paralleled by his turn to the working-class movement as the vehicle for bringing social renewal about. Yet to ally with the workers was to embrace an agenda in which antagonism toward entrepreneurial liberalism was being transformed into opposition to the capitalist system as a whole. In the context of an industrial society, such an agenda could hardly be conservative, since it raised the specter of a revolutionary transformation whose effects would have been far more destabilizing and disruptive than any of the liberal innovations it sought to retract.

As these contradictions unfolded in their lives and experiences, the Tory radicals were forced into an impossible situation: becoming adversaries of the traditions they sought to rescue and agents of the changes they were determined to resist. Trapped by this historical irony, the man who had spent his life glorifying the throne and the altar could, in the bitterness of 1838, suggest that if "the Church is no longer that of Christ... the Throne is no longer that of England... the nobles are no longer safeguards of the people.... Then, with their bitterest foes I would cry, Down with them,

---

[95] Edmund Burke, *Reflections on the Revolution in France* (New York, 1955), 35–50; Karl Mannheim, *Ideology and Utopia* (New York, 1936), 131, 200, 234.

Down with them all to the ground."[96] In the end, Richard Oastler was not really prepared to level the church, the throne, or the aristocracy, and yet, almost in spite of himself, he helped to shape the collective consciousness and spark into action the class that, in the late thirties and forties, sometimes appeared as though it would.

[96] Quoted in Driver, *Tory Radical,* 434.

16

The emergence of working-class culture and consciousness

In mid-nineteenth-century Bradford, two conflicting elite images of the worker had emerged. To the liberal he appeared through the lens of entrepreneurship as a self-improving and potentially self-reliant individual who, by imitating the entrepreneurial model, should achieve full citizenship in urban-industrial society. To the conservative whose highest values were stability and social order, the ideal worker was fundamentally a dependent being who should continue to defer to legitimate authority as long as his basic needs were met. Both bourgeois factions clung to their respective images despite mounting evidence that neither exactly fit, because they were unwilling to accept the possibility that workers had a social identity independent of their own. Proletarianization might degrade, even animalize the worker, but insofar as he retained the human attributes of consciousness and culture, these were to be interpreted in liberal or conservative terms. That workers might develop an autonomous culture or become aware that they constituted a distinctive social class was a possibility that neither bourgeois faction could seriously entertain.

So powerful and pervasive were these bourgeois images of the worker that they still color historians' views today. Modern scholarly literature on nineteenth-century workers is dominated by dichotomies between the independent and the deferential, the activist and the apathetic, and the respectable and the rough, which resemble the original antinomies of Victorian liberal and conservative views. Often seen as rooted in economic distinctions between skilled "labour aristocrats" and unskilled plebeians, these cultural dichotomies figure even in the work of historians who frame their analysis in the comprehensive terms of a classwide culture, but acknowledge the force of cultural diversity too.[1]

---

[1] E. P. Thompson, *The Making of the English Working Class* (New York, 1963) especially 711–832; R. J. Morris, *Class and Class Consciousness in the Industrial Revolution, 1780–1850* (London, 1979); G. F. A. Best, *Mid-Victorian Britain, 1850–75* (New York, 1971), 256–64: Brian Harrison, *Peaceable Kingdom* (Oxford, 1982); Patrick Joyce, *Work Society and Politics: The Culture of the Factory in Later Victorian England* (New Brunswick, 1980); Thomas Laqueur, *Religion and Respectability: Sunday Schools and Working Class Culture,*

445

The dangers of assuming that all workers constitute a homogeneous entity are now universally conceded. Every working class throughout history has consisted, to some degree, of diverse subgroups. Historians and social scientists have long recognized that different types of workers command different income levels in the labor market, either due to custom or because their work involves divergent degrees of autonomy and skill.[2]

Although this differentiation may be too elusive to substantiate arguments about a labor aristocracy superordinate to the masses, it can delineate a rougher dichotomy between the unusually privileged or skilled and those, broadly speaking, without special privileges or skills.[3] The privileged market position of specially skilled or protected workers confers substantial material advantages, inclining them toward forms of consciousness and organization narrowly limited by the interests of their particular craft. By contrast, the mass of unskilled or unprotected laborers are usually also the least educated and culturally sophisticated and frequently encounter insuperable obstacles in developing viable labor organizations because, for them, successful organization requires a much wider and more universal sense of class solidarity, more abstracted from specific workshop identities and ties.[4]

1730–1850 (New Haven, 1976); Geoffrey Crossick, *An Artisan Elite in Victorian Society: Kentish London, 1840–1880* (London, 1978); Trygve Tholfsen, *Working Class Radicalism in Mid-Victorian England* (London, 1976); Peter Bailey, *Leisure and Class in Victorian England: Rational Recreation and the Contest for Control, 1830–1885* (London, 1978); idem, "Will the Real Bill Banks Please Stand Up? Towards a Role Analysis of Mid-Victorian Working Class Respectability," *Journal of Social History*, 12 (1979); and Neville Kirk, *The Growth of Working Class Reformism in Mid-Victorian England* (Chicago, 1985).

[2] See Sidney Webb and Beatrice Webb, *The History of Trade Unionism* (London, 1913); Charles More, *Skill and the English Working Class 1870–1914* (London, 1980); Roger Penn, *Skilled Workers in the Class Structure* (Cambridge, 1985); and Raphael Samuel, "The Workshop of the World: Hand Power and Steam Technology in Mid-Victorian Britain," *History Workshop*, 3 (1977).

[3] For the debate about the labor aristocracy in Britain, see E. J. Hobsbawm, *Labouring Men* (London, 1964), 321–70; Henry Pelling, *Popular Politics and Society in Late Victorian Britain* (London, 1968), 37–61; Robert Gray, *The Aristocracy of Labour in Nineteenth Century Britain* (London, 1981); John Field, "British Historians and the Concept of the Labour Aristocracy," *Radical History Review*, 19 (1978–9); H. F. Moorehouse, "The Marxist Theory of the Labour Aristocracy," *Social History*, 3:1 (1978); Alastair Reid, "Response to Moorehouse," *Social History*, 3:3 (1978); Karl Marx, *Capital* (Moscow, 1954) 1:589–606.

[4] Hobsbawm, *Labouring Men*; John Foster, *Class Struggles and the Industrial Revolution* (London, 1974); Gareth Stedman Jones, *Languages of Class* (Cambridge, 1983); Richard Price, *Masters Unions and Men: Work Control in Building and the Rise of Labour, 1830–1914* (Cambridge, 1980); Iorwerth Prothero, *Artisans and Politics in Early Nineteenth Century London* (Folkstone, 1979).

The social foundations of working-class cohesion

In Bradford, as elsewhere, this distinction between skilled and unskilled workers was characteristic of traditional preindustrial forms of production. But the whole thrust of urban-industrial capitalism was to transform the production process in ways that broke this traditional distinction down.[5] The handicraft workers, especially the woolcombers, who constituted the majority of Bradford's adult men, saw themselves as skilled artisans whose craft was being deskilled and degraded by the spread of mechanization and by the innundation of unskilled newcomers willing to work for substandard wages. The women and adolescents who formed the bulk of the new factory operatives also defied classification in skilled–unskilled terms. Previously excluded from the wage-labor market, they were now entrusted with complex and costly machinery and earned wages much higher than they could have obtained anywhere else. Nevertheless, since their earnings were quite low compared to mens' and their work offered few chances for advancement and required little skill, they were the first exemplars of a new semiskilled category that would expand wherever mechanized production spread. Like the woolcombers, their status is captured more accurately by an analysis of their changing position within capitalist production than by any static measures of their income level or skill.[6]

Despite the impact of proletarianization, Bradford's actual working class, even at midcentury, was not entirely the sort of pure proletariat that Marxist theory specifies. In part, this was because workers themselves resisted proletarianization and retained, as far as possible, the marks of personal identity fostered outside the workplace by family and community life. More importantly, at midcentury the wholesale proletarianization of productive labor in Bradford remained incomplete. According to the data from the 1851 working-class census population, (whose compilation is described in Appendix B), factory operatives comprised 47 percent of the work force and the degraded woolcombers an additional 17 percent. Nevertheless, 15 percent were artisans skilled in traditional crafts, working mainly in the urban-service sector, which the transformation of the worsted industry had scarcely touched. Another 5 percent had skilled engineering or supervisory occu-

---

[5] Some recent work by labor historians and economists David Gordon, Richard Edwards, and Michael Reich, *Segmented Work, Divided Workers* (New York, 1982), and Charles Sabel and Jonathan Zeitlin, "Historical Alternatives to Mass Production," *Past and Present*, 108 (1985), has suggested that capitalist development may not always operate in this manner and that new forms of working-class segmentation and division can flow from the logic of capitalist production itself. On the whole, the experience of nineteenth-century Bradford corresponds far more closely to the classical Marxist view as set out by Marx in *Capital*, 1.

[6] See Chapter 13.

pations that the spread of factory production had opened up. Though a relatively small minority, these skilled workers were among the best organized and highest paid, and they constituted 39 percent of all employed adult men. Nevertheless, notwithstanding their special position in workplace, these men could never wholly constitute a labor aristocracy and always retained important links with the proletarianized masses.[7]

As indicated in Chapter 13, in addition to proletarianization within the labor process, several factors helped to level workers from many different occupations and crafts. The ill health and overcrowding that accompanied urbanization were most acute among Bradford's poorest workers, but because these effects were broadly environmental, even the more fortunate were adversely touched. Similarly, economic depression devastated not only worsted workers but also craftsmen within the secondary urban-service sector, whose welfare and security were, after 1825, governed (albeit less inexorably) by the primary industrial sphere. Finally, our examination of working-class family structure has demonstrated that living standards and income levels were not usually attributes of individual workers, but of collective family units. The families of skilled workers were, as we have seen, subject to the same economic strains inherent in the life cycle, particularly at the stage when the ratio of family dependents to wage earners was at its peak.[8]

Although skilled artisans certainly possessed material advantages that unskilled or semiskilled laborers lacked, such factors were by no means entirely decisive in determining how their families lived. Fifty-seven percent of all families headed by skilled workers in the working-class census population lived in relative comfort, as compared to 17 percent among other working-class families. During the period of danger (LCS 3 and 4 in Fig. 13–5) when the family depended most heavily on the earnings of the head, 23 percent of the families headed by skilled workers were below the minimum poverty level and only 31 percent were above the comfort line, as compared with 73 percent and 4 percent, respectively, for other working-class families. Moreover, 27 percent of the families headed by skilled workers took in lodgers to augment their family income, as compared with 39 percent of other working-class families. These statistics indicate that although real comfort was generally limited to families headed by skilled men, even in good years family poverty was a condition that could be found in every occupational sector of the urban working class.[9]

As we shall see, the market advantages of Bradford's skilled artisans did

[7] Calculated from information in HO, 107/2,308.
[8] See Chapter 13.
[9] Calculated from information in HO. 107/2308.

induce them to form labor organizations designed primarily to protect their crafts, but these did not preclude other social and political involvements that reflected wider solidarities of class. Class solidarities came naturally even to artisans during the late 1830s and early 1840s, not only because proletarianization to some extent touched them directly, but because they were well integrated into the urban working-class community at large. Residential patterns show that they were physically dispersed throughout the working-class districts and gave no evidence of constituting a caste apart. The clear-cut residential segregation between bourgeoisie and workers, documented in Chapter 4, was not accompanied by any comparable degree of intraclass residential differentiation within the working class itself. Of course, some working-class neighborhoods were better and more costly than others, but these differences correlated more closely with variations in total family income than with the occupational status of the family head. Since virtually every household headed by a skilled worker also contained a mixture of other employed laborers who were unskilled, semiskilled, deskilled, or all three, there was, almost by definition, a high level of occupational integration among workers who quite literally shared the same houses, rooms, and beds.[10]

More to the point, every working-class neighborhood contained a mixture of the entire range of urban occupations, although the exact balance between them varied from one to the next. Although the districts in which our 1851 working-class census population resided were among the poorest in town, the proportion of skilled workers in them (20 percent) is broadly similar to what the published census returns suggest for Bradford's working-class population as a whole. Moreover, within these slum neighborhoods the households headed by skilled workers did not form separate enclaves. They were usually bunched in small clusters of two to four families that were dispersed throughout a host of other families headed by woolcombers, operatives, laborers, widows, or the unemployed. Seventy-four percent of all the households headed by skilled workers in these districts had at least one next-door neighbor whose head was not skilled. Conversely, only 26 percent of all households headed by skilled workers were surrounded by families like themselves. Such figures do not indicate the presence of a closed artisanal elite.[11]

If it is not inevitable that there should be unbridgeable barriers between the proletarianized masses and the artisanal minority that still retained some

---

[10] Ordnance Survey, *Map of Bradford* (six inches to the mile) (London, 1850).
[11] Calculated from information in HO, 107/2,308

control over its work, other distinctions such as the division between English natives and Irish immigrants had more self-evidently divisive effects. Even more than the skilled–unskilled dichotomy, this ethnic distinction reflected the enduring power of traditional cultural identities, even in the face of proletarianization's homogenizing effect. Separated from native workers not only by linguistic and cultural differences, but by long-standing religious hostilities and prejudices that set them at odds, the recently arrived workers from Ireland were, in many ways, truly a caste apart. Since 96 percent of Bradford's midcentury Irish (who constituted 9 percent of the urban population) were concentrated either in woolcombing or unskilled occupations, these ethnic divisions overlapped occupational distinctions, reinforcing the potential disdain of skilled workers for the proletarianized with potent atavistic prejudices of religion and race.[12]

In a detailed study of the social geography of Bradford's Irish population, Dr. C. Richardson has shown that about 80 percent of it was concentrated in a series of seven well-defined slum enclaves within the larger proletarian residential zone. These Irish, with their alien appearance, superstitions, and peasant mores, had a reputation for brutality, intemperance, laziness, and volatility that often encouraged English workers to disdain them as class comrades and to see them as a savage and inferior breed.[13] For the most part, such racism remained submerged and silent, although, on occasion, it erupted in violent skirmishes between warring Protestant and Irish Catholic gangs. The most serious occurred in 1844, when a group of 200 to 400 Orangemen paraded with a band through an Irish neighborhood singing "Boyne Water" to celebrate the defeat of papism in 1689. Not surprisingly, the result was a full-scale riot in which several Irish were arrested and one Orangeman was killed.[14]

However, until the late forties, these ethnic antagonisms remained fairly muted and did not completely fractionalize the urban working class. Although almost all Irish workers were unskilled or proletarianized, they constituted, even in 1851, no more than about one fifth of these occupational groups. Hence ethnic hostilities were not surrogates for class fragmentation so much as obstacles that pitted the proletarianized against each other, but which both antagonists had good reason to overcome. When questioned by a visiting journalist, a group of English woolcombers at first expressed only disdain for the "shiploads of Irishmen" who "don't sleep in beds" and who "pigged together on the floor ...pulling down the wage...worse than the new machine." However, the interviewer reported, "notwithstanding this display of animosity, my guide

[12] C. Richardson, "The Irish in Victorian Bradford," *BA*, n.s. 9 (1975), 295–316; idem, "The Irish Settlement in Nineteenth Century Bradford," *Yorkshire Bulletin of Social and Economic Research*, 20:1 (1968), 41–57.

[13] Richardson, "Irish in Victorian Bradford"; *BO* June 5, 1851.

[14] *BO* May 30, June 6, July 25, 1844.

informed me that, on occasions of difference between masters and workmen, English and Irish pulled together in the most brotherly fashion."[15]

As we shall see, a solid record of interethnic cooperation in trade unions and Chartist organizations throughout the late thirties and early forties shows that, in the face of powerful impulses for class solidarity, racial or religious prejudices could be held in abeyance. Even strictly ethnic movements, like Irish nationalism and the Protestant Orange response, endowed participants with an experience of abstract causes, militant strategies, and mass organizations that, except insofar as they actively engendered hostility, may have paved the way for alternative movements and organizations based on the economic solidarities of class.

There is even evidence that, when not inflamed by demagoguery, relations between Irish and English workers were reasonably good. None of the "Irish" districts noted by Dr. Richardson were ethnic ghettos in the classic sense. Of the 88 Irish-headed households in our 1851 working-class census sample, 82 percent resided next door to at least one English-headed household, and only 18 percent were surrounded by Irish on both sides. Sixteen instances of mixed marriages were discovered, representing 20 percent of all married Irish in the group.[16]

Like differences based on skill level, those grounded in ethnicity cannot be ignored in any general account of the structure of the urban working class. At the same time, their significance should not be exaggerated, especially at the expense of other distinctions based on age, gender, and family situation, which scholars have more frequently ignored. Even such factors as education, social background, and residential location might materially affect the circumstances of any given worker and thus constitute additional coordinates that ought to be considered when his or her socioeconomic position is mapped. Since these forces were not always mutually reinforcing and often cut through one another in myriad, complex ways, they did not bifurcate Bradford's workers into clearly distinguishable sections with completely divergent or incompatible interests and experiences. Proletarianization was itself a powerfully leveling process, but even when it did not entirely homogenize workers into a uniform dehumanized lump, they were often "sewn together" by their own inner divergences, which frequently counteracted one another or cancelled each other out.[17]

Yet amidst this universe of working-class socioeconomic complexity in which proletarianization stands out as the most dominant force, there remain the

---

[15] A. B. Reach, *Yorkshire and the Textile Districts in 1849* (Blackburn, 1974), 21–2.
[16] Calculated from information in HO 107/2,308.
[17] In this argument, I adapt a notion development by Brain Harrison, *Peaceable Kingdom*, 5, 125, who uses it to make a case for commonality not within, but between, social classes.

cultural dichotomies between rough versus respectable, apathetic versus activist, and servile versus self-reliant, which left so strong an impression on contemporary observers and modern historians alike. In Bradford, however, these cultural antinomies were not so much mutually exclusive attributes of distinct individuals dividing workers into two incompatible cultural camps, as coexisting polarities within the same personality that pulled most workers in opposite directions at once. Peter Bailey has suggested that workers who appeared "rough" in one social setting might behave entirely respectably in the next. In Bradford, such cultural conflict within the individual was reinforced by the larger historical framework of urban-industrial transformation, which left workers torn between nostalgia for a vanished community and the necessity of functioning in a modern market world. Hence a fundamental ambivalence toward both the respectable values of industrial capitalism and the traditional communitarian culture that it replaced was structured into the experience of first-generation urban-proletarian life.[18]

Unlike their entrepreneurial bourgeois counterparts, Bradford's working-class immigrants could neither fully assimilate into the new competitive individualist environment nor wholeheartedly internalize its liberal ideals. Yet unlike the Anglican Tory establishment, these workers were denied the luxury of simply rejecting the values of the urban-industrial world. Deprived of paternalist protection, they could not express their distaste for liberal individualism by embracing the ideals of deferential organicism that were being offered by the purveyors of the Tory radical creed. Caught between an ideal of servility that no longer protected them and a promise of self-reliance effectively beyond their reach, the workers who emerged from the proletarianizing process had to transcend the limits of both "roughness" and "respectability," forging their own cultural synthesis in which communitarian moral values and voluntaristic modes of association were integrated and fused.

Armed with liberal ideals of independence and equality, Bradford workers now turned on the bourgeoisie who had introduced these ideals but who blocked their realization within the existing frame of capitalist social relations. Subordinated and dependent in their essential social being, workers then turned to the old traditions of communitarian protectionism to give content to their new aspirations for autonomy and advancement, casting them in collectivist, rather than individualist forms. Breaking down the liberal and conservative legacies they had inherited, Bradford's workers began to transcend both bourgeois visions of their destiny as they forged, in the crucible of their distinctive class experience, a cultural synthesis all their own. This creation of a new proletarian culture out of the materials bequeathed from

---

[18] Bailey, *Leisure and Class*, 80–91, 101; idem, "The Real Bill Banks."

the old is most evident in Bradford workers' handling of the legacy of community, a legacy that bourgeois conservatives would abstractly idealize and that bourgeois liberals would, in principle, reject.

Working-class culture and the tradition of community

In the contest between bourgeois liberals and conservatives for the allegiance of the workers, the problem of community inevitably arose. To entrepreneurial liberals who identified with competitive individualism, the legacy of a normatively grounded community transcending the free market's distributive laws necessarily appeared as an irrational atavism, a threat to both the freedom of the individual and to the welfare of the larger society in which he or she lived. When it became clear that individual freedom and opportunity had been purchased at a disastrous human and environmental cost, the way was open not only for the ideologically imagined "community" of conservatives, but for workers to remember the concrete communities from which they had originally come.[19]

Not only were these first-generation, working-class immigrants more likely than their bourgeois counterparts to have come directly from village backgrounds, they were also more inclined to remain close to rural friends and relatives, even after their arrival in town.[20] Those, particularly women, who came when they were young and unmarried, often envisaged their time in Bradford as a temporary sojourn, signaling their commitment to their families of origin by regularly sending portions of their pay back home. Even for workers who did become permanent residents, the proximity of native villages made it easy for hinterland immigrants to return home frequently and to recall the environment in which their ancestors had lived. Among the woolcombers, according to one contemporary, there was a tradition "that in hay-time and harvest he used to lay aside his woolcombs, take up his scythe ... and go to his own country a-harvesting."[21]

For such workers, the cultural baggage carried with them from the countryside not only remained a vital part of their identity as city dwellers, but fortified them with antidotes to the disorientation of the urban environment and the alienation of industrial work. As we have seen, traditional plebeian notions of community had long been animated by assumptions about a moral economy in which customary prerogatives took precedence over innovative

---

[19] See Chapters 2 and 15.
[20] See Chapter 6.
[21] William Scruton, *Bradford Fifty Years Ago* (Bradford, 1897), 95–6; Joan Scott and Louise Tilly, "Women's Work and the Family in Nineteenth Century Europe," *Comparative Studies in History and Society*, 17 (1975).

initiatives, and collective survival took priority over individual gain. Imported by working-class immigrants into the city, this residual moral economy became a kind of cultural raw material out of which entirely new notions of community could be built. Far more than the exhortations of Tory radicals or even the utopian projections of socialist visionaries, it was Bradford workers' memories of a precapitalist moral economy that enabled them to counter urban-industrial alienation and empowered some of them to envision a more humane and moral postcàpitalist world.[22]

This transmutation of traditional "moral economy" notions of community, in the crucible of industrial-capitalist development, into a workers' culture and consciousness of class is, of course, the central theme of E. P. Thompson's work. Yet Thompson's use of evidence from plebeian communities to buttress historical arguments about the formation of class has elicited considerable skepticism from scholars such as Craig Calhoun who painstakingly elaborates the explanatory problems this entails.[23]

As a sociologist concerned with matters of clarity and definition, Calhoun rightly insists that, at the conceptual level, "class" and "community" are not the same. But although such ideal type distinctions are analytically significant, the historian is concerned with the concrete reality in which they are invariably mixed. As they were actually encountered in experience, class and community were not mutually incompatible forms of solidarity, characteristic of diametrically opposite social systems and appearing alternatively in different historical times.[24] Rather, as Thompson so brilliantly demonstrates, they were, at least in nineteenth-century Britain, coexisting, complementary impulses that brought workers together from different directions at once. The process of proletarianization in an impersonal urban world compelled workers to forge more abstracted forms of consciousness based on the wider, more generalized solidarities of class. Yet in practice, class consciousness obtained concrete grounding in the dense nexus of immediate personal relationships that the older communitarian sociability preserved. Nevertheless, although class consciousness was sustained by a plebeian culture of

---

[22] E. P. Thompson, *English Working Class*, 55–101, 401–47, 711–832; idem, "The Moral Economy of the English Crowd in the Eighteenth Century," *Past and Present*, 50 (1971); idem, "Patrician Culture, Plebeian Society," *Journal of Social History*, 7:4 (1974); idem, "Eighteenth Century English Society: Class Struggle Without Class?," *Social History*, 3:2 (1978).

[23] Craig Calhoun, *The Question of Class Struggle: Social Foundation of Popular Radicalism During the Industrial Revolution* (Chicago, 1982).

[24] Calhoun, *Class Struggle*, 3–32. Calhoun's distinction draws on the classic sociological dichotomy between gemeinschaft and gesellschaft, first formulated in analytical terms by Ferdinand Tönnies, *Community and Society* (Ann Arbor, Mich., 1957).

community, the advent of urban-industrial capitalism transformed this plebeian community and its moral economy in a number of significant ways.[25]

However tenuous its underlying foundations or problematic its relationship to elites, community in protoindustrial Bradford still represented not only an ideal of social organization, but the physical environment in which most inhabitants worked and lived. In practice, elites distanced themselves from the common people and neglected the responsibilities of their paternalist role, but they never repudiated the principle of a moral economy or disputed the community's right to the protection and market regulation that was necessary for its members to subsist. At minimum, they knew that failure to provide this protection would lead to bread riots or other forms of direct action through which the community would collectively enforce the moral economy itself.[26]

As industrial capitalism created a new and fully globalized marketplace while urbanization obliterated the traditional community's physical space, the moral economy became increasingly unacceptable, even as an ideal. After welfare policy was taken hostage by free-market Benthamism and popular direct action became intolerable to the new generation of entrepreneurial elites, community had to be socially constructed, something that not only belonged uniquely to workers but that they had consciously to reinvent for themselves. With the advent of full-scale proletarianization, the very meaning of the moral economy was radically transformed. When it resurfaced in the 1820s and 1830s in trade unions, cooperatives, and short-time committees, its focus had shifted from the obvious plight of the consumer in an inflationary food market to the underlying exploitation of the producer that occurred within capitalist production itself. Actively assailed by the new entrepreneurial liberals and increasingly repudiated even by traditional elites, this fully proletarianized version of the moral economy began to underwrite a more abstracted, classwide vision of community as it assumed more militant and purposive organizational forms.[27]

Yet to refashion precapitalist traditions of community in an environment fractured by the atomizing force of competition and infused with individualistic behavioral norms was a task that was almost bound to fail. The kind of community traditionally nurtured in the protoindustrial village simply could not be imported directly into the factory town. Although the family could migrate en masse to the city and reappear as a unit of consumption

[25] Thompson, *English Working Class* 401–47, 711–832; idem, *The Poverty of Theory* (New York, 1978), 164–72.

[26] See Chapter 2 of this volume and Thompson, "Moral Economy."

[27] Thompson, "Moral Economy," 128–30; Prothero, *Artisans and Politics*, 328–40.

even after its viability as a unit of production has been undermined, preexisting communities were obliterated in Bradford's squalid, amorphous working-class slums. The 1851 census manuscripts indicate that villagers, unlike family members, showed no measurable propensity to move to Bradford in clusters or to settle down in the same place. Immigrants from particular localities were scattered throughout the working-class residential districts, not concentrated in particular neighborhoods and streets. Yet although Bradford's working-class immigrants could not exactly replicate the communities from which they had come, they exhibited a strong determination to adapt communitarian values to the proletarian conditions of their new urban world.[28]

From the start, many of the superstitions, beliefs, and practices of the old popular culture – witchcraft, wife selling, and charivari – all quickly reappeared in the new urban slum alleys and on the unenclosed grounds like Peep and Fairweather Greens, which stood just beyond the borough, outside the jurisdiction of the police. With the approach of Whitsun, Martinmas, and the Bradford Fair, there was a sharp increase in the frequency with which illicit recreations were reported in the local press. In 1835, for example, a crowd of twelve thousand was said to have gathered to witness a prize fight between "Brassey" of Bradford and "Bailey" of Leeds. With the actual arrival of Bradford and Whitsun fairs, even larger numbers regularly assembled on the nearby fairgrounds for games, music, dancing, pantomimes, and boxing matches.[29]

With their ribald disdain for the entrepreneurial values of self-discipline and their carefree atmosphere of the carnivalesque, these spontaneous celebrations were a standing embarrassment to bourgeois liberals, proof that workers' nostalgia for a bygone community could, even within the new urban setting, be reshaped to gain a new lease on life. Such rituals could be dismissed by bourgeois liberals as residual barbarisms, fragments of an outmoded way of life, but they were beginning to form a more coherent pattern of collective action and organization as industrial workers, disfigured by the scars of proletarianization, drew on old traditions with which they were familiar to construct a new class culture of their own.[30]

This flowering of new approaches to working-class community amidst the apparently hostile urban-industrial milieu was manifested most dramatically by the emergence of distinctive neighborhoods within the expanse of urban

[28] HO, 107/2,308.

[29] *BO*, Oct. 20, 1836; Oct. 19, 1837; Dec. 13, 1838; Aug. 15, 1839; Apr. 16, Nov. 5, 1840; Jan. 20, Feb. 3, 1842; Aug. 29, 1844; July 31, 1845; Apr. 26, 1849; William Cudworth, *Condition of the Industrial Classes in Bradford* (Bradford, 1887), 84; James Burnley, *Phases of Bradford Life* (Bradford, 1871), 75–85.

[30] R. W. Malcolmson, *Popular Recreations in English Society, 1700–1850* (Cambridge, 1973).

Bradford's downtown slums. This process was facilitated by the morphology of small-scale urban development on two or three acre building plots. Often located within a single development, around a few adjoining blocks, or on one larger street, these neighborhoods became more and more genuine communities with their own networks of personal interaction that were largely invisible to undiscerning elites. According to one observer who actually ventured into Silsbridge Lane, during the daytime when "the great bulk of the residents are away at work," the street would "swarm with sickly looking children in various degrees of raggedness; and slipshod females . . . and idling men smoking short pipes." However, "from eleven to twelve o'clock on a Saturday night the noise in the Lane is nearly, if not quite riotous." With crowds of men fighting, swearing, and carousing, and "a number of girls galloping down the Lane arm in arm," two outnumbered policemen "are in anxious consultation as to which part of the Lane needs their services the most."[31]

Given the poverty and overcrowding that surrounded these slum dwellers, their culture was pervasively public, enacted less at the hearth or in the club room than through the flowing life of the dramshop and open street. To sustain ongoing bonds of community amidst a culture of poverty as amorphous as this was a formidable challenge. The impermanence and insecurity of most workers' existence and the prevalence of transients made it almost impossible, especially during the 1830s and 1840s when the urban working-class neighborhood was new. Yet there was another face to this neighborhood culture, less colorful than the visible ribaldry of the street. This more prosaic public culture was focused on the beershop where residents would gather for recreation and socializing, and the corner grocery where they got their provisions and obtained credit when they fell on hard times. Often the beerseller, the grocer, or even the moneylender, with his superior education or economic status, provided a kind of informal leadership for proletarian families in the neighborhood and helped mediate relations with the outside world.[32]

Ultimately, however, the cultural integrity of the neighborhood did not depend on petit bourgeois community leaders, but on the impulses toward mutuality that the workers themselves displayed. Such collectivism was most

---

[31] Burnley, *Bradford Life*, 30.

[32] Robert Roberts, *The Classic Slum: Salford Life in the First Quarter of the Century* (Manchester, 1971), 83–7. Among the most interesting of Robert's observations on working-class community in late-nineteenth-century Salford concerns the role of a small clique of matriarchs known as the "old queens" in policing neighborhood morality and in making its constituent families cohere (pp. 26–7). How far comparable phenomena may have been at work in the less settled environment of mid-nineteenth-century Bradford is something which the evidence does not permit us to say.

instinctive among the Irish whose intense poverty and ethnic isolation created a community particularly closeknit. As one observer put it in the mid-1840s: "There always seems to exist a sort of community of dwellings among the people which I never did find among their English neighbors. The doors invariably stand open, and when I enquire about sleeping accommodations, I am invariably told that half the people whom I find crouching round the fireplace are only 'naybors.'"[33]

Yet English workers could also turn to one another in distress. In the weaving and farming villages of the Yorkshire hinterland, it had long been the custom for families to rely on their neighbors when unemployment, poverty, or ill health struck. With the heightened insecurity of proletarian living in the city, this impulse toward mutuality broadened. Here, neighbors were strangers who, at least initially, could not draw on common funds of tradition and trust. Yet mutual aid could recommend itself on grounds of self-interest, serving as a tacit policy of insurance on which a present-day benefactor might someday fall back. Whatever their motives, there is evidence that, as early as the late 1820s, urban immigrants, at least in certain parts of the town, were developing their own community assistance networks so that destitute families could obtain aid from their neighbors to avoid the stigma of elite charity or the official Poor Law.[34]

Of course, such networks were likely to break down in general depressions when informal webs of neighborhood mutuality ceased to be adequate forms of community organization for an increasingly proletarianized class. Even two or three generations later, when they had stabilized and evolved into "classic slums" – self-contained urban villages with cultural traditions of their own – they remained, as Robert Roberts and Richard Hoggart have described them, narrowly localized, inward-looking enclaves, which did not draw upon workers' hopes for transforming their condition, but reflected a passive mood of fatalistic despair.[35] Yet at least during the 1830s and 1840s, when the rigors of proletarianization were felt most keenly and the evolution of poor neighborhoods into working-class communities had only just begun, their inhabitants were not inclined to withdraw defensively into a kind of community that offered no protection against exploitation in the workplace and no antidote to the squalor of the slum. On the contrary, they worked to devise entirely new social agencies to realize the possibilities inherent in urban-capitalist social relations for mobilizing class solidarities on a wider,

---

[33] *BO*, Dec. 13, 1849.

[34] John Tester, "History of the Bradford Contest" (Bradford Archives, D.B. 3/38), 26; PP (XXIII, 1840), 565.

[35] Standish Meacham, *A Life Apart: The English Working Class, 1890–1914* (Cambridge, Mass., 1977), 30–59; Roberts, *Classic Slum;* Richard Hoggart, *The Uses of Literacy* (London, 1957).

more purposive scale. Building upon the face-to-face collectivism of the working-class neighborhood, but transcending the particularism of the "classic slum," workers strove to create entirely new social institutions organized on the abstracted principle of associational voluntarism that had so effectively served the entrepreneurial bourgeoisie.[36]

As we have seen, the mainstream bourgeois-run voluntary associations in Bradford were largely inappropriate to the situation of most workers. Addressing the predicament of the rootless individual, assisting him on his way toward salvation and self-help, the mainstream chapels, Temperance Society, and Mechanics Institute had failed to enlist the mass of workers in a liberal consensus because their program was essentially irrelevant to pro- letarianized workers' conditions of life.[37] Yet there was no inherent reason why workers could not form their own voluntary associations to promote their own class interests and ends. Shorn of its original individualist objec- tives, voluntarist culture might be radically transformed. By definition, vol- untary associations, whatever their purposes, were instruments of collective action, vehicles of social cooperation toward mutually desired ends. In the hands of the new urban-industrial workers they might become the means by which communitarian impulses could be transposed onto more purposive, self-conscious organizations that could draw on the more abstract solidarities of class.

Our study of urban religion has already demonstrated that those sects, such as the Primitive Methodists and the Prospect Street Baptists, that did attract substantial worker participation were, to a much greater extent than the bourgeois denominations, rooted in the thicket of personal connections that came from kinship and local neighborhood life. Unlike the bourgeois or socially mixed congregations, these distinctively working-class religious associations were not so much products of an open market in competing spiritualities as outgrowths of existing worker communities manifested in the new associational terms.[38]

What was true of working-class religion in Bradford became even truer of secular culture as a whole series of distinctively proletarian voluntary associations – social, economic, and ultimately political – began to proliferate during the 1830s and 1840s. Like the working-class religious sects, these secular associations all departed from Bradford's bourgeois voluntarist main- stream in rejecting the notion that the autonomous individual ought to be the central object of associational life. Like the religious groups, these secular associations channeled collective impulses inherent in the workers' condition

---

[36] Thompson, *English Working Class*, 401–47.
[37] See Chapters 10 and 11.
[38] John Bates, *A Sketch of His Life* (Queensbury, 1895). See Chapter 10.

into the kind of self-conscious, self-created community that would require voluntary associational organizational forms.

What these new working-class associations shared with one another, what they even shared with the mainstream associations of the bourgeoisie, was a common commitment to the principle of self-help. Although workers may have regarded much of the culture of entrepreneurial liberalism as inappropriate to the condition in which they found themselves, they had very clearly absorbed its underlying assumption that progress was not only desirable but possible and that independence could be everyone's goal. Indeed, it was workers' very commitment to self-help and improvement that obliged them to repudiate the egocentric core of competitive individualism that stood at the heart of the entrepreneurial creed. For Bradford's impoverished and alienated workers who were being stripped of the material foundations of independence and reduced to a common proletarianized state, self-help was not something that could be achieved by individuals; it was something that had to be collectively won for their class.[39]

Friendly societies: associational voluntarism and collective self-help

The first and always the largest of Bradford's working-class voluntary associations were the friendly societies in which a group of individuals would regularly pool their resources to shield their families against the exigencies of accident, illness, and death. Like the informal patterns of neighborhood mutuality that they institutionalized, friendly societies in Bradford can be traced back to the eighteenth century. By 1803, there were already twenty-two in the vicinity of Bradford with a total of 2,500 members.[40] However, their rapid proliferation and final evolution occurred only with the advent of urban-industrial capitalism after 1815. The first to expand were the small, isolated, localized societies like the Bradford Engineer and Millwrights Society (c. 1822) and the Miners Friendly Society (c. 1838) that were now rooted not in protoindustrial communities, but in thriving trades.[41] However, from the 1830s onward, growth tended to concentrate in the great, centralized national orders, the Oddfellows, the Ancient Foresters, and the Druids, which expanded dramatically over the next fifty years. Unlike the

[39] Geoffrey Crossick, "The Labour Aristocracy and its Values: A Study of Mid-Victorian Kentish London," *Victorian Studies*, 19 (1975–6); Raymond Williams, *Culture and Society, 1780–1950* (New York, 1958), 327–30; Hoggart, *Uses of Literacy*, 32, 51–61.

[40] John James, *History and Topography of Bradford* (Bradford, 1842), 265; H. J. Maltby, "Early Bradford Friendly Societies," *BA*, n.s. 6 (1940).

[41] *BO*, Nov. 24 1836; Dec. 27, 1838; Oct. 6, 1842.

original independent clubs, these branch societies, with their strict accounting procedures and national affiliations, offered more financial security and the right to transfer benefits to another locality when members were forced to move in search of work. At the same time, the proliferation of semiautonomous branch lodges at the local level rooted the movement in the urban neighborhood culture and insured that, as they broadened into classwide agencies, friendly societies remained rooted in the realities of working-class community life. By 1871, Bradford had 133 distinct lodges with a total of 10,016 members, as well as 3,805 unionists with friendly society benefits who, together, constituted 37 percent of the town's adult men.[42]

Although friendly societies occasionally attracted lower-middle-class members, and members rose into the lower middle class, the composition of the movement was fundamentally proletarian reaching, as the numbers indicate, well beyond the ranks of the skilled working-class elite. As long as they were not burdened down with a swarm of wageless dependents nor were chronically unemployed or abysmally underpaid, most working-class breadwinners could, theoretically, afford the 5d. weekly dues that membership generally required. Although the typical member was probably a craftsman, a stonemason, or a skilled mechanic, the Oddfellows, who constituted the elite of the movement, counted 1,700 woolcombers in their 1846 national membership, most of whom must have come from Bradford. For families that could not afford full-fledged membership, burial clubs were available that provided no sick benefits, but paid for funerals when a family member died. According to testimony given at the middle of the century, twenty thousand Bradfordians, or virtually every working-class family, participated in a benefit society of some sort.[43]

When bourgeois observers contemplated this profusion of friendly societies, their reactions were decidedly mixed. In one sense the phenomenon did seem to represent an incontrovertible triumph for the liberal, voluntarist ideal. As instruments of thrift and self-improvement, the friendly societies promised to help workers achieve self-reliance without dependence on charity or the state. Yet unlike Bradford's mainstream voluntary associations, they were not bourgeois-dominated agencies of outreach but autonomous creations of the workers themselves. Their imperviousness to elite influence and authority caused considerable bourgeois unease.

The complaint most frequently articulated was that societies failed to distance themselves from the popular culture of drink. Although there were a handful of temperance friendly societies, most benefit clubs met in a

---

[42] PP (1854, VIII), 41–2; (1874, XXIII), 2:206.
[43] P. H. J. H. Gosden, *The Friendly Societies in England: 1815–1875* (Manchester, 1961), 74–6; Crossick, *Artisan Elite*, 174–98; PP (1854, VIII), 41–2.

neighborhood tavern or beerhouse.[44] This mixing of the serious business of self-help and insurance with the wasteful culture of drink tended, the *Observer* at one point argued, to undermine those habits of frugality in whose name the friendly society had originally been formed. "In a great multitude of cases," the paper suggested, "the 'club' is mere decoy to the public house or beershop."[45] However, because the pub was the social center of the working-class community, the friendly society had to be headquartered there. Without any other available meeting rooms, workers usually welcomed the cozy atmosphere of the back barroom and looked to the landlord not only for entertainment, but sometimes for financial assistance and managerial advice.[46]

For workers whose associations grew out of their communities, there seemed no contradiction between the serious functions of providing for welfare and the displays of conviviality that were necessary to build up mutual trust. Unlike the elite-run voluntary organizations, within the working-class friendly society, collective solidarity was not simply a means to other objectives, but the fundamental end of associational life. So far from remaining severely utilitarian, the affairs of the friendly society were fraught with secret oaths, elaborate regalia, and other ritual practices pertaining to the initiation of officers and the celebration of important ceremonial events. In part because they seemed irrational throwbacks to the barbaric collectivism of a bygone era and in part because they took place in secret and might serve as a cover for conspiratorial activities, bourgeois elites disparaged such rituals as dangerous anachronisms that diminished the societies' respectability and jeopardized their ability to manage their affairs.[47]

In fact, no one was more deeply concerned than the workers that the societies into which they regularly poured their income remain solvent and that officials were competent, accountable, and honest. However, given the workers' social and economic isolation and their great difficulty in gaining access to legal redress, such rituals of mutuality were not merely decorative superfluities, but important reminders that members and officers were subject to the sanction of the community that would restrain them with an informal but binding behavioral code.

The imperviousness of friendly societies to bourgeois domination and their close links with the traditions of working-class community life made them perfect agencies for the first stage in the urban-industrial workers' quest for collective self-help. By insuring workers against the vicissitudes of

[44] PP (1874, XXIII), 2:206.
[45] *BO*, Nov. 8, 1849.
[46] Brian Harrison, *Drink and the Victorians* (London, 1971), 50–4.
[47] Thompson, *English Working Class*, 418–23; James, *History of Bradford*, 265; *BO*, Nov. 30, Dec. 7, 1848; Nov. 8, 1849.

proletarian life, the friendly society also gave them their first real opportunity for self-government in a world where they were otherwise dominated and dispossessed. As evidence that workers could successfully be organized and would act independently on the political stage, radicals in the late 1830s referred proudly to their "conduct in reference to the management of their own [friendly] societies."[48]

Yet despite their proletarian social composition, their connections with working-class culture, and their independence of the bourgeoisie, friendly societies were, by nature, unsuited to offer any direct critique of capitalist productive relations or to mount political challenges to the power of elites. The very purpose for which they had been founded, to protect workers within the wage-labor system rather than to transform or overthrow it, dictated that they be defensive rather than offensive class organizations, which, in themselves, posed no threat to the existing status quo. To ensure that the societies would not stray from this purpose, the government had instituted a system of voluntary registration that promised them legal status in return for official supervision of their finances and rules. Although most Bradford friendly societies opposed state regulation in principle, many found its benefits to be irresistible in practice. Even those that refused to register became concerned to establish reputations of respectability in informal ways.[49]

This growing preoccupation with respectability can be traced precisely in the case of the Oddfellows, the largest and most successful of the national orders in Bradford, whose local lodges contained 2,200 members in 1836 and 3,453 in 1871, or 30 percent of all society members in town. With their capacity for mobilizing large numbers of working people and their ability to raise thousands of pounds per year, the Oddfellows emerged as an extremely powerful organization whose membership and financial resources far exceeded that of the Temperance Society, the most successful of the outreach associations of the bourgeoisie.[50]

In fact, both groups seem to have been in an unspoken competition for recruits from the same social milieu. Both expanded rapidly during the 1830s, and the Temperance Hall (c. 1838) must have been, at least in part, a deliberate response to the Oddfellows Hall, which had opened in the previous year. Like the Temperance Society, the Oddfellows inaugurated their headquarters with a grand procession of 1,500, subsequently repeated as a semi-

---

[48] *BO*, Sep. 13, 1838.
[49] *BO*, Jan. 24, 1839; P H. J. H. Gosden, *Self-Help: Voluntary Associations in the Nineteenth Century* (London, 1973), 11–76.
[50] J. T. Illingworth, *The Progress of Oddfellowship in Yorkshire* (Huddersfield, 1867); *BO*, July 7, 1836; PP (1874, XXIII), 2:206.

annual event. The advent of class conflict and Chartism after 1838 did not split the Oddfellows as it did the Temperance Society, which divided internally along class lines, but it did confront the organization with a fundamental crisis whose outcome determined its future shape.[51]

What kept the Oddfellows together was that its working-class leaders, unlike the bourgeois officers of the Temperance Society, seem to have shared a common affinity with their members for the Chartist creed. Yet in their capacity as representatives of a registered friendly society, they were forbidden to assist the radical cause. Although the Oddfellows observed this proscription, they rented their hall to Chartists when the latter found other meeting places closed off. At a time of intense class conflict and distrust, the very existence of an organized, financially powerful working-class body like the Oddfellows clearly frightened the authorities. In May 1839, with very little legal justification, the magistrates summarily threatened to revoke the Oddfellows' license if they rented to the Chartists again. Angered by what they regarded as an arbitrary and illegal intervention in their affairs, the Oddfellows prepared for a confrontation, which was avoided only when the radical leaders themselves decided that the Oddfellows ought not to be exposed to the political fray.[52] For their part, the Oddfellows learned their lesson, for a year later they were holding a "grand demonstration . . . to render the principles of Oddfellowship better understood by the upper class of society." Thereafter, as class tensions eased during the 1850s and 1860s and their own membership and financial security increased, the Oddfellows edged closer to the liberal associational mainstream that dominated Bradford's mid-Victorian age.[53]

Given the institutional constraints that law and custom placed upon them, as well as their own fundamentally defensive conception of collective self-help, it was inevitable that the friendly societies would offer no satisfactory framework for the mobilization of working-class resistance to capitalism or for its assertion of political independence from the bourgeoisie. What the friendly societies gave their members was the experience of autonomous collective organization that could be applied in the formation of more aggressive types of voluntary association, like trade unions and cooperatives, which would more actively advance the workers' class interests and could, in some instances, even challenge capitalist productive relations themselves.

[51] *BO*, Feb. 18, July 7, 1836; Feb. 9, Nov. 9, 1837; Jan. 3, 1839; Apr. 2, 23, 1840; Sep. 6, 1842; Mar. 27, May 15, 1845; Apr. 12, 1849.

[52] *BO*, May 9, 1839; *Northern Star*, June 1, 1839.

[53] *BO*, Apr. 2, 1840; Illingworth, *Oddfellowship in Yorkshire;* Gosden, *Friendly Societies,* 155–210.

Trade unions: associational voluntarism
and class organization

The roots of trade unionism in nineteenth-century Bradford must be sought in the impulse toward craft organization pervasive among artisans before the industrial age. Under protoindustrial conditions, this impulse was often institutionalized in the early occupation-based friendly society, which protected members by defending customary wage levels or workshop rules wherever market conditions or employer initiatives threatened them. But since controlling wage levels or labor processes brought workers into adversarial relations with capital, the unions evolved into separate organizations as the friendly societies came under increasing pressure to accommodate themselves to the status quo.[54] Since union bargaining power was enhanced by members' ability to insure their families' long-term economic security, some unions continued to offer friendly society benefits. However, most workers found it more desirable to seek insurance under the umbrella of a large, affiliated friendly society while combining as producers in parallel organizations that were organized explicitly along trade union lines. There were already five such craft-based trade unions when the repeal of the Combination Acts conveyed a faint aura of legality to them in 1825. By 1861, a national trade union directory listed twenty-two such craft associations representing twenty different trades.[55]

Like the friendly society branches, these local craft unions generally represented the more skilled and better-paid adult male artisans and tended to affiliate together on a regional or national basis to increase the security and power of the branches and to regulate conditions throughout the trade. Nevertheless, like the friendly societies, local unions retained much autonomy, continuing to organize, govern, and finance themselves. As in the case of friendly societies, local branch activity, self-government, and internal democracy were important parts of what trade unions were about. Lodge meetings were held in neighborhood taverns and taken very seriously by groups like the woolcombers, whose rules required officers to be elected every three months.[56] In the words of a leading trade union periodical, democracy "was the fundamental principle of a Trades Union, where every brother is understood to have a voice in the management of the common affairs of his trade." Like the bourgeois parvenus who had viewed their

---

[54] Webb and Webb, *History of Trade Unionism*, 13–112; Cudworth, *Industrial Classes*, 80–2.

[55] Jack Reynolds, *The Letter Press Printers of Bradford* (Bradford, 1970), 3–11; *United Kingdom Trades Union Directory* (London, 1861).

[56] E. C. Tufnell, *The Character Objects and Effects of Trades' Unions* (London, 1834), 130.

religious congregations as the seedbeds of a wider civic democracy, articulate unionists saw their class organizations as "the only means by which universal suffrage can safely be obtained because it is obtained in practice or in the language of the trade, by serving an apprenticeship."[57]

Since the unions' success in achieving their objectives was dependent, even more than in the case of the friendly society, on mobilizing the feelings of craft solidarity that naturally emanated from the cooperation inherent in most artisanal work, it is not surprising that rituals of mutuality and patterns of conviviality were even more thoroughly interwoven into the fabric of trade union life. Completely isolated from the mainstream of bourgeois voluntarism, sometimes forced underground by employer hostility, and always obliged to compel loyalty on the part of individual members to collective decisions and union rules, groups like the woolcombers saw no difference between "uniting to cultivate friendship" and organizing as laborers "to protect our trade."[58]

Seen in this light, the secret ceremonies, mysteries, and dramatic solemnities, which appeared as barbaric superstitions to bourgeois commentators, were integral parts of a trade union culture whose very inaccessibility to outsiders rendered it particularly effective as a distinctive language of class. Not surprisingly, it was in rituals of initiation that this new language of class community was most vividly expressed. For the woolcombers, the induction of new members into the society was the occasion for a full-fledged secular sacrament in which pseudoclerical paraphernalia of bibles, robes, and surplices was combined with a concoction of pagan and masonic symbols, skeletons, battleaxes, and swords to awe and frighten "novice brethren" into "solemnly swear[ing]," on pain of death and eternal damnation, "never [to] act in opposition to the brotherhood" and always to "assist them in all lawful and just occasions, to obtain a fair remuneration for our labour."[59]

Such intricate rituals, with their elaborate regalia, sacredotal drama, and dreadful oaths, were calculated to leave a deep impression on first-generation immigrants still imbued with a magical mind-set and highly responsive to quasi-liturgical forms. At the same time, however, they legitimized novel and innovative forms of labor organization with the aura of a corporatist guild tradition (whether real or invented) that was handed down orally from one generation to the next. Thus sanctified, trade unionists could justify their self-interested strategies of collective bargaining by reference to transcendent rights and customs that history had bequeathed for the common good.[60]

---

[57] *Pioneer*, May 31, 1834.

[58] Tufnell, *Trades' Unions*, 71.

[59] Ibid., 65–75.

[60] Webb and Webb, *History of Trade Unionism*, 64–179; James Burnley, *History of Wool and*

Naturally, such claims to customary rights and protections, however framed within the traditional language of the moral economy or legitimized in the name of an organic commonweal, were bound to be increasingly unacceptable to entrepreneurial employers to whom labor was a commodity like any other, to be exchanged solely through the mechanism of supply and demand. "The working classes," the *Observer* grumbled, as it witnessed this proletarianization of voluntary association and self-help, "have as much right to confederate for the purposes of endeavoring to effect, by peaceable means, an amelioration of their lot, as they have to thrust their fingers into a blazing fire."[61]

In fact, the conflict between the employers' political economy and the trade unions' invocation of a higher moral law had a practical significance that varied markedly, depending on the particular location within the production process occupied by each specific trade or craft. Not surprisingly, those who were relatively immune from structural proletarianization were best able to organize trade unions, to protect customary wage levels and terms of work, and to function without recourse to the kind of violence, intimidation, or industrial organization which virtually invited legal repression from political elites.

These craft unions can be further subdivided into three basic types. The first consisted of traditional artisanal workers, coach builders, cabinet makers, compositors, bookbinders, and printers, who retained real power in relation to their employers because their trades were largely untouched, at least before midcentury, by the forces of economic and technological change. A second group, represented by the boilermakers, woolsorters, tinplate workers, and engineers, were privileged precisely because of their employment on the economic and technological cutting edge. Such workers were the elites of the industrial work force, often building and repairing the new power machines. Like the older crafts, these trades required genuine skill and workmanship and, because their members were in such growing demand, they often found themselves in a better bargaining position than any other sector of their class.[62]

In the case of the third category of local craft unions, the painters, the boot- and shoemakers, the stonemasons and the tailors, there was little technical foundation behind the privileged economic status that they enjoyed.

Woolcombing (London, 1889), 160–4. See also William Lovett, *Life and Struggles* (London, 1967), 19–27, for a superb account of craft unionism in London.
[61] *BO*, Apr. 24, 1834.
[62] Reynolds, *Letter Press Printers*, 7; anon., *Trades Union Directory* (1861); *BO*, Apr. 14, 1836; July 23, 1840; Apr. 2, 9, 16, 1846. For a description of local wages and working conditions in these occupations during the 1830s, see Cudworth, *Industrial Classes*, 34–40.

It was because these workers were located in the urban-service sector and benefited from the rapidity of Bradford's growth that they maintained their scarcity value as an organized elite in occupations that, in the course of feverish expansion, were drawing in an influx of unskilled and unorganized laborers who earned low wages and endured debased conditions of work. Unlike the better-placed artisanal workers, these unions upheld craft status not by organizing their entire occupation, but by protecting the privileges of a small minority at the top.[63]

Narrowly focused on serving the immediate interests of their members, all these craft unions tended to be wary of the general run of workers whom they perceived less as comrades in a struggle against capital than as competitors who were trying to take away their jobs. This "supineness and apathetic feeling" of the more "aristocratic portion of the operatives" was deeply frustrating to radical unionists like Peter Bussey who sought to promote a wider and more militant class consciousness.[64] Nevertheless, it would be wrong to exaggerate these craft impulses toward sectionalism or to ignore those that periodically impelled skilled workers in the opposite direction. If trade unions were, in many ways, "partial" and "frequently inimical to each other," they also experienced considerable counterpressure toward class solidarity that, if not "at once amalgamate[ing] the whole of these various societies into one grand stupendous aggregate," at least encouraged them to "approach as near to that point as we can."[65]

As we have seen, the advent of deep depression throughout much of the late thirties and forties threatened the incomes and employment of many skilled workers, even of those not in competition with the unskilled or with machines. Those, like shoemakers, tailors, and construction workers, who were located in the least-skilled and most cyclically sensitive consumer goods trades, were often hit almost as hard as the structurally proletarianized. Consequently, local craft unions maintained informal structures of communication and assistance, not only during depressed periods of nearly universal suffering, but during prosperous interludes such as 1834–5 and 1844–6 when a better bargaining position encouraged them to take the

---

[63] *BO*, May 16, 1844; Apr. 3, 1845; Webb and Webb, *History of Trade Unionism*, 180–232; Cudworth, *Industrial Classes*, 31–4.

[64] Quoted in J. R. Sanders, "Working Class Movements in the West Riding Textile District, 1829 to 1839, with Emphasis on Local Leadership and Organization" (Manchester, Ph.d., dissertation, 1984), 86.

[65] John Tester quoted in R. C. N. Thornes, "The Early Development of the Co-operative Movement in West Yorkshire, 1827–1863" (Sussex, D. Phil. dissertation, 1984), 80–1. For a recent sustained interpretation of working-class trade unionism along these lines, see Robert Glen, *Urban Workers in the Early Industrial Revolution* (London, 1984). I have discussed some of the problems with this approach more fully in a review of Glen's book in *Journal of Modern History*, 59:4 (1987).

offensive.[66] Although the craft unions generally kept their distance from radical political movements like Chartism, individual members were often deeply involved. Most significantly, the spread of unionism beyond the craft sector to the proletarianized textile workers ensured that trade unionism in Bradford became inextricably interconnected with wider economic and even political movements of class.[67]

Organizing out of the traditions of craft unionism with which they identified, Bradford's endangered textile handicraftsmen, the woolcombers, and, to a lesser degree, the handloom weavers were increasingly compelled to act according to the logic of the proletarians they had become. Their looming presence as Bradford's largest and most vocal occupational sector throughout the 1830s and 1840s set the tone for the local working-class movement as a whole. In particular, they served as a bridge between the narrow, sectional predispositions of organized craft unionism and the imperatives of a classwide consciousness that confronted the problem of capitalist productive relations in the widest sense.

For the weavers, the effort to harken back to a primordial craft status was largely indulgence in a consolatory myth. But for the combers, the artisanal legacy was palpably real. As the acknowledged elite of the protoindustrial worsted work force, the combers had a tradition of craft organization that dated back to the seventeenth century.[68] In the eighteenth century, their trade was organized on a national basis and successfully enforced uniform wage rates and apprenticeship regulations throughout the United Kingdom. Even a 1726 law to prevent combinations in woolen manufacturing failed to dislodge the combers' craft organization, and until the early nineteenth century, they maintained their reputation as "a discontented race, forever combining against their employers and resorting to extreme methods of coercion and restriction."[69]

With effective monopoly over an indispensable part of the production process and access to parliamentary influence and courts of law, the combers had only to look to their own occupational history for proof of their status as freeborn Englishmen. They knew they were productive citizens who made a significant contribution to the economic welfare of the nation. Even employers had to acknowledge the combers' privileged status and to concede, however grudgingly, their legitimate place within a moral economy of production that involved not only responsibilities but customary rights. Moreover, the corporatist character of the combers' relation to the production

---

[66] *BO*, Mar. 27, 1845.
[67] Ibid., A. J. Peacock, *Bradford Chartism, 1836–40* (York, 1969), 8, 18–19.
[68] Burnley, *Wool and Woolcombing*, 160; John James, *History of the Worsted Manufacture in England* (London, 1857), 262, 294.
[69] Burnley, *Wool and Woolcombing*, 164.

process that they articulated in their own secret craft rituals was openly affirmed through a tradition of public festivals mounted by the entire trade in honor of their patron saint. According to legend, the woolcomb had been invented in the fourth century by an Armenian bishop named Blaize whose birthday had been celebrated septennially ever since. In Yorkshire, Blaize festivals can be traced back into the eighteenth century, and after 1804 they had been centered in Bradford and repeated in 1811, 1818, and 1825.[70]

Because the early twenties were an Indian summer of industrial peace and prosperity – a brief interlude before the strains of urban-industrial development reached inescapable proportions – wages and profits suddenly boomed, and the bleak eras of wartime inflation and postwar depression seemed a thing of the past. Amidst this atmosphere of apparent social harmony and complacency, the 1825 Blaize festival was planned. The enormous strides that the industry had made in the previous seven years, the unequalled prosperity that it had brought to the town, would be reflected in the grandest Blaize performance ever. Its splendor would symbolize Bradford's claim to regional predominance by demonstrating the vigor and unity of its staple trade.[71]

The centrality of woolcombing in worsted manufacturing, the hierarchy implicit in industrial organization, and the reciprocity that supposedly subsisted between masters and men were all to be expressed in the Blaize ceremonies through the visual language of a processional display. Headed by the senior gentleman-capitalist Matthew Thompson, there followed an array of twenty-four equestrian woolstaplers and thirty-nine factory spinning masters with the largest, Richard Fawcett, marching in the lead. Six merchants with colored sashes came next, followed by fifty-six apprentices and masters' sons, still on horseback but separated from their elders by a row of guards. Finally, after a solid interlude of hands and effigies, the textile artisans brought up the rear – sixty woolsorters on horseback, a phalanx of 470 combers, and forty dyers following on foot.[72]

The graduated social structure of traditional manufacturing was disclosed along the streets for all to see. The organic ideal of mutual interdependence was set forth in a symbolism articulated by the masters and organizers and ratified silently by the mass of workers who contributed their bodies for the visual effect. Worsted production depended on their labor; in turn it would ceremonially acknowledge their place. Prosperity was trumpeted by pageantry and an extravagant display of useless costumery and decoration. This surfeit

[70] Ibid., 186–8; James, *Worsted Manufacture*, 322–5.
[71] Anon., *A Full and Particular Account of the Septennial Festival Held in Honor of Bishop Blaize* (Bradford, 1862); Burnley, *Wool and Woolcombing*, 186–210.
[72] Burnley, *Wool and Woolcombing*, 199–200.

of colorful finery, profusely draped over each constituent element of the procession, also served to demonstrate the multiplicity of worsted products and the skill of Bradford craftsmen in fabricating them. Finally, the festivities were capped with recitations, speeches, and a public feast for all. To John Rand, the whole affair was a dramatic affirmation that "one sentiment appears to pervade all classes of our countrymen."[73]

Although the Blaize festivities evoked an almost medieval image of stable corporate unity, Bradford's worsted trade was now entirely dominated by competitive market forces and had commenced its urban transformation to mature industrial-capitalist form. Perhaps the very extravagance of the official ceremonial betrayed a certain nervousness about the message it so self-consciously conveyed – a fear that assumptions that had hitherto been taken for granted had now to be deliberately packaged and displayed. In any case, one wonders how many of the participants could have anticipated that this would be the last public Blaize festival ever celebrated in Bradford or that the social peace that it proclaimed would be shattered only six months later by one of the most massive and protracted industrial conflicts that British society had ever known. Pitting an estimated 20,000 combers and weavers in a bitter, twenty-three-week-long strike against the combined worsted manufacturers, this event was to inaugurate a new age of protracted class conflict between labor and capital that would last for another twenty-five years.[74]

Class consciousness:
industrial conflict and the cooperative ideal

The abruptness with which Bradford's combers and weavers turned from celebrating with their masters to turning out against them should not obscure the fact that the 1825 explosion was the product of pent-up resentments that had been building for some time. The weavers, facing the imminent prospect of unskilled competition and supercession by machine were subject to the most immediate threat. But even the combers, notwithstanding their strong craft heritage and technological indispensability, feared losing control over apprenticeship and being relocated into centralized workshops and

---

73 William Smith, ed., *Old Yorkshire* (London, 1888), 2:150; James, *History of Bradford*, 165; anon., *Account of Bishop Blaize*, 12.

74 Tester, "Bradford Contest," William Scruton, "The Great Strike of 1825," *BA*, o.s. 1: (1888), 67–73; J. T. Ward, "A Great Bradford Dispute," *Journal of Bradford Textile Society* (Bradford, 1961–2), 117–32; Jonathan Smith, "The Strike of 1825," in D. G. Wright and J. A. Jowitt, eds., *Victorian Bradford: Essays in Honour of Jack Reynolds* (Bradford, 1982), 63–80.

subjected to tighter employer control. Particularly alarming was the rise of a few factory spinning capitalists whose increasing monopoly of yarn production gave them effective control over the woolcombers' trade.[75]

In 1824, the weavers took advantage of the repeal of the combination acts to form a union while they still could. The combers then revitalized old craft organizations to defend their artisanal status before it was too late. Emboldened by the same sense of the dignity of their labor that had informed their participation in the rites of Bishop Blaize, they now joined the weavers in a united front of handicraftsmen to resist the forces that threatened them both. Disappointed that the "humane speeches made by the manufacturers with regard to the condition of their workmen" had been followed by behavior that "cast a stain upon their characters," the workers felt compelled to defend the rights of labor themselves.[76]

At first the workers' demands were quite modest. Focusing on the three worst offending firms, they called for an end to undercutting and an equalization of wages. What transformed the strike into a full-scale class struggle was the employers' determination not only to resist the workers' demands, but to destroy the union. Speaking to the association of masters that was formed to combat the strike, Richard Fawcett, the largest capitalist, proclaimed that "he would go to any length rather than be dragooned by any committee of workmen, however established – he would stop his works forever and retire upon the pittance that providence had blessed him with."[77] Whether offended by the workers' challenge to their authority or determined to defend what they regarded as their private property rights, capitalists of all persuasions quickly closed class ranks. Heartened by Fawcett's "spirited and just" sentiments "coming from an individual possessing so much capital and carrying on so extensive a business," the Masters Association vowed to give the strikers no quarter, convinced "that if they remained united, they might be certain of success."[78]

It was at this point that class conflict escalated out of control. Stung by the masters' determination to crush their unions, the workers extended the strike throughout the trade. The employers then blacklisted the strikers, firing their wives and children and closing down the spinning mills in an all-out assault on the strikers' family wage. Enlisting the aid of their counterparts in Keighley, Halifax, and the Bowling Iron Company, they extended

[75] Tester, "Bradford Contest," 3; Jack Reynolds, *The Great Paternalist, Titus Salt and the Growth of Nineteenth Century Bradford* (London, 1983), 29–30.
[76] Worker quoted in R. D. Storch, "The Problem of Working Class Leisure: Some Roots of Middle Class Moral Reform in the Industrial North: 1825–50," in A. P. Donajgrodzki, ed., *Social Control in Nineteenth Century Britain* (London, 1977).
[77] Quoted in Scruton, "Great Strike," 70.
[78] Ibid.

the blacklist throughout the region and warned that continued working-class resistance would only hasten the spread of unskilled labor and machines.[79] As their employers dramatically abandoned the ideals of reciprocity embodied in the organic symbolism of Bishop Blaize, workers concluded that profit maximization mattered more than gentlemanly behavior in their eyes. It was not workers, but the greedy and unfeeling masters who had caused the downward spiral in class relations, for it was they who had undermined the status quo. The unions, they insisted, were merely defensive organizations against a capitalist conspiracy to deprive them of their legitimate rights. Even the strike was not an act of insubordination but the endangered handicraftsman's desperate last recourse against "tyrants [who would] rob them of their only marketable estate."[80]

The protection of the adult male artisan's wage was not simply a matter of his own self-interest, they argued, but an essential bulwark for the community at large. Correctly prophesying that the man whose "wages are not sufficient for the maintenance of his family" would have to set "his wife to work at home and sending his children to the mill," the strikers could even portray themselves as the ultimate defenders of patriarchy and the paternalist hierarchy that elites had permitted to collapse.[81] But to defend customary values through forms of collective action that mobilized workers into general class unions and pitted them against the capitalist producers as a group was, as the latter contended, to pose a revolutionary threat to law and order and a fundamental challenge to the system as a whole. In moving from a specific avowal of grievances to a universal struggle for the rights of labor, the strike inevitably raised doubts about the sanctity of private property and the right of capitalists to appropriate the surplus value generated in their plants.[82]

Although this ideological challenge to capitalism remained largely latent throughout the strike, the struggle itself was a consciousness raising experience, generating a wider sense of working-class solidarity and a greater steadfastness in pursuing common aims. As the industrial conflict deepened, working working-class demands grew more insistent, anger mounted, and the stakes were raised. In mobilizing a mass membership, the unions themselves began to change. Craft exclusiveness was replaced by a more democratic spirit, and decisions that had hitherto been taken in the privacy of the committee room were openly debated by the rank and file.[83] To survive, the unions had to seek support not only from workers throughout the worsted

[79] Tester, "Bradford Contest," 9–11, 15; *Bradford Courier*, Sep. 15, 1825; Burnley, *Wool and Woolcombing*, 167–73.
[80] Scruton, "Great Strike," 71.
[81] *Bradford Courier*, Nov. 3 1825.
[82] Smith, "Strike of 1825," 72–6.
[83] Tester, "Bradford Contest."

industry, but from craft unionists in other localities and trades. To sustain over 2,658 participant families at a cost of more than £900 per week, the unions augmented their meager funds with nearly £16,000 in contributions from other workers, 90 percent from outside Bradford itself.[84] Indeed, the combers' and weavers' struggle to resist proletarianization struck a chord with artisans throughout the United Kingdom who recognized in the textile handicraftsmen's actions a cause that might someday become their own. For trade unionists throughout the nation, the Bradford contest, as it was known, became a symbol of the larger struggle for the rights of labor and a milestone in the transmutation of traditional craft loyalties into a wider, anticapitalist consciousness of class.[85]

The tenacity of the weavers and combers and the outpouring support they received, permitted the strikers to hold out against the combined power of capital for twenty-three long weeks. Nevertheless, resistance could not continue indefinitely. By November, when declining trade undermined their bargaining position and financial reserves began to dry up, the unions were compelled to capitulate, virtually accepting the employers' terms. The latter, infuriated by their workers' insubordination, were not inclined to be charitable. Over the next few years, under cover of deepening depression, they were able to insist that all employees renounce trade unionism, and they continued to deny former activists work.[86]

The weavers were the worst affected as mechanization proceeded, unemployment spread rapidly, and wages dropped by at least a third.[87] As an occupation, woolcombing was not hit so badly, but the combers' union was forced underground when one thousand two hundred ex-strikers were permanently blacklisted and an additional one thousand eight hundred were left temporarily without work.[88] But the combers, with their strong belief in the skill and dignity of their labor, continued to maintain secret organizations, which surfaced periodically and continued to draw on the aid of those other craft unions whose greater sense of security might otherwise have led them to eschew class consciousness and opt for a narrower, sectional approach. Applying their artisanal mentality to their proletarianized condition, the woolcombers played a critical mediating role among the skilled, the semiskilled, the unskilled, and the deskilled, ensuring that the types of workplace organization pioneered by the former would at least periodically become translated into the latter's terms. As a result, the trade union movement, which

---

[84] Ibid.

[85] Thompson, *English Working Class*, 282–5; Prothero, *Artisans and Politics*, 159–60.

[86] *Bradford Courier*, May 23, 30, Aug. 24, 1826; Burnley, *Wool and Woolcombing*, 173–5.

[87] William Scruton, "History of a Bradford Riot," *BA*, o.s. 1 (1888), 131–5; *Bradford Courier*, May 4, 1826.

[88] Ward, "Bradford Dispute," 120.

evolved in Bradford during the next two decades, developed a dual focus that linked the particular concerns of occupations with the wider and more systemic problems of a proletarianized class.[89]

The first organization formed for this purpose was the Bradford Order, an association of worsted workers, mostly combers and weavers, which sought to reconstitute, under the adverse conditions of the early thirties, the handicraftsmans' traditional status and power. In this organization, a new generation of working-class leaders, who had served their union apprenticeship during the 1825 strike, sought to organize worsted workers not only in Bradford, but throughout the nation. Although never entirely successful in this objective, the Bradford Order, like its counterpart in the woolen trade, the Yorkshire Trades Union centered in Leeds, represented a pioneering experiment in general unionism that abandoned traditional strategies of monopolizing craft privileges, seeking instead to organize an entire labor market so as to equalize conditions throughout the trade.[90]

To accomplish this purpose, the traditional craft practice of individual branch autonomy was modified to permit a more centralized superstructure, operating at the regional level through district delegate committees and at the national level through an executive grand lodge, which was empowered to audit the accounts of the branches and had final authority over local decisions to strike. The main point of this system was to strengthen local branches in their dealings with large capitalist employers, enabling them to draw on the resources of the entire trade. Although the rules specified that a branch "shall keep its own money," it was pledged "to advance such sums of money as may be required to assist any other... which may come in collision with their employers." Conversely, local members engaged in an authorized strike could, in return for their own 3d. weekly contribution, draw a 7s. maintenance stipend with another 1s. for every family dependent out of work. In 1833, a five-month strike in the village of Dolphinholme put this system to the test and £2,058 was raised to sustain a few hundred workers, £1,823 from Bradford alone.[91]

According to Peter Bussey, who played a leading role in the Bradford Order, such general unions, despite their large scale and novel appearance, simply reflected, under modern conditions of industry, the workers' exercise of basic rights of mutual aid and voluntary association, which nobody ques-

[89] The basic source for the history of the general trade union movements of this period is G. D. H. Cole, *Attempts at General Union* (London, 1953). More detailed examination of specific aspects of the movement can be found in Prothero, *Artisans and Politics*, 159–310, and R. G. Kirby and A. E. Musson, *The Voice of the People: John Doherty, 1798–1854* (Manchester, 1975), 9–319.

[90] Sanders, "Working Class Movements," 13, 20.

[91] Tufnell, *Trades' Unions*, 126–34.

tioned when practiced by other social groups. Indeed, by "partly destroying the all-devouring monster home competition," these unions could even contribute to the stabilization of the capitalist system, "placing the manufacturer operating from principle on an equality with those who through the means of low wages were underselling them in the market," thus promoting, in a more liberal and egalitarian fashion, the infusion of social responsibility into economic entrepreneurship, which conservatives sought to inculcate by paternalist means.[92]

However, the events of the 1829–34 period suggest that the spread of general unionism permanently institutionalized the class struggles initiated during the 1825 conflict and posed a more profound challenge to capitalism and private property than Bussey was openly prepared to admit. Trade union consciousness moved another step closer to class consciousness in 1830 when John Doherty's Manchester-based National Association for the Protection of Labour organized a Bradford branch. Designed, like the Bradford Order, to provide a national network of strike solidarity, this association encompassed not only worsted workers but other industrial laborers in the iron industry as well as artisans like tailors and building workers in the more vulnerable crafts. With a local membership of 5,000 in 1832, this association seems to have gained at least the nominal allegiance of almost half of Bradford's adult male workers.[93]

Of course, the simultaneous appearance of equally popular movements, like the Tory radical campaign for factory regulation and the liberal struggle for parliamentary reform, demonstrates that, during this period, economic class consciousness was not inconsistent with the pursuit of social or political alliances with reform-minded elements of the bourgeoisie.[94] Moreover, economic class consciousness, although adversarial in its immediate relations with capital, was not necessarily anticapitalist in its ultimate aims. But within their sphere, the general unions constituted impressive experiments in class-wide consciousness and organization. Moreover, as they became increasingly threatened with repression, they necessarily moved in directions that set them in opposition to the capitalist system as a whole.

This dynamic can be detected in the development, after 1829, of a series of trade-union-inspired cooperatives that, more than any other type of working-class voluntary association, channeled inherited plebeian communitarian traditions into deliberately anticapitalist collectivist forms.[95] Grounded in

[92] *Leeds Mercury,* Aug. 31, 1833.
[93] Sanders, "Working Class Movements," 64, 109; Kirby and Musson, *John Doherty,* 257; Peacock, *Bradford Chartism, 7–8.*
[94] See Chapters 12 and 15.
[95] By 1830, nine loosely affiliated societies were operating in the Bradford area, four within

existing neighborhood communities whose members shared a common interest as consumers, the cooperators began modestly by starting small, collectively owned and operated retail establishments to obtain cheap, quality goods. From the outset, however, this mundane, day-to-day work of collectivist shopkeeping was informed by far-reaching Owenite and Ricardian socialist ideals. The ostensible purpose of the retail cooperatives was to accumulate money for the foundation of a system of producer cooperatives that would enable participating workers to opt out of the labor market and ultimately to transcend the capitalist system itself.

The theorists who articulated this cooperative, socialist vision, Thomas Hodgskin, William Thompson, and later John Francis Bray, themselves represented a new breed of radical political economist, often of artisanal background. From the almost universally acknowledged postulate that labor was the source of all value, these men deduced the highly controversial conclusion that the investing capitalist, no less than the rentier landlord, was a superfluous parasite who made no real contribution to the realm of productive work. As a result, they argued that the capitalists' profit was just as illegitimate and socially dysfunctional as the aristocrats' unearned rent. Rejecting the entrepreneurial belief that capital was necessary to organize labor, these Ricardian socialists insisted that the workers could more effectively run their own enterprises and that the entire product of their labor properly belonged to them alone.[96]

This idea had first been taken up by London artisans who left their employers and organized their own labor exchanges in which individual producers directly traded the products of their work by means of a system of labor–time notes.[97] In the industrial North, such a system of direct labor exchanges was deemed impractical since the work force was concentrated in a few specialized occupations, and production was increasingly located in

the town itself. Sanders, "Working Class Movements," 251; Thornes, "Co-operative Movement," 20.

[96] Thomas Hodgskin, *Labour Defended against the Claims of Capital* (London, 1825); William Thompson, *An Inquiry into the Principles of the Distribution of Wealth Most Conducive to Human Happiness* (London, 1824); *Labour Rewarded: The Claims of Capital Conciliated* (London, 1827); J. F. Bray, *Labour's Wrongs and Labour's Remedies* (Leeds, 1839); R. L. Meek, *Studies in the Labour Theory of Value* (London, 1973); Elie Halévy, *Thomas Hodgskin* (London, 1956); and E. Lowenthal, *The Ricardian Socialists* (New York, 1924). For an introduction to Robert Owen's social thought, see Robert Owen, *A New View of Society* (London, 1927), and J. F. C. Harrison, *Quest for the New Moral World: Robert Owen and the Owenites in England and America* (New York, 1969). In addition are two new studies of the Ricardian socialists that have recently appeared, Noel Thompson, *The People's Science: The Popular Political Economy of Exploitation and Crisis* (Cambridge, 1985), and Gregory Claeys, *Machinery, Money, and the Millennium* (Princeton, 1987).

[97] Lovett, *Life and Struggles*, 33–40.

large factories, which proletarianized workers could not easily establish on their own. Thus the retail trading cooperatives were envisioned as mechanisms to surmount this impasse through the accumulation of a collectively owned fund that, in addition to giving workers day-to-day experience in cooperation, would finance large projects of industrial production and ultimately free both handicraftsmen and factory workers from capitalist control.[98]

Judged by this standard, Bradford's cooperatives failed. None succeeded in establishing a producers community. Even as limited retailing collectives, only a small minority of the town's workers took part. Although they can be seen as precursors of the more successful retail cooperatives that proliferated in the mid-Victorian age, few of these initial experiments survived the depressions of the late thirties, and those that did set in abeyance their ulterior socialist goals. To retain rank-and-file participation over an extended period, it was found necessary to create incentives by paying out collective profits as individual dividends, thus effectively transforming this harbinger of a New Jerusalem into another self-help savings scheme.[99] Although a minority of cooperators remained committed in principle to their original socialist vision, after 1835, these were segregated in a tiny Owenite sect. Here, in an increasingly sectarian community, they were able to cultivate a rich and autonomous counterculture of meetings, discussion groups, anniversaries, and teas, but only by separating themselves from the prevailing world of cultural alienation and dysfunction that beset the overwhelming bulk of their class.[100]

But if these early socialist cooperatives had only a limited direct impact, they did make a more permanent and far-reaching contribution by inculcating into the rank and file of the trade union movement a new and distinctively collectivist vision for a postcapitalist restructuring of the urban-industrial world. Urban-industrial workers, however skeptical of specific socialist schemes and organizations, were instinctively receptive to the underlying message that cooperation, as one local leader put it, "was likely to gain for them all those advantages competition had robbed them of." Such assertions made sense as ideological propositions because they explicitly formulated a set of conclusions inherent in the workers' daily

---

[98] Sidney Pollard, "Nineteenth Century Co-operation: From Community Building to Shopkeeping," in Asa Briggs and John Saville, eds., *Essays in Labour History* (London, 1960), 74–112.

[99] Pollard, "Nineteenth Century Co-operation," 74–112; Thornes, "Co-Operative Movement," 114–5, 125.

[100] Thornes, "Co-operative Movement," 192–5; Eileen Yeo, "Robert Owen and Radical Culture," in Sidney Pollard and John Salt, eds., *Robert Owen: Prophet of the Poor* (London, 1971), 84–114; *BO*, Aug. 23, Dec. 13, 1838; Nov. 21, Dec. 12, 1839; Feb. 16, 23, 1843; *Northern Star*, Feb. 24, Mar. 3, Apr. 28, Aug. 11, 1838.

experience of life. Thus they fostered a more studied and uncompromising sense of social equity that could insist on maximum wages and optimal working conditions and even depict unemployment relief or charity as "an act of justice" that merely "give[s] back to the poor man what had been wrung from him."[101]

For a brief moment in 1834, this socialist conviction that economic tendencies that had to be resisted also constituted a flawed social system that could be replaced appeared within the very heart of the general trade union movement. This occurred when the essentially defensive Association for the Protection of Labour suddenly metamorphosed into the aggressive Grand National Consolidated Trades Union (GNCTU), some of whose leaders looked beyond the limits of collective bargaining to envision a new quasi-syndicalist role for the general trade union as initiator and organizer of a new moral, cooperative world.[102]

Although Bradford was not in the forefront of these stirring developments, at every key juncture, the town's unionized workers played a role. Here, as elsewhere, the unification of several craft unions in the building trade seems to have sparked a more generalized leftward turn. Striking to eliminate the system of general contracting that threatened the status of traditional construction trades, the builders were joined by the tailors and textile handicraftsmen in openly embracing Owenite cooperative schemes. Early in the year, striking building workers initiated their own construction projects including a trades hall that, had it been completed, would have been the first public building in town. Even more portentously, the professedly socialist Bradford Regeneration Society was established by local union leaders to wrest an eight-hour working day from all employers by organizing for a general strike.[103]

The fusion of the Regeneration Society's radical objectives with the GNCTU's numbers and organizational strength seemed to presage the unfolding of a great confrontation that would determine whether entrepreneurial capital or collectivized labor would become masters of the emerging urban-industrial world. Perhaps it was naive to imagine that even universal trade unionism would, in the words of the leading trades' journal, "gradually draw into its vortex all the commercial interest of this

---

[101] Thornes, "Co-Operative Movement," 88–114; Prothero, *Artisans and Politics*, 247–57. The woolcomber George Flinn quoted in David Ashforth, "The Poor Law in Bradford, c. 1834–71" (Bradford, Ph.D. dissertation, 1979), 357.

[102] For the best general discussion of the movements of this period, see Cole, *General Union;* W. H. Oliver, "The Consolidated Trades Union of 1834," *Economic History Review,* 17 (1964); and John Saville, "J. E. Smith and the Owenite Movement, 1833–4," in Pollard and Salt, eds., *Robert Owen,* 115–44.

[103] Kirby and Musson, *John Doherty,* 286; Peacock, *Bradford Chartism,* 8–22.

country and in so doing, it will become a most influential, we might almost say dictatorial, part of the body politic."[104] However, with workers increasingly organized into one big union with its own rituals, associational culture, regulations, and bylaws, the union, with its counterhegemonic institutions of lodges, courts, and parliaments, might well appear as a prototype for postcapitalist forms of social organization that the cooperatives had hitherto projected only in the abstract. Although there were considerable differences of opinion within the GNCTU, both locally and nationally, as to how far the union ought to go, radical leaders, soaking up the heady atmosphere of the period, began to act as though the new collectivist forms of industrial production and distribution that the cooperatives had vainly sought by voluntaristic and evolutionary means might be instantly achieved by a universal cessation of wage labor in which the workers would give a dramatic and practical demonstration that labor really was the source of all wealth.

There is a considerable question as to how far the rank and file would have pursued an open declaration of class warfare or how elites and property owners would have responded given their ultimate legal and military control within the state. In any event, the matter was never put to the test. In 1835, as worsted markets tightened and as a spate of local strikes depleted union funds, the employers initiated a two-pronged counteroffensive using the courts to prosecute unionists for secret organization and oath taking, and their own economic powers of blacklisting to coerce employees into renouncing union membership and strikes. By 1836, it was clear that, so far from bringing down capitalism, the general union structures painstakingly erected by Bradford's workers during the 1829–34 period had been reduced to a state of bankruptcy and collapse. Of course, working-class radicalism and organization did not utterly dissipate in this debacle, but with the onset of protracted depression and mass unemployment after 1837, it was redirected into political movements like Chartism. General unions of the type that dominated the earlier period appeared to have become a thing of the past.[105]

Nevertheless, this shift from orientation toward exploitation in the workplace to countering oppression on a wider experiential plane preserved much of the instinctive anticapitalism and explicit class consciousness that the general trade unions had brought to the fore. Thus in 1839, when Bradford's Chartists formed in procession, many of them marched as members of constituent trades. Such links between a primordial, underlying identity as

---

[104] *Pioneer*, May 31, 1834.
[105] Sanders, "Working Class Movements," 109–12; Thornes, "Co-operative Movement," 69–81; Peacock, *Bradford Chartism*, 8–9.

wage laborers and the manifest Chartist politics of class became even clearer in August 1839 and again in August 1842, when at least part of the movement revived the general strike weapon as a means of obtaining its universal male suffrage goal.[106]

Just as trade union tactics were enlisted in the cause of political radicalism, so the heightened militancy and mobilization that the latter made possible eventually breathed new life into trade unionism too. At least this became clear during the brief 1843–5 boom when the organized trades, acting under Chartist auspices, sought to benefit from their advantageous bargaining position by organizing an umbrella, called the United Trades. Although structured more loosely than the general unions of the thirties, this body proved more effective in maintaining some links between the skilled and the proletarianized, serving as a more militant and activist precursor to the trades councils of the mid-Victorian age.[107]

In 1845, a spate of successful strikes by colliers, tailors, and joiners showed how skilled artisans could benefit from such arrangements. Even more striking was the way that they permitted the woolcombers to revive their union organization and temporarily arrest the decline of conditions within their own trade. Pooling 10 percent of each member's weekly income into a joint agitational and strike reserve, the Combers Protective Society worked not only to advance their own trade interests, but to reactivate the spirit of classwide solidarity without which the proletarianized could not effectively organize.[108] In 1843, the union successfully struck for a wage increase against the large employer William Walker who capitulated within a week. Two years later, similar actions were threatened against Thomas Willett and mounted against Christopher Waud as well as John and William Rand.[109]

But the new generation of leaders who refurbished the combers' union knew that they could not indefinitely depend on their temporary advantages in a tight labor market. In the long run, their interests could only be protected through a renewal of the kind of general trade unions that they had tried to build a decade before. Facing "an accursed competition which...if not checked, [would] involve them in still greater privation," these new leaders, George White, George Fletcher, Robert Mullen, and Henry Burnett, knew that their first task was to cultivate "a deep indignation for the sufferings of those whose situation was even more intolerable than their own."[110] As a first step in this errand of fraternal aid, the combers attempted to organize

---

[106] *Northern Star*, Oct. 13, 1838; Sep. 25, 1839; *BO*, Aug. 11, 18, 25, 1842; *Bradford Herald*, Aug. 18, 25, 1842.
[107] *BO*, Mar. 27, Apr. 10, 1845.
[108] *BO*, Sep. 4, 1845.
[109] *BO*, May 23, 1844; May 8, July 3, 10, 17, 24, 1845; Reynolds, *Great Paternalist*, 123.
[110] *BO*, Sep. 4, 1845.

the female powerloom weavers who constituted a substantial proportion of the factory workers in town. Although this weavers' union never drew more than a tiny minority, the combers proposed a series of further measures to help proletarianized workers everywhere to defend themselves.[111]

Most impressive among these was an initiative to resurrect the schemes of cooperative production that had promised an alternative to capitalist exploitation in earlier years. In the early forties, the combers' union even allocated its own funds to establish workshops that would operate according to the principle of the labor exchange. However, since they were unable to elicit the participation of other artisans, they had to dispose of their goods in the open marketplace where they faced, as independent producers, the same competitive pressures that had undermined their position as wage laborers.[112]

With the return of depression in 1846, the combers' cooperative scheme succumbed to insolvency, and within a year or two, the union itself had collapsed. By then, woolcombing was a dying occupation beset not only by an overstocked labor market, but by the irresistible competition of a perfected machine. With the woolcombers' final demise after the middle of the century, a distinct era in the relations between labor and capital drew to a close. During the mid-Victorian period, Bradford's labor force became increasingly divided between a skilled, adult male, artisanal minority, fundamentally constrained by sectional craft concerns, and a largely silent, unorganized, and increasingly feminized mass of industrial operatives isolated within the confines of the factory's walls.[113]

Under these circumstances, general unions embracing all categories of wage labor, indeed class-conscious mass movements of any sort, became increasingly difficult to sustain. However, during the 1825–50 period when proletarianized adult, male, handicraft workers had constituted the largest single category of wage earners in town, a very different social pattern had prevailed. Acting as intermediaries between the skilled craftsmen with whom they identified and the hapless industrial proletarians to whose ranks they were being reduced, these textile handicraftsmen facilitated the evolution of a militant anticapitalist working-class consciousness that spread to other workers in the town. Beginning with the 1825 strike and with increasing intensity over the next twenty years, these economically essential but socially unassimilable workers played a critical role in transforming indigenous plebeian

[111] *BO*, Mar. 27, 1845.
[112] Aug. 27, 1840; Aug. 1, 1844; Apr. 10, 1845.
[113] See Chapter 18.

traditions of craft and community into new forms of collective association based on wage laborers' common interests as a class.

During the first decade after 1825, this new organizational framework of class consciousness was forged in the series of general trade unions that arose in response to the predicament of proletarianization. As institutions that confronted capitalist exploitation at its source in the workplace, these general unions, together with the cooperative experiments that they spawned, inevitably fostered a sense of worker self-consciousness that, at least momentarily in 1834, began to assume explicitly anticapitalist forms. But in the more troubled second half of the 1830s, these voluntary associations of working-class consciousness were increasingly isolated, disarmed, and ultimately suppressed. As a result, the workers who had organized them began to realize that, behind the capitalist economy of production and distribution, stood an even more deeply entrenched system of social and political power. Thereafter, the central thrust of Bradford's working-class movement, between the late 1830s and its collapse at midcentury, shifted from the economic associations in which class consciousness had been incubated into a new and even more inclusive mass movement in which the impulse to transcend capitalist productive relations reappeared as a crusade for political reform.

17

The challenge of Chartism

The initial entry of Bradford's workers into the political arena reflected, as we have seen, less an independent class consciousness than the struggle between bourgeois liberals and Tories, who were driven by their own mutual antagonisms to enlist the aid of popular allies. Yet in calling up the political energies of the workers, bourgeois politicians unleashed a potentially explosive force. By the mid-1830s, the popular politics inspired by liberal and Tory reformers was patently slipping out of bourgeois party control. Sinking ever deeper into mutual recrimination, each party unmasked the other in working-class eyes. Bull and Oastler stimulated the workers' hostility toward entrepreneurial capitalism by playing on their instinctive anticapitalist values and beliefs. At the same time, the democratic aspirations that radical liberalism had nurtured tended to immunize them against the Tory radical alternative that was hostile, in principle, to popular rule.

Amidst all this came the rise of an autonomous working-class culture, incubated in the communitarianism of the urban slum neighborhood and developed through the new worker voluntary associations. Ever more deeply enmeshed in the vortex of proletarianization, the spirit of working-class consciousness could scarcely be nurtured in the benefit club, the trade union, or the cooperative without also engendering a distinctive political class identity too. Finally, in 1837, after the exhaustion of the liberal reform and Tory factory campaigns, Bradford's workers declared their political independence, initiating mass movements like the struggle against the Poor Law and the agitations for universal suffrage and an unstamped press, which openly broke with the policies of both bourgeois parties and evoked only hostility from either camp. A year later, these separate strands coalesced under the banner of Chartism, which remained the primary vehicle of organized working-class politics for a decade.[1]

[1] For the best studies of Chartism, see Dorothy Thompson, *The Chartists* (New York, 1984); David Jones, *Chartism and the Chartists* (London, 1975); Asa Briggs, ed., *Chartist Studies* (London, 1959); F. C. Mather, *Public Order in the Age of the Chartist* (Manchester, 1959); G. D. H. Cole, *Chartist Portraits* (London, 1940); Mark Hovell, *The Chartist Movement* (Manchester, 1970); and R. G. Gammage, *History of the Chartist Movement* (London, 1894).

Chartism and the development of the working-class movement

This absorption of proletarian politics within the general fabric of Chartism marked a decisive moment for social relations in Bradford and a high point of working-class mobilization in the town. This was not primarily because of the movement's focus on universal suffrage, which had, after all, been on the popular political agenda for some time. What made the turn to Chartism particularly significant was that it signaled the emergence of a form of mass protest that, even more than the trade unions or cooperatives that preceded it, looked beyond the limits of capitalist economic relations to contest the political roots of capitalist state power. Moreover, in adding a political overlay to the struggle between capital and labor, Chartism betokened the infusion of these economic class antagonisms into the very heart of the political realm. It served notice, in the words of a local spokesman, that "only that which has direct relation to the interests of the great family of workers...can awaken the popular interests." Although "the political evils under which we groan are, indeed, immense," Chartism as a political movement undergirded by class consciousness would insist that "the real cause of the disease which is consuming us is to be found in our social relations."[2]

What made such statements particularly significant was that the general trade unions and cooperatives, in which class consciousness had first crystalized, though perhaps more self-conscious about their explicit class basis, had been disinclined to comprehend class oppression in this way. Indeed, during the 1825 strike, the combers and weavers had expressly forbidden the introduction of political discussions into deliberations about union affairs. Similarly, the general unions and cooperative societies, even in their most militant anticapitalist phase, insisted that the New Jerusalem was a social and economic Arcadia that could not be built by political means. Only in the second half of the 1830s, when full-scale proletarianization had seriously sapped the workers' economic class institutions, were they compelled to look behind the immediate menace of market competition to the underlying structures of political domination and property rights that underwrote a massive expansion of capital, while the value of labor was allowed to decay. The role of political privilege in sustaining class oppression had already been demonstrated by the liberal, antiaristocratic critique. Now, following the lead of the Ricardian socialists, workers began to question whether the capitalists' profit might not turn out to be the same sort of parasitic monopoly that bourgeois liberalism had originally diagnosed in the landlord's rent.[3]

---

[2] *BO*, Sep. 9, 1847.
[3] Thomas Hodgskin, *Labour Defended against the Claims of Capital* (London, 1825).

By the late thirties, the notion that industrial workers could effectively advance their class interests through voluntary action, collective bargaining, or even a universal withdrawal of labor in the economic sphere, was widely recognized as a dangerous illusion that ignored the political realities of class compulsion and state power. In Bradford, the woolcombers, who had hitherto eschewed political involvement, now became "almost without exception rabid politicians . . . enthusiastic adherents" of the Chartist movement whose "one book of study was the *Northern Star*."[4]

As Gareth Steadman Jones has persuasively argued, this turn toward politics on the part of the working-class movement can be seen as a direct response to the altered character of the postreform Whig liberal state. The transparent class basis of the 1832 franchise, which brought the bulk of the middle class into the political process while leaving virtually all workers outside, was followed in quick succession by a series of measures – the 1833 Irish Coercion Act, the 1834 "Malthusian" Poor Law, the reaffirmation of "knowledge taxes," and the various acts reforming and strengthening the police – that could easily be construed as attacks on popular working-class rights. Conversely, the refusal to protect textile outworkers and the unceremonious defeat of the ten-hours bill merged with the pattern of trade union repression to convince workers that the state, which had hitherto served the interests of aristocrats, had now fallen under capitalist control.[5]

This convergence of preexisting forms of working-class consciousness and organization into a mass political movement that was radical democratic in its immediate objectives but anticapitalist in its underlying aims can be clearly seen in the career of Peter Bussey, who had emerged as Bradford's most important working-class leader during the 1830s and dominated local Chartism during its early years. Bussey began as a woolcomber in the 1820s and got his first taste of class activism through participation in the 1825 strike. Rising to a leadership position in the trade union movement five years later when the Bradford Order was formed, Bussey was drawn into the political fray by the parliamentary reform struggle, and after the organization of the Bradford Political Union, he emerged as the main spokesman for the working-class rank and file.[6]

However, Bussey's 1830 political alliance with the entrepreneurial liberals did not prevent him from joining forces a year later with Tory radicals like

---

[4] Frank Peel, *The Risings of the Luddites, Chartists and Plug Drawers* (London, 1880), 329–43; G. D. H. Cole, *Attempts at General Union* (London, 1953).

[5] Gareth Stedman Jones, *Languages of Class* (Cambridge, 1983), 128–62; Thompson, *Chartists*, 11–36.

[6] A. J. Peacock, *Bradford Chartism, 1838–40* (York, 1969), 8–9; *The Charter*, May, 5 1839; J. Schofield, *Peter Bussey, Once a Noted Bradfordian* (Bradford, 1895). For a more critical view of Bussey's character, see *BO*, Jan. 31, 1839.

Bull and Oastler in the campaign for a ten-hours act. His work as a leading organizer of the short-time committees further sensitized him to the pitfalls of entrepreneurial capitalism and convinced him of the necessity for workers to organize collectively to further their own class ends. In 1834, as sponsor of the socialist Regeneration Society and secretary of the local GNCTU, Bussey secured his position as the most important local advocate of independent working-class action to resist capitalist encroachments into the labor process and to pave the way for a future cooperative world.[7] However, with the repression of the GNCTU nationally and the local Regeneration Society's precipitous collapse, working-class leaders were forced to turn their attention to the coercive role of the state. In 1835, the trial of the Dorchester laborers, which became a *cause célèbre* locally, focused attention squarely on the power of the law. At a mass meeting of ten thousand held to protest their conviction, the verdict was portrayed not as a mere miscarriage of justice, but as a "trial of the strength of the working classes."[8]

Convinced that workers would never achieve any of their other objectives until the strength that they naturally possessed in numbers was translated into democratic state power, Bussey returned, in 1836, to the working-class political agenda, organizing the Bradford Radical Association, which immediately began agitating for a free press and constitutional reform. However, from the outset he insisted that this working-class return to politics would not, as in the earlier period, operate within either the liberal or conservative party framework. Hitherto, he admitted, "we have assisted in these struggles" and "the contending parties have made use of us to answer their own ends." However, now, having "been cast on one side by both factions when they had no further need of us," the workers were determined to pursue an independent course.[9] Immediately signaling their departure from the political mainstream by holding a festival on the birthday of Tom Paine, Bussey's radicals went beyond the neo-Jacobin Paineite tradition and "formed themselves into a branch of the Socialists who not only require to be emancipated from their political disabilities but seek also to free themselves from those disadvantages which attach to their dependence on and servitude of landlords and capitalists."[10]

As long as such sentiments were confined to the articulate minority on

[7] J. C. Gill, *The Ten Hour's Parson* (London, 1959), 136–42; *BO*, Mar. 13, 20, 1834.

[8] J. R. Sanders, "Working Class Movements in the West Riding Textile District, 1829 to 1839, with Emphasis on Local Leadership and Organization" (Manchester, Ph.D. dissertation, 1984), 411–13.

[9] Quoted in Sanders, "Working Class Movements," 467.

[10] *Northern Star*, May 5, 1838; Sanders, "Working Class Movements," 36. For an account of similar developments in the nearby village of Queensbury, see John Bates, *A Sketch of His Life* (Queensbury, 1895).

the trade union or cooperative fringe, they might be seen as posing no more than a rhetorical challenge to capitalist authority. However, when they erupted in mass movements like the anti-Poor Law campaign amidst the heightened tensions of a massive depression year, they might well appear as ominous forshadowings of some desperate and violent revolutionary outrage. Although Bussey, at least openly, disclaimed revolution, he eagerly seized on popular fears of the workhouse to amplify his club of radicals into a crusading mass movement under the aegis of Feargus O'Connor's protean Great Northern Union, which became the midwife of Chartism in the industrial North. Now, amidst a climate of widespread poverty and unemployment, when workers' bargaining power in the marketplace had reached its nadir, class consciousness had to find refuge in political radicalism as the latter finally secured a uniquely working-class base. Interweaving the legacies of all previous worker organizations and movements, Chartism, in the summer and fall of 1838, crystallized a new, radical collectivist vision in which it was the disenfranchisement of the worker as citizen, his dispossession in the political sphere, that was seen as the single most critical impediment to redressing all the specific afflictions and grievances of those who found themselves economically proletarianized.[11]

Of course, by thus focusing on the political manifestations of class oppression, Chartism evolved into a movement whose appeal was not restricted to wage laborers, but extended to small shopkeepers and other petty propertyowners, who, being disenfranchised by the existing £10 property qualification, could embrace the cause of popular sovereignty as their own. Indeed, there is a strong temptation to exaggerate the significance of this self-employed, lower-middle-class component, which, because of its members' higher levels of education and relative immunity from employer coercion and recrimination, contributed a disproportionate share of the movement's local leadership. Nevertheless, petit bourgeois Chartists never constituted more than about 5 percent of all rank-and-file activists, and membership statistics not only demonstrate the movement's working-class social foundations, but suggest that it represented, at least until the midforties, a fairly accurate cross section of the entire adult male work force of the town.[12]

Given the predominance of textile handicraftsmen within the overall working-class population, it is not surprising that they dominated local Chartism too. A roster of the Great Horton Charter Association in 1840–2 reveals that 76 percent of the 113 individuals listed worked within the staple trade.

---

[11] The charismatic O'Connor himself played a considerable role in whipping up local enthusiasm, visiting Bradford at least five times in the space of these two years. *BO*, Jan. 12, Sep. 21, 1837; Jan. 11, Sep. 13, 1838; *Northern Star*, Nov. 3, 1838.
[12] Thompson, *Chartists*, 152–74.

Nearly half were weavers, a third were woolcombers, and a mere 8 percent were skilled mechanics or artisans. Perhaps a more accurate estimate of the composition of the movement can be gleaned from the occupational distribution of the forty-seven Bradford Chartists who were arrested during the riots of 1842. Fifty-one percent were combers, 26 percent were unskilled laborers, and 17 percent were skilled workers of various sorts. If hinterland workers are also included, the proportion of weavers and unskilled laborers is substantially increased. Perhaps the only occupational sector of the work force relatively underrepresented in the movement was that of the factory operatives, the majority of whom were female and integrated into Chartism through auxiliary organizations of their own.[13]

Although Chartism, like the general unions that preceded it, rested largely on the mass of disaffected, proletarianized handicraftsmen who constituted the numerical bulk of its strength, these figures indicate that its success, no less than that of its trade union forerunners, hinged on its ability to encompass within the same movement a significant core of the less vulnerable urban-artisanal workers whose greater capacity for sustained organization and action facilitated the channeling of impulses of protest and resentment into positive programs of reconstruction and reform.[14] Since economic depressions, with their widespread poverty and unemployment, always provided optimal conditions for expressions of solidarity between the proletarianized whose labor was being systematically devalued and the skilled who, though vulnerable to cyclical oscillations, remained, in structural terms, secure, it is not surprising that Chartism in Bradford ebbed and flowed with the trade cycle, reaching its moments of greatest strength and visibility in 1839, 1842, and 1848, when economic depression was worst.[15]

The highest apogee of Bradford Chartism came during the first of these periods, when the movement posed its most serious and sustained political challenge and a high point of working-class mobilization and solidarity was reached. In 1839, as never before or after, the Chartist cause drew unqualified support and enthusiasm from all sectors of the working population of the town. In the crucible of deep depression, skilled artisans joined forces with the much larger mass of woolcombers and hinterland weavers whose economic position had been deteriorating for some time. For a full year,

---

[13] *Bradford Herald*, Aug. 16, 1842; "Membership Book, Great Horton Chartist Association" (mss., Bradford Archives, D.B. 1/4).

[14] See J. F. C. Harrison, "Chartism in Leeds," in Briggs, ed., *Chartists Studies*, 65–98.

[15] For narrative accounts of Chartism in Bradford see Peacock, *Bradford Chartism;* D. G. Wright, "Politics and Opinion in Nineteenth Century Bradford" (Leeds, Ph.D. dissertation, 1966), 188–307; and Jack Reynolds, *The Great Paternalist: Titus Salt and the Growth of Nineteenth Century Bradford* (London, 1983), 122–63.

despite numerous pitfalls and several outside challenges from Tory radicals and the liberal Anti-Corn Law League, Chartism continued to act as a force of cohesion binding together the wide range of different social groups and political factions within Bradford's organized working class.

A determination to obtain the People's Charter, "peaceably if we can, forcibly if we must," became the common thread that united the entire working-class movement and guided the strategies that it successively adopted. At this point, there was no real distinction between advocates of physical and moral force. Initially, all hoped that the massive Chartist petition to Parliament would be sufficient to achieve their goal. However, when the petition was summarily rejected, few were prepared to give up and admit defeat. Even John Jackson, a shoemaker who represented the movement's most moderate and "aristocratic" artisanal wing, recognized the need for ulterior measures involving some degree of compulsion, if any real concessions from above were to be obtained.[16]

The logic of embracing ulterior measures, in the spring and summer of 1839, forced Chartists of all constituent working-class strata to recognize the true character of their movement and to acknowledge, even if only implicitly, that they constituted a potentially revolutionary force. By May, there were frequent reports of secret drilling, and in June, several hundred Bradford Chartists were reported to be armed. Even those who eschewed violence opted for more gradualist forms of compulsion that would demonstrate working-class economic muscle through exclusive dealing with sympathetic shopkeepers, boycotts of excisable articles, and a run on the banks. Naturally, the logical culmination of this strategy was for the workers to withhold their labor and to go out on strike. By the summer, there was considerable local support for this option, far more than in many other Chartist strongholds. The failure of the work stoppage that was planned for August and was known as the "sacred month" appears to have been the precipitating factor in the establishment of a local secret underground organization under Bussey's leadership that began to prepare for an insurrectionary *coup de main*.[17]

In September, plans appear to have been made for a national rising, although Bussey's insistence that this project be postponed insured that the small group of Welsh revolutionaries who marched on Newport would not get the reinforcements from the Yorkshire militants that they appear to have expected. Fearing assassination from those who regarded him as a traitor, Bussey disappeared and went into hiding, and in December, the Yorkshire insurrection was rescheduled for January of the following year. This new

[16] *BO*, Oct. 13, 1838; Mar. 1, Aug. 1, 1839.
[17] *BO*, Aug. 1, 1839; *Northern Star*, July 27, Aug. 3, 10, 17, 1839.

conspiracy, however, was infiltrated by government informers, and on the night of January 26, when a band of armed Chartists in Bradford attempted to seize various strategic points downtown, the authorities were waiting to meet them and the whole venture ignominiously collapsed.[18]

The second phase of Chartism in Bradford commenced amidst the confusion that followed these unfortunate events. With the leadership decimated by arrests and defections and with demoralization rampant among the rank and file, the movement spent 1840 recovering and reorganizing according to O'Connors' National Charter Association plan. By 1842, the next trough of depression, it had, at least superficially, revived.[19] Certainly, the spontaneous outbreak of a general strike in August and the application of quasi-syndicalist tactics in support of the Chartist political cause seemed to indicate that urban-industrial capitalism would continue to be confronted with a united, politicized, and fundamentally unassimilable proletariat so long as it remained vulnerable to wholesale economic crisis and so long as its own social and ideological contradictions remained unresolved.[20]

Nevertheless, this recourse to obdurate forms of industrial militancy, which challenged capitalism as a total system and contained, at least implicitly, a socialistic thrust, alarmed Chartist moderates, including many skilled craftsmen like John Jackson, who reaffirmed their comittment to orthodox political economy and eagerly grasped at the initiatives of the United Reform Club to merge the campaign for the People's Charter with the liberal cause of free trade. As long as depression persisted, such efforts were doomed to failure. However, with the revival of trade in 1843, fissures began to appear within the working-class movement's ranks. That spring, when Feargus O'Connor spoke, he was openly criticized by local Chartist moderates who dismissed his land plan as "bastard socialism" and identified themselves as staunch free traders who would not be driven to the absurdity of advocating protectionism simply because they remained wary of the anti-Corn Law bourgeoisie.[21]

Over the next two years, as disagreements over Corn Law repeal, home colonization, and a series of local issues which will be examined in the next chapter, split Bradford's Chartists into two increasingly incompatible camps, these political divisions were exacerbated by the economic effects of prosperity, which tended to divide skilled workers from the structurally prole-

---

[18] Peacock, *Bradford Chartism*, 25, 29–53.
[19] *BO,* Jan. 2, June 25, 1840; *Northern Star,* Apr. 4, 11, 1840.
[20] See Chapter 12.
[21] *BO,* Feb. 2, 23, 1843. For an analysis of a comparable process in the very different social and economic environment of Leeds, see Harrison, "Chartism in Leeds," 65–98, and Alexander Tyrell, "Class Consciousness in Early Victorian Britain: Samuel Smiles, Leeds Politics, and the Self-Help Creed," *Journal of British Studies* 11:2 (1970).

tarianized and to undermine that sense of commonality that had hitherto underwritten their consciousness of themselves as a single, unified class. Consequently, the revival of proletarian militancy that the 1846–8 depression sparked inaugurated what turned out to be the final stage of Chartism as the crucible of crisis, so far from forging class cohesion, split the skilled and proletarianized decisively apart.[22]

At first, in the spring and summer of 1848, Chartism seemed to be repeating, in an even more ominous manner, the revolutionary potential it had first displayed a decade before, as petitions and mass meetings gave way to secret arming and ulterior measures that then led to Continental-style conspiracies and abortive uprisings in the slum streets. In the event, however, it was the marked differences between the two moments of Chartist challenge that was most dramatically revealed. In sharp contrast to the 1839 insurgency, when the high-water mark of working-class solidarity was reached, 1848 witnessed the last gasp of the economically moribund handicraft stratum that had been spawned by the initial stages of industrial development but would find no permanent place in the future urban-capitalist world. Largely abandoned by the skilled artisans and best-paid factory workers who used the developments of that year to strengthen their links with radical liberalism and to seek integration into Bradford's emerging mid-Victorian milieu, the 1848 insurgency was almost exclusively the work of the desperate but dwindling woolcombers and unskilled laborers. Many of these were recent Irish immigrants who were ill equipped to implement, on an on-going basis, the new social democratic and egalitarian class ideals. Not surprisingly, events proved that these 1848 insurgents would be even less successful than their 1839 counterparts, and when the authorities finally restored order by late summer, Chartism as a mass movement was dead.[23]

As this brief narrative of events clearly demonstrates, the rise and fall of mass Chartism in Bradford is largely the story of the fate of the working-class alliance between the skilled and the proletarianized that was forged in the general unions of the 1830–5 period and whose roots can be traced back to the great strike of 1825. In the late thirties, when the bonds of this alliance were strengthened by depression, the movement was politicized and Chartism arose. After the midforties, however, the united political movement began to disintegrate as the working-class alliance began to unravel in the

---

[22] *BO*, Jan. 4, Feb. 22, 1844; Joy MacAskill, "The Chartist Land Plan," in Briggs, ed., *Chartist Studies*, 304–41.
[23] See Chapter 18.

changed economic conditions of the end of the decade. Nevertheless, even at its greatest moment of initial triumph, Chartism was riven with cultural and ideological ambiguities that implicitly belied the staunch independence and firm sense of common purpose that its working-class participants so impressively displayed.

These cultural and ideological ambiguities were, in fact, almost inevitable by-products of the politicization of class consciousness and the attempt to wield the weapons of class struggle in a field that was broader than the industrial workplace. When they translated the class solidarities that had been forged by trade unions into the open-ended imperatives of political action, workers found themselves operating within an arena subject to a multitude of pressures, not all of which were reducible to a strict economic logic of class. More significantly, in the realm of political behavior, acts gained significance within a preexisting framework of discourse in which the languages of bourgeois liberalism and conservatism continued to be felt.[24] Liberalism and conservatism, whatever their limitations, were not only bourgeois class ideologies, but broadly cultural, political, and theoretical constructs in which the particular interests of the social groups that espoused them were reflected by being cast in a universalistic language in which they could be identified with the interests of society as a whole.

As elites who were engaged in the practice of social dominance and needed to legitimize their rule, this sort of abstract, hegemonic thinking came naturally to Bradford's liberal and Tory bourgeoisie. But for working-class Chartists, it was considerably more difficult to devise their own positive, reconstructive social vision, so long as their fundamentally subordinate condition pressed them naturally into a politics of opposition through which they were inclined to define themselves negatively with reference to the larger power structures that they were against.[25] As we have seen, the general unions and early cooperatives contained the germ of a social and economic practice on which such ideological hegemony might have been built. But the utopian character of these first socialist experiments and their evaporation in the face of capitalist political power disclosed their inadequacy as vehicles for a uniquely proletarian vision of the world.

To be sure, in shifting the locus of class exploitation from dispossession in the workplace to disenfranchisement within the state, Chartism, in its own way, pointed toward a new conception of citizenship in which equality in

---

[24] Jones, *Languages of Class*, 90–178. For an interpretation that highlights the Tory component in Chartism, see R. N. Soffer, "Attitudes and Allegiances in the Unskilled North," *International Review of Social History*, 10:1 (1965). For an interpretation that highlights the liberal component, see Brian Harrison and Patricia Hollis, "Chartism, Liberalism, and the Life of Robert Lowery," *English Historical Review*, 82:324 (1967).

[25] Karl Mannheim, *Ideology and Utopia* (New York, 1936).

the realm of politics presupposed the equitable distribution of social and economic goods. But this embryonic impulse to redefine politics through a language of social democracy was only erratically and incompletely realized. All too often the Chartist goal of universal suffrage, instead of underwriting an integrative program for the reorganization of a postcapitalist state and society, remained little more than an enabling measure, the glue that held together a diverse collection of ideological strands and social constituencies by posing as the common precondition for their distinct individual goals.[26]

Coming at a moment of deep social crisis, before entrepreneurial capitalism was so entrenched as to appear politically irremovable, when it was scarcely viable even in purely economic terms, Chartism seemed, albeit nebulously and uncertainly, to prefigure a postliberal form of social relations that would transcend both hierarchical and competitive principles and reorganize society in an egalitarian, cooperative way. Yet most Chartists consistently denied the subversive implications of the activities that they mounted or the revolutionary character of the ideas they embraced. Moreover, since the movement failed to achieve even the most limited of its stated objectives, Chartism must ultimately be judged a failure even in its own self-professedly reformist terms. From one perspective it appears as the culminating moment of an anticapitalist working-class consciousness and insurgency that had been building in Bradford for three decades. From another it might be dismissed as the last gasp of a demoralized traditional proletariat, soon to be replaced by more limited, but realistic, class organizations that would be more assimilable and better integrated into Bradford's mature urban-industrial space.[27]

In fact, it is not possible to understand Chartism unless we recognize that it was a transitional movement that accurately reflected the worldview of the generation of workers who were undergoing the trauma of proletarianization for the first time. Involuntarily thrust by the imperatives of the competitive market from the protoindustrial cottage and countryside into the factory and foetid city slum, this first generation of urban-industrial workers lived its life caught between the legacy of a world that was dying and the harsh realities of one that had scarcely been born. This transitional nature of these workers' lives and experience had a profound impact on their outlook and behavior and goes a long way toward explaining many of the peculiarities of the mass movement that they formed.

For a small but critical minority of artisans whose labor was, as yet, untouched by technological transformation and who were able, despite mar-

---

[26] Hovell, *Chartist Movement*, 98–115.
[27] *BO*, June 1, 8, 15, 22, 29, July 20, 27, Aug. 10, 17, 24, Sep. 14, 1848.

ket pressures, to keep their craft status relatively intact, proletarianization was largely experienced as an intermittent danger associated with the great cyclical cataclysms that periodically wreaked havoc on local social and economic life. However, even among groups like the weavers and woolcombers, who were condemned to proletarian status as a lifelong fate, the bitter memory of a time when things had been different shaped the character of worker response. Unlike subsequent generations of fully industrialized workers, those who became Chartists could envision wholesale alternatives to capitalism, at least in part, because, for all their suffering, they possessed firsthand experience of a less alienating way of life. Yet the very impoverishment and demoralization to which proletarianization subjected them to some degree stripped them of the material and organizational capabilities that their generally more prosperous and less militant descendants possessed. Ironically, these men and women may have acquired the presumption to assault the capitalist citadel precisely because they underestimated its strength and tenacity, naively viewing it not as a permanent world-historical structure, but as some aberrant innovation that might easily be brought down.[28]

Yet although the Chartist vision of an alternative to capitalism was rooted in traditional values and institutions derived from the rural protoindustrial past, it would be wrong to portray the movement as a backward-looking, atavistic relic that provided no model for the future tasks of working-class organization in the new urban-industrial milieu. Under new circumstances, the old forms had to assume new meanings, as standards that had their roots in traditional ideals of community were transformed by the experience of struggle into entirely novel aspirations to seek hitherto unimagined democratic forms. The fact that the Chartists' idealized image of an egalitarian, cooperative future was drawn from a memory of their own preindustrial past may have been a source of weakness for the movement, but it endowed their struggle against the dehumanization that surrounded them with a concrete richness and vitality that turned out to be the movement's greatest source of strength.[29]

---

[28] See Jones, *Languages of Class*, 90–178, for elaboration of a similar argument.

[29] It is striking that virtually every aspect of Chartist ideology and activity in Bradford drew deeply upon the traditions of working-class community and on the customary values of the popular culture that this generation of recent immigrants held close their hearts. Dorothy Thompson, in her magisterial survey *The Chartists*, 108–9, has stressed the extent to which the movement was rooted in the ecology of traditional manufacturing communities where, despite widespread economic development and the abdication of traditional elites, working-class culture remained essentially the face-to-face culture of traditional village life. Yet the same features that made Chartism attractive to the hinterland weaver also made it attractive to the woolcomber, the artisan, or even the factory operative who had recently moved to the city from exactly the environment that Thompson

Chartism and the politicization of working-class culture

As a movement that encompassed both city dweller and villager, bridging the experiences of industrial and protoindustrial life, the great genius of Chartism lay in its ability to generate multivalent symbols in which potentially revolutionary new forms of action and consciousness could be expressed in a more traditional language which drew on the older, communitarian values and norms. To be sure, Chartism's underlying class character and social democratic content were not simply constructs that historians have formulated from hindsight. They were also facts of which the movement's leaders were themselves well aware. Yet when Peter Bussey protested the New Poor Law by refusing, in 1838, to pay his rate, he acted out of a logic that came from Hodgskin and Carlile, but it was Blackstone and the Bible that he cited in his defense. A year later, when he "recommended that every man shall be in possession of a musket," he justified this as "the means by which their ancestors had secured their liberty in the time of King Alfred."[30]

Indeed, in the context of the great agitational conjunctures of the spring and summer of 1839, virtually every element in the Chartist tactical repertoire was tantamount to a subversive act. Yet all could still be justified on the basis of traditional precedents as no more than the freeborn Englishman's natural right. The very name, "People's Charter," became a synonym for democratic radicalism, yet it conjured up the memory of another great charter that had scarcely been democratic in its aims. The original Chartist plan of petitioning Parliament was, perhaps, the most classic example of a time-honored method of popular protest that raised the inevitable specter of more militant action after it failed to have effect. Although every ulterior measure that the Chartists considered after the rejection of the petition – exclusive dealing, boycott of excisable articles, and the work stoppage known as the "scared month" – represented revolutionary challenges to the established power structure, they were all conceived not as uncompromising gestures of class struggle, but in the tradition of previous political protest movements that had mobilized the "people" to bring "old corruption" to heel. Even insurrection could be thus defended if it were portrayed not as violence, but as the people acting in their self-defense.[31]

This harkening back to traditional values, which drew radical inspiration

---

describes; for Bradford Chartism was not an urban, but a regional phenomenon in which city dwellers united in the same organizations and activities with those who still lived in the hinterland villages beyond.

[30] *BO*, Nov. 15, 1838; Jan. 19, 1839.

[31] Iorwerth Prothero, "William Benbow and the Concept of the General Strike," *Past and Present*, 63 (1974); T. M. Parssinen, "Association, Convention, and Anti-Parliament, British Radical Politics, 1771–1848," *English Historical Review*, 88:348 (1973).

from the "poetry of the past," can be seen most clearly through an examination of the role in the movement that religious traditions and influences
played. Not surprisingly, with its emphasis on legitimizing notions of right
and justice, Chartism, even as a secular phenomenon, drew on many of the
same popular cultural traditions that had nurtured traditional evangelicalism
too. Indeed, for those who sought the sanction of the gospel to support their
claims for the rights of the poor, the movement actually encompassed a
religious revival that channeled the plebeian spiritual energies that had once
fueled Methodism and millenarianism into the campaign for political
reform.[32]

This politicization of popular religion had been unwittingly prepared by
the evangelical Tory radicals and rhetorically inflated during the Poor Law
crisis by the renegade Wesleyan J. R. Stephens, who preached increasingly
violent sermons against "those abodes of guilt" that the liberals "have reared
to violate all Law and God's book."[33] Although Stephens abandoned the
movement when it turned to Chartism, other charismatic preachers such as
Ben Rushton, William Arran, and William Thornton, the last whom O'Connor humorously proposed as archbishop of York, quickly emerged to take
his place. To the *Observer*, such men seemed mere "hypocrites who mask
themselves in religion," but with their emphasis on the blessedness of the
humble and meek, and their conviction that they would inherit the earth,
these radical preachers articulated a dimension of Christianity that the salvation-centered sects of bourgeois Nonconformity either minimized or forgot. Excluded from most existing preaching rooms and aware of the existence
of a potential constituency for a radical brand of Christianity based on
collectivist principles, these men organized an alternative Chartist congregation with a chapel of its own.[34]

The vision of Christianity as a religion of the poor and downtrodden
rather than as a rationalization for worldly prosperity and success not only
inspired a few experiments in Chartist sectarianism, but was implicitly embraced by the vast majority of workers except for the minority of atheists
who rejected religion in all forms. Although this populist, plebeian vision of
Christianity could hardly be expected to recommend itself to the neo-Calvinist denominations of bourgeois dissent, many workers entertained hopes
that it might be reactivated within the framework of the national church.

Tory radicalism had long instructed Bradford's workers to look to An-

---

[32] H. U. Faulkner, *Chartism and the Churches* (New York, 1916).
[33] Gammage, *History of the Chartist Movement*, 58–9.
[34] Thompson, *Chartists*, 182–3, 344. See also Faulkner, *Chartism and the Churches*, although
the best study of this plebeian strain of Christianity is Deborah Valenze, *Prophetic Sons
and Daughters: Female Preaching and Popular Religion in Industrial England* (Princeton,
1985), which focuses on the late eighteenth and early nineteenth centuries.

glicanism for the ideal of a paternalist community in which the poor would be cared for by the benevolent rich. Yet even after Tory radicalism had revealed its bankruptcy, the Chartists, in their quest for their own symbols of community, found themselves periodically driven back to the old parish church. Thus, on two successive Sundays in August 1839, several thousand Chartists proceeded en masse to attend morning service, reclaiming this symbol of communion as their own. Astounded at such plebeian gestures of defiance in the guise of deferential returns to the fold, the vicar was clearly taken aback. Pleased to see so many habitual nonattenders, he was concerned that the church could not accommodate all of them and worried that their numbers might intimidate the regular pewholders. The same uncertainty was generated a few months later when a demoralized crowd of the unemployed determined "to let the people of Bradford see their numbers and to petition the authorities of the town to provide them with employment or food," marched in desperation to the vicar's rectory, unclear about whether they had come to attack him as a class enemy or to request his intercession with the magistrates on their behalf. In the end, they went away with a stern admonition about their threatening demeanor and a promise of a sermon on the subject of their plight.[35]

This tendency to fall back on traditional symbols of community, even in moments of angry class revolt, can be seen most clearly in the monster radical demonstrations when tens, perhaps hundreds of thousands of Chartists gathered from all over the West Riding to declare their solidarity in an overwhelming show of strength. Not only were these mass mobilizations held on the same hinterland moorlands to which popular festivals like Whitsun had been relegated, but, in two instances in 1837 and 1839, they were deliberately scheduled to coincide with Whitsun itself.[36]

At these moments, all the theatricality and conviviality of traditional wakes and festivities was explosively embodied in a mass demonstration of collective anger that served to propel the radical political campaign. The booths, concession stands, rough sports, and gambling that customarily graced the old Whitsun festivities were simply incorporated into these giant protest gatherings in which the somber tones of angry rhetoric were punctuated by a lighter, carnivalesque air. Well accustomed to the liberal entrepreneurial mentality that treated both popular recreations and radical protests as subversive, radical workers saw absolutely no contradiction in articulating opposition to urban-industrial capitalism through such exuberant, holiday-like festivals of the oppressed. If tired and beleaguered workers could best contest

---

[35] William Scoresby, *What Shall We Do? or the Enquiry of the Destitute Operatives Considered* (London, n.d.); *BO*, Aug. 8, 15, 22, 29, 1839.
[36] *BO*, May 18, 1837; May 23, 1839; *Northern Star*, May 25, 1839.

capitalism during brief moments of leisure, they found that leisure itself had become a political act.[37]

This use of traditional communitarian functions to express more abstract solidarities can be seen in the revival of public processions that accompanied the radical festivals held on Peep Green. Public processions, which had fallen into desuetude as general expressions of community within the entire population, were now dramatically resurrected as distinctively proletarian phenomena, enlisted by the Chartist political campaign. Indeed, the order of march adopted by the Bradford contingent to the monster demonstration of October 1838 can be read as a metaphor for the transformation of inherited, face-to-face bonds of community into broader, self-conscious solidarities of class. Early in the morning, six hundred Chartists left the town center "headed by Peter Bussey on horseback, followed by an open carriage drawn by four grey horses, in which there were some of the leading radicals of the town." In the contingent that followed were the members of the newly formed Northern Union and the component groups of the Bradford United Trades. As these groups wended their way through suburbs and hinterland villages, "they were joined by large numbers from different quarters" who swelled into a surging throng of 12,000 before merging into the sea of 100,000 faces, thousands of banners, and dozens of marching bands that had, by the afternoon, assembled on the moor.[38]

Yet as this parade of working men and women from diverse neighborhoods and social backgrounds, encompassing the full range of local occupations and trades, gathered together at the Chartist mass meetings to demonstrate its collective solidarity as a class, its participants pressed the limits of the traditional communitarian rituals that they had chosen to serve their larger political aims. This became particularly clear in the aftermath of the last great Peep Green Whitsun demonstration, which was held on May 21, 1839. Coming at a critical juncture in Chartism's history when the movement was forced to face the implacability of elites, the meeting was intended not only to politicize Whitsun, but to serve as a gargantuan forum in which convention delegates could report back to their constituents and plumb the sentiments of the rank and file. Moreover, the Peep Green meeting was only one of a series of similar demonstrations held simultaneously throughout the country that were intended as a flexing of muscles to show the authorities the extent of Chartist unity and strength.[39]

The official reaction was predictable enough. When workers sponta-

[37] *BO*, May 18, 1837; Oct. 18, 1838; May 23, 1839; *Northern Star*, Oct. 20, 1838; May 25, 1839.
[38] *BO*, Oct. 13, 20, 1838; *Northern Star*, Oct. 13, 20, 1838.
[39] Gammage, *History of the Chartist Movement*, 105–21.

neously gathered on Peep Green to celebrate Whitsun, it made local elites very nervous. When these gatherings were harnessed to political protests, nervousness turned to fear. Now, as these mass political festivals were co-ordinated to occur simultaneously as part of an organized agitational plan, it was obvious that they had to be stopped. In May, the government had already begun by proscribing torchlight processions. In July, however, a group of local property owners discovered a more permanent and liberal-minded solution when they joined forces to obtain an enclosure act that would divide up and parcel out the open space of Hartshead Moor. Thus, what the logic of rising property values had originally initiated, the imperatives of political order now finally secured. In August, the Chartists attempted to move their meeting ground to Fairweather Green, but in November this too was divided up and enclosed so that, according to the *Observer*, "radicals and others who have long resorted to that spot will have to seek another." Indeed, by the beginning of 1840, in the vicinity of Bradford virtually no open spaces were left. Thus it was that, in the heat of bitter class conflict, private property achieved its final triumph in Bradford over the legacy of communal space. As a result, the Chartists lost one of their most effective techniques of protest, while the spontaneous plebeian celebrations of Whitsun, were finally rendered, in Bradford, a thing of the past.[40]

Cooperation and democracy in the Chartist associations

If the great open-air protest demonstrations of the 1830s reflect the convergence of a wide range of plebeian neighborhoods and occupations into a broader, more cohesive, proletarian stream, their precipitous demise in the crisis of 1839–40 symbolizes the acute difficulty that workers experienced in translating the traditional, particularistic values of community into vehicles for collective class organization. Destroyed not only by a political authority that suppressed them, but by an urban-industrial process that undercut their space, these demonstrations seemed to point toward newer, self-consciously democratic forms of cooperation that would require a much more structured organizational base.

Indeed, to become more than intermittent explosions of collective nostalgia, desperate recapitulations of a half-mythical popular culture of the past, Chartism, like the friendly societies, the trade unions, and the coop-

---

[40] *BO*, July 4, Aug. 1, Nov. 7, 1839; Gammage, *History of the Chartist Movement*, 98–9. By midcentury, one mill manager was pleased to report that "Peckover Walks (1.5 acres), formerly a place where Chartist and other public meetings were held, [had been] made into a most beautiful garden, chiefly occupied by the middle classes and gentlemen." (1850, XXIII), 48.

eratives, had to develop its own permanent voluntary associations and offer a viable, ongoing alternative culture to that of Bradford's bourgeois liberal voluntarist mainstream. As a classwide movement of social and political insurgency, which sought to perpetuate the militant union of all sectors of workers that had been forged in the period 1825–39, the Chartists promised to do considerably more. That they ultimately failed in their most ambitious undertakings should not obscure their very real achievement in initiating within the limits of their own organizations that experiment in practical social democracy that they were unable to extend to the society as a whole.

Although the vast bulk of Bradford's workers gave some clear expression of Chartist sympathies, either by signing the Chartist petition or by attending mass demonstrations, only a small minority were prepared to make the more strenuous commitment that day-to-day involvement in the work of permanent associations would bring. Membership in the Bradford Northern Union in 1839 and in the Bradford Charter Association in 1841 both seem to have peaked at about two thousand.[41] Although this figure probably leaves out organizational auxiliaries as well as the more distant hinterland branches, it indicates that Chartism as an organized movement drew in only a fraction of those who could, in moments of crisis, be rallied to the cause. Nevertheless, Chartist associational life plays a part in the movement's history far greater than a mere numerical accounting would suggest. Here, the strategy of the larger movement was formulated, and leadership cadres began to emerge.[42]

As advocates of democratization within society, these Chartists, to an even greater degree than other organized workers, actively drew on the democratic traditions of voluntary association that liberal Nonconformity had bequeathed. Yet as participants in a militant class movement of political confrontation, the Chartists, even more than the members of trade unions or benefit societies, had to adapt these liberal democratic values and practices to a distinctively proletarian set of social conditions and needs. Indeed, the need to transmute the liberal quest for individual self-help and salvation into a collective movement for advancement as a class was experienced with a heightened sense of urgency by Chartists who, in organizing to redress the injustices of the present, had also somehow to prefigure the new and more egalitarian kind of social relationships on which the future classless society might ultimately be based.[43]

Since it was not often easy to combine these two objectives, the Chartists

---

[41] Peacock, *Bradford Chartism*, 18; Thompson, *Chartists*, 344.

[42] Eileen Yeo, "Some Problems of Chartist Democracy," in J. A. Epstein and Dorothy Thompson, eds., *The Chartist Experience* (London, 1982).

[43] John Bates, *A History of His Life* (Queensbury, 1895).

developed an approach to internal democracy that diverged significantly from the hyperindividualist, ultravoluntarist forms of organization pioneered by the liberal bourgeoisie. Both because it was a movement of proletarianized workers whose strength lay in union and because it was an organized political insurgency in which local initiatives had to be reconciled with larger national strategies and aims, Chartism exhibited a style of democratic practice wherein the quest for autonomy that would empower its constituents was constantly tempered by an imperative toward centralization that was required for it to operate effectively as a collectivized force. This tension was reflected in the tendency for Chartist organization, like that of the general trade unions, only to a greater degree, to occur simultaneously at several different levels, ranging from a centralized executive where overall strategy was formulated to the grass roots, local neighborhood branch where the scope for participatory democracy was most great. If the former was necessary to give the movement coherence, the latter was always the core of Chartism's organizational strength. Here, within the confines of protoindustrial villages like Clayton, Queenshead, Thornton, Oakenshaw, North Bierley, and Great Horton, and in urban working-class slum neighborhoods like George Street, Pitt Lane, White Abbey, Bowling Lane, Wapping, and Nelson Court, Chartist organization appeared to grow most organically out of preexisting community life.[44]

Although Chartism's status as an indigenous working-class movement embodying the sentiments of the rank and file rested largely on the vitality of these branch associations, its viability as an organized political movement depended on their ability to coordinate effectively under a more centralized infrastructure of leadership and control. In 1839, the development of a spontaneous and virtually frictionless symbiosis between these different organizational levels was a key source of the movement's early success. At this point, when the spirit of class unity was felt most powerfully, Bradford's two dozen or so neighborhood radical associations required little prompting to affiliate together under the umbrella of the O'Connorite Great Northern Union and to coordinate activities in delegate meetings that were held every few days in Peter Bussey's home. Here, important policy questions were framed and debated while demonstrations and agitational tactics were planned. Petitioning, delegate election, and movement fund-raising were all largely organized at this townwide level, which, later in the year, became the primary unit for secret conspiratorial planning too.[45]

---

[44] Yeo, "Chartist Democracy."

[45] Although this constituted the most important level of Chartist organization, to the historian it remains the most opaque. Meeting, like unions or friendly societies, in neigh-

For obvious reasons, participatory democracy was more difficult to practice at this level, but regular meetings of a steering committee of branch delegates ensured considerable input from the grass roots. Moreover, in 1839, the Bradford Northern Union held regular public meetings, during the spring every few weeks, during the summer every night. As a convention delegate, Bussey made it a regular practice to return to Bradford to report to his constituents at regular intervals, and unlike the Peep Green demonstrations, at these smaller meetings, where he and other leaders spoke, there seems to have been genuinely open discussion as to the proper course for the movement to take.[46]

Thus the most important function of the Bradford district association was to serve as a bridge between local rank-and-file activists and the movement's regional and national leadership, which was centered in London, in the National Convention that acted as a Chartist counter-Parliament, and in Leeds, in the editorial offices of O'Connor's *Northern Star*. With the dispersal of the National Convention, and even more, with the collapse in early 1840 of the movement's embryonic underground, this bridge between local and national organization was sundered, and the spontaneous fusion between grass-roots initiative and centralized leadership was permanently lost. For a time, concerted efforts were made to revitalize the connection and to institutionalize early Chartism's multilayered organizational structure in the National Charter Association. But the spirit of 1839 could never be recaptured, and even in the subsequent moments of movement revival, 1842 and especially 1848, Chartist unity was impaired by a growing gap between center and periphery that was itself at least an indirect product of the deepening fissures in the movement's social base.[47]

Here again, Chartism's subsequent record of failure only underlines its early promise of success, not only in effecting a symbiosis among different organizational levels, but in weaving the ideological strands of political and economic radicalism together within a single crusade. In 1839, when class consciousness reached its apogee, the links between the two seemed entirely

borhood pubs or beershops, occasionally in small plebeian chapels or even in private homes, the great issues of the movement were discussed and debated, funds were collected, and Chartist papers, particularly the *Northern Star*, were regularly read. Other activities like teas and anniversaries were occasionally reported, and in the spring and summer of 1839, much secret arming and drilling also took place. Thompson, *Chartists*, 344; *Northern Star*, May 4, Aug. 17, 1839; *BO*, Dec. 6, 1838; Sanders, "Working Class Movements," 36–49, 563–70.

[46] *Northern Star*, Sep. 8, Oct. 20, Nov. 15, 22, 29, 1838; Apr. 20, June 15, July 6, 13, 1839; *BO*, Jan. 31, Sep. 20, 1838.

[47] *BO*, Mar. 1, Aug. 1, 1839; *Northern Star*, June 15, July 6, 13, 1839; Apr. 4, 11, 1840.

self-evident as political exclusion became a metaphor for socioeconomic dispossession, and the campaign for the vote became a powerful vehicle for demanding enfranchisement in the fullest sense.[48] The early Chartists themselves experienced little of the difficulty expressed by some modern historians in disentangling the language of freeborn Englishmen from a subterranean desire for social citizenship, regarding it as axiomatic that the redress of their political grievances simply implied resistance to the traumas of proletarianization that bound them together as an exploited class.[49] No doubt, such easy assimilation of economic to political relationships contributed to the Chartists' ideological woolliness and evaded as many problems as it resolved. But such difficulties did not trouble activists amidst the high hopes of 1839 when their adaptation of the traditions of radical political insurgency seemed to have raised the class struggle to a more generalized plane.

This recognition of the necessity of political organization as a foundation for the advocacy of economic objects can be seen in the behavior of the surviving trade unions that quickly established informal and often illegal connections with the Chartism that greatly benefited the movement in 1839 and resurfaced in 1842 and 1845. Equally revealing of the interpenetration of political with economic activism was the distinctive contribution to the larger movement that the Chartist women's auxiliaries made. Recent studies have emphasized the importance of women within Chartism, and in Bradford, their role was unusually great.[50] In March 1839, the official Female Radical Association was founded, although informal organizations had probably existed for some time. By mid-1839, the Female Radical Association had at least six hundred members and was divided into at least five neighborhood branches.[51] Unlike the women's auxiliaries of the chapels and temperance societies, these Female Radical Association branches were not simply adjuncts to fundamentally male-dominated enterprises, but quasi-autonomous organizations in their own right. They were run by women and explicitly repudiated any need for male leadership or control. Chartist women participated in virtually every aspect of the movement, and certain activities were recognized as their special sphere.[52]

Nevertheless, despite their impressive independence and autonomy, Bradford's female Chartists were not feminists, and they loyally supported

[48] Thompson, *Chartists*, 91–105; J. A. Epstein, *The Lion of Freedom* (London, 1982).

[49] Jones, *Languages of Class*, 90–178.

[50] Thompson, *Chartists*, 120–51.

[51] Ibid., 344; *Northern Star*, Aug. 18, 1838; Mar. 2, 9, 1839; *BO*, Nov. 22, 1839.

[52] By 1841, they had secured a significant place within Chartism's institutional structure with two representatives on the steering committee of the West Riding Charter Association. Thompson, *Chartists*, 134–6; *Northern Star*, Aug. 18, 1838; Mar. 2, 9, Apr. 6, Aug. 3, 1839.

the demand for universal male suffrage without ever making claims for their own political rights. Indeed, they tended to view politics from their perspective as housewives, and what inspired them to take so public and political a stand was not the wrongs of women, but the domestic plight of the working-class family that capitalist exploitation and class legislation had brought about. Even before the People's Charter had formally been adopted, the female radicals organized to mount a boycott protesting an increase in the price of milk. Although later they involved themselves in all aspects of Chartism and proved to be invaluable in fund-raising work, their main task was to organize and sustain the Chartist boycott of petit bourgeois shopkeepers who refused to give the movement their support. This culminated in a grand procession of female radicals, in August 1839, who marched through the streets to protest the plight of their families and to indicate their determination to boycott all retailers who did not agree to endorse their cause.[53]

Hence, although the Chartist women's associations included many female factory operatives among their members, it was as consumers, not as producers, that they were moved to act. No doubt, if 28 percent of all wage earners in Bradford's primary productive industrial sector had not been women, it is doubtful that they would have been able to achieve a public status and gender autonomy far beyond what their bourgeois counterparts, at the time, ever claimed. Still, the primary contribution they made to local Chartism was not to raise its gender consciousness, but to sharpen its class focus by emphasizing all the ways in which capitalism and corruption had eroded the living standards of the proletarian family and all the ways in which the struggle for political enfranchisement was also a social and economic struggle for a better way of life.[54]

As their day-to-day agitational activities forced them to deploy political reform tactics attacking economic class oppression, many Chartists inevitably looked beyond the limited goals of improving consumer living standards and turned again toward the wholesale critique of competitive capitalism that had first surfaced in the early Owenite cooperatives and the quasi-syndicalist unions of 1834. In fact, many local Chartist leaders who had lived through the early thirties had themselves gone through a definite socialist phase. Although, by 1838, they had become critical of Owenite sectarianism, with its blind imperviousness to political realities, they were still drawn to the vigorous indictment of competitive individualism and to the moral appeal of the cooperative vision that had been nurtured within the Owenite fold.

---

[53] *Northern Star*, Aug. 18, 1838; Aug. 3, 1839.
[54] The most insightful discussion of the relationship between class and gender consciousness among working-class women in early-nineteenth-century Britain is Barbara Taylor, *Eve and the New Jerusalem, Socialism and Feminism in the Nineteenth Century* (New York, 1983), 75–82.

According to the local Owenite Samuel Bower, "a large section" of the Chartists "are favorable to, at least, the economic views of the socialists, and seek political power merely as an effective instrument for removing the competitive principle from society." Conversely, many socialists, among whom he counted himself, believed "that had we universal suffrage, greater facilities would thereby be gained for the formation of [socialist] communities."[55]

Even without the People's Charter, Bradford's socialists clearly benefited from the wave of popular radicalism that the advent of Chartism had called forth. Several times in 1838–9, they initiated public lecture series to try to stimulate interest in their creed. So nervous did this make local elites, both liberal and Tory, that on four separate occasions clergymen were drafted to give their own sets of antisocialist discourses in response.[56] The Chartists, in their turn, when forming their own associations, borrowed heavily from the calendar of organized branch activities, teas, soirees, lectures, and outings that had done so much to enrich and stabilize Owenite associational life. However, Owenism's most important legacy to Chartism was its concrete ideological program of socialist transformation that suggested how the popular energies of traditional plebeian communitarianism might be mobilized into self-conscious, egalitarian cooperatives that could build a new, moral working-class world.

Here, the Owenites went far beyond the rather vague official positions of Chartism, and men like Bower, arguing from an explicitly socialist perspective, were able to subject working-class political radicalism to a searching critique. Even if universal suffrage was enacted and a Chartist government was actually formed, he insisted that it would have little success in alleviating the plight of the workers so long as competitive capitalism remained in place. "The wealth and political position of your opponents," he warned, "will always enable them to detach a considerable number from your party," and their "greater advantages . . . could scarcely fail to practically destroy the assumed political equality" of even a formally democratic state.[57]

At best, populist legislation to regulate capital and prevent its concentration might be passed. But under the technical conditions of modern industry, this would simply lead to the substitution of a few wealthy industrialists by a mass of petty shareholders with their capital combined. "The great disproportion which had always previously existed between the numbers

---

[55] *BO*, Mar. 13, 20, 1834; Schofield, *Peter Bussey;* Samuel Bower, *The Peopling of Utopia, or the Sufficiency of Socialism For Human Happiness* (Bradford, 1838), 4; idem, *A Sequel to the Peopling of Utopia* (Bradford, 1838), 11.

[56] *Northern Star*, Aug. 11, 1838; *BO*, June 27, Nov. 21, 28, Dec. 12, 19, 26, 1839; May 28, 1840.

[57] Bower, *Utopia*, 14.

of masters and servants" would now, to the workers disadvantage, "no longer exist"; for as the masters grew more numerous, their political power would intensify, and the workers would find themselves ever more isolated and dependent in the face of an increasingly united and homogeneous propertied middle class. Moreover, in a particularly prescient analysis, Bower suggested that the natural tendency of industrial capitalism might actually diminish rather than increase the numerical superiority of the manual working class. "Is not the province of manual labour continually being inundated by the spirit of contrivance, and wealth and numbers added to the classes which already have more of both than is compatible ... with the freedom and happiness of their fellow men?"[58]

By beginning with the complete abolition of competitive capitalism and private ownership, socialists like Bower, in contrast to the Chartists, promised to resolve the problem of proletarianization by eliminating its source:

> It is now, then, contended that no other social arrangement than community of possession can fairly respond either to the long recognized principle of co-equality of rights, or the newly discovered principle of the all-powerful nature of circumstances not within the control of the individual in forming the human character, it being utterly incompatible with the institution of private property, under any form, to guarantee to everyone freedom of access to the land and its productions, or to effect the constant repartition of the benefits derived from the gathered knowledge of past generations, to which all men are joint heirs.[59]

Identifying the principles of communitarianism with both progress and morality, and associating their spread with the inevitability of scientific law, Bower deployed the same kinds of universalistic arguments in defense of socialism that had been developed to glorify liberal capitalism by the ideologues of the entrepreneurial bourgeoisie. All the technological and environmental features of modern industrial society that bourgeois ideologists had linked to the spread of competitive individualism, Bower, like Owen, saw as the determinate material underpinnings that would make possible the future collectivist social world.[60]

The complexity and interdependence of modern economic relationships, and the concentration of population and the intensification of communication that the growth of cities and the development of railways had brought forth, would both promote and necessitate new social arrangements that would replace the anarchy of unrestrained competition with a logical, planned, cooperative approach. "In community," in which social wealth would be

[58] Ibid., 5–7; idem, *Sequel*, 8.
[59] Bower, *Utopia*, 11.
[60] Robert Owen, *A New View of Society and Report to the Country of Lanark* (London, 1970), 201–69.

rationally and equitably distributed, "there will be plenty of good food and clothing with comfortable dwellings for all...Labour" fully recognized as the source of all value, would be evenly distributed throughout the population, becoming "light and pleasant" for any given individual as its productive powers were augmented by scientific knowledge collectively pooled. "The inhabitants of community will not fear want," for in a rational society "the knowledge to produce cannot with them regress." Finally transcending the realm of necessity and bringing to all the freedom and leisure that had hitherto been confined to a privileged few, "science, the fine arts and literature will be cultivated to an extent hitherto unknown."[61] Hence, although socialism was a system that peculiarly benefited the workers and universalized an experience uniquely their own, its rationale, no less than that of bourgeois liberalism, rested on its effectiveness as an agent of general progress that could promote the improvement of society as a whole.

Like the Chartists, Bower was critical of the initial socialist enthusiasts who, in the early thirties, through schemes like the labor exchanges and syndicalist trade unions, had attempted to build the New Jerusalem overnight. Erroneously "attempting to apply to the present generation principles applicable only to a much higher state of intellect and morality," they had neglected the important truth on which Robert Owen had insisted, that the triumph of socialism would have to be a gradualist phenomenon occurring entirely by nonviolent means.[62] Although he sympathized with the motives that had drawn working-class radicals to Chartism, Bower insisted that universal suffrage would not be enough. Fearful that physical-force militants would provoke a conflagration that would leave the working-class movement in defeat, he urged that at least some of the energies devoted to obtaining the vote be rechanneled into the creation of model communities and associations of cooperative producers whose moral and economic superiority would serve as an irresistible example to everyone else:

> A successful Community, say in Lancashire or Yorkshire, would instantly become an object of universal interest and attraction. The unequalled facilities of transport we possess would bring it within the actual observation of immense numbers of classes....What we now see take place in relation to improvement in physical science would happen in relation to this, namely, the time of its general adoption would be regulated by its importance and value. As the manufacturer supplants imperfect and costly methods of production by more improved and cheaper ones, so would the labourers abandon their benefit...sick and burial societies, draw out of the coffers of the government their £16,000,000

[61] Bower, *Sequel*, 12–13.
[62] Samuel Bower, *Competition in Peril* (London, n.d.), 6.

of money, and apply their enormous capital to the production of superior comfort and happiness in communities."[63]

Although attracting workers through their promise of prosperity and independence, the burgeoning socialist cooperatives, like their primitive predecessors, the friendly societies, would mollify elite fears of working-class organization with their promise to put an end to the burden of pauperism and provide property-owning ratepayers with tax relief. Indeed, the high interest rates that could be offered by the productive cooperators who owed no profit to capitalists and retained the full surplus value of their work would, in Bower's view, provide an irresistible attraction to the propertied investor whose loans would enable those workers with insufficient resources to organize producers cooperatives of their own. Eventually, with "owners of houses losing their tenants – employers their workpeople – shopkeepers their customers," the individual producers cooperatives would affiliate in a grand confederation that, without any violence or revolutionary expropriation, would simply engulf the existing society and state.[64]

Bower's grandiose and compelling vision of how the proliferation of communities organized as voluntary producers cooperatives could regenerate society and transform the world seemed, at least in theory, to offer a means of achieving the kind of social democracy that was eluding the electoral reform campaign. Clearly, it attracted many of the Bradford activitists whom his writings sought to convince and convert. However, there were other features of Bower's socialist program that caused considerable Chartist skepticism and doubt. The Owenite attack on conventional marriage and Christianity often seemed little more than a gratuitous diversion that not only unnecessarily offended bourgeois proprieties, but also violated many of the most deeply rooted values of traditional working-class culture too. Antisocialist lecturers facing working-class audiences had the sense to ignore the socialists' economic programs and scored points by attacking the unpopular rationalist doctrines that always kept socialist societies both sectarian and small.[65]

However, even the socialist social and economic program of building socialism through gradualist voluntary associational means, although gen-

---

[63] Bower, *Competition*, 11.
[64] Bower, *Sequel*, 15–18.
[65] *BO*, Jan. 12, 1843. For evidence that local Owenites practiced consensual divorce, sometimes to the disadvantage of women, see *BO*, Dec. 13, 1838. However, see also Taylor, *Eve and the New Jerusalem*, for a persuasive argument that the Owenite critique of the nuclear family and sexual inequality was an essential feature of the entire early socialist worldview.

uinely appealing to many working-class activitists, was by no means as straightforward or unproblematic as Bower thought. As we have seen, when particular groups of workers did attempt to form themselves into the sort of exemplary islands Bower projected, infiltrating the competitive capitalist world, they usually succumbed to the same sort of economic pressures that had made them vulnerable in the industrial labor market. Clearly under-estimating elites' hostility to such cooperatives and greatly exaggerating their chances of economic success, Bower's program of cooperative production was really viable for only the small minority of skilled craft artisans whose relatively protected position within the labor market made them the least likely to take it up. In fact, Bradford Owenites were no more successful than the early cooperators of the 1830s in establishing model communities or even lasting producers cooperatives in the capitalist town. Hence, their col-lectivist impulses had to be channeled inward toward the cultivation of their own branch associational life. Activities like retailing, fund-raising, convivial gatherings, and educational work, which had been intended as mere means to the New Jerusalem, became, increasingly, socialist ends in themselves. Marked by their peculiar rituals, cultural self-containment, and unorthodox, generally unpopular, beliefs, the Owenites found themselves separated not only from official bourgeois voluntarism, but from the mainstream of urban-industrial working-class life. As it withdrew from the society it had intended to revitalize, Owenism lost its character as a proletarian class movement and instead of providing an ideological alternative to capitalism, settled down into a sectarian counterculture of consolation and escape.[66]

With their active involvement in the political process and their willingness to keep within the cultural mainstream, Bradford's Chartist associations were more resistant than their socialist counterparts to the logic that pushed them toward this fate. Nevertheless, as they also passed through the ordeal of repression and suffered successive political defeats, the Chartist associations began to show a similar tendency to become divorced from their urban-industrial mass constituency and increasingly to concentrate on the culti-vation of their own associational life. This trend became most obvious in the final stages of Chartism as the mass following drifted away into silence and the working class itself fragmented and split. However, its roots can be traced back to the movement's formative period when official efforts at isolation and harassment forced the Chartists to build an increasingly sep-aratist culture outside the urban-voluntarist mainstream.

The most obvious way the authorities could segregate the Chartists was by denying them access to public halls and meeting places like the Exchange

---

[66] Eileen Yeo, "Robert Owen and Radical Culture," in Sidney Pollard and John Salt, eds., *Robert Owen; Prophet of the Poor* (London, 1971), 84–114.

rooms and later the Oddfellows and Temperance Halls. Although small committee meetings or neighborhood district gatherings could always be held in sympathetic pubs, the blacklist on large meeting rooms forced the Chartists, after a brief unsatisfactory spell when they rented from the socialists, to acquire a political headquarters of their own. In August 1839, a large room in Butterworth's buildings was left and more ambitious plans to erect a workingman's hall with shops, committee rooms, and a lecture theater seating two thousand were commenced. By October, designs were being considered and 100 shares were taken out. Although this building was never constructed, and after the debacle of 1840 the project was given up, virtually all the Chartist enterprises and activities that were to have been centered there were initiated, even if they were never physically housed under one roof.[67]

As we have seen, Bradford's Chartists, and groups closely allied with them, established their own alternative working-class offerings in every sphere of cultural activity that mainstream bourgeois voluntarism had involved itself. As against official Nonconformity, Chartists could join their own Chartist chapel or congregate in working-class denominations like the Primitive Methodists or send their children to Chartist Sunday schools where they would be inoculated against the dogmas of the orthodox sects. Chartist or neo-Chartist temperance advocates formed their own Long Pledged Teetotal Association, and Chartist autodidacts found radical alternatives to the Mechanics Institute in the Chartist library, the Great Horton Chartists' reading room, or in rationalist discussion groups and academies like M. de St. Hilaire's People's Educational Institute.[68] However, the Chartists were not content merely to provide their own versions of bourgeois cultural activities but followed the example of the socialists and trade unionists and began to establish cooperative retailing outlets of their own. In May 1840 a Chartist cooperative store was opened with Joseph Alderson, a local teetotaling radical, as secretary, which continued in operation for at least ten years.[69]

With Chartist religion, education, temperance, and groceries, with their own social calendar of events and radical holidays like the birthday of Tom Paine, the committed Chartist activist, if he or she wished, after the workday was over, could live in a virtually self-contained Chartist social world. Insofar as this constellation of autonomous Chartist culture offered an alternative

---

[67] *Northern Star*, Oct. 19, Nov. 2, 1839; *BO*, Aug. 15, 1839.

[68] *Rules of Bradford Secular Improvement Society* (Bradford, n.d.); *Northern Star*, Oct. 26, 1839; *BO*, June 20, 1844; Apr. 10, June 27, 1845; Sep. 20, 1849; Bates, *His Life*.

[69] *Northern Star*, May 2, 9, 1840; R. C. N. Thornes, "The Early Development of the Cooperative Movement in West Yorkshire, 1827–1863" (Sussex, D.Phil. dissertation, 1984), 170–4.

to bourgeois-inspired forms of leisure or bourgeois-run agencies of associational life, it undoubtedly contributed to workers' sense of independence and autonomy and promoted class consciousness of a most thoroughgoing sort. However, insofar as it simply catered to an activist minority it may have had the opposite effect, actually widening the gap between the spontaneous plebeian culture of the demoralized slum dweller and the collective self-help culture of a movement elite. Unlike the inchoate culture of poverty – the culture of the beer house, the slum street, and the fair – Chartist culture, no less than bourgeois agencies of cultural voluntarism, purveyed a kind of personal identity and commitment that was inaccessible to the thoroughly demoralized and debilitated, to those so completely fatalistic about their lot as to be incapable of envisioning a significantly better future.

Perhaps, if the movement had not been organizationally decimated in 1840 and if its social base had not collapsed after 1846, it might have bridged the gap with the popular culture and extended its associational nexus on a more universal plane. As it was, the new values of cooperation and democracy that Chartism proffered abstractly as a working-class political demand became real and ongoing social experiences for only a small minority of movement leaders and activitists to whom Chartism meant not only marches, petitions, boycotts, strikes, and uprisings, but a partially lived vision of how urban-industrial society might be reorganized beyond the anarchy of the competitive marketplace into a more humane and habitable way of life.

Conclusion

In developing their own indigenous culture, in reorganizing their social life, insofar as they controlled it, along cooperative and democratic lines, Bradford's Chartists, no less than the socialists before them, posed an implicit challenge to the Tory values of hierarchy and the liberal ideology of competitive individualism that dominated the urban-industrial cultural mainstream. However, to go beyond simply challenging liberal and Tory ideologies to actually contesting the power of the liberal and Tory elites would have required that these values of cooperation and democracy be elevated from the internal practice of the Chartist associations to the movement's program of mass social and political insurgency in which they could be projected as universal principles of social organization and imposed on the larger urban-industrial world.

Yet despite their impressive array of enthusiasm and numbers, this the Chartists were consistently unable to do. At the moment when their prospects for success were brightest, in the spring and summer of 1839, the movement proved incapable of sustaining even a coherent agitational strategy, much less of formulating a viable social and political program for the reconstruction of the urban-industrial world. When this insurgency reached its climax in the fall and winter, the insurrectionary paradigm on which it drew owed less to the socialist vision of a future industrial commonwealth than to the neo-Jacobin conspiratorial republican traditions of 1792–5.

After the smoke had cleared from this revolutionary debacle, the stalwart minority that persevered in Chartist associations found itself increasingly trapped in a self-contained, sectarian culture, which, like Owenism, represented not so much an alternative to capitalism as a partial escape from the harsh realities that capitalism had successfully imposed. Focused inward on its own counterattractions, this Chartist culture found it increasingly difficult to engage with the most significant forces that impacted on workers from the world beyond. Now constrained within the prevailing framework of bourgeois electoral machinery, Chartist politics, by the General Election of 1841, were reduced to an essentially negative, "spoiler" role. Several thousand Chartists did gather at the hustings, wearing their own distinctive color green, to "elect" their candidate, William Martin, at the symbolic show of hands. Nevertheless, in the actual poll of electors, they had to content themselves with indirectly assisting the Tory Hardy, so that at least the hated Whig incumbent, Busfield, would temporarily be kicked out.[70] By the end of the decade, many of those who still called themselves Chartists had become deeply involved in the work of the newly formed municipal town council, advocating a program that was only slightly more radical than that of the council's liberal, Nonconformist mainstream. After midcentury, even radical religion, education, and teetotalism became almost indistinguishable, in content and increasingly in form, from the corresponding cultural offerings of the official chapels, Sunday schools, mechanics institutes, and temperance societies of the liberal, associational status quo.[71]

Of course, there were temporary revivals of the militant mass movement during the social and economic crises of 1842 and 1848. Yet the Chartism that was generated in the heat of these conjunctures was essentially contingent in character, a response to forces and developments that threatened Bradford's workers but that were fundamentally beyond their control. Ironically, the moments when Chartism posed its greatest political challenge were the moments when it represented not the organized politics of the voluntary association, but the spontaneous, largely uncoordinated politics of the beerhouse, the mass rally, the radical festival, and the street. Thus in 1848, Chartists could momentarily seize the streets and neighborhoods that

---

[70] Wright, "Politics and Opinion," 229–34; *BO*, July 1, 1841.
[71] Adrian Elliott, "The Establishment of Municipal Government in Bradford" (Bradford, Ph.D. dissertation, 1976), 337; see Chapter 8.

they lived in, much as they had "occupied" the open greens and public fairgrounds a decade before. However, in neither instance could the workers permanently control the space that they had wrested from their bourgeois, property-owning, entrepreneurial adversaries who possessed precisely the power that the working-class Chartists lacked. By contrast, the entrepreneurial bourgeoisie was never content merely to occupy space. It always strove to redefine and fundamentally to transform physical reality according to its own privatized, environmental vision, which it thereby imposed on the larger urban-industrial world. Workers could seize and temporarily close down the factories, as they did during the plug plots of 1842, but the failure of their experiments in cooperative production suggests that they could not run them on a permanent basis, so as to redirect their surplus value in more socially desirable ways.

In August 1848, as the new police and municipal authorities swept through the back alleys of Adelaide Street and Silsbridge Lane, it became clear that the Chartists had not only lost the open fields and factories, but that control had passed to the ascendant bourgeois liberals, even in their own urban neighborhood slums. During the decade that preceded this mopping-up operation, radical working-class politics in Bradford rose and fell. Amidst the traumas of early urban-industrial capitalism, particularly in 1839–42, the worst crisis years, an aggressively anticapitalist working-class challenge had threatened the hegemony of the liberal entrepreneurial bourgeoisie even as its triumph over the old Anglican Tory establishment remained incomplete. Yet even in the worst moments of conflict and crisis, this organized and aggressive proletariat, in sharp contrast to its entrepreneurial antagonist, failed to develop a viable vision of urban-industrial social organization and was, in spite of its overwhelming majority status, unable to exercise its own forms of class rule.

As a first-generation proletariat, the men and women who swelled the ranks of Bradford Chartism possessed both the strengths and weaknesses of their transitional state. Unlike their more subdued and "realistic" successors, they had no difficulty in imagining a world beyond capitalism or in revolting against the tyranny of its economic laws, for they possessed in their own personal experience the memory of a world in which the local community rather than the global free market had stood at the center of social life. Yet their very preoccupation with the evils of market tyranny, with the surface dislocations that unfettered competition had wrought, tended to obscure the deeper structures of productive relations in which the underlying mold of class oppression was set. Indeed, as Gareth Stedman Jones has persuasively demonstrated, none of the working-class movements of the 1830s and 1840s, neither the Chartists nor the socialists, fully penetrated the logic of capitalist productive relations and, thus, were deflected by the abuses of corruption or the evils of the marketplace from the sort of focused program of social transformation that might have grappled more effectively with the actual realities of urban-industrial life.[72]

As a result, the vague collectivist strivings of Bradford's working-class radicals were no match for the resonant individualist ideals of the ascendant entrepreneurial bourgeoisie. Bourgeois liberalism was an ideology whose abstract notions of freedom had been forged in the concrete experiences of domination over men and nature and engendered by the fact of entrepreneurial power. At every stage in the development of liberal thought and culture there was an actual, if never total, correspondence between the liberal theory and the urban-industrial world that it had wrought. As we have seen, it was the very function of liberalism to make sense of this world to the entire population and to justify the new inequalities of wealth and power that it generated by depicting them as necessary for general social prosperity and progress.

By contrast, Bradford's early-nineteenth-century working-class challenge never fully transcended its original character as a defensive response. Workers were the victims, not the architects, of urban-industrial capitalism, and their image of a just, stable, and egalitarian society was essentially a negation of the unstable, unjust, and unequal environment in which they found themselves condemned to live. Abstracted from their social reality, an imagined inversion of their actual proletarian state, the social visions that they constructed tended to assume timeless, utopian forms. Whether refracted through the memory of a bygone, traditional community or cast in the future promise of some cooperative new moral world, these utopian visions could never fully engage with the harsh realities of proletarianization or escape the pervasive debility of contemporary urban life. Unable to bridge the gap between practice and theory, the working-class insurgency declined into a culture of consolation that had no real remedies for the ills of the existing world.

To be sure, for a brief moment, the dysfunctions of urban-industrial crisis did appear to provide the workers with a historical breach through which this imagined utopian vision, in the words of Karl Mannheim, "breaks out suddenly, takes hold of the outer world and transforms it."[73] Yet these momentary explosions of chiliastic insurgency were no match for the constant dialectic of theory with practice that habitually linked the development of liberal action and thought. The working-class radicals, like the elite con-

---

[72] Jones, *Languages of Class,* 107–58.
[73] Mannheim, *Ideology and Utopia,* 192–219.

servatives before them, could point out the contradictions of entrepreneurial capitalism. For a brief moment they could even threaten to bring down the capitalist social and political order in a way that traditional conservatives neither would nor could. But in devising concrete, practical alternatives for the reconstruction of urban-industrial life, the workers were no more successful than the traditional oligarchs and, like them, were obliged, once the crisis had receded, to recast their own utopian ideals and pursue their class interests within the general framework that liberal voluntarism had set. Yet could liberal voluntarism, the product of the individual entrepreneurial experience, really be broadened not just in theory, but in practice to encompass the experiences and aspirations of nonentrepreneurial social groups? By the midforties, the most prescient of Bradford's bourgeois liberals, sobered by the critical barrage of their antagonists and reeling from the constant crises of the previous five years, were determined that their original program be reformulated and reconstituted in such a manner that it could better integrate the entire urban population into the basic structures of industrial-capitalist life.

18

The foundations of the mid-Victorian liberal consensus

In 1842, Bradford's bourgeois liberals had every reason to regard their prospects as bleak. Two decades of traumatic urban-industrial development capped by five years of economic crisis and social strife seemed to deny the viability of urban-industrial society as organized along entrepreneurial capitalist lines. Challenged from the right by a revivified Tory paternalism and from the left by proletarian radicalism with a collectivist creed, liberalism's quest for a progressive consensus within the framework of the competitive marketplace was exposed as a hopeless utopian dream. Repudiated by the angry, unenfranchised masses, it increasingly lost the confidence of Bradford's propertied electorate who doubted its ability to secure public order or to underwrite the legitimacy of capitalist elites.

Yet by 1850, the situation had dramatically changed. Amidst a stable climate of economic growth and prosperity, the liberal ideal of a voluntary, progressive consensus seemed less a utopian pipe dream than a sober fact. As the challenges of Tory paternalism and proletarian collectivism had faltered and encountered contradictions of their own, a new and revivified liberal vision of urban-industrial society seemed to arise out of the ashes of the old. Now uniformly triumphant in local elections, Bradford's liberals not only dominated preexisting offices and institutions, but had successfully created a whole series of new agencies of local governance, both municipal and voluntary, which appeared spontaneously to emanate from the kind of competitive urban society that was naturally predisposed toward liberal rule. Secured in the economic buoyancy of the early 1850s and developed in mid-Victorian Bradford over the next twenty years, this liberal consensus nevertheless had its roots in the dark years of the 1840s when the experience of social crisis and political challenge had forced entrepreneurial liberalism to confront its contradictions, to shed its illusions, and to compromise with its enemies – in short, to transform itself in significant ways.[1]

---

[1] This transformation of bourgeois liberalism in the late 1840s and 1850s from a narrowly entrepreneurial to a broadly consensual creed has never been fully studied. Asa Briggs's *Victorian People* (Chicago, 1955) sensitively explores a number of different individual

Ideologically chastened, Bradford's insurgent liberals were obliged during the 1840s to pursue in practice at least some of the cultural and economic benefits to the entire community that entrepreneurial liberalism had hitherto offered only as abstract ideals. Conversely, having failed to bring down the entrepreneurial edifice and unable to reorganize urban-industrial society outside its competitive market terms, nonentrepreneurial social groups like traditional elites and workers were compelled to accept the new reformist liberalism and even to contribute to making it work. In this final chapter, these interrelated processes will be examined as we trace the roots of the mid-Victorian stabilization of urban-industrial Bradford in the early Victorian experience of social crisis and class revolt.

The transformation of entrepreneurial liberalism

In 1842, bourgeois liberalism in Bradford had, by all measures, reached its nadir. After two decades of economic instability and social tension capped by five years of open class revolt, most Bradfordians had lost faith in the promise of entrepreneurial leadership and began to dismiss the tenets of market freedom and self-help individualism as empty ideals. The failure, in that year, of the United Reform Club and the Complete Suffrage movement seemed to sound the death knell of the reforming alliance that had first formed twelve years earlier when a popular movement for progress and democracy had become fused by the heat of antiaristocratic rhetoric to a bourgeois program of voluntarism and free trade. In the face of the intractable social problems and open class divisions that had appeared during the intervening years, it became obvious that such a coalition between capital and labor was no longer possible, at least not in classical liberalism's ideological terms.

And yet the bourgeois reform initiatives that were set forth in the unpropitious climate of 1842 also revealed the first stirrings of a new voice among Bradford's entrepreneurial liberals – one prepared to recognize the reality of class differences, if not the inevitability of class antagonisms, and willing to acknowledge that their creed would never command widespread acceptance so long as it was associated exclusively with the particular interests

pathways into mid-Victorian liberalism as well as the limits and possibilities of the consensus that it sustained. However, in approaching the problem through a succession of particular, biographical case studies, Briggs's astute assessments provide only hints of the kind of general interpretations that might be derived from a survey of the consensus as a whole. Useful beginnings in this direction can be found in Trygve Tholfsen, *Working Class Radicalism in Mid-Victorian England* (London, 1976), 124–55; and Harold Perkin, *The Origins of Modern English Society, 1780–1880* (London, 1969), 271–407.

of capitalists and was perceived as incompatible with the basic needs of other social groups. The most important of these new liberal voices was that of W. E. Forster, the future cabinet minister and deputy party leader who later became famous as Gladstone's political lieutenant and author of the 1870 Education Act. In 1842, however, Forster was a young Bradford industrialist, just beginning to make his fortune and to involve himself in political debate.

Always a somewhat reluctant businessman, Forster consciously resisted the single-mindedness and mental rigidity that entrepreneurship seemed to engender in those who embraced it as a life's calling. Nevertheless, like others, he accepted the lot of a capitalist as his destiny and resolved to devote whatever energies he could spare from his business to forge a new and more inclusive liberalism, still fundamentally entrepreneurial, but able to encompass all that was not reactionary within the establishment and all that was respectable within the working class.[2] Deeply influenced by the writings of Thomas Arnold, whose daughter he later married, and Thomas Carlyle, who spent three weeks visiting in his home, Forster began to move away from the narrow Quaker antislavery culture in which he had been reared. According to his biographer,

> The old feelings on the subject of slavery were not, indeed, dismissed from his mind; but now that an active life in a great manufacturing community brought him in daily contact with the working classes the current of his thoughts began to change. The claims of the poor at his own door began to press upon him more closely... and overshadowed those purely philanthropic projects which had absorbed his interests hitherto.[3]

Impressed by the Chartist Thomas Cooper, whom he also befriended, Forster was one of the initiators of the United Reform Club. He enthusiastically endorsed the Complete Suffrage alliance, expressing complete sympathy with the workers' democratic political demands. However, after the collapse of these ill-fated ventures, Forster, unlike most of the entrepreneurial liberals, began to realize that such efforts to reactivate popular liberalism would have to incorporate at least elements of the workers' social and economic program too. Reflecting on his own experience as an employer, he was deeply troubled by the pattern of periodic unemployment dictated by the tyranny of the trade cycle, which seemed to condemn whole sectors of the urban work force to destitution every few years. A visit to Ireland at the height of the potato famine further convinced him that doctrinaire adherence to laissez-faire principles could, in

---

[2] T. Wemyss Reid, *The Life of the Right Honourable William Edward Forster* (London, 1888), 1:74–94, 115–46.
[3] Ibid., 81.

some circumstances, have disastrous results. Although he disparaged the radical socialist alternatives all of which "have within them, more or less concealed, a damning desire to shirk work," Forster became convinced of the necessity of a much more active policy of social amelioration on the part of the state.[4]

Although he did not object to regulation of the factories, Forster was more concerned with the debilitating effects of working-class poverty and sought to devise positive schemes of state intervention that could promote true independence and respectability among workers in a way that the purely negative Poor Law had not. In his view, surplus labor was a real social problem that the authorities should not dogmatically dismiss. Thus in 1849, Forster got himself elected to the Bradford Board of Guardians and became a leader of the new faction of advanced liberals who sought to supplement the old remedies of the workhouse, and test labor with official subsidies to support emigration to the colonies and spade husbandry at home.[5] Nevertheless, it was in the establishment of a national system of popular education that Forster saw the most extensive and positive role for the state. Since "private efforts were inadequate to the task of education," it was the government's duty to undertake this activity that could not be provided in any other way. Moreover, education was a particularly desirable benefit for government to offer, since, by curing the worker of his "want of self-denial and self-control," it would actually improve his subsequent prospects for independence and lay the groundwork for the sort of society in which workers really could become full individuals capable, without assistance, of standing on their own.[6]

Of course, Forster's great prestige three decades later makes it easy to overestimate his influence during the 1840s. Both then and later, his statist leanings were considered anathema by many of Bradford's other entrepreneurial liberals, whereas his youthful propensity for ultraradical enthusiasms elicited even more mistrust. Nevertheless, his ideas did not go entirely unheeded, and after 1842, William Byles, the editor of the *Observer* and a close friend of Forster, took over sole proprietorship of the newspaper from the clique of liberal capitalists who had founded it and began to convey the new message in a more subtle way.[7]

---

[4] Ibid., 137; *BO*, Dec. 11, 1847; Oct. 12, 1848.

[5] *BO*, Dec. 4, 1849. Forster was, in fact, deeply ambivalent about emigration as a solution to the problem of unemployment and regarded it, at best, as a regrettable last resort. Indeed, he dismissed the whole Malthusian approach of blaming the victim and argued that the workers would only begin to practice thrift and prudence when they received wages sufficient to give them realistic grounds for exercising initiative and hope. William Cudworth, *Condition of the Industrial Classes, in Bradford* (Bradford, 1887), 27–30.

[6] Reid, *Forster*, 1:143–5; *BO*, Oct. 12, Dec. 9, 1848.

[7] David James, "William Byles and the *Bradford Observer*," in D. G. Wright and J. A.

Like Forster, Byles recognized that Bradford's liberals needed to be awakened from their dogmatic slumbers and taught that, in fulfilling their social responsibilities, competitive individualism was not enough. "We say not a word against political economy, or free trade, or machinery," he acknowledged, for "they are all based on law which cannot be violated without injury to the material interests of the community.... But this we say, that all of them together can never bless a nation; can never raise it from the depths of poverty. Ideas of duty and of brotherhood, of sympathy and benevolence" would also be necessary if entrepreneurs were to be accepted as legitimate community leaders and if liberalism were to attract nonentrepreneurial social groups. By 1848, the paper could even momentarily acknowledge that "the laws of political economy by their natural operation, do not always direct the industry of the country in the channels which lead to the greatest amount of national happiness."[8]

A decade earlier, such a concession would have been inconceivable although, even then, Byles, in an uncharacteristic gesture, had once permitted the appearance of an anonymous letter criticizing "the merchant [who] in the amassing of gold recedes towards barbarism," who is "in the opinion of less selfish society, endowed with a sort of half-humanity."[9] As bourgeois liberals became convinced during the early 1840s that "the opinion of less selfish society" would have to be taken into account, they were troubled to learn that entrepreneurship was increasingly viewed not as a font of social vision and virtue, but as an occupation which, unless tempered by the dictates of a higher morality, was calculated to produce men of dangerously "contracted views."[10]

One measure of the extent to which Bradford's liberal entrepreneurs were beginning, during the forties, to absorb such criticisms is their response to Lord Ashley's 1846 revival of the campaign to enact a ten-hours factory law. By this time, at least half a dozen of the most successful rising liberal manufacturers, including Henry Ripley, Titus Salt, John Priestman, and Henry Forbes, had achieved a higher level of wealth and economic security than the factory movement's Tory benefactor, John Wood, had possessed fifteen years earlier when the campaign had begun. Although such men might have little enthusiasm for state regulation, they were in a position to countenance legislative interference at a time when it no longer constituted a serious personal threat.[11]

Jowitt, eds., *Victorian Bradford; Essays in Honour of Jack Reynolds* (Bradford, 1982), 115–36,

[8] Quoted in David Ashforth "The Poor Law in Bradford, c. 1834–71" (Bradford, Ph.D. dissertation, 1979), 361.

[9] *BO*, Dec. 9, 1837.

[10] Ibid.

[11] See Appendix C.

From the start, the *Observer* suggested that, although economic imperatives might necessitate caution, the moral soundness of the case against child labor could no longer be plausibly or honorably cast into doubt.[12] In March, a meeting of the leading liberal industrialists revealed that they were half inclined to agree. Titus Salt and others expressed the usual fears of foreign competition from those "who ran their mills fourteen hours a day." But the meeting concluded that "the prolonged agitation of the question of hours of labour in the factories tends to keep alive a spirit of jealousy and alienation between employer and workpeople" and that "a middle course might be adopted which would heal divisions and settle the question upon a permanent basis: and would recommend an Eleven Hours Bill as likely to secure so desirable an object."[13] However, in 1847, when they were presented with a more implicit compromise in which the Corn Laws would be sacrificed by the aristocratic establishment in return for entrepreneurial acceptance of a ten-hours act, most Bradford industrialists were favorably disposed. At least they were disinclined to protest when Ashley's bill, almost anticlimactically, passed into law.[14]

This willingness to acquiesce in factory regulation, which they had so bitterly opposed only a decade before, indicates that, by the midforties, Bradford's leading entrepreneurial liberals were prepared to go some distance to placate an aroused and organized working class. Nevertheless, direct state interference in capitalist production was, at best, a concession that such men could grudgingly tolerate, not a cause that they could enthusiastically embrace. Unaccompanied by their own constructive, reforming alternatives clearly rooted in the principles of the liberal creed, such concessions to the Tory or even socialist visions would be taken as tantamount to a confession of intellectual bankruptcy – a tacit admission that the contradictions of urban-industrial capitalism could not be confronted within liberal individualist terms. There, in a nutshell, was the liberals' dilemma: How could they devise liberal solutions to a social crisis that had been generated, in the first instance, by the very competitive market forces out of which liberalism naturally grew? Could the traumas of proletarianization be substantially alleviated by means other than regulating the marketplace or reforming the factory? In the 1840s, the more forward-looking of Bradford's entrepreneurial liberals sought to prove that, by devising a program of wholesale civic improvement, social recon-

---

[12] *BO*, Apr. 25, 1844; May 28, 1846.
[13] Quoted in Jack Reynolds, *The Great Paternalist; Titus Salt and the Growth of Nineteenth Century Bradford* (London, 1983), 130–1.
[14] William Cudworth, *The Ten Hours Bill, was it Passed by a Liberal or a Tory Government?* (Bradford, n.d.), 16–17.

struction and economic progress would be placed back on the liberal agenda through the reform of the urban environment itself.

Entrepreneurial liberalism and urban reform

If urban reform became the focus of Bradford liberals' efforts during the forties to forge a more popular and socially responsible creed, this was because it had always been an important element in their original antiaristocratic critique. From the start, liberal attacks on parasitic rural landlords had been accompanied by assaults on oligarchical urban elites. "While we profess a sincere regard for the interests of mankind at large," insisted the *Observer*, "we do not forget that 'charity begins at home.' "[15] Having "the welfare and prosperity of our good town of Bradford very much at heart," the paper could not but look with dismay at the incompetent, illogical tangle of ancient local authorities – parish, manor, township, and magistracy – all irrelevant to the administration of the urban-industrial environment and dominated by elites who were insensitive to its needs."[16]

In particular, as we have seen, the Improvement Commission, which prevented improvement by stinting on the development of public services and by sanctioning environmental neglect, became a special target of liberal ire. Even though Bradford, as an unincorporated borough, would obtain no direct benefit from the 1835 government proposal for municipal reform, the *Observer* endorsed it in the strongest language for the general benefit to liberalism that it was likely to bring: "We know of no measure of modern times, not even the Reform Bill itself, so momentous in its consequences to the stability of the government and the concord, the prosperity, the moral and we will add, the religious welfare of the people."[17]

By concentrating their fire on the Old Regime's urban outworkings, where the forces of progress were most powerful and the bastions of reaction most weak, liberals might realistically hope to achieve, within a local context, the total elimination of feudalism that had been denied them at the national level by the 1832 compromise. The liberal landslide of town councils all over England in the first postreform election of 1835 seemed to presage the kind of permanent ascendancy in the municipalities that still eluded the party in the parliamentary world: "No housemaid ever demolished a cobweb so

[15] *BO*, Sep. 15, 1836.
[16] Ibid.
[17] Feb. 6, 1834. For general assessments of the social and political consequences of the Municipal Reform Act, see G. B. A. M. Finlayson, "The Politics of Municipal Reform, 1835," *English Historical Review*, 81 (1966), 673–92; and Derek Fraser, *Power and Authority in the Victorian City* (Oxford, 1979).

ruthlessly as the householders have swept away the accumulated filth of ages from those styes of Toryism, the now defunct Corporations."[18]

Municipal reform had made incorporation "the most important auxiliary in the improvement of any community – and in proportion to its size, the commerce and wealth of the community, its importance is enhanced." Bradford, being destined to become one "of the largest communities existing in the kingdom," had particularly powerful reasons in "the present generation to secure that kind of legislative machinery which will enable them to leave to their posterity a worthy legacy – not an ill built cramped up dirty town, full of courts and alleys and narrow streets."[19] Yet the same municipal machinery that could transform Bradford's alleys into thoroughfares would first have to transform the irrational tangle of local politics, replacing the Improvement Commission with an efficient municipal corporation, curbing the role of the vestry, and reining in the arbitrary power of the unpaid Tory magistracy that was "more opposed to popular principle" than any other part of government – "more unsuited to the spirit of the day."[20]

In an 1837 speech to the Reform Society and in the columns of the *Observer*, Byles argued that, if Bradford's liberals were to play their part in the coming drama of national regeneration and remain on their party's ideological cutting edge, they would have to obtain for their own borough those "municipal institutions" that constituted veritable "schools of political science," within which in its natural habitat of the new industrial city, the liberal approach to government could be perfected before being universalized throughout society at large. "When men had learnt to manage their own affairs well," he concluded, "they must necessarily be competent to form a judgement on the affairs of the nation."[21]

With its wide, quasi-democratic franchise encompassing both urban property owners and the respectable, rate-paying working class, a municipal corporation could institutionalize the reforming alliance of the people, elevating it from the transience of an antiaristocratic insurgency to the permanence of an urban community whose governmental forms would be derived from the same voluntaristic principles of self-development that governed the actions of individuals as well. Since "the middle and working classes are those most interested in good local government – they have the closest and most permanent connexion with the well being of a town."[22]

---

[18] *BO*, Dec. 31, 1845.

[19] *BO*, Sep. 15, 1836; Oct. 12, 1837.

[20] *BO*, Oct. 19, 1839. The general structure of early-nineteenth-century local government in Britain is detailed in Derek Fraser, *Urban Politics in Victorian England: The Structure of Politics in Victorian Cities* (Leicester, 1976).

[21] *BO*, Mar. 2, 1837.

[22] *BO*, Aug. 14 1845.

Self-interest would naturally draw them together toward a common program of progressive administration to run the environment with which, as individuals, they had cast their lots. For the bourgeois, local government would provide an essential opportunity to eliminate "the reproach of our nation that the middle classes are not educated for public life.... The formation of town councils will compel the members of that class to fit themselves for public life." As for the workers, "they will come to the consideration of other and higher affairs with a sounder judgement, with less prejudice, and with a loftier public spirit. They will feel, in the exercise of their privileges as electors, a social dignity which has heretofore been unknown to them." In either case, the transmutation of individual self-help into collective self-government would teach both that the personal qualities that fostered success in the industrial city would prove equally "good for communities as well."[23]

Yet this entire analysis was based on the thoroughly questionable assumption that to grant workers political rights within an urban-capitalist framework would automatically bind them to its liberal individualist values and induce them to play by the rules of the entrepreneurial game. As long as the liberal approach to government remained essentially negative, focusing the collective will on the elimination of corruption and monopoly but then relying on competition and individual enterprise to accomplish the rest, the new, liberal municipality, however progressive, was no better equipped to resolve the contradictions of urban-industrial capitalism than the old, oligarchical approach of benign neglect. As workers articulated their own vision of community in which laissez-faire was subordinated to collective human purpose and cooperation was glorified as an end in itself, progressive liberals were forced to question whether market forces really could spontaneously generate social integration and whether a viable urban community really could be constructed with only the voluntaristic principles of supply and demand.

"What is a town?" asked one of the *Observer's* more thoughtful readers amidst the social crises and class conflicts of 1838. Perhaps it was, in the first instance, but "a mere money-making aggregation of human beings." But harsh experience had brought with it the revelation that "intelligent, industrious, sober, contented, cheerful men and women who fear God and love one another are the best moneymakers." If nothing else, then, the very aims of entrepreneurship "to facilitate the creation of wealth" seemed to necessitate a more robust sense of community in which the town would be conceived as more than a marketplace, as "a body – a moral though not perhaps a legal corporation the various members of which are destined to minister

---

[23] *BO*, Mar. 29, 1838; Aug. 14, 1845.

to its wants, add to its comforts, and promote its highest welfare and happiness."[24]

Of course, this liberal assimilation of the idea of community to the dynamism of the urban-industrial space could be dismissed as a mere rhetorical gesture by a bourgeoisie that had momentarily lost its self-confidence and had allowed, on the political agenda, a few orotund phrases from alien ideologies whose substance it continued to dismiss. Nevertheless, certain aspects of the entrepreneurs' own situation also made them susceptible during the late thirties and forties to give priority to their quest for a dynamic and stable urban community over their instincts to adhere dogmatically to the letter of the original free-market creed.

As we have seen, the boom of the midthirties had already lifted a handful into affluence, and by the midforties, at least one or two dozen had achieved considerable success. Unlike much of the rank and file of small manufacturers, merchants, slumlords, and shopkeepers who were still struggling for survival, the most successful industrialists could now depend on substantial profits entirely drawn from surplus labor in industry and had no need to engage in sharp practices such as rack-renting cottages or maintaining a truck shop to obtain an adequate financial return.

Hence, the self-interests of Bradford's leading entrepreneurial liberals began to diverge in certain ways from those of the small property owners who populated the lower reaches of the urban bourgeoisie. With their economies of scale, their managerial efficiencies, and their innovative and attractive export products that were marketed all over the world, the leading entrepreneurs could afford to disdain petty profiteering on which many small manufacturers still depended and which pervaded the intensely competitive environment of the secondary-service sphere. From the commanding heights of Bradford's industrial economy, such men possessed both the resources and the strongest incentives to confront the contradictions of capitalism and to isolate those that were inherent in the system from those that were amenable to amelioration or reform.[25]

Although these contradictions all had their roots in the relations of capitalist production, we have seen that many of their most fearful consequences were environmental, exacerbated by violent swings in the trade cycle or by a secondary, ecological drift toward urban decay. Detached from their roots in the logic of capitalist expansion and conceptualized more narrowly as social problems in their own right, these secondary manifestations could be diagnosed as the growing pains of a society whose industrial core had sprouted so rapidly that the surrounding environment had not yet been able

[24] *BO*, Mar. 1, 1838; Feb. 10, 1842.
[25] See Chapter 3.

to catch up. According to this view, a modicum of analysis and planning would suffice to restore the overall equilibrium of development by distinguishing inherent contradictions from remediable difficulties and by bringing the latter under conscious control.[26]

The real problem of class as seen from this perspective was not the existence of fundamental inequities within the production process but the emergence of lags and imbalances within the sphere of consumption that prevented the distribution of goods and services to those who most needed them and whom it was in the larger interests of the system to support. Not surprisingly, this rendering of social crisis and contradiction in the language of urban dysfunction and delay had an instinctive appeal to Bradford's leading industrial magnates. They grasped, if only intuitively, its enormous potential for alleviating some of the worst by-products of proletarianization, not so much by regulating industry, but by improving public services and by guiding the pattern of spontaneous urban growth. When the structural problems of industrial-capitalist development were redefined as transitory traumas of urbanization, their deep roots in low wages and labor exploitation could be papered over by an assault on the visible symptoms of overpopulation, overcrowding, poor sanitation, and ill health. Regulating the urban environment might, then, become a safety mechanism to insure that, within the primary sphere of production, capitalist free enterprise would continue to prevail.[27]

It was in something like this frame of mind that the *Observer* suddenly discovered, in 1840, that there existed a form of landlordism within the heart of the city that posed a far greater long-term threat to the future of liberalism than the monopolies of the distant agrarian rentier:

> ...if men of property will not live in society as those who have an
> interest in its welfare they must be taught that it is not enough for them

---

[26] This characterization of social problems as the growing pains of modernity rather than as the contradictions of capitalism, which was initially devised in places like mid-nineteenth-century Bradford, albeit in an embryonic and unsystematic form, was, in important ways, a precursor of the kind of "modernization" theory that was formulated explicitly two generations later by Ferdinand Toennies, *Community and Society* (Michigan, 1957); Emile Durkheim, *The Division of Labor in Society* (New York, 1933); Max Weber, *Economy and Society*, in two volumes (Berkeley, 1978), and which remains an intellectual lynchpin of mainstream academic sociology today.

[27] Similarly, these rudimentary insights into the possibilities for urban reform presage a long tradition of subsequent efforts throughout the capitalist world, from progressivism to the Great Society, which have sought to sustain the basic viability of the free-wage labor system and to alleviate the suffering of the dependent poor and proletarianized by focusing on the environmental manifestations of their plight. See David Harvey, *Social Justice and the City* (London, 1978); F. F. Piven and R. A. Cloward, *Regulating the Poor: The Public Functions of Welfare* (New York, 1971).

to draw weekly rents for the badly accommodated abodes of their wretched tenants and to leave them to perish in the stench of a putrid atmosphere.[28]

Of course, the notion that, to justify its rights, property had to accept its responsibilities had, up to a point, been implicit in entrepreneurial liberalism from the start. However, if the entrepreneur could glory in the benefits that allegedly accrued to the community as a consequence of his own personal gain, the slumlord, like the aristocrat, was essentially a parasite who made no contribution to the production process. He benefited only by subjecting others to substandard housing at exorbitant rents. Could the model of self-reliance and respectability that the entrepreneur had offered to the worker really have a positive effect when the slumlord condemned him to an animal existence in which it was "physically impossible for him to persevere un-polluted in the moral sense"?[29] Byles and the *Observer* now concluded it could not: "It is rendered most appallingly evident that the filthy state of a neighborhood creates dirty homes and habits of indolence in wives who have no encouragement to clean their houses; and hence arise domestic discomfort and quarrels which lead to drunkenness, immorality and crime."[30]

Perhaps urban workers were not, after all, entirely responsible for the poverty, ignorance, and barbarism they displayed. In Byles's new social analysis, the habitual liberal instinct, so evident in the Nonconformist chapels and the Temperance Society, to attribute physical suffering to individual moral failing was now suddenly and dramatically reversed. Now it was the physical environment with which workers were involuntarily surrounded that was assigned primary responsibility for their moral inadequacies and their failure to live up to the entrepreneurial ideal. "Where wives of the labouring poor are surrounded by puddles and mud for want of drainage and water, and constantly met with the offensive exhalations of exposed cesspools and privies," he discovered, "they have not a single encouragement to strive for cleanliness and health." This "has a great effect in degrading the characters and feelings. . . . Nor can there be any doubt that the filthy abodes of many of the poor in our large towns is the direct and immediate cause of their demoralization by drunkenness. . . . Many," he concluded, "are led to it by seeking in dram-drinking a stimulus to relieve them from the faint and nauseous feelings which they experience, from constantly inhaling an im-pregnated, if not a foetid atmosphere. . . . Others by want of all comfort at home are driven to the pothouse."[31]

[28] *BO*, Sep. 24, 1840.
[29] *BO*, Nov. 27, 1851.
[30] *BO*, Sep. 24, 1840.
[31] *BO*, Dec. 24, 1840.

Here was the real source not only of workers' immorality but of the angry class consciousness that made them hate and threaten the bourgeoisie:

> Disaffected towards public order and reckless of character, their [the slums'] inhabitants view the possessors of superior comforts with envy, and acquire the notion that might gives right. Regarding the superior circumstances of those above them as the result of partial laws or injustice, their indolence and vice stimulates them to plunder and murder without regret.[32]

Not even Byles and the progressive entrepreneurs whose views he articulated were so naive as to accept all the logical consequences of this argument. The working-class drunkenness, immorality, and anticapitalist extremism that the chapels, the temperance movement, and the liberal party had failed to cure would not be instantly extirpated by the improvements in sanitation and public service that could come from a general program of municipal reform. Nevertheless, the *Observer* continued to repeat this analysis, particularly in the years after 1842, when its editor enjoyed a freer reign. The appearance in 1840 of Edwin Chadwick's *Report on the Sanitary Conditions of the Labouring Population of Great Britain,* followed in 1844 by the reports of the Royal Commission on the State of Large Towns, and by the formation of the Health of Towns Association in 1845 no doubt further educated local liberals about the importance of decent housing and sanitation. They began to see that their popular appeal would be greatly enhanced if they formulated a positive program of urban renewal and reform.[33] The decision of the woolcombers' leaders, in their 1845 social survey, to stress the environmental over the specifically occupational hazards associated with their trade, must have further convinced many liberals that urban reform was precisely the sort of issue that was both consistent with the entrepreneurial economic agenda and compatible with the workers' social critique.[34]

However, even without these visible incentives, slum conditions increasingly impinged on day-to-day bourgeois consciousness, not only because they fueled worker disaffection, but also because they posed hazards to public health. For some time local elites had been aware that disease, much more surely than economic depression or social disorder, would spread beyond its original slum breeding grounds to strike every urban neighborhood and social group. As early as 1825, such anxieties had contributed to the establishment of an infirmary, but before 1840, early urbanization did not engender overt fears of an epidemic. In 1832, cholera produced only a handful

---

[32] Ibid.
[33] S. E. Finer, *The Life and Times of Edwin Chadwick* (London, 1952), 209–42; M. J. Cullen, *The Statistical Movement in Early Victorian Britain* (New York, 1975).
[34] "Woolcombers' Report," *BO*, June 12, 1845.

of local cases, and in 1838, an unspecified contagious disease was reported but never spread beyond the slums.[35]

Nevertheless, as conditions worsened throughout the forties – as the slums expanded and their density increased – bourgeois elites began to view them as tinderboxes of contagion that threatened their own more comfortable and protected semisuburban world. Finally, in May 1847, a serious outbreak of typhus among "the poorer classes" spread "to the middle classes in their comfortable houses." Then, two years later the town experienced a major outbreak of cholera that engendered a full-scale public health crisis that lasted eight months.[36]

The first fatal case, an Irish laborer, was recorded in March 1849, but by the summer, the death toll was rising every week. Up to this point, cases seem to have been confined to slum neighborhoods where inadequate water supply was blamed for the disease's spread. In some of these districts, the waterworks company had not even laid pipes. However, the sultry heat of August made the entire town a zone of contagion. Cases were now reported in the middle-class neighborhood of Hanover Square and in Manningham. By September, the weekly death toll had risen to sixty-five and victims were distributed all over town. Finally in October, as the weather cooled, the death count tapered off, and the epidemic ended leaving a total of four hundred dead.[37]

Of course, the wealthiest capitalists could escape the danger of epidemic simply by moving their families into the suburbs. As we have seen, however, in 1850, such individuals constituted no more than 10 percent of Bradford's bourgeoisie. For the ordinary bourgeois property owners, the epidemics of the late forties were simply graphic confirmation of what the *Observer* had been telling them for years. "There is nothing arbitrary in such a judgement," the paper insisted when typhus broke out:

> When by a long and systematic violation of the moral and social laws we have reduced millions of our fellow creatures to the lowest sort of food; or when by a disregard of the laws of industry and prudence and economy, people have reduced themselves to poverty and destitution – a judgement follows as a matter of course.[38]

[35] Benjamin Godwin, "Autobiography" (mss., Bradford Central Library), 554; R. J. Morris, *Cholera, 1832, the Social Response to an Epidemic* (London, 1976). Charles Creighton, *A History of Epidemics in Britain* (Cambridge, 1894), 2:822, records thirty deaths in Bradford. *BO*, Feb. 1, 1838.

[36] *BO*, May 13, June 3, 1847.

[37] *BO*, Apr. 1, June, 14, 21, 28, July 12, 26, Aug. 2, 23, 30, Sep. 6, 13, 20, 27, Oct. 4, 11, 18, 1849.

[38] *BO*, Apr. 27, 1847.

By imposing the physical reality of a microbiologically connected collectivity in which the sufferings of the poor could endanger the lives of the rich, epidemics simply exacted as punishment what social obligation ought to have acknowledged from the start, that the urban environment was not just a self-adjusting marketplace but a human community – a corporate entity, sewn together literally by organic bonds. Its members had to learn not only how to compete but how to cooperate in order to provide for the common welfare of all. "This terrific visitor," editorialized the *Observer* after Bradford had buried its cholera dead, has "at length awakened men from their stolid slumbers, convincing them by a new though fearful argument that 'cleanliness is next to godliness'.... The necessity of local improvements must, ere long become the question of questions. In vain do the rich and powerful lavish wealth unknown upon their own individual habitations. One and the same atmosphere exists for high and low."[39]

The struggle for liberal municipal reform

Six years before the cholera epidemic thrust the new liberal vision of an urban community upon even the most complacent, dogmatic, and self-seeking elements of the bourgeoisie, Bradford's leading entrepreneurial liberals had begun working to create the civic institutions around which such a vision could take shape. Devastated by the failure of the Complete Suffrage movement and the collapse of its populist alliance on a national plane, the Bradford United Reform Club shifted its focus to the local arena, seeking, in 1843, to reconstruct the bourgeois liberal/respectable worker consensus around a campaign for the incorporation of the town.[40]

In March, the Reform Club formally presented its incorporation proposal at a public meeting of ratepayers at which it resolved that "a corporate body [was] superior to any other government . . . because it combines the purposes of improvement with the principle of liberty . . . resting on the representative basis." Although the liberals seem to have expected widespread support for this measure, the resolution was voted down by those in attendance, and several speeches made it clear that virtually all confirmed Tories, many small suburban ratepayers, and a large section of the Chartist workers were strenuously opposed to municipal incorporation.[41]

---

[39] *BO*, Oct. 18, 1849.

[40] Adrian Elliott, "The Incorporation of Bradford" *Northern History*, 15 (1979), 156–75; idem, "The Establishment of Municipal Government in Bradford" (Bradford, Ph.D. dissertation, 1976), 79–84.

[41] *BO*, Dec. 7, 1843.

Objections were offered on several distinct grounds. In the first place, it was argued that municipal government would create a costly and unnecessary administrative bureaucracy. At worst, this would provide leading entrepreneurial liberals with a lucrative patronage outlet. At best, it would enable them to fall back on the general body of ratepayers to resolve problems of urban decay and industrial pollution that their own factories had been primarily responsible for creating. Although these arguments were most frequently articulated by Tory politicians, they had particular appeal, as Dr. Elliott has shown, to the small ratepayer, especially those who feared that (as in the case of the Poor Law) they would be called upon to finance solutions to problems that they had done nothing to create.[42]

These Tory and lower-middle-class doubts that municipal incorporation would really offer the fair, effective, and democratic local government that its bourgeois liberal advocates claimed, were shared by many working-class Chartists who added a few others peculiarly their own. Although the municipal ratepayer franchise was wider than the £10 parliamentary franchise, its exclusion of all who did not meet a three-year residency requirement, of all nonratepayers, and of all who defaulted on their rates, was bound to leave out virtually all structurally proletarianized workers as well as some of the more respectable and skilled ones. Even in the prosperous early fifties, Dr. Elliott has estimated that only 54 percent of Bradford's householders were qualified to vote in municipal elections, and in the depressed conditions of the 1840s, far more would have been at least periodically disenfranchised.[43] Recalling their experience a decade earlier in the aftermath of the political reforms of 1832, many workers feared that to join bourgeois liberals in seeking municipal government, so far from promoting social consensus and compromise, would simply consolidate entrepreneurial dominance, creating institutions from which workers would be effectively excluded but which would become new bastions of oppressive class rule.

What brought these feelings out with particular intensity was the knowledge that the first, indeed the only certain consequence of municipal incorporation would be the application of the metropolitan model to create a

---

[42] Elliott, "Establishment of Municipal Government," 107–14. Nevertheless, Bradford's urban problems were so serious that small ratepayers in the town center generally favored incorporation despite the inequities inherent in the rating system. In general, however, both Dr. Elliott and I have found that support for and opposition to the incorporation issue broke down along liberal and conservative party lines. See also, Theodore Koditschek, "Class Formation and the Bradford Bourgeoisie" (Princeton, Ph.D. dissertation, 1981), 854–5.

[43] In July 1848, 40 percent of the municipal electorate was disenfranchised for nonpayment of rates. Elliott, "Establishment of Municipal Government," 83–4, 267, 286.

new and more efficient borough police. The explosive pace of Bradford's urban development and the deepening demoralization and disaffection of the new working class made all middle-class people extremely sensitive to the danger of public disorder. Much more than its failure to improve housing and sanitation, it was the Improvement Commission's inability to protect urban property that inspired many rank-and-file property owners to swallow their fear of higher rates and to support the liberals' incorporation campaign.[44]

From the start, the *Observer* had acknowledged that an efficient police force was one of the most important benefits a municipal corporation would bring, but it indignantly denied that this would involve class oppression, insisting that workers, so long as they were respectable and law-abiding, would benefit equally with all other citizens from the public order and stability that the police would promote. The paper contrasted the rational administrative order that it sought with a municipal police force from the brutalizing reign of reaction and terror associated with the army, which had hitherto kept the peace.[45]

To be sure, in the insurrectionary atmosphere of the late 1830s, even bourgeois liberals had felt a reluctant gratitude toward the army, which stood as a bulwark against anarchy and revolt. But the army and the yeomanry, which were under the control of Tory landowners and magistrates, always made bourgeois liberals nervous. In 1841, the decision to build a permanent barracks, just as the danger of insurrection seemed to be winding down, evoked widespread disapproval among leading liberals who feared the moral as well as the political dangers of permanently quartering a debauched and arrogant soldiery in the vicinity of the town. "What in the name of all that's good," queried the *Observer*, "do we want with a yeomanry force in this neighborhood? To preserve the peace and prosperity of the country. From whom?"[46]

At best, the tyrannical, aristocratic military was a necessary evil whose violent mode of repression would be rendered superfluous by an effective police force that would uphold law and order under the control of the self-governing municipal institutions of the town. Whereas the army was an alien imposition on a hostile community – a desperate antidote to be applied only during moments of crisis when "order" depended on the musket and sword – the police would be permanent members and servants of the community, who, by engaging in preventative law enforcement on an ongoing basis while

---

[44] Elliott, "Establishment of Municipal Government," 73–114; *BO*, Aug. 1, 1839.
[45] *BO*, Nov. 3, 1842; May 4, 18, 1843.
[46] Reynolds, *Great Paternalist*, 105–6; *BO*, May 18, 1843.

respecting individual civil liberties and rights, would promote a more lasting and meaningful kind of public order and eliminate any legitimate grounds for revolt.[47]

Whereas an army ignored criminality and exacerbated immorality in the name of repressing political dissent, the police would concentrate on these ordinary transgressions. Clamping down on the thieves, gamblers, prostitutes, and drunkards, the police would enforce a law and order peculiarly rooted in liberal entrepreneurial values by monitoring the incorrigibles and regulating the reprobates who would not voluntarily adhere to respectable behavioral norms. Convinced that these norms were class neutral, one pro-corporationist indignantly denied that they violated the rights of Bradford's workers, who, he suggested, ought only to feel "insulted" at Tory insinuations that they might be "afraid of the very sight of a policeman," since "honest men should not be so."[48]

Rebutting Tory propaganda and assuaging working-class anxieties between 1843 and 1845, the agitation for municipal incorporation was buttressed by a new liberal interest in taking control of the existing government institutions of the town. In 1842, victory in the church-rates controversy and the election of a Nonconformist churchwarden had already demonstrated that liberals could control the vestry. In the following year, they again asserted their power to elect a liberal Board of Surveyors under the provisions of the 1835 Highway Act. The oligarchic Tory Improvement Commission proved a somewhat tougher nut to crack. In 1843, liberals constituted only a small minority within this closed and self-selecting body, yet over the next four years, they took advantage of the Tory commissioners' apathy and nonattendance to co-opt an additional twenty-one liberal commissioners so that, by 1845, they had obtained a bare majority within the bastion of local privilege that they had pledged to destroy.[49]

At this stage, the incorporation campaign entered its final stages as the liberals circulated a mass petition among the ratepayers, obtaining 8,715 legitimate signatures representing property valued at £70,512. Nevertheless, the opponents of incorporation mustered larger numbers and greater wealth, in a counterpetition that garnered 10,716 legitimate signatures representing

---

[47] After incorporation, constables were officially instructed that their job was to protect, not to oppress. Nevertheless, they were also told to "watch narrowly all persons having no visible means of subsistence," and to apprehend all vagrants and beggars. *Bradford Court House: General Instructions to Constables* (Bradford, 1849).

[48] Procorporation Handbill quoted in Elliott, "Incorporation of Bradford," 170.

[49] Ibid., 166–74.

property worth £96,432.[50] In response to this apparent expression of local opinion, the request to the Privy Council for a municipal charter was denied. "They have, in effect, declared," the *Observer* morosely lamented, "that Bradford which is the dirtiest, filthiest, and worst governed town in the kingdom, shall continue to be the dirtiest, filthiest, worst governed town in the kingdom."[51]

Convinced that their opponents had no alternative solutions to the problems of urban government, the liberals refused to accept this negative verdict and reopened the issue with another petition in the following year. Lacking both the requisite financial and organizational resources and the determined sense of purpose necessary for a new petition campaign, the anticorporationists abruptly conceded the fight that they had won a year earlier. In April 1847, a municipal charter was officially granted, a burgess roll was quickly prepared. Council elections were held, and as anticipated, the liberals swept 76 percent of the forty-two seats.[52] On August 19, the *Observer* could inform the municipality that had hitherto been "a body without a head" that its organic unity was now complete as "the sun will rise to-day for the first time on the Bradford Corporation." However, the relationship of the municipality to its urban-industrial constituency was, perhaps, depicted more tellingly in the design of the official corporate seal – a woolcomb and a horn of plenty, with the figure of Justice seated atop a pile of woolsacks, surrounded by an alpaca goat and a factory in the distance. Underneath, the motto read, Labor Omnia Vincit.[53]

Over the next few years, Bradford's liberals used their overwhelming majority on the Town Council to dominate the institutions of local government and to reward those liberal entrepreneurs whose private success had contributed to the development of the community with public offices of municipal trust. Indeed, participation in Bradford's municipal government, at least during its first decade, closely mirrored the social structure of the ascendant entrepreneurial elite. Second-ranked industrialists and the town's leading liberal professionals and tradesmen manned the council, whereas the more honorific positions of alderman and mayor (selected annually from among the aldermen) were reserved for the most prominent among the new entrepreneurs. The inaugural mayoralty of Robert Milligan was followed by those of Titus Salt, Henry Forbes, William Rand, and the dyer Samuel Smith.

[50] William Cudworth, *Historical Notes on the Bradford Corporation* (Bradford, 1881), 101.
[51] *BO*, Aug. 14, 1845.
[52] *BO*, Apr. 29, June 17, 24, Aug. 12, 19, 1847.
[53] "Labor conquers everything." Cudworth, *Bradford Corporation*, 107.

After some initial Tory opposition, names were submitted for a borough magistracy, and the twelve candidates eventually selected by the lord chancellor included the seven most eminent liberal aldermen and five prominent Whig and Tory notables to counterbalance their weight.[54]

In Bradford, unlike some other cities, municipal government was not left to shopkeepers, but was considered both the perquisite and the duty of those who dominated the community in social and economic terms. Although a few leading liberal entrepreneurs eschewed or limited their involvement in the affairs of the council, and a few others, as Tories, were excluded from leadership roles, all the leading figures in municipal politics during the forties and fifties, with the exception of the professional "improvers" Joseph Farrar and the physician Thomas Beaumont, were leading entrepreneurial capitalists for whom municipal office represented an official reflection of underlying economic power.[55]

Not surprisingly, a Town Council whose composition was so massively bourgeois responded most quickly and effectively to those aspects of the overall liberal program of urban improvement that directly served the interests of the bourgeoisie. By law, a watch committee and police force were immediately established, consisting of a chief constable, eight officers, and fifty-eight constables hired at the meager rate of 17s. per week. It was clear that police work was the council's top priority, absorbing 49 percent of the entire municipal budget in the first year. A few years later, the corporation took over fire fighting from private insurance companies, and street lighting was extended, though not to most working-class sections of town.[56]

Obviously, what was completely lacking from this minimal program was any serious interest in the sanitary and environmental improvements that had figured so heavily in the *Observer's* original municipal reform creed. In part, this was because municipal corporations did not automatically combine "the principles of self-government" with "the purpose of improvement" and, like most liberal political institutions, were administratively neutral, designed to eliminate Old Regime structures, but possessing no inherent blueprint for constructing the new. To obtain the necessary powers to raise money and intervene actively in reshaping urbanization necessitated a private parliamentary bill – a procedure which maximized the opportunities for

---

[54] Ibid., 110, 227–8.

[55] Ibid., 227–8; Elliott, "Establishment of Municipal Government," 199–231. In Leeds, the social composition of the Town Council was similar to that in Bradford at midcentury. In Birmingham, the council was dominated by smaller businessmen who were more popular among the household suffrage electors than the town's wealthiest economic elites. E. P. Hennock, *Fit and Proper Persons; Ideal and Reality in Nineteenth Century Urban Government* (London, 1973), 12–30, 191–227.

[56] Cudworth, *Bradford Corporation*, 105–10.

opponents and other vested interests who could afford the legal expenses to emasculate any proposal through amendments and delays.[57]

However, inaction was also attributable to the fact that Bradford liberals' commitment in principle to a program of positive urban reform was not matched by any concrete sense of how this might be embodied in practical measures that were neither so costly as to be rejected by the ratepayers or so restrictive of competitive individualism as to be incompatible with the general precepts of the entrepreneurial ideal. As one "disappointed rate payer" put it, "It is too bad that we should be living in darkness and dirt whilst a body of men elected to serve the borough and vested with the necessary powers, consume their time and exhaust the patience of their constituents with endless idle speeches."[58]

Nevertheless, after 1849, a social program for the liberal municipality did, belatedly, begin to take shape. In the first place, the cholera finally impressed the seriousness of Bradford's environmental crisis on even the most dogmatic and constricted bourgeois minds. Second, the combination of full employment and the passage, in 1850, of the Small Tenements Rating Act, which, for the first time, enfranchised householders who did not pay their own rates, had the effect of virtually doubling the municipal electorate. As a result, Bradford's adult male skilled and respectable workers gained something close to the sort of voice in local government that radical liberalism had always, in theory, prescribed. Between 1849 and 1854, at least four neo-Chartists were elected to the Town Council. It became clear that even mainstream liberals were coming under electoral pressure to embrace at least some measure of social reform.[59] Thus, in 1850, the liberal leaders proposed an improvement bill that replicated most of the provisions of the General Public Health Acts while giving the council some additional powers in relation to housing and rates. For several months, the bill was tied up by Tory opponents of improvement and fearful out-township ratepayers who wished to be exempted from its provisions – an unholy alliance the *Observer* denominated "the minority of muck." In July, however, it finally passed, and the Town Council assumed the functions of the old Board of Surveyors, while adding new ones through committees on buildings and improvements, and public health.[60]

Although the 1850 Improvement Act initiated the Town Council's entry into the field of urban and sanitary reform, it was, in itself, only an enabling

---

[57] Fraser, *Power and Authority*, 151–73.

[58] *BO*, Sep. 23, Oct. 7, 1852.

[59] Elliott, "Establishment of Municipal Government," 115–31.

[60] Cudworth, *Bradford Corporation*, 114–17; *BO*, Jan. 24, Apr. 25, June 20, 27, July 11, Aug. 29, Sep. 12, 1850; Adrian Elliott, "Municipal Government in Bradford in the Mid-

measure – merely a precondition for substantive programs in particular problem fields. It was here that the liberal model of urban improvement succumbed to its inherently contradictory project of trying to erect a genuine urban community upon the underlying competitive capitalist foundations of Bradford's urban-industrial milieu. Although urban dysfunction manifested itself in a series of interrelated environmental crises involving public health, sanitation, housing, pollution, and public utilities, in only one area did the town council initiate bold and decisive action when, in 1853, it undertook to municipalize the hitherto privately owned water supply.[61]

Of course, the 1849 cholera had driven home the importance of a pure and abundant supply of water, not only to those who could afford to pay for it, but for every inhabitant of the town. Yet we have seen that the private waterworks company that supplied the middle class inadequately and the poor not at all had long demonstrated that it was unable to do this job. During a severe water shortage in the summer of 1852, aldermen Beaumont and Farrar and the neo-Chartist councillor John Rawson contrasted the company's 9.5 percent dividend to its shareholders with its abdication of a public trust. Since water supply, like most public utilities, was almost bound to be organized as a monopoly operation, it ought, they argued, to be removed from private interests and placed under municipal operation and control. As one correspondent argued, "The corporation being a public body ... having solemn obligations to perform towards their [sic] citizens," could not, like a private company, "be supposed to be actuated by sordid motives of gain to their own individual purses."[62]

From the start, this call for even limited municipal action evoked a virulent storm of opposition, not only from prominent Tories like William Walker and Joshua Pollard who were leading shareholders and directors of the waterworks company, but from liberal capitalists like William Rand or Henry Ripley who argued that, since private enterprise was the best and most efficient way to provide economic goods and services, there was no reason to treat water supply any differently. Ripley even proposed to begin selling water himself.[63]

Nevertheless, after much reflection and with a degree of nervousness, the bulk of the town's entrepreneurial liberals concluded that, given the economic inequalities inherent in the community, the technical complexity of tapping, storing, transporting, and purifying distant sources of

Nineteenth Century," in Derek Fraser, ed., *Municipal Reform and the Industrial City* (Leicester, 1982), 117–23.

[61] *BO*, Sep. 30, 1852.

[62] *BO*, Nov. 11, 1853.

[63] Cudworth, *Bradford Corporation*, 130–2; *BO*, Nov. 4, 11, Dec. 23, 1852; Aug. 18, Oct. 6, 20, 1853.

water, as well as the explosive rapidity of Bradford's urban growth, an adequate supply of water would never become available unless the municipality took the business into its own hands. Thus after much heated wrangling and legalistic posturing, an agreement with the company was finally reached and the corporation was authorized to raise £240,000 to buy the company and to bring Bradford's water supply under public control.[64]

Although it would be wrong to underestimate the significance of this pioneering instance of "municipal socialism" two decades before Joseph Chamberlain made the phrase fashionable, subsequent events demonstrated that it would not automatically resolve all urban water-supply problems, nor would it become a viable model for comparable action in other spheres. Indeed, the only reason why the municipalization of the water supply could even be contemplated, in light of its great complexity and enormous cost, was the prospect that it would someday become a profitable business that would not only repay the loans required to finance it, but become a source of municipal income and permit a reduction in the taxpayers' rates.[65]

Other collective projects in which the potential for long-run profitability was either dim or nonexistent could not be undertaken by the municipal authority except in the most halting and inadequate way. Even improvements such as street widening and extension, and downtown renewal, which would have benefited worsted entrepreneurs and tradesmen economically, had to be kept to an absolute minimum because the high costs of construction and compensation always raised the danger of a ratepayers' revolt.[66] Despite the unsatisfactory state of Bradford's streets and the absence of adequate downtown thoroughfares, only a handful of street improvements were undertaken during the fifties.[67] Even harder to justify were fancy public buildings, which might have endowed Bradford's chaotic urban jumble with a genuine civic focus. Although municipal inaction in this area was, to some extent, compensated by a series of ambitious voluntaristic ventures during the prosperous years of the early

---

[64] Cudworth, *Bradford Corporation*, 133; Elliott, "Establishment of Municipal Government," 164–98; *BO*, Jan. 26, Mar. 16, July 20, 1854.

[65] Barbara Thompson, "Public Provision and Private Neglect: Public Health," in Wright and Jowitt, eds., *Victorian Bradford*, 137–64.

[66] *BO*, July 14, 28, 1853.

[67] *BO*, July 14, 1853; May 17, 1855; June 10, 1858; June 14, 1860. Even during the sixties, when the council began to evolve a more comprehensive downtown plan, work had to be scaled back, delayed, and undertaken piecemeal to prevent the expense from becoming prohibitive, *BO*, Aug. 21, Sep. 11, 1862; Feb. 26, Sep. 24, Nov. 26, 1863; Nov. 2, 1865; and Cudworth, *Bradford Corporation*, 152.

1850s, which financed the construction of an impressive downtown concert hall (St. George's Hall) in 1853 and a large fifty-six-acre public park (Peel Park) in 1856, these facilities were built entirely by private subscription, and the Bradford Corporation took no official part in them.[68] Indeed, for the first twenty-seven years of its existence, the corporation did not even possess its own office headquarters, and it was only at the highest tide of mid-Victorian prosperity, during the economic boom of 1869–73, that the Town Council dared to authorize the construction in the city center of a ratepayer-financed municipal Town Hall.[69]

The limits of mid-Victorian municipalization are, however, most fully exemplified, not by its neglect of civic centers, which could sometimes be constructed by private enterprise, but by its inability to provide the system of public drainage and sewerage that had constituted the central plank of the original sanitary program and could only be accomplished by municipal government. The connection between morbidity and inadequate disposal of surface effluence was very well documented and, if anything, overestimated by prevailing "miasmic" theories of contagion and disease. Hence, the council acted quickly after acquiring public health powers to authorize a detailed survey of the town. Nevertheless, it was not until the 1870s that an infrastructure of arterial sewerage was effectively put into place. Although a paltry £13,000 was allocated in 1854, serious work did not begin until after the disastrous flood of 1859 when, according to Barbara Thompson, "the foul and filthy waters of Bradford Beck caused thousands of pounds' worth of damage . . . and even reversed

---

[68] For St. George's Hall, see *BO*, Dec. 20, 1849; Feb. 28, Sep. 12, 1850; Aug. 7, Sep. 25, 1851; July 28, Sep. 8, 1853; and Asa Briggs, *Victorian Cities* (New York, 1963), 153–7. For Peel Park see, *BO*, Aug. 15, Sep. 12, 1850; Jan. 30, 1851; Feb. 10, 17, Apr. 28, Sep. 1, 1853; Nov. 1, 8, 1855; Apr. 24, July 3, 17, 24, Aug. 14, Sep. 11, Oct. 2, 1856; May 8, 1862. Although both St. George's Hall and Peel Park experienced financial difficulties during the economic recession of the late 1850s and, in 1863, the park was turned over to the municipality, after prosperity returned during the early 1860s, leading local capitalists raised shares to purchase choice downtown property and to erect an imposing Gothic Wool Exchange. In 1864, Prime Minister Palmerston laid the foundation stone for the Exchange, which was opened in 1867, and dominated Bradford's downtown with its lofty clock tower until 1873, when it was surpassed by the even larger and more imposing clock tower of the municipal Town Hall. *BO*, Feb. 13, 20, 27, 1862; Aug. 11, Sep. 8, 1864; Mar. 16, 1867; Igor Webb, "The Bradford Wool Exchange: Industrial Capitalism and the Popularity of Gothic," *Victorian Studies*, 20: 1 (1976), 45–68.

[69] For the construction of the Bradford Town Hall, see *BO*, Aug. 24, Sep. 7, Nov. 16, 23, Dec. 7, 21, 1867; Jan. 19, May 28, 1868; Sep. 10, 11, 1873; and Cudworth, *Bradford Corporation*, 166–70. Other municipal amenities such as libraries, bath houses, city parks, and recreational facilities were not even begun until the late Victorian era. *BO*, June 23, 1853; Oct. 9, 1856; and Cudworth, *Bradford Corporation*, 187–9, 191–4.

the flow of some of the few existing sewers."[70] Even then, sewers proved to be of little practical value as long as most houses were not connected to them and little was done to improve the treatment and disposal of wastes. Thus thwarted by its inability, before the late-Victorian period, to confront the major cause of pollution and ill health, the council tended to concentrate on smaller projects, like the closing of downtown church and chapel grave-yards and the diversion of burials to a new cemetery built in a bucolic setting at Undercliffe, beyond the borders of the town.[71]

If the council was hampered by its inability to mount expensive projects or to create a full infrastructure of municipal public works, it also suffered from the extreme reluctance of the entrepreneurs who dominated it to implement bylaws or regulations, which, even when they cost the ratepayer nothing, interfered with market competition or private property use. Most striking, in this regard, was the systematic refusal of the council to enact regulations to limit air pollution, which was exacerbated by the constant increase in the number of factory chimneys in the low-lying, atmospherically inverted town. Although the "smoke nuisance" was, arguably, the most serious of Bradford's public health problems, any attempt to alleviate it would have necessitated restricting the operation of factories or at least required the installation of costly smoke-burning apparatuses that would limit the fuel efficiency of mill engines. Not surprisingly, whenever this issue was raised in the Town Coun-cil, it was immediately shelved.[72]

Of course, a substantial measure of urban improvement could be sought through the regulation of those in the secondary-service economy – retailers, food preparers, builders, and developers – who were less powerful than the dominant industrialists and involved in enterprises whose profitability was less essential to the urban population as a whole. From the start, the coun-cillors took seriously the powers that they had obtained through the Im-provement Act for inspecting and approving all building plans. However, the earliest building codes required little more than the provision of a privy for every two working-class cottages. At least before the 1860s, Bradford's councillors proved extremely reticent about enacting regulations that might constrain urban enterprise in any other way. Even slaughterhouses were not

[70] Thompson, "Public Provision," 14; Reynolds, *Great Paternalist*, 237–42; W. T. Mc-Gowen, *The Sewage of Manufacturing Towns* (Bradford, 1873).

[71] Stuart Rawnsley and Jack Reynolds, "Undercliffe Cemetery, Bradford," *History Workshop*, 4 (1977).

[72] *BO*, Feb. 22, Aug. 2, 1849; Feb. 17, 1853; Sep. 18, 1856; Feb. 19, Sep. 3, 1857; Mar. 13, 1862; Oct. 29, 1863; June 15, 1865; Nov. 2, 1867.

regulated in the 1850s, and the number of prosecutions of retailers and food adulterers in Bradford magistrates' court was disproportionately low even by regional standards.[73]

From all this, it is difficult to avoid the conclusion that the sort of progressive, positive, municipal government that the leading liberals had envisioned in the 1840s, dedicated to a systematic program of urban and sanitary reform, proved, in practice, to be largely incompatible with the underlying free-enterprise, capitalist structures of Bradford's mid-Victorian urban-industrial milieu. Of course, municipal incorporation itself was a major achievement providing the leading liberal businessmen with public status and political office in which their entrepreneurial prowess could be translated into political authority and power. Moreover, the Bradford Corporation, at least after midcentury, did provide a vehicle for institutionalizing their vision of social consensus, providing a symbolic focus for the development of civic consciousness and a way of fostering a sense of urban community that was consistent with the competitive entrepreneurial ideal. Nevertheless, as a social agency for urban reform and reconstruction, the mid-Victorian municipality, though not completely ineffective, fell far short of the full-scale environmental improvement that the crisis of the forties had seemed to require.[74]

Fortunately, the ability of Bradford's bourgeois liberals to sustain social

---

[73] Thompson, "Public Provision," 151–2. Finally, in 1860, the council made an uncharacteristic attempt to improve working-class housing by forbidding the ubiquitous back-to-back. Although obviously self-serving, the outcry of builders that their business would be ruined and that construction capital would flee the town turned out, in the event, to contain a grain of truth; for, although a downturn in construction was likely to have occurred for other reasons, the drop, in the early sixties, from over a thousand to under two hundred new units per year, was, in large measure, a consequence of the inability of most working-class families to pay the 5–7s. weekly rental that owners of full-length cottages expected. The result was a housing shortage by the middle of the decade and a tendency for increased residential crowding to counteract whatever benefits might have been gained through the building code in terms of improved ventilation and more open space. Consequently, in 1865, under pressure from the builders, the council repealed its earlier bylaw and permitted renewed back-to-back construction, albeit in modified form. The result was a massive housing boom that resulted in the construction of more houses over the next two decades than existed in Bradford at the time. BO, Mar. 2, Oct. 19, 1865; Mar. 22, June 7, 1866; Cudworth, Bradford Corporation, 145–6. See Bradford Corporation Council, Annual Reports (Bradford, 1854–85).

[74] See Theodore Koditschek, "The Dynamics of Class Formation in Nineteenth Century Bradford," in A. L. Beier, David Cannadine, and James Rosenheim, eds., The First Modern Society: Essays in Honour of Lawrence Stone (Cambridge, 1989), 544–6; Thompson, "Public Provision," 157.

and political hegemony in the economically expansive mid-Victorian years depended, not so much on the practical success of their urban improvement program, but on the willingness and ability of nonentrepreneurial social groups to abandon alternative visions of urban-industrial reorganization – to give up their quest for paternalist or collectivist utopias and to effect limited but pragmatic solutions to their predicaments by seeking concessions within a broadly liberal, entrepreneurial framework.

The collapse of political conservatism in Bradford

Perhaps the most remarkable feature of Bradford's incorporation was the sudden acquiescence of the local Tory leadership only a year after it had mobilized a majority of ratepayers and a preponderance of real property to resist the liberals' municipal campaign. This evaporation of conservative opposition to liberal forms of urban government was, in fact, part of a larger Tory collapse. By 1847, Bradford's liberals had not only gained firm control of all aspects of local government, but had triumphed in parliamentary politics too. Twelve years earlier the party had been soundly defeated when it offered the electorate an ideologically orthodox candidate. Now, with the divisive issues of free trade and factory reform behind them and firmly ensconced in local government institutions, the liberals could safely nominate Perronet Thompson, the famous Anti–Corn Law ideologue who perfectly embodied their renewed commitment to reconcile popular demands for democracy with the dictates of their entrepreneurial creed. To secure their right flank within the existing electorate the liberals renominated William Busfield, the colorless local gentleman who had represented the borough since 1837. When Busfield showed insufficient enthusiasm for religious voluntarism and expressed support for education grants from the state, the militant Nonconformists wanted to dump him but were prevailed upon to exercise forbearance in the name of party unity. The resulting Whig liberal ticket became unbeatable, accumulating a 53 percent majority on election day.[75]

Four years later, when Busfield died, liberal dominance became complete when his seat was taken by Robert Milligan who had achieved comparable local status as an entrepreneur. With its control of local government institutions now complemented by command of both parliamentary seats, progressive liberals had acquired a virtual political monopoly in which Whig

[75] D. G. Wright, "Politics and Opinion in Nineteenth Century Bradford" (Leeds, Ph.D. dissertation, 1966), 277–330; J. A. Jowitt, "Dissenters Voluntaryism and Liberal Unity: The 1847 Election," in J. A. Jowitt and R. K. S. Taylor, eds., *Nineteenth Century Bradford Elections* (Bradford, 1979), 7–23; *Pollbook* (Bradford, 1847).

moderates became increasingly irrelevant and conservative diehards were rendered impotent, relegated to the margins of political life.[76]

Insofar as Bradford's conservative party was rooted in the town's traditional Anglican oligarchy, its atrophy was no more than an inevitable consequence of the economic and demographic disappearance of this group. Progressively diminished by death and departure, its numbers dwindled, dwarfed by the tide of ascendant entrepreneurial immigrants who, throughout the forties, were establishing themselves.

Nevertheless, no less than liberalism, political conservatism in Bradford had always looked beyond its permanent constituency, taking advantage of the discomfiture of its antagonists and reaching out to other social groups. As we have seen, even after the failure of Tory radicalism, Bradford's conservatives were able during the 1838–43 crisis to patch together an electoral alliance based on the fears of small property owners disillusioned with the collapse of the liberal dream. Nevertheless, as the incorporation controversy demonstrated, this conservative coalition was built upon liberalism's failure and lacked any viable urban reform program of its own. Certainly, there was some truth in the *Observer's* contemptuous claim that the commissioners who had opposed the municipality had, "by their notorious inattention to the duties of office, rendered themselves ineligible to give an opinion on the question."[77]

After liberalism began to change in the mid- and late forties, seeking to stabilize society in more realistic ways, conservatism lost much of its popular appeal. With liberals now appearing to offer their own version of urban collectivism and acquiescing in such disagreeable necessities as factory reform, even responsible Anglican elites like the mill-owning Rand brothers acknowledged that their former antagonists had now embraced social policies and political programs containing some of the best features of their own. At the same time such men could not help but be conscious that conservatism, as a distinctive political party and philosophy, had little to offer the urban-industrial milieu. Once inspired by the Oastlerite vision of factory paternalism, events now obliged them to recognize, if only im-

---

[76] Even within the magistracy, the creation of a predominantly liberal Municipal Court broke the final stranglehold of the hinterland Tory squirearchy on Bradford's internal urban affairs. Wright, "Politics and Opinion," 330–445; Jack Reynolds, "The General Election of 1859, Bradford," in Jowitt and Taylor, eds., *Nineteenth Century Bradford Elections*, 35–49.

[77] Cudworth, *Bradford Corporation*, 100. Periodic expressions of interest in a new improvement act for the old Commission were transparently defensive gestures that tended to be advanced only at moments when the procorporationists seemed to be attracting popular support. Elliott, "Incorporation of Bradford," 170–1.

plicitly, the incompatibility of a creed based on hierarchy and tradition with an environment whose essence was constant mobility and change.

Despite his own opposition to municipal incorporation, John Rand was troubled by the failure of his fellow conservatives to offer their own solutions to the social and environmental problems that the liberal sanitary campaigns had raised.[78] Even more alarming was the staunch commitment of the Tory party leadership to agricultural protectionism, notwithstanding the protracted depressions and poor harvests that jeopardized the economic welfare of the industrial world. Up to the twenties, "protectionism" might still be a class-neutral doctrine embraced not only by landlords, but by many worsted industrialists too. But once industry became dependent on international markets and secure in its dominance of global trade, even conservatives, insofar as they remained linked to Bradford and its industry, found it difficult to justify an agrarian monopoly that spelled only disaster for the urban-industrial world. Torn between traditional political loyalties and his economic self-interest, John's brother William Rand broke with the Tory establishment and even joined the Anti–Corn Law League.[79]

Finally, in 1846, Peel's conversion to free trade and the consequent split in national Toryism opened the floodgates locally for a mass exodus of conservatives from their traditional party identity and creed. Although many of these men hesitated openly to join with the liberals, their politics became indistinguishable from the consensus liberalism of the mid-Victorian age. For two decades, only a small, diehard minority remained in Bradford's orthodox Tory camp.

But paradoxically, Toryism left its most enduring political legacy in Bradford only after the midforties when its ideology and party organization had collapsed. Though conservatives and the traditional establishment they represented could no longer govern in their own right, the more responsible among them who were willing to work with liberals quickly discovered that they could make an indispensable contribution to the consensus of the mid-Victorian age. In particular, their abandonment of diehard political reaction was often accompanied by a turn to new forms of social action that they initiated within the framework of a revivified Anglican Church. In Bradford, this Anglican revival occurred under the aegis of Vicar William Scoresby who served between 1839 and 1846.

Scoresby came out of the same evangelical tradition that produced Rich-

---

[78] *BO*, Aug. 21, 1847.
[79] Cudworth, *Bradford Corporation*, 129–30; *BOB*, May 5, 1906, *BO*, Dec. 11, 1868.

ard Oastler and Parson Bull, and he frequently invoked the language of corporatism and paternalism that they had pioneered. Yet Scoresby lacked the ideological predispositions of his Tory radical predecessors, and an examination of his actual aims and activities reveals some sharp departures from the original paternalist vision that had cast the church as a clerical adjunct to the authority of a benevolent industrial squire. In the first place, Scoresby quickly discovered that few such industrial paternalists actually existed. Moreover, as the vicar of a large subdiocesan parish, Scoresby had no intention of being anyone's surrogate and saw himself not only as chief administrator of local Anglican operations, but as a moral leader of the community at large. Although this exalted self-image seems to have made him numerous enemies even within his own church, it enabled Scoresby to do what no other churchman had hitherto accomplished – transforming discredited ideas and institutions into vital agencies of urban-industrial stabilization to insure that some elements of the traditional Anglican heritage would be grafted onto the social and political consensus over which Nonconformist liberals were destined to preside.[80]

Scoresby's first and greatest achievement was in the realm of elementary education, perhaps the one field of social provision in which the failure of liberal voluntarism had been most conspicuous and complete. Although it was widely recognized that the Sunday schools alone were inadequate agencies for the education and socialization of the emerging generation of urban-industrial workers, there were many reasons why day schools could not be provided on a mass basis by the same purely voluntaristic means. In the first place, before 1833, the ubiquitousness of child labor was an insuperable barrier to any elementary day school education for most working-class youths. Thereafter, the attempt to solve the problem of education by making paternalism obligatory through factory laws either drove the millowners to open disobedience or, at best, induced them to replace young children with adolescents over the age of eighteen for whom educational provision not was required. In 1844, there were only 745 factory scholars in Bradford, or about 8 percent of the nine- to thirteen-year-olds in town.[81] The gradual removal of preadolescents from direct factory labor made some form of day schooling both possible and necessary. In light of the millowners' refusal to take on this responsibility, the main difficulty was to find alternative agencies on whose shoulders the burden of financing and organizing elementary education could be placed.

---

[80] R. E. Scoresby-Jackson, *The Life of William Scoresby* (London, 1861); Tom and Cordelia Stamp, *William Scoresby Arctic Scientist* (Whitby, Yorkshire, 1975), 140–95.

[81] *PP* (1836, XLV), 10; (1844, XXVII), 8; (1845, XXV), 51–3; (1850, XXIII), 62–5; (1866, XXIV), 36–9; (1868–9, XIV), 11–17, 76; (1873, XIX), 56–9.

Because of their remarkable success in creating the Sunday school infrastructure, the voluntary religious sects seemed logical candidates to assume responsibilities for this task. However, day schools, which required costly permanent structures and necessitated the employment of trained, full-time staff, required resources far beyond what the religious denominations' voluntary subscriptions (even if supplemented by nominal pupil tuition charges) could have raised. The cost-effective monitorial system reduced expenses by adapting industrial production techniques to the business of education by having the paid schoolmaster concentrate on teaching the most advanced students who would, in turn, instruct the rest. But even this could not reduce costs to the point where voluntarism, unaided, could support a system that elites would finance and workers could afford.[82]

By the end of the thirties very little had been done. Outside the dame schools, most of which were useless, the only elementary schools accessible to Bradford's 55,000 workers were an experimental Quaker operation and two small establishments attached to the church. Yet if bourgeois elites needed any reminding, the advent of Chartism rudely reminded them of the enormous danger of popular educational neglect. Perhaps there was little hope of influencing the older generation of working-class immigrants, but now a new working-class generation was emerging, born and bred in the city and molded by the experience of industrial capitalism itself. Unless the bourgeoisie acted, they would be socialized by the workers' own indigenous culture or, worse, by the political radicals who were all too ready to do the job. Troubled by these disquieting developments, a group of dissenting ministers met in 1839 to consider adding day school instruction to their Sunday school infrastructure so that basic literacy, numeracy, the truths of religion, the principles of political economy, and the values of respectability could be inculcated into the broad ranks of the urban working class. But when they faced the gap between costs and resources, the ministers discovered that there was little they could do. The only concrete result of their efforts was that the Congregationalists joined the Quakers in opening their own experimental schools.[83]

---

[82] The parallels between the organization of these elementary schools and the factory have frequently been drawn. Although this doubtless reflects some underlying and unconscious belief that working-class children had to be "processed" like the commodities they were being raised to produce, these similarities between the "production" techniques of schools and factories are more self-evidently explained by the fact that the same rigid imperatives of cost efficiency pertained to both. See S. Frith, "Socialization and Rational Schooling: Elementary Education in Leeds before 1870," in Phillip McCann, *Popular Education and Socialization in the Nineteenth Century* (London, 1977), 78; S. J. Curtis and M. E. A. Boultwood, *An Introductory History of English Education Since 1800* (Cambridge, 1960), 10–12.

[83] G. W. Fenn, "The Development of Education in an Industrial Town (Bradford) during

Yet what the Nonconformists could not do in the name of voluntarism, Vicar Scoresby began to accomplish in relatively short order, working under the aegis of the church. Over the next five years, nine Anglican day schools were opened capable of enrolling up to 1,400 pupils at any given time (which represented about 12 percent of all the ten- to fourteen-year-olds in town). As his accounts demonstrate, the secret of Scoresby's success was his ability to draw on financial resources, which the Nonconformists could not or would not acquire. Although £1,418 was raised by local subscription and about another £1,000 was contributed by tuition fees levied on the scholars themselves, this constituted less than half of the schools' total budget, 33 percent of which came from the coffers of the Anglican National Education Society and 16 percent of which came directly from central government grants under the auspices of the education committee of the Privy Council.[84]

Although local voluntarism alone might be ineffective in providing major social services and goods, Scoresby's work had demonstrated what could be accomplished when it was judiciously supplemented by outside contributions, particularly by grants-in-aid from the state. Of course, in the conflict-ridden forties, most Nonconformist liberals saw Scoresby's success less as an example to be emulated than as unfair competition, which they had to combat. Seeing state aid as specially privileging their Anglican Tory antagonists, the leading Nonconformist liberals, with a few exceptions like Forster, only became more dogmatic in their insistence on a strict policy of educational laissez-faire, at a time when, in other areas like public health and the urban environment, they were beginning to countenance a more positive governmental role.[85]

However, by the fifties, as ideological contestation was replaced with a more down-to-earth concern that the educational job be properly done, Scoresby's pragmatic blend of private initiative with public action began to seem more attractive to the liberals who were, after all, seeking a similar balance in their municipal reform program, which sought to reconcile the collective needs of an urban community with free enterprise's competitive individualist thrust. Indeed, it might be argued that Scoresby's abandonment of ideological purism in favor of a pragmatic administrative approach provided liberals with the sort of concrete model for urban-industrial social provision that their own progressive program seemed to necessitate, but

the Nineteenth Century," *University of Leeds Institute of Education Researches and Studies* (1952, 1953), 34; anon., *The State of Popular Education in England* (London, 1861), 2:175–241; *BO*, Oct. 27, 1842.

[84] William Scoresby, *Records of the Bradford Parochial Schools, 1840–6* (Bradford, 1846).

[85] *BO*, May 28, 1835; June 20, 1844; Mar. 20, 1845; Feb. 28, Mar. 4, 25, Apr. 15, 1847; Apr. 26, 1849; June 13, 1850.

which, because of residual ideological commitments, they were unable to initiate on their own.

Certainly, Nonconformists were not about to leave the elementary education of workers entirely to the Anglicans. During the fifties and sixties, as they developed their own day school infrastructure, they found that state subsidies, so far from vitiating their efforts at educational voluntarism, were essential to facilitating them on the requisite scale. Indeed, this reliance on government subsidies to supplement large projects that had been initially established by voluntary means became a paradigm for the organization of social services in urban-industrial society during the long interlude between the mid-Victorian age of equipoise and the final twentieth-century triumph of the centralized welfare state.[86]

Turning his attention from the education of factory children to the condition of the female factory operatives who were replacing them, Scoresby sponsored yet another social reform initiative within the framework of Anglicanism that would subsequently contribute to the mid-Victorian social and political consensus over which Nonconformist liberals were destined to preside. Concern about female millworkers, like the earlier interest in factory children, initially flowed from traditional Tory preoccupations with the breakdown of the family, the plight of dependent women and children, and the paternalist responsibilities of male elites.

In 1844, Scoresby visited Lowell, Massachusetts, to examine the system whereby millowners, in recruiting millgirls from the countryside, undertook to provide them not only with wages but with decent accommodation, proper moral supervision, and some domestic training to fit them for future housewifely roles. Publishing the results of his investigation, Scoresby found much that Bradfordians could emulate although he recognized that Lowell "paternalism" was, in large measure, a capitalist response to conditions of labor shortage, which would require significant modification in Bradford where there was an abundance of available hands. Nevertheless, Scoresby concluded, there was no reason why decent boarding houses could not be supplied by the marketplace. If they were not, as in Lowell, to be provided

---

[86] N. B. Roper, "The Contribution of the Nonconformists to the Development of Education in Bradford in the Nineteenth Century," (Leeds, M.Ed. thesis, 1967); anon., *Popular Education in England*; anon., *Education in Bradford Since 1870* (Bradford, 1970), 38–72. For a general discussion of the development of an elementary educational infrastructure in early-nineteenth-century Britain, see Brian Simon, *The Two Nations and the Educational Structure, 1780–1870* (London, 1974), 126–76, 337–68; and Richard Johnson, "Educational Policy and Social Control in Early Victorian England," *Past and Present*, 49 (1970).

by paternalism, they could be run for profit and partly subsidized by voluntary charitable work.[87]

Although Scoresby found that many of the existing lodging houses were "clean, comfortable [and] well conducted," either "furnished by steady and virtuous families... [or] kept by widows and elderly people of approved character from whom it would be cruel to withdraw the means of support which their lodgers supply," he also encountered some disreputable establishments where there was no attempt to provide positive moral influence, and proper standards were not maintained. To raise the general tone of the lodging houses, Scoresby appointed a committee to raise funds and organize a few model establishments that would be run along exemplary lines. Meanwhile the committee urged the millgirls "to shun low and disorderly houses and cheerfully to submit to the rules of a well conducted family... to consider such restraint as an advantage, and perfect freedom as unfavorable to the cultivation of domestic feelings and the formation of a delicate female character."[88]

In contrast to his work in education, Scoresby kept this movement free of the political and sectarian conflicts that had beset so many bourgeois efforts at social reform. He was careful to include leading Nonconformists within his lodging house committee, and by 1847, the local political atmosphere had become sufficiently harmonious that "ministers of the Gospel of various denominations stood together on the platform and called one another brother." Perhaps more importantly, the movement drew in not only bourgeois men but their wives and daughters who "mingled familiarly with the humble mill girls as sisters with sisters" for "the purpose of raising them up to a higher and happier region of life."[89]

Of course, elite women had always played a critical role in charitable activities, but now the elevation of the condition of working-class women into a major question of public discussion and debate also brought them into the public arena for the first time. They began to speak at meetings on the subject, to organize their own committees, and even to open a female educational institute that offered evening classes to the millgirls in town. Here was a new and politically neutral arena in which the vast energies of women's voluntarism could be mobilized without the legacy of sectarian divisiveness or the restraints of market competition that so often had vitiated voluntaristic endeavors among the male bourgeoisie. Preoccupied with their endless quest for profitability, male industrialists might have little choice but to abdicate paternalist obligations, but the task of creating surrogate families for their young female employees flowed quite easily from the "maternalism"

[87] William Scoresby, *American Factories and their Female Operatives* (London, 1845).
[88] *BO*, Jan. 14, 1847.
[89] *BO*, June 24, 1847.

of bourgeois wives and daughters, hitherto confined within the nuclear family, which now sought wider public responsibilities and roles.

By training future working-class housewives in those domestic virtues that they had perfected within their own households, "the kind attentions and trifling self-denials which tend to soften and refine the manners," bourgeois women could discharge their responsibilities to their less fortunate sisters while making a significant contribution to inculcating within the working-class family the same values of moral probity, work discipline, and respectability, which they had so successfully instilled within their own.[90] The full contribution of elite women to the bourgeois program of working-class socialization would not emerge for several decades until they obtained greater scope for public action in the final years of the Victorian age. Nevertheless, the female factory movement of the 1840s presaged some of these latent possibilities whereby the gender solidarities and concerns of women were appropriated to buttress the liberal consensus, to flesh out its social vision of progress, and to help heal the divisions of politics and class.[91]

Here again, in discarding discredited paternalist pieties and in mobilizing the energies of bourgeois women to recast voluntarism in an ideologically unexceptionable way, Scoresby's Anglicans showed greater flexibility and creativity than their liberal Nonconformist counterparts in confronting the crises of early industrial capitalism. Here too, Scoresby's initiatives contributed a good deal to insuring that the liberal consensus of the mid-Victorian decades would be broad enough to encompass women and Anglicans and would not degenerate, as it had during the thirties, into a male, Nonconformist, entrepreneurial preserve. In retrospect, even the liberal leaders acknowledged the service that pragmatic conservatives had performed. In 1855, at the apogee of their triumph, when they had to choose a name for Bradford's first public park, they selected not their own heroes, Bright, or Cobden, but the renegade Tory Sir Robert Peel, whose conversion to free trade opened the path to liberal ascendancy and who, more than anyone, symbolized the transformation of conservatism from a virulent, aristocratic, class ideology into a neutral, bureaucratic, administrative creed.[92]

The end of militant working-class consciousness

The creation, by midcentury, of a broad coalition of property owners that joined most bourgeois factions and social strata, women, petite bourgeoisie,

[90] Ibid.,
[91] LeeAnn Whites, "Southern Ladies and Millhands: Class Politics and the Domestic Economy; Augusta, Georgia, 1870–90" (Irvine, Ph.D. dissertation, 1982).
[92] *BO*, Nov. 1, 8, 1855.

professionals, and most Anglicans under the leadership of the ascendant entrepreneurial elite, must be accounted a considerable achievement, but it was not consensus liberalism's most formidable task. Notwithstanding the intensity of intraelite conflict in early Victorian Bradford, the coalescence of property owners was no novel accomplishment, since it had occurred spontaneously in the late thirties and forties in response to the emergence of working-class consciousness and what was perceived as a proletarian revolutionary threat.

This social configuration of the 1839–42 period, when bourgeois unity was a temporary by-product of a much more profound social fissure in which class was ranged against contending class, had marked not the triumph of consensus liberalism, but its lowest ebb of discredit and defeat; for the liberal project entailed a more positive, universal kind of consensus in which the entire urban-industrial community would play a part. Liberalism would be of little value if the political reconciliation of elite parties and factions it effected were not part of a larger process of social reconciliation that closed the rift dividing Bradford's workers from all sections of the bourgeoisie. Unless it could reclaim a substantial portion of the hitherto alienated urban workers, eliciting their voluntary acquiescence in the conditions of industrial-capitalist life, liberalism would not long underwrite the consensus of property holders for whom social order and stability took precedence over liberal, entrepreneurial ideals.

As we have seen, liberals had actively courted respectable workers through the United Reform Club since 1842. After 1843, when urban reform gained top billing with the inauguration of the municipal incorporation campaign, their efforts finally began to bear fruit. Although a majority of Bradford's workers probably opposed incorporation and feared the introduction of a borough police, the 1845 petitions show that, among the minority who were sufficiently well off to be ratepayers, opinion was about evenly split.[93] In 1847, when the liberals nominated Col. Thompson as their parliamentary candidate, officially embracing household suffrage as a liberal party goal, working-class resistance further evaporated, and even the most militant Chartist leaders temporarily laid aside their hostility to join in the liberal radical cause. By the early fifties, the widening of the municipal franchise and the presence of moderate Chartists within the dominant liberal camp demonstrated that working-class politics, insofar as it remained viable, was now conducted under the broad umbrella of a mid-Victorian liberal party machine.[94]

[93] "Petitions for and against Incorporation" (Bradford Archives, D.B. 69/2–3).

[94] Mid-Victorian working-class radicalism as a general phenomenon is examined in John Vincent, *The Formation of the British Liberal Party, 1857–68* (London, 1966), 112–60.

Of course, this remarkable political reconciliation between organized workers and bourgeois liberals was underpinned by the economic boom that brought full employment and prosperity for three years in the middle of the decade, and again, more permanently, after 1849. In particular, many of the 39 percent of adult male artisans and factory workers outside the structurally declining textile handicraft trades experienced these years as a period of rising incomes. Trade union initiatives under favorable market conditions enabled them to improve their living standards substantially without attacking the fundamental structures of capitalist social and economic life.[95]

By the midforties, the rising incomes of skilled and unionized male workers were beginning to produce visible results. In particular, the woolsorters, who were among the best paid of industrial Bradford's new working-class elite, purchased a large field on the outskirts of town in 1844. Part of this was divided into small garden plots, which the woolsorters cultivated. The rest was turned into a pleasure garden to which the general public was admitted for a modest charge. The woolsorters garden, as it came to be known, became instantly popular, especially during the first decade of its existence, which was, in terms of provision for popular recreation, a dismal interlude, before the appearance of new public parks constructed under the aegis of the municipality, but after the old open moors and traditional fairgrounds had been turned into speculative builders plots.[96]

For groups like the woolsorters and other well-paid workers who could afford to use their recreational facilities, the half-decade after 1842 marked a dramatic contrast with the preceding half-decade when cyclical depression and wholesale unemployment had subjected all but the most privileged to the perils and insecurities of proletarianization. Now, however, as conditions improved significantly, many among the skilled began to consider the possibility that limited, incremental reforms were possible and that they were more likely to benefit from progressive coalitions that operated within the existing system than from apparently vain mass movements of militant protest that sought to transform competitive capitalism from without. Amidst an economic environment affording them some share in prosperity and a political climate in which bourgeois liberals conceded many of their demands, it made sense for those workers who thought they could benefit to cultivate their place within the voluntaristic community of urban-industrial capitalism rather than to pursue the utopian aspirations that had hitherto possessed them, to fully collectivize industrial production or to reorganize the capitalist city in a radically social democratic way.[97]

95 See Chapter 16.
96 *BO*, Aug. 22, 1844.
97 The integration of skilled and respectable workers into the new mid-Victorian liberal

However, with the return of depression in 1847, this new working-class impulse toward reformism and respectability threatened to come to a premature end. As unemployment and mass poverty mounted, radical Chartism recovered its former, strident voice. By March 1848, as their brethren on the Continent were taking to the barricades, Bradford's Chartists held a series of mass open-air meetings to inaugurate a new agitational campaign.[98] Suddenly faced, not only with an economic crisis, but with the potential collapse of the working-class consensus they had painstakingly built up, Bradford's liberal leadership bent over backward to express their sympathy for the workers and their willingness to press for legitimate working-class demands. Now, when the unemployed held meetings, leading entrepreneurs put in appearances, and resolutions were passed expressing "unfeigned sorrow" at "the circumstances of destitution and misery into which so large a portion of Bradford is plunged."[99] Although the Town Council itself could do little, the liberal Board of Guardians initiated the more innovatory approach to relieving poverty that was outlined in Chapter 14.

Most importantly, however, liberal politicians sought a rapprochement with the working-class movement for constitutional reform. Now, instead of heaping insults on the Chartists, liberal politicians outdid one another in affirming their own support for popular suffrage demands. So far from suppressing Chartist rallies, liberal elites, now ensconced in municipal office, attempted to tame and co-opt them, even delegating bourgeois sympathizers like W. E. Forster to take the chair. Even drilling and pike selling, which, in 1839, had occurred clandestinely, were now tacitly permitted, and in May,

consensus has been considered on a general level by Perkin, *Modern English Society*, 271–407; Briggs, *Victorian People*, 168–231; Trygve Tholfsen, *Working Class Radicalism;* idem, "The Transition to Democracy in Victorian England," in Peter Stansky, ed., *The Victorian Revolution: Government and Society in Victorian Britain* (New York, 1973), 169–98; Sidney Pollard, "Nineteenth Century Co-operation: From Community Building to Shopkeeping," in Asa Briggs and John Saville, eds., *Essays in Labour History* (London, 1960), 1:74–112; John Foster, *Class Struggle and the Industrial Revolution: Early English Capitalism in Three Towns* (London, 1974), 203–50; Royden Harrison, *Before the Socialists: Studies in Labour and Politics 1861–1881* (London, 1965), 78–136; Brian Harrison, *Peaceable Kingdom: Stability and Change in Modern Britain* (Oxford, 1982), 123–56; and Neville Kirk, *The Growth of Working Class Reformism in Mid-Victorian England* (Urbana, Ill., 1985). For a study that stresses the early and pre-Victorian origins of respectable working-class liberalism, see Brian Harrison and Patricia Hollis, "Chartism, Liberalism, and the Life of Robert Lowery," *English Historical Review*, 82:324 (1967). For a work that emphasizes the uniquely working-class character of artisanal liberalism during the Mid-Victorian age, see Geoffrey Crossick, "The Labour Aristocracy and its Values: A Study in Mid-Victorian Kentish London," *Victorian Studies*, 19:3, (1976).

[98] *BO*, Mar. 16, 23, 30, Apr. 6, 13, 20, 27, May 4, 11, 25, 1848.

[99] Quoted in Reynolds, *Great Paternalist*, 139.

when Chartists were reported gathering in military formation, the municipal authorities did nothing to stop them.[100]

The Chartist moderates, mostly skilled artisans and factory workers who could weather the depression with their memories of earlier gains, were impressed with the liberal elites' conciliatory behavior, which contrasted so sharply with the official repression that had characterized the elite response of a decade before. Physical force would no longer be necessary, a Chartist cobbler now asserted, since "Bradford had recently sent a friend of the Charter to parliament; there were councillors and aldermen who supported its principles and so they would go step by step, till the principles of the Charter were ratified by the House of Commons."[101]

If skilled workers and industrial operatives were generally amenable to a political alliance with bourgeois liberals in 1848, under economic privations that six or nine years earlier had aroused them to violent class revolt, this was, in no small measure, because one of the most pressing of their social and economic grievances had been addressed a year earlier with the passage of the Ten Hours Factory Act – a measure that bourgeois liberals had certainly not initiated, but which most of them were now prepared, at least grudgingly, to accept. Aptly described by Marx and Engels as the first victory of a nascent working-class political economy over the orthodox political economy of the bourgeoisie, the new law required employers to reduce the hours of all women and children to the legal limit by May 1, 1848.[102] Though the full effect of the Factory Act was somewhat delayed by the depression, which necessitated temporary reductions in hours (and wages) on economic

---

[100] *BO*, Mar. 23, Apr. 13, May 4, 11, 25, June 1, 8, 1848.
[101] *BO*, Mar. 16, May 4, 1848, quoted in Reynolds, *Great Paternalist*, 135. Such attitudes form a marked contrast to those expressed by skilled workers during the 1839–41 period, even in a less proletarianized city like Birmingham, where the liberal radical–respectable worker reforming alliance was much more firmly established and had been longer in place. See Trygve Tholfsen, "The Chartist Crisis in Birmingham," *International Review of Social History* 3, (1958).
[102] Karl Marx and Friedrich Engels, "Address to the Central Committee of the Communist League," in Robert Tucker, ed., *The Marx Engels Reader* (New York, 1972), 517; Marx, *Capital* (Moscow, 1954), 1:264–71. After the implementation of the Ten Hours Act of 1847, widespread employer resistance and obstruction necessitated a further compromise in 1850, which raised hours for women and children to ten and a half on weekdays, while lowering them to seven and a half on Saturdays. The result was effectively to eliminate the notorious relay system, which had hitherto enabled masters to reduce working hours for young children while extending them for legally unprotected adults. Marx, *Capital*, 1:272–81.

grounds, workers understood that, when wage rates recovered during the next wave of prosperity, working conditions would be permanently improved.

Indeed, two years later, when the Factory Inspector R. J. Saunders interviewed workers about the effects of the Ten Hours Act, he found that they were generally satisfied. Although by no means resolving all problems of capitalist exploitation, the new act, as most operatives and their relatives acknowledged, had done much to equalize employment, to enhance their workplace environment and safety, and to increase the possibilities for achieving domestic order and for establishing a normal home and family life. According to one old woman, it had enabled her daughters to acquire domestic skills and to assist with the housework, while her husband had been freed to take up gardening, growing vegetables for the family to eat.[103] Indeed, several employers who had been, one way or another, influenced by the ideals of industrial paternalism, responded to the new legal order in the factory by renting parcels of unused or underused land to select groups of employees for use as garden plots. By 1850, 75 acres had been divided up in this fashion and leased to 834 individual occupiers at a moderately remunerative average rental of £6 7s. per acre. Although 60 percent of these occupiers were skilled or supervisory workers, a not insignificant minority were families of the industrial rank and file. To such people, the advent of a ten-hour workday clearly indicated that, at least now, in the depths of depression, they would be able to obtain through intervention by the state some small measure of those new opportunities for enhanced leisure and domestic economy that had accrued a few years earlier through the natural workings of a tight labor market to the small, aristocratic, male worker elite.[104]

Unfortunately, however, such benefits could not be anticipated by the mass of beleaguered woolcombers who were experiencing the full brunt of structural proletarianization at the very moment when factory work was being brought under the effective protection of the state. In 1848, the combers' labor was rapidly being superseded by the newly developed combing machine. Nevertheless, Bradford's magistrates and manufacturers rejected a proposal for regulating mechanization or delaying its introduction to protect the livelihoods of the handicraftsmen who could not compete. With their trade obliterated by that march of progress that promised other sectors of Bradford's working class a better deal, the woolcombers had little incentive to embrace the liberal urban-industrial consensus in which they themselves obviously had no place.[105]

---

[103] *PP* (1850, XXIII), 47–9.

[104] *Ibid.*, 46–7; *BO*, Mar. 28, 1850.

[105] *BO*, May 18, 1848; James Burnley, *The History of Wool and Woolcombing* (London, 1889), 183–5.

Yet when woolcombers sought to reactivate the spirit of militant class consciousness that had once united workers from a range of diverse occupations and crafts they found that, in the context of the 1848 depression, this spirit was virtually impossible to conjure up. Increasingly estranged from the dominant thrust of artisanal, collective, self-help associations that formed the core of working-class voluntarism in the town, the hapless woolcombers, just when their situation grew bleakest, found themselves with diminishing access to the ideological and organizational resources that had buoyed them during the late twenties and thirties, when they had formed the lynchpin of a classwide alliance between aroused and angry proletarianized masses and effectively organized handicrafts elites.

Even during the early 1840s, the Combers' Protective Society began to demonstrate diminished capacity for that proud and purposive self-assurance that had characterized their behavior during the early industrial age. In 1840, Henry Burnett, the society's secretary, advocated the establishment of an official chamber of commerce to regulate local working conditions and to fix a minimum wage. For a union whose members, a decade earlier, had stood in the forefront of the recasting of older, plebeian, communitarian traditions into modern, openly anticapitalist, collectivist forms, this retreat toward a traditional corporatist vision, in which the moral economy was no longer independently won by the workers but graciously granted by paternalist elites, suggests a deepening despair over the combers' ability to save themselves.[106]

Although the prosperity of the midforties obviously benefited the combers, their gains proved far more tenuous than was the case with more favorably placed elements within the urban working class. Thus the combers continued to lose self-possession and composure, fluctuating recklessly between impotent outbursts of anger and pathetic appeals to the benevolence of elites. Even a sophisticated and articulate leader like George White, who emerged as the preeminent local spokesman for political and economic radicalism during the forties, tended, in contrast to Peter Bussey, his counterpart a decade earlier, to display a certain ambivalence as he alternated between a militant and a supplicant stance.

According to the Chartist chronicler R. G. Gammage, White was "noted for his inflexible perseverance" and was "ever ready for whatever work fell to his lot." Although "quite at home" in the art of "battering the head of a policeman," and well known for his defiant, physical-force advocacy and his shadowy links with Irish revolutionaries abroad, White was also accused of being in the pay of the Tories and indisputably emerged as the most effective propagandist in mobilizing working-class opposition to the liberal incor-

[106] BO, Aug. 27, 1840; Burnley, *Wool and Woolcombing*, 175–83.

poration campaign.[107] In fact, notwithstanding the occasional violence of his speeches, White betrayed a strain of nostalgic longing for what he usually acknowledged to be an anachronistic paternalism. Thus when local conservatives responded favorably to his report on the sanitary conditions of the slum districts, "he was grateful to the gentlemen who had come forward to assist them" and would do them "justice to say that no men on earth could have expressed themselves or acted more generously toward the working men than they had."[108] Nevertheless, a few months later, when the limits of elite paternalism became manifest, he resumed his more typical stream of "poignant sarcasms" and, a year later, summarily dismissed the capitalists as "an unfeeling class of men."[109]

During the 1846–8 depression, as their trade was inundated by a swarm of starving Irishmen, as their wages sank below the level of subsistence, and as their trade union organization completely collapsed, the combers' oscillation between cringing servility and angry defiance became even more pronounced. Finally, in 1848, the introduction of a fully cost-effective mechanical woolcomb brought demoralization to its lowest ebb. Our study of the 1851 census manuscripts clearly shows that the woolcombing remnant still present within Bradford's urban working population was, by then, degenerating into a separate subproletarian caste. In contrast to most other working-class occupations whose members were becoming increasingly residentially dispersed, the combers' extreme poverty was forcing them to concentrate ever more intensively in the four or five worst downtown slums. Even more striking were the ways in which the combers' nativity and ethnic composition had now diverged dramatically from the overall working-class norm. By 1851, only 13 percent of the woolcombers were Bradford natives, as compared with 45 percent for the entire population, while the Irish, who constituted 9 percent of all Bradfordians, accounted for 36 percent of all woolcombers in town.[110]

Increasingly separated from other skilled artisanal occupations by their declining status, diminishing incomes, and ever more alien ethnic cast, the woolcombers began to lose touch with their own powerful craft legacy, and the struggles and class institutions of the late twenties and thirties became vague legends for the vast majority who had only recently entered the trade. Now uniquely victimized by the final phase of proletarianization in which a much wider range of workers had once felt themselves enmeshed, the

[107] R. G. Gammage, *A History of the Chartist Movement, 1837–1854* (London, 1961), 154.
[108] Dorothy Thompson, *The Chartists* (New York, 1984), 228–30; *BO*, July 21, 1845.
[109] *BO*, Dec. 24, 1846; Gammage, *Chartist Movement*, 154.
[110] Calculated from information in HO, 107/2,308.

⸴

combers were now isolated by ethnic, occupational, and residential stigmata that had hitherto been submerged in the wider solidarities of class.

As the woolcombers' position continued to deteriorate and as they became ever more predominant within Chartism's radical wing, the more "English" traditions of collective self-help voluntarism that had been ascendant during the movement's vital early stage now began to give way to the more "Irish" traditions of subterranean neo-Jacobinism that had hitherto constituted a subordinate strain. In the late forties, just over half of the 806 Bradfordians who participated in the Chartist Land Company were woolcombers as compared with the third who belonged to the Great Horton Charter Association early in the decade.[111] Under these circumstances, the resilient tone of early Chartist radicalism, with its richly textured counterhegemonic aspirations and its immersion within a cooperative culture of class, degenerated into a groan of explosive desperation from men who had nothing to lose but their chains. "I would sooner just now go to gaol than to my cottage," declared one comber who described himself as "a starving man." "There I should have bread and water, but at my house there is nothing but water.... Let every man beg from door to door," he concluded, "for the means to get a pike...to force tyranny from its damnable throne."[112]

By May, it was evident that many others were beginning to follow his advice as the slum districts teemed daily with crowds and excitement, and radical blacksmiths like Isaac Jefferson did a brisk trade in pikes. Although there is some evidence of involvement by tailors, whose trade was also becoming debased, these activities were overwhelmingly dominated by woolcombers and their wives.[113] With the industrialization of the old hinterland villages and the enclosure of the traditional fairgrounds on which working-class radicals from the entire region had gathered a decade before, the fully urbanized Chartists of 1848 were thrown back almost entirely on their own resources and confined to their downtown residential slums. Here, at least, amidst the self-contained impenetrability of their own communities where the writ of the liberal municipality did not yet run, they could defiantly reenact the gestures of control over their lives and environment that they had ceased to exercise within the larger framework of capitalist life. Seizing the most notorious of the downtown slum neighborhoods, especially the districts around White Abbey and Adelaide Street where the largest concentrations of woolcombers lived, Chartist militants set up their own de facto community networks of authority and forced the police and other municipal

[111] Thompson, *Chartists,* 217. See Chapter 17.
[112] Quoted in Reynolds, *Great Paternalist,* 138.
[113] *BO,* May 4, 11, 25, June 1, 8, 1848.

emissaries to keep out."[114] "If you wish to have the Charter," the *Northern Star* exulted, "then let every district do openly what Bradford has so nobly done. The middle classes were not alarmed; the police are idle, the soldiers have nothing to do and the magistrates know not what to do."[115]

In fact, with their well-developed law and order instincts, and one eye focused on events in France, the Tory magistrates knew exactly what they wanted to do. However, for weeks they remained hamstrung by the inaction of the liberal municipal authorities who were caught between their desire to maintain good relations with the workers and their need to demonstrate that they could fulfill their newfound responsibilities as a governing elite. Armed with evidence collected by Home Office agents that the woolcombers' leaders George Flynn and George White had abandoned peaceable methods of agitation and, perhaps acting under the heady inspiration of Paris, had involved themselves in revolutionary plots, Tory magistrates like Joshua Pollard strenuously argued for the necessity of a preemptive strike. Stung by Tory accusations of irresponsibility and ineptitude, Mayor Milligan could hardly ignore White's open boast that he had no fear of official crackdown in Bradford, which would be "a dead letter for they had declared a republic there."[116]

As White's woolcombers coordinated their insurrectionary conspiracies with political radicals elsewhere and forged close ties with Irish revolutionary groups, the municipal liberals reluctantly concluded that a military confrontation had become inevitable and that unless they quickly took the initiative, the army would be sent in behind their backs.[117] Nevertheless, before they finally acted, Bradford's liberals ensured that they would not be left to suppress Chartist militancy alone. They were determined to seek assistance not only from the trigger-happy Tory magistrates who were always ready to bathe subversives in blood, but from moderate and respectable groups among the workers who found the violent invective of the militants inimical to an order in which they, too, now hoped to share. Anxious to preserve their hard-won gains of the midforties and to realize the vision of orderly progress that now seemed to offer so much, many of these working-class moderates were now prepared not only to repudiate the radical rebels, but to join the party of order that would put them down. As early as April, the municipal authorities had sworn in over 1,500 special constables, deliberately including

[114] *BO*, June 1, 8, 15, 1848; H. McCarthy, *Chartist Recollections*, (n.p., n.d.). In June, George White claimed that there were 15,000 Chartists organized in Bradford. *BO*, June 29, 1848.

[115] Quoted in Elliott, "Establishment of Municipal Government," 211.

[116] Quoted in Reynolds, *Great Paternalist*, 144.

[117] *BO*, May 25, June 1, 8, 15, 1848; Elliott, "Establishment of Municipal Government," 206–31.

not only petit bourgeois property owners. but a goodly portion of artisans, overlookers, warehousemen, and woolsorters, who, having turned their backs on the physical-force fantasies of the demoralized, now conclusively sealed their alliance with bourgeois liberalism by legally placing themselves under municipal command.[118]

Armed with such assurances of respectable working-class loyalty, Milligan and the liberals prepared to act. After an abortive early-morning foray into the Manchester Road slum district, when a thousand stone-throwing residents beat back one hundred officers, an armed body of fifteen hundred was quickly assembled. It was headed by policemen who were followed by special constables with a contingent of dragoons bringing up the rear. On the afternoon of June 5, this force marched from the courthouse to the slum districts with Mayor Milligan and the arch-Tory magistrate Joshua Pollard leading the charge. After a pitched battle, in which neither policemen nor specials were able to gain control of the crowds, order was finally restored by the army, although the warren of backstreets offered an effective escape route for resisters and few arrests of ringleaders could be made. For a time thereafter, working-class crowds continued to have the run of their neighborhoods, harboring agitators like White or David Lightowler who continued their insurrectionary rumblings for the next two months. In the end, however, militant Chartism's back had been broken, as one by one, leaders were captured and police control within the slum districts was restored.[119]

Conclusion

Although less dramatic and bloody than their Parisian counterpart, Bradford's 1848 "June days" marked an equally decisive turning point in the history of social relations within the town. As in Paris, the specter of a proletarian social revolution had left radical workers isolated and defeated by a coalition of respectability acting under the banner of law and order that included virtually every other urban social group. For Karl Marx, the defeat of the forces of social revolution at the hands of a conservative coalition that momentarily united all sections of the propertied elite signaled a necessary, but only temporary, setback for an immature but ultimately ascendant proletariat. Forced back entirely on its own class resources, taught the futility of seeking its salvation within the framework of bourgeois liberalism, and

[118] BO, Mar. 16, 1848; Reynolds, Great Paternalist, 135–6. With a masterful ambiguity, Bradford's moderate Chartist leaders urged their respectable followers to enroll as special constables, not to protect their employers' property, but to defend their own. BO, Apr. 13, 1848.

[119] BO, June 1, 8, 15, 1848; McCarthy, Chartist Recollections.

faced with the necessity of forging an alternative socialist framework all its own, Marx saw the June days as a painful but salutary moment of clarification when the true character of capitalist social relations had been bared.[120]

Examination of the events in Bradford, however, suggests an insurgency whose social constituency was much narrower than the Marxist proletariat and whose long-term prognosis was far more bleak. For here, at least, the 1848 charge to the barricades represented not the first flowering of the industrial workers of the future, but the last gasp of a dying generation of proletarianized artisans who were deskilled and degraded by the triumph of capitalist productive relations but whose visions of a more humane, communitarian social alternative remained trapped within the now bankrupt values of a bygone protoindustrial past. Similarly, the united front of respectability that so decisively defeated them was not, as in 1838, the mere patched-together coalition of frightened property owners that Marx had envisioned, but a more positive and enduring social alliance led not by law-and-order conservatives, but by entrepreneurial liberals who were able to attract not only property owners, but those among the more respectable workers, mechanics, and skilled craftsmen who Marx expected to find on the other side. As for the true factory proletarians on whose labor capitalist production now depended, they consisted, for the most part, of adolescents and young adults, especially unmarried and/or childless women who, though by no means inherently quiescent politically, tended to respond less from their class position as productive laborers than from the vantage of their temporary position in the life cycle or from the permanent perspective of their feminine gender roles. Generally mollified after 1847 by effective government regulation, which addressed their specific labor and domestic concerns, Bradford's factory proletarians would contribute little to class-conscious activism for the next forty years.

It would be easy to ascribe this discrepancy between Marx's prophecy of deepening class contradiction and the more complex social patterns and trajectories that Bradford's 1848 crisis actually disclosed to the fallacy of treating real social classes as philosophical categories: as entities whose concrete course of historical development must inevitably divulge their ultimate meaning as receptacles for the realization of theoretically inspired ideals. Although it is certainly an error to conflate history and theory in this manner, it is no less mistaken to regard them as unconnected phenomena that can be understood outside the dialectic in which they interact. It is, of course, vain to imagine that social classes and ideologies, considered as abstractions, can ever remake history in their own image. But history can

---

[120] Karl Marx, *Class Struggles in France* (Moscow, 1972); idem, *The Eighteenth Brumaire of Louis Bonaparte* (New York, 1963).

be rendered comprehensible only by the realization that they do act as real forces of social transformation, significantly impacting on the actual course of events. If the pattern of social relations revealed in Bradford's 1848 crisis seems to obscure these deeper structures of historical determination, the pattern of crisis manifested a decade earlier displays a close, if never total, congruence with the dualism of the Marxist model in which class appears ranged against contending class.

As we have sought to demonstrate in the course of this study, this at least provisional correspondence between history and theory was the result of a long-term process that gradually inscribed the logic of competitive capitalism as a material force within Bradford's social development, profoundly influencing the actual course of local history itself. If the visible impact of this capitalist dynamic remained muted throughout the protoindustrial period, for the generation that came of age after 1825 it appeared as a palpable and increasingly inescapable social reality – a social reality that was experienced differentially by those it embourgeoised and those it proletarianized, in the form of radically alienated, depersonalized forms of industrial labor, and novel, competitive, rationalistically purposive modes of urban life. For those with access to property or productive resources, these novel social forms signaled the opening of fresh opportunities in which uncertainties and risks were eventually vindicated by greater prospects for self-realization and success. However, for those who experienced the urban-industrial capitalist transformation without these advantages, it often appeared as no more than a bewildering ordeal of dehumanization and dispossession, to which they were being involuntarily subject.[121]

Directly undermining the mass of Bradford's adult male handicraftsmen, periodically threatening the town's skilled artisans and factory laborers and blighting all working-class domestic life, this proletarianized version of the urban–industrial experience proved an insuperable obstacle to the realization of the liberal entrepreneurial social vision that the bourgeois experience had originally inspired. So long as tens of thousands were impoverished, demoralized, and subjected to periodic bouts of hunger and disease, the image of urban-industrial civilization as a progressive voluntary association of autonomous individual producers spontaneously integrated by the invisible hand of the market could never even begin to materialize.[122]

Indeed, the contradiction between these soaring aspirations of ideological liberalism and the grim reality of Bradford's early urban-industrial age not only sparked nostalgia among conservatives for a "golden age" of paternalism, but underwrote the emergence of a powerful and increasingly self-

[121] See Chapters 1–12.
[122] See Chapters 13 and 14.

conscious working-class movement in which beleaguered plebeian traditions of community were drawn upon to forge entirely new collectivist forms. Rejecting both liberal and conservative paradigms during the thirties, when the movement reached its peak, it began to transform indigenous communitarian legacies into cooperative experiments in social democracy that seemed to prefigure postcapitalist societal forms.

Nevertheless, this incipient counterhegemonic vision, which the contest with capital had tentatively raised up, was always overshadowed by a more deeply rooted strain of defensive traditionalism among the workers – a strain that reflected the ambivalence of a generation of proletarianized producers whose ability to project a postcapitalist future was constrained by their longing for a precapitalist past. Working-class consciousness, even at its moment of greatest vitality, notwithstanding the vigor of its anticapitalist critique, was no more successful than Tory radicalism in devising viable alternatives to the emerging entrepreneurial world. Abandoned, in the end, by the better-off artisans who saw more hope in reforming industrial capitalism from within, working-class radicalism became the province of dying handicraftsmen. Reduced to a state of hopeless desperation, this remnant of the proletarianized class fell back upon anachronistic notions of moral economy or utopian visions that could not possibly be realized.[123]

This failure on the part of Bradford's organized working-class movement to liquidate the nascent entrepreneurial social order, at a time when crisis rendered it dysfunctional and weak, gave bourgeois liberals some badly needed breathing space to shed their own ideological illusions and to implement the more limited but more effective reformist program that this chapter has traced. In the end, their project of social progress was partly realized, but not until it had been thoroughly tested and refined in the class conflicts that deflated its claims to universality by revealing its irrelevance to the overwhelming majority who lived within the urban-industrial world. Indeed, the seeds of entrepreneurial liberalism's mid-Victorian triumph were, ironically, contained in its very experience of early Victorian defeat. In particular, the chastening experience of the 1840s taught the most prescient of its defenders that, although class could never be eliminated from capitalist society, it might satisfactorily be tempered and tamed. Redirected into regular channels of negotiation and compromise, the class antagonisms that had once loomed as ideological death struggles might be rendered more limited and manageable once they were institutionalized in the form of interest-group politics within a regulatory, reformist governmental frame.

Of course, the creation of a genuine social consensus in Bradford during the 1840s depended not only on the emergence of a more pragmatic and

---

[123] See Chapters 15–17.

genuinely inclusive entrepreneurial liberalism, but on the appearance of a comparable shift from absolutist engagement to opportunist pursuit of limited objects on the part of both the most respectable and best organized section of the workers and the most vigorous and responsible portion of the traditional Anglican Tory elite. Moreover, given its tentative, haphazard, and ultimately contradictory character, such a consensus could only provide the basis for a long-term stabilization of urban-industrial society in the context of the long wave of generalized economic prosperity that began with the boom of 1849 and lasted, with a few brief interruptions, throughout the mid-Victorian age. Nevertheless, as Bradford's "June Days" graphically demonstrated, the basic social constituents that would go into the making of this more enduring consensus were already in place during the depression of 1848. In that year, as Bradford experienced one final episode of acute economic crisis and social strife, it became clear that the class struggle of the previous decade, so far from foreshadowing some final conflagration, had actually opened people's eyes to the necessity of compromise and had thus begun to lay the foundations for a new and enduring era of relative social peace. The reformist legacy of popular liberalism which Marx associated with capitalism's infancy and which he imagined the growing pains of June to have left behind suddenly and spectacularly resurfaced in Bradford to underwrite a more lasting consensus in which entrepreneurial capitalism could stabilize and mature.

Epilogue

In 1874, a local writer named James Burnley published a novel that took the reconciliation of Bradford's social classes at midcentury as its theme. In *Looking for the Dawn*, the rebellious workers, exemplified by the attractive daughter of a Chartist weaver, are alternately wooed by the son of a parvenu entrepreneurial capitalist named Thomas Ayrton and by Hugh Trafford, the heir of an irascible, reactionary, factory-hating squire. Young Ayrton, an immoral degenerate who has been corrupted from the stolid virtues of his honest, hard-working father by "the mysteries of metropolitan gaieties and university high life", attempts to ensnare the unsuspecting mill girl by falsely implicating her father and working-class suitor as instigators of a revolutionary Chartist plot.[1] Predictably enough, her heart is won by the noble young Trafford, who risks the ire of his magistrate father by undertaking the innocent workers' defense. However, to perform the role of social reconciliator in which he is both literally and figuratively cast Trafford must first abdicate the privileges that aristocratic heredity has bequeathed him, earning for himself in the competitive marketplace the position of wealth and social authority that the ideology of entrepreneurial liberalism had promised, but had failed to provide.

Coming "to a determination to fling his ancient name and all the pride of family distinction behind him, and at once rush into the world of business," young Trafford "was possessed of a burning desire to be a worker, to join the pioneers of commerce, and to win something more than the heritage of a landed estate and a pedigree." Embracing the entrepreneurial creed that "earned wealth [was] . . . twice as valuable as inherited wealth," he cast his lot with the industrial city, concluding that it was "worthier to be a developer of new inventions, a large employer of labour, and an instrument of public usefulness, than to live in idleness, the world administering to his wants with a ready hand, and he contributing nothing in return to the well being of the community."[2]

Indeed, in Burnley's account, young Trafford's personal renunciation of aristocratic privilege in favor of the new entrepreneurial virtues becomes the

---

[1] James Burnley, *Looking For the Dawn; A Tale of the West Riding* (London, 1874), 34.
[2] Ibid., 207–8, 241, 280.

narrative thread through which the entire story of social reconciliation unfolds. "The people could warmly appreciate the act which had brought Hubert to their own level, and merchants and spinners were glad to do business with the new man who had stepped down from his aristocratic exclusiveness to be one of them."[3] But having "cast aside the prejudices which had previously kept him aloof from the great world of commerce which he now found to be full of enchantment and delight," Hubert was driven farther to "also cast aside the prejudices which had made the factory girl a meaner being than her employer." Having "already set the county families an example of stepping down with advantage onto a lower round of the social ladder; he would now set the employer the further example of placing himself on an equality with his workpeople."[4]

Indeed, by wooing his working-class sweetheart, Trafford was merely pursuing the logical consequences of entrepreneurial liberalism – acting out the egalitarian program of social harmony and progress that had been disregarded by the actual entrepreneurial bourgeoisie. Having exchanged the false nobility of aristocratic parasitism for the true nobility of self-realization through competitive entrepreneurship, he could now complete the symbolic circle of social reconciliation, openly revealing his inner virtue and character by uniting his fortunes with that which was most virtuous within the working class.

Throughout the traumas of 1848, Trafford's aims were repeatedly obstructed by circumstances, but after the return of prosperity and the end of Chartism, with the onset of the mid-Victorian age, his dreams of social fusion were realized at last. Finally marrying the wronged daughter of the downtrodden proletariat, Trafford restored the honor of the entire *dramatis personae* by assuming the hitherto unconsummated legacy of the old honest industrialist whose own offspring had now destroyed himself and the family business through unbridled egotism and lust.[5] With his demise, the dark side of competitive capitalism was finally buried, and entrepreneurial liberalism could fully assume its rightful hegemonic mantle personified by a new type of leader who successfully combined the nobility of character and blood. With her unassimilable former proletarian suitor conveniently shipped off to America and her respectable ex-Chartist father happily promoted to a factory manager's job, our working-class heroine could acknowledge the

---

[3] Ibid., 267.

[4] Ibid., 269.

[5] Although Burnley does not explicitly draw the link between the unrestrained sensual egotism of young Tom Ayrton and the unrestrained acquisitive egotism of the radical individualist philosophy of which he is an abortive product, this connection was made with marvelous acuity by Charles Dickens, *Hard Times* (London, 1969), 105, in his portrayal of young Tom Gradgrind, on whom Burnley's character is obviously based.

inauguration of a new era. At last she could agree to the cross-class alliance after obtaining the consent of her aristocratic father-in-law, whose own realization that the workers no longer threatened the social order enabled him to relinquish his traditional attachment to privileges and hierarchies and to reconcile himself to the competitive egalitarianism that characterized the new urban-industrial world.

As the novel ends, this social resolution becomes permanently hypostatized when the new Trafford union gives birth to a child in whom aristocracy, bourgeoisie, and proletariat are organically fused. Here, with the arrival of a truly classless generation that "shall start life," in the words of his father, "unhampered by the follies and prejudices that made such a darkness of our former lives . . . shall have instilled into his heart a sense of the dignity of labour" and will know that every individual is worth no more or less than "what he makes himself worth," Burnley can finally allow the curtain to fall. Now that "love has hallowed everything," the age of conflict and crisis is over, "the dawn has broken at last."[6]

In Burnley's romance of social reconciliation, the reader of this study will recognize elements of the actual dynamics of class conflict and stabilization in mid-nineteenth-century Bradford intermixed with strong infusions of ideological fantasy and myth. As a chronicler with direct access to men and women who actually participated in the traumas of early industrial capitalism on which he based his allegorical account, Burnley, on one level, was well aware of the real historical pattern of events. Nevertheless, in transposing them onto a fictional format in which individual actors with caricatured relationships are made to personify the complex historical processes and interactions of collective social groups, what was, in reality, an arduous task of consensus building is effortlessly reified into a transcendent utopia in which every social distinction is magically obliterated and every historical disharmony is unconditionally resolved. Written at the height of mid-Victorian complacency for an admiring audience of now established entrepreneurial elites, Burnley's story simply consigned the conflicted relationships out of which stability had been constructed to an imagined fictional world of prehistory in which it was "love" rather than the practical necessity for compromise that "hallowed everything." The task of historical explanation was simply replaced with an inevitable "happy ending" that substituted literary convention for social analysis.[7]

---

[6] Burnley, *Looking For Dawn*, 390.

[7] James Burnley was a Victorian writer from Bradford who seems to have built his career almost entirely on bourgeois patronage. Certainly, he devoted his pen to a succession of

Not surprisingly, it was in the characters of the novel's two main pro-
tagonists that Burnley's reification of the actual historical process had its
most serious and distorting effect. By personifying Bradford's workers as a
victimized virgin whose search for a viable place in the new urban-industrial
society inevitably pointed toward an alliance with one or another dominant
male, Burnley simply erased from historical memory the reality of the independent, self-conscious working-class movement that, as Chapters 16 and
17 demonstrated, constituted the actual challenge against which all bourgeois
conciliatory gestures were framed. To be sure, the possibility of a union
between the mill girl and her angry, proletarianized suitor seemed a real
possibility at the beginning of the novel and was not entirely ruled out until
the end. Nevertheless, from the outset he was portrayed as an unworthy
partner, capricious, imprudent, and ultimately ineffectual, who could be
redeemed at the final moment only by being removed.

Nevertheless, Burnley's most striking violation of the actual course of
Bradford's history was his choice of the renegade aristocrat Hugh Trafford
as the proper agent for actively reformulating the liberal entrepreneurial
ideal. Ironically, young Trafford, who was loosely modeled on the indus-
trialist-inventor Samuel Cunliffe Lister, was, of all the characters in the
novel, the only one actually drawn from life.[8] Nevertheless, as Chapter 9
contended, Lister was a highly atypical figure – the Anglican exception within
the ascendant capitalist generation whose affirmation of intensely competitive
attitudes and behavior confirmed the reality of the liberal entrepreneurial
rule.

As we have shown in Chapter 18, the reform of entrepreneurial liberalism,
its transformation from a sectional bourgeois party ideology into a genuinely
inclusive, hegemonic urban-industrial creed, was not a magical sleight of
hand that could be performed by some ex-aristocratic sorcerer without any
practical sacrifice or ideological cost. To be sure, the liberal consensus would
not become fully viable until moderate Whigs like Lister, or even outright
Tories, could be convinced to embrace it and even to contribute residual
elements of their now defunct paternalism to the creation of a more ecu-

works in which he wrote what he imagined they wanted to hear. After *Looking for the
Dawn* and two other semifictionalized accounts of local life published in the 1870s, *Phases
of Bradford Life* (London, 1871) and *West Riding Sketches* (London, 1875), Burnley wrote
The History of Wool and Woolcombing (London, 1889), as well as several celebratory works
in the Smilesean tradition whose content is sufficiently indicated by their titles: *The Romance
of Modern Invention* (London, 1886), *The Romance of Modern Industry* (London, 1888), and
*Summits of Success: How they have been reached, with sketches of the careers of some notable
climbers* (London, 1901).

[8] Although Trafford was clearly modeled on the real-life Lister, his literary function as
social synthesizer seems to have been at least partly plagiarized from Benjamin Disraeli's
Sybil (Oxford, 1926), whose aristocratic character Egremont performs a similar role.

menical social reformist program. But the actual task of self-consciously reformulating liberalism into a social vision around which a real consensus might be sustained was, in reality, a painful and ultimately contradictory mission undertaken directly by bourgeois liberals, not out of any coherent sense of purpose, but because the early Victorian crisis in class relations obliged them to act.

As the one social group that required both an economic environment sufficiently open to remain profitable and a social order sufficiently stabilized to be viable in cultural and political terms, Bradford's liberal entrepreneurial bourgeoisie was uniquely qualified to establish the new hegemonic framework in which a proper balance between regulation and competition could be struck. Once they abandoned their vain resistance to the workers' demand for a modicum of protection, they quickly found that they could command general assent to a system that not only served as the source of their own profits, but for the first time, genuinely appeared as the foundation of future progress and prosperity for the urban-industrial population as a whole. But the consensus that crystallized around this new awareness was not the work of some supernatural synthesizer; it was the product of actual historical experience, the outcome of a tacit negotiation between a new capitalist elite that was determined to dominate and a larger nonentrepreneurial majority who exacted a commitment to a minimal level of social security as the price for their acquiescence to entrepreneurial rule.

Given Burnley's own position as an ideologue for entrepreneurial capitalism and a spokesman for Bradford's mid-Victorian liberal bourgeoisie, his neglect of their active role during the crisis of the forties appears, at first sight, to be rather odd. Yet this denigration of liberal bourgeois agency was necessary to sustain a deeper denial, shared by bourgeois liberals themselves, of the historical memory of class conflict and class consciousness, which stabilization could never entirely obliterate but which ideology could seek to repress. By making the idealized Trafford the author of consensus, ignoring the role of a fumbling and reluctant bourgeoisie, social harmony itself could be presented as a timeless, transcendent, ultimately inscrutable blessing, a providential accident of the market's invisible hand, when it was, in reality, a fragile, humanly achieved equilibrium that had constantly to be reestablished in order to be maintained.[9]

Of course, neither Burnley nor the bourgeois liberals whose position he articulated were alone in seeking to project their particular class experience

---

[9] The best general account of the whole mid-Victorian period, especially with reference to the underlying socioeconomic dynamics on which its high tides of economic prosperity and bourgeois liberalism were based, is E. J. Hobsbawm, *The Age of Capital, 1848–1875* (New York, 1975).

in ultimate, transcendent, universalized terms. As we have seen, the same utopian impulses can be detected in the thought and behavior of Bradford's traditional elites and proletarianized workers, even though they proved far less successful in putting such impulses into effect. However, in the end, the entrepreneurial liberals no less than the social groups they dominated were forced, at least implicitly, to recognize that in real history no abstract ideology can ever materialize absolutely, in an unconditional way.

Every social group in mid-nineteenth-century Bradford contributed to making its own history, although none were able to make it exactly as they chose. From the vantage of the mid-Victorian age of equipoise, it might momentarily appear as though the urban-industrial environment had, in fact, metamorphosed into a liberal entrepreneurial utopia – a classless, individualistic society regulated by the voluntaristic workings of the marketplace and dominated not by a bourgeois class of industrial capitalists, but by a natural order of self-made elites. Nevertheless, even at the moment when it appeared most plausible, this ideological reading of social relations cast in the distorting language of market exchange masked the underlying reality of a culturally fragmented, economically divided society that had been formed not only by the impersonal flows of supply and demand forces, but by the self-conscious interaction of contending social groups.

This concrete historical pattern of class formation and conflict in the crucible of early industrial-capitalist crisis and change set the stage for the stabilization of social relations around midcentury that Burnley chose to obscure and mythicize, but which this book has endeavored to delineate and explain. As we have argued, during the social and economic crises of the late 1830s and 1840s, Bradford's bourgeoisie itself was forced by circumstances to confront this reality of capitalist class conflict and to acquiesce, at least partly, in a new vision of stabilization that they never could have provided entirely on their own. Indeed, the experience of social crisis was a learning experience that compelled bourgeois liberals to look beyond their own class situation and, if only momentarily, to see, from the vantage of the proletarianized worker, what the ideal of market freedom really meant. As a result they were motivated, if only for self-preservation, to accept a modicum of government regulation so that the larger entrepreneurial framework could survive.

Nevertheless, with the onset of sustained economic prosperity during the 1849–74 period, the necessity of collectivist reforms began to seem less obvious and, forgetting the lessons that crisis had taught them, bourgeois liberals tended to fall back on their original entrepreneurial vision of a fully competitive, voluntaristic society in which cultural integration and social provision was not managed by government or corporatist compromise but occurred spontaneously through the natural workings of the marketplace. The material underpinnings of this liberal, voluntarist ideological revival, in which social class was displaced even as a conceptual category, were laid in the economic boom of 1849. Suddenly, a pent-up demand for worsted products sparked an orgy of production in which the volume of stuff exports rose 32 percent over the levels that had prevailed during the depression of 1848. But unlike previous booms, which had gone bust after three or four years, this one inaugurated a long wave of economic growth and industrial expansion that sustained generally high levels of profit and employment for the next twenty-five years.[10]

Naturally, this long wave of growth did not pass entirely without interruption, and in 1857 and 1868, there were serious (albeit temporary) checks. Then consumer demand softened and the entire financial superstructure of Bradford's industrial organization shuddered under the accumulated weight of nearly a decade of almost limitless credit and consequent speculative excess.[11] Nevertheless, unlike the depressions of the 1830s and 1840s, those of the 1850s and 1860s did not lead to widespread unemployment and destitution for whole sectors of the urban-industrial working class. Moreover, once marginal competitors were eliminated, full production was quickly able to resume. In the free-trade, cotton-starved conditions of the early 1860s the Bradford trade benefited, as it did in the French political crisis of the early 1870s, when what was becoming an increasingly formidable foreign competitor was temporarily rendered economically prostrate.[12]

Although the mere experience of sustained economic prosperity did much to facilitate social consensus in Bradford, the process of stabilization was even more profoundly influenced by the qualitative restructuring of labor and industrial organization that followed in the wake of simple quantitative growth. In particular, high profits, sustained over a very long period, permitted widespread investment in technologically advanced machinery, making the entire period of the 1850s and 1860s not only a time of vastly augmented output when spindle and loom capacity for the entire industry increased between three and fourfold, but also an era of significant improvement in labor productivity in the face of a work force that grew by only 67 percent.[13] In Bradford itself, these patterns were even more striking as the industrial and mercantile boom of the 1850s was actually accompanied by a 34 percent decline in the size of the worsted work force – and it was

[10] John James, *History of the Worsted Manufacture in England* (London, 1857).
[11] E. M. Sigsworth, *Black Dyke Mills* (Liverpool, 1958), 55–75.
[12] Ibid.
[13] Ibid., 121–2.

not until the early 1880s that the 1851 employment levels in the local industry were again reached.[14]

These improvements in labor productivity were of decisive importance since they tended to make industrial prosperity virtually self-reinforcing, creating an environment in which consistently high profits and gradually increasing wages (especially during the 1860s) could be sustained simultaneously with the gradually declining commodity prices that were necessary if market volume were continuously to expand. Evidence of increasing productivity can be found during this period at virtually every stage in the worsted production process including the established factory processes of spinning and weaving, for which the widespread adoption of the fastest and most automatic modern machinery caused average output per worker to increase by at least 75 and 97 percent, respectively, between 1850 and 1867.[15] However, the most important advances in labor productivity were generated through the final elimination of the hand woolcombers and their replacement by a much smaller complement of female factory operatives who tended self-acting combing machines. As we have seen, this process had been well underway since the late 1840s, and by 1856, it was substantially complete.[16]

It is scarcely possible to overestimate the significance of this shift from hand to machine woolcombing or the contribution that it made to the process of labor reorganization and social stabilization in mid-Victorian Bradford. The complete elimination of the last remnant of the proletarianized, textile handicraftsmen who had served as the backbone of the militant working-class movement for three decades obviously constituted a precondition for the full triumph of consensus liberalism. During the 1830s and 1840s, the presence of large numbers of such angry, dispossessed, and impoverished workers had virtually ensured the development of militant working-class consciousness. Hence, their disappearance during the early 1850s opened the way for the atrophy of proletarian militancy and for the relegation of any kind of class consciousness from a dominant to a subordinate working-class strain.

Of course, during the final stages of crisis in the late 1840s, this painful demise of the proletarianized handcomber had itself been a source of social division, but because the process was completed amidst the environment of generalized economic prosperity during the 1850s, its disruptive consequences were greatly eased. As we have seen, during the depressed and

---

[14] Calculated from information in *PP* (1852–3, LXXXVIII), 2:720–32; *PP* (1863, LIII), 2:722–9; and *PP* (1883, LXXX), 408–15.

[15] Calculated from information in Sigsworth, *Black Dyke*, 121–2.

[16] *BO*, Feb. 9, 23, Mar. 2, 1854; E. M. Sigsworth, "An Episode in Woolcombing," *Journal of the Bradford Textile Society* (1956–7), 113–25.

volatile 1840s, the worst social consequence of the woolcombers' precipitous decline was the dearth of remunerative forms of alternative employment for adult men of the working class. In addition to the ordeal directly borne by the hapless comber, this dearth of viable employment for working-class male breadwinners had the effect, as Chapter 13 demonstrated, of forcing the vast majority of working-class families into a dangerous dependence on the low-paid factory labor of their women and children as an antidote to that state of chronic poverty and destitution to which economic depression and/ or the stages of the family life cycle would periodically reduce them in any case.[17]

By contrast, the generalized prosperity of the early 1850s facilitated the gradual emergence of a more balanced and diversified local economy in which the disappearance of abysmally paid jobs in the textile handicrafts was at least partly compensated by the proliferation of comparatively more skilled and higher paid forms of adult male employment. As an increasingly prosperous local populace began to increase the range and volume of its own consumer demands, other industries like construction or various types of retailing, began to provide an increasing number of jobs.

These striking changes in the structure of male employment can be traced quite precisely through the published returns of the census, which show that, in 1851, 45.2 percent of all male workers in Bradford had been employed in worsted manufacturing, while only 14.4 percent had jobs in other industries, 8.4 percent worked in construction, and 25.4 percent were in other urban-service craft and retail trades.[18] By contrast, ten years later, only 25.4 percent were employed in worsted manufacturing (mostly in skilled or supervisory occupations), while 27.6 percent had jobs in other industries, 9.3 percent worked in construction, and 30.1 percent were in other urban-service craft and retail trades.[19]

These new opportunities for remunerative male employment that changes in the mid-Victorian urban economy wrought had far-reaching social consequences, not only for the adult men who were their direct beneficiaries, but for the entire working-class family whose living standards were significantly raised. As a result, a whole range of new possibilities for the augmentation and enhancement of domestic life were opened up. Indeed, the shift from a comparatively low-waged to a comparatively high-waged structure of male employment goes far to account for the indisputable improvement in the collective living standard of the working-class family during the

[17] See Chapter 13.
[18] Calculated from information in *PP* (1852–3, LXXXVIII), 2:720–32; *PP* (1863, LIII), 2:722–9; and *PP* (1883, LXXX), 408–15.
[19] Ibid.

1850s, a mildly inflationary decade when real wages for individuals in virtually every occupation either stagnated or registered only the most modest gains.[20]

Of course, this evolution of a more diversified urban economy, which afforded more remunerative forms of employment for an increasing number of adult working-class men, could not instantly absorb the thousands of desperate woolcombers and ex-woolcombers who were forced to leave town in search of work. This rapid exodus of unemployed woolcombers, together with the removal to the suburbs of several large businesses (most notably that of Titus Salt) and the increasing capital intensivity of factory labor in town, resulted in a startling demographic reversal during the 1850s. The population of Bradford Borough, which had risen eightfold during the first half of the nineteenth century and increased by 56 percent during the forties alone, virtually ceased to grow between 1850 and 1860. Indeed, a comparison of population with statistics on fertility and mortality indicates that demographic growth during the decade was well below the level of natural increase. Hence, in striking contrast to the 1840s when a net in-migration to the borough of about 30,000 persons occurred, during the 1850s, there was a net out-migration of about 8,000 persons.[21]

Although this demographic reversal surprised many contemporaries who had learned to equate demographic with economic growth, it also made a significant contribution to the stabilization of mid-Victorian society in Bradford both by removing much of the surplus labor population that had arrived during the inundations of the late 1840s and by easing the dangerous overcrowding of the downtown slum districts where most of the woolcombers and their families had been compelled to live. Simultaneously, as downtown slum districts were noticeably thinning, the construction of 4,919 new houses in Bradford Borough during the 1850s, generally in the more salubrious semisuburban residential neighborhoods that were being developed on what was then the edges of town (see Figure 4–3), provided a range of more attractive housing alternatives for the growing numbers of respectable working-class and lower-middle-class families whose rising incomes enabled them to escape from the congested downtown.[22] Although the persistence of high mortality rates until the

[20] James, *Worsted Manufacture*, 400–16, 441; A. L. Bowley, "Statistics of Wages in the United Kingdom," *Journal of the Royal Statistical Society*, 65 (1902), 104–13; William Cudworth, *Condition of the Industrial Classes in Bradford* (Bradford, 1887).

[21] Theodore Koditschek, "Class Formation and the Bradford Bourgeoisie" (Princeton, Ph. D. dissertation, 1981), 86. Calculated from information in Registrar General, *Annual Reports* (1841–60); *PP* (1852–3, LXXXVIII), 2:677; and *PP* (1863, LIII), 157.

[22] Calculated from information in *PP* (1852–3, LXXXVIII), 2:677; and *PP* (1863, LIII), 157.

1870s attests to the failure of municipal provision for public health and
sanitary reform, the overall reduction of housing density in Bradford Borough during the course of the 1850s, from 5.5 to 4.7 persons per house,
indicates the limited but real possibilities for environmental improvement
that flowed, even in the absence of effective local government, from the
spontaneous workings of the competitive marketplace.

Not surprisingly, this experience during the 1850s and 1860s of rising living
standards, diminished class tensions, and environmental improvement – all
apparently achieved without self-conscious planning as an automatic outcome of supply and demand – reinforced the laissez-faire instincts of Bradford's bourgeois liberals that the harsh lessons of the 1840s had compelled
them to doubt. Once again, they now felt free to follow their own experience
and to conclude that there was no contradiction between private interest
and collective welfare, indeed, that the very goal of social progress and
collective advancement, ultimately required individual initiative and competitive enterprise.

Indeed, no sooner had overt signs of working-class suffering and militancy
evaporated in the boom conditions of 1849 than Bradford's leading entrepreneurial liberals engineered a marked retreat from the environmentalist
diagnosis of urban poverty and class division that, during the previous five
years of crisis, had fueled their campaign for urban and municipal reform.
As full employment suddenly appeared to eliminate immediate grounds for
concern over Bradford's physical condition, a committee of notables was
formed under Mayor Salt's chairmanship to investigate the moral condition
of the town. When this group issued its report twelve months later, it focused
almost entirely on the problem of working-class irreligion and on the role
of personal disorderliness and immorality in causing environmental disame-
nity and economic distress. As such, it constituted a resounding reassertion
of that hyperindividualist, ultravoluntarist approach to the problem of working-class dysfunction that, a decade earlier, the *Observer* had repudiated in
the face of mass Chartism and wholesale depression. Now this old approach
suddenly seemed more appropriate in a world where market competition
appeared to be solving its own worst problems and where those who remained
poor had only themselves to blame.[23]

In fact, this influential document established a whole new agenda for liberal
voluntarism in Bradford that would, in the course of the economically expansive 1850s, extend it far beyond the narrow grooves of sectarian religion,
temperance, and autodidacticism in which it had hitherto been contained.

[23] *BO*, June 21, 28, 1849; Mar. 7, 1850.

The result was the sudden appearance of a host of new associations and agencies that endeavored to provide, by purely voluntary methods, a broad range of further popular educational and cultural services and even went so far as to assume responsibility for some parts of the 1840s urban and environmental reform program, which the Town Council had now abandoned as too ambitious for municipal government to undertake.[24]

The committee's recommendation for the establishment of a permanent, nonsectarian Town Mission, "in which the representatives of all denominations, both clerical and lay, shall cordially unite," was adopted without delay. This was soon followed by the employment of "two or three town missionaries – men whose specific and exclusive duty is to visit the poor in their own houses for the purpose of imparting religious instruction and consolation, and perpetually [to] explore as messengers of truth and mercy, the retreats of vice and wretchedness [that] have long been at work within the town."[25] Over the next few years, the Town Mission sponsored a wide range of different nondenominational, charitable, and proselytizing activities and generated a series of other ecumenical spin-off associations such as the Bradford Charitable Inquiry Society for "the suppression of mendicant imposture and the promotion of the judicious distribution of private charity within the Borough of Bradford."[26] Even more significant was the Bradford Female Educational Institute, partly run by bourgeois women, which sought to teach domestic skills to Bradford's female factory operatives while also promoting basic literacy and numeracy within their ranks.[27]

Nevertheless, the ultimate triumph of bourgeois voluntarism in midcentury Bradford was its success in financing and managing major public facilities, most notably a large park that promised "to substitute manly and open air exercises for vicious and enervating pleasures," while promoting "the health and happiness of both old and young." Also planned were an even more expensive and elaborate downtown concert hall that would not only serve as a symbol of civic identity and provide an arena for public meetings, but also constitute a site for "such amusements and recreations as tend to refine and elevate, not debase and sensualize our natures."[28] Over the next seven years, £16,000 in £10 shares was raised by voluntary subscription for an imposing, classical, colonnaded edifice, the 3,100 seat St. George's Hall. At the same time, a further £10,000 was collected, not only

---

[24] *BO*, Mar. 7, 1850.
[25] *BO*, Mar. 7, 1850; and also Apr. 3, 1851; Mar. 16, 24, 1853; Mar. 15, 22, 1855; Feb. 21, 28, Apr. 3, 1856; Mar. 23, 1867; and "Journal of William Fletcher, Bradford Town Missionary, 1870–75" (uncatalogued mss., Bradford Archives).
[26] *BO*, Dec. 1, 1859.
[27] *BO*, Nov. 20, 1856; June 4, 1857; Feb. 11, 1858; Nov. 17, 1859; Feb. 6, 1862.
[28] *BO*, Mar. 7, 1850.

through the pounds and guineas of the bourgeois capitalists who then found themselves awash in boom market profits, but also from the increasingly well paid and comfortable skilled workers who contributed their pence and shillings to the purchase and landscaping of the new Peel Park, also promoted entirely by voluntary means.[29]

"In these contemporaneous projects," prophesied the *Observer*, "the dawning of better things is perceivable. First, social *unity*. All classes meet together; all classes subscribe together. Together they will greet in the park; together they will sit in the public concert or town's gathering. Party feeling will be undermined, and a fresh ... confidence will be gradually established in the various grades of social and political life." In addition to these manifest social benefits, the two projects also promised to promote individual advancement, and while the paper could not promise "that parks and music halls will exterminate vice, ... we do think they will eminently tend to the moral improvement of the people."[30]

In the face of such impressive and widespread displays of civic purpose, class consensus and political fusion, not to mention enlightened self-interest and individual self-help, bourgeois liberals might well be pardoned for imagining that the park and concert hall movements represented mere foretastes of a whole new mode of voluntaristic social action. Henceforth, they might conclude that there was no social object that could not be accomplished privately by entrepreneurial or voluntary associational means. Indeed, these early years of mid-Victorian social calm and prosperity did witness a veritable explosion of creative, new voluntary associations and initiatives in Bradford to promote working-class savings, cooperative retailing, home ownership, freehold landowning, political enfranchisement, competitive sportsmanship, choral harmony, domestic economy, horticulture, adult education, personal character building, and every imaginable form of self-help.

Like the temperance and religious sects on which they were modeled, these new voluntary associations all sought to negate class distinctions by bridging the barriers of culture and communication which separated workers from the entrepreneurial bourgeoisie. However, unlike their early-nineteenth-century predecessors, these mid-Victorian ventures did prove significantly more successful in translating liberal individualism into a working-class language that even workers who valued their autonomy and independence might, within limits, voluntarily choose to embrace. Insofar as this actually happened, it occurred because the new voluntarism, operating in a propitious economic climate, genuinely succeeded where the old voluntarism had but

---

[29] For sources on the financing and construction of St. George's Hall and Peel Park, see Chapter 18, note 68.

[30] *BO*, Aug. 15, 1850.

vainly aspired, in extending the material and psychological benefits of self-discipline and self-reliance from the entrepreneurs who had originally formulated them to hitherto inaccessible nonentrepreneurial groups.

Nevertheless, this apparent triumph of liberal voluntarism in midcentury Bradford, for all its highly visible achievements, proved in some respects to be remarkably superficial and short lived. Even when most successful, it never encompassed everybody, and if it was able to integrate many better-off workers, it aggressively marginalized those who remained unrespectable and poor. Most significantly, however, it depended far too heavily on the indefinite continuation of the long wave of industrial expansion and economic prosperity that characterized the quarter-century after 1849. Even during the brief recessions of 1857 and 1868, the voluntarist groundswell suddenly dwindled to a trickle as projects that depended on large contributions for purposes other than charitable relief found themselves in serious financial difficulty. Far more devastating, then, were the long-term consequences during the last quarter of the nineteenth century when the era of automatic prosperity finally ceased.

This "great depression," as contemporaries termed it was (as the phrase abundantly indicates) a period of generally stagnant or declining profits that adversely affected British industry as a whole. In the Bradford worsted trade, these problems were significantly compounded by a rising tide of protectionism in America and Germany, by changing fashions in women's dress clothing, and by the rise of a formidable French worsted industry whose designs and workmanship were generally considered superior to those that the Bradford capitalists were able or willing to produce. Having exhausted the productivity gains of mechanization, Bradford's capitalists suddenly found themselves in a new and far more sophisticated international marketplace. In the face of far superior French products, consumers, who had learned to be more discriminating, became less and less interested in the old mixed-worsteds with which the Bradford trade had triumphed a generation before.[31]

As they increasingly found themselves in the unfamiliar position of being losers rather than winners in the competitive market game, Bradford's now established and increasingly postentrepreneurial bourgeois liberals were again forced, this time in their own direct self-interest, to reexamine the orthodox laissez-faire creed. Although the results of this reexamination differed depending on the individual and only a minority completely abandoned the faith, there was a noticeable diminution in the ideological conviction that everything was reducible to a market calculus and that all problems could be resolved entirely by voluntarist means.[32]

---

[31] Sigsworth, *Black Dyke*, 75–132.

[32] There are no good, accessible, modern historical studies of Bradford during the later

At the same time as declining sales and diminished profits forced employers to cut workers' wages, to switch to short time, and to impose layoffs, class tensions within the industry began to resurface, and a new kind of proletarian class consciousness arose.[33] Frightened by this prospect of renewed class conflict and increasingly aware of the squalor and poverty that continued to fester in Bradford's slums, the town's capitalists began to redirect their attention back to the public institutions and reformist social practices that they or their predecessors had devised during the forties to confront those problems that remained unresolved (and often even unformulated) when viewed exclusively within a voluntaristic conceptual frame.

Of course, the social problems of the 1880s and 1890s were very different from those of the 1830s and 1840s, and there was never any return to the full-scale crises and unconditional class conflicts that had devastated Bradford during the early industrial age. However, one important reason why conditions did not completely deteriorate under the social and economic pressures of the late-Victorian era was that Bradfordians of all classes were now deeply committed to the modes of compromise and traditions of consensus that had been first established in the crisis of the late 1840s, when the specter of total chaos had seriously loomed. Most importantly, Bradfordians of the late nineteenth century were able to fall back on those governmental institutions that had been established by their. predecessors during the era of factory reform and municipal incorporation. Quietly, these institutions had been extending their regulatory powers and administrative competence even amidst the laissez-faire hyperbole of the mid-Victorian age. With the increasing professionalization of all forms of public service and the advent of

nineteenth century, although political developments are well covered in D. G. Wright, "Politics and Opinion in Nineteenth Century Bradford, 1832–1880," (Leeds, Ph.D. dissertation, 1966); W. D. Ross, "Bradford Politics, 1880–1906," (Bradford, Ph.D. dissertation, 1977); and J. A. Jowitt and R. K. S. Taylor, *Nineteenth Century Bradford Elections* (Bradford, 1979); and in the controversy which followed the appearance of M. Hurst, "Liberal versus Liberal: The General Election of 1874 in Bradford and Sheffield," *Historical Journal*, 4:4 (1972), 669–713; D. G. Wright, "Liberal versus Liberal, 1874: Some Comments," *Historical Journal*, 6:3 (1973), 597–603; M. Hurst, "Liberal Versus Liberal, 1874: A Rebuttal," *Historical Journal*, 7:1 (1974), 162–4; and M. R. Temmell, "Liberal versus Liberal, 1874: W. E. Forster, Bradford, and Education," *Historical Journal*, 8:3 (1975), 611–22.

[33] See Jack Reynolds and Keith Laybourn, "The Emergence of the ILP in Bradford," *International Review of Social History* 20 (1975), 313–46; Cyril Pearce, *The Manningham Mills Strike: its importance in Bradford History* (Hull, 1975); E. P. Thompson, "Homage to Tom Maguire," in Asa Briggs and John Saville, eds., *Essays in Labour History* (London, 1960), 1:276–316; J. A. Jowitt and R. K. S. Taylor, eds., *Bradford 1890–1914: The Cradle of the ILP* (Bradford, 1980); M. Ashraf, *Bradford Trades Council* (Bradford, 1972); and Fenner Brockway, *Socialism over Sixty Years: The Life of Jowett of Bradford, 1864–1944* (London, 1946).

new layers of local and central authority, especially in the fields of education and public health, the stage was set for a further expansion of the role of government, once the prod of popular mobilization and fear of social disorder finally aroused elites to react.[34]

Thus, in the harsher economic climate of the late nineteenth century, the challenge of social problems became more insistent, and the infrastructure of government regulation was again increased. Voluntaristic fantasies about the possibilities of a seamless, frictionless, fully entrepreneurial society, which, a few years earlier, might have seemed on the verge of fulfillment, began, once again, to give way to hegemonic realism. Forced again to confront formidable threats to their economic dominance and social authority, Bradford's elites relearned the lessons of the 1840s, that the surest foundation for capitalist stability was not cultural universalism or some economic miracle, but a carefully designed program of reform and regulation that supplemented the basic framework of the market society with a pragmatic mixture of social welfare provision, organized political negotiation, and class compromise.

In this book, we have concluded our story of Bradford's urban-industrial development by anatomizing this process of social stabilization whereby the massively crisis-ridden and unconditionally divided city of the early Victorian period was transformed by an ideologically tempered and institutionalized liberalism into the more orderly urban community of the mid-Victorian age. Considerable attention has been devoted to the details of this process because it represents the local instance of an epochal watershed that, occurring cumulatively in other times and places, was a major milestone in the making of the modern world.

In places like nineteenth-century Bradford, for the first time in history, a fully capitalist society was compelled to confront its contradictions – to devise strategies for forestalling that "mutual ruin of the contending classes" that Marx predicted as the only alternative to socialism but that we now

---

[34] Pat Thane, *The Foundations of the Welfare State* (London, 1982), 38–46; William Cudworth, *Historical Notes on the Bradford Corporation* (Bradford, 1881), 173–226; Bradford Corporation, *Annual Reports* (1854–85); Barbara Thompson, "Public Provision and Private Neglect: Public Health," in D. G. Wright and J. A. Jowitt, eds., *Victorian Bradford: Essays in Honour of Jack Reynolds* (Bradford, 1981), 137–64; idem, "Infant Mortality in Nineteenth Century Bradford," in Robert Woods and John Woodward, *Urban Disease and Mortality in Nineteenth Century England* (London, 1984), 120–47; A. J. Evans, "A History of Education in Bradford during the Period of the Bradford School Board, 1870–1904" (Leeds, M.A. thesis, 1947); G. W. Fenn, "The Development of Education in an Industrial Town 'Bradford,' During the Nineteenth Century," *University of Leeds Institute of Education Research and Studies* (1952–3), 24–75; Bradford Corporation, Educational Services Committee, *Education in Bradford since 1870* (Bradford, 1970).

know to be at least provisionally avoidable, within a (duly modified) capitalist frame.[35] Watching nineteenth-century Bradfordians of all social classes as they took their first halting steps in this direction, I was motivated to retrace their path for the reader, at least in part, out of a recognition that theirs was one of the first documented journeys along a road that we are still traveling today. By examining their traumatic experience of class crisis and resolution in a time and place where industrial capitalism was still embryonic and unformed, it is my hope to shed some light on the still ongoing process of social reconstruction whereby capitalist societies learn to survive their own infancy by acquiring the necessary skills of self-understanding and self-control.

No doubt, the task of comprehending these more mature forms of capitalism requires conceptual tools and a historical focus somewhat different from the one that has been employed in this book. The very impact of the early capitalist crisis we have studied, the extraordinary success of the reformist reaction whose origins we have traced, have insured that in subsequent capitalist societies, class boundaries have become more permeable, class conflict has generally been more muted, and class consciousness has proved less decisive in shaping the overall history of the age. Nevertheless, advancing capitalism, for all its self-reforms and transformations, has retained much of its original character, even as it has developed and spread.

In today's world, a fortunate, not inconsiderable minority has actually achieved a level of material prosperity and existential liberation of which nineteenth-century Bradfordians could only dream. Yet a far greater and probably increasing majority finds itself even more profoundly dispossessed – unconditionally estranged from vastly augmented and now fully globalized forces of production that have become even more oppressive and inescapable as they have been concentrated in the hands of an even narrower economic elite. Moreover, in spite of its far greater technological resources and capabilities and not withstanding the sophisticated reformist machinery at its command, our contemporary system of modified capitalism still remains subject to its own inexorable, destabilizing, ultimately uncontrolled logic of ecological dislocation and competitive excess. Indeed, today's most intractable social problems – poverty, pollution, ignorance, unemployment, rootlessness, family breakdown, drug addiction, and labor unrest – would be instantly recognizable, at least in broad outline, to any of the characters who have appeared in this book. So long as our world remains, in this fundamental sense, capitalist, subject to contradictions that Bradfordians first encountered and open to solutions that they first tentatively explored, we can be sure that our experience will continue to echo their own.

---

[35] Karl Marx and Friedrich Engels, *Manifesto of the Communist Party* (New York, 1932), 9.

Appendixes

Appendix A: A note on the 1851 bourgeois census population

The 1851 bourgeois census population and its related subpopulations are the products of an extensive effort to generate as much quantitatively analyzable information as possible on wealth, occupation, age, nativity, property holding, business structure, political affiliation, family structure, residential location, and consumption patterns on as many of the bourgeois households as possible within Bradford Borough at the middle of the nineteenth century.[1]

The main population (bourgeois census population) was generated from the 1851 census manuscripts for Bradford Borough (HO 107/2305–10), and contained the 1,259 households that fulfilled at least one of the following criteria: (1) At least one full-time coresident domestic servant (excluding members of the nuclear family) was employed in the household. In the case of innkeepers, a minimum of two servants was required. In all cases, every effort was made to exclude productive workers and to consider only true domestics in this category. (2) The households of all accredited members of the medical and legal professions and of all clergymen were included whether they kept servants or not. (3) In cases in which the household head reported himself an employer of labor and (a) if it was a craft or retail enterprise and he had at least ten or more employees, or (b) if it was an industrial enterprise and he had twenty or more employees, the household in question was included whether or not it contained live-in domestics. (4) The households of all farmers who worked at least twenty acres of land were included whether or not they kept domestic servants. Finally, in an effort to include as many local elites as possible, the census manuscripts for the surrounding townships outside Bradford Borough (HO 107/2303, 2311–2, 2385, and 2397) were examined to isolate individuals who were known to have worked in town. Thirty-seven households were included on this basis.

This census-based method of quantitative class analysis is not ideal. In

---

[1] A detailed discussion of this research project and the strategy behind it are contained in Appendix A of my Ph.D. dissertation, "Class Formation and the Bradford Bourgeoisie" (Princeton, Ph.D. dissertation, 1981), 902–28, which should be consulted for technical information that the following discussion does not provide.

particular, its heavy reliance on servant holding as a prime basis for inclusion within the bourgeoisie isolates a class defined not so much in terms of wealth or relation to production as consumption level – itself one of the dependent variables that the project aimed to analyze in class terms. The main reason, therefore, for employing this procedure is that the alternatives would have been worse.

The most logical approach would have been to ground the population in Ibbetson's *Bradford Directory* (Bradford, 1850) and then to link the names, addresses, occupations, and business affiliations obtained in this manner with information from the census manuscripts and other sources. The *Directory*, with its 6,390 entries (representing about 34 percent of all households in town) offers the most comprehensive listing of the entire propertied urban middle class.[2] Of course, to handle such a large number of cases would have been difficult, given the investigator's limited resources, and it would have been absolutely impossible (both because of problems of logistics and imperfections in the data) to link them successfully with the information from other sources on wealth, consumption, family structure, and political affiliation that would have made the project worthwhile.

The pollbooks (or electoral registers) with their lists of £10 borough householders might have provided a more manageable alternative, generating a population of about two thousand substantial property holders, which would have excluded most of the petit bourgeoisie.[3] Nevertheless, because of the limited resources available to the researcher and the difficulties of record linkage described below, this approach was also rejected in favor of a strategy that would generate a bourgeois population directly through the census manuscripts – a source that provides a comprehensive survey of the entire urban population and directly includes more relevant information on age, occupation, nativity, residence, family and household structure, and consumption than any other single source. To isolate a bourgeois population from the 1851 census manuscripts, it was, at first, thought best simply to adopt W. A. Armstrong's occupation-based stratification scheme.[4] However, it quickly became evident that this would not do, for the census occupation categories make no distinction even between masters and employees, much less between the wealthy and powerful entrepreneurs who were on the cutting edge of their occupation and the mass of small struggling stragglers and

---

[2] Calculated from information in James Ibbetson, *Directory of Bradford* (Bradford, 1850), and *P.P.* (LIII, 1863), 1:612.

[3] In addition to the electoral registers, which provide names, residential and business addresses, and occupations, pollbooks exist for the 1835 election with names, addresses, and occupations; and for the 1841, 1847, and 1859 elections with names and partial addresses only. *Pollbook* (Bradford, 1835, 1841, 1847, 1859).

[4] W. A. Armstrong, "The Use of Information about Occupation," in E. A. Wrigley, ed., *Nineteenth Century Society* (Cambridge, 1972), 191–223.

middle-range or even small businessmen below them on the income scale. As Figure 4–2 has demonstrated, particularly in highly competitive trades like the worsted industry, such distinctions were of critical significance and cannot be ignored in any discussion of class.[5]

Consequently, in the basic compilation of the bourgeois census population, the criteria of servant holding inevitably emerged as the primary distinguishing tool, although strenuous efforts were made to eliminate, as far as possible, the distortions inherent in this procedure by using the above stated criteria of professional occupation, work force size, and farming acreage to insure that those properly bourgeois householders who did not keep servants were brought into the population by other means. Indeed, 13 percent of the population kept no servants at all.

Although the census itself contains a wealth of information for examining the relationship among class and other variables, additional efforts were made to link the members of the bourgeois census population with data from other sources on social background, religion, politics, and wealth. Although church and chapel records, newspaper sketches, obituaries, and miscellaneous sources provided indispensable information about the social origins, education, and religion of many individuals, such sources proved too fragmentary and limited to permit linkage with the whole bourgeois census population or, indeed, to sustain systematic quantitative analysis of any kind. They do, however, figure heavily in the qualitative analysis of Chapters 6,7,8, and 10.[6]

Fortunately, the availability of pollbooks and petitions for and against municipal incorporation opened the way for record linkage to correlate political identity with the social structural variables that the census disclosed.[7] Although the indifferent quality of the 1847 pollbook complicated the linkage process, the political identities of 677 (54 percent) of the bourgeois census householders were found – thereby generating the politics-linked sample of the bourgeois census population that is analyzed in Chapter 12.[8]

Unfortunately, results were less satisfactory with regard to wealth holding, a (if not the) central characteristic of social stratification on which the census provides no information at all. Quite apart from the inherent difficulties of measuring wealth in a capitalist society in which it constantly changes and

---

[5] For a further discussion of this issue, see Koditschek, "Bradford Bourgeoisie," 294–7, 905–7.

[6] Most of the sources for this information can be found in the footnotes to Chapter 6.

[7] *Electoral Register* (Bradford, 1846); *Pollbook* (Bradford, 1841, 1847, 1859); "Petitions for and Against Incorporation" (mss., Bradford Archives D.B. 6912–3).

[8] The party political distribution of the politics-linked sample of the 1851 bourgeois census population (54 percent liberal, 46 percent Tory) roughly mirrored that of the entire electorate (53 percent liberal, 47 percent Tory) in the 1847 parliamentary election. See Koditschek, "Bradford Bourgeoisie," 326–9.

assumes different forms (a difficulty exacerbated in a place like nineteenth-century Britain where income taxation was rudimentary and some assets were not legally subject to reporting at all), the sources for wealth measurement in early-nineteenth-century Bradford were notably deficient.[9]

Wills and probate valuations provided invaluable information on the real (nonlanded) assets of the wealthy at time of death, and this material has been analyzed both qualitatively and quantitatively in Chapter 5.[10] But for various reasons, the effort to use such data as a supplement to the 1851 bourgeois census population produced only fragmentary results. Consequently, rating figures for urban real estate (houses, shops, factories, and warehouses) provided the only basis on which a systematic analysis of bourgeois wealth holding could be correlated with the other relevant social structural variables that the bourgeois census population enabled us to investigate.[11]

Obviously, property tax assessments give a skewed profile of urban-industrial wealth holding, understating the significance of entrepreneurial capital and exaggerating that of rentier forms. Thus although they can sustain general conclusions about the relative affluence of different individuals (and, to a degree, that of different bourgeois strata), it would be foolhardy to use them as accurate measures of absolute wealth. Moreover, the actual results of record linkage proved unexpectedly disappointing, as the ratable values of only 390 (31 percent) of the 1851 bourgeois census householders could definitively be traced.

This meager result was the result of several factors. (1) Since no borough-wide rate books appear to have survived from the early nineteenth century, the only systematic source of ratable values are the petitions for and against incorporation, which are sometimes illegible and provide only imprecise and sometimes inaccurate information on occupations and addresses.[12] As a result, it was often difficult to make firm identifications, even with the aid of city directories. Moreover, this difficulty was further exacerbated by the six-year interval between the petitions and the census, the propensity of town dwellers (even bourgeois town dwellers) frequently to change their residence,[13] and, most importantly, the extraordinary predominance of a handful

---

[9] J. C. Stamp, *British Incomes and Property* (London, 1916), 2.

[10] *Calendar of Yorkshire Wills* (mss., Borthwick Institute), 20–29 (1838–57).

[11] Some of this information, gathered from "Registers of Wills and Probate" (mss., Somerset House, 1860–1906), is presented in Koditschek, "Bradford Bourgeoisie," 915–6.

[12] Koditschek, "Bradford Bourgeoisie," 917–23, and Adrian Elliott, "The Establishment of Municipal Government in Bradford, 1835–55" (Bradford, Ph.D. dissertation, 1976), 107–14.

[13] Even as late as 1858, a study showed that 12 percent of all householders in Bradford

of common West Riding surnames such as Ackroyd, Barraclough, Clough, Firth, Sutcliffe, and Wilkinson, and Christian names such as Joseph, William, and John.[14]

As a result of these problems the correlation of bourgeois wealth holding with other social structural variables was not pursued as far as originally had been hoped. Nevertheless, unreported findings from the analysis of the rating-linked sample inform the arguments at various points throughout the text,[15] and the sample itself has explicitly been used to establish the occupational differentials in the balance between wealth and consumption that support the argument of the section of Chapter 8 concerned with underconsumption and the domestic economy.

had occupied their dwellings less than one year. Twenty-nine percent had been on the premises less than three years. *BO*, Dec. 10, 1858.

[14] Koditschek, "Bradford Bourgeoisie," 923–5. An analysis of the alphabetical listing of 6,390 names in Ibettson's 1850 *Directory* showed that virtually every surname listed appeared more than once. There were 25 surnames that had twenty-five or more individual listings under them, representing 13 percent of all individuals in the *Directory*. In some cases, such as that of thirteen John Smiths, thirteen Joseph Woods, seven William Ackroyds, and seven John Harrisons, positive identification was completely ruled out. For a discussion of these and other problems involved in record linkage, see the articles in E. A. Wrigley, ed., *Identifying People in the Past* (London, 1973).

[15] Many of these findings are reported in Koditschek, "Bradford Bourgeoisie," 297–308, 313, 320, 327–32.

Appendix B: A note on the 1851 working-class census sample

To provide a data base for the quantitative study of Bradford's workers comparable to that described in Appendix A for the study of the bourgeoisie, a population referred to as the "1851 working-class census sample" was compiled. In a manner comparable to the 1851 bourgeois census population, this working-class sample, which was based on the same census manuscripts, provided direct access to information on age, occupation, nativity, residential location, and family relationship for a select group of 1,641 gainfully employed Bradford workers in 479 households, which represented 3 percent of all the gainfully employed workers in town.[1]

Although this group is called a sample, it is not a random sample of all workers or working-class households in Bradford Borough, but a comprehensive survey of those workers and working-class households located in the two specific slum districts that are mapped in Figure B-1.[2] Although these slums, encompassing the alleys of Black Abbey and those between Longlands Street and Silsbridge Lane, were not the very worst in Bradford (as measured by reputation and housing densities) they were, by all measures, very poor neighborhoods where living conditions, even by working-class standards, were grim. They were deliberately chosen because our emphasis on crisis and dysfunction as the key experiences of Bradford's early urban-industrial workers made it desirable to concentrate on areas where these experiences were particularly visible so as to provide the basis for investigating the strategies that workers developed in response to the strains of proletarianization. In addition, it was thought desirable to focus the study on two particular, well-defined neighborhoods so as to profile statistically an actual community, which would have been impossible if random sampling methods had been used. This proved particularly valuable in the study of neighboring patterns, which, as John Foster has cogently demonstrated, offer

[1] Calculated from information in *PP* (1852–3, LXXXVIII), 2:720–5; and HO, 107/2,308.
[2] Specifically, the districts in question are the census enumerators' districts 22, 23, 24, and 30 for Bradford West. HO, 107/2,308. As in the case of the bourgeois census population, the household is the basic unit of analysis for purposes of the quantitative study whose results are reported in the text.

one important quantifiable measure of class consciousness, particularly in testing the degree of integration or segregation that obtains among different occupational sectors of the working class.[3]

Nevertheless, this procedure raises legitimate questions concerning the representativeness of the districts under study in generating conclusions about the working class as a whole. Although doubts about this cannot be dispelled entirely, the occupational distribution of the districts investigated differs only slightly from that which can be culled from the published census returns for the urban working class as a whole. Thus although woolcombers are almost certainly overrepresented in the sample, textile and factory workers, as a general category, constituted 69 percent of both groups. Construction workers, who comprised 7 percent of all workers in the sample, constituted 5 percent of the entire work force. Tailors and shoemakers, who constituted 4.8 percent of the workers in the sample, represented 4.4 percent of all workers.[4] Examples could be multiplied. Moreover, as the analysis in Chapter 16 indicates, there are further reasons for believing that, although these districts contained a disproportionate number of the poorest and most vulnerable working-class families, they were neither ethnic nor occupational ghettos and their general socioeconomic structure did not differ markedly from that of the urban working class as a whole.

As with the bourgeois census population, the main purpose of this working-class census sample was to generate a data base of quantifiable information on the residential location and occupational structure of working-class households, the age, nativity, and family relationship of members, and to connect this information with such other data as was available for mapping the socioeconomic structure of the class. For the workers, information on education, religion, politics, probate assets, or ratable values was either not relevant or not available except in unusual cases. Nevertheless, although no efforts at record linkage were attempted, extensive information about prevailing local wage rates in a wide variety of occupations was used systematically to assign wage estimates to all occupied workers in the sample and thus to estimate the collective income of each working-class family as a consumption unit.

The wage rates used in constructing these estimates are given in Table B-1. Household incomes were adjusted in the case of lodgers on the assumption that, in households of five or less inhabitants, each lodger paid a weekly 1.3s. in rent, whereas, in households of six or more inhabitants, he or she paid .9s. per week. The resulting estimates of family income were

---

[3] John Foster, *Class Struggles and the Industrial Revolution; Early Industrial Capitalism in Three English Towns* (London, 1974), 125–31, 263–4.

[4] Calculated from information in *PP* (1852–3, LXXXVIII), 2:720–5; and HO, 107/2,308.

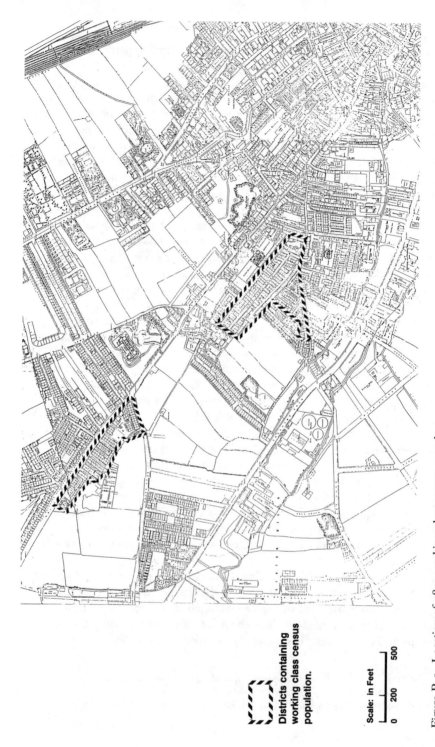

Districts containing
working class census
population.

Scale: in Feet

0   200   500

Figure B-1. Location of 1851 working-class census samples.
Drawn from OS, Map of Bradford (six inches to the mile) (Bradford, 1850); and information in HO, 107/2,308.

Table B-1. *Weekly wage rates in mid-nineteenth-century Bradford (in shillings)*

Textile workers	Wage rate	Other occupations	Wage rate
Skilled		*Skilled*	
Warehousemen	20	Artisans and craftsmen	30
Overlooker	25	Boot and shoemaker	18
Mechanic	25	Bricklayer	21
Woolsorter	20.6	Blacksmith	33
Warp dresser	31.6	Cabinetmaker	18
Millwright	35	Carpenter and joiner	16.6
Engineer	20	Plasterer	20
Stuff maker-up	23	Plumber	19
		Printer	28
Semiskilled		Sawyer	27.6
Stoker	13.6	Stonemason	21
Packer	18	Tailor	30
Washer	14.9	Tinplate worker	17
Dyer	15		
Power loom weaver	10	*Unskilled*	
Machine comber	10.6	Carter	16
Spinner	5.6, 7.9	Domestic	6,[a] 14[b]
Handloom weaver	7	Laborer	14
Hand woolcomber	8	Miner	17
Unskilled		*Self-employed*	
Unspecified women	9	In city directory	70
Unspecified children	6	Not in city directory	40

[a]Under age 14.
[b]Age 14 or over.
Source: The information on wage rates presented here and used in the study was obtained primarily from the following sources: A. L. Bowley, "Statistics of Wages in the United Kingdom," *Journal of the Royal Statistical Society*, 65 (1902), 104–6; John James, *A History of the Worsted Manufacture in England* (London, 1857), 400–16, 441; William Cudworth, *Condition of the Industrial Classes in Bradford* (Bradford, 1887); and E. M. Sigsworth, "An Episode in Woolcombing," *Journal of the Bradford Textile Society* (Bradford, 1956–7, 113–16).

then compared with projected expenditures to provide an assessment of family living standards and to ascertain whether the family was likely to have been living in relative comfort, at or above the bare subsistence minimum, or languishing in a state of utter destitution below the minimum poverty line. The Rowntree estimates were adapted for this purpose, although, since family sizes varied greatly from one case to another, this factor was explicitly incorporated into our expenditure calculation, which Rowntree, in his estimates, did not do.[5]

To live in relative comfort, it was assumed that a given family would require a weekly income equal to or greater than 12s. for the head, 8s. for each additional adult over age 14, and 5s. for each child aged 14 or under. To live above the minimum poverty line, it was assumed that a given family would require a weekly income of 6s. for the head, 5s. for each additional adult over age 14, and 4s. for each child aged 14 or under.

[5] B. S. Rowntree, *Poverty: A Study in Town Life* (London, 1902), 136–43.

Appendix C: leading Bradford textile firms, 1833–1851

Appendix C: Leading Bradford textile firms, 1833–1851

Name (founding date)	Horse power, 1833	Number employed, 1834	Number of spindles, 1839 (spinning)	Number employed, 1850–1 (name or location of factory)
Wood & Walker (1812)	184	527	19,200	3,000 (Bridge St.)
Rouse & Co. (1815)	96	438	16,320	2,200 (Bradford)
Waud & Co. (1819)	20	105	7,776	2,400 (Brittania)
Richard Garnett (1815)	83	387	7,488	1,150 (Union St.)
Rand & Co.	45	—	6,720	1,278 (Horton Ln.)
Wade & Co. (1815)	20	130	4,992	— (Victoria)
Addison & Co. (1819)	30	155	4,800	800 (Hall Ln.)
Turner & Mitchell	34	—	4,608	1,017 (Manchester Rd.)
W. Pearson	30	165	4,320	[b]
Thos. Hollings	40 [a]	176 [a]	4,224	— (Mill St.)
S. C. Lister (1836)	—	—	3,840	—
Joshua Wood	— [a]	—	3,648	
Salt & Co. (1824)	— [a]	— [a]	3,456	3,000+ (Union St.) [b]
Chas. Smithies	[a]	[a]	3,456	
J. & S. Mitchell	20	—	2,880	— (Stowells)
Illingworth & Co. (1825)	60 [c]	221	2,688	300+ (Providence)
Cousen & Co. (1827)	50	166	2,688	— (Gt. Horton)
Cowling Ackroyd	16	—	2,304	— (Gt. Horton)
Swithin Anderton (1818)	15	—	2,304	800 (Eastbrook)
Robt. Ackroyd	16	—	2,112	1,000
Calvert & Clapham	[a]	[a]	1,920	— (Thornton Rd.)
Chapman & Lofthouse	[a]	[a]	1,920	— (Bridge St.)
Bottomley & Wilkinson	[a]	[a]	1,728	— (Marshall's)
Nathan Bentley	— [a]	— [a]	1,728	— (Legrams)
Thos. Willett	[a]	[a]	1,536	— (Clarence St.)

Firm				
Oxley & Co.	[a]	[a]	[a]	[b]
Buck & Holmes	15	—	1,536	600 (Pennyoaks)
Roberts & Lupton	[a]	[a]	1,536	[b]
Shepherd & Rhodes (1820)	102	74	1,536	[b]
Wm. Chambers	[a]	[a]	1,536	[b]
John Anderton (1823)	16	44	1,536	—
Milnes & Brown (1830)	36	47	1,536	—
Tremell & Co.	[a]	[a]	[a]	1,400 (Fieldhead)
Hudson Clough	[a]	[a]	[a]	940 (Globe)
Joseph Leach	[a]	[a]	[a]	700 (Phoenix)
W. & E. Smith (1831)	—	—	—	660 (Allands?)
Horsfall & Co.	—	[a]	[a]	600 (Northwing)
James Drummond (1849)	[a]	[a]	—	537 (Manningham)
Lythall & Haigh	[a]	[a]	[b]	400 (Caledonia)
Margerison & Peckover (1820)	—	301	[b]	[b]
Matthew Thompson (1801)	30	106	[b]	[b]
John Hutton (1816)	—	72	[b]	[b]
Thomas Holdsworth (1833)	—	62	[b]	[b]
J. W. & W. Knowles (1799)	—	61	[b]	[b]
Billingsley & Tankard (1831)	—	61	—	— (Bradford Moor)
John & Wm. Terry (1833)	—	47	—	— (Dudley Hill)
W. & E. Smith (1831)	—	45	[b]	[b]
John Aked (1820)	—	28	[b]	[b] (Horton)

[a] Firm not yet founded.

[b] Firm no longer in business.

[c] Illingworth assets represent one-half of these totals for the Illingworth, Murgatroyd partnership, which broke up in 1834.

Source: Main Sources incude John James, History of Bradford, Continuations and Additions (Bradford, 1866), 225–6; PP (XX, 1834), Yorkshire, 98–122; "List of Bradford Spinning Firms, 1839," (mss., Bradford Archives D.B. 17/24); "Bradford Census Enumerators' Manuscripts (HO, 107/2305–10); Bradford Observer, Oct. 31, 1850; William White, Directory of Leeds and Clothing Districts (Leeds, 1830); idem. (Leeds, 1842); Pigot's Directory (Manchester, 1834); James Ibbetson, Directory of Bradford (Bradford, 1850); anon., Businessmen and Mercantile Interests, Leeds & Bradford (n.p. 1889); anon., The Century's Progress: Yorkshire Industry and Commerce (London, 1893). Slight changes in firm name and partnerships are recorded in this table.

Index